W9-DAT-940

THE PAPERS OF ALEXANDER HAMILTON

Alexander Hamilton, 1792. Oil portrait by John Trumbull

Yale University Art Gallery

ST. MARY'S COLLEGE OF MARYLAND
ST. MARY'S CITY, MARYLAND

43234

THE PAPERS OF

Alexander Hamilton

VOLUME XIII

NOVEMBER 1792–FEBRUARY 1793

HAROLD C. SYRETT, EDITOR

JACOB E. COOKE, ASSOCIATE EDITOR

Assistant Editors

JEAN G. COOKE
CARA-LOUISE MILLER
DOROTHY TWOHIG
PATRICIA SYRETT

COLUMBIA UNIVERSITY PRESS

NEW YORK AND LONDON, 1967

FROM THE PUBLISHER

The preparation of this edition of the papers of Alexander Hamilton has been made possible by the support received for the work of the editorial and research staff from the generous grants of the Rockefeller Foundation, Time Inc., and the Ford Foundation, and by the far-sighted cooperation of the National Historical Publications Commission. To these organizations, the publisher expresses gratitude on behalf of all who are concerned about making available the record of the founding of the United States.

Copyright © 1967 Columbia University Press
Library of Congress Catalog Card Number: 61-15593
Printed in the United States of America

PREFACE

THIS EDITION of Alexander Hamilton's papers contains letters and other documents written by Hamilton, letters to Hamilton, and some documents (commissions, certificates, etc.) that directly concern Hamilton but were written neither by him nor to him. All letters and other documents have been printed in chronological order. Hamilton's legal papers are being published under the editorial direction of Julius Goebel, Jr., George Welwood Murray Professor Emeritus of Legal History of the School of Law, Columbia University. The first volume of this distinguished work, which is entitled *The Law Practice of Alexander Hamilton,* was published by the Columbia University Press in 1964.

Many letters and documents have been calendared. Such calendared items include routine letters and documents by Hamilton, routine letters to Hamilton, some of the letters or documents written by Hamilton for someone else, letters or documents which have not been found but which are known to have existed, letters or documents which have been erroneously attributed to Hamilton, and letters to or by Hamilton that deal exclusively with his legal practice.

Certain routine documents which Hamilton wrote and received as Secretary of the Treasury have not been printed. The documents that fall within this category are warrants or interest certificates; letters written by Hamilton acknowledging receipts from banks, endorsing margins of certificate of registry, and enclosing sea letters; letters to Hamilton transmitting weekly, monthly, and quarterly accounts, or enclosing certificates of registry and other routine Treasury forms; and drafts by Hamilton on the treasurer. Statements of facts from the judges of the District Courts on cases concerning violations of the customs laws and warrants of remission of forfeiture issued to Hamilton have generally been omitted unless they pertain to cases discussed in Hamilton's correspondence.

The notes in these volumes are designed to provide information concerning the nature and location of each document, to identify Hamilton's correspondents and the individuals mentioned in the text, to explain events or ideas referred to in the text, and to point out textual variations or mistakes. Occasional departures from these standards can be attributed to a variety of reasons. In many cases the desired information has been supplied in an earlier note and can be found through the use of the index. Notes have not been added when in the opinion of the editors the material in the text was either self-explanatory or common knowledge. The editors, moreover, have not thought it desirable or necessary to provide full annotation for Hamilton's legal correspondence. Perhaps at this point it should also be stated that arithmetical errors in Hamilton's reports to Congress have not been corrected or noted. Finally, the editors on some occasions have been unable to find the desired information, and on other occasions the editors have been remiss.

GUIDE TO EDITORIAL APPARATUS

I. SYMBOLS USED TO DESCRIBE MANUSCRIPTS

AD	Autograph Document
ADS	Autograph Document Signed
ADf	Autograph Draft
ADfS	Autograph Draft Signed
AL	Autograph Letter
ALS	Autograph Letter Signed
D	Document
DS	Document Signed
Df	Draft
DfS	Draft Signed
LS	Letter Signed
LC	Letter Book Copy
[S]	[S] is used with other symbols (AD[S], ADf[S], AL[S], D[S], Df[S], L[S]) to indicate that the signature on the document has been cropped or clipped.

II. MONETARY SYMBOLS AND ABBREVIATIONS

bf	Banco florin
V	Ecu
f	Florin
₶	Livre Tournois
medes	Maravedis (also md and mde)
d.	Penny or denier
ps	Piece of eight

£	Pound sterling or livre
Ry	Real
rs vn	Reals de vellon
rdr	Rix daller
s	Shilling, sou or sol (also expressed as /)
sti	Stiver

III. SHORT TITLES AND ABBREVIATIONS

Annals of Congress, I, II, III, IV	*The Debates and Proceedings in the Congress of the United States; with an Appendix, Containing Important State Papers and Public Documents, and All the Laws of a Public Nature* (Washington, 1834–1849).
Arch. des Aff. Etr., Corr. Pol., Etats-Unis	Transcripts or photostats from the French Foreign Office deposited in the Library of Congress.
Archives Parlementaires	*Archives Parlementaires de 1787 à 1860* (Paris, 1868–).
ASP	*American State Papers, Documents, Legislative and Executive, of the Congress of the United States* (Washington, 1832–1861).
Atton and Holland, *The King's Customs*	Henry Atton and Henry Hurst Holland, *The King's Customs: An Account of Maritime Revenue & Contraband Traffic in England, Scotland, and Ireland, from the Earliest Times to the Year 1800* (New York, 1908).
Boyd, *Papers of Thomas Jefferson*	Julian P. Boyd, ed., *The Papers of Thomas Jefferson* (Princeton, 1950–).
Davis, *Essays*	Joseph Stancliffe Davis, *Essays in the Earlier History of American Corporations* ("Harvard Economic Studies," XVI [Cambridge, 1917]).

Duvergier, *Lois*	J. B. Duvergier, *Collection Complète des Lois, Décrets, Ordonnances, Réglemens, et Avis du Conseil-d'Etat, Publiée sur les Editions Officielles du Louvre; de L'Imprimierie Nationale, Par Baudouin, et Du Bulletin des Lois* (Paris, 1824).
Ford, *Writings of Jefferson*	Paul Leicester Ford, ed., *The Writings of Thomas Jefferson* (New York, 1892–1899).
GW	John C. Fitzpatrick, ed., *The Writings of George Washington* (Washington, 1931–1944).
Hamilton, *History*	John C. Hamilton, *Life of Alexander Hamilton, a History of the Republic of the United States of America* (Boston, 1879).
Hamilton, *Intimate Life*	Allan McLane Hamilton, *The Intimate Life of Alexander Hamilton* (New York, 1910).
Hamilton, *Life*	John C. Hamilton, *The Life of Alexander Hamilton* (New York, 1840).
HCLW	Henry Cabot Lodge, ed., *The Works of Alexander Hamilton* (New York, 1904).
Hogan, *Pennsylvania State Trials*	[Edmund Hogan], *The Pennsylvania State Trials: Containing the Impeachment, Trial, and Acquittal of Francis Hopkinson, and John Nicholson, Esquires* . . . (Philadelphia, 1794).
Isambert, *Recueil Général des Anciennes Lois Françaises*	*Recueil Général des Anciennes Lois Françaises, Depuis L'An 420 Jusqu'à La Révolution de 1789, par MM. Jourdan, Docteur en droit, Avocat à la Cour royale de Paris; Isambert, Avocat aux Conseils du Roi et à la Cour de Cassation; Decrusy, ancien Avocat à la Cour royale de Paris* (Paris, 1821–1833).

James, *Clark Papers*	James Alton James, ed., *George Rogers Clark Papers, 1781–1784* ("Collections of the Illinois State Historical Library," XIX, Virginia Series, IV, [Springfield, 1926]).
JCC	*Journals of the Continental Congress, 1774–1789* (Washington, 1904–1937).
JCH Transcripts	John C. Hamilton Transcripts. These transcripts are owned by Mr. William H. Swan, Hampton Bays, New York, and have been placed on loan in the Columbia University Libraries.
JCHW	John C. Hamilton, ed., *The Works of Alexander Hamilton* (New York, 1851–1856).
Journal of the House, I	*Journal of the House of Representatives of the United States* (Washington, 1826), I.
JPP	"Journal of the Proceedings of the President," George Washington Papers, Library of Congress.
Knopf, *Wayne*	Richard C. Knopf, ed., *Anthony Wayne: A Name in Arms; Soldier, Diplomat, Defender of Expansion Westward of a Nation; the Wayne-Knox-Pickering-McHenry Correspondence* (Pittsburgh, 1960).
Laws of the State of New York, III	*Laws of the State of New York Passed at the Sessions of the Legislature Held in the Years 1789, 1790, 1791, 1792, 1793, 1794, 1795 and 1796, inclusive, Being the Twelfth, Thirteenth, Fourteenth, Fifteenth, Sixteenth, Seventeenth, Eighteenth and Nineteenth Sessions* (Albany, 1887), III.
Macpherson, *Annals of Commerce*, IV	David Macpherson, *Annals of Commerce, Manufactures, Fisheries, and Navigation, with*

	Brief Notices of the Arts and Sciences Connected with Them. Containing the Commercial Transactions of the British Empire and Other Countries, From the Earliest Accounts to the Meeting of the Union Parliament in January 1801; and Comprehending the Most Valuable Part of the Late Mr. Anderson's History of Commerce . . . (London, 1805), IV.
Miller, *Treaties,* II	Hunter Miller, ed., *Treaties and International Acts of the United States of America* (Washington, 1931), II.
"Minutes of the S.U.M."	MS minutes of the Society for Establishing Useful Manufactures, City of Paterson, New Jersey, Plant Management Commission, Successors to the Society for Establishing Useful Manufactures.
Mitchell, *Hamilton*	Broadus Mitchell, *Alexander Hamilton* (New York, 1957–1962).
Moreau de St. Méry, *Loix et Constitutions des Colonies Françoises*	Mederic Louis Elie Moreau de St. Méry, *Loix et Constitutions des Colonies Françoises de l'Amérique sous le Vent* (Paris, 1784–1790).
Morris, *Diary of the French Revolution*	Gouverneur Morris, *A Diary of the French Revolution,* ed. by Beatrix Cary Davenport (Boston, 1939).
Pennsylvania Archives, 2nd ser., IV	*Pennsylvania Archives,* 2nd ser., IV (n.p., 1876).
PRO: F.O., or PRO: C.O.	Transcripts or photostats from the Public Record Office of Great Britain deposited in the Library of Congress.
PRO: F.O., or PRO: C.O. (Great Britain)	Public Record Office of Great Britain.
"Reynolds Pamphlet"	Alexander Hamilton, *Observations on Certain Documents Contained*

in No. V and VI of "The History of the United States for the Year 1796," in which the Charge of Speculation against Alexander Hamilton, Late Secretary of the Treasury, is Fully Refuted. Written by Himself (Philadelphia: Printed for John Fenno, by John Bioren, 1797).

Saintoyant, *La Colonisation Française pendant la Révolution* — J. Saintoyant, *La Colonisation Française pendant la Révolution, 1789–1799* (Paris, 1930).

Setser, *Commercial Reciprocity* — Vernon G. Setser, *The Commercial Reciprocity Policy of the United States, 1774–1829* (Philadelphia, 1937).

Simcoe Papers — E. A. Cruikshank, ed., *The Correspondence of Lieut. Governor John Graves Simcoe, with Allied Documents Relating to His Administration of the Government of Upper Canada* (Toronto, 1923–1931).

1 *Stat.* — *The Public Statutes at Large of the United States of America* (Boston, 1845).

6 *Stat.* — *The Public Statutes at Large of the United States of America* [Private Statutes] (Boston, 1856).

Turner, "Correspondence of French Ministers" — Frederick J. Turner, ed., "Correspondence of the French Ministers to the United States, 1791–1797," *Annual Report of the American Historical Association for the Year 1903* (Washington, 1904), II.

IV. INDECIPHERABLE WORDS

Words or parts of words which could not be deciphered because of the illegibility of the writing or the mutilation of the manuscript have been indicated as follows:

1. ⟨-----⟩ indicates illegible words with the number of dashes indicating the estimated number of illegible words.
2. Words or letters in broken brackets indicate a guess as to what the words or letters in question may be. If the source of the words or letters within the broken brackets is known, it has been given a note.

V. CROSSED-OUT MATERIAL IN MANUSCRIPTS

Words or sentences crossed out by a writer in a manuscript have been handled in one of the three following ways:

1. They have been ignored, and the document or letter has been printed in its final version.
2. Crossed-out words and insertions for the crossed-out words have been described in the notes.
3. When the significance of a manuscript seems to warrant it, the crossed-out words have been retained, and the document has been printed as it was written.

VI. TEXTUAL CHANGES AND INSERTIONS

The following changes or insertions have been made in the letters and documents printed in these volumes:

1. Words or letters written above the line of print (for example, 9th) have been made even with the line of print (9th).
2. Punctuation and capitalization have been changed in those instances where it seemed necessary to make clear the sense of the writer. A special effort has been made to eliminate the dash, which was such a popular eighteenth-century device.
3. When the place or date, or both, of a letter or document does not appear at the head of that letter or document, it has been inserted in the text in brackets. If either the place or date at the head of a letter or document is incomplete, the necessary additional material has been added in the text in brackets. For all but the best known localities or places, the name of the colony, state, or territory has been added in brackets at the head of a document or letter.

4. In calendared documents, place and date have been uniformly written out in full without the use of brackets. Thus "N. York, Octr. 8, '99" becomes "New York, October 8, 1799." If, however, substantive material is added to the place or date in a calendared document, such material is placed in brackets. Thus "Oxford, Jan. 6" becomes "Oxford [Massachusetts] January 6 [1788]."
5. When a writer made an unintentional slip comparable to a typographical error, one of the four following devices has been used:
   a. It has been allowed to stand as written.
   b. It has been corrected by inserting either one or more letters in brackets.
   c. It has been corrected without indicating the change.
   d. It has been explained in a note.
6. Because the symbol for the thorn was archaic even in Hamilton's day, the editors have used the letter "y" to represent it. In doing this they are conforming to eighteenth-century manuscript usage.

THE PAPERS OF ALEXANDER HAMILTON

1792

From Tobias Lear[1]

United States, 1st Novr. 1792.

By the Presidents' command T. Lear has the honor to return to the Secretary of the Treasury, the authenticated copy of the Contract for the last Loan made in Holland, which has been submitted to the president; [2] & to inform the Secretary, that as soon as he shall have prepared the form of the ratification, the President will execute it.

T. Lear.
S. P. U S.

LC, George Washington Papers, Library of Congress.

1. Lear, a native of Portsmouth, New Hampshire, and a graduate of Harvard, was Washington's secretary.

2. See H to George Washington, October 31, 1792.

From Thomas Smith[1]

[*Philadelphia*] *November 1, 1792.* Forwards information required by the Senate order of May 7, 1792.[2]

LC, RG 53, Pennsylvania State Loan Office, Letter Book, 1790–1794, Vol. "615-P," National Archives.

1. Smith was commissioner of loans for Pennsylvania.

2. See "Treasury Department Circular," September 13, 1792. For the Senate order, see "Treasury Department Circular to the Collectors of the Customs," August 31, 1792.

To Joseph Whipple[1]

[*Philadelphia, November 1, 1792.* On November 30, 1792, Whipple wrote to Hamilton: "I have to acknowledge the receipt of your letter of the 1st. instant." *Letter not found.*]

1. Whipple was collector of customs at Portsmouth, New Hampshire.

To Otho H. Williams[1]

Treasury Department
November 1st. 1792

Sir

The Post of to day brought me your letter of the 29th of October, which I immediately communicated to the President, and hasten to make known to you his consent to your undertaking the voyage recommended to you. It is not doubted that due care will previously be taken to secure the proper management of the public business in your absence.

My most sincere and cordial wishes for the restoration of your health will accompany you.

With great consideration & esteem I remain Sir Your obed servant
Alex Hamilton

Otho H Williams Esqr

ALS, Maryland Historical Society, Baltimore.

1. Williams was collector of customs at Baltimore.

To Thomas Jefferson

Treasury Department
November 2d. 1792

The Secretary of the Treasury presents his respects to the Secretary of State; incloses a contract for a loan lately concluded which has been submitted to the President and approved.[1] It is now transmitted in order that a ratification in the usual form may be prepared and executed.

AL, Thomas Jefferson Papers, Library of Congress.

1. See H to George Washington, October 31, 1792, and Tobias Lear to H, November 1, 1792.

From Gouverneur Morris[1]

Paris 2d. November 1792

Dear Sir

I sent you on the twenty fifth of September my Correspondence with Mr. Short respecting the Debt of the United States to this Country. I now transmit a Letter from Mr. Le Brun[2] with my Answer of the twenty seventh and twenty eighth of September which were not forwarded with my other Correspondence on that Subject to Mr. Jefferson. It is not necessary to make thereon any Comment.

[ENCLOSURE]

Pierre Henri Hélène Marie Lebrun-Tondu to Gouverneur Morris[3]

Paris le 27. Septembre 1792.
L'an ler. de la Republique.

J'ai reçu, Monsieur, la lettre que vous m'avez fait l'honneur de m'écrire le 20. de ce mois, pour m'annoncer que les difficultés élevées à la Haye par M. Short sur le païement de seize cent vingt cinq mille florins de Banque avoient été applanies le 9. du courant, et que vous espérez qu'il ne résultera aucon inconvénient d'un délai de quelques jours.[4]

Après avoir réfléchi sur le motif qui vous a déterminé à donner votre assentiment au païement de la somme ci-dessus, je juge, Monsieur, que vous n'êtes fondé ni en justice ni en raison à vous refuser de faire tenir à notre disposition à Philadelphie les quatre cent mille Dollars nécessaires pour l'approvisionnement de nos Colonies.[5] Il me

LC, Gouverneur Morris Papers, Library of Congress.

1. Morris had been appointed United States Minister Plenipotentiary to France in January, 1792.

2. Pierre Henri Hélène Marie Lebrun-Tondu, French Minister of Foreign Affairs from August 12, 1792, to June 2, 1793. See enclosures.

3. LS, Columbia University Libraries.

4. For the problem concerning the payment of the installment due on the French debt in the summer of 1792, see the correspondence between Morris and William Short enclosed in Morris to H, September 25, 1792. See also Short to H, September 25, 1792.

5. This reference by Lebrun concerns the plan to use money owed France by the United States as payment on the French debt for the purchase of supplies

for the relief of Santo Domingo. For the background of these advances, see Jean Baptiste de Ternant to H, September 21, 1791, February 21, March 8, 10, August 22, 1792; H to Ternant, September 21, 1791, February 22, March 8, August 22, 1792; Short to H, December 28, 1791, January 26, April 22, 25, May 14, June 28, August 6, 1792; H to Short, April 10, 1792.

The proposal to use the debt owed France by the United States for the relief of Santo Domingo had been advanced as early as October, 1791, and in March, 1792, the Assembly authorized the sum of six million livres for aid to Santo Domingo, but this decree was not implemented to involve the American debt (*Archives Parlementaires*, XL, 577–78). On June 26, 1792, however, the French Assembly voted the sum of four million livres "imputables sur la dette americaine" to be used for the purchase of supplies for the relief of Santo Domingo and authorized the French Ministry to open negotiations with the United States Minister in France (*Archives Parlementaires*, XLV, 594). Before this decree, in March, 1792, the United States had agreed to the request of Jean Baptiste de Ternant, French Minister to the United States, to make advances on the French debt for the purchase of supplies for Santo Domingo, even though Ternant had no formal authorization from the French government on this matter. H and Ternant worked out an agreement by which the sum of four hundred thousand dollars would be advanced to the French Minister at stated intervals during 1792. See Ternant to H, March 8, 10, 1792; H to Ternant, March 8, 1792.

For two months after the passage of the June 26 decree the French Ministry made no attempt to negotiate with Morris. On August 16 he wrote to Jefferson that "the minister of the marine, altho' authorized to treat with me for Supplies to the colony of St. Domingo, has done nothing in that affair. Two ministers have occupied that place since the Decree. Each has given me various rendezvous, but neither has appeared at the time and place. . . ." See Morris to Jefferson, August 16, 1792, printed as an enclosure to Jefferson to H, October 31, 1792. On August 29, however, Morris was summoned to an interview with Lebrun, Gaspard Monge, the Minister of Marine, and Etienne Clavière, Minister of Finance, "at the Hôtel of foreign Affairs. They wish me to enter into a Contract to furnish $400,000 in America for the Use of St. Domingo. I shew them many reasons why I cannot and among others tell them that I am not authoriz'd to treat with them. This touches them unpleasantly. I add that I will write and recommend the Matter strongly to the Ministers of the United States but that is not what they want. Clavière is much vexed (Morris, *Diary of the French Revolution*, II, 518). In a letter to Jefferson dated August 30, 1792, Morris wrote as follows concerning the ministers' proposal:

"A few Days since Mr Monge the present ⟨M⟩inister of the Marine desir'd an Interview and at our Meeting ⟨pres⟩ented me a regular Contract for Payment of 800000 Dollars as being Equivalent to the 4,000,000 ₶ of livres which the Assembly ⟨had⟩ appropriated as abovemention'd. I will not trouble you with the Conversation because it ended in a Request on his Part to me⟨et⟩ Mr Lebrun . . . and Mr Claviere. . . . This Meeting took Place yester⟨day⟩ by their Appointment. The same form of Agreement was ag⟨ain⟩ produced and Mr Claviere who was principal Spokesman men⟨tioned⟩ my signing it as a Thing of Course. I told him that I had been authorized to settle with the late Government the Exchange of one Half of that Sum already paid and paying on this very Account. He spoke of such Settlement as the easiest thing in the World and advancd on the Subject exactly those Principles which Mr Short had refusd to be govern'd by; and rejected as visionary those which Mr Short had stated as just, and which I think ⟨are⟩ reasonable and right. The great object however was to get the M⟨oney,⟩ and *Congress* was to fix the Exchange. I told them (which is very ⟨true)⟩ that I felt a very sincere Desire to furnish Aid to that unhappy Colony and had done every Thing in my Power to comply with ⟨the⟩ Wish of the Legislature in that Respect but in Vain. That at last our Bankers in Holland being extremely anxious to discharge ⟨t⟩hemselves of the large Sums which had for Months been lying ⟨in⟩ their Hands, Their own Commissaries of the Treasury being also ⟨des⟩irous to receive, Mr Short (to whom the Management of that business had been committed by the United States) being also ⟨so⟩licitous that the Payments should be made, I had desired him ⟨to⟩ place in the Hands of the Bankers named by the Commissaries ⟨a⟩n Equivalent of 6000000 of livres by which Means the Installments of our Debt already due were overpaid. That of Course ⟨a⟩ny Advances now made must be on Account of those Installments ⟨w⟩hich are to become due hereafter. That I have no Instructions ⟨re⟩specting them, for Reasons I had already assign'd, and that of ⟨con⟩sequences if I should enter into the Agreement they wish'd I ⟨sho⟩uld probably be blamed for exceeding the Line prescribd to me. ⟨That⟩ there remain'd however another Point worthy of their Attention ⟨whi⟩ch was that my Agreement would be in itself void because I ⟨ha⟩d no Powers to treat with the present Government. It follow'd ⟨ther⟩efore that the Ministers of the United States would feel them⟨se⟩lves as much at Liberty as if Nothing had been done and act according to their own Ideas of the Object distinctly from m⟨y⟩ Engagements; that it would be equally usefully to them, and more proper in me, to state the whole Matter to you in the first Instance, and that I would add my earnest Request to mak⟨e⟩ the desired Payment. This however did not at all suit th⟨eir⟩ Ideas. Mr. Claviere made many Observations on the Nature of ou⟨r⟩ Debt and the Manner in which it had accrued. He said th⟨at⟩ the United States would certainly act in a different Manner towards the present Government than the Monarchs of Europe did. That it was impossible I should have any Difficulty if I inclin'd to do what they ask'd, and then concluded by asking me peremptorily whether I would or would not. His Language & Manner was such as naturally to excite some little Indignation, altho I could pardon much to a Man whose Stockjobbing Life had not much qualified him for a Station in which Delicacy of Manner and Expression are almost essential; Yet I could not submit to an Indignity in my Person towards the Country I repre⟨sent.⟩ I told him therefore that I did not understand what he meant to say. My Countenance I believe spoke the Rest of my Sentiment a⟨nd l⟩ed him to say in Explanation that it was necessary for them to ⟨h⟩ave some positive Engagement because otherwise they must make ⟨pro⟩vision for the Service from another Source, and then he again ⟨exp⟩rest his Conviction that the United States would recognize them, ⟨an⟩d at any Rate would not disavow the Engagements which I might make. I told him that it was not proper for me (a ⟨Serva⟩nt) to pretend to decide on what would be the Opinion of my ⟨Mas⟩ters. That I should wait their Orders, and obey them when ⟨recei⟩v'd. That the present Government might collect my Senti⟨me⟩nts from my Conduct. That I could not possibly take on me ⟨to ju⟩dge Questions of such Magnitude. That I would do every⟨thing⟩ I could with Propriety: and again repeated my offer which ⟨they⟩ would not listen to, and I left them not a little displeased ⟨if I⟩ may judge from Appearances by no Means equivocal." (ALS, RG 59, Despatches from United States Ministers to France, 1789–1869, June 17, 1792–March 7, 1794, National Archives.)

An exchange of letters between Morris and Lebrun followed Morris's refusal, culminating in the United States Minister's threat to leave France. Although Morris's departure was averted by a conciliatory statement from Lebrun, the French Ministry continued to press its plan for the payment on behalf of Santo Domingo. On September 19 and 27 Morris transmitted to

semble, Monsieur, qu'il y a une contradiction évidente dans la manière dont vous envisager ce dernier objet qui ne différe en rien du premier. Les deux sont les mêmes pour nous. J'ai l'honneur de vous observer, que dans aucun cas vous ne pouviez vous dispenser de faire à M. Short remplir son engagement pour les quatre cent mille Dollars, puisque, de votre aveu, il a agi par votre impulsion pour les seize cent vingt cinq mille florins de Banque.

Vous connoissez, Monsieur, les besoins de nos Colonies et tous les titres que nous avons pour reclamer l'assistance d'un peuple à qui nous sommes unis d'amitié et par principe, et pour la prospérité de qui nous faisons toujours des voeux les plus sincères. Toutes ces considérations devroient être d'un grand poids auprès du Ministre des Etats-unis, à qui une formalité d'etiquette ou des pouvoirs un peu moins, ou un peu plus étendus ne devroient par interdire la faculté d'agir, surtout lorsqu'il s'agit de remplir une obligation aussi

---

Jefferson copies of his correspondence with Lebrun on the matter and stated his views of the Ministry's plan: "I had good Reason to beleive that a private Speculation was at the Bottom of the Proposals made to me, and the extreme Urgency which was exhibited by one of the Conferees, who had been designated to me as concerned therein, tended not a little to confirm the Information I had receivd. The Wrath excited by the Unwillingness on my Part to jump over all the Bounds of my Powers and Instructions, did by no means lessen, but came in Support of the same Idea. Since that Period I have been asked by a Person who said he was offered a Bill drawn by the Government her⟨e⟩ on the Treasury of the United States, whether such Bill would be paid. I exprest my Surprize there at, and was told that ⟨this⟩ Bill would be for the Sum decreed by the Assembly to be employd in purchasing Supplies for the Colony of St Domingo. I observd thereon, that it seemed a strange Procedure either to sell or buy such a Bill: because the Vender could only employ the Money in Amer⟨ica,⟩ and of Course need not risque a Draft; and the Purchaser, who mu⟨st⟩ make the Expenditure thereof, could not I suppos'd find his Account in the Transaction. This led to an Explanation. The Bill was to be paid for in Assignats at Par, six or nine Months hence, and the Produce was to be employ'd in purchasing Manufactures suitab⟨le⟩ to the Colony in this Country. I told the Person who applied to me that I did not think this would be consider'd in America as falling within the Decree, and that no good Reason could be assign'd for paying under great *Disadvantages* in Philadelphia, what could be paid with great *Advantage* in Paris, when the Sum paid was not to be expended in the *United States* but in *France*. At length the true Object of this Application to me came out. I discover'd that it was meerly a Scheme of Speculation ⟨to⟩ be carried into Effect if I could be induced to recommend the Payment, under what was known to be a favorite Idea ⟨w⟩ith me, viz the expending *in America* what we owe to France; *for the Support of the Colony of S Domingo*. As my Concurrence could not be hop'd for, I beleive that the Plan is abandon'd, but perhaps it is only abandon'd in Appearance" (Morris to Jefferson, September 27, 1792, ALS, RG 59, Despatches from United States Ministers to France, 1789–1869, June 17, 1792–March 7, 1794, National Archives).

See also Morris, *Diary of the French Revolution*, II, 519–31, 542–47.

solemnellement contractée et de donner à nos possessions en Amérique des secours très-urgents dans l'état où elles se trouvent.

Le Ministre des affaires étrangères.
Le Brun

M. Morris

[ENCLOSURE]

Gouverneur Morris to Pierre Henri Hélène Marie Lebrun-Tondu[6]

Paris le 28 Septembre 1792.

Monsieur Le Brun
Monsieur

J'ai reçu hier ausoir le lettre que vous m'avez faite l'honneur de m'ecrire le 27. Il me semble que dans la multitude des affaires qui vous occupent, vous avez oublié Monsieur, ceque j'ai eu l'honneur de vous mander le premier du Courant sur le paiement qui vient de s'effectuer à Amsterdam; puisque vous supposez que Monseur Short à agi par mon impulsion. Au contraire, Monsieur, dans tout cela je n'ai fait que de me conformer au desirs de Monsieur Short lui même. Car quoi que ce paiement convenu avec Messieurs les Commissaires de la Tresorerie le six aout, n'ait été effectué que le cinq de September, il n'avoit été cependant reglé que d'apres les demandes de Monsieur Short. Juger d'apres cela Monsieur, s'il y a lieu de croire qu'il déféreroit à un arrangement pris sans son aveu. Faites attention, aussi, je vous prie Monsieur que dans le Cas, que la totalité de la somme de quatre millions eut été tenue à votre Disposition à Philadelphie, le paiement à Amsterdam auroit été d'autant plus faible— Au reste si vous le jugez a propos, je ferai part à Monsieur Short de la reclamation que vous venez de faire à l'égard des quatre cent mille Dollars; Et loin le croire qu'il y ait une difference entre cette somme et celle déja payée à Amsterdam, je trouve comme je viens d'avoir l'honneur de vous exposer, Monsieur, qui il y a même identité puisque l'une devoit toujours faire partie de l'autre.

Depuis que j'ai eu l'honneur de vous ecrire sur ce sujet j'ai encore eu de nouvelles preuves que notre Gouvernement ne veut pas que je me méle de cette affaire, car Monsieur Short m'a annoncé avoir encore reçu des instructions de Monsieur Hamilton à cet égard.[7]

6. LC, Governeur Morris Papers, Library of Congress.
7. See H to Short, June 14, 1792.

Dans cet etat de choses tout se que je puis faire c'est d'appuyer aupres de notre Gouvernement les démarches du Ministre de la france. Les paiemens qui se font actuellement á Philadelphie, sur les instances de Monsieur Ternant, nous donnent la certitude, Monsieur, que notre Gouvernment fera tour les efforts possibles pour le Soulagement de votre Colonie. L'emploi de la somme dont il s'agit doit etre fait en Amerique non seulement d'apres les propres Termes du Decret mais par la nature même des Choses, qui en obligeant la france de tirer de l'etranger des Subsistances et du bois de Construction pour elle même, la force imperativement de prendre chez nous les fournitures de ses Colonies occidentales: il me semble donc, Monsieur, qu'on ne risque rien en s'addressant pour cet objet au Gouvernement des Etats Unis, puisque dans le cas ou il lui seroit impossible de fournir à votre ministre la somme plus ou moins grande qu'exigent les besoins de la Colonie, il pourra toujours y faire face par les mêmes moyens qui sont mis en usage pour procurer des fournitures à la Metropole.

From William Short[1]

The Hague Nov. 2. 1792

sir

I had the honor of recieving yesterday your letter of the 28th. of August. Being desirous from its nature to answer it in the speediest manner possible, I do it immediately (without waiting for the account, for which I wrote yesterday to the commissioners,[2] in the instant of recieving your letter) this day's English post being the last which will be in time for the New-york packet of Wednesday next.

You inform me that the accounting officers of the treasury here represented to you that a regular account from me of the monies which I have recieved & those which have been paid by my order, will be requisite in the adjustment of the accounts of the commis-

ALS, letterpress copy, William Short Papers, Library of Congress.

1. Short was United States Minister Resident at The Hague. Since 1790 he had been in charge of the reimbursement of the foreign debt and had carried on negotiations in Europe for contracting new loans for the United States.

2. Short to Willink, Van Staphorst, and Hubbard, November 1, 1792 (ALS, letterpress copy, William Short Papers, Library of Congress).

sioners. You observe that no account of the monies which I have recieved has been rendered lower down than the 24th of Sep. 1789.

The only monies I have recieved were my salary & the contingencies of stationery postage &c. paid me, as to the other foreign agents, by order of the Secretary of State, who directed me, as I suppose he did them, also to transmit to his department a regular acct. of these monies, terminating annually on the 1st. of July. His first letter to me on the subject,[3] informed me that the salary of Chargé des affaires was raised to take place from July 1. 1790. & directed me to state my acct down to that day, which was accordingly done & transmitted. After the 1st. of July 1791. my account was stated in like manner & sent from Paris in the beginning of October following.[4] On my return to Paris in Jany last I recieved a letter from the Sec. of State informing me that my letter inclosing that acct & to which I had referred in subsequent letters, had not been recieved & desiring me to send it again & in future to do it by duplicates immediately after the 1st. of July.[5] Accordingly I immediately transcribed the acct & transmitted it by two separate conveyances in Jany last. In like manner I stated my acct. up to the 1st. of July last & transmitted it by three separate conveyances to the department of State in the months of July & August. This account contained the sums paid for the two golden medals ordered by the same department for Mess. de la Luzerne & de Moustier[6]—although no part of the money passed through my hands—the several artists having been paid by M. Grand[7] & he re-imbursed by my bill on the bankers at Amsterdam. The medal with its chain for

3. Jefferson to Short, July 26, 1790 (LC, Papers of the Continental Congress, National Archives).

4. ALS, letterpress copy, William Short Papers, Library of Congress. This letter is dated October 6, 1791.

5. Jefferson to Short, January 5, 1792 (LC, RG 59, Diplomatic and Consular Instructions of the Department of State, 1791–1801, January 23, 1791–August 16, 1793, National Archives).

6. On April 30, 1790, Jefferson wrote to Short: "It has become necessary to determine on a Present proper to be given to Diplomatic Characters on their taking Leave of us; and it is concluded that a Medal and Chain of Gold will be the most convenient" (LC, Papers of the Continental Congress, National Archives). Short had been ordered to supervise the engraving of these medals in France. Anne César, Chevalier de La Luzerne, and Eleanor François Elie, Comte de Moustier, had both served as French ministers to the United States.

7. Ferdinand Le Grand, the Paris banker who handled the accounts of France.

De Moustier was delivered to himself—that for de la Luzerne, to M. de Montmorin[8] as appears by their respective letters written to me. The dye was left with the engraver to be taken care of with the others belonging to the U.S. & placed at the disposition of M. Morris.[9]

Before I quit this head, I should repeat perhaps what I formerly mentioned to you—that M. Jefferson on his departure from Paris left with me bills of exchange to the amount of I think 66,000 ₶. This was destined to a particular object with which you are acquainted.[10] He expected it would be immediately applied & therefore wished me to be the instrument instead of deposing it in a banker's hands, to avoid the commission. When the term of these bills arrived, finding less probability of their being immediately applied & not chusing to keep by me such a sum at my risk in an house which was robbed regularly two or three times a year, I gave the bills to M. Grand to recieve their amount & hold it appropriated to the object in question. It remains still in his hands having never been called for. I wrote more than once respecting it on finding the depreciation commencing—but never recieved an answer.[11] It remains

8. Armand Marc, Comte de Montmorin Saint-Herem, who had served as French Minister of Foreign Affairs from July 15, 1789, to November 27, 1791.

9. Gouverneur Morris.

10. On July 18, 1787, the Continental Congress authorized Jefferson to take any steps necessary to redeem American captives at Algiers and instructed the Board of Treasury "to provide ways and means for enabling Mr. Jefferson to defray the said expences, either by remitting money from hence or by a Credit in Europe" (*JCC,* XXXII, 364–65). The Board of Treasury accordingly instructed Willink, Van Staphorst, and Hubbard, the bankers of the United States in Amsterdam, to honor Jefferson's "drafts to the amount of 30,000 florins for the purpose of executing a certain act of Congress of the 18th. of July 1787" (Boyd, *Papers of Thomas Jefferson,* XV, 41). On October 12, 1787, "On a report of the board of treasury in consequence of the Act of 18 July.

"*Resolved,* That the balance of the appropriation for the Barbary treaties of the 14 february 1785 not hitherto applied to that Object be and it is hereby constituted a fund for redeeming the American captives now at Algiers and that the same be for this purpose subject to the direction of the Minister of the United States at the court of Versailles.

"That the Acts of Congress of the 14 february 1785 and such part of the resolves of the 18th. July 1787 as directs provision to be made for the above object be and they are hereby repealed." (*JCC,* XXXIII, 664.)

See *JCC,* XXXIII, 441–43, for the "Report of Board of Treasury on money to redeem captives."

11. Short is mistaken. Jefferson wrote to him on this subject on January 23, 1791 (ALS, letterpress copy, Thomas Jefferson Papers, Library of Congress). Short acknowledged receipt of this letter in his letter to Jefferson of March 30, 1791 (LC, RG 59, Despatches from the United States Ministers to France, 1789–1869, January 16, 1791–August 6, 1792, National Archives).

now to be considered whether you would chuse to recieve it in its present depreciated state—or wait for the change of circulating medium in France.

These are all the monies within my present recollection which have ever been at my disposition except those which you have from time to time directed me to have paid and of the loans made by me. These I come now to speak of & which I have ever considered as under totally different circumstances. I have made a point of never allowing one single farthing of it to pass through my hands & of course had no account to keep respecting it. I knew the commissioners were in direct correspondence with the department of the treasury & they told me they transmitted their accounts regularly. I therefore did not see that there would be any occasion for my intervention. It appeared to me from the nature of the business & from the part I took in it that there would be no chasm in its final & complete adjustment, by my being left out of the question—nor indeed do I see how I could have entered into the account, as no part of the money passed through my hands, without rendering it less simple than at present.

The loans as made, which have been regularly announced to you, shew the cash which the U.S. have in the hands of the commissioners—the payments they make, & which they state in their accts of course, if properly vouched, complete the acct. it seems to me, & shew whether there is error. The payments made by my directions which I have transmitted to the commissioners as recieved from you, are the bills which you have directed to be drawn on them—the interest accruing on the loans at Amsterdam—& the debt to France. The two first carry their own proofs in themselves & nothing that I could do could add to them—the proofs of the third consist in the reciepts or bills which they recieve from the French treasury & which they hold, & transmit to you, as I imagine, doubles.

The commissioners of the treasury formerly gave me a copy of the sums they have recieved from the commissioners & which is as conformable to one the commissioners gave me last winter at Amsterdam. No payment has been since made by them except the 1625m florins agreed for by M. Morris as already often mentioned to you.[12] This conformity of the accts. gave me all the presumption I had occasion for, of its justness—but as the commissioners had other

12. See Short to H, August 30, September 25, October 27, 1792.

payments to make also on public acct. which were not within my control, such as the monies paid to other foreign agents & the bills from America whose amount were unknown to me, I could no[t] ascertain the accuracy of the total of their transactions—which could be done only at the original source to which all the branches of the acct. were carried, the Treasury.

This has been the light in which I have ever recieved the subject & which prevented me from considering myself as involved in the comptability of the business. Your letter of yesterday however makes me fear you have viewed it differently—as you say my account will be considered as an essential guide in the settlement which is contemplated. Should the acct. for which I have written to Amsterdam be not adequate to this purpose (& I own I do not see how it can be more complete than that which I imagine the commissioners send regularly) I must beg you Sir to inform me in what it shall be defective, & to give me your orders fully on the business, having it above everything at heart to give you the most perfect satisfaction in every business you confide to me & particularly one of this kind. I have so full a reliance on its having been properly transacted by the commissioners & of their having taken all the proper vouchers, that I have no objection to be placed in the account, although I did not consider myself as any thing more, as to the payments, than the chanel of your orders for the purpose.

If it has been your expectation & is still your desire that I should enter into this kind of comptability I beg you to be so good as to say in what way you desire it & what kind of an account you wish me to transmit you. I hope it will not be your wish that I do actually recieve the money from the commissioners & pay it to its several destinations. I think I mentioned to you from the beginning, when you ordered the first payment to France, how inadequate I was to that kind of manutention, & how sollicitous I was to be excused from it.

I have already transmitted to you the acct. of the Antwerp payments as sent to me by M. de Wolfe.[13] The duplicate of the reciepts he took from the French agent were forwarded to me at Paris. I left them with M Morris, that he might compare them with the acct to be recieved from the commissaries. The part remitted by bills of

13. John Charles Michael de Wolf. See Short to H, August 6, 1792.

exchange like that paid in the same way from Amsterdam, is justified in like manner, by the conformity of the commissaries acct. For greater certainty I shall send this letter by duplicate & it shall be followed immediately by the acct. expected from Amsterdam—repeating my prayer, that if it should leave you unsatisfied with respect to my part however inconsiderable or if your satisfaction should not be complete in every respect, that you would be so good as to mention it, & enable me to procure the eclaircissement, which may be necessary. I have the honor to be most respectfully, Sir, your most obedt & most humble servt. W Short

The Honble Alexander Hamilton Secretary of the Treasury

From William Channing, John S. Dexter, and Jeremiah Olney[1]

[*Providence, November 3, 1792.* On December 12, 1792, Hamilton wrote to Channing, Dexter, and Olney: "I have yet to reply to your letter of the 3d. ultimo." *Letter not found.*]

1. Channing was United States attorney for the District of Rhode Island; Dexter was supervisor of the revenue for Rhode Island; Olney was collector of customs at Providence.

From Henry Knox

[*Philadelphia, November 3, 1792.* In a letter to Anthony Wayne, dated November 24, 1792, Knox referred to "my letter of the 3d. instant to the Secretary of the Treasury."[1] *Letter not found.*]

Knopf, *Wayne*, 140.

1. Knox's letter concerned directions to be given to Robert Elliot and Elie Williams, Army contractors, for an advance supply of rations (Knox to George Washington, November 3, 1792, LS, George Washington Papers, Library of Congress).

To John F. Mercer[1]

Philadelphia Novr 3d 1792

Sir

The Post two days since, brought me your letter of the 16th of October.

I deemed it incumbent on me previous to a more particular notice of its contents to forward a copy of it, and of the documents which accompany it, as far as they regard your public discourses to Major Ross.

With due consideration I am Sir Your Obedt Servt A H

John F Mercer Esq
Annapolis

Copy, Hamilton Papers, Library of Congress.

1. Mercer was a member of the House of Representatives from Maryland. For background to this letter, see the introductory note to H to Mercer, September 26, 1792. See also H to David Ross, September 26, 1792; Ross to H, October 5–10, 1792; Mercer to H, October 16–28, 1792.

To David Ross[1]

Philadelphia Novr 3d 1792.

Sir

Two days since, I received a Letter from Mr Mercer dated the 16th of Octr in answer to mine of the 26 of September, to him. A Copy of his letter and of the documents accompanying it, as far as they regard his public Speeches, is herewith sent; in order that your comments, as to the facts which are in question, may enable me to judge what further Step I ought to take.

I remain with perfect consideration & esteem Sir your Obed Servt A H

David Ross Esq
Bladensburg Maryland

Copy, Hamilton Papers, Library of Congress.

1. Ross had served during the American Revolution as a major in Grayson's Additional Continental Regiment. After the war he had practiced law and managed his family's extensive estates in Frederick County. From 1786 to 1788 he was a delegate to the Continental Congress from Maryland.

For background to this letter, see the introductory note to H to John F. Mercer, September 26, 1792. See also H to Ross, September 26, 1792; Ross to H, October 5–10, 1792; Mercer to H, October 16–28, 1792; H to Mercer, November 3, 1792.

To Otho H. Williams

Treasury Department
November 3d. 1792

Sir

I received by the hands of Mr. Richmond your letter on the subject of the stock standing in your name on the public books.[1]

Though, according to the letter of the law, the prohibition to *dispose* appears to be retrospective as well as future, I am of opinion that it is consistent with sound legal construction to confine the latitude of the expression, so as to admit of the alienation and transfer of stock, which was previously owned.[2] A different supposition makes the law an invasion of the right of property previously acquired, possibly to the ruin of the party, or his exclusion from office, and could not be within the intention of the law-makers. Nor ought in my opinion, expressions merely general to be construed so as to produce such a consequence.

But in giving this opinion I ought to apprize you that it differs from that of the Attorney General,[3] which was sometime since taken at the request of another public officer.[4] I need not observe, that my opinion could not exempt you from any penalties which by the true construction of the law, if different from mine, would follow.

With much consideration I am Sir Your obedient servant

Alex Hamilton

Otho H Williams Esqr
Collector &c

ALS, Maryland Historical Society, Baltimore.

1. Williams to H, October 30, 1792. Christopher Richmond, Williams's agent, had delivered this letter.

2. See Williams to H, October 30, 1792, and Edmund Randolph to H, June 26, 1792.

3. See Randolph to H, June 26, 1792.

4. William Heth, collector of customs at Bermuda Hundred, Virginia. See H to Heth, June 26, 1792.

From Francisco de Miranda[1]

Paris Novr. the 4th. 1792.
the 1t. year of the Republic.

My dear friend,

The affairs & Success of france take a happy turn in our favour. I mean in favour of our dear Country America, from the North to the South. The official Communications from the new appointed Minister of france,[2] & the Information our friend Col. Smith shall give to you, will Shew how things are grown ripe & into maturity for the Execution of those grand & beneficial projects we had in Contemplation, when in our Conversation at New Yorck the love of our Country exalted our minds with those Ideas, for the sake of unfortunate Columbia.

I am sincerely yours M.

Copy, Academia Nacional de la Historia, Caracas, Venezuela.

1. For Miranda's earlier career and his friendship with H, see H to Miranda, January–July, 1784, and the introductory note to H to Miranda, November 23, 1784.

After leaving New York, where in 1784 he had met H, Miranda in 1785 went to Europe and toured the Continent with William S. Smith, John Adams's son-in-law. In 1789 he visited England where he made an unsuccessful attempt to secure the British ministry's support for his plans for a revolution in Spain's Latin American colonies. Early in 1792 he went to France to place his proposals before that country's Revolutionary government. He met with some success in France, for he attracted the interest of Pierre Henri Hélène Marie Lebrun-Tondu, Minister of Foreign Affairs during the first months of the Convention, and Jean Pierre Brissot de Warville, leader of the Girondists and a member of both the Committee for the Constitution and the Diplomatic Committee during the opening days of the Convention. According to a later statement by William S. Smith, who had been in Paris in 1792, French officials at that time were drawing up plans for fomenting a revolution in the Spanish territories in South America. Included in such plans was a proposal that Miranda command an expeditionary force which would be supported by forty-five ships of the line (Ford, *Writings of Jefferson*, I, 216–17).

2. Edmond Charles Genet had served as translator in the French Office of Foreign Affairs during the American Revolution. In 1787 he was appointed secretary to the French Minister at St. Petersburg, and in October, 1789, he became chargé d'affaires at that post. Expelled from Russia because of his adherence to the French Constitution of 1791, he returned to Paris during the summer of 1792 and was appointed Minister Plenipotentiary to the United States. He did not arrive in the United States until April 8, 1793, for he was detained at Paris by the Girondists, who had hoped up until the time of the King's execution that the royal family might accompany Genet to the United States.

To the President and Directors of the Bank of the United States[1]

[*Philadelphia, November 5, 1792.* In a letter to the president and directors of the Bank of the United States on November 28, 1792, Hamilton referred to "my letter of the 5th Instant." *Letter not found.*]

1. Thomas Willing was president of the Bank of the United States.

Contract with James and Shoemaker[1]

[Philadelphia, November 5, 1792]

On behalf of Messrs. Nicholas Low and Abijah Hammond of New York,[2] I promise to pay to Messrs. James and Shoemaker or their order on demand such sums as may be advanced to John Campbell[3] by them or their Agents for any machinery tools or utensils for a Stocking Manufactory which shall be shipped by the said John Campbell or by his order per the Ship Glasgow from any part of Great Britain to the United States consigned either to the said Nicholas Low or Abijah Hammond or to the said James and Shoemaker and for the freight of the said articles and the passage money of any persons who shall be embarked on board the said Ship for the United States, being makers of such machinery or Manufacturers in the Stocking Branch, together with five per Cent Commission on the amount thereof provided the said sums do not exceed Eight hundred Pounds current money of Pensylvania.

Witness my hand at Philadelphia the fifth day of November 1792.

ADf, Hamilton Papers, Library of Congress.

1. The merchant firm of James and Shoemaker was located at 25 North Water Street in Philadelphia.

2. On October 12, 1792, Nicholas Low had been elected governor and Abijah Hammond a director of the Society for Establishing Useful Manufactures ("Minutes of the S.U.M.," 72).

3. On October 13, 1792, the directors of the society recorded the receipt of "a Letter from John Campbell of Philadelphia, proposing the establishment of a stocking manufactory." On the following day the directors "proceeded to Inquire into the business of the Stocking Weaving which was dismissed for the present" ("Minutes of the S.U.M.," 73).

To Thomas Jefferson

Treasury Department Novr. 5th. 1792.

Sir,

I have only considered the principal subject of the extracts from Mr. Morris's letters, which you did me the honor to send me,[1] namely the adjustment or liquidation of the payments to France, and am of Opinion, that the Idea which appears to be that of Mr. Morris is the safest now to be pursued vizt.—to ascertain the rate of exchange between Paris and Amsterdam, at each period of payment, as an eventual guide, and to leave the liquidation open till the completion of the entire reimbursement shall furnish an equitable rule, upon all the circumstances of the case. While the United States do not wish to profit by any disorder in the affairs of France, neither ought they to suffer any loss in consequence of it. As further payments have been suspended till further order, there will be time for further consideration, before the payments recommence.

The Accounts furnished by the French Treasury have been committed to the Comptroller, with direction to make a full and critical examination, and to prepare all statements, and documents, which may be necessary completely to enlighten Mr. Morris.

The affair of the payment of the debt due to the French officers has been arranged. In your absence from the Seat of Government I wrote a letter to Mr. Morris[2] on the subject of which the enclosed is a Copy.

With great respect, I have the honor to be, Sir, Your obedient servant. Alexander Hamilton.

The Secretary of State.

Copy, Columbia University Libraries; letterpress copy, Thomas Jefferson Papers, Library of Congress.

1. See Jefferson to H, October 31, 1792.
2. H to Gouverneur Morris, September 13, 1792.

To Thomas Pinckney[1]

Philadelphia November 5th 1792

The Secretary of the Treasury presents his respectful compliments to the Minister Plenipotentiary of the united States at the court of

Great Britain, requests the favour of his particular care of the enclosed letter to Messrs Willink & van Staphorst Amsterdam.[2]

L, in an unidentified handwriting, Pinckney Family Papers, Library of Congress.
1. This letter was enclosed in H to William Seton, November 5, 1792.
2. H to Willink and Van Staphorst, November 5, 1792.

To William Seton[1]

Treasury Department Novemb 5th 1792

Sir

Enclosed is a letter to our Ambassador at the Court of Great Britain[2] which I request you will please to forward by the November Packet as usual.

I am with great consideration Sir Your Obedt Servt

Alexander Hamilton

William Seton Esqr
New York

LS, The Andre deCoppet Collection, Princeton University Library.
1. Seton was cashier of the Bank of New York.
2. H to Thomas Pinckney, November 5, 1792.

To William Short

Treasury Department
November 5th, 1792.

Sir:

The last letter which I have had the pleasure of receiving from you is dated the 6th of August. By letters from Mr Morris to the Secretary of State, down to the 16th of that month, it appeared that he had, on the 6th, ordered a payment, to the French Treasury, of one million six hundred and twenty five thousand B. florins. But nothing is said which can enlighten me as to his opinion whether the last change in the affairs of France, namely the suspension of the King, ought to suspend further payments on account of the United States to the government of that country.[1] Hence, though I enter-

JCH Transcripts.
1. For the controversy concerning this payment, see the correspondence between Short and Gouverneur Morris enclosed in Morris to H, September 25, 1792. See also Short to H, September 25, 1792; Jefferson to H, October 31, 1792.

tain a persuasion, as mentioned in my letter of the 1st of October, a fourth copy of which is inclosed, that no further payments after that event will have been deemed proper, and, consequently that a considerable sum of money will have been left undisposed of in the hands of our Commissioners, yet the want of some certain indication on that point is a cause of perplexity to me.

The dispositions heretofore announced contemplated the payment of interest on the foreign debt to individuals only up to the end of the present year out of funds accruing in Europe, and render it possible that all others might be applied in payments to France. Yet, under present circumstances, to add, by remittances from this country, to the considerable funds which probably are already on hand there unemployed, and a part of which has been so long in that situation, would be too disadvantageous to the United States.

Upon the whole, I elect to forbear, till further advices, any remittances from hence, considering that on any emergency you will be able to procure either a temporary or permanent loan equal to the demand. On the 1st of January 1793 there will be due in Hollund 120000 florins for interest, on the 1st of February £30000 for interest and 100000 for premium, on the 1st of March 125000 for interest, on the first of June 470000 for interest and 1000000 for the first instalment of the 5000000 loan.[2]

For facing these engagements it appears adviseable that you endeavour to contract a loan for 2000000 of florins. In the present state of French affairs it is proper to postpone any further borrowing with a view to reimbursements there.

Should it appear, as I expect from your future advices, that there will remain moneys unapplied and subject to dispositions from hence, I shall take care so to regulate the drafts which may be made as to leave at your disposal at least a sufficient sum for paying the interest in January and February, so as to afford time for such further operations as may be requisite.

I am now anxious, as soon as possible, to adopt a regular plan for paying the interest on our foreign debt by remittances from this country. On full reflection I have concluded that the doing of it by means of bills of exchange is preferable to any other mode. But

2. This was the Holland loan of 1782. For a description of this loan, see Willink, Van Staphorst, and Hubbard to H, January 25, 1790, note 15.

for this purpose some auxiliary arrangement is necessary. Bills are not always to be had at the moment they are wanted. If I am to depend wholly on a casual supply I shall often be obliged to force the market or remit specie. To avoid being pressed at any time I have conceived that it would be eligible to adopt the following plan: To stipulate with some competent house for a *contingent* credit, equal to the sums payable for interest at the several periods, that is, the house to be obliged to furnish the sums when due, if required so to do, for a certain term of credit, say six months, upon the conditions of receiving, absolutely, a small premium, whether the money be called for or not, with a certain rate of interest if called for on the sum actually advanced, from the time of its being advanced to the time of its reimbursement.

Suppose the contract were made and the premium stipulated ½ per cent, the rate of interest five per cent, the operation of the plan would be as follows: On the first of January next there is a sum of 120000 florins payable, on account of interest. It would be in my option to remit the sum at the period or not. If I remitted it the contractor would then be entitled only to ½ per cent of the 120000 florins. If I remitted no part of it, he would be obliged to advance the money at the time it became due, and would be entitled to ½ per cent by way of premium, and at the rate of five per cent per annum on the 120000 florins from the time it was advanced to the time it was reimbursed, the term of reimbursement not to exceed six months. If I remitted a part but not the whole, he would be obliged to advance the residue, and would be entitled to ½ per cent premium on the entire sum, say 120000 florins and at the rate of five per cent per annum, as before, on *the sum actually advanced,* as that should happen to be. And so from period to period through the year.

I have supposed that the rate of premium and interest which have been mentioned would obtain the credit desired. And I will thank you, if it can be done, to effect the arrangement to begin after the 1st of June next. I should not wish it, in the first instance to extend beyond a year. Offers of a similar credit have been intimated to me from London, but, as the payments are to be made in Amsterdam, I deem it preferable to simplify the business by a direct operation.

I shall endeavor to engage the Bank of the United States to undertake the payment of our foreign interest, combining it with a plan for keeping our foreign exchange within certain determinate limits; a measure which will unite a moderate profit to the Bank with the advantage to trade of a steady course of exchange and to the government of a convenient and oeconomical mode of remitting its foreign interest. But some little time will be requisite to mature mens ideas on the subject.

With respectful consideration, I have the honor to be, Sir, Your obedt Servant Alexander Hamilton

William Short Esquire
Minister Resident from the United States, at
The Hague.

To Wilhem and Jan Willink, Nicholaas and Jacob Van Staphorst[1]

Triplicate

Treasury Department
Philadelphia Novr. 5. 1792.

Sir

I have to acknowledge the receipt of your letter of the 24th. of August last[2] enclosing an authenticated copy of the Contract for the last three million Loan, which Contract is now before the President for his ratification.[3] If it should be completed in the course of the day, it will be herewith transmitted; if not, it will be forwarded to you by the next opportunity.

Enclosed is a letter to Mr. Short which I request you will forward to him.[4] But if contrary to my expectation, Mr. Short should be absent from Holland, and it should appear from the State of the funds in your hands, that the sums in your possession would be insufficient to pay the Interest, which will fall due on the several Loans to the 1st. of February next ensuing inclusively, including one hundred thousand Guilders premium, I authorize you to open Mr. Shorts letter, and to adopt the arrangement therein proposed, in order that no deficiency may arise in regard to those payments.

With great consideration & esteem I am Gentlemen Your Obedt servant A Hamilton

P.S. The Presidents ratification of the Contract alluded to in the foregoing letter is herewith inclosed.

Messrs. Willinks & Van staphorsts.
Amsterdam

LS, Short Family Papers, Library of Congress.

1. The Willinks and Van Staphorsts were members of the banking firm of Willink, Van Staphorst, and Hubbard, the bankers of the United States in Amsterdam.

2. Letter not found.

3. See H to Washington, October 31, 1792; H to Jefferson, November 2, 1792.

4. H to Short, November 5, 1792.

From William Ellery[1]

Colles Office [Newport, Rhode Island]
Novr. 6th. 1792

Sir,

I have recd. your circular letter of the 12th of the last month, and will pay a due regard to the request contained in the first paragraph thereof, and to your opinion on the case stated in the second.

A Vessel bound to a foreign port is compelled by distress of weather to put into the port of Newport, and it is necessary in order to repair her, or to procure supplies for the crew; or because she has perishable articles on board that part of her cargo should be sold, is she liable to the tonnage duty? Or if a vessel bound to a foreign port should put into this port for an harbour, continue herein forty eight hours, and not dispose of any part of her cargo, would the tonnage duty in this case be demandable? Instances of the case last mentioned have occurred, and will probably again occurr. Please to favour me with an answer to these questions.

I am, Sir, Yr. most obedt. servant Wm Ellery Collector

A Hamilton Esqr
Secry Treasury

LC, Newport Historical Society, Newport, Rhode Island.

1. Ellery was collector of customs at Newport.

From Uriah Forrest[1]

Georgetown [Maryland] 7. Nov. 1792

Dear Sir:

Inclosed is the copy of what Mr. William Bayley lately gave Dr. Steuart to forward to the President of the United States in consequence as Steuart told Bayley of a letter from the President requesting it the Doctor having before mentioned to him the circumstances to which it alluded.[2] I only heard of it yesterday and sent today to Bayley who furnished me a copy he is a man of fair character and on no account would intentionally misrepresent but he not the most attentive and exact man. There is no doubt you are privy to and I dare say caused the application through the President yet no harm can arise from sending the copy.

I considered all that was said respecting your public Agency not worth any other regard than merely stating facts in conversation when it happened to be the subject which was very frequent during the rage of Electioneering. Because there are not three men of reputation even in the district where so much has been said who think ill of you and nothing is believed injurious to your Fame had there been a probability of your Character being any way affected you should have had the earliest information. I wish not to be mentioned in the business but there is one circumstance which may eventually be useful should Mr. Sterett[3] not return soon from Europe. He informed me that he had called with Colo. Mercer at your office when the Colo. applied for payment of a horse which he had killed during the war I think in Virginia. He related to me the conversation that passed and mr. mercers observation to him at leaving you. I am pretty certain I have the whole correct on my memory and if necessary will readily furnish it.

If there is any thing in which you can make me useful you will make me happy being with the greatest esteem & respect Dr. Sir yrs.[4]

Uriah Forrest

ALS, Hamilton Papers, Library of Congress.

1. Forrest, who had served as a delegate from Maryland to the Continental Congress in 1786 and 1787, was elected in 1792 to the House of Representatives as a Federalist.

For background to this letter, see the introductory note to H to John F. Mercer, September 26, 1792. See also H to Mercer, November 3, 1792; Mercer to H, October 16–28, 1792; H to David Ross, September 26, November 3, 1792; Ross to H, October 5–10, 1792.

2. For this enclosure, see H to Mercer, September 26, 1792, note 16.

3. Presumably Samuel Sterrett of Baltimore.

4. On the envelope of this letter, H wrote "Answered April 5, 1793 with thanks &c." H's reply has not been found.

From Tobias Lear

United States, November 7, 1792. Transmits "a statement of the administration of the funds appropriated to certain foreign purposes, as the same has been submitted to the President by the Secretary of State." [1]

LC, George Washington Papers, Library of Congress.

1. On November 3, 1792, Thomas Jefferson had submitted to the President two statements concerning funds appropriated for the State Department and an explanatory letter (LS, letterpress copy, Thomas Jefferson Papers, Library of Congress). The closing paragraph of the letter reads as follows: "I had presented to the auditor [Richard Harrison] the Statement No. 1. with the vouchers, and also the special accounts rendered by the several persons who have received these monies, but, on consideration, he thought himself not authorized, by any law, to proceed to their examination. I am, therefore, to hope, Sir, that authority may be given to the auditor, or some other person to examine the general account and vouchers of the Department of State, as well as to raise special accounts against the persons into whose hands the moneys pass, and to settle the same from time to time on behalf of the public."

The problems in settling accounts for transactions abroad, as well as the secret nature of some of the State Department accounts, caused delays and difficulties in accounting for these funds at the Treasury Department. On November 7, 1792, Washington communicated Jefferson's letter with its enclosures to Congress. In response to Jefferson's letter, Congress included provisions for settlement of these accounts in "An Act to continue in force for a limited time, and to amend the act entitled 'An Act providing the means of intercourse between the United States and foreign nations'" (1 *Stat.* 299–300 [February 9, 1793]). Section 2 of this act reads as follows: "*And be it further enacted,* That in all cases, where any sum or sums of money have issued, or shall hereafter issue, from the treasury, for the purposes of intercourse or treaty, with foreign nations, in pursuance of any law, the President shall be, and he hereby is authorized to cause the same to be duly settled annually with the accounting officers of the treasury, in manner following, that is to say; by causing the same to be accounted for, specifically, in all instances, wherein the expenditure thereof may, in his judgment, be made public; and by making a certificate or certificates, or causing the Secretary of State to make a certificate or certificates of the amount of such expenditures, as he may think it advisable not to specify; and every such certificate shall be deemed a sufficient voucher for the sum or sums therein expressed to have been expended" (1 *Stat.* 300).

From Jeremiah Olney [1]

Custom House
District of Providence 7th November 1792

The refusal of Credit to Mr. Edward Dexter on the Sixth Instant for the amount of the duties on the Cargo of the Brigantine Neptune (Consisting of one Hundred and Twenty Two Hogsheads and Twenty Three Teirces of Melasses &c.) Stephen Peirce Master, which entered at my office on the Said Sixth Instant, from Surinam, being the Property of Welcome Arnold Esquire and which was by him Transferred to the said Edward Dexter on the Fifth Instant—was founded on the Ground of Probability that said Transfer was Collusive and made with intent to effect a Further Credit in evasion of the Law, 1st. Because Mr. Arnold had a Bond then in Suit and remained unpaid which *by Law*[2] deprived him of a Further Credit during his delinquency—2ndly as Mr. Arnold had previously to this (in the month of September 1792) effected a Further Credit (His said bond being then in Suit) in three Instances, by Similar Transfers, one to Mr. Stephen Dexter of the Brigantine Samuel with all her Cargo,[3] and the other Two to Edward Dexter for the Cargoes of the Brigantine Harriot[4] and Sloop Sally—which Cargoes after being unladen were deposited in Mr. Arnolds Stores and himself and Clerks generally attended the unlading—3rdly. that Mr. Arnold Suffered considerably for the want of Melasses (being reduced to the Necessity of borrowing from Several Persons) to work his Distillery in order to Compleat a Cargo of Rum for the Brigantine Betsey bound for Copenhagen and now awaiting with Eighty Six Hogsheads and Two Barrels of Rum, as part of her Cargo, on Board—4thly. the improbability that Mr. Arnold would make a *Real* Sale of a Cargo of Melasses which he so much wanted for immediate use, to Mr. Edward Dexter, who has but lately opened a Store in this Town, and could not, in all probability, have occasion for (or means in his power to make a real purchase of) upwards of Fourteen Thousand gallons of Melasses which at half a Dollar a Gallon being the lowest price, would amount to upwards of Seven thousand Dollars, and lastly that it is very unusual for Merchants to buye or Sell whole Cargoes of Merchandize by the lump.

To Shew the Probability that the Transfer of the Brigantine Samuels Cargo to Mr. Stephen Dexter, was also Collusive, it is proper further to observe, that he expected a Ship of 231 Tons burthen from the same place, with a larger quantity of the same Kind of Merchandize; and which did actually arrive here in about Three Weeks after the Samuel. Jereh. Olney Collr.

ALS, Rhode Island Historical Society, Providence; ADfS, Rhode Island Historical Society, Providence.

1. For background concerning the problem of collusive transfers, see William Ellery to H, September 4, October 9, 1792; Olney to H, September 8, second letter of September 13, October 4, 25, 1792; H to Olney, September 19, 24, October 12, 1792.

2. See Ellery to H, September 4, 1792, note 2.

3. See Olney to H, September 8, 1792.

4. See Olney to H, September 13, 1792.

From David Porter[1]

[*November 7, 1792.* "I am now obliged to report Mr. James Forbes, third mate, to your notice for the following reasons: 1 Neglect of duty—2 Slanderous reproach on Authority—3 Ill treatment to the men, the latter is designed to retard duty to answer private purposes in my opinion, besides his situation is generally such that renders him incapable of duty or trust which is occasioned by intemperance; those are what I alledge against him and for such have suspended him. I choose to do his duty myself as I have done before, rather than put up with him. I have coolly and deliberately considered on what I have here said, for some time past, and now transmit the same to your notice, and pray that he may not be ordered to this Cutter more."[2] *Letter not found.*]

1. Porter was captain of the Maryland revenue cutter *Active.*

2. This extract was enclosed in H to Otho H. Williams, November 21, 1792.

From Tench Coxe[1]

[Philadelphia, November 8, 1792]

Dear Sir

I consider it as a duty to communicate the substance of a conversation, which I had this Evening with a intelligent citizen of Philada. on whose veracity I rely, and who, in common affairs is far from inaccurate. He informed me that his Catholic Majestys Commissioners[2] were lately sitting with him, when a gazette was brought in; which contained the accot. of the Indian Movements in the Southern quarter, to which account a suggestion was added that the Governor of New Orleans, and an Indian Trader in the Spanish territory, were the causes of those hostile movements by their Instigations & Supplies.[3] Having been unaccustomed to the restraints and reserves of political life he did not hesitate to ask Mr. Jaudines, whether he thought the suggestion founded, and he pursued a conversation on the subject with him for some time in the Presence of Mr. Viar. In the Course of the Conversation Mr. Jaudines took occasion to observe, that the U. S., in all their treaties with the indians, had introduced clauses by which the tribes had been made to submit themselves to the U. S and that a consequent protection of them had been held up and promised on our part—that similar engagements had subsisted between Spain and the Southern Indians (parties to the Treaty made at New York with Mr. McGilivray) *prior* to that Treaty—that he would not say the Governor of New Orleans had supplied them with Arms and stores, but that it would be best that the U. S. should not attempt to run the line contemplated in the Treaty of New York, for, that if they did, Spain would support the Indians in preventing it.[4] The Citizen remarked that such a procedure would, as it appeared to him, produce a disagreement and probably a rupture between the U. S. and Spain; to which Mr. Jaudenes answered in terms implying, that such a circumstance would be very disagreeable, but that such interposition would in the event mentioned, certainly take place.

There was present at the conversation a Mr. Bryan of Georgia (who, I understand, is a Student in the Office of the Attorney Genl.) [5] between whom & Mr. Jaudines some warm discussion took place. It is probable therefore, that he may remember the precise language of the Commissioner of Spain. Should you think it well to ask Mr. Randolph to converse wtih him, I wish, that the young Gentleman may be cautioned not to mention the Enquiry, as the citizen is desirous from personal reasons, that a guarded use may be made of the information. He is not unwilling however, if it be desired that his name be known to you, and in any other place where you may think it necessary.

I have the honor to be, your respectful humble Servant

Tench Coxe

Walnut Street
Thursday Evening 8th. Novr. 92

ALS, Thomas Jefferson Papers, Library of Congress.

1. Coxe was commissioner of the revenue.

Although this letter is unaddressed, the cover is directed to H and is endorsed in Thomas Jefferson's handwriting "Coxe Tenche to mr Hamilton."

2. The Spanish commissioners to the United States were Josef de Viar and Josef de Jaudenes.

3. On November 3, 1792, both the [Philadelphia] *National Gazette* and the [Philadelphia] *Gazette of the United States* printed excerpts from an article that had appeared in the *Knoxville Gazette* concerning an attack on "John Buchanan's station, four miles south of Nashville . . . by a party of Creeks and Lower Cherokees." The newspaper article stated: "It is an undoubted Truth . . . that the Baron D'Corrondolet, governor of Louisiana . . . [has] opened the stores of the king of Spain, in West Florida, to the Creeks and Cherokees, and delivered them arms and ammunition in abundance, advising and stimulating them to go to war against the frontier inhabitants of the United States. . . . These are the fruits of the advice of the Baron D'Corrondolet . . . and it is due to Mr [William] Panton, their chief instrument, to add, he has well acted his part" (*Knoxville Gazette*, October 6–10, 1792).

Francisco Louis Hector, Baron de Carondelet, succeeded Esteban Miró as governor and intendant of Louisiana and West Florida on December 30, 1791. Panton had been a member of a British trading firm in the Floridas before the American Revolution. Through his friendship with the Creek chief, Alexander McGillivray, and with the aid of the Spanish before 1795, he developed a monopoly of the Indian trade in the Spanish possessions east of the Mississippi.

4. The Spanish had objected to Article 2 of the Treaty of New York signed in 1790 with the United States by Alexander McGillivray. This article acknowledged the sovereignty of the United States Government over those territories in which Creeks resided and which were within the boundaries of the United States. In order to settle the question of the disputed boundary between Georgia and Creek territory, Article 5 of the treaty provided for a survey by a surveyor appointed by the United States and assisted by a group of Creeks (*ASP, Indian Affairs*, I, 81–82). The Spanish authorities insisted that these articles were in violation of a treaty signed by the Creeks with the Spanish at Pensacola in 1784, and in 1792 Carondelet sent an agent, Pedro Olivier, to the Creek Nation with instructions to prevent the running of the boundary and to induce McGillivray to repudiate the Treaty of New York. As a result of Olivier's activities, McGillivray signed a treaty on July 6, 1792, with the Spanish at New Orleans which virtually abrogated the Treaty of New York (John Walton Caughey, *McGillivray of the Creeks* [Norman, Oklahoma, 1939], 285–86, 329–30). The Spanish made similar objections to a treaty which the United States signed with the Cherokee in 1791.

5. John Bryan was one of three young men who studied law under Edmund Randolph at Philadelphia. The other two students were Lawrence Washington, the President's nephew, and John Randolph of Roanoke.

From Joseph Nourse

Treasury Department
Registers Office 8th: November 1792

Sir

I have the Honor to enclose the several Estimates for which Appropriations will be necessary for the Services of the Year 1793.—vizt.

Civil List[1] .... Dollars 352.466.39/100
War Department[2] 1.089.473.73
Invalid Pensioners[3] 82.245.32
Extraordinaries[4] .... 92.599.66.

The foregoing Estimates are accompanied with particular Statements of the Application of Two Several Sums vizt:

Of 50,000 Dollars[5] } Granted by Several Acts
And of 5,000 do.[6] } for the Purpose of discharging

such Demands on the United States not otherwise provided for as shall have been ascertained and admitted in due Course of Settlement at the Treasury and which are of a Nature according to the Usage thereof to require Payment in Specie.

With much Respect I am sir, Your mo: ob. & mo: hb: Servt.

J: N: Regr.

Honourable
Alexander Hamilton Esqr.
Secretary of the Treasury

LC, RG 53, Register of the Treasury, Estimates and Statements for 1793, Vol. "135-T," National Archives.

1. "Estimate of the Expenditure for the Civil List of the United States for the Year 1793 together with the incidental and Contingent Expences of the several Departments and Offices" (DS, RG 53, Register of the Treasury, Estimates and Statements for 1793, Vol. "135-T," National Archives).

2. "Estimate, of the Expences of the War-department, for the Year 1793" (D, RG 53, Register of the Treasury, Estimates and Statements for 1793, Vol. "135-T," National Archives).

3. "Invalids, for the annual allowance to the Invalids of the United States from the fifth day of March, One thousand seven hundred and Ninety three to the fourth day of March, One thousand seven hundred ninety four" (D, RG 53, Register of the Treasury, Estimates and Statements for 1793, Vol. "135-T," National Archives).

4. "An Additional Estimate for making good Deficiencies for the Support of the Civil List Establishment—For aiding the fund appropriated for the payment of Certain Officers of the Courts, Jurors & Witnesses—For the Support of Light Houses and for the Establishment of Ten Cutters and for other purposes" (DS, RG 53, Register of the Treasury, Estimates and Statements for 1793, Vol. "135-T," National Archives).

5. "A particular Statement of the Application of Fifty thousand Dollars granted by an 'Act making certain Appropriations therein mentioned' passed the 12th August 1790, for the purpose of Discharging such Demands on the United States, not otherwise provided for as shall have been ascertained and admitted in due Course of Settlement at the Treasury and which are of a Nature according to the Usage thereof, to require payment in Specie" (DS, RG 53, Register of the Treasury, Estimates and Statements for 1793, Vol. "135-T," National Archives).

6. "A particular Statement of the Application of five Thousand Dollars

granted by an Act making Certain Appropriations therein mentioned passed the 8 May 1792 (& included in Appropriation of 34.497. Dollars 90 Cents) for the purpose of discharging such Demands on the United States not otherwise provided for as shall have been ascertained and admitted in due Course of Settlement at the Treasury and which are of a nature according to the Usage thereof to require paymt. in Specie" (DS, RG 53, Register of the Treasury, Estimates and Statements for 1793," Vol. "135–T," National Archives).

Agreement with John Campbell and Receipt from John Campbell[1]

[Philadelphia, November 9, 1792]

Agreement between Alexander Hamilton on behalf of Nicholas Low & Abijah Hammond of the one part and John Campbell on the other part.

The said John Campbell agrees to proceed forthwith to Scotland in the Kingdom of Great Britain there to endeavor to purchase and to ship from thence to the united States on account of the said Nicholas Low & Abijah Hammond the following articles, Eight Stocking frames, one finishing press, and tools or impliments for four workmen to be employed in making frames.

The said John Campbell further engages to endeavour to procure and send to the United States from Scotland aforesaid for the service of the said Nicholas Low & Abijah Hammond in carrying on a manufactory of Stockings the following persons. Eight Stocking frame Knitters three frame Smiths & one repsetter.

Which persons shall if possible be under contract to serve the said Nicholas Low & Abijah Hammond in the capacities aforesaid for a term not less than three years upon compensations by way of wages or for peice worke not exceeding by ten pr Cent the rates which are usually allowed where they are engaged the Said Low & Hammond defraying their passages to the United States.

The said Alexander Hamilton in behalf as aforesaid engages to repay the amount of the sumes which shall be expended for the purchase of the said articles, for the freight thereof to the united States, & for the passages of the said workmen, And further that the said Nicholas Low & Abijah Hammond upon the arival of said macheenery & workmen in the United States shall advance for carrying on a Manufactory of Stockings under the management of the said John Campbell at such place within the United States as they shall think proper the Sum of [three thousand] [2] Dollars.

The said John Campbell on his part further engages that he will Superintend for the said Nicholas Low & Abijah Hammond the Said manufactory of Stockings for the term of [seven] years for the consideration of one third of the neat profits thereof, in ascertaining which neat profits besides the expence of carrying on the business there shall be a deduction for the benefite of the Said Nicholas Low & Abijah Hammond of five pr Centum pr Annum on the whole sum which shall have been by them advanced & paid towards the purposes aforesaid.

It is understood that if the said Nicholas Low & Abijah Hammond shall think fit to extend the Capital for carrying on the said Manufactory the said allowance of one third to the said John Campbell shall be computed on the whole Capital employed.

As James & Shoemaker have agreed to advance the Sum requisite for procuring and sending out the said macheenery & workmen, it is understood in such case the reimbursement is to be emmediatly to them.[3]

In witness whereof the parties aforesaid have to these presants subscribed & set their hands and seals the [Ninth] Day of November in the year of our lord 1792.

Alexander Hamilton
[on behalf as aforesaid]
John Campbell

[Sealed & Delivered
in presence of]
John Meyer

[Philadelphia November 9th 1792 of Alexander Hamilton One hundred & Fifty Dollars on account of the foregoing Agreement.]

John Campbell

DS, Hamilton Papers, Library of Congress.

1. For background to this document, see "Contract with James and Shoemaker," November 5, 1792.

2. Material within brackets is in the handwriting of H.

3. In the Hamilton Papers, Library of Congress, there is an undated bill from James and Shoemaker to H for "Cash advanced John Campbell in Greenock including Passage of himself, his Wife & Workmen in the Ship Glasgow" in the amount of £726.10.2.

["C"] [1]

[Philadelphia, November 10, 1792]

[Philadelphia] *Gazette of the United States*, November 10, 1792.

1. Philip Marsh has written: "In November, 'C.' taunted Freneau, the translator-editor, for publishing a French poem without translating it. Hamilton, who as 'T. L.' and 'An American' had called attention to Freneau's lack of translating ability, may well have taken this opportunity to point out the editor's awkward situation" (Philip Marsh, "Hamilton's Neglected Essays, 1791–1793," *The New-York Historical Society Quarterly*, XXXII [October, 1948], 296). Despite Marsh's statement that H may have been the author of "C," there is no conclusive evidence that H wrote this article.

From Tench Coxe

Treasury Department, Revenue Office, November 10, 1792. "I have the Honor to inform you, that the Supervisor of North Carolina [1] has communicated to me the Resignation of William Wynne, John Baker and Edmund Sawyer Esquires, as Inspectors of the Revenue for the ports of Wynton, Bennets Creek Bridge and Pasqustank River Bridge, of which ports they were also Surveyors. . . ."

LC, RG 58, Letters of Commissioner of Revenue, 1792–1793, National Archives.

1. William Polk.

From Tench Coxe

Treasury Department, Revenue Office, November 10, 1792. Encloses "for the purpose of submission to the President, two contracts between the Superintendent of the light House at New London and Daniel Harris and Nathl. Richards." [1] Discusses the cost of the contract. States that he has sent a circular letter to the superintendents of the lighthouses "calculated to draw from them a report comprehending all the material facts in regard to their construction, present condition and past and present supplies and management, with a view to embracing by general measures cheaper and better supplies." [2]

LC, RG 58, Letters of Commissioner of Revenue, 1792–1793, National Archives.

1. Copies of these contracts may be found in RG 26, Lighthouse Deeds and Contracts, National Archives.

2. Coxe is referring to his circular to the superintendents of the lighthouses, dated October 23, 1792. In this circular Coxe requested answers to thirty-five questions concerning the construction and maintenance of the lighthouses under their supervision (LC, RG 58, Letters of Commissioner of Revenue, 1792–1793, National Archives).

From Richard Morris[1]

New York, November 10, 1792. "I anxiously wait to hear from you for tho I should submitt willingly to Expend my own time and money I do not wish to incur the Expence that will Necessarily fall on me for the Clerk, Stamper, Office Rent, fuel, and the Unavoidable Expences of Marking and Guageing the Stills in the Remote Counties. . . . I hope when the President Reconsiders this Business he will direct the Clk, the Stamper of Certificates, Office Rent, Fuel and the Expence of Guageg. and Marking the Stills in the Remote Counties to be paid as Contingencies. . . ."

ALS, Hamilton Papers, Library of Congress.

1. Morris was supervisor of the revenue for the District of New York.

Report on the Receipts and Expenditures of Public Monies to the End of the Year 1791[1]

[Philadelphia, November 10, 1792
Communicated on November 12, 1792] [2]

[To the Speaker of the House of Representatives]

An account of the Receipts and Expenditures of the United States commencing with the establishment of the Treasury Department under the present Governmt, and ending on the thirty first day of December 1791, stated in pursuance of the standing order of the

D, signed by Oliver Wolcott, Jr., and Joseph Nourse, RG 233, Original Report of the Secretary of the Treasury, 1792, National Archives; copy, RG 39, Reports to Congress, Account of Receipts and Expenditures, National Archives.

1. The copy in RG 39, Reports to Congress, Account of Receipts and Expenditures, National Archives, was printed in 1793 by Francis Childs and John Swaine. Material within broken brackets in the document printed below has been taken from the printed copy.

2. *Journal of the House*, I, 618. The communicating letter, dated November 9, 1792, may be found in RG 233, Reports of the Treasury Department, 1792–1793, Vol. III, National Archives.

House of Representatives of the United States passed on the thirtieth day of December 1791, of which the following is a copy.

In the House of Representatives of the United States.

Friday the 30 of December 1791.

Resolved, that it shall be the duty of the Secretary of the Treasury to lay before the House of Representatives on the fourth Monday of October in each Year, if Congress shall be then in session, or if not then in session, within the first week of the session next following the said fourth Monday of October, an accurate Statement and account of the receipts and expenditures of all public monies down to the last day inclusively of the Month of December immediately preceding the said fourth monday of October, distinguishing the amount of the receipts of each State or District, and from each Officer therein, in which statement shall also be distinguished the expenditures which fall under each head of appropriation, and shall be shewn the sums, if any, which remain unexpended, and to be accounted for in the next statement of each and every of such appropriations.[3]

3. *Journal of the House*, I, 484.

A STATEMENT SHOWING THE AMOUNT OF DUTIES ON IMPORTS TONNAGE, OF FINES PENALTIES AND FORFEITURES, OF PAYMENTS DRAWBACKS ON MERCHANDIZE, AND BOUNTIES ON SALTED FISH PROVISION EXPORTED, AND OF THE EXPENSES ON COLLECTION OF REVENUE FROM THE COMMENCEMENT OF THE PRESENT GOVERNM

			Gross amount of			Payn	
States	Districts	Collectors	Duties on Merchandize.	Duties on Tonnage.	Fines Penalties and Forfeitures.	Drawbacks on Merchandize exported.	Bounties on salted Fish
New Hampshire	Portsmouth	Joseph Whipple	55,770.30½	4,212.42	22.53	344.19	855
Massachusetts	Newbury Port	Stephen Cross	85,849.90½	2,535.52	......	642.42	4,369
	Gloucester	Epes Sargent	26,660.58½	1,170.42	......	......	2,132
	Salem	Joseph Hiller	175,341.93½	3,290.03	308.18½	10,265.17	8,600
		Richard Harris	......	......	......	......	...
	Marblehead		20,798.70¼	1,379.92	......	......	3,361
		Samuel R. Gerry	......	......	......	......	...
	Boston	Benjamin Lincoln	635,148.44¾	24,861.49⅔	2,845.97⅔	7,564.57⅓	4,626
	Plymouth	William Watson	6,572.37½	743.99	......	......	645
	Barnstable	Joseph Otis	2,351.73½	722.80½	......	......	...
	Nantucket	Stephen Hussey	3,136.68½	1,384.91½	......	......	22
	Edgartown	John Pease	635.46	188.44	......	......	88
	New Bedford	Edward Pope	3,919.63	996.84	......	......	137
	Dighton	Hodijah Baylies	3,024.15	681.59	......	......	102
	York	Richard Trevett	1,646.23	194.14	......	......	102
	Biddeford	Jeremiah Hill	9,734.22½	968.85	......	......	84
	Portland	Nathaniel F. Fosdick	32,529.09½	3,779.88	139.50	⟨658.02½⟩	677
	Bath	William Webb	5,548.44	1,354.49⅓	200.	......	15
	Wiscassett	Francis Cook	8,975.49½	2,580.66	......	......	28
	Penobscot	John Lee	647.29	956.84	......	......	41
	Frenchman's Bay	Melatiah Jordan	1,317.17¾	1,389.56	......	......	10
	Machias	Stephen Smith	1,262.25	2,677.55	......	......	...
	Passamaquody	Lewis F. De Lesdernier	874.63½	46.12	......	......	...
Rhode Island	New Port	William Ellery	49,624.91½	1,825.01½	334.02½	445.52	876
	Providence	Jeremiah Olney	103,511.84	1,312.08¾	......	76.35	1,051
Connecticut	New London	Jedediah Huntington	150,857.56	7,016.70½	......	......	929
	New Haven	Jonathan Fitch	49,323.63¼	1,603.62	......	......	273
	Fairfield	Samuel Smedley	14,086.55	467.20½	......	......	76
		John Gelston	......	......	......	......	...
New York	Sagg Harbour		1,479.15¼	182.61	......	......	16
		Henry P. Dering	......	......	......	......	...
	New York City	John Lamb	1,354,585.23	59,202.34	......	22,289.20	366
New Jersey	Perth Amboy	John Halsted	10,562.70½	750.64	......	......	7
	Burlington	John Ross	2,327.13	85.54	......	......	...
	Bridgetown	Eli Elmer	1,432.67½	187.59	......	......	...
	A Great Egg Harbour	Daniel Benezet	1,057.05	45.55	......	......	...
Pennsylvania	Pennsylvania	Sharp Delany	1,475,428.20	60,404.24	138.22	8,976.17	...
Delaware	Delaware	George Bush	40,299.22	3,247.34	......	138.32	...

TO THE LAST DAY OF DECEMBER 1791, AGREEABLY TO THE ACCOUNTS SETTLED AT THE TREASURY; EXHIBITING ALSO THE MONIES PAID INTO THE TREASURY BY THE SEVERAL COLLECTORS OF THE CUSTOMS DURING THE PERIOD AFORESAID, AND THE BALANCES DUE BY THEM RESPECTIVELY ON THE FIRST DAY OF JANUARY 1792.

for			Balances in the hands of Collectors.			Monies received by the Treasurer		
Expenses on Collection of the Duties.	Expenses attending Prosecutions.	Net amount of Duties on Imports and Tonnage, and of Fines Penalties and Forfeitures.	Bonds uncollected.	Cash on hand.	Total amount.	For Warrants included in his accounts to Decemr 31, 1791, not passed to the credit of the Collectors on that day.	For Warrants included in his accounts to Decr. 31, 1791, for which the collectors received credit on that day.	For Warrants credited the Collectors previous to January 1, 1792, which are stated in the Treasurers subsequent accounts.
5,772.47½	....	53,033.15	14,456.72½	5.533.42½	19 990.15	......	29,087. "	3,956. "
7,551.10½	....	75,822.65¼	21,525.14¼	......	21,525.14¼	......	54,297.51	......
2,844.44½	28.45	22,825.43	5,924.71	382.72	6,307.43	......	16,518. "	......
10,131.49	3.12½	149,939.44	35,729.83½	212.60½	35 942.44	......	113,997. "	......
......	....	......	......	55.48¾	55.48¾	......	3,874. "	......
2,534.33¾	....	16,282.75¾						
......	....	......	5,517.60¾	911.74½	6,429.35¼	......	5,923.92	......
26,987.47	....	623,677.80¾	175 651.98½	50,490.77¼	226,142.75¾	4,345.67	357,535.05	40,000. "
751.91	....	5,918.66	531.13	307.53	838.66	......	5,080. "	......
210.42	....	2,864.12	......	231.32	231.32	......	2,632.80	......
373.21½	....	4,126.28½	......	182.81½	182.81½	......	3,943.47	......
156.52	....	578.58	......	178.58	178.58	......	400. "	......
434.24	....	4,344.68	198.90	25.78	224.68	......	4,120. "	......
297.12	88.26	3,218.31	318.84	599.47	918.31	......	2,300. "	......
170.66½	....	1,567.08½	117.46	49.62½	167.08½	......	⟨1,400.⟩"	......
857 88½	....	9,760.74	1,851.40	475.91	2,327.31	......	⟨7,433.43⟩	......
3,056.39½	21.78	32,034.71¼	10,919.08	3,865.99¼	14,785.07¼	668...	⟨17,249.64⟩	......
380.88⅓	....	6,706.94½	2,126.27½	926.67	3,052.94½	......	⟨3,654.⟩	......
1,237.33	....	10,289.92½	2,363.69	1,317.38½	3,681.07½	......	⟨6,392⟩.85	216. "
242.08	....	1,320.85	......	920.85	920.85	......	⟨400...⟩	......
377.11¾	....	2,319.62	......	1,271.28	1,271.28	......	⟨1,048.34⟩	......
203.79	206.09	3,529.92	606.56	718.20	1,324.76	......	2,205.16	......
133.04	....	787.71½	......	576.87½	576.87½	......	210.84	......
3,719.55	....	46,742.33½	14,368.18½	2,016.48	16,384.66½	......	23,357.67	7,000...
3,899.90¾	....	99,796.08¾	58,748.88¾	130.87	58,879.75¾	......	39,466.52	1,449.81
11,916.88	....	145,028.22	29,249.29½	14,569.82½	43,819.12	......	91,147.50	10,061.60
2,634.23	....	48,019.92¼	8,417.16½	7,765.96¾	16,183.13¼	......	31,836.79	......
844.16½	....	13,633.49	2,349.85	906.64	3,256.49	......	10,377.	......
......	....	......	......	......	......	......	507.85	......
231.67¾	....	1,413.88½						
......	....	......	269.88¾	236.14¾	506.03½	......	400.	......
28,035.33	....	1,363,096.45	423,700.37	16,444.08	440,144.45	......	922,952.	......
402.41	11.93	10,892. ½	3,468.63	204.50½	3,673.13½	......	7,218.87	......
350.79	....	2,061.88	......	241.88	241.88	......	1,820.	......
622.42	....	997.84½	......	......	......	......	1,039.94	......
150.34	....	952.26	122.50	86.73	209.23	......	743.03	......
35,970.88	....	1,491,023.61	405,743.15	6,499.37	412,242.52	......	1,078,781.09	......
2,404.79	77.69	40,925.76	7,782.10½	1,464.77½	9,246.88	......	30,292.83	1,386.05

States	Districts	Collectors	Gross amount of			Paym	
			Duties on Merchandize.	Duties on Tonnage.	Fines Penalties and Forfeitures.	Drawbacks on Merchandize exported.	Bounties on salted Fish and Provision exported.
Maryland	Baltimore	Otho H. Williams	570,036.54	29 644.33	35,34⅔	13,530.29	14.
		John Scott	......	......	......	......	....
	Chester		272.21	369.89	......	......	....
		Jeremiah Nicols	......	......	......	......	....
	Oxford	Jeremiah Banning	83.28	260.59½	......	......	....
	B Vienna	John Muir	928.47	247.69	......	......	....
	Snowhill	John Gunby	715.63	212.73	......	......	....
	Nottingham	George Biscoe	20,856.48½	2,523.22	......	......	....
	Annapolis	John Davidson	5943.91½	528.26	......	......	....
	Cedar Point	John C. Jones	8,421.39	1,445.99	......	......	....
	George Town	James M. C. Lingan	34,387.99¼	3,378.52½	......	54.64¾	....
Virginia	Norfolk	William Lindsay	363,157.65	40,720.29	22.96	461.66.	27.
	Bermuda Hundd.	William Heth	228,664.44	12,578.85	176.88	......	....
		Jacob Wray	......	......	......	......	....
	Hampton		62.50	59.38	......	......	....
		George Wray	......	......	......	......	....
	York Town	Abraham Archer	9,238.10	1,446.14	......	......	....
	Tappahannock	Hudson Muse	63,385.13	6,334.01	......	......	....
	Yeocomico river	Vincent Redman	1,631.13	76.22	......	......	....
	Dumfries	Richard M. Scott	15,788.23½	1,141.40	......	......	....
	Alexandria	Charles Lee	122,135.66	10,312.44	3.83½	443.02	....
	Foley Landing	William Gibb	582.75	78.69	......	......	....
		George Savage	......	......	......	......	....
	Cherry Stone		539.46	49.80	......	......	....
		Nathaniel Wilkins	......	......	......	......	....
	South Quay	Thomas Bowne	702.39	21.17	......	......	[illegible]
North Carolina	Wilmington	James Read	49,534.95	9,082.18¼	......	29.45¼	....
	Newbern	John Daves	24,290.34¾	2,430.90	......	......	83.
	Washington	Nathaniel Keais	7,572.83½	1,110.35	......	......	....
	Edenton	Thomas Benbury	20,565.98	2,301.60	7.50	......	58.
	Camden	Isaac Gregory	4,729.74	398.98	......	......	....
South Carolina	Georgetown	C John Cogdell	3,231.12	973.04	......	......	....
		George Abbot Hall	......	......	......	......	....
	Charleston		522,614.24½	34,055.84	......	3,684.78	....
		Isaac Holmes	......	......	......	......	....
	Beaufort	Andrew Agnew	......	......	......	......	....
Georgia	Savannah	John Habersham	77,116.20¾	20,368.91	......	202.06	....
	D Sunbury	Cornelius Collins	491.54½	419.78	......	......	....
	Brunswick	Christopher Hillary	......	79.12	......	......	....
	E Saint Mary's	James Seagrove	224.48	226. “	......	......	....
			6,494,225.42	375,323.28½	4,234.95⅚	69,805.85 1/12	29,682.

A The accounts settled to June 30, 1791 only.
B Ditto to Septem 30, 1790.
C Ditto to June 30, 1791.
D Ditto to Septem 30, 1791.
E Ditto to June 30, 1791.

t			Balances in the hands of Collectors.			Monies received by the Treasurer		
Expenses on Collection of the Duties.	Expenses attending Prosecutions.	Net amount of Duties on Imports and Tonnage, and of Fines Penalties and Forfeitures.	Bonds uncollected.	Cash on hand.	Total amount.	For Warrants included in his accounts to Decemr 31, 1791, not passed to the credit of the Collectors on that day.	For Warrants included in his accounts to Decr. 31, 1791, for which the collectors received credit on that day.	For Warrants credited the Collectors previous to January 1, 1792, which are stated in the Treasurers subsequent accounts.
2,803.32⅙	....	563,368.10	142,325.10¾	14,138.74¼	156 463.85	......	406,904.25	......
......	....	......	......	46.	46...	......	336.	......
101.74	....	540.36						
......	....	......	......	158.36	158.36	......	......	......
276.75	....	67.12½	......	67.12½	67.12½	......	......	......
12.51	....	1,163.65	250.54	613.11	863.65	......	300.	......
86.89	....	841.47	216.96	84.51	301.47	......	540.	......
904.65½	....	22,475.05	3,656.85	1,249.45	4 906.30	......	17,568.75	......
232.71	....	6,239.46½	764.49	848.52½	1,613.01½	......	2,826.45	1,800.
281.50	....	9,585.88	......	3,185.88	3,185.88	......	6,400. "	......
972.92	....	36,738.95	9,297.90	572.50	9,870.40	400.	26,868.55	......
4,217.18	28.86	389,166.	91,077.31	39,667.81	130,745.12	24,700.	253,790.28	4,630.60
4,539.40½	....	236,880.76½	72,864.14	11,757.40½	84,621.54½	443.	148 059.22	4,200.
......	....	......	......	10.38	10.38	......	......	......
63. "	....	58.88						
......	....	......	......	48.50	48.50	......	......	......
154.91	....	10,529.33	4,994.92	1,557.14	6,552.06	1,400.	3,977.27	......
2,141.06	....	67,578.08	16,021.43	6,288.51	22,309.94	2,050.	44,013.47	1,254.67
129.10	....	1,578.25	1,478.25	......	1,478.25	......	100.	......
339.49½	....	16,590.14	4,861.56	847.58	5,709.14	300.	10,881.	......
3 937.23½	....	128,071.68	28,631.97	11,293.71	39,925.68	8,000.	88,146.	......
172.94	....	488.50	152.37	336.13	488.50	......	......	......
......	....	......	......	23.58	23.58	......	......	......
187.37	....	401.89						
......	....	......	......	378.31	378.31	......	......	......
148.85	....	574.01	......	324.01	324.01	200.	250.	......
2,817.42¼	....	55,770.25¾	16,323.84¼	12,289.08½	28,612.92¾	7,000.	27,157.33	......
1,616.60¾	....	25,021.64	4,409.63¼	4,311.76¾	8,721.40	2,150.	15,800.24	500.
645.61½	....	8,037.57	1,210.49½	4,142.07½	5,352.57	2,000.	2,685.	......
1,501.12	....	21,315.36	3,300.89	1,803.71	5,104.60	1,350	14,545.76	1,665
262.80	....	4,865.92	947.75	2,128.17	3,075.92	700.	1,790.	......
204.45	....	3,999.71	521.60	2,178.11	2,699.71	2,000.	1,300.	......
......	....	......	......	5,781.09	5,781.09	......	275,075.83	1,851.93
3,201.40½	....	534,783.90						
......	....	......	172,625.20	36,934.43	209,559.63	27,751.88	38,575.97	3,939.45
......	....	......	......	......	......	......	......	......
6,233.62¾	24.44	91,024.99	20,296.71	26,220.84	46,517.55	3,566.	42,396.87	2,110.57
84.01	....	827.31½	......	385.83½	385.83½	......	441.48	......
.76	....	78.36	......	......	......	......	74.62	3.74
382.37	....	68.11	......	68.11	68.11	......	......	......
9.541.03¼	490.62½	6,534,263.84	1,828,289.28¼	309,542.79¾	2,137,832.08	89,024.55	4,310,448.44	86,025.42

tal amount of balances in the hands of Collectors 2,137,832.08

om which deduct the amount of a balance due to he Collector of the District of Bridgetown in the State of New Jersey on the 31 day of December 1791, being so much over paid by him into the Treasury, prior to that day 42.09½

2,137,789.98½

A SUMMARY STATEMENT OF MONIES RECEIVED INTO THE TREASURY TO DECEMBER 31, 1791, INCLUSIVELY.

From the Collectors of the Customs agreeably to the first and second columns of the preceding statement entitled "Monies received by the Treasurer."	4,399,472.99	
From Clement Biddle Marshal for the District of Pennsylvania, for Fines and Forfeitures arising under the Act entitled "An Act for the punishment of certain crimes against the United States."[4]	311.	
Gained by a remittance of 10,000 Dollars in gold from Philadelphia to New York.	6.28	
From sundry persons for interest due on their notes.	17.54	
		4,399,807.81

FUNDS ARISING FROM BALANCES FOUND DUE ON ACCOUNTS WHICH ORIGINATED UNDER THE LATE GOVERNMENT.

From Nathaniel Gilman, late receiver of continental taxes for the State of New Hampshire	3,225.70	
From James Blanchard, Paymaster to the late second Regiment of New Hampshire	394.10	
From Horatio Clagget, Paymaster to the late Maryland line	1,480.30	
From Thomas McWhorter, in the Department of the Commissary of Hides	17.20	
From Joseph Carleton, late Secretary in the War Office	155.52	
From Reading Howell Executor to the Estate of Cornelius Sherriff deceased, in the Quartermasters Department	31.55	
From Benjamin Hitchbourne Attorney to the Administrator to the Estate of Thomas Chase deceased, in the Qr. Mrs. Department	5,682.14	
From Lynde Catlin, Clerk in the Office of the acting Paymaster	14.60	
		11,001.11

TEMPORARY DOMESTIC LOANS.

From the President Directors and Company of the bank of North America	90,008.81	
From the President Directors and Company of the bank of New York	155,000.	
From Joseph Howell acting Paymaster	1,600.	
		246,608.81

FOREIGN LOANS.

From the President Directors and Company of the bank of North America, being the produce of bills of Exchange drawn on the Agents for negotiating foreign Loans in Holland	229,269.47	
From the President Directors and Company of the bank of New York, being the produce of bills of Exchange drawn on the Agents aforesaid	132,121.87	
		361,391.34

4. 1 *Stat.* 112–19 (April 30, 1790). Biddle's account, dated December 10, 1791, states that the fines were imposed for assault and battery and for contempt of court (DS, RG 217, Miscellaneous Treasury Accounts, 1790–1894, Account No. 1834, National Archives).

REPAYMENTS IN CONSEQUENCE OF ADVANCES PREVIOUSLY MADE.

From Sharp Delany Agent for paying Invalid pensions	3,000.	
From Frederick A. Muhlenberg Speaker of the House of Representatives of the first Congress	2,979.50	
From Nathaniel Appleton Commissioner of Loans	28,785.83	
From John Hopkins Commissioner of Loans	6,012.	
		40 777.33
Total amount of Receipts, and Repayments, into the Treasury		5,059,586.40

THE FOLLOWING SUMS WHICH ARE DEDUCTED IN THE ACCOUNT OF EXPENDITURES UNDER THEIR RESPECTIVE HEADS, IN ORDER TO SHEW THE TRUE AMOUNT THEREOF; ARE TO BE DEDUCTED ALSO FROM THE AMOUNT OF THE RECEIPTS AND REPAYMENTS, VIZT.

In page	55 a repayment by Frederick A, Muhlenberg	2,979.50	
"	91 Ditto by Jeremiah Olney	36.08	
"	92 Ditto by Sharp Delany	3,000.	
"	95 the amount of a Loan obtained by the Secretary of the Treasury from the President Directors & Company of the bank of New York	155,000.	
"	95 the same from the President Directors and Company of the bank of North America including an overcharge in their interest account	90,008.81	
"	95 the same from Joseph Howell, acting Paymaster	1,600.	
"	109 a repayment by Nathaniel Appleton	28,785.83	
"	112 Ditto by John Hopkins	6,012.	
"	135 Ditto by Joseph Nourse Register of the Trey	529.75	
"	137 Ditto by do	292.	
			288,243.97
	Amount carried to the credit of a General Account of the receipts and expenditures, in page 142[5]		4,771,342.43

5. This page number and the page numbers cited above refer to the pagination in the original document. The material which appears on these manuscript pages may be found on the corresponding pages in this volume: 68, 87, 88, 90, 96, 98, 108, 109, 114.

FOR DISCHARGING WARRANTS ISSUED BY THE LATE BOARD OF TREASURY

Warrants issued by the late Board of Treasury		Warrants drawn by the Secretary of the Treasury for payment of those issued by the late Board of Treasury.			
Date	No.	Date	No.	To whom payable	Amount
1789 March 3	1101	1789 Novemr. 23	94	Royal Flint Contractor, for Clothing supplied the Army	3000
"	1105	Decemr. 11	143	Ditto for do.	3449 82
1788 April 14	317	16	148	Henry Knox Secretary at War	1000
"	318				
1789 May 13	1148	1790 January 4	163	Patrick Ferrall	22 36
1788 Decemr. 19	1038	5	164	Patrick Ferrall Atty to Edward Chinn	1262 79
24	1039				
"	1040				
1786 October 10	522	7	168	William Henderson Atty to Samuel Engs	351 16
1788 Novemr. 18	450	19	184	Joseph Nourse Attorney to Richard Gridley	444 40
26	451	21	189	Jonathan Burrall Assignee of John White	705 35
Septemr 27	420	"	190	Ditto do	600
1789 June 2	1168	23	193	Paul Richard Randall	700
1787 October 5	219	30	199	Ebenzer Thayer Assignee of Doctor Joseph Waldo	252
1789 May 23	1161	Februy 1	201	Dominick Lynch Assignee of Arthur St. Clair	2068 07
"	1158	3	205	Joseph Nourse Assignee of do.	1867
1789 July 7	1191	8	208	James Livingston	500
Februy 17	1083	"	211	Robert Watts Atty to Stephen Moore	437 50
August 1	1198	10	213	John Cochran	261 62
Februy 10	1081	12	215	John Meyer Assignee of George Stanton	112 49
May 16	1151				
23	1160	15	218	William Seton Assignee of Arthur St. Clair	2000
March 26	1116	"	219	William Smith Assignee of Wm. Winder	193 16
"	482	17	221	John Murray Assignee of Michael Hillegas	791 80
1788 Novemr 6	444	19	223	Joseph Howell Junior Assignee of do.	2000
1787 Decemr. 31	264	23	227	Samuel Meredith Assignee of John Wagner	500
1788 July 5	380	1790 Februy 24	228	Royal Flint Assignee of Mat McConnell	557 17
1789 January 19	471	"	229	Ditto Assignee of Thomas Halt	960
May 27	1162	March 2	234	Thomas Bazen Assignee of Joseph Bindon Attorney to Joseph Traversee	60
1787 August 21	181	4	238	William Constable Assignee of Richd. Butler	250
Novemr 22	242	"	239	Ditto Assignee of Patrick Ferrall	250
1789 May 26	1163	"	240	Ditto Assignee of Richd. Butler	538 35
"	1164	"	241	Ditto Assignee of do	1611 75
June 18	1173	"	242	Ditto Assignee of Arthur St. Clair	1220 83

1787 Novemr	19	237		5	244	Royal Flint Assignee of Michl. Hillegas	1937	49
	"	241		"	245	Ditto Assignee of do	1100	
	"	240		6	246	Ditto Assignee of do	1500	
1788 April	14 " " " " " "	320 321 342 343 344 345 346		8	248	Henry Knox Secretary at War Assignee of Michael Hillegas	3000	
	" " " " "	347 348 349 350 351		9	249	Ditto Assignee of do.	2000	
1789 March	26 "	1114 1115		10	250	John Henry Assignee of William Winder	1000	
1787 Septemr.	10	202		13	252	Royal Flint Assignee of Stephen Bruce	669	38
1786 October	10	522		15	253	Nicholas Lemmerman	38	
1789 June	18	1172	1790 March	20	255	Frederick Augustus Muhlenberg Assignee of Arthur St. Clair	779	16
1788 Novemr	6	443		31	274	Joseph Howell Junior	2000	
March	28	290	April	5	358	Henry Knox Secretary at War	1600	33
April	14	353		"	359	Ditto	400	
Novr.	7	450		9	397	Thomas T. Tucker Assignee of Michael Hillegas	416	66
Decemr.	31	1044		12	411	Joseph Howell Junior	6000	
1789 August	3	1199		15	430	John Jay late Secretary for Foreign Affairs	57	24
January	19	470		29	463	Alexander Thompson Agent of Thomas Holt	350	
1788 Novemr	6	442	May	1	467	Joseph Howell Junr. Assignee of Michael Hillegas	2000	
April	14 "	319 352		12	479	Henry Knox Assignee of Michl. Hillegas	900	
March	31	293		"	480	Ditto Assignee of do	960	
Novemr	16	438		21	488	Joseph Howell Junr. Assignee of do	1000	
	6 "	440 441		24	492	Ditto Assignee of do	2000	
1787 Decemr.	21	257	June	3	500	James OHara Assignee of do	920	
	"	258		"	501	Ditto Assignee of do	1000	
1788 May	22	366		14	512	Theodosius Fowler & Co. Assignees of do	58	
Septemr.	10	412		23	519	Robert Gilchrist Assignee of do	115	42
1789 March	26	1109		29	522	Reuben Burnley Assignee of Wm. Winder	101	83
	"	1111		"	523	Ditto Assignee of do	23	96
1788 Decemr.	31	1045	July	9	554	Joseph Howell Junior	6000	
1787 August	28	191		19	562	William Constable Assignee of Philip Audebert	2000	
1789 May	19	1154		"	563	Ditto Assignee of James OHara	4223	32
	20	1157		"	564	Ditto Assignee of do	2133	63
1788 Decemr.	31	1046	1790 August	18	615	Joseph Howell Junr.	6000	
	"	1047		21	626	Ditto	6000	
Novemr	6	447		31	641	Ditto Assignee of Michl. Hillegas	4000	

	Decemr.	31	1049		Septemr.	4	649	Ditto	6000
		"	1048			6	653	Ditto	6000
		"	1050			13	661	Ditto	4000
	Februay	28	1085						
		"	1086						
		"	1087						
		"	1088						
		"	1089			24	667	Ditto	22,681 37
		"	1090						
		"	1091						
		"	1092						
	Decemr.	31	1043			27	668	Ditto	6000
	Novemr	6	439		October	1	674	Ditto	3000
		"	445						
1789	March	26	1110			8	702	Joshua Pain Assignee of William Winder	22 37
1788	Decemr.	31	1051			11	708	Joseph Howell Junior	2363 50
1789	Februay	28	1093						
		"	1094						
		"	1095		Novemr	23	750	Ditto	17320 60
		"	1096						
		"	1097						
1788	Decemr.	6	457	1791	July	6	1146	Abijah Hammond Assignee of M. Hillegas	150
								Total amount	157,789 94

FOR THE SUPPORT OF THE CIVIL LIST UNDER THE LATE AND PRESENT GOVERNMENT.

IN RELATION TO THE LATE GOVERNMENT.

FOR DEFRAYING THE EXPENSES OF THE HOUSEHOLD OF THE LATE PRESIDENT OF CONGRESS.

1790 April	21	To Rachael Reed for Wages as a Servant in the Family, Warrt. No.	445	45.	
"	"	" Candes Lewis for the same	446	20.	
"	"	" Henry Rhieman for do	447	36.	
	23	" Henry Arcularius for bread for the use of the Family	448	17.	
August	19	" Walter Nichols for groceries for the use of the Family	619	22.12	
"	"	" Cobus Myers for Wood for do	620	13.84	
Septemr	10	" Richard Phillips Steward for his own salary and that of Palsey Phillips housekeeper, and for sundry expenditures on account of the Family	659	234.22	
					388.18

John R. Livingston for his salary as Secretary to the late President of Congress.

1790 April	22	To Warrant No. 457	102.52

James Hallet for repairs done to the Presidents Chariot in the Year 1788.

1790 May	29	To Warrant No. 497	92.83

Roger Alden late deputy Secretary to Congress for his own and Clerks salaries and sundry contingent expenses.

1790 April	5	To Warrant No. 334	623.70		
	15	" do 429	250.		
					873.70

TREASURY DEPARTMENT.

For compensation to the Commissioners of the late Board, their Secretary and Clerks, and for Office rent.

1789 Novemr	30	To Warrant No. 107	1895.82	
Decemr.	1	" do 122	162.50	
				2058.32

Joseph Nourse Register for his own and Clerks salaries.

1789 Novemr.	30	To Warrant No. 105	670.83

		Joseph Hardy Accountant for his own and Clerks salaries.				
1789 Novemr.	30	To Warrant No. 108			418.05	
		For compensation to sundry Persons Clerks in the Department.				
1789 Novemr	30	To Henry Kuhl	Warrant No. 109	88.56		
1790 April	1	" Christopher Banker	do 293	62.87		
	12	" George Nixon	416	62.37		
					213.80	
						3361.

DEPARTMENT OF FOREIGN AFFAIRS.

		For compensation to the Secretary his Clerks and Messenger and for sundry contingent expenses of the Office.			
1789 Novemr.	30	To Warrant No. 116		1088.87	
"		" do	117	266.07	
1790 May	18	" do	485	53.54	
					1408.48

DEPARTMENT OF WAR.

		For compensation to the Secretary his Clerks and Messenger.	
1789 Novemr.	30	To Warrant No.112	768.04
		Joseph Howell acting Paymaster General and Commissioner of Army accounts, for his own and Clerks salaries and the contingent expenses of his Office.	
1789 Novemr.	30	To Warrant No. 110	1328.21
		For compensation to the Commissioners for settling the accounts between the United States and Individual States their Clerks and Messenger.	
1789 Decemr.	1	To Warrant No. 124	1400.47
		Jonathan Burrall late Commissnr. for adjusting the accounts in the Commissary and Quarter Masters Departmts. for his own and Clerks Salaries.	
1790 March	31	To Warrant No. 275	1010.55
		Benjamin Walker late Commissioner for the Marine Clothing and Hospital Departments, and for settling the accounts of the late secret and commercial Committees for his own and Clerks salaries.	
1790 April	7	To Warrant No. 376	174.90

John White late Commissioner of accts. for the States of Pennsylvania, Delaware and Maryland for his own and Clerks salaries, pursuant to a resolution of Congress passed the 29 of September 1789.[6]

1790 March	30	To Joshua Dawson,	Warrt. No.	268	155.		
April	1	" John Wright	do	289	155.		
July	30	" John White	do	575	430.40		
							740.40

Guilliam Aertsen late Commissioner for adjusting the accounts of the States of South Carolina and Georgia.

1790 April	8	To Warrant No. 385	637.83

Robert Smith Chaplain to the southern Hospital in pursuance of an Act of Congress passed Septemr. 12, 1786.[7]

1790 April	3	To Warrant No. 316	345.

William Kinnan late Copperplate Printer to the United States, for a balance due to him.

1790 April	5	To Warrant No. 363	514.17

Joseph King late Paymaster and Agent to Colonel Baldwins Regiment of Artificers.

1790 May	8	To Warrant No. 474	583.10

Hugh Smith late Postmaster at the head quarters of the Army, for a balance due to him.

1790 August	20	To Warrant No. 624	120.65

For arrearage of salary due to the following Loan Officers.
Nathaniel Appleton late Commissionr of Loans for the State of Massachusetts.

1790 April	3	To Warrant No.	314	2645.73	
June	4	" do	504	2038.04	
					4683.77

William Ellery late Commissioner of Loans for the State of Rhode Island.

1790 March	20	To Warrant No.	254	300.	
April	1	" do	287	400.	
	14	" do	423	300.	
June	28	" do	521	460.26	
1791 February	1	" do	861	84.63	
					1544.89

6. 1 *Stat.* 98. 7. *JCC*, XXXI, 646.

John Cochran late Commissioner of Loans for the State of New York.

1790 March	27	To Warrant No. 263		507.38

James Ewing late Commissioner of Loans for the State of New Jersey.

1790 April	26	To Warrant No. 459		298.12

Thomas Smith late Commissioner of Loans for the State of Pennsylvania.

1790 February	2	To Warrant No. 203	750.	
April	27	" do 461	1200.	
Decemr.	14	" do 774	1100.	
1791 March	7	" do 931	700.	
				3750.

James Tilton late Commissioner of Loans for the State of Delaware.

1791 May	5	To Warrant No. 1055		295.39

William Skinner late Commissioner of Loans for the State of No. Carolina.

1791 January	21	To Warrant No. 849		730.46

John Neufville late Commissioner of Loans for the State of South Carolina.

1790 July	19	To Warrant No. 561	1500.	
October	14	" do 729	700.	
1791 Februy	12	" do 892	596.90	
				2796.90

Richard Wylly late Commissioner of Loans for the State of Georgia.

1790 March	8	To Warrant No. 247	300.		
April	12	" do 412	400.		
July	2	" do 530	678.28		
August	19	" do 622	804.26		
				2182.54	
					16,789.45

For compensation due to the Officers of the Government of the Northwestern Territory.
Arthur St. Clair, Governor.

1789 Novemr.	30	To Warrant No. 114		388.89

Winthrop Sargent, Secretary.

1790 January	29	To Warrant No. 197	740.		
April	1	" do 312	467.88		
				1207.88	

John Cleves Symmes one of the Judges.

1790 Februy	13	To Warrant No. 216		556.52	
					2153.29

INDIAN DEPARTMENT

1790 April	9	To Thomas Tudor Tucker Agent for Richd. Winn, on account of Salary due to the said Winn as superintendant of Indian affairs in the southern Department, from the 29 August 1788 to the 29 November following Warrant No. 398	125.
1790 August	14	To Tench Coxe Attorney for Richard Butler Executor to the Estate of William Butler deceased, for the said William Butlers pay as deputy Superintendant of Indian Affairs for the Northern Department from March 17, 1787 to October 14, 1788 Warrant No. 603	788.35
	15	To Tench Coxe Attorney for Richard Butler late Superintendant of Indian Affairs Northern department for a balance due to the said superintendant for supplies furnished to Indians and for the pay of an Interpreter &c Warrt. No. 604	337.67
	16	To Thomas Tudor Tucker Agent for Richd. Winn late Superintendant of Indian Affairs in the southern department for a balance due to the said Richd. Winn Warrant No. 607	75.
	21	To Matthias Ogden Assignee of Albion Cox for a pair of dyes furnished for the purpose of striking Indian Medals by direction of the late Board of Treasury Warrant No. 625	140.
1790 August	23	To William Edgar Assignee of James Rankin Attorney for Isaac Williams, for the said Williams pay as Interpreter to the Wyandot Indians from the 20 March 1788 to the 14 October following Warrt No. 627	416.
		To William Edgar Assignee of James Rankin for the said Rankins pay and expenses as Messenger to the Indian Nations from the 22 of January 1788 to the 14th. of October following Warrt. No. 628	878.78
Septemr.	2	To Edmond Prior Attorney for William Wilson for the said Wilsons pay as Messenger to the Indian Nations, and for sundry other charges from February 8, 1788 to the 14 October following Warrt. No. 645	958.80
Decemr.	7	To Henry Knox Assignee of James OHara Attorney for George Loveless, for services performed by the said Loveless in the Indian Department from the 8 Februy to the 14 October 1788 Warrt. No. 765	209.77

1790 Decemr. 7	To Henry Knox Assignee of James OHara Attorney for Joseph Nicholson, for pay and Horse hire due to the said Nicholson as Indian Interpreter from the 11 Feby to the 14 October 1788 Warrant No. 766	255.73	
1791 July 28	To Thomas McEuen Attorney to Joseph Martin late Agent for the Cherokee and Chickasaw Nations of Indians, for the said Martins salary from the 20 July 1788 to the 20 March 1789, pursuant to Acts of Congress passed the 19 of June and the 20 August 1788 [8] Warrt. No. 1197	333.33	
			4 518.43
	Total in relation to the late Government		37,311.20

IN RELATION TO THE PRESENT GOVERNMENT, VIZT.

FOR THE COMPENSATION OF
THE PRESIDENT OF THE UNITED STATES.

1789 Septemr.	26	To Warrant No.	75	on account	1000.
October	5	" do	77	do	2000.
	6	" do	78	do	1000.
	14	" do	80	do	3500.
	15	" do	81	do	200.
	28	" do	83	do	300.
Novemr	24	" do	95	do	1000.
Decemr.	7	" do	140	do	1000.
	18	" do	149	do	2000.
	23	" do	151	do	500.
	31	" do	157	do	2000.
1790 January	12	" do	169	do	500.
	20	" do	185	do	1066.66
	29	" do	198	do	1000.
February	2	" do	202	do	1680.
March	2	" do	233	do	2000.
	23	" do	256	do	1000.
	31	" do	273	do	1000.
April	8	" do	384	do	2253.34
May	4	" do	470	do	1000.
	22	" do	490	do	1000.
	28	" do	490	do	1000.
June	5	" do	505	do	2000.
	24	" do	520	do	1000.
July	9	" do	555	do	1000.
	22	" do	566	do	500.
August	4	" do	587	do	1500.
	16	" do	609	do	1000.
	25	" do	637	do	1000.
	31	" do	640	do	2000.
Septemr	6	" do	652	do	1000.
	22	" do	665	do	1000.
October	9	" do	705	do	1500.

8. *JCC*, XXXIV, 241, 433.

	Novemr. 1	" do	732	do	500.	
	16	" do	738	do	2000.	
	Decemr. 10	" do	772	do	2000.	
1791	January 1	" do	793	do	1000.	
	20	" do	848	do	1000.	
	February 8	" do	876	do	1000.	
	22	" do	909	do	601.64	
	28	" do	918	do	398.36	
	"	" do	919	do	1650.	
	March 19	" do	944	do	1000.	
	22	" do	947	do	500.	
	30	" do	958	do	1000.	
	April 15	" do	1024	do	1000.	
	May 7	" do	1060	do	1000.	
	June 3	" do	1089	do	1000.	
	21	" do	1106	do	1500.	
	July 13	" do	1178	do	1000.	
	August 4	" do	1206	do	1000.	
	19	" do	1228	do	1000.	
	Septemr 10	" do	1242	do	2500.	
	21	" do	1254	do	1000.	
	29	" do	1263	do	1500.	
	October 13	" do	1314	do	500.	
	15	" do	1320	do	1000.	
	22	" do	1326	do	1000.	
	Novemr 14	" do	1354	do	1000.	
	29	" do	1361	do	1000.	
	Decemr. 16	" do	1367	do	500.	
	27	" do	1383	do	500.	
						72150.

EXPENSES INCURRED FOR THE TEMPORARY ACCOMMODATION OF THE PRESIDENT OF THE UNITED STATES.

1789	Decemr. 1	To Royal Flint Warrt. No.	118	5000.	
	5	" do do	136	500.	
	7	" do do	141	1000.	
	16	" do do	147	1500.	
1790	April 7	To Samuel Osgood do	381	5677.83	
					13,677.83

FOR THE COMPENSATION OF THE VICE PRESIDENT OF THE UNITED STATES.

1789	October 28	To Warrant No.	84	on account	1000.
	Novemr. 13	" do	91	do	2000.
	Decemr. 14	" do	144	do	300.
	29	" do	155	do	700.
1790	February 8	" do	210	do	1000.
	May 17	" do	484	do	1000.
	July 9	" do	553	do	500.
	August 2	" do	580	do	500.
	7	" do	589	do	1000.
	Septemr 25	" do	666	do	1000.

Novemr. 18	" do	740	do	1000.		
1791 March 1	" do	921	do	1000.		
April 27	" do	1038	do	1000.		
30	" do	1045	do	1000.		
October 27	" do	1335	do	1000.		
					14,000.	
						99,827.83

JUDICIARY DEPARTMENT

For the compensations of the Judges, the Attorney General, the Marshals, the District Attornies and Clerks of the Circuit and District Courts.

John Jay Chief Justice of the United States.

1789 Decemr. 1	To Warrant No.	119	54.79	
1790 January 15	" do	175	666.66	
April 6	" do	366	333.34	
7	" do	375	1000.	
July 17	" do	560	1000.	
October 4	" do	686	1000.	
1791 January 22	" do	851	1000.	
April 2	" do	973	1000.	
August 2	" do	1201	1000.	
October 12	" do	1312	1000.	
				8 054.79

John Rutledge one of the associate Judges of the Supreme Court.

1790 January 15	To Warrant No.	171	500.	
March 29	" do	265	422.55	
April 15	" do	431	875.	
July 13	" do	557	875.	
October 1	" do	676	875.	
1791 January 5	" do	801	875.	
April 9	" do	1009	622.22	
				5 044.77

James Wilson one of the associate Judges of the Supreme Court.

1790 January 15	To Warrant No.	183	500.	
March 26	" do	257	422.55	
April 16	" do	438	875.	
July 7	" do	544	875.	
October 1	" do	677	875.	
1791 January 6	" do	804	875.	
April 7	" do	1006	875.	
July 6	" do	1152	875.	
October 5	" do	1293	875.	
				7 047.55

John Blair one of the associate Judges of the Supreme Court.

1790 February 11	To Warrant No. 214	500.		
April 15	" do 427	875.		
"	" do 428	422.55		
July 23	" do 569	875.		
October 1	" do 673	875.		
1791 February 22	" do 906	875.		
April 11	" do 1012	875.		
July 6	" do 1155	875.		
October 6	" do 1297	875.		
			7 047.55	

William Cushing one of the associate Judges of the Supreme Court.

1790 February 17	To Warrant No. 222	500.	
April 6	" do 365	422.55	
7	" do 373	875.	
August 3	" do 585	875.	
1791 February 8	" do 873	1750.	
April 11	" do 1015	875.	
August 1	" do 1199	875.	
October 6	" do 1295	875.	
			7 047.55

James Iredell one of the associate Judges of the Supreme Court.

1790 May 13	To Warrant No. 481	486.11	
August 7	" do 592	875.	
October 4	" do 687	875.	
1791 January 5	" do 799	875.	
April 6	" do 994	875.	
July 6	" do 1147	875.	
October 3	" do 1277	875.	
			5,736.11

David Sewall Judge for the District of Maine.

1790 January 25	To Warrant No. 195	133.33	
April 6	" do 370	130.25	
July 9	" do 552	500.	
1791 January 7	" do 812	500.	
October 27	" do 1334	750.	
			2 013.58

John Sullivan Judge for the District of New Hampshire.

1790 February 15	To Warrant No. 220	166.66
April 21	" do 449	346.92
July 6	" do 540	250.
Decemr. 8	" do 770	250.
1791 January 7	" do 816	250.

April	7	" do	997	250.	
July	7	" do	1162	250.	
October	7	" do	1302	250.	
					2 013.58

John Lowell Judge for the District of Massachusetts.

1790 April	9	To Warrant No.	392	616.30	
1791 Februy	14	" do	894	900.	
					1 516.30

Henry Marchant Judge for the District of Rhode Island.

1791 January	17	To Warrant No.	839	395.65	
April	11	" do	1013	200.	
July	7	" do	1157	200.	
October	1	" do	1303	200.	
					995.65

Richard Law, Judge for the District of Connecticut.

1790 February	10	To Warrant No.	212	166.66	
April	6	" do	371	96.92	
	9	" do	393	250.	
July	7	" do	524	250.	
October	11	" do	709	250.	
1791 January	5	" do	800	250.	
June	1	" do	1083	250.	
October	3	" do	1278	500.	
					2 013.58

Nathaniel Chipman Judge for the District of Vermont.

1791 October	22	To Warrant No.	1324	400.	
Decemr.	1	" do	1363	62.22	
					462.22

James Duane Judge for the District of New York.

1790 April	9	To Warrant No.	391	770.38	
October	13	" do	715	750.	
1791 February	8	" do	874	375.	
April	11	" do	1016	375.	
Novemr	4	" do	1346	750.	
					3 020.38

David Brearly, Judge for the District of New Jersey.

1790 January	22	To Warrant No.	191	166.66	
April	12	" do	410	250.	
	13	" do	417	96.92	
July	8	" do	548	250.	
1791 Novemr.	24	" do	1359 to August 16, 1790	127.71	
					891.29

Robert Morris Judge for the District of New Jersey.

1791 February	17	To Warrant No.	899	342.39	
May	30	" do	1079	250.	
July	6	" do	1153	250.	
October	16	" do	1318	250.	
					1 092.39

Francis Hopkinson Judge for the District of Pennsylvania.

1790 January	27	To Warrant No.	196	266.66	
April	8	" do	369	155.08	
	15	" do	434	400.	
July	13	" do	556	400.	
October	2	" do	681	400.	
1791 January	6	" do	803	400.	
April	14	" do	1021	400.	
July	11	" do	1171 to May 8. 1791	167.03	
					2 588.77

William Lewis Judge for the District of Pennsylvania.

1791 October	25	To Warrant No.	1327		343.48

Gunning Bedford Judge for the District of Delaware.

1790 July	27	To Warrant No.	571	610.86	
1791 April	9	" do	1007	600.	
					1 210.86

William Paca Judge for the District of Maryland.

1790 May	20	To Warrant No.	487	415.76	
July	27	" do	573	375.	
October	15	" do	730	375.	
1791 January	10	" do	824	375.	
April	27	" do	1039	375.	
July	22	" do	1192	375.	
Octr.	7	" do	1300	375.	
					2 665.76

Cyrus Griffin Judge for the District of Virginia.

1790 March	12	To Warrant No.	251	166.30	
April	15	" do	433	450.	
July	6	" do	539	450.	
October	6	" do	692	450.	
1791 January	7	" do	817	450.	
April	7	" do	999	450.	
July	11	" do	1158	450.	
October	7	" do	1301	450.	
					3 316.30

Harry Innes Judge for the District of Kentucky.

1790	April	27	To Warrant No.	461	250.	
	June	14	" do	510	250.	
	August	3	" do	583	13.58	
	"		" do	584	250.	
	October	12	" do	710	250.	
1791	January	7	" do	810	250.	
	April	6	" do	995	250.	
	July	5	" do	1145	250.	
	October	3	" do	1279	250.	
						2 013.58

John Stokes late Judge for the District of North Carolina, deceased.

1791	May	23	To Warrant No. 1076 to October 11,1790	287.67

John Sitgreaves Judge for the District of North Carolina.

1791	April	18	To Warrant No.	1027	423.91	
	July	5	" do	1143	375.	
	October	4	" do	1286	375.	
						1173.91

William Drayton Judge for the District of South Carolina.

1790	March	2	To Warrant No.	236	215.21	
	April	13	" do	420	450.	
	Septemr	7	" do	654 to May 18, 1790	237.36	
						902.57

Thomas Bee Judge for the District of South Carolina.

1790	October	13	To Warrant No.	713	450.	
1791	January	6	" do	802	534.06	
	April	4	" do	980	450.	
	July	11	" do	1172	450.	
	October	5	" do	1292	450.	
						2 334.06

Nathaniel Pendleton Judge for the District of Georgia.

1790	January	15	To Warrant No.	177	266.66	
	April	9	" do	396	128.72	
		12	" do	409	375.	
	July	8	" do	549	375.	
	October	6	" do	698	375.	
1791	January	10	" do	825	375.	
	April	14	" do	1020	375.	
	July	11	" do	1168	375.	
	October	19	" do	1321	375.	
						3 020.38

Edmund Randolph Attorney General of the United States.

1790 Februy	8	To Warrant No.	209	250.	
April	15	" do	432	375.	
August	2	" do	578	145.38	
"		" do	579	375.	
October	1	" do	675	375.	
1791 Februy	1	" do	862	375.	
April	7	" do	1005	407.22	
July	6	" do	1156	475.	
October	6	" do	1296	475.	
					3 252.60

John Parker Marshal for the District of New Hampshire.

1791 July	8	To Warrant No. 1165, for attending several Sessions of the Circuit and District Courts from December 1789 to May 1791, for the compensations of grand and petit Juries, and for sundry contingent expenses	358.30

Thomas Lowry Marshal for the District of New Jersey.

1791 May	21	To Warrant No. 1074, for attending the several Sessions of the Circuit and District Courts, for the compensations of Jurors and Witnesses, and for sundry contingent expenses from November 1789 to May 1791	622.42

Pierpont Edwards Attorney for the District of Connecticut.

1791 June	15	To Warrant No.	1100	75.20	
	16	" do	1103	106.25	
					181.45

George Read Attorney for the District of Delaware.

1791 June	2	To Warrant No. 1085	33.60

William Hill Attorney for the District of North Carolina.

1791 October	19	To Warrant No. 1322	40.

Jonathan Steele Clerk of the Circuit and District Courts for the State of New Hampshire.

1791 July	11	To Warrant No. 1169	103.60

Sundry Persons Clerks of the Circuit and District Courts for the State of Connecticut.

1791 May	2	To Mark Leavenworth, Warrt. No.	1050	137.80	
		" Simeon Baldwin do	1078	69.20	
					207.

Robert Troupe Clerk of the Circuit and District Courts for the State of New York.

1791 April	7	To Warrant No. 1001	223.

Sundry Persons Clerks of the Circuit and District Courts for the State of New Jersey.

1791 May	2	To Robert Boggs,	Warrt. No. 1066	90.		
June	10	" Jonathan Dayton	do 1096	89.		
					179.	

Mathew Pearce Clerk of the Circuit and District Courts for the State of Delaware.

1791 June	2	To Warrant No. 1086	103.60

Joshua Barney Clerk of the Circuit and District Courts for the State of Maryland.

1791 May	31	To Warrant No. 1082	174.28

Venables Bond Clerk of the Circuit and District Courts for the State of Georgia.

1791 June	17	To Warrant No. 1105	134.

Samuel Bayard Clerk of the Supreme Court.

1791 Septemr	27	To Warrant No. 1259	24.	
				79,491.48

LEGISLATIVE DEPARTMENT

For compensation to the Senators and members of the House of Representatives, their Officers and Clerks, and for the contingent expenses of both houses.

SENATE.

First Session of the first Congress.

1789 Septemr. 29 To Warrant No. 1, for compensation due to the under mentioned Senators. . . . .

Vizt.

Richard Bassett	1101.
Pierce Butler	1238.
Charles Carroll	1170.
Tristram Dalton	1194.
Oliver Ellsworth	1345.
Jonathan Elmer	966.
William Few	1709.
William Grayson	996.

James Gunn	1618.
John Henry	1139.
William S. Johnson	1304.
Ralph Izard	1580.
Rufus King	402.
John Langdon	1254.
Richard Henry Lee	1290.
William Maclay	1266.
Robert Morris	1131.
William Patterson	1131.
George Read	1110.
Caleb Strong	1127.
Philip Schuyler	489.
Paine Wingate	1449.
	26 009.

Second Session of the First Congress.

1790 April	1	To Benjamin Hawkins	Warrt. No.	309	147.
"	"	" Ralph Izard	do	310	796.
	5	" Richard Bassett	do	338	496.50
	"	" Pierce Butler	do	339	796.
	"	" Charles Carroll	do	340	186.
	"	" Tristram Dalton	do	341	612.
	"	" Oliver Ellsworth	do	342	546.50
	"	" Jonathan Elmer	do	343	414.
	"	" William Few	do	344	833.50
	"	" John Henry	do	345	596.50
	"	" William S. Johnson	do	346	544.
	"	" Samuel Johnston	do	347	534.
	"	" Rufus King	do	348	522.
	"	" John Langdon	do	349	618.
	"	" William Maclay	do	350	585.
	"	" Robert Morris	do	351	430.50
	"	" William Paterson	do	352	514.50
	"	" George Read	do	353	195.
	"	" Caleb Strong	do	354	575.50
	"	" Philip Schuyler	do	355	571.50
	"	" Paine Wingate	do	356	616.50
	"	" Benjamin Hawkins	do	357	468.
May	21	" John Walker	do	489	114.
July	6	" Joseph Stanton	do	536	62.
	"	" Benjamin Hawkins	do	537	546.
	16	" James Gunn	do	558	866.
	17	" Ralph Izard	do	559	636.
	22	" Pierce Butler	do	567	636.
	23	" William Maclay	do	568	759.
	27	" Richard Bassett	do	572	754.50
August	5	" Theodore Foster	do	588	285.
	9	" John Langdon	do	595	876.
	11	" Richard Bassett	do	598	78.
	"	" Pain Wingate	do	599	886.50
	18	" Jonathan Elmer	do	614	924.

Septemr. 7	To Warrant No. 655 in favor of Samuel Meredith Agent for the following Senators Vizt.			
	Pierce Butler		441.90	
	Charles Carroll		876.	
	Tristram Dalton		894.	
	Oliver Ellsworth		846.30	
	William Few		1115.40	
	Theodore Foster		135.	
	James Gunn		494.	
	John Henry		878.40	
	Benjamin Hawkins		405.	
	William S. Johnson		825.90	
	Samuel Johnston		972.	
	Ralph Izard		441.90	
	Rufus King		804.	
	Richard Henry Lee		954.	
	Robert Morris		832.50	
	William Paterson		706.50	
	George Read		843.	
	Philip Schuyler		853.50	
	Joseph Stanton Junr.		355.50	
	John Walker		882.	
				14,556.80
"	To William Maclay	Warrant No. 656		18.
"	" Caleb Strong	do 657		834.

Third Session of the First Congress.

1790 Decemr. 17	To Ralph Izard	Warrant No. 779		243.90
23	" Pierce Butler	do 784		243.90
24	" James Monroe	do 786		86.70
1791 January 8	To Warrant No. 821 being for compensation due to the undermentioned Senators on the 31 day of Decemr. last.			
	Richard Bassett		76.50	
	Pierce Butler		157.50	
	Tristram Dalton		272.10	
	Philemon Dickinson		165.	
	Oliver Ellsworth		225.30	
	Jonathan Elmer		159.	
	William Few		443.40	
	Theodore Foster		181.50	
	Benjamin Hawkins		273.90	
	William S. Johnson		164.70	
	Samuel Johnston		288.60	
	Ralph Izard		157.50	
	Rufus King		184.50	
	John Langdon		278.70	
	William Maclay		193.50	
	James Monroe		156.	
	Robert Morris		36.	
	George Read		154.20	

		Joseph Stanton Junr.	192.30	
		Caleb Strong	226.50	
		Philip Schuyler	192.	
		Paine Wingate	277.20	
				4 455.90
1791 March	25	To Warrant No. 956 being compensensation due to the undermentioned Senators on the 4th. instant.		
		Richard Bassett	322.50	
		Pierce Butler	623.40	
		Charles Carroll	342.	
		Tristram Dalton	488.10	
		Philemon Dickinson	387.	
		Oliver Ellsworth	447.30	
		Jonathan Elmer	387.	
		William Few	659.40	
		Theodore Foster	473.10	
		James Gunn	862.20	
		Benjamin Hawkins	495.90	
		John Henry	427.80	
		William S. Johnson	428.70	
		Samuel Johnston	510.60	
		Ralph Izard	623.40	
		Rufus King	406.50	
		John Langdon	504.30	
		Richard Henry Lee	258.	
		William Maclay	409.50	
		James Monroe	458.70	
		Robert Morris	378.	
		George Read	388.20	
		Philip Schuyler	450.	
		Joseph Stanton Junr.	522.30	
		Caleb Strong	454.50	
		Pain Wingate	502.80	
				12,211.20
April	7	To Samuel A. Otis Agent for Richard Henry Lee, Warrant No. 1002		30.

First Session of the Second Congress.

1791 Novemr.	12	To Samuel Meredith Agent for the undermentioned Senators, Warrant No. 1352, being their compensation for travelling to the Seat of Governmt.		
		Richard Bassett	22.50	
		Aaron Burr	28.50	
		Pierce Butler	245.40	
		George Cabot	109.50	
		Charles Carroll	39.	
		Philemon Dickinson	9.	
		Oliver Elsworth	69.30	
		William Few	287.40	
		Theodore Foster	95.10	
		James Gunn	284.10	

		Benjamin Hawkins	117.90	
		John Henry	45.90	
		Samuel Johnston	132.60	
		Ralph Izard	245.40	
		Rufus King	28.50	
		John Langdon	124.50	
		Richard Henry Lee	75.	
		James Monroe	86.70	
		George Read	10.20	
		John Rutherford	24.	
		Roger Shearman	55.50	
		Joseph Stanton Junr.	90.30	
		Caleb Strong	82.50	
		Pain Wingate	123.	
		Moses Robinson	88.50	
			2,520.30	
1791 Decemr.	3	To Samuel A. Otis, to enable him to pay the compensation due to the Senators, Warrt. No. 1364	* 5 256.	
				85 487.20

Samuel Provost Chaplain to the Senate in New York.

1789 Novemr	30	To Warrant No.	102	188.57	
"	"	" do	103	26.02	
1790 August	16	" do	608	295.80	
					510.39

William White Chaplain to the Senate in Philadelphia.

1791 March	19	To Warrant No. 940	120.49

Samuel A. Otis Secretary to the Senate.

1789 Septemr.	29	To Warrant No.	61	1069.17	
1790 April	3	" do	318	926.05	
July	7	" do	545	375.	
August	24	" do	629	268.	
Novemr.	24	" do	751	375.	
1791 January	6	" do	807	375.	
	8	" do	822	52.	
March	15	" do	936	† 756.	
April	5	" do	985	375.	
July	2	" do	1133	‡ 678.	
October	3	" do	1276	375.	
					5 624.22

* The expenditure of this sum will appear in the next statement.
† This Warrant includes the salaries of the Clerks, Doorkeeper and Messenger.
‡ This Warrant includes the salary of the Chief Clerk.

Benjamin Bankson Principal Clerk in the Office of the Secretary to the Senate.

1789 Septemr. 29	To Warrant No.	63	435.	
1790 March 31	" do	271	288.	
April 7	" do	378	261.	
August 24	" do	630	402.	
				1 386.

Robert Heysham engrossing Clerk in the Office of the Secretary of the Senate.

1789 Septemr 29	To Warrant No.	65	202.	
1790 March 31	" do	272	100.	
April 7	" do	379	174.	
August 24	" do	631	268.	
1791 January 8	" do	822	78.	
				822.

Samuel A. Otis Junior engrossing Clerk in the Office of the Secretary to the Senate.

1791 January 8	To Warrant No.	822	72.	
May 30	" do	1069	52.	
				124.

James Mathers Doorkeeper to the Senate.

1789 Septemr. 29	To Warrant No.	67	630.	
1790 April 3	" do	330	96.	
May 25	" do	493	261.	
August 24	" do	632	402.	
1791 January 8	" do	822	78.	
				1 467.

Cornelius Maxwell Messenger to the Senate.

1789 Septemr 29	To Warrant No.	69	350.	
1790 April 7	" do	380	174.	
August 24	" do	633	268.	
1791 January 8	" do	822	52.	
				844.

Contingent expenses of the Senate.

1790 March 31	To Samuel A. Otis Secretary, Warrt. No.		276	2300.	
June 15	" do	do	513	400.	
August 3	" do	do	582	1500.	
October 30	" do	do	728	300.	
1791 March 2	" do	do	924	2000.	
April 29	" do	do	1041	300.	
May 2	" do	do	1048	345.	
16	" do	do	1071	52.	
					7,197.
					103,582.30

HOUSE OF REPRESENTATIVES

First Session of the First Congress.

1789 Septemr. 29	To Frederick A. Muhlenberg Speaker of the House	Warrt. No.	2	2418.
"	" Lambert Cadwallader	do	3	1125.
"	" Isaac Coles	do	4	1455.
"	" Peter Silvester	do	5	1050.
"	" John Brown	do	6	1182.
"	" Daniel Hiester	do	7	1212.
"	" Jonathan Trumbull	do	8	1182.
"	" John Page	do	9	1446.
"	" Fisher Ames	do	10	1416.
"	" Thomas Hartley	do	11	1071.
"	" Peter Muhlenberg	do	12	1332.
"	" Andrew Moore	do	13	1440.
"	" Thomas Fitzsimmons	do	14	1233.
"	" George Clymer	do	15	1047.
"	" Michael Jenifer Stone	do	16	1005.
"	" Thomas Scott	do	17	1344.
"	" Alexander White	do	18	1239.
"	" George Gale	do	19	1290.
"	" George Thatcher	do	20	1479.
"	" Daniel Carroll	do	21	1213.
"	" Josiah Parker	do	22	1254.
"	" William Floyd	do	23	990.
"	" Abiel Foster	do	24	474.
"	" Samuel Livermore	do	25	1116.
"	" James Jackson	do	26	1599.
"	" Abraham Baldwin	do	27	1599.
"	" George Partridge	do	28	1242.
"	" Thomas Sinnickson	do	29	978.
"	" James Schureman	do	30	1041.
"	" George Leonard	do	31	1050.
"	" Benjamin Goodhue	do	32	1425.
"	" Jereh. Van Rensselaer	do	33	960.
"	" John Hathorn	do	34	960.
"	" Henry Wynkoop	do	35	1092.
"	" William Smith	do	36	1281.
"	" Thomas Sumpter	do	37	1278.
"	" Elbridge Gerry	do	38	1413.
"	" Thomas Tudor Tucker	do	39	1806.
"	" Joshua Seney	do	40	1140.
"	" William Smith	do	41	1578.
"	" Jonathan Grout	do	42	1056.
"	" Elias Boudinot	do	43	1134.
"	" Theodorick Bland	do	44	1428.
"	" Richard Bland Lee	do	45	1362.
"	" Roger Sherman	do	46	1266.
"	" Benjamin Contee	do	47	804.
"	" George Mathews	do	48	1266.
"	" Jeremiah Wadsworth	do	49	1161.
"	" Benjn. Huntington	do	50	1350.
"	" Daniel Huger	do	51	1578.
"	" Ædanus Burke	do	52	1578.

"	"	Samuel Griffin	do	53	1443.
"	"	James Madison Junr.	do	54	1410.
"	"	John Vining	do	55	990.
"	"	Egbert Benson	do	56	1092.
"	"	John Laurence	do	57	1050.
"	"	Nicholas Gilman	do	59	1447.20
"	"	Theodore Sedgwick	do	60	576.
"	"	Jonathan Sturges	do	58	1107.
1790 February	20	"	Theodore Sedgwick	do	224	18.
March	2	"	George Leonard	do	232	168.

Second Session of the First Congress.

	31	To	Thomas Hartley	Warrt. No.	278	582.
April	1	"	Henry Wynkoop	do	280	522.
	"	"	Samuel Livermore	do	281	624.
	"	"	Benjamin Goodhue	do	282	600.75
	"	"	John Brown	do	284	792.
	"	"	Peter Muhlengberg	do	285	558.
	"	"	Elias Boudinot	do	288	522.
	"	"	Jonathan Grout	do	294	585.
	"	"	George Thatcher	do	295	631.80
	"	"	Daniel Huger	do	296	798.
	"	"	Ædanus Burke	do	297	798.
	"	"	Thomas Scott	do	298	648.
	"	"	Alexander White	do	299	610.50
	"	"	Andrew Moore	do	300	621.90
	"	"	Benjamin Huntington	do	301	519.
	"	"	George Gale	do	302	453.
	"	"	Peter Sylvester	do	303	456.
	"	"	William Smith	do	304	534.
	"	"	Roger Sherman	do	305	549.
	"	"	Thomas Sumpter	do	306	444.
	"	"	Michl. Jenifer Stone	do	307	615.
	"	"	William Smith	do	308	798.
	"	"	Daniel Carroll	do	320	633.33
	"	"	Fredh. A. Muhlenberg, Speaker		321	1108.50
	"	"	Nicholas Gilman	do	322	615.60
	"	"	Theodorick Bland	do	323	471.
	"	"	Josiah Parker	do	324	573.
	"	"	Isaac Coles	do	325	679.50
	"	"	Elbridge Gerry	do	326	603.
April	8	"	James Jackson	do	336	786.
	"	"	Theodore Sedgwick	do	360	543.
	"	"	John Laurence	do	361	552.
	"	"	John Hathorn	do	362	540.
	"	"	Samuel Griffin	do	364	682.50
	"	"	Abiel Foster	do	382	618.
	"	"	George Leonard	do	386	525.
	"	"	John Page	do	387	675.
	"	"	Jonathan Trumbull	do	388	537.
	"	"	Thomas T. Tucker	do	389	798.
	"	"	Jeremiah Wadsworth	do	390	453.
	9	"	Jeremiah Van Renselaer	do	394	600.
	"	"	James Madison Junr.	do	399	585.

	12	"	Richard Bland Lee	do	407	570.
	"	"	Timothy Bloodworth	do	413	216.
	"	"	Egbert Benson	do	414	606.
	"	"	John Baptist Ash	do	415	192.
	13	"	Hugh Williamson	do	422	287.
	15	"	William Floyde	do	424	513.
	"	"	Abraham Baldwin	do	425	912.
	"	"	Joshua Seney	do	426	708.
	"	"	John Vining	do	436	303.
	17	"	Fisher Ames	do	441	690.
	21	"	Thomas Sinnickson	do	444	606.
	22	"	George Gale	do	453	207.
	"	"	George Clymer	do	454	646.50
	30	"	John Steel	do	465	204.
May	1	"	Isaac Coles	do	466	168.
	3	"	Josiah Parker	do	469	327.
	4	"	George Partridge	do	471	804.
	5	"	James Schureman	do	472	712.50
	8	"	Benjamin Contee	do	475	474.

To Frederick Augustus Muhlenberg Speaker, to enable him to pay the compensations due to the Members, their Officers and Clerks.

1790 May	11	"	Warrant No.	478	12000.	
June	23	"	do	518	12000.	
July	21	"	do	565	8000.	
August	10	"	do	596	12000.	
	"	"	do	597	15911.69	
						59,911.69

For which he has accounted by the following payments Vizt.

To Samuel Livermore	894.
" Abiel Foster	882.
" Elbridge Gerry	864.
" Fisher Ames	780.
" George Leonard	759.
" Jonathan Grout	855.
" Benjamin Goodhue	878.25
" George Thatcher	900.80
" Theodore Sedgwick	759.
" Jonathan Trumbull	765.
" Roger Sherman	819.
" Peter Sylvester	834.
" Egbert Benson	756.
" William Floyd	759.
" John Laurence	762.
" Thomas Scott	918.
" George Clymer	658.50
" Peter Muhlenberg	828.
" Thomas Hartley	648.
" Henry Wynkoop	756.
" John Vining	753.
" Daniel Carroll	808.47
" Michael J. Stone	780.

" Joshua Seney	714.
" George Gale	666.
" Benjamin Contee	588.
" Estate of Theodorick Bland	495.
" Samuel Griffin	892.50
" Alexander White	880.50
" Andrew Moore	921.90
" Richard Bland Lee	894.
" Isaac Coles	757.50
" John Brown	1026.
" Josiah Parker	612.
" John Page	873.
" John Babtist Ash	960.
" John Steel	888.
" Hugh Williamson	905.
" Timothy Bloodworth	978.
" John Sevier	795.
" Ædanus Burke	1068.
" Daniel Huger	1068.
" William Smith	1068.
" Thomas Sumpter	1098.
" Abraham Baldwin	1026.
" James Jackson	1086.
" George Matthews	1920.
" Thomas Fitzsimons	1269.
" Lambert Cadwalader	1191.
" Daniel Hiester	1350.
" Nicholas Gilman	885.60
" George Partridge	672.
" Benjamin Huntington	837.
" Jonathan Sturges	1335.
" Jeremiah Wadsworth	741.
" John Hathorn	762.
" Jeremiah Van Renselaer	792.
" Elias Boudinot	762.
" James Schureman	592.50
" Thomas Sinnickson	714.
" James Madison Junr.	879.
" Thomas T. Tucker	1068.
" William Smith	852.
" Frederick A. Muhlenberg	1576.35
	56,875.87
" William Linn, Chaplain	180.82
" John Beckley, Clerk	889.
" Joseph Wheaton Sergeant at Arms	528.
" William Lambert principal Clerk to Mr. Beckley	396.
" Bernard Webb engrossing Clerk	382.
" Gifford Dally, Doorkeeper	396.
" Thomas Claxton assistant Doorkeeper	264.
	59,911.69

Third Session of the First Congress.

To Frederick Augustus Muhlenberg Speaker, for the same purpose.

1790 August 13	To Warrant No. 600	670.	
Decemr. 21	" do 782	12 000.	
1791 January 28	" do 857	12 000.	
March 2	" do 926	25 388.	
	50,058.		
	From this sum deduct the amt. of a Warrant No. 50 dated the 26 May 1791, on the Speaker in favor of the Treasurer, being for a balance which remained unexpended	2 979.50	
			47,078.50

For which he has accounted by the following payments . . . Vizt.

Two days compensation paid the Members and Doorkeepers, due the 11th. and 12th. of August 1790	664.
To Abiel Foster	783.
" Nicholas Gilman	774.
" Samuel Livermore	804.
" Fisher Ames	744.
" Elbridge Gerry	738.
" Benjamin Goodhue	732.
" Jonathan Grout	714.
" George Leonard	783.
" George Partridge	753.
" Theodore Sedgwick	690.
" George Thatcher	804.
" Benjamin Huntington	678.
" Roger Sherman	640.
" Jonathan Sturges	618.
" Jonathan Trumbull	654.
" Jeremiah Wadsworth	636.
" Egbert Benson	630.
" William Floyd	624.
" John Hathorn	570.
" John Laurence	585.
" Jeremiah Van Renselaer	642.
" Peter Sylvester	672.
" Elias Boudinot	576.
" Lambert Cadwallader	546.
" James Schureman	564.
" Thomas Sinickson	520.50
" George Clymer	444.
" Thomas Fitzsimmons	528.
" Thomas Hartley	528.
" Daniel Hiester	543.60
" Frederick A. Muhlenberg	1 068.
" Peter Muhlenberg	540.
" Thomas Scott	720.
" Henry Wynkoop	540.
" John Vining	536.

Date		Item	Amount	Total	Grand total
	"	Daniel Carroll	480.		
	"	Benjamin Contee	306.		
	"	George Gale	389.		
	"	Joshua Seney	582.		
	"	William Smith (M)	576.		
	"	Michael Jenifer Stone	561.		
	"	John Brown	1 023.50		
	"	William B. Giles	702.		
	"	Samuel Griffin	726.		
	"	Richard Bland Lee	630.		
	"	James Madison Junr.	578.		
	"	Andrew Moore	719.10		
	"	Josiah Parker	726.		
	"	Alexander White	636.		
	"	John Babtist Ash	738.		
	"	Timothy Bloodworth	904.		
	"	John Sevier	868.		
	"	John Steel	792.		
	"	Ædanus Burke	984.		
	"	Daniel Huger	1 014.		
	"	William Smith (S. C.)	1 020.		
	"	Thomas Sumpter	564.		
	"	Thomas T. Tucker	1 008.		
	"	Hugh Williamson	792.60		
	"	Abraham Baldwin	1 104.		
	"	James Jackson	1 092.		
	"	George Matthews	1 086.		
	"	Benjamin Bourne	652.20		
			44,839.50		
	"	Samuel Blair, Chaplain	125.		
	"	John Beckley, Clerk	551.		
	"	Jonathan Wheaton, Sergeant at Arms	352.		
	"	Bernard Webb, principal Clerk to Mr Beckley	279.		
	"	William Clairborn, engrossing Clerk	368.		
	"	Reuben Burnley, do	124.		
	"	Gifford Dally, Doorkeeper	264.		
	"	Thomas Claxton assistant Doorkeeper	176.		
			47,078.50		

First Session of the Second Congress.

Date		Item	Amount	Total	Grand total
	To	Jonathan Trumbull Speaker to enable him to pay the compensations due to the Members their Officers and Clerks.			
1791 Novemr. 2	"	Warrant No. 1345	12000.		
Decemr. 18	"	do 1368	12000.		
				* 24,000.	239,715.77

* The expenditure of this sum will appear in the next statement.

William Linn Chaplain to the House of Representatives in New York.

1789 Septemr.	29	To Warrant No.	72	208.	
1790 April	23	" do	458	113.70	
					321.70

John Beckley Clerk to the House of Representatives.

1789 Septemr.	30	To Warrant No.	76	1 114.	
1790 March	31	" do	279	924.	
Decemr.	4	" do	763	379.	
1791 June	6	" do	1091	375.	
July	22	" do	1189	* 275.	
October	3	" do	1280	375.	
					3,442.

Joseph Wheaton Sergeant at Arms to the House of Representatives.

1789 Septemr.	29	To Warrant No.	62	564.	
1790 April	7	" do	377	348.	
					912.

William Lambert principal Clerk in the Office of the Clerk of the House of Representatives.

1789 Septemr.	29	To Warrant No.	64	546.	
1790 April	3	" do	328	549.	
Novemr	30	" do	756	60.	
					1 155.

George Sutton engrossing Clerk in said Office.

1789 Septemr.	29	To Warrant No.	66	248.	
1790 April	1	" do	290	70.	
					318.

Bernard Webb engrossing Clerk in said Office.

1790 Decemr.	4	To Warrant No.	764	224.	
1791 June	6	" do	1092 as principal Clerk	267.	
					491.

Reuben Burnley engrossing Clerk in said Office.

1791 June	6	To Warrant No. 1093			178.

* This Warrant includes the salaries due to his Clerks.

Gifford Dally Doorkeeper to the House of Representatives.

1789 Septemr	29	To Warrant No. 68	645.66		
1790 April	3	" do 327	357.		
				1 002.66	

Thomas Claxton Assistant Doorkeeper.

1789 Septem	29	To Warrant No. 71	358.		
1790 April	3	" do 331	174.		
				532.	

Cornelius Maxwell Messenger.

1789 Septemr	29	To Warrant No. 70		62.	

Contingent expenses of the House of Representatives.

1790 March	31	To John Beckley	Warrt. No.	277	3657.85		
April	21	" do	do	450	1000.		
June	22	" do	do	517	888.80		
	31	" do	do	576	1000.		
Septemr	3	" do	do	647	1500.		
1791 March	15	" do	do	937	2500.		
April	6	" do	do	990	1500.		
August	29	" do	do	1234	800.		
						12,846.65	
							364,559.08

TREASURY DEPARTMENT

For compensation to the Officers, Clerks and Messengers, and for the contingent expenses of the Department.

Alexander Hamilton Secretary of the Treasury, his Assistant, Clerks and Messenger.

1789 Decemr.	1	To Warrant No.	134	361.08	
1790 January	20	" do	186	1625.	
April	6	" do	367	198.09	
	13	" do	419	1895.84	
July	2	" do	529	1764.28	
August	31	" do	642	71.42	
October	2	" do	683	2050.	
1791 January	4	" do	794	1964.37	
March	25	" do	955	27.77	
April	2	" do	976	2253.03	
May	23	" do	1077	21.98	
July	2	" do	1132	2309.32	
October	3	" do	1270	2562.50	
					17,104.68

Nicholas Eveleigh Comptroller of the Treasury, his Clerks and Messenger.

1789 Decemr.	1	To Warrant No.	132		230.	
	26	" do	153		60.	
1790 January	15	" do	179		565.	
April	1	" do	291		112.50	
"		" do	292		64.81	
	5	" do	335		135.	
	12	" do	402		1125.24	
July	3	" do	531		1138.73	
Septemr.	13	" do	663		103.26	
October	1	" do	678		1130.43	
1791 January	5	" do	797		1262.49	
	13	" do	832		50.	
April	2	" do	975		2084.99	
					8062.45	

Oliver Wolcott Junr. Comptroller his Clerks and Messenger.

July	2	To Warrant No.	1134	1717.30		
August	9	" for a part of	1222	32.61		
October	3	" Warrant	1275	2025.		
Novemr	1	" do	1342	14.94		
	19	" do	1356	61.14		
					3850.99	
						11 913.44

Samuel Meredith Treasurer of the United States, his Clerks & Messenger.

1790 January	15	To Warrant No.	172		784.23	
April	13	" do	418		650.	
July	7	" do	543		650.	
October	6	" do	691		650.	
1791 January	6	" do	806		650.	
April	2	" do	972		793.89	
July	6	" do	1151		775.	
October	4	" do	1285		775.	
						5 728.12

Oliver Wolcott Junior Auditor of the Treasury, his Clerks and Messenger.

1789 Decemr.	1	To Warrant No.	133		92.87	
1790 January	6	" do	167		108.50	
	15	" do	170		846.57	
April	5	" do	333		34.24	
	12	" do	401		2106.92	
	26	" do	460		32.96	
July	2	" do	527		2470.03	
October	5	" do	690		2525.	

	Novemr	19	" do	741	21.73	
	"		" do	742	57.06	
	"		" do	743	42.11	
1791	January	5	" do	796	2150.	
	March	2	" do	925	83.33	
		4	" do	927	165.	
	April	2	" do	974	2223.31	
		30	" do	1043	34.34	
	May	2	" do	1047	6.87	
		9	" do	1067	6.86	
	July	2	" do	1140	2472.65	
	August	26	" do	1233	57.61	
	October	5	" do	1290	2012.50	
	Novem	5	" do	1347	46.95	
						17,597.41

Joseph Nourse Register of the Treasury, his Clerks and Messengers.

1789	Novemr.	30	To Warrant No.	106	194.44	
1790	January	15	" do	173	875.	
	April	12	" do	403	1119.43	
	July	3	" do	533	1312.50	
	October	2	" do	680	1311.14	
1791	January	5	" do	795	1690.22	
	April	2	" do	970	2884.84	
		5	" do	987	72.	
		"	" do	988	72.	
	July	2	" do	1136	3132.12	
		28	" do	1195	43.33	
	Septemr.	12	" do	1243	250.	
	October	3	" do	1271	3192.28	
						16 149.30

David Henley and Isaac Sherman Clerks in the Treasury Department, employed in counting Bills of credit of the old and new emissions and Indents of Interest.

1791	February	1	To David Henley	Warrt. No.	863	125.	
		"	" Isaac Sherman	do	864	70.65	
	April	6	" David Henley	do	991	125.	
		"	" Isaac Sherman	do	992	125.	
	July	6	" Ditto	do	1141	125.	
		"	" David Henley	do	1149	125.	
	October	4	" Ditto	do	1284	125.	
		5	" Isaac Sherman	do	1289	125.	
							945.65

Henry Kuhl, for examining Bills of credit of the old emissions for the purpose of discovering counterfeits.

1791	May	30	To Warrant No. 1080	50.

Contingent expenses of the Treasury Department.

1789	October	15	To John Meyer	Warrant No.	82	200.	
	Novemr.	2	" do	do	85	200.	
		13	" Joseph Hardy	do	89	200.	
		30	" Joseph Stretch	do	97	150.	
	Decemr.	1	" John Ramsay	do	123	62.50	
		4	" John Meyer	do	135	150.	
1790	April	1	" Joseph Nourse Register,	do	286	1422.59	
		6	" Ditto	do	368	450.	
		19	" Samuel Meredith Treasurer,	do	442	500.	
		21	" Joseph Nourse Register	do	451	190.30	
		"	" Ditto	do	452	500.	
	July	7	" Ditto	do	546	17.31	
		"	" Ditto	do	547	517.39	
	Septem	3	" Ditto	do	648	500.	
	October	13	" Ditto	do	716	700.	
		30	" Ditto	do	731	336.77	
1791	Februy	22	" Ditto	do	907	563.90	
		"	" Ditto	do	908	49.71	
		25	" Ditto	do	915	1800.	
	March	19	" Samuel Meredith Treasr.	90	942	100.	
		31	" Tench Coxe for Rent	do	961	341.71	
	April	26	" Joseph Nourse Register	do	1037	500.	
	May	4	" William Simmons	do	1053	40.	
	June	3	" Joseph Nourse Register	do	1088	500.	
		6	" Ditto	do	1094	200.	
	July	19	" Ditto	do	1184	479.69	
	Septemr.	27	" Samuel Meredith Treasr.	do	1260	400.	
		"	" Ditto	do	1261	160.	
							11,231.87

80,720.47

DEPARTMENT OF STATE

Thomas Jefferson Secretary of State, for his own compensation and that of his Clerks, Interpreter and Messenger.

1790	April	5	To Warrant No.	337	650.	
		22	" do	455	537.50	
	July	9	" do	551	1584.72	
	August	31	" do	643	22.25	
	Septemr	6	" do	651	302.75	
	October	4	" do	688	1504.16	
1791	January	6	" do	805	1547.32	
	April	2	" do	969	1596.66	
	July	2	" do	1131	1563.34	
	October	3	" do	1274	1546.67	
						10,855.37

Contingent expenses of the Office of the Secretary of State.

1789 Novemr. 13	To Warrant No.	90	50.		
1790 April 30	" do	464	250.		
October 2	" do	679	300.		
Decemr. 31	" do	790	354.		
1791 March 31	" do	962	500.		
August 10	" do	1223	150.		
				1 604.	
					12,459.37

DEPARTMENT OF WAR

Henry Knox Secretary at War, for his own compensation and that of his Clerks and Messenger.

1789 Novemr. 30	To Warrant No.	113	263.84		
1790 January 15	" do	182	1156.50		
April 6	" do	372	31.		
12	" do	408	1252.77		
July 2	" do	528	1295.98		
October 2	" do	684	1288.03		
1791 January 5	" do	798	1312.50		
April 2	" do	971	1394.44		
July 2	" do	1135	1437.50		
October 3	" do	1273	1437.50		
				10,870.06	

Joseph Howell acting Paymaster General and Commissioner of Army accounts, for his own and Clerks salaries, and certain contingent expenses of his Office.

1789 Novem 30	To Warrant No.	111	375.35		
1790 Januay 15	" do	180	1557.71		
April 12	" do	404	1551.75		
August 7	" do	590	1628.13		
October 6	" do	695	781.94		
1791 January 29	" do	859	125.		
April 16	" do	1026	136.85		
May 4	" do	1054	43.75		
July 7	" do	1163	179.57		
October 7	" do	1304	138.61		
				6,518.66	
					17,388.72

For compensation to the Commissioners for adjusting the accounts between the United States and Individual States, their Clerks and Messenger.

1789 Decemr. 1	To Warrant No.	125	477.88
1790 Januay 15	" do	176	1937.50
April 12	" do	405	2162.79
July 3	" do	532	2275.

	October	6	" do	693	2336.92	
	"	"	" do	694	420.66	
1791	Januy	7	" do	808	2525.29	
	"	"	" do	809	198.25	
	April	5	" do	986	2936.40	
	July	2	" do	1138	2883.37	
	October	3	" do	1281	2925.54	
						21,079.60

Contingent expenses of the Office of the Commissioners for adjusting the accounts between the United States and Individual States.

1789	Novem	7	To Patrick Ferrall	Warrt. No.	87	200.		
1790	April	8	" do	do	383	125.		
	August	7	" do	do	591	29.51		
		18	" do	do	617	300.		
	Novemr	10	" do	do	735	100.		
1791	Februy	26	" do	do	917	150.		
	May	7	" do	do	1064	300.		
	Novem	10	" do	do	1350	100.		
							1,304.51	
								22,384.11

GOVERNMENT OF THE WESTERN TERRITORY.

District northwest of the River Ohio.

Arthur St. Clair Governor, for his compensation.

1789	Novemr.	30	To Warrant No.	115	111.11	
1790	January	15	" do	181	500.	
	April	22	" do	456	500.	
	July	3	" do	535	500.	
	October	4	" do	689	500.	
1791	January	24	" do	853	500.	
	April	7	" do	1003	500.	
	July	8	" do	1164	500.	
	October	13	" do	1317	500.	
						4,111.11

Winthrop Sargent Secretary, for his compensation.

1790	April	1	To Warrant No.	313	228.26	
		15	" do	435	187.50	
	August	19	" do	621	187.50	
	October	6	" do	696	187.50	
1791	January	7	" do	813	187.50	
	April	12	" do	1017	187.50	
	July	22	" do	1187	187.50	
	Novemr.	1	" do	1344	125.	
						1 478.26

Contingent expenses of the Office of the Secretary.

1791 March 25	To William Poyntell Warrt. No. 954	64.20	
October 6	" John Mills Attorney to Winthrop Sargent Warrant No. 1299	200.	
			264.20

George Turner one of the Judges, for his compensation.

1790 January 15	To Warrant No.	174	241.30	
July 23	" do	570	158.70	
August 19	" do	618	241.30	
1791 January 7	" do	814	400.	
May 23	" do	1075	200.	
August 1	" do	1200	200.	
October 25	" do	1328	200.	
				1 641.30

John Cleves Symmes one of the Judges, for his compensation.

1790 Februy 13	To Warrant No.	217	243.48	
August 2	" do	581	400.	
1791 January 18	" do	842	200.	
February 25	" do	916	200.	
July 22	" do	1188	200.	
				1 243.48

Samuel Parsons one of the Judges deceased, for his compensation.

1790 June 18	To Warrant No.	515	304.32

Rufus Putnam one of the Judges, for his compensation.

1791 February 7	To Warrant No.	871	200.	
"	" do	872	400.	
April 18	" do	1028	200.	
Septemr. 12	" do	1244	200.	
				1 000.

District south of the River Ohio.

William Blount Governor, for his compensation.

1790 October 13	To Warrant No.	712	500.	
1791 January 17	" do	841	626.37	
April 2	" do	978	500.	
August 3	" do	1202	500.	
October 28	" do	1337	500.	
				2 626.37

Daniel Smith Secretary, for his compensation.

1791 March	19	To Warrant No.	943	422.39	
April	2	" do	979	187.50	
August	3	" do	1203	187.50	
October	29	" do	1338	187.50	
					984.89

David Campbell one of the Judges, for his compensation.

1790 Decemr.	4	To Warrant No.	762	200.	
1791 January	10	" do	823	200.	
April	14	" do	1019	50.54	
	16	" do	1025	200.	
July	6	" do	1148	200.	
October	10	" do	1306	200.	
					1 050.54

John McNeery one of the Judges, for his compensation.

1791 April	23	To Warrant No.	1033	650.55	
October	28	" do	1339	400.	
					1 050.55

Joseph Anderson one of the Judges, for his compensation.

1791 June	10	To Warrant No.	1095	75.55		
July	11	" do	1174	200.		
October	6	" do	1298	200.		
					475.55	
						16 230.57

FOR COMPENSATION TO THE LOAN OFFICERS
AND THEIR CLERKS, AND
FOR STATIONARY PURCHASED BY THEM
FOR THE USE OF THEIR SEVERAL OFFICES.

Nathaniel Appleton Commissioner of Loans for the State of Massachusetts.

1791 January	14	To Warrant No.	834	599.18	
June	2	" do	1087	375.	
July	2	" do	1139	873.66	
August	8	" do	1221	375.	
Decemr.	13	" do	1366	375.	
					2 597.84

Jabez Bowen Commissioner of Loans for the State of Rhode Island.

1791	January	17	To Warrant No.	838	239.67	
	May	4	" do	1051	150.	
	July	5	" do	1144	150.	
	October	26	" do	1333	150.	
						689.67

William Imlay Commissioner of Loans for the State of Connecticut.

1790	October	6	To Warrant No.	699	149.45	
1791	January	7	" do	811	250.	
	May	4	" do	1052	250.	
	July	11	" do	1173	250.	
	October	5	" do	1288	250.	
						1 149.45

John Cochran Commissioner of Loans for the State of New York.

1790	October	6	To Warrant No.	700	224.18	
1791	Januy	12	" do	829	375.	
	April	7	" do	996	375.	
	July	6	" do	1154	375.	
	October	22	" do	1325	375.	
						1 724.18

James Ewing Commissioner of Loans for the State of New Jersey.

1791	January	12	To Warrant No.	830	281.52	
	June	4	" do	1090	175.	
	July	28	" do	1196	175.	
						631.25

Thomas Smith Commissioner of Loans for the State of Pennsylvania.

1791	February	2	To Warrant No.	867	599.18	
	May	14	" do	1070	375.	
	July	21	" do	1185	375.	
	October	26	" do	1332	375.	
						1 724.18

James Tilton Commissioner of Loans for the State of Delaware.

1791	January	17	To Warrant No.	836	89.67	
		"	" do	837	150.	
	May	5	" do	1056	150.	
	October	3	" do	1272	150.	
	Novemr	23	" do	1357	150.	
						689.67

John Hopkins Commissioner of Loans for the State of Virginia.

1791 August	26	To Warrant No.	1232		1 348.63	

William Skinner Commissioner of Loans for the State of No. Carolina.

1791 January	18	To Warrant No.	844	399.45		
April	2	" do	977	250.		
Novemr	9	" do	1349	500.		
					1 149.45	

John Neufville Commissioner of Loans for the State of So. Carolina.

1791 Februy	17	To Warrant No.	898	399.45		
April	4	" do	981	250.		
July	7	" do	1160	250.		
October	13	" do	1316	250.		
					1 149.45	

Richard Wylly Commissioner of Loans for the State of Georgia.

1791 January	25	To Warrant No.	854	279.62		
April	28	" do	1040	175.		
July	22	" do	1190	175.		
Novemr	23	" do	1358	175.		
					804.62	
						13,658.66

PENSIONS, ANNUITIES AND GRANTS

Elizabeth Bergan for a pension allowed her by an Act of Congress passed the 24 of August 1781.[9]

1789 Novemr.	15	To Warrant No.	92	8.54	
	"	" do	93	2.91	
1790 January	15	" do	178	13.33	
April	12	" do	406	13.33	
July	6	" do	538	13.33	
October	6	" do	697	13.33	
1791 January	10	" do	826	13.33	
April	11	" do	1014	13.33	
July	15	" do	1181	13.33	
Novemr	1	" do	1343	13.33	
					118.09

9. *JCC*, XXI, 908.

P. Dominique L. Eglize for a pension granted by an Act of Congress passed the 8th day of August 1782.[10]

1789 Novemr	30	To Warrant No.	98	23.33	
	"	" do	99	6.67	
1790 January	20	" do	187	30.	
April	15	" do	437	30.	
July	2	" do	526	30.	
October	9	" do	706	30.	
1791 January	12	" do	831	30.	
April	12	" do	1018	30.	
July	11	" do	1175	30.	
October	12	" do	1311	30.	
					270.

Joseph Traversie, pursuant to an Act of Congress passed August 8, 1782.[11]

1789 Novemr.	30	To Warrant No.	100	53.33	
	"	" do	101	6.67	
1790 January	20	" do	188	30.	
July	3	" do	534	60.	
1791 April	7	" do	998	60.	
May	2	" do	1046	30.	
August	30	" do	1235	30.	
					270.

For the education of George M. White Eyes an Indian Youth, pursuant to the respective Acts of the 13 October 1781 and the 21 September 1787.[12]

1789 Novemr	30	To Warrant No.	104	110.72

John Paulding, pursuant to an Act of the 30 of November 1780.[13]

1789 Novemr	30	To Warrant No.	120	71.04	
	"	" do	121	10.95	
1790 March	2	" do	235	50.	
April	3	" do	329	50.	
July	2	" do	525	50.	
October	8	" do	704	50.	
1791 May	7	" do	1061	100.	
					381.99

10. *JCC*, XXII, 457. 11. *JCC*, XXII, 456–57.

12. *JCC*, XXI, 1051. Although a letter from Ebenezer Hazard concerning this account was read in Congress on September 21, 1787, there is no evidence in *JCC* that an act was passed on that date (*JCC*, XXXIII, 513). On November 7, 1788, however, a warrant was drawn "for sundries supplied Geo. M. White Eyes an Indian Youth agreeable to Act of Congress of 21st Sept. 1787" (RG 39, Blotters of the Register of the Treasury, 1782–1810, National Archives).

13. *JCC*, XVIII, 1009–10.

James McKenzie, pursuant to an Act of Congress passed Septemr. 15, 1783.[14]

1789 Decemr.	1	To Warrant No.	128	17.78	
	"	" do	129	2.22	
1791 March	16	" do	938	50.	
Novemr	17	" do	1355	30.	
					100.

Joseph Brusselle, pursuant to an Act of the 15 September 1783.[15]

1789 Decemr.	1	To Warrant No.	130	17.78	
	"	" do	131	2.22	
1790 Decemr.	30	" do	789	40.	
1791 April	7	" do	1000	20.	
July	26	" do	1194	10.	
Novemr	11	" do	1351	10.	
					100.

David Williams, pursuant to an Act of the 3 of November 1780.[16]

1789 Decemr.	7	To Warrant No.	137	70.44	
	"	" do	138	11.10	
1790 Januay	22	" do	192	50.	
1791 Februy	24	" do	911	200.	
					331.54

Richard Gridley, pursuant to the Acts of Novemr. 17, 1775, and February 26, 1781.[17]

1789 Decemr.	24	To Warrant No.	152	444.40	
1790 July	28	" do	574	444.40	
1791 July	15	" do	1180	444.40	
					1 333.20

The Youngest Children of the late Major General Warren pursuant to an Act of Congress passed July 1st. 1780.[18]

1789 Decemr.	28	To Warrant No.	154	450.	
1790 April	13	" do	421	450.	
Novemr	20	" do	746	450.	
1791 July	7	" do	1161	450.	
					1 800.

For the education of the Eldest Son of the late Major General Warren pursuant to the Acts of Congress of the 8 April 1777 and June 4 1788.[19]

1790 Februy	1	To Warrant No.	200		400.

14. *JCC*, XXV, 568–69.
15. *JCC*, XXV, 568–69.
16. *JCC*, XVIII, 1009–10.
17. *JCC*, III, 358–59; XIX,197.
18. *JCC*, XVII, 581.
19. *JCC*, VII, 243; XXXIV, 199.

Isaac Van Wart, pursuant to an Act of Congress passed November 3, 1780.[20]

Year	Month	Day		Warrant No.	Amount	Total
1790	June	10	To Warrant No.	509	200.	
	April	20	" do	1030	182.42	
						382.42

Lieutenant Colonel de Touzard pursuant to an Act of Congress passed the 27 October 1778.[21]

Year	Month	Day		Warrant No.	Amount	Total
1790	June	14	To Warrant No.	511		1 440.

Lewis Joseph de Beaulieu pursuant to an Act passed August 5, 1782.[22]

Year	Month	Day		Warrant No.	Amount	Total
1790	March	29	To Warrant No.	264	200.	
1791	Februy	24	" do	910	200.	
						400.

For the education of the Youngest Son of the late General Hugh Mercer pursuant to an Act of the 8 of April 1777.[23]

Year	Month	Day		Warrant No.	Amount	Total
1790	August	3	To Warrant No.	586	400.	
1791	May	7	" do	1059	800.	
						1 200.

Frederick William Baron de Steuben, pursuant to an Act of Congress passed June 4, 1790.[24]

Year	Month	Day		Warrant No.	Amount	Total
1790	August	13	To Warrant No.	601	1250.	
	October	2	" do	682	625.	
1791	Januy	12	" do	827	625.	
	April	5	" do	984	625.	
	July	5	" do	1142	625.	
	October	4	" do	1287	625.	
						4 375.

John Jordan pursuant to an Act of Congress passed September 15, 1783.[25]

Year	Month	Day		Warrant No.	Amount	Total	Grand Total
1790	Decemr.	17	To Warrant No.	778	50.		
1791	Januay	21	" do	860	10.		
	April	9	" do	1008	10.		
	July	2	" do	1137	10.		
	October	25	" do	1330	10.		
						90.	
							13,102.96
					Total amount of the Civil List		757,134.45

20. *JCC*, XVIII, 1000–10.

21. On October 27, 1778, Lewis Tousard was granted a pension for life (*JCC*, XII, 1068).

22. *JCC*, XXII, 428–29.

23. *JCC*, VII, 243.

24. "An Act for finally adjusting and satisfying the claims of Frederick William de Steuben" (6 *Stat.* 2 [June 4, 1790]).

25. *JCC*, XXV, 568–69.

WAR DEPARTMENT

Henry Knox Secretary at War, for monies advanced for the use of the War Department.

1790	June	10	To Warrant No.	508	12,400.	
	August	24	" do	634	1 300.	
1791	Februy	23	" do	868	10 000.	
						23,700.

Joseph Howell Junior Acting-Paymaster General and Commissioner of Army accounts for monies advanced to be by him applied towards the support of the Military Establishment of the United States.

1789	October	10	To Warrant No.	79	24 177.54	
1790	March	30	" do	269	2 242.	
	June	5	" do	506	2 500.	
	August	17	" do	612	811.	
	Septem	8	" do	658	8 438.	
		15	" do	662	1 906.20	
	October	13	" do	714	500.	
	Novem	1	" do	733	3 000.	
		"	" do	734	10 000.	
		13	" do	737	3 000.	
		16	" do	739	10 926.	
	Decemr.	15	" do	775	15 000.	
		24	" do	785	5 000.	
1791	Januy	14	" do	835	6 000.	
	Februy	9	" do	877	5 000.	
	March	4	" do	929	10 000.	
		"	" do	930	11 002.20	
		11	" do	935	10 000.	
		23	" do	949	15 000.	
	April	5	" do	982	10 000.	
		11	" do	1011	18 500.	
		21	" do	1031	22 500.	
		30	" do	1044	8 000.	
	May	9	" do	1065	40 000.	
		31	" do	1081	20 000.	
	June	14	" do	1099	13 387.44	
		17	" do	1104	32 000.	
	July	9	" do	1167	7 500.	
		19	" do	1183	4 000.	
	Augst.	5	" do	1220	7 000.	
		22	" do	1229	2 554.59	
		24	" do	1231	5 000.	
	Septem	7	" do	1240	5 000.	
		13	" do	1246	8 296.53	
		17	" do	1248	1 500.	
						349,741.50

Robert Elliott and Eli Williams Contractors for the supply of the Army on the western Frontiers.

1789 Septem	29	To Warrant No.	73	4 000.	
Novem	5	" do	86	2 000.	
Decem	7	" do	139	2 000.	
	31	" do	159	2 000.	
1790 May	19	" do	486	20 000.	
August	24	" do	635	15 000.	
1791 March	8	" do	933	30 000.	
June	15	" do	1102	15 000.	
	22	" do	1116	15 000.	
Septem	13	" do	1247	6 000.	
					111,000.

William Hill Contractor for Clothing, for the use of the Army.

1789 Novem	24	To Warrant No.	96	6 500.	
Decem	7	" do	142	5 000.	
	22	" do	150	1 500.	
1790 January	2	" do	162	2 200.	
	5	" do	165	1 500.	
	"	" do	166	1 323.59	
1791 June	1	" do	1084	10 000.	
					28,023.59

For Provision supplied the Troops at West Point and New York.

1789 Decemr.	1	To Smith and Wyckoff	Warrt. No.	126	938.67	
	"	" do	do	127	52.55	
	15	" do	do	145	175.51	
	"	To Melancton Smith	do	146	71.99	
1790 Januay	25	" do	do	194	141.77	
March	27	" do	do	258	227.30	
	"	" do	do	261	399.42	
April	10	" do	do	400	761.37	
May	10	" do	do	477	58.46	
June	18	" do	do	516	58.54	
July	8	" do	do	550	55.44	
Septemr	6	" do	do	650	57.28	
	30	" do	do	671	57.28	
Novem	20	" do	do	745	55.44	
	"	" do	do	747	57.28	
Decemr.	28	" do	do	787	52.41	
1791 Januay	22	" do	do	850	52.08	
April	5	" do	do	989	106.20	
May	13	" do	do	1068	109.80	
July	22	" do	do	1191	105.39	
October	13	" do	do	1315	106.02	
Novem	14	" do	do	1353	107.28	
						3,807.48

For Supplies furnished the Troops at Springfield, including some provisions issued in Boston.

1789 Decemr.	29	To William Smith	Warrt. No.	156	800.	
1790 Februay	27	" do	do	230	52.34	
March	27	" Melancton Smith	do	259	310.10	
"		" do	do	260	47.53	
"		" do	do	262	328.70	
April	16	" William Smith	do	439	46.37	
	19	" Melancton Smith	do	443	29.12	
						1 614.16

Stephen Moor for the Rent and Purchase of West Point.

For Rent.

1790 March	4	To Warrant No.	243	400.		
Novem	24	" do	752	380.16		
Decem	10	" do	771	37.50		
					817.66	

For the Purchase.

Novem	25	To Warrant No.	755	6196.75		
Decem	16	" do	777	5000.		
					11,196.75	
						12,014.41

Royal Flint Contractor, for Clothing furnished the Army.

1790 April	1	To Warrant No.	283	6 000.	
	3	" do	315	2 000.	
Septem	17	" do	664	6 000.	
October	12	" do	711	5 750.	
1791 Januay	7	" do	815	993.58	
					20,743.58

John Habersham Agent for supplying the Troops in the State of Georgia.

1790 Novemr.	30	To Warrant No.	758	337.45	
1791 October	15	" do	1319	78.79	
1792 Januay	17	" do	1485	99.86	
					516.10

Theodosius Fowler Contractor for supplying the Troops in the Western Territories.

1791 March	22	To Warrant No.	946	10,000.	
April	7	" do	1004	15,000.	
	25	" do	1036	15 000.	
May	7	" do	1063	20 000.	
July	13	" do	1179	10 000.	
					70,000.

John Shepherd and Robert Smith Contractors, for Clothing supplied the Army.

1791 April	29	To Warrant No. 1042	11,000.	

Samuel and John Smith for supplies furnished Capt. Alexander Trumans Company of federal Troops from the 22 day of July 1790 to the 28 day of Decemr. following, pursuant to instructions from the Secretary at War.

1791 Januay	18	To Warrant No. 843		643.21

MONIES ADVANCED TO AGENTS FOR THE PURPOSE OF PAYING PENSIONS DUE TO INVALIDS.

State of New Hampshire.

1791 Februy	9	To William Gardner,	Warrt. No.	878	4074.67	
August	4	" do	do	1208	2040.	
						6,114.67

State of Massachusetts.

1791 Februy	9	To Nathaniel Appleton,	Warrt.	879	12586.75	
August	4	" do	do	1209	6294.	
						18,880.75

State of Rhode Island.

1790 Februy	4	To Jeremiah Olney,	Warrt. No.	206	900.	
	22	" do	do	226	500.	
May	15	" do	do	483	1454.	
					2854.	
		From which deduct the amount of Warrant No. 60 date Feb. 27, 1792 being so much repaid into the Treasury			36.08	
					2817.92	
1791 Februy	9	To Jabez Bowen,	Warrt. No.	880	2981.	
August	4	" do	do	1210	1490.	
						7,288.92

State of Connecticut.

1791 Februy	9	To William Imlay	Warrt. No.	881	8048.86	
August	4	" do	do	1211	4024.	
						12,072.86

State of New York.

1790 March	3	To John Lamb,	Warrt. No.	237	8000.	
August	9	" do	do	594	5656.68	
Septemr.	30	" do	do	670	2137.32	
1791 Februy	9	To John Cochran	do	882	17280.	
August	4	" do	do	1212	8640.	
						41,714.

State of New Jersey.

1790	March	1	To John Halsted	Warrt. No.	231	1700.	
	May	27	" do	do	494	2500.	
1791	Februy	9	To James Ewing	do	883	4534.27	
	August	4	" do	do	1213	2267.	
							11,001.27

State of Pennsylvania.

1790	Februy	22	To Sharp Delany,	Warrt. No.	225	8300.	
	June	3	" do	do	503	8250.	
						16,550.	
			From which deduct the amount of Warrant No. 17 dated Mar 19, 1790 being so much			3 000.	
						13 550.	
1791	Februy	9	To Thomas Smith,	Warrt. No.	884	16 767.45	
	August	4	" do	do	1214	8 383.	
							38,700.45

State of Delaware.

1790	June	17	To George Bush,	Warrt. No.	514	1008.	
	July	31	" do	do	577	1008.	
1791	Februy	9	To James Tilton,	do	885	2136.	
	August	4	" do	do	1215	1068.	
							5,220.

State of Maryland.

1791	Februy	9	To Thomas Harwood,	Warrt. No.	886	4140.56	
	August	4	" do	do	1216	2070.	
							6,210.56

State of Virginia.

1790	Februy	5	To William Heth	Warrt. No.	207	2500.	
	June	3	" do	do	502	2188.33	
	August	7	" do	do	593	4033.33	
1791	Februy	9	To John Hopkins	do	887	9513.33	
	August	4	" do	do	1217	4757.	
							22,991.99

State of North Carolina.

1790	Februy	9	To John Haywood	Warrt. No.	204	300.	
	May	15	" do	do	482	420.	
1791	Februy	9	To William Skinner	do	888	886.	
							1,606.

State of South Carolina.

1791 Februy	9	To John Neufville	Warrt. No. 809		3,000.	

State of Georgia.

1791 Februay	9	To Richard Wylly,	Wart. No. 889	674.41		
August	4	" do	do 1219	338.		
					1,012.41	
						175,813.88
			Total amount			808,617.91

FOR DEFRAYING THE EXPENSES OF NEGOTIATIONS OR TREATIES OF PEACE WITH THE INDIAN TRIBES.

Henry Knox Commissioner for effecting Negotiations or Treaties with the Indian Tribes, for monies advanced to him in pursuance of the respective Acts of Congress passed August 7, 1789[26] and July 12, 1790.[27]

1789 Septem	29	To Warrant No.	74	20,000.
1790 August	17	" do	613	7,000.
		Total amount		27,000.

FOR THE REIMBURSEMENT OF TEMPORARY LOANS OBTAINED BY THE SECRETARY OF THE TREASURY, AND PAYMENT OF INTEREST DUE THEREON.

				No.		
1789 Novem	11	To Joseph Howell Junior,	Warrt.	88		1,600.
Decemr	31	To the President Directors and Compy. of the bank of North America,	Wart.	158	50,940.	
1790 April	3	" do	do	319	39,060.	
June	8	" do	do	507	886.28	
						90,886.28
1789 Decemr.	31	To the President Directors and Company of the bank of New York	Wart.	160	38,402.94	
"	"	" do	do	161	10,000.	
1790 April	1	" do	do	311	53,132.80	
May	8	" do	do	476	43,405.15	
	22	" do	do	491	11,779.76	
						156,720.65
						249,206.93

26. "An Act to establish an Executive Department, to be denominated the Department of War" (1 *Stat.* 49–50).

27. "An Act providing for holding a Treaty or Treaties to establish Peace with certain Indian tribes" (1 *Stat.* 136) was approved on July 22, 1790.

From this deduct the amount of the sums borrowed Vizt.

From the President Directors and Compy. of the bank of New York.

1789 Septemr.	13	Received on Warrant No. 1	20,000.		
	14	do do 3	30 000.		
October	1	do do 5	20 000.		
Decemr.	1	do do 7	10 000.		
1790 February	17	do do 14	20 000.		
May	29	do do 20	30 000.		
April	3	do do 21	25 000.	155,000.	

From the President Directors and Company of the bank of North America.

1789 Septem	21	Received on Warrant No. 2	50,000.		
October	10	do do 4	20,000.		
Decr.	2	do do 8	20 000.		
		And this sum for an over charge in their interest account	8.81		
				90,008.81	
1789 October	18	From Joseph Howell on Warrt. No.6		1,600.	
					246,608.81
		Total amount of expenditure under this head			2,598.12

FOR THE SUPPORT OF MINISTERS OF THE UNITED STATES AT FOREIGN COURTS.

Thomas Jefferson Secretary of State, for monies advanced to him in pursuance of the Act entitled "An Act providing the means of intercourse between the United States and foreign Nations." 28

1790 August	14	To Warrant No. 605	500.
Decem	20	" do 780	1,233.33
		Total amount	1,733.33

FOR THE PURPOSE OF EFFECTING A RECOGNITION OF THE TREATY OF THE UNITED STATES WITH THE NEW EMPEROR OF MOROCCO.

Thomas Jefferson Secretary of State for an advance made to him pursuant to the Act entitled "An Act making an Appropriation for the purpose therein mentioned." 29

1791 May	7	To Warrant No. 1062	13,000.

28. 1 *Stat.* 128–29 (July 1, 1790). 29. 1 *Stat.* 214 (March 3, 1791).

George Wray Collector for the port of Hampton in the State of Virginia, for an advance made, to be by him applied towards the building and equipment of the Revenue Cutter for the Virginia Station, in pursuance of the Act entitled "An Act to provide more effectually for the Collection of the duties imposed by Law on Goods, Wares and Merchandize imported into the United States and on the Tonnage of Ships or Vessels".[30]

1791 Septemr	1	To Warrant No. 1236	570.

TOWARDS DISCHARGING CERTAIN DEBTS CONTRACTED BY ABRAHAM SKINNER LATE COMMISSARY OF PRISONERS.

1790 October	13	To Doctor James J. Van Beuren for Medicine and attendance on sundry Officers of the late Army whilst in captivity on Long Island Warrt. No. 717		306.92
	"	To Rutgert Van Brunt and Richard Stilivell Agents for the under-mentioned persons, for the amount of sundry orders drawn by Officers of the late Army for their subsistence whilst in captivity on Long Island Vizt. Warrt. No. 718.		
		Isaac Denyse	309.94	
		Charity Ryder	339.99	
		William Johnson	163.12	
		Joost Stilwell	325.99	
		Hendrick Van Cleef	163.14	
		Rem Van Cleef	235.40	
		Rutgert Stilwell	22.	
		Samuel Gerretsen	386.50	
		William G. Van Dyker	302.73	
		Court Jansen	49.75	
		Daniel Lake	433.25	
		Lawrence Ryder	369.27	
		John Boyce Junr.	141.69	
		Bemardus Ryder	500.74	
		Stephen Voorhees	405.72	
		Ferdinandus Van Sicklen	413.97	
		Hendrick Wyckoff	232.54	
		Albert Terhune	90.33	
		Richard Stilwell Junr.	80.14	
		Sarah Emmens	193.69	
		Abraham Emmens	85.	
		John Foorhest	321.99	
		John Boyce Senr.	399.97	
		Cornelius Emmens	116.57	
		John Emmens	163.43	
		Albert Voorhees	267.12	

30. 1 *Stat.* 145–78 (August 4, 1790).

	Richard Stilwell	328.57	
	Charles Van Cize	276.53	
	Nicholas Stilwell	327.13	
	Daniel Boies	30.28	
	John Glean	264.86	
	Rutgert Van Brunt	221.72	
	Anna Stilwell	35.12	
			7,998.19
1790 October 13	To William Couvenhoven Agent for the undermentioned persons for amount of sundry orders drawn by Officers of the late Army, for their subsistence whilst in captivity on Long Island, Warrt. No. 719 Vizt.		
	Estate of Garret Kouvenhoven	29.14	
	Ditto of Peter Kouvenhoven	314.25	
	Abraham Voorhis	290.87	
	Estate of Roelof Voorhis	320.71	
	Do of Joost Wyckoff	330.56	
	Do of Thomas Whitlock	19.44	
	Nicholas Schenck	254.56	
	Eida Stryker	345.67	
	Johannes Stoothoff	137.43	
	Barent Johnson	228.28	
	Mary Stoothoff	196.43	
	Elias Hubbard	350.70	
	Johannes Remsent	343.13	
	Garret Wyckoff	353.98	
	Thomas Elsworth	273.18	
	Peter Vander Bilt	287.14	
	Ulpianus Van Sinderen	409.57	
	Martin Schenck	339.70	
	Joost Van Nuys	331.43	
	Peter Wyckoff	282.53	
	Peter Lott	201.88	
	Willemtie Ammerman	290.38	
	Folkert Sprong	298.58	
	Wilhemus Stoothoff	175.14	
	Estate of W. Stoothoff Senr.	160.30	
	Isaac Slover	120.53	
	Estate of Hendrick Lott	368.87	
	Derick Remsen	334.81	
	Johannes Ditmars	500.51	
			7,889.70
1790 October 13	To John Vanderveer and Johannes I. Lott Agents for the undermentioned persons, for amount of sundry orders drawn by the Officers of the late Army for their subsistence whilst in captivity on Long Island Warrt. No. 720 Vizt.		
	John Vander Veer	528.25	
	Garret Boerum	378.25	
	Roeloff Lott	181.13	
	Stephen Ryder	279.98	
	Johannes Boerum	279.44	
	Dominicus Vander Veer	243.50	
	Jacob Snedicker	303.	

Nicholas Wyckoff	11.12	
Isaac Snedicker	230.28	
Hendrick Wyckoff	314.84	
Cornelius Wyckoff	319.99	
Jacob Cozine	30.	
Isaac Eldert	56.	
Johannes Eldert	50.58	
Femmetic Eldert	50.57	
Jacob Field	143.70	
Nicholas Williamson	344.22	
John Williamson	262.85	
Anne Van Cleef	129.68	
Mauris Lott	48.57	
Joseph Howard	216.	
Johannes Lott	338.34	
Daniel Rapalje	332.58	
Hannah Lefferts	64.	
Margaret Cornell	248.56	
		5,385.43

1790 October 13 To Nicholas Cowenhoven, Simon Cortelyou and Adrian Hageman Agents for the undermentioned persons, for amount of sundry orders drawn by Officers of the late Army, for their subsistence whilst in captivity on Long Island Warrt. No. 721 Vizt.

Anne Denyse	314.85	
Adrian Hageman	268.29	
Jacques Denyse	28.	
Isaac Cortelyou	125.80	
Casper Cropsey	50.57	
Hendrick Johnson	85.71	
Helmus Van Nuys	57.41	
John Vankerk Van Nuys	330.57	
Ferdinand Johnson	114.	
John Blake	94.08	
Rem Van Pelt	90.	
Ast Van Pelt	129.44	
Peter Van Pelt	244.56	
Johannes Cowenhoven	313.08	
Garret Cowenhoven	355.12	
Evert Suydam	257.50	
Adrian Van Brunt	256.86	
Nicholas Gronendyck	276.63	
Wilhelmus Van Nuys	184.	
William Van Brunt	83.44	
Mary Emans	177.46	
William Barre	347.72	
Peter Vander Bilt	219.24	
John Van Duyn	173.71	
Isaac Van Brunt	94.28	
		4,672.32

1790 October 13 To Aquila Giles and Johannes E. Lott Agents for the undermentioned persons, for amount of sundry orders drawn by Officers of the late Army, for their subsistence whilst in captivity on Long Island

Warrant No. 722 Vizt.

Jacob Lefferts	252.28
Geashe Bergen	219.12
Jeremiah Vander Bilt	508.53
Martha Garrison	22.
Leffert Lefferts	324.08
Garret Marteson	360.79
Philip Nagle	281.14
Rem Hageman	94.12
Rem Vander Bilt	234.28
Sytie Hageman	362.84
Peter Lefferts	330.36
Jacobus Vander Veer	129.17
Hendrick Vander Veer	214.53
Adrian Voorhees	375.67
Jacob Suydam	456.53
Marrietta Lott	276.18
Johannes E. Lott	240.28
Hendrick Suydam first	368.27
Hendrick Suydam second	308.57
Cornelius Vander Veer	741.68
Johannes Ditmars	368.05
Cornelius Van Duyn	330.53
John Van Duyn	347.36
Garret A. Mortense	312.86
John Bennem	247.29
Gabriel Ellison	145.12
Peter Antonidas	94.27
John Striker	352.55
Michael Striker	224.
Johannes Van Sicklen	374.59
Hendrick L. Suydam	245.65
Peter Wyckoff	221.14
Wynant Bennett	124.27
Wynant Van Pelt	68.
John A. Hageman	242.85
Peter Nefus	333.38

10,132.33

1790 October 13 To Samuel Hubbard Agent for the undermentioned persons for amount of sundry orders drawn by Officers of the late Army, for their subsistence whilst in captivity on Long Island

Warrant No. 723 Vizt.

Samuel Hubbard	36.
James Hubbard	315.13
Rem Williamson	107.77
Samuel Striker	102.56
Cornelius Striker	42.

603.46

1790 October 13 To Peter Vandervoort Agent for Joseph Smith for an order drawn by Ebenzer Carson late a Lieutenant in the tenth Pennsylvania Regiment, for his subsistence whilst in captivity on Long Island Warrt. No. 724 — 58.28

	"	To Denyse Van Duyn administrator to the Estate of Garret Van Duyn, for amount of sundry orders drawn by Officers of the late Army for their subsistence whilst in captivity on Long Island Warrt. No. 725	215.62	
	"	To Aquila Giles Assignee of John Cowenhoven Executor to the Estate of Garret Cowenhoven deceased for amount of an order drawn by Elihu Hall late an Ensign in the first Maryland Regiment, for his subsistence whilst in captivity on Long Island Warrt. No. 726	163.12	
1790 October	13	To Nathaniel Lawrence Assignee of Dominicus Vander Veer for amount of an order drawn by Nathaniel Lawrence late a Lieutenant in the second North Carolina Regiment, for his subsistence whilst in captivity on Long Island Warrant No. 727	42.	
1790 Decemr.	2	To William Boyd Agent for Johannes Lott Administrator to the Estate of Hendrick A. Lott, for amount of sundry orders drawn by Officers of the late Army, for their subsistence whilst in captivity on Long Island, Warrt. No. 761	244.	
	11	To William Rogers on behalf of Joseph Winter Agent for the undermentioned persons, for amount of sundry orders drawn by Officers of the late Army, for their subsistence whilst in captivity on Long Island Warrant No. 773 Vizt.		
		Peter Cornell 371.84		
		Garret Striker 270.72		
			642.56	
	31	To Aquila Giles Agent for Sarah Van Nuys, for amount of sundry orders drawn by Officers in the late Army for their subsistence whilst in captivity on Long Island—Warrant No. 791	311.14	
1790 Decr.	31	To Aquila Giles Agent for Jeremiah Vander Bilt for a balance due on an order drawn by Captain de Utrecht, for his subsistence whilst in captivity on Long Island. Warrant No. 792	18.06	
		Total amount		38,683.13

TOWARDS DISCHARGING CERTAIN DEBTS CONTRACTED BY COLONEL TIMOTHY PICKERING LATE QUARTERMASTER GENERAL.

1790 Decemr.	22	To Charles Bitters Assignee for John Dill, for a balance of pay and subsistence due to the said John Dill as Clerk in the Quarter Master Generals Office from the first of June 1782 to the 31 of October 1784. Warrant No. 783	363.
1791 Januay	7	To Michael Connelly Assignee of Mary Mandevil, for damage done to her Farm in the Year 1781 Warrant No. 818	34.36
		To Michael Connelly Assignee of Mary Dusenberg, for Officers Quarters and damage done to her Lands in the Year 1782. Warrant No. 819	126.04

April	14	To William Graham Attorney for David Wolfe late Assistant Deputy Quarter Master under Hugh Hughes Deputy Quarter Master for the State of New York, for his pay from the first of January to the 16 of October 1782, and for sundry disbursements during the same period; Wart. No. 1022	930.68	
		Total amount		1,454.08

FOR PAYING INTEREST ON THE DOMESTIC DEBT OF THE UNITED STATES.

William Gardner Comissioner of Loans for the State of New Hampshire, for monies advanced to be by him applied towards paying the interest due on the 6 and 3 ℔ cent Stock standing on the books in his Office.

1791 June	25	To Warrant No.	1107	2400.	
Septemr	8	" do	1241	4000.	
1792 Januy	13	" do	1458	6000.	
					12,400.

Nathaniel Appleton Commissr. of Loans for the State of Massachusetts for monies advanced to be by him applied towards paying the interest due on the 6 and 3 per cent Stock standing on the books in his Office.

1791 March	5	To Warrant No.	923	10,000.	
April	9	" do	1010	2 500.	
June	21	" do	1108	50,000.	
Septem	12	" do	1256	60 000.	
October	12	" do	1307	30 500.	
1792 Januy	14	" do	1463	25 000.	
	"	" do	1464	2 000.	
	"	" do	1465	3 600.	
	"	" do	1466	500.	
	"	" do	1467	17 200.	
				201,300.	
		From which deduct the amount of a repayment into the Treasury by Warrant No. 51 dated June 21, 1791		28,785.83	
					172,514.17

Jabez Bowen Commissioner of Loans for the State of Rhode Island for monies advanced to be by him appli'd towards paying the interest due on the 6 and 3 per cent. Stock standing on the books in his Office.

1791 June	21	To Warrant No.	1109	3500.	
Septemr	10	" do	1249	4950.	
October	12	" do	1308	450.	
1792 Januay	14	" do	1461	3000.	
	"	" do	1462	4400.	
					16,300.

William Imlay Commissioner of Loans for the State of Connecticut for monies advanced to be by him applied towards paying the interest due on the 6 and 3 per cent Stock standing on the books in his Office.

Year	Month	Day		No.	Amount	Total
1791	June	21	To Warrant No.	1110	8200.	
	Septem	6	do	1239	7700.	
	October	12	do	1309	1200.	
1792	Januay	16	do	1469	400.	
		"	do	1471	3000.	
		"	do	1472	2900.	
						23,400.

John Cochran Commissioner of Loans for the State of New York for monies advanced to be by him applied towards paying the interest due on the 6 and 3 per cent Stock standing on the books in his Office.

Year	Month	Day		No.	Amount	Total
1791	June	21	To Warrant No.	1114	26 250.	
		25	" do	1127	55 000.	
	Septem	27	" do	1257	60 000.	
	October	1	" do	1269	30 000.	
	Decemr.	23	" do	1371	90 000.	
						261,250.

James Ewing, Commissioner of Loans for the State of New Jersey, for monies advanced to be by him applied towards paying the interest due on the 6 and 3 per cent Stock standing on the books in his Office.

Year	Month	Day		No.	Amount	Total
1791	March	24	To Warrant No.	950	5 000.	
	Septem	20	" do	1252	10 000.	
		27	" do	1258	10 000.	
	Decem	23	" do	1370	7 000.	
						32,000.

Thomas Smith Commissr. of Loans for the State of Pennsylvania for monies advanced to be by him applied towards paying the interest due on the 6 and 3 per cent Stock standing on the books in his Office.

Year	Month	Day		No.	Amount	Total
1791	March	31	To Warrant No.	964	12,961.97	
		"	" do	965	2 735.40	
	June	28	" do	1128	32 000.	
	Septem	30	" do	1267	33 000.	
	Decem	30	" do	1402	33 791.28	
						114,488.65

James Tilton Commissioner of Loans for the State of Delaware for monies advanced to be by him applied towards paying the interest due on the 6 and 3 per cent Stock standing on the books in his Office.

Year	Month	Day		No.	Amount	Total
1791	June	21	To Warrant No.	1113	170.	
	Septem	20	" do	1253	2 000.	
	Decem	23	" do	1372	500.	
						2,670.

Thomas Hardwood Commissioner of Loans for the State of Maryland, for monies advanced to be by him applied towards paying the interest due on the 6 and 3 per cent Stock standing on the books in his Office.

1791	June	21	To Warrant No.	1111	6 400.	
	Septem	20	" do	1251	21 150.	
	October	12	" do	1310	25 000.	
	"	"	" do	1313	3 000.	
1792	Januay	16	" do	1473	2 550.	
						58,100.

John Hopkins Commissioner of Loans for the State of Virginia, for monies advanced to be by him applied towards paying the interest due on the 6 and 3 per cent Stock standing on the books in his Office.

1791	June	21	To Warrant No	1115	12 000.	
	Septemr.	1	" do	1237	8 626.	
1792	Januay	16	" do	1474	9 900.	
					30,526.	
			From which deduct the amount of Warrant No. 52 dated June 21, 1791, being so much repaid into the Treasury		6,012.	
						24,514.

William Skinner Commissioner of loans for the State of North Carolina, for monies advanced to be by him applied towards paying the interest due on the 6 and 3 per cent Stock standing on the books in his Office.

1791	June	21	To Warrant No.	1112	100.	
	Septem	20	" do	1250	200.	
1792	Januay	17	" do	1482	1 000.	
						1 300.

John Neufville Commissioner of Loans for the State of South Carolina for monies advanced to be by him applied towards paying the interest on the 6 and 3 per cent Stock standing on the books in his Office.

1791	August	3	To Warrant No.	1204	3 000.	
1792	Januay	17	" do	1481	3 500.	
						6,500.

Richard Wylly Commissioner of Loans for the State of Georgia for monies advanced to be by him applied towards paying the interest due on the 6 and 3 per cent Stock standing on the books in his Office.

1791	Septem	5	To Warrant No.	1238	250.	
1792	Januay	17	" do	1478	1 000.	
		"	" do	1479	349.39	
						1,599.39

Tench Francis Cashier of the Bank of North America for monies advanced to pay the interest due on the Funded and Unfunded Registered Debt standing on the books of the Treasury.

1791 March	31	To Warrant No.	959	20,612.98 9/10	
	"	" do	960	5,982.23 5/10	
June	30	" do	1130	63,998.56	
Septem	29	" do	1264	95,174.80	
	30	" do	1268	113,000	
Decem	30	" do	1401	114,036.76	
					412,805.34

For Interest payable on Certificates issued to Non-subscribers.

1791 March	31	To Thomas Smith Commissioner of Loans for the State of Pennsylvania—Warrt. No. 966	335.65
		Total amount	1,140,177.20

INTEREST ON THE DUTCH LOANS.

For the purchase of Bills of Exchange amounting to one hundred thousand current Guilders, remitted to W. and J. Willink, N. and J. Van Staphorst and Hubbard of Amsterdam, for the purpose of paying Interest on the Dutch Loans.

1790 March	29	To Le Roy and Bayard	Warrt. No.	266	20 000.
April	3	" do	do	317	3 000.
	9	" do	do	395	7 000.
	17	" do	do	440	2 000.
Septem	30	" do	do	672	3 087.71
		Total amount			35,087.71

INTEREST DUE ON LOAN OFFICE CERTIFICATES.

For paying Bills of Exchange drawn on the late Commissioners at Paris, for Interest due on Loan Office Certificates.

1790 March	31	To Jeremiah Wadsworth	Warrt. No.	270	288.
April	5	" Comfort and Joshua Sands	do	332	180.
May	7	" James Williams	do	473	162.
August	25	" Shedden Patrick and Compy	do	636	200.
	26	" Thomas Leaming Junior	do	638	36.
Septem	28	" Benjamin Harrison Junr.	do	669	24.
October	6	" George Joy	do	701	12.
Novem	20	" John Mitchell Junr.	do	744	24.
1791 Januay	12	" Jeremiah Wadsworth	do	828	72.
	14	" John Harback	do	833	168.
	17	" Jacob Lawerswyler	do	840	30.

	19	"	Richard Adams	do	846	40.
	"	"	do	do	847	20.
Februy	1	"	Thomas Tillyer	do	865	54.
	"	"	Robert Patterson	do	866	18.
	16	"	Samuel A. Otis Agent for John Hurd	do	897	48.
	17	"	Edward Fox	do	900	30.
	"	"	Andrew Porter	do	901	24.
	"	"	Joseph Mercier	do	902	18.
	24	"	Samuel Dunn	do	912	108.
	"	"	Joshua Sands	do	913	42.
	"	"	Josiah Hews	do	914	108.
March	1	"	Willing Morris and Swanwick in behalf of Samuel Ingliss and Co	do	922	825.
	4	"	Willing Morris and Swanwick	do	928	12.
June	24	"	George Tudor	do	1121	30.
	24	"	Lewis Deblois Agent for James F. Sebor	do	1122	12.
	"	"	Mark Pichard	do	1123	120.
	"	"	James Glentworth	do	1124	186.
	"	"	Cornelius Barnes Agent for Alexander Kieth & Co	do	1125	30.
	"	"	Thomas G. Pollard	do	1126	60.
July	11	"	Joseph Hopkinson Executor to the Estate of Frans. Hopkinson deceased	do	1170	120.
	21	"	James Gibson Attorney for Anne Gibson Executrix to the Estate of John Gibson	do	1186	156.
August	19	"	Henry Drinker Junior Executor to the Estate of Richard Vaux deceased	do	1227	36.
October	4	"	George Mead	do	1282	60.
	"	"	William Irvine	do	1283	84.
	5	"	John White Agent for John Templeman	do	1291	12.
Novem	9	"	Jonathan Sturgess	do	1348	48.
Decemr.	7	"	Charles Jarvis	do	1365	36.
			Total amount			3,533.

FOR THE SUPPORT AND REPAIRS OF LIGHT HOUSES, BEACONS, BUOYS AND PUBLIC PIERS.

Benjamin Lincoln Superintendant of the Light houses in the State of Massachusetts.

1790 Novem	30	To Warrant No.	757		4,345.67⅓

Thomas Randall Superintendant of the Light house at Sandy Hook.

1790 May	28	To Warrant No.	495	1670.90
June	1	" do	499	266.10
August	17	" do	611	415.80
October	8	" do	703	268.63

1791 Februay	11	" do	891	184.75	
April	23	" do	1034	555.31	
July	12	" do	1176	202.97	
October	28	" do	1336	264.06	
					3,828.52

William Allibone Superintendant of the Light House at Cape Henlopen, and of the beacons, buoys and public piers in the Bay and River Delaware.

1790 May	3	To Warrant No.	468	4000.	
Novem	30	" do	759	1000.	
1791 March	22	" do	945	800.	
June	29	" do	1129	940.	
Septem	28	" do	1262	640.	
Decem	26	" do	1374	425.	
					7,805.

John McComb Junior on account of his contract with the Secretary of the Treasury, for erecting a light house on Cape Henry in the State of Virginia.

1791 Decem	22	To Warrant No. 1369	6,000.

Edward Blake Superintendant of the Light house, beacons, buoys and public piers in the State of So. Carolina.

1791 March	8	To Warrant No. 932	612.75
		Total amount	22,591.94

FOR DEFRAYING THE CONTINGENT CHARGES OF GOVERNMENT.

1790 August	17	To Peter R. Maverick for sundry Seals furnished for the use of the supreme and circuit Courts; Warrt. No. 610	91.08
	27	" Royal Flint Agent for Jeremiah Wadsworth, for the amount of an account against the United States, for apprehending the Cranes and other persons concerned in counterfeiting public securities Warrant No. 639	1,061.
	31	" Mark Leavenworth Agent for Amos Doolittle for a Seal made by the said Doolittle for the District Court of Connecticut, Warrant No. 644	8.
Septem	2	" Peter R. Maverick for a Seal for the District Court of Rhode Island, Warrant No. 646	5.50
October	4	" Cyrus Griffin for a seal and an iron screw procured by him for the use of the circuit and district Courts of the State of Virginia, Warrant No. 685	19.33
1791 Januay	26	" George Thatcher, for so much paid by David Sewall for a Seal for the use of the District Court of Main, Warrant No. 855,	9.
July	12	" Andrew G. Fraunces Agent for Peter R. Maverick, for a Seal furnished by the said Maverick for the use of the District Court of New York, Warrant No. 1177	11.79

1791 Septem	13	" John Sitgreaves of Philadelphia Attorney for John Sitgreaves Judge for the District of North Carolina, for a seal made by William Johnston for the use of the Court of said District, Warrt. No. 1245	10.
October	21	" John Brown Assignee of Harry Innes Judge for the District of Kentucky for amount of a seal made by David Humphreys for the use of said District, Warrant No. 1323	10.
		Total amount	1,225.70

FOR THE REDUCTION OF THE PUBLIC DEBT.

For monies advanced to sundry persons Agents for the President of the Senate, the Chief Justice, the Secretary of State, the Secretary of the Treasury and the Attorney General, who, by virtue of the Act entitled "An Act making provision for the reduction of the Public Debt" [31] are impowered to make purchases of the Debt of the United States.

1790 Decemr.	15	To Samuel Meredith Treasurer,	Warrt. No.	776	200,000.	
1791 January	26	" do	do	856	50,000.	
Septem	29	" do	do	1265	149,984.23	
						399,984.23
Februy	5	To Benjamin Lincoln Collector for the District of Boston	do	869		50,000.
	"	To William Heth Collector for the District of Bermuda hundred	do	870		50,000.
Septem	29	To William Seton Cashier of the Bank of New York	do	1266		200,000.
		Total amount				699,984.23

ENUMERATION OF THE INHABITANTS OF THE UNITED STATES.

For compensation to the Marshals and their Assistants for taking the number of Inhabitants within their respective Districts, in pursuance of the Act entitled, "An Act providing for the enumeration of the Inhabitants of the United States." [32]

1791 Februay	14	To Jonathan Jackson Marshal for the District of Massachusetts, Warrant No. 893	2,892.18
	15	To John Cochran on account of the expenses incurred by the Marshal for the District of New York. Warrt. No. 895	1,000.
April	25	To Henry Knox Agent for Edward Carrington Marshal for the District of Virginia, Warrant No. 1035	3,300.
May	18	To Thomas Lowrey Marshal for the District of New Jersey, Warrt. No. 1072	1,300.
	20	To Allen McLane Marshal for the District of Delaware, Warrt. No. 1073	377.

31. 1 *Stat.* 186–87 (August 12, 1790).

32. 1 *Stat.* 101–03 (March 1, 1790).

June	14	To William S. Smith Marshal for the State of New York, Warrt. No. 1098	1,000.
	15	To Hezekiah B. Pierpont Attorney for Philip B. Bradley Marshal for the District of Connecticut, Warrt. No. 1101	1,584.
July	8	To Tobias Lear Agent for John Parker Marshal for the District of New Hampshire, Warrant No. 1166	1,030.
	23	To Clement Biddle Marshal for the District of Pennsylvania, Warrant No. 1193	2,500.
	28	To Nathaniel Ramsey Marshal for the District of Maryland, Warrt. No. 1198	1,960.
August	4	To John Skinner Marshal for the District of North Carolina, Warrant No. 1205	1,730.
	"	To Robert Forsyth Marshal for the District of Georgia, Warrant No. 1207	1,080.
	10	To William Peck Marshal for the District of Rhode Island, Warrant No. 1224	376.
October	25	To John Brown Assignee of Samuel McDowell Senior Attorney for Samuel McDowell Junior Marshal for the District of Kentucky, Warrt. No. 1329	250.
	29	To James Sawyer one of the Assistants to Lewis R. Morris Marshal for the District of Vermont Warrt. No. 1340	211.53
		Total amount	20,590.71

FOR SATISFYING MISCELLANEOUS CLAIMS IN RELATION BOTH TO THE LATE AND PRESENT GOVERNMENT.

UNDER THIS HEAD ARE ALSO INCLUDED. THE EXPENSES INCURRED IN CONSEQUENCE OF REMOVING THE SEAT OF GOVERNMENT FROM NEW YORK TO PHILADELPHIA. THE DISTRIBUTION OF PRIZES CAPTURED BY THE SQUADRON UNDER THE COMMAND OF JOHN PAUL JONES. THE COST OF HYDROMETERS FOR THE USE OF THE OFFICERS OF THE CUSTOMS. THE EXPENSE OF CERTIFICATES PREPARED FOR THE FUNDED DEBT, AND, PAYMENTS MADE FOR EXECUTING THE SURVEYS DIRECTED BY AN ACT OF CONGRESS PASSED JUNE 6, 1788.[33]

1790 April	7	To William S. Smith, Egbert Benson and Daniel Parker late Commissioners for superintending the evacuation of the City of New York by the British Troops, for a balance due to them—Warrt. No. 374	1,000.	
June	1	To Royal Flint Attorney for Catherine Greene Assignee of P. G. J. Ludovicus Baron de Glaubeck, for one fifth of the amount of the said Barons pay as a Captain in the service of the United States, allowed by an Act of Congress passed Septemr. 29, 1789[34]—Warrant No. 498	140.26	

33. *JCC*, XXXIV, 203.
34. "An Act to allow the Baron de Glaubeck the pay of a Captain in the Army of the United States" (6 *Stat.* 1).

July	7	To Jehoiakim McTocksin for his services as Interpreter and Guide in the expedition commanded by Major General Sullivan in the Year 1779, pursuant to an Act of Congress passed the 26 March last[35]—Warrt. No. 541	120.
	"	To John McCord in full for his claims and demands against the United States, pursuant to an Act of Congress passed the first Instant[36]—Warrant No. 542	1,309.71
August	13	To Francis Christopher Mantel Attorney to Le Ray de Chaumont the younger Attorney to Le Ray de Chaumont, the elder towards discharging certain demands of the said Le Ray de Chaumont the elder on the United States; Warrant No. 602	9 051.33
	14	To Seth Harding for services on board the Alliance Frigate during the late War pursuant to an Act of Congress passed the 11 Instant[37]—Warrant No. 606	200.
	20	To Constant Freeman of the Province of Quebeck for a bill of exchange dated Quebeck Augst. 5, 1776 drawn by William Thompson, Wm. Irvine, Christopher Green, John Lamb, Timothy Bigelow and Daniel Morgan on Meredith and Clymer for 1677 70/100 Dolls with Interest and sundry charges thereon; Warrant No. 623	3 123.28
Septemr.	11	To Israel Ludlow for a balance due to him for executing a survey of a tract of Country sold to Messrs. Cutler and Sargent by the late Board of Treasury; Warrt. No. 660	541.75
October	11	To Thomas Franklin Junior for his commission as Auctioneer on the sale of lands in the Western Territory by order of the late Board of Treasury—Warrt. No. 707	48.
Novemr.	11	To James O'Hara late Contractor for supply the Troops on the Western Frontier, for provisions seized from him after the expiration of his contract by the commanding Officer at Post St. Vincennes; Wart. No. 736	1 755.42
	22	To Israel Ludlow for his expenses in bringing forward to the Seat of Government a return of surveys made of a tract of Country sold to Messrs. Cutler and Sargent, and for executing four draughts of the same by direction of the Secretary of the Treasury—Warrant No. 748	249.
	"	To Israel Ludlow Agent for Absalome Martin, for executing a survey in the Year 1788 of the Western boundry line of the tract of Country sold to Messrs. Cutler and Sargent—Warrant No. 749	365.50

35. Section 6 of "An Act making appropriations for the support of government for the year one thousand seven hundred and ninety" (1 *Stat.* 105 [March 26, 1790]).

36. "An Act to satisfy the claims of John McCord against the United States" (6 *Stat.* 2 [July 1, 1790]).

37. Section 6 of "An Act for the relief of disabled soldiers and seamen lately in the service of the United States, and of certain other persons" (6 *Stat.* 4 [August 11, 1790]).

	25	To Joseph Nourse Assignee of Samuel Baird for executing a survey of the land at Post Vincennes granted to the Inhabitants of said place pursuant to the Act of Congress of the 29th of August 1788 [38]—Warrant No. 753	120.
Decemr	7	To Henry Knox Assignee of James OHara for sundry charges made by the said O Hara in his account of rations of provisions delivered at Muskingum, between the first of December 1787 and the 30 of June 1788; Warrant No. 767	2,876.45
	"	To Henry Knox Assignee of James OHara for supplies furnished by the said OHara to the Troops at Post St. Vincennes, Fort Harmar and the Rapids of the Ohio in the Year 1788—Warrant No. 768	1 197.34
	"	To John Leamy Agent for Joseph Ignatius Viar Attorney for Joseph Gardoqui and Sons of Bilboa, for a balance due to the said Gardoqui and Sons on the books of Thomas Barclay late Commissioner for adjusting accounts in Europe; Wart. No. 769	502.86
	21	To Caleb Brewster late a Lieutenant in the service of the United States pursuant to an Act of Congress passed the eleventh day of August last [39]—Warrant No. 781	348.57
1791 Januay	18	To Benjamin Goodhue Agents for Francis Dana for the service and expense of a private Secretary employed by the said Francis Dana whilst on his embassy at the Court of Petersburgh, pursuant to an Act of Congress passed the 2nd. of October 1787 [40]—Warrant No. 845	2 410.03
	24	To William Bell Attorney for J. Henry Laurens, Administrator to the Estate of Lieutenant Colonel Laurens deceased for a balance due to the said Lieutenant Col. Laurens as special Minister from the United States to the Court of Versailles in the Year 1781—Warrant No. 852	6 017.31
Februy	17	To Richard Platt Agent for Elnathan Haskell late Commissioner of accounts for the Eastern District for sundry contingent expenses of the said Commissioners Office which accrued in the Years 1787 and 1788—Warrant No. 904	47.57
	18	To Samuel Baird for executing surveys of the lands at Post Vincennes granted to the Inhabitants of said place, pursuant to an Act of Congress of the 29 of August 1788 [41]—Warrant No. 905	80.
March	1	To Samuel Meredith Treasurer of the United States for charges of protests on three bills of exchange drawn on James Hunter and for commissions on deposits lodged in the Bank of Massachusetts—Warrt. No. 920	178.73

38. *JCC*, XXXIV, 472–74.
39. Section 2 of "An Act for the relief of disabled soldiers and seamen lately in the service of the United States, and of certain other persons" (6 *Stat.* 4 [August 11, 1790]).
40. *JCC*, XXXIII, 588–89.
41. *JCC*, XXXIV, 472–74.

	19	To John M. St. Clair for laying off and drawing a plan of the Town of Cahokia by direction of the Governor of the Western Territory—Warrant No. 941	60.
	31	To Nicholas Gilman Agent for Simon Knowles and John Whittor late Soldiers in the second New Hampshire Regiment, for services performed in the Year 1783—Warrant No. 968	13.32
April	6	To Nicholas Gilman Agent for James Sinkler and William Hill late Soldiers in the second New Hampshire Regiment for services performed in the Year 1783; Warrant No. 993	16.66
June	24	To Andrew G. Fraunces for expenses incurred in fitting out a barge for the late Board of Treasury, Secretary for foreign Affairs and Secretary at War in order to attend the President of the United States at Elizabeth Town, by order of the said Board of Treasury; Warrant No. 1117	30.92
August	17	To M. Jean de Ternant Minister Plenipotentiary of the Court of France at the United States Attorney for the heirs or representatives of the late P. C. J. B. Tronson du Coudrai deceased, pursuant to a Resolve of Congress dated September 25, 1781 [42]—Warrant No. 1225	2 977.24
	19	To John Fenno, for printing done for the Office of the Secretary of the Treasury in the months of June and July last—Warrant No. 1226	81.35
	22	To Antoine Rene Charles Mathurin de la Forest Vice Consul General of France to the United States, on account of a debt due to the French Government for supplies furnished in the West Indies by the Navy Department of France to sundry Ships of War of the United States; Warrant No. 1230	20,000.
Decemr.	26	To Thomas Motley keeper of the Gaol in Portland Massachusetts, for the maintenance of three prisoners from the 23rd. of July 1789 to the 4 of June 1790, committed on a charge of piracy and felony on the high Seas—Warrant No. 1377	256.

55,118.60

EXPENSES INCURRED IN CONSEQUENCE OF REMOVING THE SEAT OF GOVERNMENT FROM NEW YORK TO PHILADELPHIA, IN PURSUANCE OF THE RESPECTIVE ACTS THE ONE ENTITLED, "AN ACT FOR ESTABLISHING THE TEMPORARY AND PERMANENT SEAT OF THE GOVERNMENT OF THE UNITED STATES" AND THE OTHER ENTITLED "AN ACT IN ADDITION TO AN ACT, ENTITLED, AN ACT FOR ESTABLISHING THE SALARIES OF THE EXECUTIVE OFFICERS OF GOVERNMT, WITH THEIR ASSISTANTS AND CLERKS".[43]

1790 Novemr	25	To John Inskeep Agent for J. N. Cumming, for the transportation of public books and papers from New York to Philadelphia—Warrant No. 754	236.25

42. *JCC*, XXI, 1014.
43. 1 *Stat.* 130 (July 16, 1790); 1 *Stat.* 216 (March 3, 1791).

1791 January	29	To Joseph Howell for the expenses of removing the books and papers of the late Office of Commissioner of Army accounts, from New York to Philadelphia—Warrant No. 858	98.26	
March	31	To William Simmons Attorney to sundry persons Clerks in the public Offices attached to the Seat of Government, for their expenses incurred by the removal from New York to Philadelphia—Warrant No. 963	1,011.28	
	"	To Edward Jones Clerk in the Comptrollers Office for his expenses incurred by the removal from New York to Philadelphia Warrant No. 967	103.80	
April	5	To John Stagg Junior, R. J. vanden Broek and Constant Freeman Clerks in the War Office, for their expenses incurred by the removal from New York to Philadelphia—Warrant No. 983	122.20	
June	24	To Isaac Sherman Clerk in the Treasury Department for his expenses incurred by the removal from New York to Philadelphia—Warrant No. 1118	12.	
	"	To Robert Heysham principal Clerk in the Office of the Secretary of the Senate for his expenses incurred by the removal from New York to Philadelphia—Warrant No. 1119	12.	
	"	To Benjamin Bankson Clerk in the Office of the Secretary of the Senate, for expenses attending the transportation of public papers under his care from New York to Philadelphia—Warrant No. 1120	7.66	
July	6	To David Henly Clerk in the Treasury Department for his expenses incurred by the removal from New York to Philadelphia—Warrant No. 1150	18.	
	15	To John Meyer Agent for George H. Remsen late a Clerk in the Office of the Secretary of the Treasury for expenses incurred by the said Remsen in consequence of the removal from New York to Philadelphia; Warrant No. 1182	12.	
August	9	To Joseph Hardy late principal Clerk in the Comptrollers Office for his expenses incurred by the removal from New York to Philadelphia—Warrt. No. 1222	30.	
				1,663.45

DISTRIBUTION OF PRIZES CAPTURED BY THE SQUADRON UNDER THE COMMAND OF JOHN PAUL JONES IN THE NORTH SEAS, IN PURSUANCE OF AN ACT OF CONGRESS PASSED THE ELEVENTH DAY OF OCTOBER 1787.[44]

1790 Decemr.	29	To Joseph Brussells late a boy on board the Ship Bon Homme Richard for his proportion of said prizes—Warrant No. 788	13.16
1791 Februay	8	To Mary Winter Attorney for Thomas Jones late a Seaman on board the Ship Bon Homme Richard, for his proportion of the said prizes—Warrant No. 875	52.66

44. *JCC*, XXXIII, 663.

	15	" To Robert Troup Attorney for Matthew Parke Administrator to the Estates of sundry persons late of the Ships Alliance and Bon Homme Richard deceased, for their respective shares of the said prizes—Warrant No. 896	818.74	
March	17	To Margaret Hall Administratrix to the Estate of William Phisick deceased, for his proportion of the said prizes; Warrt. No. 939	52.66	
April	14	To Samuel A. Otis Attorney for Mary Taylor Administratrix to the Estate of John Combs late a Seaman on board the Ship Alliance deceased, for the said John Combs's proportion of the said prizes; Warrant No. 1023	35.14	
May	2	To Thomas Dupey late a boy on board the Alliance, for his proportion of the said prizes—Warrant No. 1049	36.25	
	5	" To Mary Morrison Administratrix to the Estate of Elijah Middlton late a boy on board the Ship Bon Homme Richard deceased, for his proportion of the said prizes—Warrant No. 1058	6.03	
July	7	To Joseph Frederick late a Boatswains Mate on board the Ship Alliance for his proportion of the said prizes; Warrt. No. 1159	36.25	
October	5	To Nathan Dane Attorney to Josiah Batchelor Junior Administrator to Nathanl. Porter late a Seaman on board the Ship Alliance deceased, for the said Porters proportion of the said prizes—Warrant No. 1294	36.25	
				1,087.14

MONIES ADVANCED FOR THE PURPOSE OF PAYING FOR HYDROMETERS PROCURED FOR THE USE OF THE OFFICERS OF THE CUSTOMS.

1791 March	10	To Joseph Nourse Register of the Treasury Warrant No. 934	250.	
	30	" do do 957	568.41	
June	10	" do do 1097	200.	
			1,018.41	
		From which deduct this sum repaid into the Treasury, being the amount of a Warrant No. 61 dated March 14, 1792	529.75	
				488.66

PAYMENTS AND ADVANCES MADE ON ACCOUNT OF CERTIFICATES PREPARED FOR THE FUNDED DEBT, PURSUANT TO THE ACT ENTITLED, "AN ACT MAKING PROVISION FOR THE DEBT OF THE UNITED STATES".[45]

1791 March	22	To Mark Wilcox for 229¼ Reams of Certificate paper—Warrant No. 948	764.16	
	25	To Thomas Mendenhall and John Wilson for superintending the making of Certificate paper from the 9 day of Septemr, 1790 to the 18 day of December following; Warrant No. 951	149.32	

45. 1 *Stat.* 138–44 (August 4, 1790).

"		To William Govett for his services in forwarding to the several Commissioners of Loans books of printed Certificates; Warrant No. 952	350.78	
"		To John Wharton, William Govett, Joseph Bullock and Archibald Woodside, for superintending the press for printing Certificates from the 13 day of Septemr, 1790 to the 12 day of March 1791—Warrant No. 953	1 000.	
April	19	To James Muir for binding [46] books of certificates—Warrant No. 1029	258.26	
May	5	To Nathan and David Sellers for making moulds for certificate paper; Warrt. No. 1057	74.50	
Septem	25	To Joseph Nourse Register of the Treasury to be by him applied towards defraying the expense of printing the several discriptions of Treasury and Loan Office Certificates—Warrant No. 1255 .	300.	
October	10	To Thomas Dobson for binding 75 books of Certificates for the Register of the Treasury—Warrant No. 1305	30.	
Novemr	1	To Mark Wilcox for 29½ Reams of certificate paper —Warrant No. 1341	98.33	
Decemr.	1	To Joseph Nourse Register of the Treasury to be by him applied towards defraying the expense of stamping the several species of Treasury and Loan Office Certificates—Warrant No. 1362	524.28	
			3 549.63	
		From which deduct the amount of Warrt. No. 62 dated the 14th. day of Mar 1792, being so much repaid into the Treasury by Joseph Nourse Register	292.	
				3 257.63

PAYMENTS MADE FOR EXECUTING THE SURVEYS DIRECTED BY CONGRESS IN THEIR ACT OF JUNE 6, 1788, AND A CONCURRENT RESOLUTION PASSED THE 26 DAY OF AUGUST 1789.[47]

1790 March	30	To Andrew Ellicott Surveyor Warrt. No. 267	1 234.78	
August	18	To Joseph Howell Junior Agent for Andrew Ellicott Surveyor, Warrant No. 616	1 200.	
Decemr.	2	To Andrew Ellicott Surveyor, Warrt. No. 760	200.	
1791 Januay	8	" do do 820	662.	
Februy	17	To Caleb Strong Agent for Israel Chapin, for sundry expenses incurred by the said I. Chapin, under Andrew Ellicott, Warrt. No. 903	34.32	
April	23	To Andrew Ellicott Surveyor, Warrt. No. 1032	718.75	
				4,049.85
		Total amount		65,665.33

46. Space left blank in MS.

47. *JCC*, XXXIV, 203; 1 *Stat.* 96.

A GENERAL STATEMENT OF THE APPROPRIATIONS MADE BY LAW IN RELATION TO THE EXPENDITURES OF THE UNITED STATES FROM THE COMMENCEMENT OF THE PRESENT GOVERNMENT TO THE LAST DAY OF DECEMBER 1791, INCLUSIVELY.

		Dates and titles of the Acts of Appropriations	For discharging the Warrants
1789 August	20	An Act providing for the expenses which may attend Negotiations or Treaties with the Indian Tribes, and the appointment of Commissioners for managing the same.	. .
Septemr.	29	An Act making Appropriations for the service of the present Year.	190,0
1790 March	26	An Act making Appropriations for the support of Government for the Year 1790.	. .
July	1	An Act providing the means of intercourse between the United States and foreign Nations.	. .
	"	An Act to satisfy the Claims of John McCord against the United States.	. .
	22	An Act providing for holding a treaty or treaties to establish peace with certain Indian Tribes.	. .
August	4	An Act making provision for the Debt of the United States.	. .
	"	An Act to provide more effectually for the Collection of the Duties imposed by Law on Goods, Wares and Merchandize imported into the United States, and on the Tonnage of Ships or Vessels	. .
	10	An Act authorizing the Secretary of the Treasury to finish the Light House on Portland Head in the District of Main.	. .
	11	An Act for the relief of disabled Soldiers and Seamen lately in the service of the United States, and of certain other persons	. .
	12	An Act making certain Appropriations therein mentioned.	. .
	"	An Act making provision for the Reduction of the Public Debt.	. .
1791 Februay	11	An Act making Appropriations for the support of Government during the Year 1791 and for other purposes.	. .
March	3	An Act making an Appropriation for the purpose therein mentioned.	. .
	"	An Act providing compensations for the Officers of the Judicial Courts of the United States and for Jurors and Witnesses, and for other purposes.	.
	"	An Act for raising and adding another Regiment to the Military Establishment of the United States, and for making farther provision for the protection of the Frontiers.	. .
		Aggregate of Appropriations	190,0
		Recapitulation of the Expenditures	157,7
		Balances unexpended, to be accounted for in the next Statement	32,2

Government; page 11 to 83.[49]	For the support of the Army of the United States; page 83 to 90.[50]	For paying the pensions due to Invalids; page 91 to 93.[51]	For defraying the expenses of negotiaitons or treaties of peace with the Indian Tribes; page 94.[52]	For paying interest due on temporary loans obtained by the Secretary of the Treasury; page 95.[53]	For the support of Ministers &c of the United States at foreign Courts; page 96.[54]	For effecting a recognition of the treaty of the United States with the new Emperor of Morocco; page 97.[55]	For the building, equipment and support of ten Revenue Cutters; page 98.[56]	Towards discharging certain debts contracted by Abraham Skinner late Commissary of Prisoners; page 99 to 107.[57]
....	......	......	20,000.	......	......	......	......	......
00.	137,000.	96,000.	......	......	......	......	......	......
3.16 7.28	155,537.72	96,979.72	......	5,000.	......	......	......	......
....	......	......	......	......	80,000.	......	......	......
....	......	......	......	......	......	......	......	......
....	......	......	20,000.	......	......	......	......	......
....	......	......	......	......	......	......	......	......
....	......	......	......	......	......	......	10,000.	......
....	......	......	......	......	......	......	......	......
....	......	......	......	......	......	......	......	......
58.70	39,207.10	......	......	......	......	......	......	38,892.75
....	......	......	......	......	......	......	......	......
26.53	302,735.94	87,463.60	......	......	......	......	23,327.50	......
....	......	......	......	......	......	20,000.	......	......
55.33	......	......	......	......	......	......	......	......
....	312,686.20	......	......	......	......	......	......	......
41.	947,166.96	280,443.32	40,000.	5,000.	80,000.	20,000.	33,327.50	38,892.75
34.45	632,804.03	175,813.88	27,000.	⟨2,5⟩98.12	1,733.33	13,000.	570.	38,683.13
06.55	314,362.93	104,629.44	13,000.	⟨2,⟩401.88	78,266.67	7,000.	32,757.50	209.62

48. These page numbers and subsequent page references in the headings of this statement refer to the pagination in the original document. For the material which appears on the manuscript pages cited here, see pages 42–44 in this volume.

49. See pages 45–83 in this volume.
50. See pages 84–87 in this volume.
51. See pages 87–89 in this volume.
52. See page 89 in this volume.
53. See pages 89–90 in this volume.
54. See page 90 in this volume.
55. See page 90 in this volume.
56. See page 91 in this volume.
57. See pages 91–95 in this volume.

		Dates and titles of the Acts of Appropriations	Towards discharging certain debts
1789 August	20	An Act providing for the expenses which may attend Negotiations or Treaties with the Indian Tribes, and the appointment of Commissioners for managing the same.[67]	. . .
Septemr.	29	An Act making Appropriations for the service of the present Year.[68]	. . .
1790 March	26	An Act making Appropriations for the support of Government for the Year 1790.[69]	. . .
July	1	An Act providing the means of intercourse between the United States and foreign Nations.[70]	. . .
	"	An Act to satisfy the Claims of John McCord against the United States.[71]	. . .
	22	An Act providing for holding a treaty or treaties to establish peace with certain Indian Tribes.[72]	. . .
August	4	An Act making provision for the Debt of the United States.[73]	. .
	"	An Act to provide more effectually for the Collection of the Duties imposed by Law on Goods, Wares and Merchandize imported into the United States, and on the Tonnage of Ships or Vessels [74]	. . .
	10	An Act authorizing the Secretary of the Treasury to finish the Light House on Portland Head in the District of Main.[75]	. . .
	11	An Act for the relief of disabled Soldiers and Seamen lately in the service of the United States, and of certain other persons [76]	. . .
	12	An Act making certain Appropriations therein mentioned.[77]	40,00
	"	An Act making provision for the Reduction of the Public Debt.[78]	. . .
1791 Februay	11	An Act making Appropriations for the support of Government during the Year 1791 and for other purposes.[79]	. . .
March	3	An Act making an Appropriation for the purpose therein mentioned.[80]	. .
	"	An Act providing compensations for the Officers of the Judicial Courts of the United States and for Jurors and Witnesses, and for other purposes.[81]	. .
	"	An Act for raising and adding another Regiment to the Military Establishment of the United States, and for making farther provision for the protection of the Frontiers.[82]	. .
		Aggregate of Appropriations	40,00
		Recapitulation of the Expenditures	1,45
		Balances unexpended, to be accounted for in the next Statement	38,54

A The expenses arising from and incident to the sessions of Congress which happened in the course of the Year 1790 amount to 203,167 28/100 Dollars, which being added to the specific sums appropriated by said Act, constitutes the total amount as extended, marked B.
C The amount of interest on the Domestic Debt of the United States for the Year 1791, agreeably to the dividend accounts settled at the Treasury to that period.
D The surplus of Duties on Merchandize and Tonnage on the last day of December 1790.
E The net sum arising from Fines Penalties and Forfeitures to Decemr. 31, 1791.

Domestic Debt of the United States; page 109 to 114.[59]	For paying the Interest due on the Dutch Loans; page 115.[60]	For paying Bills of Ex drawn on the late Commissioners at Paris, for interest due on Loan Office Certificates; page 116 to 117.[61]	For the support and repairs of Light Houses, Beacons, Buoys and Public piers; page 118 to 119.[62]	For defraying the Contingent charges of Government; page 120 to 121.[63]	For the Reduction of the Public Debt; page 122.[64]	For defraying the expenses of the Enumeration of the Inhabitants of the United States; page 123 to 124.[65]	For satisfying miscellaneous Claims, which include all other expenditures; page 125 to 138.[66]	Total amount.
......	......	......	......	......	......	......	......	20,000.
......	......	......	......	......	......	......	......	639,000.
......	32,000.	1,000.	45,380.38	10,000.	......	......	11,060.73	B 754,658.99
......	......	......	......	......	......	......	......	80,000.
......	......	......	......	......	......	......	1,309.71	1,309.71
......	......	......	......	......	......	......	......	20,000.
9,630.14	......	......	......	......	......	......	......	1,369,630.14
......	......	......	......	......	......	......	......	10,000.
......	......	......	1,500.	......	......	......	......	1,500.
......	......	......	......	......	......	......	548.57	548.57
......	3 087.71	2,685.38	2,372.14	......	......	21,850.	55,566.19	233,219.97
......	......	......	......	...... D	1,374,656.40	......	......	1,374,656.40
......	......	......	16,428.57	......	......	......	10,750.46	740,232.60
......	......	......	......	......	......	......	......	20,000.
......	......	......	......	......	......	......	......	4,055.33
......	......	......	......	......	......	......	......	312,686.20
9,630.14	35,087.71	3,685.38	65,681.09	10,000.	1,374,656.40	21,850.	79,235.66	5,581,497.91
0,177.20	35,087.71	3,533.	22,591.94	1,225.70	699,984.23	20,590.71	65,665.33	3,797,436.78
9,452.94		152.38	43,089.15	8,774.30	674,672.17	1,259.29	13,570.33	1,784.061.13

pages 95–96 in this volume.
pages 96–99 in this volume.
page 99 in this volume.
pages 99–100 in this volume.
pages 100–01 in this volume.
pages 101–02 in this volume.
page 102 in this volume.
pages 102–03 in this volume.
pages 103–09 in this volume.

67. 1 *Stat.* 54.
68. 1 *Stat.* 95.
69. 1 *Stat.* 104–06.
70. 1 *Stat.* 128–29.
71. 6 *Stat.* 2.
72. 1 *Stat.* 136.
73. 1 *Stat.* 138–44.
74. 1 *Stat.* 145–78.

75. 1 *Stat.* 184.
76. 6 *Stat.* 3–4.
77. 1 *Stat.* 185–86.
78. 1 *Stat.* 186–87.
79. 1 *Stat.* 190.
80. 1 *Stat.* 214.
81. 1 *Stat.* 216–17.
82. 1 *Stat.* 222–24.

GENERAL ACCOUNT OF RECEIPTS AND EXPENDITURES OF THE PUBLIC MONIES TO THE LAST DAY OF DECEMBER 1791, INCLUSIVELY.

DR.		CR.	
To total amount of Expenditures, as stated in page 140[83]	3,797,436.78	By amount of Receipts, as stated in page 5[84]	4,771,342.43
Balance in the Treasury on the 31 day of December 1791	973,905.65		
	4,771,342.43		4,771,342.43

The Treasurer having been overcharged in the statement of his accounts at the Treasury for the quarter ending June 30, 1790, on Warrant No. 249 drawn on Sharp Delany, nine cents; and the omission of fractional parts, amounting to one cent, in the account of monies received from Collectors, will account for the difference between the balance of this statement and that of the Treasurers account settled for the last quarter of the Year 1791, in which he is held accountable for the sum of 973,905 75/100 Dollars.

Treasury Department, Registers Office Novemr. 10, 1792.
Stated from the Records of the Treasury.
Joseph Nourse Regr.

Comptrollers Office Novemr. 10, 1792.
Examined by.
Oliv: Wolcott Jr. Compt.

83. This page number refers to the pagination of the original document. For the material cited, see page 113 in this volume.

84. This page number refers to the pagination of the original document. For the material cited, see page 41 in this volume.

From Otho H. Williams

Baltimore 10th November 1792.

Sir,

In consequence of your communication of the 3d Instant I have resolved for the present to postpone the disposal of my Stock in the funds.

I would not offend against the most rigid construction of the most unjust *Law* while it is in force. It cannot be doubted that some sensible and liberal Member of the Legislature will take to himself the merit of repealing an act replete with injustice, before the expiration of this session of Congress.

I have been obliged to adopt a very disadvantageous expedient to avoid the necessity of trespassing in this Instance.

You will permit me to use this opportunity for thanking you for the permission obtained of the President to avail myself of the advice of my Physicians.[1]

Tomorrow I depart for Barbadoes. Accept, Sir, my best thanks for your very friendly sentiments respecting my health.

With very sincere regard and respect. I am, Sir, Your Most Obedt. Servt.

Alexander Hamilton Esqr.

ADf, Maryland Historical Society, Baltimore.

1. See H to Williams, November 1, 1792.

From James Reynolds[1]

[*Philadelphia, November 13–15, 1792.* On July 19, 1797, Henry Seckel attested that sometime between November 13 and 15, 1792, "the said James Reynolds requested this Deponent to carry a letter for him to Alexander Hamilton . . . that this Deponent carried the said letter as requested." *Letter not found.*]

"Reynolds Pamphlet," August 31, 1797.

1. Seckel's deposition is printed as document No. XXIII in the appendix of the "Reynolds Pamphlet," August 31, 1797.

Seckel's deposition concerned the second phase of the Reynolds affair. The first phase of that affair resulted in H's paying blackmail to his mistress's husband, James Reynolds. For background to these payments, see Reynolds to H, December 15, 17, 19, 22, 1791, January 3, 17, March 24, April 3, 7, 17, 23, May 2, June 3–22, 23, 24, August 24, 1792; H to Reynolds, December 15, 1791, April 7, June 3–22, 24, 1792; Maria Reynolds to H, December 15, 1791, January 23–March 18, March 24, June 2, 1792.

The second phase of the affair began with the prosecution of Reynolds and Jacob Clingman, a clerk employed by Representative Frederick A. C. Muhlenberg of Pennsylvania, for attempting to defraud the United States Government. The scheme worked out by the two men was to make themselves executors of the estate of a claimant against the United States. To achieve this, Reynolds and Clingman had persuaded a third person, John Delabar, to commit perjury. Early in November, 1792, the fraud was detected, and Oliver Wolcott, Jr., comptroller of the Treasury, had Clingman imprisoned. On November 13, 1792, Reynolds was also apprehended. Once in prison, Reynolds requested Henry Seckel, a Philadelphia merchant who earlier had employed Clingman as a bookkeeper, to carry to H the letter mentioned in Seckel's deposition. Reynolds now began to hint that he had information which, if disclosed, would discredit a certain head of a department, obviously H. When Wolcott heard of Reynolds's threats, he informed H who advised him "to take no step towards a liberation of Reynolds, while such a report existed and remained unexplained" ("Reynolds Pamphlet," August 31, 1797). Reynolds and Clingman, however, soon found a way to secure their release from prison. In return for Wolcott's promise to drop the prosecution against them, they gave him a list of creditors of the United States which they had obtained from the Treasury Department. According to Clingman, the list had been furnished by William Duer, former Assistant Secretary of the Treasury, a charge which Wolcott refuted. On or shortly after December 4, 1792, Clingman was released from jail, and on December 12 Reynolds was also set free.

In mid-November, 1792, shortly after his imprisonment, Clingman had asked Muhlenberg for help. Muhlenberg agreed to assist Clingman, but declined to aid Reynolds on the ground that he was not "particularly acquainted" with him. For the next three weeks, according to Muhlenberg, "Clingman, unasked, frequently dropped hints to me, that Reynolds had it in his power, very materially to injure the secretary of the treasury, and that Reynolds knew several very improper transactions of his" ("Reynolds Pamphlet," August 31, 1797). The reiteration of these charges disturbed Muhlenberg, and on December 12 he shared them with his fellow-Congressmen, James Monroe and Abraham Venable. Monroe and Venable immediately called on Reynolds, who repeated the accusations against H. Their suspicions were heightened when on the evening of the same day, December 12, Mrs. Reynolds corroborated her husband's story. Clingman contributed to the mounting evidence against H by handing over to the Congressmen a number of letters from H to James Reynolds.

On the morning of December 15, Muhlenberg, Monroe, and Venable called on H and informed him of the charges which Clingman and Reynolds had made. H told the three men that it was in his "power by written documents to remove all doubt as to the real nature of the business, and fully to convince, that nothing of the kind imputed to me did in fact exist" ("Reynolds Pamphlet," August 31, 1791). It was agreed that this documentary evidence should be submitted at a meeting to be held at H's house on the evening of the same day. At H's request, Wolcott was invited to attend the meeting. The three Congressmen decided that President Washington should be told of the Reynolds affair. On December 13, 1792, they wrote to Washington: "We think it proper to lay before you, some documents respecting the conduct of Colo. Hamilton, in the Office of Secretary of the Treasury." But they added: "We were, however, unwilling to take this step without communicating it to the gentleman, whom it concerns, that he might make the explanation, he has it in his power to give" (copy, Lehigh University). H's accusers obviously planned to send this letter to the President only after they had talked with H. After hearing H's explanation, they presumably decided not to send it.

In a joint statement, Muhlenberg, Venable, and Monroe described the meeting at H's house as follows: "Last night we waited on Colo. H. when he informed us of a particular connection with Mrs. R; the period of its commencment & circumstances attending it. His visiting her at Inskeeps—the frequent supplies of money to her & her husband on that acct. His duress by them from the fear of a disclosure & his anxiety to be relieved from it and them. To support this he shewed a great number of letters from Reynolds & herself commencing early in 1791. He acknowledged all the letters in a disguised hand, in our possession, to be his. We left him under an impression our suspicions were removed. He acknowledged our conduct toward him had been fair & liberal. He could not complain of it. We brot. back all the papers even his own notes, nor did he ask their destruction. . ." (D, in the handwriting of James Monroe, Lehigh University).

To Henry Knox[1]

Treasury department November 14. 1792

Sir,

In answer to your letter of this day I observe

I recalled your having spoken to me at the period to which you allude, concerning the contract which you were then about to make with Mr. Duer and the making of which by you was agreeable to former practice in similar cases.

You stated that you had adjusted with Mr. Duer the terms of the Contract; that an advance upon it of four thousand dollars was asked by him; that a question occurred whether it was necessary to take sureties of him for its performance; that it had not been your practice to demand sureties in other similar cases and that you felt some ⟨– – – –⟩ and concluded with asking my opinion whether it was essential to do it.

I replied that as it had not been your practice in other like cases —as the object could not be of much necessary magnitude—as the current supply would ⟨–⟩ away the proposed advance which was not large in no very long time—as any deficiency which might happen could not be of material consequence to the public service being ⟨–⟩ by you I thought the taking of Sureties could not be deemed essential ⟨and⟩ that a ⟨–⟩ bond in some adequate penalty ⟨might suffice.⟩

At this time Mr. Duer was in high Credit and it appeared to me that such a mode of proceeding might be ⟨pursued⟩ consistently with a due regard to caution. There is no law requiring ⟨it or⟩ any uniform usage commanding the taking of ⟨Sureties⟩ in all cases. It has consequently been deemed matter of discretion and the thing has been done or omitted according to the magnitude of the object, the course of the business to be executed and the circumstances of the parties.

With respectful consideration I have the honor to be Sir your obedient servant Alexander Hamilton

The Honble. Henry Knox, Esq. Secretary at War.

Copy, Massachusetts Historical Society, Boston.

1. For background concerning William Duer's agency as contractor for the Army during the campaign of Major General Arthur St. Clair in the fall of 1791, see "Contract for Army Rations," October 28, 1790; H to Duer, April 7, 1791; Joseph Nourse to H, May 1, 1792, note 1; H to Richard Harison, August 30, 1792.

This letter concerns the contract concluded with Duer on March 26, 1792, after the October 28, 1790, contract with Theodosius Fowler had been assigned to Duer. The letter is part of a report sent by Knox to the committee of Congress appointed to consider the report of an earlier committee, dated May 8, 1792, concerning the failure of St. Clair's campaign. In his report Knox introduces this letter from H as follows: "At the time of forming the Contract in question a conversation occurred with the Secretary of the Treasury upon the point of requiring collateral security the purport of which is contained in his letter of the 14th November 1792 . . ." (copy, Massachusetts Historical Society, Boston).

Report on Estimates of the Expenditures for the Civil List of the United States for the Year 1793

[Philadelphia, November 14, 1792
Communicated on November 14, 1792] [1]

[To the Speaker of the House of Representatives]

The Secretary of the Treasury respectfully reports to the House of Representatives the Estimates herewith, marked A, B and C.

The first relating to the Civil List, or the expenditures for the support of Government, during the year 1793, (including the incidental and contingent expenses of the several departments and offices amounting to Dollars, 352.466.39.

The second, relating to certain deficiencies in former appropriations for the support of government, to a provision in aid of the fund heretofore established for the payment of certain Officers of the Courts, Jurors, Witnesses &c. to the support of the light houses, beacons, buoys and public piers, and to certain other purposes 92.599.66

Copy, RG 233, Reports of the Treasury Department, 1792–1793, Vol. III, National Archives.

1. The communicating letter may be found in RG 233, Reports of the Treasury Department, 1792–1793, Vol. III, National Archives.

The third, relating to the War-department, shewing the probable expenditure of that department, for the year 1793, including a sum of 82.245 dollars and thirty two cents, for pensions to Invalids 1.171.719. 5.

Amounting together to, dollars, 1.616.785.10

The funds, out of which, appropriations may be made for the foregoing purposes, are—1st. the sum of 600.000 dollars reserved annually for the support of government, out of the duties on imports and tonnage, by the Act making provision for the debt of the United States.[2] 2d. The surplus, which may remain unexpended, of the sums appropriated to the use of the War department, for the year 1792. 3d. The unappropriated surplus of the existing revenues to the end of the year 1793; which funds, it is believed, will prove adequate to the object; as illustrated in the Schedule herewith transmitted, marked D.

But, as some deficiencies may possibly happen, and as partial anticipations of the revenue will probably be requisite to face the demands for the public service, as they accrue, it appears essential, that a power to borrow should accompany the grant.

The Secretary begs leave also to present for the information of the House of Representatives, two Statements (marked E and F.) of the expenditure of two several sums; One of 50.000 dollars, and the other of 5,000 dollars, heretofore appropriated 'towards discharging such demands on the United States, not otherwise provided for, as should have been ascertained and admitted in due course of settlement at the treasury, and which should be of a nature, according to the course thereof, to require payment in specie.' [3]

All which is humbly submitted Alexander Hamilton,
Secretary of the Treasury.

Treasury Department,
November 14th. 1792.

2. 1 *Stat.* 138–44 (August 4, 1790).

3. This provision was made by "An Act making certain Appropriations therein mentioned" (1 *Stat.* 185–86 [August 12, 1790]).

[A]

ESTIMATE OF THE EXPENDITURE FOR THE CIVIL LIST OF THE UNITED STATES, FOR THE YEAR 1793, TOGETHER WITH THE INCIDENTAL AND CONTINGENT EXPENSES OF THE SEVERAL DEPARTMENTS AND OFFICES.

	Dollars. Cts.	Dollars. Cts.	Dollars. Cts.
For compensation to the President of the United States		25.000.	
That of the Vice President		5.000.	
Compensation to the Chief Justice		4.000.	
Ditto of five Associate Judges, at 3.500 dollars per annum each		17.500.	
Ditto, the Judges of the following districts, Viz:			
Maine		1.000.	
New Hampshire		1 000.	
Vermont		800.	
Massachusetts		1.200.	
Rhode Island		800.	
Connecticut		1 000.	
New York		1 500.	
New Jersey		1 000.	
Pennsylvania		1 600.	
Delaware		800.	
Maryland		1 500.	
Virginia		1 800.	
Kentucky		1 000.	
North Carolina		1 500.	
South Carolina		1 800.	
Georgia		1 500.	
Attorney General		1 900.	
Members of the Senate and House of Representatives and their Officers.			
To the Speaker of the House of Representatives for his compensation to the 3d. March, 1793, 119 days at 12 dollars per day	1 428.		
Also for compensation to the Speaker of the 3d. Congress for the residuary time, so as to estimate for six months attendance in one year, at 12 dollars per day	762.		
		2 190.	
To 98 members to 3d. March, 1793, 119 days, at 6 dollars per day	69.972.		
For compensation to 134 members of the 3d. Congress, for the residuary time, so as to estimate for six months attendance in one year, at 6 dollars per day each	42.744.		
		112.716.	
Travelling expenses to and from the seat of government		20.000.	
To the Secretary of the Senate for one year's salary	1 500.		
Additional allowance estimated for 6 months at 2 dollars per day	365.		
		1 865.	

		Dollars. Cts.	Dollars. Cts.
Principal Clerk to the Secretary of the Senate for same time, at 3 dollars per day		547.50	
Engrossing Clerk to ditto, estimated do. at 2 dollars per day		365.	
Chaplain to the Senate estimated for same time at 500 dollars per annum		250.	
Doorkeeper to the Senate, one year's salary		500.	
Assistant doorkeeper to do. do.		450.	
Clerk of the House of Representatives for one year's salary	1 500.		
Additional allowance estimated for six months at 2 dollars per day	365.		
		1 865.	
Principal Clerk in the Office of the Clerk of the House of Representatives estimated for six months, at 3 dollars per day		547.50	
Engrossing Clerk estimated for same time at 2 dollars per day		365.	
Chaplain to the House of Representatives, estimated for six months, at 500 dollars per annum		250.	
Serjeant at Arms for same time at 4 dollars per day		730.	
Doorkeeper of the House of Representatives, estimated one year's salary		500.	
Assistant doorkeeper for do. one year's salary		450.	
			143.591.

TREASURY DEPARTMENT.

		Dollars. Cts.	Dollars. Cts.
Secretary of the Treasury		3 500.	
Two principal Clerks, at 800 dollars each		1 600.	
Six Clerks, at 500 dollars each		3 000.	
Messenger and Office keeper		250.	
			8 350.
Comptroller of the Treasury		2 400.	
Principal Clerk		800.	
Twelve Clerks at 500 dollars each		6 000.	
Messenger and doorkeeper		250.	
			9.450.
Treasurer		2 400.	
Principal Clerk		600.	
Two Clerks at 500 dollars each		1 000.	
Messenger and Office keeper		100.	
			4 100.
Commissioner of the Revenue		1 900.	
Three Clerks on the business of the revenue &c.		1 500.	
One do. on the business of the lighthouses, beacons, buoys, public piers and stakeage		500.	
Messenger and Office keeper		200.	
			4.100.
Auditor of the Treasury		1 900.	
Principal Clerk		800.	
Fifteen Clerks, at 500 dollars each		7 500.	
Messenger and Office keeper		250.	
			10.450.

	Dollars. Cts.	Dollars. Cts.
Register of the Treasury	1.750.	
Three Clerks on the impost, tonnage and excise accounts	1 500.	
Two Clerks on the books and accounts relative to exports	1 000.	
Two do. on do. of receipts and expenditures of public monies, at 500 dollars	1 000.	
One do. for recording ships registers and licences	500.	
Three do. for drawing out, checking, issuing and taking receipts for certificates of the domestic and assumed debts	1 500.	
Four do. on the books of the general and particular Loan Offices, comprehending the interest accounts and unclaimed dividends at the several Loan-Offices	2 000.	
Seven do. on the books and records, which relate to the public creditors, on the several descriptions of stock and transfer	3 500.	
Four Clerks on the books and records of the registered debt, including the payment of its interest	2 000.	
Two do. to complete the arrangement of the public securities	1 000.	
Two do. on the books of the late Government	1 000.	
One transcribing do.	500.	
Two Office keepers incident to the several Offices of the Register, at 175 dollars	350.	
	17 600.	
Two Clerks appointed to count and examine the old and new emissions of continental money and indents, at 500 dollars each	1 000.	
		18.600.
		55.050.

DEPARTMENT OF STATE.

The Secretary of State	3 500.	
One Chief Clerk	800.	
Three Clerks, at 500 dollars each	1 500.	
Clerk for foreign languages	250.	
Messenger and Office keeper	250.	
		6 300.

DEPARTMENT OF WAR.

Secretary for the department	3 000.	
Principal Clerk	800.	
Six Clerks at 500 dollars each	3 000.	
Messenger and Office keeper	250.	
		7 050.

	Dollars. Cts.		Dollars. Cts.
Accountant to the War department	1 200.		
Six Clerks, (one on the principal books—two on the accounts of the late Army—two on the accounts of the present Army—and one on the books of the late paymaster General, and Commissioner of Army accounts) at 500 dollars each	3 000.		
		4 200.	
			11.250.

BOARD OF COMMISSIONERS FOR THE SETTLEMENT OF THE ACCOUNTS BETWEEN THE UNITED STATES AND THE INDIVIDUAL STATES.

Three Commissioners at 2250 dollars, each	6 750.		
One Chief Clerk at 800 dollars	800.		
Eleven do. at 500 dollars each	5 500.		
Messenger and Office-keeper	250.		
			13.300.

LOAN OFFICERS

For New Hampshire	650.		
Massachusetts	1 500.		
Rhode Island	600.		
Connecticut	1 000.		
New York	1 500.		
New Jersey	700.		
Pennsylvania	1 500.		
Delaware	600.		
Maryland	1 000		
Virginia	1 500.		
North Carolina	1 000.		
South Carolina	1 000.		
Georgia	700.		
			13.250.

GOVERNMENT OF THE WESTERN TERRITORY

District North-west of the River Ohio.

Governor, for his salary as such, and for discharging the Duties of Superintendant of Indian Affairs, northern department	2 000.		
The Secretary of said District	750.		
For Stationery, Office rent, and printing patents for land &c.	350.		
Three Judges, 800 dollars each	2 400.		
		5 500.	

District South west of the river Ohio.

Governor, for his salary as such, and for discharging the duties of Superintendant of Indian Affairs, southern department	2 000.		

		Dollars. Cts.	Dollars. Cts.
Secretary of said District	750.		
Stationery, Office-rent &c. &c.	350.		
Three Judges at 800 dollars each	2 400.		
		5 500.	
			11 000.

PENSIONS GRANTED BY THE LATE GOVERNMENT.

Isaac Van Voert, John Paulding, David Williams — a pension of 200 dollars per annum, pursuant to an Act of Congress of 3d. November 1780 [4]		600.	
Dominique L'Eglize, per Act of Congress of 8th. August 1782 [5]		120.	
Joseph Traversie, per ditto		120.	
Youngest son of General Mercer, per Act 8th. April 1782 [6]		400.	
Youngest children of the late Major General Warren, per Act 1st. July 1780 [7]		450.	
James McKenzie, Joseph Brussells, John Jordan, — per Act of 10th. September 1783,[8] entitled to a pension of 40 dollars each per annum		120.	
Elizabeth Bergen, per Act of 21st. August 1781 [9]		53.33.	
Joseph De Beauleau, per Act of 5th. August 1782 [10]		100.	
Richard Gridley, per Acts of 17th. November 1775, and 26th. February 1781 [11]		444.40	
Lieutenant Colonel Tousard, per Act 27th. October 1788 [12]		360.	
			2 767.73

GRANT TO BARON STEUBEN.

His annual allowance by Act of Congress [13]			2 500.

FOR INCIDENTAL AND CONTINGENT EXPENSES, RELATIVE TO THE CIVIL LIST ESTABLISHMENT.

Under this head are comprehended, Firewood, Stationery, together with printing work, and all other contingent expenses of the two Houses of Congress, rent and Office expenses of the three several departments Viz: Treasury, State and War, and of the General Board of Commissioners.

Secretary of the Treasury, his estimate		3 000	
Clerk of the House of Representatives his do. to 3d. March 1793,	4 152.		
Provisionary for the 3d. Congress	2 400.		
		6 552.	
			9 552.

4. *JCC*, XVIII, 1009–10.

5. Congressional authorization for this account and the following one may be found in *JCC*, XXII, 456–57.

6. *JCC*, VII, 243.

7. *JCC*, XVII, 581.

8. *JCC*, XXV, 568–69.

9. *JCC*, XXI, 908.

10. *JCC*, XXII, 428–29.

11. *JCC*, III, 358–59; XIX, 197.

12. *JCC*, XII, 1068.

13. "An Act for finally adjusting and satisfying the claims of Frederick William de Steuben" (6 *Stat.* 2 [June 4, 1790]).

TREASURY DEPARTMENT.

	Dollars. Cts.	Dollars. Cts.
Secretary of the Treasury, per estimate	500.	
Comptroller of the Treasury, per do.	600.	
Treasurer per do.	450.	
Auditor of the Treasury, per do	300.	
Register of the Treasury, including books for the public stocks, per do.	2 000.	
Rent of the Treasury	650.	
Do. for a house taken for a part of the Office of the Register	200.	
Do. for a House for the Office of the Commissioner of the Revenue, and for part of the Office of the Comptroller, and part of the Office of the Register	266.66	
Do. of a house for the Office of the Auditor, and a small store for public papers	373.33	
Wood for the department (Treasurer's excepted) candles &c.	1 200.	
		7 139.99.

DEPARTMENT OF STATE.

Including the expense attending the collection of the laws of the several States—for publishing the laws of the second Session of the second Congress of the United States, and printing an edition of the same to be distributed agreeably to law—for the collection of newspapers from the different States, and gazettes from abroad		1 851.67.

DEPARTMENT OF WAR.

Secretary at War per estimate	600.	
Accountant to the War department	300.	
		900.
General Board of Commissioners, per estimate		814.
Dollars,		352.466.39

Treasury Department, Register's Office, 8th. November 1792.

Joseph Nourse, Register.

B.

AN ADDITIONAL ESTIMATE FOR MAKING GOOD DEFICIENCIES FOR THE SUPPORT OF THE CIVIL LIST ESTABLISHMENT, FOR AIDING THE FUND APPROPRIATED FOR THE PAYMENT OF CERTAIN OFFICERS OF THE COURTS, JURORS AND WITNESSES; FOR THE SUPPORT OF LIGHTHOUSES; AND FOR THE ESTABLISHMENT OF TEN CUTTERS, AND FOR OTHER PURPOSES.

For the Salaries of certain Officers, by an Act making alterations in the Treasury and War Departments.[14]

Salary of the Commissioner of the revenue, from 8th. May 1792, to 31st. December following, at 1900 dollars per annum	1 238.93.	
Do. three Clerks on the business of the Revenue, same time, at 500 dollars, per annum each	978. 9.	
Do. one do. on the business of the lighthouses, beacons, buoys public piers, and stakeage, at 500 dollars per annum for same time	326. 3.	
Do. messenger, at 200 dollars per annum, for do.	130.41.	
Contingent expenses for procuring desks and other furniture, stationery &c.	200.	
Salary of the Accountant to the War Department, from 8th. May, to 31st. December following, at 1200 dollars per annum	782.46.	
Do. of his Clerk, from 23d. July to do. at 500 dollars	220.10.	
Contingent expenses for his Office	163.33.	
Salary of each of the two principal Clerks to the Secretary of the Treasury, at 800 dollars per annum each, for the same period	1 043.28	
Do. of a Clerk to the Treasurer, from the 18th. June to 31st. December 1792, at 500 dollars per annum	269.86.	
For the encreased Salary of the Comptroller of the Treasury, from 8th. May 1792, to 31st. December following, at 400 dollars per annum	260.82	
For the encreased salary of the Auditor of the Treasury, from 8th. May 1792, to 31st. December following, at 400 per annum	260.82	
Salary of the Treasurer, from 8th. May 1792, to 31st December following, at 400 dollars per annum	260.82.	
Do. of the Register, for same time, at 500 dollars	326. 3.	
Do. of the Attorney General, same time, at 400 dollars	260.82.	
Do. of the chief Clerk in the Department of War, same time, at 200 dollars	130.41.	
		6 852.21.
To make good deficiencies for the support of the Civil List, Viz:		
To the Clerk of the House of Representatives, for amount of his estimate	320.	
And for the pay of Bernard Webb, his principal Clerk, from 1st. July, to 1st. October 1792—92 days at 3 dollars, per day	276.	
		578.

14. 1 *Stat.* 279–81 (May 8, 1792).

For so much short estimated for the contingent expenses of the Office of the Secretary of State		93.34
Do. for the contingent expenses of the Treasury department, the payments whereof, to the 30th. Sept. 1792, having exceeded the said Appropriations, by the sum of	1 500.	
Estimated amount of expenses to 31st. December 1792	900.	
		2 400.
For so much short appropriated, for the Office of the Register of the Treasury, the estimate for 1792 having been for only one Office keeper, whereas, from the encreased number of Offices, and their being kept in separate houses, two Office keepers were required and have been employed, at 175 dollars each	350	
Deduct appropriation for one	250	
		100.
For the salaries of the doorkeepers, and Assistant doorkeepers, to the Senate and House of Representatives, under the Act for their compensation, passed the 12th. April 1792.[15]		
For the salary of the doorkeeper of the Senate, from the 9th. May 1792, to the 31st. December following, at 500 dollars per annum	324.65.	
For do. same time, for doorkeeper of the House of Representatives, at 500 dollars per annum	324.65.	
For do. to the Assistant doorkeeper to the Senate, for same time, at 400 dollars per annum	292.19.	
For do. to the Assistant doorkeeper to the House of Representatives for same time, at 400 dollars per annum	292.19.	
		1 233.68.
Commissioners of Loans, in the several States for the salaries of their Clerks, and for Stationery, under the Act passed the 8th. May 1792.[16]		
By their Accounts rendered to 31st. December 1791, an additional appropriation is requisite, of	1 650.	
From their Accounts already rendered, for the present year, the following sums are estimated, for each Office, to 31st. December 1792; the aggregate whereof is calculated sufficient to cover all the demands to that period, Viz:		
William Gardner, New Hampshire	650.	
Nathaniel Appleton, Massachusetts	4 781.52	
Jabez Bowen, Rhode Island	1 073.24	
William Imlay Connecticut,	1 984.	
John Cochran, New York	7 577.68	
James Ewing, New Jersey	500.	
Thomas Smith, Pennsylvania	2 209.34.	
James Tilton, Delaware	200.	
Thomas Harwood, Maryland	1 013.70.	
John Hopkins, Virginia	3 714.56.	

15. "An Act for fixing the compensations of the Doorkeepers of the Senate and House of Representatives in Congress" (1 *Stat.* 252).

16. "An Act for making compensations to the Commissioners of Loans for extraordinary expenses" (1 *Stat.* 284).

William Skinner, North Carolina	844.44.	
John Neufville, South Carolina	1 500.	
Richard Wylley, Georgia	364.80.	
To extend their allowance for said expenses, to 31st. March 1793, in conformity with said Act	7 000.	
		35.063.28.
Clerks of Courts, Jurors, Witnesses &c. the fund arising from fines, forfeitures and penalties, having last year proved insufficient for the discharge of the accounts of Clerks of Courts &c. to which they were appointed; a sum for the present year is estimated, in order to provide against a similar contingency, of		12.000.
For the maintenance and support of lighthouses, beacons, buoys, public piers, and stakeage of channels, bars and shoals; and for occasional improvements in the construction of the lanthorns, and of the lamps and materials used therein,		20.000.
For the establishment of ten Cutters, deficiency in the appropriation heretofore made for building and equipping ten cutters		3 000.
For the purchase of hydrometers for the use of the Officers of the Customs, and Inspectors of the Revenue, for the year 1793	1 500.	
And to make good so much short estimated for 1792	610.10.	
		2 110.10
For the expenses towards the safe keeping and prosecution of persons committed for offences against the United States		4 000.
For the payment of Robert Fenner, late Agent for the North Carolina line, his commission of 1 per cent on 16.905$\frac{38}{100}$ths, paid to the Officers of the said line, for their pay and subsistence for the years 1792, and 1793		169.
For the discharge of such demands against the United States, not otherwise provided for, as shall have been ascertained and admitted in due course of settlement at the Treasury, and which are of a nature, according to the usage thereof, to require payment in specie		5 000.
		90.599.66.

Treasury Department, Register's Office, 8th. November 1792.

Joseph Nourse, Register.

C.

ESTIMATE OF THE EXPENSES OF THE WAR-DEPARTMENT, FOR THE YEAR 1793

THE LEGION OF THE UNITED STATES.

General Staff.

1 Major General	at 166.	dollars, per month	1 992.
4 Brigadier Generals	104.	" "	4 992.
1 Major Commandant of Artillery	55	" "	660.

1	Major of Dragoons	55	dollars, per month		660.
1	Quarter Master General	100.	" "		1 200.
1	Paymaster at Head Quarters	60.	" "		720.
1	Adjutant General to do the duty as Inspector,	75.	" "		900.
1	Chaplain	50.	" "		600.
1	Surgeon of the Staff	70.	" "		840.
1	Deputy Quarter Master	50.	" "		600.
2	Aids de Camp to the Major General in addition to their pay in the line	24.	" "		576.
4	do. 1 for each of the Brigadiers, in addition to their pay in the line	24.	" "		1 152.
4	Brigade Majors to act as Deputy Inspectors in addition to their pay in the line	24.	" "		1 152.
6	Surgeons-Mates for the Hospitals for the Western and Southern frontiers	30.	" "		2 160.
1	Principal Artificer	40.	" "		480.
1	Second Artificer	26.	" "		312.

The first Sub-Legion.

	Field.				
3	Majors	50.	" "		1 800.
	Staff.				
1	Sublegionary paymaster	10.	" "	120.	
1	Sublegionary Quarter Master	8.	" "	96.	
3	Battalion Quarter Masters	8.	" "	288.	
3	Adjutants	10.	" "	360.	
1	Sublegionary Surgeon	45	" "	540.	
3	Battalion Surgeon's mates	30.	" "	1 080.	
3	Sergeant Majors	7.	" "	252.	
3	Quarter Master Sergeants	7.	" "	252.	
					2 988.
	One Company of Artillery.				
1	Captain	40.	" "	480.	
2	Lieutenants	26.	" "	624.	
4	Sergeants	6.	" "	288.	
4	Corporals	5.	" "	240.	
10	Artificers	8.	" "	960.	
40	Privates	3.	" "	1 440.	
2	Musicians	4.	" "	96.	
					4 128.
	One Troop of Horse				
1	Captain	40.	" "	480.	
1	Lieutenant	26.	" "	312.	
1	Cornet	20.	" "	240.	
6	Sergeants	6.	" "	432	

6 Corporals	5.	dollars, per month		360.	
1 Farrier	8.	"	"	96	
1 Saddler	8.	"	"	96.	
1 Trumpeter	4.	"	"	48.	
65 Privates	3.	"	"	2 340.	
					4 404.
Eight Companies of Infantry.					
8 Captains	40.	"	"	3 840.	
8 Lieutenants	26.	"	"	1 920.	
8 Ensigns	20.	"	"	1 920.	
48 Sergeants	6.	"	"	3 456.	
48 Corporals	5.	"	"	2 880.	
1 Senior Musician	6	"	"	72.	
15 Musicians	4	"	"	720.	
648 privates	3	"	"	23 328.	
					38.712.
Four Companies of Riflemen.					
4 Captains	40.	"	"	1 920.	
4 Lieutenants	26	"	"	1 248.	
4 Ensigns	20	"	"	960.	
24 Sergeants	6	"	"	1 728.	
24 Corporals	5	"	"	1 440.	
4 Buglers	4	"	"	192.	
328 Privates	3.	"	"	11.808.	
					19.296.
				Dollars,	71.328.

Amount of Pay of the Legion of the United States.

General Staff	18.996.
The first Sub-legion	71.328.
The second Sub-legion, to the same amount	71.328.
The third Sub legion do.	71.328.
The fourth Sub legion do.	71.328.

SUBSISTENCE.

1 Major General	at 15	rations	per day	5 475	rations
4 Brigadier Generals	12	"	"	17.520.	"
14 Majors	4	"	"	20.440.	"
1 Adjutant	6.	"	"	2 190.	
1 Paymaster at Head Quarters	4	"	"	1 460.	
1 Quarter Master	6.	"	"	2 190	
1 Deputy Quarter Master	3.	"	"	1 095.	
1 Surgeon to the Staff	6.	"	"	2 190.	
4 Surgeons	3.	"	"	4 380.	
12 Surgeon's mates	2	"	"	8 760.	
6 do. for Garrisons	2	"	"	4 380.	
1 principal Artificer	3.	"	"	1 095.	
1 Second Artificer	2.	"	"	730.	
56 Captains	3.	"	"	61 320.	
60 Lieutenants	2.	"	"	43 800.	
48 Ensigns	2.	"	"	35 040.	
4 Cornets	2.	"	"	2 920.	
				214.985.	rations.

Or money in lieu thereof, at the option of the Officers at the contract price at the posts respectively where the rations shall become due.

240. Non commissioned and privates, Artillery.			
320. do.	do. Cavalry.		
4560. do.	do. Infantry.		
5120, Men,	at 1 ration per day	1,868.800.	
		2.083.785	rations.
2.083.785 rations at 15 cents per rations,		Dollars,	312.567.75.

FORAGE.

1	Major General	at 20	dollars per month		240.	
4	Brigadier Generals	16	"	"	768.	
13	Majors	10	"	"	1 560.	
1	Paymaster at Head Quarters	10	"	"	120.	
1	Adjutant General	12	"	"	144.	
1	Quarter Master General	12	"	"	144.	
1	Deputy Quarter Master General,	10	"	"	120.	
6	Aids de Camp	10	"	"	720.	
4	Brigade Majors	6	"	"	288.	
4	Adjutants	6	"	"	288.	
1	Surgeon to the Staff	12	"	"	144.	
4	Surgeons	10	"	"	480.	
12	Surgeons Mates	6.	"	"	864.	
6	do. for the Garrisons	6	"	"	432.	
4	Paymasters	6	"	"	288.	
12	Quarter Masters	6.	"		864.	
						7 464.
	Cavalry, unprovided for in the Year 1792.					
1	Major	10	"	"	120.	
4	Captains	10	"	"	480.	
4	Lieutenants	6.	"	"	288.	
4	Cornets	6.	"	"	288.	
						1 176.
	For the Year 1793.					
1	Major	10	"	"	120.	
4	Captains	10	"	"	480.	
4	Lieutenants	6	"	"	288.	
4	Cornets	6	"	"	288.	
320	Non commissioned and privates	6	"	"	25 040.	
						26.216.
						34.856.

CLOTHING.

240	non commissioned and privates,	Artillery.	
320,	do.	Cavalry.	
4 560,	do.	Infantry.	
5.120.			
480.	Contingencies.		
5.600	Suits, at 20 dollare per suit		112 000.

EQUIPMENTS FOR CAVALRY.

Boots, Horseman's Caps, and such articles, as may be lost or worn Conjectural	5 000.

HORSES FOR CAVALRY.

To replace the horses which may die or become unfit for service, ditto	5 000.

BOUNTY.

	To complete the number in lieu of discharged soldiers, those rendered unfit for duty, and deserters, conjectural, 500 soldiers, including premium of 10 dollars each	5 000.
	Additional Bounty, for which no provision was made, but allowed by the Act passed March 5th. 1792.[17]	
952	non commissioned and privates in service, at 2 dollars	1 904.
4168.	do. to be raised, being estimated in former estimate at dols. 8, including premium the Act of the 5th. March 1792,[18] allowing dols. 10, is for the difference, 2 dollars	8 336
	Dollars,	15.240.

DEFENSIVE PROTECTION OF THE FRONTIERS.

Pay &c. of the Militia and Scouts, estimated at	50.000.

HOSPITAL DEPARTMENT.

For medicines, instruments, furniture and stores for the Hospital, for the garrisons and posts on the western and southern frontiers; also the pay and subsistence of a purveyor, assistants and nurses in the Hospitals, conjectural	25.000.

QUARTER-MASTER'S DEPARTMENT.

Pack horses and forage, tents, boats &c. also the transportation of the recruits, Ordnance and Military Stores, and all the articles of the Quarter Master's department, the purchase of axes, camp kettles, pack-saddles, iron, fuel, board, nails, paint company books, stationery &c. Also the pay and subsistence of Artificers employed in the said department,—Conjectural,	100.000.

17. Section 5 of "An Act for making farther and more effectual Provision for the Protection of the Frontiers of the United States" (1 *Stat.* 242).

18. Section 6 of "An Act for making farther and more effectual Provision for the Protection of the Frontiers of the United States" (1 *Stat.* 242).

INDIAN DEPARTMENT.

The expenses in this Department amount, in the year 1792, as per Accounts rendered, at dollars	44 207.98	
Accounts allowed, which will be shortly stated	5 500.	
	49.707.98.	
Provided for in the year 1792	25.000.	
Dollars,	24 707.98.	
The surplus has been paid from the general Contingencies of the War Department.		
The expenses of the year 1793 may probably amount to		50.000.

N: B. It is impossible to foresee the events which may occasion expenses in this department, so as to reduce them to particulars. The sums of the present year in the accounts settled at the treasury, may serve to form some idea of the expenses for the year 1793.

ORDNANCE DEPARTMENT.

For the Salaries of the Storekeepers at the several Arsenals

Springfield	Massachusetts	480.
Fort Rensselaer and its dependencies	New York	172.
West Point	ditto	480.
Philadelphia	Pennsylvania	500.
Carlisle	ditto	60.
Fort Pitt	ditto	360.
New London	Virginia	430.
Manchester	ditto	50.
Charleston	South Carolina	100.
One Assistant at Springfield		240.
Two ditto at Westpoint		480.
One Clerk of military Stores, Philadelphia		480.
	Dollars,	3 832.

Rents.

Philadelphia	666.66.	
New London	350.	
Manchester	66.66	
		1 083.32.
Laborers at the Arsenals	400.	
Coopers, Armorers and Carpenters employed occasionally	600.	
10 Armorers at 10 dollars per month	1 200.	
2 Conductors of Military stores at 30 dollars per month	720.	
		2 920.
500 rifles purchased in 1792, and not included in former estimates		6 000.
Repairing of Arms, equipments of Cannon, cartridge-boxes, swords, and every other article in this department,—Conjectural,		10.000.
Dollars,		23.835.

INVALIDS.

For the annual allowance to the invalids of the United States, from the 5th. day of March, one thousand seven hundred and ninety three, to the fourth day of March, one thousand seven hundred and ninety four.

New Hampshire	3 810.68.	
By the Circuit Court	409.12.	
		4 219.80.
Massachusetts	11.941.75.	
By the Circuit Court	1 336.45.	
		13.278.20
Rhode Island	2 899.	
By the Circuit Court	196.	
		3.095.
Connecticut	7.682. 3.	
By the Circuit Court	795.80	8.477.83.
Vermont	......	
By the Circuit Court	510.64.	
		510.64.
New York		15.972.66.
New Jersey	4.094.26.	
By the Circuit Court	76.	
		4.170.26.
Pennsylvania		16.642.64
Delaware		1.884.
Maryland		4 328.56.
Virginia		7.761.33.
North Carolina		886.
Georgia		1.018.40.
		82.245.32.

LEASE,

Of the buildings occupied for the use of the War Office, and the Office of the Accountant of the War Department.

The amount of the lease for the term of four years, as per Indenture thereof with James Simmons — 1.666.66.

CONTINGENCIES OF THE WAR DEPARTMENT.

For maps, hiring expresses, allowances to Officers for extra expenses, printing, loss of stores of all kinds, advertising and apprehending deserters &c.—Conjectural — 50.000.

N:B. It is to be observed, upon this article, as well as every other of this Statement, that for every cent expended in pursuance thereof vouchers must be produced at the Treasury, excepting, perhaps, the sums which may be expended for secret intelligence, where the names might be important to be concealed; but for the propriety of the small sums, which might be so expended, the reputation of the Commanding Officer is pledged to the public.

RECAPITULATION.

Pay of the Legion of the United States	304.308.
Subsistence	312.567.75.
Forage	34.856.
Clothing	112.00.
Equipments for Cavalry	5.000.
Horses for Cavalry	5 000.
Bounty	15.240.
Defensive protection of the frontiers by Militia	50.000.
Hospital Department	25.000.
Quarter Master's Department	100.000.
Indian Department	50.000.
Ordnance Department	23.835.32.
Invalids	82.245.32.
Lease of the buildings occupied for the War Office &c.	1.666.66.
Contingencies of the War department	50.000.
	1.171.719. 5.

War Office, October 26th. 1792.

H. Knox,
Secretary of War.

Treasury Department,
Register's Office, November 8th. 1792.

I certify that the foregoing is a true Copy of the Original filed in this Office.

Joseph Nourse, Register.

The above Dollars,	1.171.719. 5.
Deduct for Invalids	82.245.32.
Leaves Dollars,	1.089.473.73.

D.

COMPARATIVE STATEMENT OF EXPENDITURE AND REVENUE, TO THE END OF THE YEAR 1793.

EXPENDITURE.

Amount from the commencement of the year 1791, to the end of the year 1792, as stated in a report to the House of Representatives of the 23d. January last[19]	7.082.197.74
Additional Appropriation for the War department, per Act of the 2nd. of May, 1792,[20] for raising a farther sum of money for the protection of the frontiers &c.	673.500.
Appropriations by an Act of the 8th. of May 1792, intitled "An Act making certain appropriations therein specified."[21]	84.497.90.
Monies requisite by estimate for the current service of 1793.	1.616.785.10.
Interest on the public debt for the same year	2.849.194.73.
Total Expenditure	12.306.175.47.

19. "Report on Estimates of Receipts and Expenditures for 1791–1792," January 23, 1792.

20. Section 15 of "An Act for raising a farther sum of money for the protection of the frontiers, and for other purposes therein mentioned" (1 *Stat.* 262).

21. 1 *Stat.* 284–85.

WAYS AND MEANS.

Net product of duties on Imports and Tonnage, for the year 1791, as ascertained	3.403.195.18
Ditto for the year 1792, as estimated (a)	3.900.000.
Ditto for the year, 1793, (b)	4.000.000.
Ditto of duties on home made spirits for one half year of 1791, (c)	150.000.
Ditto for 1792 (c.)	400.000.
Ditto for 1793 (c.)	400.000.
Surplus, which will probably remain unexpended of the sums appropriated for the War department for 1792. (d.)	140.000.
Total Ways and Means,	12.393.195.18.

Notes.

(a) This sum is estimated by adding to the ascertained product of the year 1791, an ascertained excess of the product of the first two quarters of the year 1792, beyond the product of the first two quarters of the year 1791, being 252.319 dollars, and eleven cents, and the estimated product, for a half year of the additional duties on imports, laid during the last Session of Congress, and commencing on the first of July last, being 261.750 dollars. According to the information hitherto received at the Treasury, there is every probability that the amount of the duties, for the last half year of 1792, will fully equal this calculation of their product; if in the ratio of the first half year, will exceed it.

(b) This Estimate proceeds on the basis of the product of 1792, making a compromise of two considerations; one, an increase, which may be expected, equal to the difference between a whole and a half year's product of the additional duties above mentioned; the other, a decrease, which may arise, from a defalcation of the duties on foreign spirits, in consequence of the increase of domestic distillation. There is good ground to conclude, that the sum stated will rather fall short of, than exceed the actual product.

(c.) This branch of the revenue is not yet in complete order; but enough is ascertained by actual returns, to afford a moral certainty, that the product cannot be materially less than is here stated.

(d.) This surplus is thus deduced:

The total Appropriation for the War department for the year 1792, is		1.081.146.68.
The total expenditure to the 27th. of October, was	690.796.	
The sum at that time estimated by the Secretary at War, to be further necessary to the end of the year, exclusive of provision supplies, is	218.950.	
For provisions and contingencies, may be stated a farther sum of	30.000.	
		939.746.
Balance which will probably remain unexpended		141.400.68.

Some inconsiderable appropriations for particular purposes are unnoticed, because certain casual funds will probably, nearly, if not altogether balance them.

Treasury Department, November 14th: 1792.

Alexander Hamilton

E.

A PARTICULAR STATEMENT OF THE APPLICATION OF FIFTY THOUSAND DOLLARS, GRANTED BY AN ACT MAKING CERTAIN APPROPRIATIONS THEREIN MENTIONED, PASSED THE 12TH. AUGUST 1790, FOR THE PURPOSE OF DISCHARGING SUCH DEMANDS ON THE UNITED STATES, NOT OTHERWISE PROVIDED FOR, AS SHALL HAVE BEEN ASCERTAINED AND ADMITTED IN DUE COURSE OF SETTLEMENT AT THE TREASURY, AND WHICH ARE OF A NATURE, ACCORDING TO THE USAGE THEREOF, TO REQUIRE PAYMENT IN SPECIE.[22]

Warrant No. 660, dated September 11th: 1790, in favor of Israel Ludlow, a balance due him for executing a survey in 1788, (by direction of Thomas Hutchins, late Geographer to the United States) of the north and south boundaries of the tract of country sold Cutler and Sargent, by the late Board of Treasury	341.75.
Warrant, No. 694, dated October 8th. 1790, in favor of William Irvin, T: Gilman and John Kean, Commissioners for adjusting the accounts of the several States against the Union, in full for their own, Clerks and Messenger's salaries, from 1st. July to 30th. September 1790	420.66.
Warrant, No. 736, dated November 11th. 1790, in favor of James O'Hara, late Contractor for supplying the troops in the western Territory, for provisions seized from him after the expiration of his contract, by the commanding Officer at Post St. Vincennes, including sundries delivered in August 1787, under the contract, amounting to 14:48 cents, for the use of the troops at said Post	1 755.42
Warrant, No. 748, dated November 22d. 1790, in favor of Israel Ludlow, for his expenses in bringing forward to the seat of Government, a return of the surveys made of the tract of country sold Cutler and Sargent, and for executing four draughts of the same, per direction of the Secretary of the Treasury	249.
Warrant, No. 749, dated November 22d. 1790, in favor of Israel Ludlow, as agent for Absalom Martin, balance due to said Martin, for executing a survey, in the year 1788, of the western boundary of the tract of country sold Cutler and Sargent, by order of Thomas Hutchins, late Geographer of the United States	365.56.
Warrant, No. 755, dated November 25th. 1790, in favor of Stephen Moore, for the purchase of land, called West Point, in pursuance of the Act of Congress, of 5th. July 1790,[23] excluding the sum of 5000 dollars, due to Eleazer Levy for a mortgage thereon	6 196.75.
Warrant, No. 753, dated November 25th. in favor of Joseph Nourse, Assignee of Samuel Baird, for a survey made by said Baird, by order of the Secretary of the western Territory, of the land at Post St. Vincennes, granted to the inhabitants of said place, pursuant to the Act of Congress of 29th. August 1788 [24]	120.
Warrant, No. 754, dated November 25th, in favor of John Inskeep, Agent for John N: Cumming, for the transportation of public papers from New York to Philadelphia	236.25

22. 1 *Stat.* 185–86.

23. "An Act to authorize the purchase of a tract of land for the use of the United States" (1 *Stat.* 129).

24. *JCC*, XXXIV, 472–73.

Warrant, No. 769, dated December 7th. in favor of John Leamy, Agent for Joseph Ignatius Viar, Attorney for Joseph Gardoqui and sons, of Bilboa, for balance due to said Joseph Gardoqui and sons, on the books of Thomas Barclay, late Commissioner for adjusting the accounts in Europe, and an advance made by direction of John Adams to sundry American seamen who had been captured by the British 502.86.

Warrant, No. 777, dated December 16th. in favor of Solomon M: Cohen, Attorney for Eleazer Levy, for the amount of a bond of mortgage in favor of said Levy (signed by Stephen Moore) on the lands called Westpoint, certified by the Secretary of War, to be lodged in his Office, which sum is the final balance, for the purchase of said land agreeably to contract 5 000.

Warrant, No. 781, dated December 21st. 1790, in favor of Caleb Brewster, for this amount, allowed him by Act of Congress of the 11th. August last,[25] for his sustenance and medical assistance, including interest to 1st. July, 1790 348.57.

Warrant, No. 809, dated January 8th. 1791, in favor of Wm. Irvin, T: Gilman, and John Kean, Commissioners &c. for the balance of salary due to said Commissioners, their Clerks and messenger, from 1st. October to 31st. December 1790 198.25.

Part of Warrant, No. 846, dated January 20th. 1791, in favor of Richard Adams, in part for Bills of Exchange, drawn on the late Commissioners at Paris, for interest due on money borrowed, and which remained unpaid 36.

Warrant, No. 847, dated January 20th. 1791, in favor of Richard Adams, for the balance due to the said Adams, for the purposes above mentioned 20.

Warrant, No. 845, dated January 20th. 1791, in favor of Benjamin Goodhue, agent for Francis Dana, for the services and expense of a private Secretary, by him, the said Francis Dana, employed, from 1st. July 1781, to 21st. April 1783, whilst on his embassy at the Court of St. Petersburg, Russia, pursuant to an Act of Congress of 2nd. October 1787[26] 2 410. 3

Warrant, No. 865, dated February 3d. 1791, in favor of Thomas Tillyer, for Bills of exchange, drawn on the late Commissioners at Paris, for interest due on monies borrowed by the United States, and which remained unpaid 54.

Warrant, No. 866, dated February 3d. 1791, in favor of Robert Patterson, for the purposes above mentioned 18.

Warrant, No. 897, dated February 21st. 1791, in favor of Samuel A: Otis, Agent for John Hurd, for 2 setts of Exchange, No. 806 and No. 1494, drawn by M: Hillegas, for the purposes above mentioned 48.

Warrant, No. 901, dated February 21st. in favor of Andrew Porter, for a sett of Exchange No. 5, drawn by Francis Hopkinson, for the purposes above mentioned 24.

Warrant, No. 902, dated February 21st. in favor of Joseph Mercier, for a sett of Exchange, No. 63, drawn by Francis Hopkinson, for the purposes above mentioned 18.

Warrant, No. 903, dated February 21st. 1791, in favor of Caleb Strong, Agent for Israel Chaping, for sundry expenditures incurred

25. Section 2 of "An Act for the relief of disabled soldiers and seamen lately in the service of the United States, and of certain other persons" (6 *Stat.* 4).

26. *JCC*, XXXIII, 588–89.

by him under Andrew Ellicott, in executing the surveys directed by Act of Congress of August 26th. 1789[27] 34.32.

Warrant, No. 905, dated February 21st. 1791, in favor of Samuel Baird, for executing surveys by order of the Governor of the western territory, of the land at Post St. Vincennes, granted to the inhabitants of said place, pursuance to an Act of Congress of 29th. August 1788[28] 80.

Warrant, No. 904, dated February 21st. 1791, in favor of Richard Platt, Agent for Elnathan Haskell, late Commissioner of accounts for the eastern district, for sundry contingent expenses of said Commissioner's Office, which accrued in the years 1787 and 1788 47.57.

Warrant, No. 912, dated February 25th. 1791, in favor of . . . [Dutilh] and Wachsmuth, Agents for Samuel Dunn, for three setts of exchange, No. 309 and 310, drawn by Francis Hopkinson, and No. 1253, drawn by Michael Hillegas, on the Commissioners at Paris, for interest due on monies borrowed by the United States, which remained unpaid 108.

Warrant, No. 913, dated February 25th. 1791, in favor of Joshua Sands, for two setts of exchange, No. 805 and 1342, drawn by M: Hillegas, on the Commissioners at Paris, for interests due on monies borrowed by the United States, which remained unpaid 42.

Warrant, No. 914, dated February 25th. 1791, in favor of Josiah Hewes, for three setts of Exchange, No. 788, 955, and 1390, drawn by Francis Hopkinson on the Commissioners at Paris, for interest due on monies borrowed by the United States, which remained unpaid 108.

Warrant, No. 922, dated March 2nd. 1791, in favor of Willing, Morris and Swanwick, in behalf of the late House of Samuel Inglis & Co. for two setts of exchange, No. 331, drawn on the Commissioners at Paris, and No. 801, on the Commissioner at Madrid 825.

Warrant, No. 928, dated March 5th. 1791, in favor of Willing Morris and Swanwick, for a sett of exchange No. 520, drawn by Michael Hillegas, late Treasurer of the United States, on the Commissioners at Paris, for interest due on monies borrowed by said States 12.

Part of Warrant, No. 920, dated March 8th. 1791, in favor of Samuel Meredith, for carriage of money, and for commissions on deposits of money, in the Bank of Massachusetts 137.26.

Warrant, No. 941, dated March 21st. 1791, in favor of John M: St. Clair, for laying off and drawing a plan of the town of Cahokia; by direction of the Governor of the western territory 60.

Warrant, No. 963, dated March 31st. 1791, in favor of William Simmons, Attorney for several persons, clerks in the Offices attached to the Seat of Government—monies due to the said Clerks, for their expenses, incurred by the removal of Congress from New York to Philadelphia; which expenses are authorised by an Act of Congress of March 3d. 1791[29] 1 011.28.

27. On August 26, 1789, the President approved a joint resolution requiring the appointment of a surveyor at five dollars per day to complete the survey directed by Congress on June 6, 1788 (1 *Stat.* 96).

28. *JCC*, XXXIV, 472–73.

29. "An Act in addition to an act intituled 'An act for establishing the salaries of the Executive officers of Government, with their assistants and clerks'" (1 *Stat.* 216).

Warrant, No. 961, dated March 31st. 1791, in favor of Tench Coxe, Assistant to the Secretary of the Treasury, rent of the houses occupied, as Offices for the Secretary, Comptroller, Auditor and Register, from 12th. May to 31st. December 1790 341.71.

Warrant, No. 967, dated March 31st. 1791, in favor of Edward Jones, Clerk in the Comptroller's Office, his expenses incurred by the removal of Congress from New York to Philadelphia, which expenses were authorised by Act of Congress, of March 3d. last 103.80.

Warrant, No. 968, dated April 4th. 1791, in favor of Nicholas Gilman, Agent for Samuel Knowles, and John Whitter, balance due them for services performed in the second New Hampshire regiment, in the months of January and February 1783 13.32.

Warrant, No. 983, dated April 7th. 1791, in favor of John Stagg, junr, R: J.: Van Den Broeck, and Constant Freeman, for their expences incurred by the removal of Congress from New York to Philadelphia per act of March 3d. last 122.20.

Warrant, No. 993, dated April 7th. 1791, in favor of Nicholas Gilman, Agent for James St. Clair and William Hill, for services performed by them, being soldiers in the second New Hampshire regiment, in the months of January and February 1783. 16.66.

Warrant, No. 1032, dated 23d. April 1791, in favor of Andrew Ellicott, for a balance due him for pay, from 24th. May to 17th. December 1790 718.75.

Warrant, No. 1095, dated June 10th. 1791, in favor of John Inskeep, Attorney for Joseph Anderson, one of the Judges of the territory south of the Ohio, for said Judges salary, from 26th. February, to 31st. March 1791 75.55.

Warrant, No. 1117, dated June 25th. 1791, in favor of Andrew G: Fraunces, for expenses incurred in fitting out a barge, for the late Board of Treasury, Secretary of foreign affairs and Secretary at War, in order to wait on the President of the United States, at Elizabeth Town point, by Order of the late Board of Treasury. 30.92.

Warrant, No. 1118, dated June 25th. 1791, in favor of Isaac Sherman, Clerk, for expenses incurred by him in consequence of the removal of Congress from New York to Philadelphia, agreeably to an Act of Congress of 3d. March 1791 12.

Warrant, No. 1119, dated 25th. June 1791, in favor of Robert Haysham, Clerk, for the same purposes as above mentioned 12.

Warrant, No. 1120, dated June 25th. 1791, in favor of Benjamin Bankson, Clerk, for the same purposes as above mentioned 7.66.

Warrant, No. 1121, dated June 25th. 1791, in favor of George Tudor, for a sett of Bills of Exchange, No. 27, drawn by M: Hillegas, on the Commissioners of the United States at Paris, for interest due on monies borrowed by said States, which remained unpaid 30.

Warrant, No. 1122, dated June 25th. 1791, in favor of Lewis De Blois, Agent for James F. Sebor, for a sett of Exchange No. 663, drawn by Michael Hillegas on the Commissioners of the United States at Paris, for the purposes above mentioned 12.

Warrant, No. 1123, dated June 25th. 1791, in favor of Mark Pickard, for the 2d. 3d. and 4th. bills of exchange of six setts, numbered 319, 320, 321, 322, 385, and 386, drawn by M. Hillegas on the Commissioners of the United States at Paris, for the purposes above mentioned 120.

Warrant, No. 1121, dated June 25th. 1791, in favor of James Glentworth, for seven setts of Exchange, No. 192, 981, 1302, 1303, 1304, 2319, and 2377, drawn by Michael Hillegas on the Commissioners of the United States at Paris, for the purposes above mentioned 186.

Warrant, No. 1125, dated June 25th. 1791, in favor of Cornelius Barnes, Agent for Alexander Keith & Co. for the 1st. 3d. and 4th. bills of a sett of exchange, No. 38, drawn by Michael Hillegas, on the Commissioners of the United States at Paris, for the purpose above mentioned 30.

Warrant, No. 1126, dated June 25th. 1791, in favor of Thomas G: Pollard, for a sett of exchange, No. 865, drawn by F. Hopkinson, on the Commissioners of the United States at Paris, for interest due on monies borrowed by the United States, which remained unpaid, for the purposes above mentioned 20.

Part of Warrant, No. 976, dated June 30th. 1791, in favor of Tench Coxe, Assistant to the Secretary of the Treasury, for balance of salaries in the office of the Secretary of the Treasury 32.22.

Part of Warrant, No. 1132, dated July 2d. 1791, in favor of Tench Coxe, Assistant Secretary, for balance due for salary of the Secretary his Assistant, Clerks and Messenger 100.

Part of Warrant, No. 1134, dated July 2d. 1791, in favor of Oliver Wolcott, junior, Comptroller, for a balance of salaries due sundry Clerks, messengers &c. employed in his Office, from 1st. April to 30th. June 15.38.

Part of Warrant, No. 1136, dated July 2d. 1791, in favor of Joseph Nourse, Register, for the purpose above mentioned 62.50.

Part of Warrant, No. 1137, dated July 2d. 1791, in favor of Henry Knox, Secretary at War, balance of salaries due sundry Clerks, messenger &c employed in his Office, from 1st. April to 10th. June 125.

Part of Warrant, No. 1140, dated July 2d. 1791, in favor of Oliver Wolcott, junior, Auditor, balance due for same purpose as above 100.54.

Warrant, No. 1139, dated July 2nd. 1791, in favor of Matthew Mc.-Connell, Assignee of Nathaniel Appleton, Commissioner of loans, for the balance of said Commissioner's salary, from 1st. January to 31st. March 1791; likewise for sundry contingent expenses of his Office, and for his Clerks salaries from various periods, up to 31st. March 873.66.

Warrant, No. 1150, dated July 8th. in favor of David Henley, Clerk, for expences incurred by him, in consequence of the removal of Congress from New York to Philadelphia, agreeably to their Act, passed 3d. March 1791 18.

Part of Warrant, No. 1156, dated July 8th. 1791, in favor of Samuel Meredith, agent for Edmund Randolph, for a balance of salary due him, from 1st. April, to 30th. June 1791 100.

Warrant, No. 1163, dated July 8th. 1791, in favor of Joseph Howell, for the salary of Lynde Catlin, clerk, employed under him in arranging the accounts of the late Office of Army Accounts 179.57.

Warrant, No. 1174, dated July 11th. 1791, in favor of John Inskeep, Attorney for Joseph Anderson, one of the Judges of the territory south of the Ohio, for the said Judge's salary, from the 1st. day of April, to 30th. of June 1791 200.

Warrant, No. 1170, dated July 11th. 1791, in favor of Joseph Hopkinson, executor to the estate of Francis Hopkinson, for a sett of Bills of exchange, No. 1165, drawn by Michael Hillegas, on the late Commissioners at Paris, for interest due on monies borrowed, by the United States, which remain unpaid 120.

Warrant, No. 1182, dated July 16th. 1791, in favor of John Meyer, Agent for George H: Remsen, late a Clerk &c. for expenses incurred in consequence of the removal of Congress from New York to the seat of government, per Act of the 3d. March 1791 12.

Warrant, No. 1186, dated July 23d. 1791, in favor of James Gibson, Attorney for Anna Gibson, executrix to the estate of John Gibson, for two setts of exchange, No. 45 and 108, drawn on the Commissioners at Paris, for interest due on monies borrowed by the United States, and which remained unpaid 156.

Warrant, No. 1197, dated July 28th. 1791, in favor of Thomas Mc.-Ewen, Attorney for Joseph Martin, late agent for the Cherokee and Chickasaw Indians, for the said Martin's Salary, from 20th. July 1788, to the 20th. March 1789, agreeably to an Act of Congress of June 19th. and 20th. August, 1788 [30] 333.33.

Part of Warrant, No. 1222, dated August 10th. 1791, in favor of Joseph Hardy, Clerk, for his salary, from 1st. to 15th. July 1791, and for the expenses incurred by himself and family, from New York to Philadelphia, allowed by Act of Congress of 3d. March last 30.

Warrant, No. 1226, dated August 10th. 1791, in favor of John Fenno, printing work done for the Office of the Secretary of the Treasury, in June and July last 81.35

Warrant, No. 1227, dated August 27th. 1791, in favor of Henry Drinker, junior, executor to the estate of Richard Vaux, for two setts of exchange, No. 1978, and 2054, drawn by Francis Hopkinson on the late Commissioners of the United States at Paris, for interest due on monies borrowed by said States, which remain unpaid 36.

Warrant, No. 1230, dated August 22d. 1791, in favor of Antoine R: C: M: De la Forest, Vice Consul General of France, part of the amount due to his most Christian Majesty, for supplies furnished in the West Indies, by the Navy department of France, to sundry ships of War of the United States, agreeably to a settlement made at the Treasury, on 28th. February last 20.000.

Warrant, No. 1282, dated October 13th. 1791. in favor of George Meade, for the first Bills of two setts of exchange, No. 2701, and 2702, drawn on the late Commissioner at Paris, for interest due on monies borrowed by the United States, which monies remain unpaid 60.

Warrant, No. 1283, dated October 13th. 1791, in favor of William Irvine, for the fourth bills of three setts of exchange, No. 73, 857 and 858, drawn on the late Commissioners at Paris, for the above purposes 84.

Warrant, No. 1291, dated October 13th. 1791, in favor of John White, Agent for John Templeman, for a sett of bills of Exchange, No. 1259, drawn on the late Commissioners at Paris, for the purposes above mentioned 12.

Warrant, No. 1324, dated October 26th. 1791, in favor of Nathan Osgood, Agent for Nathaniel Chipman, District Judge of Vermont, on account of said Chipman's salary from 4th. March, 1791, to the 30th. September following 400.

Warrant, No. 1340, dated October 31st. 1791, in favor of James Sawyer, Assistant to Lewis R: Morris, Marshall for the district of Vermont, on account of the compensation due to the said L: R: Morris, for himself and Assistants, in taking the enumeration of the inhabitants of Vermont 211.53.

Part of Warrant, No. 1296, dated November 2d. 1791, in favor of Edmund Randolph, Attorney General, for his salary from 1st. July to 30th. September 1791 100.

30. *JCC*, XXXIV, 241, 433.

Warrant, No. 1296, dated November 2d. 1791, in favor of John Inskeep, Attorney for Joseph Anderson, one of the Judges of the western territory, for said Anderson's salary, from 1st. July to 30th. September 1791 200.

Warrant, No. 1304, dated November 2d. 1791, in favor of Joseph Howell, for the salary of Lynde Catlin, from 1st. July to 30th. September 1791 138.61.

Part of Warrant, No. 1270, dated November 2d. 1791, in favor of Tench Coxe, Assistant Secretary, for balance of salaries in his Office, from 1st. July to 30th. September 1791 100.

Part of Warrant, No 1271, dated November 2d. 1791, in favor of Joseph Nourse, Register, for the same purposes as above 62.50.

Part of Warrant, No. 1273, dated November 2d. 1791, in favor of Henry Knox, Secretary at War, for the same purposes as above 125.

Part of Warrant No. 1275, dated November 2d. 1791, in favor of Oliver Wolcott, junior, Comptroller of the Treasury, for the same purposes as above 100.

Part of Warrant, No. 1281, dated November 2d. 1791, in favor of Kean and Irvine &c. Commissioners for settling State accounts, for the same purposes as above 38.

Warrant, No. 1348, dated November 11th. 1791, in favor of Jonathan Sturges, for two setts of exchange, No. 575 and 27 3, drawn by Francis Hopkinson, Treasurer of Loans, on the late Commissioners of the United States at Paris, for interest due on monies borrowed by said States 48.

Warrant, No. 1363, dated December 2d. 1791, in favor of Israel Smith, Agent for Nathaniel Chipman, Judge of the district of Vermont, balance of an account due to him for his salary, as adjusted at the Treasury, the 21st. October last 62.22

Warrant, No. 1365, dated December 18th. 1791, in favor of Charles Jervais, for a sett of Exchange, No. 1540, drawn by Michael Hillegas on the late Commissioners at Paris, for the payment of interest on monies borrowed by the United States, which remain unpaid 36.

Part of Warrant, No. 1409, dated January 19th. 1792, in favor of Tench Coxe, Assistant to the Secretary of the Treasury, for part of the Salary of the Secretary, Assistant Secretary, their Clerks, and Messenger &c. from 1st. October to 31st. December 1791 418.46.

Part of Warrant, No. 1410, dated January 19th, 1792, in favor of Oliver Wolcott, Comptroller of the Treasury, part of his own, Clerks and Messenger's salary, from do. to do. 100.

Part of Warrant, No. 1411, dated January 19th. 1792, in favor of Richard Harrison, Auditor, part of his own, Clerks and Messenger's salary, from do. to do. 35.86.

Part of Warrant, No. 1412, dated January 19th. 1792, in favor of Joseph Nourse, Register, part of his own, Clerks and Messenger's salary, from do. to do. 302.70.

Part of Warrant No. 1414, dated January 19th. 1792, in favor of Henry Knox, Secretary at War, part of his own, Clerks and Messenger's salary from do. to do. 527.78.

Part of Warrant, No. 1429, dated January 19th, 1792, in favor of Samuel Meredith, Agent for Edmund Randolph, in part of his salary as Attorney General of the United States, from do. to do. 100.

Warrant, No. 1477, dated January 19th, 1792, in favor of Joseph Howell, for the salary of Lynde Catlin, a Clerk employed in the Treasury department, by direction of the Secretary, in arranging the accounts of the late Office of Army accounts, and for sundry contingent expenses, from October to 31st. December 1791 | 137.86.

Warrant, No. 1487, dated January 19th. 1792, in favor of Henry Kuhl, for his services as a Clerk employed in the Treasury department, to examine bills of credit of the old emissions for loan, in order to detect counterfeits, from 1st. April, to 30th. September 1791 | 100.

Warrant, No. 1503, dated January 30th. 1792, in favor of David Allison, agent for Robert King and Richard Fields, for their compensation in going express to the Chiefs of the Cherokee nation, in October 1788 | 64.

Part of Warrant, No. 1512, dated February 10th. 1792, in favor of A: C: M: De la Forest, Consul of France, balance of an account due to his most Christian Majesty, for supplies furnished out of the king's magazines, to sundry American ships of War, in the West Indies, from 1781 to 1783, agreeably to a certificate | 9.

Warrant, No. 1587, dated March 19th. 1792, in favor of Joseph Nourse, Register, for expenses incurred in removing the books, papers and furniture of the several Offices of the Treasury department, from New York to the Seat of government, in October 1790 | 554.70.

Part of Warrant, No. 1614, dated April 2d. 1792, in favor of Tench Coxe, Assistant to the Secretary of the Treasury, in part of the salary of the Secretary, the Assistant, his Clerks and Messenger, from January 1st. to March 31st. 1792 | 68.13.

Part of Warrant, No. 1627, dated April 3d. 1792, in favor of Joseph Nourse, Register, in part of the salaries of said Register, his Clerks and Messengers, from January 1st. to March 31st. 1792 | 37.29.

Part of Warrant, No. 1618, dated April 3d. 1792, in favor of Henry Knox, Secretary at War, part of the salary of himself, Clerks and Messenger, from do. to do. | 49.45.

Part of Warrant, No. 1631, dated April 3d. 1792, in favor of William Irvine, and Woodberry Langdon, Commissioners for settling State accounts, in part of chief Clerk's salary from do. to do. | 37.90.

Warrant, No. 1652, dated April 6th. 1792, in favor of Benjamin Goodhue, for the two first bills of two setts of exchange, No. 570 and 1625, drawn by Michael Hillegas, on the late Commissioners of the United States at Paris, for interest due on monies borrowed by said States, and which remained unpaid | 84.

Warrant, No. 1672, dated April 10th. 1792, in favor of Fisher Ames, for the second bills of two setts of exchange, drawn by Michael Hillegas, on the late Commissioners of the United States, at Paris, for interest due on monies borrowed by said States, and which remained unpaid | 36.

Part of Warrant, No. 1741, dated May 11th. 1792, in favor of Joseph Nourse, Assignee of Thomas Tredwell, for two setts of exchange, No. 1672 and 1673, drawn by Francis Hopkinson, Treasurer of loans, on the Commissioners of the United States, at Paris, for interest due on monies borrowed by said States, and which remained unpaid.

Dollars, 50.000.

Treasury Department,
Register's Office, November 8th, 1792.

I certify, that the foregoing is a true extract from the Treasury Books.

Joseph Nourse, Register.

F.

A PARTICULAR STATEMENT OF THE APPLICATION OF FIVE THOUSAND DOLLARS, GRANTED BY AN ACT MAKING CERTAIN APPROPRIATIONS THEREIN MENTIONED, PASSED THE 8TH. MAY 1792,[31] (INCLUDED IN APPROPRIATION OF 34.497 DOLLARS 90 CENTS) FOR THE PURPOSE OF DISCHARGING SUCH DEMANDS ON THE UNITED STATES, NOT OTHERWISE PROVIDED FOR, AS SHALL HAVE BEEN ASCERTAINED AND ADMITTED IN DUE COURSE OF SETTLEMENT AT THE TREASURY, AND WHICH ARE OF A NATURE, ACCORDING TO THE NATURE THEREOF, TO REQUIRE PAYMENT IN SPECIE.

Part of Warrant, No. 1741, dated May 11th. 1792, in favor of Joseph Nourse, Assignee of Thomas Tredwell, in part of two setts of exchange, No. 1672 and 1673, drawn by Francis Hopkinson, late Treasurer of Loans, on the Commissioners of the United States at Paris, for interest due on monies borrowed by said States, and which remained unpaid	15.62.
Warrant, No. 1748, dated 12th. May 1792, in favor of George Walker, for his travelling expenses, going to and returning from Edenton, North Carolina, and for his pay for extra-services in assisting the Commissioner of Loans in North-Carolina, in the execution of his Office	304.59.
Warrant, No. 1763, dated May 16th. 1792, in favor of John Cleves Symmes, and George Turner, Judges of western Territory, for expenses incurred by them, in sending an express, and in purchasing a boat to go the Circuit in 1790	66.59.
Warrant, No. 1794, dated May 25th. 1792, in favor of William Peery, late one of the Commissioners for treating with the southern Indians, for forty six days attendance, as Commissioner aforesaid at Charleston, South Carolina, in the year 1785	299.
Warrant, No. 1819, dated June 4th. 1792, in favor of Stephen Keys, for sundry expenditures incurred by him, in executing and procuring surveys of the north-west part of Lake Champlain, in October 1791, for the purpose of ascertaining a proper position for a Custom-house, per direction of the Secretary of the Treasury	44.55.
Warrant, No. 1829, dated June 7th. 1792, in favor of James Burnside, Attorney for James Ewing, Commissioner of Loans, New Jersey, for sundry Acts of the State of New Jersey, furnished by him, for the use of the Treasury department, in Septembeer 1791	19.18.
Part of Warrant, No. 1881, dated July 2nd. 1792, in favor of Alexander Hamilton, Secretary of the Treasury, in part of his own, Clerks and Messenger's salary, from 1st. April to 30th. June 1792	57.12.
Part of Warrant, No. 1882, dated July 2d. 1792, in favor of Oliver Wolcott, junior, Comptroller, for additional salary of said Wolcott, from April 1st. to June 30th. 1792	59.34.
Part of Warrant, No. 1883, dated July 2d. 1792, in favor of Richard Harrison, Auditor, for the same purpose	59.34.
Part of Warrant, No. 1892, dated July 3d. 1792, in favor of Joseph Nourse, Register, for the same purpose	74.17.
Part of Warrant, No. 1897, dated July 5th. in favor of Samuel Meredith, Treasurer of the United States, for the same purpose	59.34.

31. 1 *Stat* 284–85.

Part of Warrant, No. 1906, dated July 6th. 1792, in favor of Samuel Meredith, Treasurer of the United States, as Agent for Edmund Randolph, Attorney General of the United States, for account of his salary, from April 1st. to June 30th. 1792 59.34.

Part of Warrant, No. 1912, dated July 7th. 1792, in favor of Henry Knox, Secretary at War, for additional salary of himself, Clerks and messenger, from April 1st. to June 30th. 1792 81.73.

Part of Warrant, No. 1916, dated July 8th. 1792, in favor of Joseph Howell, Accountant to the department of War, for part of his Salary, from May 9th. to June 30th. 1792 174.72.

Warrant, No. 1918, dated July 8th. 1792, in favor of Tench Coxe, Commissioner of the revenue, for his own and Clerks salaries from May 9th. to June 30th. 1792 459.59.

Warrant, No. 1932, dated July 12th. 1792, in favor of Cornelius Ten Broeck, executor to the estate of Jacques Vooheese, for a sett of Bills of exchange, No. 20, and for the first, third and fourth bills of a sett No. 1919, drawn by Michael Hillegas on the late Commissioners at Paris, for interest due on monies borrowed by the United States, and which remained unpaid. 90.

Part of Warrant, No. 1934, dated July 13th. 1792, in favor of George Taylor, Junior, agent for Thomas Jefferson, Secretary of State, for account of the contingent expense of the Office of said Secretary of State 2.

Warrant, No. 1966, dated July 23d. in favor of John Wilcox, agent for Rawleigh Colston, for the first Bills of two setts of exchange, No. 549 and 976, and three complete setts of exchange, No. 1070, 1074, and 1643, drawn by Francis Hopkinson, Treasurer of Loans, on the late Commissioners of the United States at Paris, for interest due on monies borrowed by said States, and which remained unpaid 132.

Warrant, No. 1999, dated August 8th. 1792, in favor of Arnold Welles, for a balance due from the United States, on account of a Bill of exchange, in his favor, drawn by William Thompson, William Irvine, Christopher Greene, Timothy Biglow, John Lamb, and Daniel Morgan, dated Quebec, August 5th. 1776, on Messrs. Meredith and Clymer, and which Bill remained unpaid 594.50.

Warrant, No. 2049, dated September 10th. 1792, in favor of James and Shoemaker, for sundry buoys with their appurtenances, procured and forwarded by them, for the use of the harbor of Charleston, South Carolina, by direction of the Secretary of the Treasury, agreeably to an Act of Congress, of the 12th. April, 1792[32] 1 319. 7.

Warrant, No. 2056, dated September 17th. 1792, in favor of Jonathan Williams junior, for a sett of exchange, No. 2687, drawn by F. Hopkinson on the late Commissioners at Paris, for interest due on monies borrowed, which remained unpaid 12.

Warrant, No. 2074, dated September 27th. 1792, in favor of William Allibone, for his services and expenses on a visit of examination and survey of the Light house, erecting at Bald Head, and navigation of the river Cape Fear, in the State of North-Carolina, by direction of the Secretary of the Treasury 212.

Warrant, No. 2077, dated September 28th. 1792, in favor of William Bell, for sundry Bills of exchange, Viz: the second Bills of 484, 485, 1041, 1043, 1171, 1173, and 1344; the third Bill of No. 486; and the

32. "An Act supplementary to the act for the establishment and support of lighthouses, beacons, buoys, and public piers" (1 *Stat.* 251).

fourth bill of No. 584, drawn by Michael Hillegas, late Treasurer of the United States, on the Commissioners at Paris, for interest on monies borrowed by said States, and which remain unpaid 168.

Part of Warrant, No. 2096, dated October 1st. 1792, in favor of Oliver Wolcott, junior, Comptroller, in part for his own, Clerks and Messenger's salaries, from July 1st. to September 30th 100.

Part of Warrant, No. 2099, dated October 1st. 1792, in favor of Henry Knox, Secretary at War, in part of do. from do. to do. 50.

Part of Warrant, No. 2102, dated October 2d. in favor of Joseph Nourse, register, in part of his own, Clerks and Messenger's salaries, from July 1st. to September 30th 125.

Part of Warrant, No. 2104, dated October 2d. 1792, in favor of Richard Harrison, Auditor, in part of do. from do. to do. 100.

Part of Warrant, No. 2105, dated October 2d. 1792, in favor of Thomas Jefferson, Secretary of State, in part of do. and for rent, from do. to do. 46.67.

Part of Warrant, No. 2107, dated October 2d. 1792, in favor of James Mathers, doorkeeper to the Senate, for balance of his salary, from July 1st. to September 30th. 1792 37.30.

Part of Warrant, No. 2108, dated October 2d. 1792, in favor of Thomas Claxton, assistant-doorkeeper to the House of Representatives, for balance of his salary, from do. to do. 71. 2.

Part of Warrant, No. 2112, dated October 2d. 1792, in favor of Gifford Dalley, doorkeeper to the House of Representatives, for balance of his salary, from do. to do. 37.30.

Warrant, No. 2160, dated October 13th. 1792, in favor of John Templeman, for a sett of Bills of exchange, No. 1447, drawn by Francis Hopkinson, Treasurer of Loans, on the late Commissioners of the United States, at Paris, for interest on monies borrowed, and which remained unpaid 12.

Warrant, No. 2188, dated October 26th. in favor of Edmund Randolph, Attorney General of the United States, for his expenses to and from York Town in Pennsylvania, to attend the Circuit and District Court, which was held at said place, on the 11th. instant, by order of the President of the United States 54.

Dollars, 4 997. 8.

Treasury Department, Register's Office
November 8th, 1792.

I certify that the foregoing is a true Extract from the Treasury Books,
Joseph Nourse, Register.

Conversation with George Hammond[1]

Philadelphia [November 15–December 3, 1792]

In a recent conversation which I have had with Mr Hamilton, that Gentleman informed me that this government has in its possession the most indisputable proofs of an active interference on the part of the Spanish government in exciting the Creeks and Cherokees to war against the United States.[2] He added that Baron Corrondolet,

Governor of West Florida,[3] had furnished the Indians with considerable supplies and ammunition for carrying into effect their hostile purposes. A confidential communication of these circumstances has been made to the two houses of Congress,[4] but as during the reading of those papers, the doors were shut, I have not yet been able to ascertain the precise extent of the information submitted.

D, PRO: F.O., Series 4, Vol. 16, Part V.

1. Hammond had served as chargé d'affaires at Vienna from 1788 to 1790 and in 1791 as Minister Plenipotentiary at Madrid. In September, 1791, he was appointed British Minister Plenipotentiary to the United States.

This conversation has been taken from Hammond to Lord Grenville, December 4, 1792, Dispatch No. 41.

2. On July 6, 1792, the Creek Indians and the Spanish signed a treaty which guaranteed the Creeks possession of their lands and promised them Spanish aid in case of attack. On August 15, 1792, George Washington sent to Henry Knox dispatches received from James Seagrove, agent of the United States to the Creek Nation, and at the same time requested "that the Secretary of the Treasury would also consider them attentively" (*GW*, XXXII, 116). These dispatches described Spanish efforts to arouse the Indians against the Americans and included information that in October, 1792, a six-man delegation from the Cherokee Nation had gone to New Orleans, where plans for a defensive alliance between Spain and the Cherokee Nation were made. The dispatches, together with other papers concerning the southern Indians and their relations with Spain, were sent by Knox to Congress on November 7, 1792, and are printed in *ASP, Indian Affairs,* I, 225, 295–318. On November 7 Washington also sent to Congress a message and papers "relative to Spanish interference with the Indians" (*ASP, Foreign Relations,* I, 138–39).

3. Don Francisco Louis Hector, Baron de Carondelet, Spanish Governor and Intendant General of the Provinces of Louisiana and West Florida. On October 14 Jefferson wrote to William Carmichael and William Short, United States commissioners to Spain: "That the Baron de Carondelet their chief Governor at New Orleans has excited the Indians to war on us; that he has furnished them with abundance of arms and ammunition, and promised them whatever more shall be necessary I have from the mouth of him who had it from his own mouth. In short, that he is the sole source of a great and serious war now burst out upon us, and from Indians who we know were in peaceable dispositions towards us, till prevailed on by him to commence the war, there remains scarcely room to doubt" (Ford, *Writings of Jefferson,* VI, 118–19). Jefferson again wrote to Short and Carmichael on this subject on November 3, 1792 (Ford, *Writings of Jefferson,* VI, 129–30). On December 4, 1792, Hammond wrote to Lord Grenville: "I have however learnt from another quarter that Baron Corrondolet justifies his interposition upon the principle that part of the Creeks comprehended in the treaty settled at New York in the year 1790, reside within the limits of Spain, are subjects of that Crown, and consequently not competent to enter into any sort of separate agreement with any other power" (PRO: F.O., Series 4, Vol. 16, Part V). See also Tench Coxe to H, November 8, 1792.

4. See note 2.

From Benjamin Lincoln[1]

Boston, November 15, 1792. "Your Circular letter to the Collectors of the Customs under the date of Octr 25 has been received by me. In that letter I am requested to furnish you as early as possible with an estimate of the amount of bounties payable in this district on fishing vessels. It is out of my power to comply with the request with any degree of Exactness as we have not more than ten or fifteen vessels which make their fish in this district. Our merchants here are interested in vessels in different districts where they make their fish. Whether they will apply for the bonds there or here where the supplies are received I know not. I am persuaded that no evil will arise to individuals or to the public from this state of uncertainty as I am always in cash to pay all such bounties as can be demanded from me. . . ."

LC, Massachusetts Historical Society, Boston; LC, RG 36, Collector of Customs at Boston, Letter Book, 1790–1797, National Archives; copy, RG 56, Letters from the Collector at Boston, National Archives.

1. Lincoln was collector of customs at Boston.

From Jeremiah Olney

Providence, November 15, 1792. "Agreeable to your circular Letter of the 25th of Octr. I enclose an Estimate of the Amot. of Bounty wch. . . . fishing Vessels belonging to this District, will be entitled to on the last Day of Decemr. next. . . ."

ADfS, Rhode Island Historical Society, Providence.

From Jeremiah Olney

[*Providence, November 15, 1792.* On November 27, 1792, Hamilton wrote to Olney: "Your letter of the 15th instant has been duly received . . . in relation to the Brig Neptune." *Letter not found.*]

From Jean Baptiste de Ternant[1]

Philade. 15 Nove. 1792
l'an 4 de la libé. fre.

En conformité de nos arrangemens, je vous prie de faire payer au citoyen Laforest[2] Consul general de france ou à son ordre la somme de 2,358 piastres au 15 du present, et celle de 8997, au lr. decembre suivant, lesquelles ⟨deux⟩ sommes completteront le 3e. payement à effectuer par les Etats unis.[3] T

LC, *Arch. des Aff. Etr., Corr. Pol., Etats-Unis,* Supplement Vol. 20.

1. Ternant was French Minister Plenipotentiary to the United States.
2. Antoine René Charles Mathurin de La Forest.
3. This was the third payment from a grant of four hundred thousand dollars from which payments were to be made on the debt owed France. In an exchange of letters on March 8, 1792, Ternant had made arrangements with H for this grant, and a change in the dates on which payments were to be made was arranged in August, 1792. See Ternant to H, August 22, 1792.

To Thomas Jefferson

[Philadelphia, November 17, 1792]

The Secretary of the Treasury presents his respectful Compliments to The Secretary of State and sends two Copies of the Report of the Trustees of the Sinking Fund agreed upon last night with the requisite documents for each.[1] This is the last day for presenting them; so that even if either House should not sit it will be proper to forward the Report to the Presiding Officer.[2]

The S of the T. will wait upon the Secretary of State at two OClock to day, if he hears nothing to the contrary, to adjust finally, the affair of Mr. Ternants application for the supply of St Domingo.[3]

November 17th 1792

AL, Thomas Jefferson Papers, Library of Congress.

1. "Report of the Commissioners of the Sinking Fund," November 17, 1792.
2. November 17 fell on a Saturday, and neither the House of Representatives nor the Senate met on that date (*Journal of the House*, I, 621; *Annals of Congress*, III, 615).

Section 9 of "An Act supplementary to the act making provision for the Debt of the United States" provided "That quarter yearly accounts of the application of the said fund shall be rendered for settlement, as other public accounts, accompanied with returns of the sums of the said debt, which shall have been from time to time purchased or redeemed; and a full and exact report of the proceedings of the said commissioners, including a statement of the disbursements, which shall have been made, and of the sums which shall have been purchased or redeemed under their direction, and specifying dates, prices, parties, and places, shall be laid before Congress, within the first fourteen days of each session which may ensue the present, during the execution of the said trust" (1 *Stat.* 283 [May 8, 1792]).

3. See H to George Washington, November 19, 1792.

To Thomas Jefferson

[Philadelphia, November 17, 1792]

Mr. Hamilton regrets extremely that an unexpected occurrence has detained him so much beyond the hour mentioned to Mr. Jefferson, that he should fear interrupting him by calling. He requests Mr. Jefferson to mention some other early time convenient to him for the Interview.

Saturday near 3 oClock

AL, Thomas Jefferson Papers, Library of Congress.

To Benjamin Lincoln

Treasury Department, November 17, 1792. "The Collector of Frenchmans Bay in his letter to me dated October the 1st,[1] which has just come to hand, applies for some blank certificates of Registry. I have informed him in the enclosed letter[2] that he will be supplied from your office in the usual course. This I request may be done without loss of time . . . ."

L[S], RG 36, Collector of Customs at Boston, Letters from the Treasury and Others, 1789–1809, National Archives; copy, RG 56, Letters to the Collector at Boston, Vol. 1, National Archives; copy, RG 56, Letters to Collectors at Small Ports, "Set G," National Archives.

1. Meletiah Jordan's letter to H has not been found.

2. Letter not found.

Report of the Commissioners of the Sinking Fund

[Philadelphia, November 17, 1792
Communicated on November 19, 1792][1]

[To the Speaker of the House of Representatives and the President of the Senate]

The Vice President of the United States and President of the Senate, The Chief Justice, The Secretary of State, The Secretary of the Treasury and the Attorney General respectfully report to The Congress as follows—

That pursuant to the Act intitled An Act making provision for the reduction of the Public Debt [2] and in conformity to resolutions agreed upon by them and severally approved by the President of the United States they have since their last Report [3] caused purchases of the said Debt to be made through the Agency of Samuel Meredith Treasurer of the United States and William Seton Cashier of the Bank of New York respectively to the amount of Three hundred and twenty five thousand three hundred and seventy eight dollars and sixty two Cents, for which there have been paid Two hundred and forty two thousand, six hundred and eighty eight dollars and thirty one Cents in Specie as will more particularly appear by the several documents herewith submitted marked A, B, C.[4]

That pursuant to the Act intitled "An Act supplementary to the Act making provision for the Debt of the United States" [5] and in conformity to resolutions agreed upon by them and severally approved by the President of the United States they have also caused purchases of the said debt to be made through the Agency of Samuel Meredith Treasurer of the United States to the amount of Thirty eight thousand seven hundred and fourteen dollars and fifty one Cents; for which there have been paid Twenty five thousand nine hundred and sixty nine dollars and ninety six Cents in specie as will more particularly appear by the document herewith submitted marked D:

An Abstract of the whole of which purchases is contained in the Statement E, herewith also reported amounting to Three hundred and sixty four thousand and ninety three dollars and thirteen Cents; for which there have been paid Two hundred and sixty eight thousand six hundred and fifty eight dollars and twenty seven Cents in specie.

That the said several documents marked A, B, C, D (which are submitted as part of this report) shew in detail the places where, the times when, the prices at which, and the persons of whom the purchases aforesaid have been made.

That the purchases now and heretofore reported amount together to One Million, four hundred and ninety five thousand, four hundred and fifty seven dollars and eighty nine Cents; for which there have been paid Nine hundred and sixty seven thousand, eight hundred and twenty one dollars and sixty five Cents in specie; and for which credits have been passed on the Books of the Treasury, as will be more particularly seen by the Certified Statement herewith also submitted marked F.

On behalf of the Board
Th: Jefferson

D, signed by Thomas Jefferson, RG 46, Second Congress, 1791–1793, Reports of the Commissioners of the Sinking Fund, National Archives.

1. *Annals of Congress*, III, 615; *Journal of the House*, I, 621. The communicating letter is dated November 17, 1792, and is addressed to "The President pro temp. of the Senate" (ALS, in Jefferson's handwriting, RG 46, Second Congress, 1791–1793, Reports of the Commissioners of the Sinking Fund, National Archives).

2. 1 *Stat.* 186–87 (August 12, 1790).

3. "Report of the Commissioners of the Sinking Fund," November 7, 1791.

4. D, signed by Joseph Nourse, RG 46, Second Congress, 1791–1793, Reports of the Commissioners of the Sinking Fund, National Archives. The enclosures for this document are printed in *ASP, Finance*, I, 163–71.

5. Section 7 of this act provided that interest on the redeemed or purchased debt of the United States should be used for sinking fund purchases and gave rules for sinking fund purchases of Government securities (1 *Stat.* 281–83 [May 8, 1792]).

Report on Several Petitions Seeking Indemnification for Various Sums of Paper Money Received During the Late War

[Philadelphia, November 17, 1792
Communicated on November 22, 1792] [1]

[To the Speaker of the House of Representatives]

The Secretary of the Treasury, to whom were referred the several petitions specified in the list herewith transmitted,[2] respectfully submits the following Report thereupon.

These petitions seek indemnifications upon various sums of paper money received from the public, during the late war, by the respective petitioners on account of claims arising upon transactions of that period.

There is no subject, upon which the special interposition of the Legislature, for relief of particular individuals, can be more delicate and dangerous, than that of depreciation. The infinite multitude of cases, in which claims of this nature might, with equal or nearly equal degrees of equity, be supported; the impossibility, from the extraordinary circumstances of the times when those claims originated, of doing general justice, the inextricable confusion, and incalculable expense, of an attempt to redress all the grievances and hardships of that kind, which unavoidably took place, afford considerations of the most powerful nature for leaving every question of depreciation, where the rules and principles of settlement at the Treasury have left it.

If the claim of either of the petitioners is within those rules, and not barred by the Acts of limitation,[3] no interposition of the Legislature is necessary. If not within those rules and barred by the Acts of limitation, such an interposition would, in point of precedent, be of the most inconvenient tendency. The magnitude and extreme delicacy of the matter, in question, appear to render it advisable to adhere to the Acts of limitation, as well as the rules of settlement at the Treasury, in this particular, with peculiar caution and strictness.

Such was the policy of the United States in Congress assembled, and a perseverance in that policy is recommended, by a variety of weighty reasons.

The Secretary understands, that an allowance of depreciation, in either of the cases mentioned in the petitions, would be contrary to the rules and principles, which have governed in public settlements.

All which is humbly submitted Alexander Hamilton
Secry. of the Treasry.

Treasury department
November 1792.

Copy, RG 233, Reports of the Treasury Department, 1792–1793, Vol. III, National Archives; copy, RG 233, Messages from the President, Second Congress, National Archives.

1. *Journal of the House*, I, 625–26. The communicating letter, dated November 21, 1792, may be found in RG 233, Reports of the Treasury Department, 1792–1793, Vol. III, National Archives.

2. H accompanied this report with a "List of petitions referred to in the report of the 17th of November 1792," including the names of ten petitioners. Thomas Barclay and Jacob Winey petitioned for an allowance of depreciation for payment made by Congress for freight and valuation of two ships chartered during the American Revolution for public service and later cap-

tured by the British. Their petitions were read in the House and referred to H on February 12, 1791 (*Journal of the House*, I, 376).

The petition of John Nicholason (Nicholson), Indian interpreter and guide, was referred to H on February 17, 1791 (*Journal of the House*, I, 381).

On April 16, 1792, the House had referred to H the petition of John Wereat of Georgia for money advanced to American troops during the American Revolution (*Journal of the House*, I, 578).

Abraham Van Alstine's petition concerned the depreciation of money which had been held for public use over a period of years since some time during the American Revolution. The full value of the money when it was received by him was charged against him in the public accounts, although in 1792 the same money still held by him was worthless. The petition was referred to H on June 27, 1790 (*Journal of the House*, I, 177, 250).

An earlier petition of Jacob Garrigues, "a former employee in the Quartermaster General Department, for compensation for depreciation notwithstanding the settlement of his account" had been read in Congress on May 11, 1785 (*JCC*, XXVIII, 350*n*). No record of a report on this petition has been found. On February 16, 1791, a similar petition of Garrigues was referred to H (*Journal of the House*, I, 380).

The petition of Lemuel Cravath of Connecticut was referred to H on April 27, 1790 (*Journal of the House*, I, 142, 203).

The petition of John Griffith, Jr., was referred to H on July 30, 1790 (*Journal of the House*, I, 285).

The petition of John Spaulding was referred to H on March 19, 1792 (*Journal of the House*, I, 539–40).

No reference to the petition of William Browner has been found.

3. The general acts of limitation may be found in *JCC*, XXIX, 866; XXXIII, 392. See also "Report on Sundry Petitions," April 16, 1792.

To the Senators and Representatives of the State of Georgia

Treasury Department
Novemr. 17th 1792

Gentlemen

The Commissioner of the Revenue has transmitted to me the enclosed instrument as a draught of a deed of Conveyance for the Tybee light House intended to be executed by the Senators and Representatives of the State of Georgia.[1]

On considering together the proviso in the first Section of the Act of Congress of the 7th. day of August 1789 for the establishment and support of light Houses &ca.[2] and the second proviso in the Act of the Legislature of Georgia,[3] recited in the proposed conveyance I have the honor to inform you that it appears to me, that this deed cannot be accepted by an executive Officer of the United States because it would carry a clear tho implied engagement for the continuance of a Law, which it is in the power of the Legislature alone to make.

I have the Honor to be with great Respect, Gentlemen, Your most obedient Servt.

Alexander Hamilton
Secretary of the Treasury

The Honble
The Senators & Representatives of the State of Georgia in the Congress of the United States

LS, Montague Collection, MS Division, New York Public Library.

1. On November 9, 1792, Tench Coxe wrote to the Senators and Representatives of Georgia enclosing a copy of his letter to John Habersham, superintendent of the Tybee Island lighthouse in Georgia, dated November 7, 1792. In this letter he suggested that they inform interested members of both houses of the Georgia legislature of the requirements concerning cessions of land needed to qualify for Federal support for the maintenance of lighthouses after July 1, 1793 (LC, RG 58, Letters of Commissioner of Revenue, 1792–1793, National Archives).

On November 17, 1792, Coxe wrote to Habersham: "I find that an Act has been passed by the legislature of Georgia for the cession of the Tybee light House and that the Instrument is prepared for Execution by the Senators and Representatives" (LC, RG 58, Letters of Commissioner of Revenue, 1792–1793, National Archives).

2. "An Act for the establishment and support of Lighthouses, Beacons, Buoys, and Public Piers" (1 *Stat.* 53–54).

3. "An Act to empower the senators or one senator and two representatives from this state in the Congress of the United States, to sign, seal, and deliver a deed of cession of the light house on Tybee island, and five acres of land belonging thereto to the United States" states:

"*Be it enacted by the Senate and House of Representatives of the State of Georgia in General Assembly met,* That from and immediately after the passing of this act, it shall be lawful for the Senators of this state in the Congress of the United States, or for one of the said Senators, with any two of the Representatives of this state to the said Congress, to sign, seal, and deliver a deed of cession to the United States on behalf of this state, of the light house on Tybee Island, of the property and jurisdiction of this state, of, in and to the same, and of five acres of land nearest adjoining and belonging thereto, to hold the same and every part thereof to the said United States forever. *Provided always,* That the act allowing three pence per ton for clearing and removing wrecks and other obstructions in the River Savannah, be continued until the same shall be completely cleared" (Georgia sessions laws, December, 1791, p. 17, Microfilm Collection of Early State Records, Library of Congress). This act was passed on December 15, 1791.

From James McHenry[1]

Annapolis 18th Novr. 1792

My dear Sir

We have scattered in air the long string of amendments that had been proposed to be incorporated into our constitututíon by those who were no friends to the U.S.'s constitution,[2] so we remain a free people and a tolerably virtuous people.

There are three or four bills before the house and to come before the house in which I feel an interest and which will detain me here perhaps two weeks.[3] I shall then take my station at my little farm with my little wife, where if my health returns, I shall envy no man's happiness. Before I leave this however I wish you could say something to me respecting Mr. Perry.[4] The supervisorship of the excise of the Eastern shore I suggested to you long since. His exertions in a late election has been uncommon. The opponent of Mr. Hindman[5] tho' connected with good federalists is nevertheless the disciple of Mercer[6] and would have been his implicit and devoted follower. This was known to his friends, but it became a family affair, and of course Hindmans friends were obliged to make use of all the means in their power. It fell heaviest on Perry. Give me some comfort for him—and destroy this letter.

Yours affectionately James McHenry

ALS, Hamilton Papers, Library of Congress.

1. At this time McHenry was attending the 1792 session of the Maryland Senate, of which he was a member.

2. *The constitution and form of government, as proposed to be amended by a committee appointed by the House of Delegates at the last session* (Annapolis: Printed by Frederick Greene, printer to the State [1792]).

3. McHenry attended the session of the Senate until November 23, 1792. He returned in December and took an active part in subsequent proceedings of the Senate.

4. On November 19, 1791, McHenry had suggested William Perry as "an officer in the Revenue," and in the summer of 1792 he had described Perry's efforts in the election campaign of 1792. See McHenry to H, November 19, 1791; August 16, 1792.

5. William Hindman, who was Perry's brother-in-law, had recently been elected to the House of Representatives from the upper district of the Eastern Shore of Maryland. His opponent in the election was James Tilghman.

6. For John F. Mercer's views on public credit which H criticized, see H to Edward Carrington, May 26, 1792, note 18. For Mercer's controversy with H growing out of the 1792 election campaign, see the introductory note to H to Mercer, September 26, 1792.

To the President and Directors of the Bank of the United States

Treasury Department
November 19, 1792

Sir

I should be glad as early as may be, after to day, of an interview with the President and Directors of the Bank of the United States on a subject of some importance.[1]

I have the honor to be with respectful consideration Sir Your most Obed servant Alexander Hamilton

The President of The Bank of The United States

ALS, Hamilton Papers, Library of Congress.

1. See H to the President and Directors of the Bank of the United States, November 20, 1792.

From Tench Coxe

Treasury Department, Revenue Office, November 19, 1792. "I have the honor to inclose to you a statement of the substance of the two Acts of the President of the United States of the 4th. of August and 29th of October last relative to the compensations and expences in the Business of the Revenue, together with the estimates E and A refered to therein.[1] Also a draught of a communication from the President to the Legislature, applicable to the present occasion, and similar to that of the last year." [2]

LC, RG 58, Letters of Commissioner of Revenue, 1792–1793, National Archives.

1. For background to this letter, see George Washington to H, October 1, 1792; H to Washington, September 22, first letter of October 31, 1792; Coxe to H, first letter of July 25, September 12–18, October 20, 1792.

2. Coxe is referring to Washington's letter of November 1, 1791, to Congress transmitting the arrangements made under "An Act repealing, after the last day of June next, the duties heretofore laid upon Distilled Spirits imported from abroad, and laying others in their stead; and also upon Spirits distilled within the United States, and for appropriating the same" (1 *Stat.* 199–214 [March 3, 1791]). See H to the Senate and the House of Representatives, October 31, 1791.

From John Fenno[1]

[Philadelphia, November 19-December 3, 1792]

Sir,

In lieu of a narrative in my own writing the enclosed paper,[2] with the marginal addition, contains all the facts. I would have transcribed it, but have not time.

You will please Sir, to note the enclosed Account.

Monday Morning

AL, Hamilton Papers, Library of Congress.

1. Fenno was the editor of the [Philadelphia] *Gazette of the United States.*

2. H endorsed this letter: "Mr. Fenno concerning his application to inspect certain letters." See "A Plain Honest Man," October 30–November 17, 1792, note 5.

From William Heth[1]

Collectors Office
Berma Hundred [Virginia] 19th Novr. 92

Dr Sir

Enclosed you have copy's of a letter from me to the United States Atty for this District,[2] with his answer, which are transmitted at his request.

Finding that, several weeks after my first letter—process had not been served upon Horton,[3] I wrote again, repeating the information & beging to know whether my first had been recd—some days ago, I saw him in Richmond, when he gave me the answer, of which the enclosed is a copy,[4] & which had been laying some time for an opportunity of conveying it to this place. I satisfyd him, that he was mistaken as to the *five cases* in which you had remitted in "*cases like that of the Abigail*"—Allyn's[5] being the only one—and *this,* was not

ALS, Hamilton Papers, Library of Congress.

1. Heth was collector of customs at Bermuda Hundred, Virginia.

2. Alexander Campbell, United States attorney for the District of Virginia, had earlier criticized H's interpretation of the section of the Coasting Act which concerned fees. See Heth to H, November 20, 1791.

3. Samuel Horton was master of the ship *Abigail.*

4. See the enclosures to this letter.

5. Presumably William Allin, who had been a Richmond printer.

publickly known—i.e.—it was not enterd on record. However, he mentioned some cases wch arose in the Norfolk District in which you had remitted, & which, with the decision on *Hunts* case [6]—produced the determination in the present Instance. I hope I shall not be considered as exceeding the bounds of my duty, if I add that Mr. Campbell's opinion & sentiments on this subject, are precisely those, of the other officers of this District Court—and, for my own part candor obliges me to declare that, if I did not feel myself indispensibly bound by my oath, to direct process to be instituted in all cases where the laws are violated & where, I have no discretionary powers, I should certainly not have given any notice to the Attorney in the present case. For, as I told you in person, the decision on Hunts case filld every body with astonishment, except those, who offerd bets upon the petition being presented, that he would be relieved. Had I been a sporting man I would have risqued *my all* that he would not. With Lyle & McCredies case [7] upon record—I

6. Charles Hunt, a merchant of Williamsburg, Virginia, had been indirectly involved in the case of the *United States* v *Goods in the Sloop Friendship John.* He was the owner of six pipes of wine and four hogsheads of rum and the shipper of a set of used type which had belonged to William Allin and which now was being sold by Ashley Adams, Allin's executor, for the benefit of Allin's heirs. When the *Friendship John* arrived in the District of Bermuda Hundred on December 13, 1791, John Carter, the master of the sloop, had neither manifest nor permit. On June 26, 1792, H had signed the remission of forfeiture for Ashley Adams. On July 16, 1792, H had also remitted the fine and forfeiture for Carter and Adams. No remission of the forfeiture in the case of the wine and rum owned by Hunt appears in the record book of the Virginia District Court (Records of the District Court of Virginia, Archives Division, Virginia State Library, Richmond).

7. Lyle and McCredie were part owners of goods brought from Norfolk to Manchester in the sloop *Non Pareil,* Benjamin Forrester, master. A libel was filed in the District Court at Richmond on December 22, 1790. H rejected the petitions of both Lyle and McCredie and George Yuiville and Company (copy, Records of the District Court of Virginia, Archives Division, Virginia State Library, Richmond).

Heth took several depositions concerning the case, and Lyle and McCredie submitted a letter dated December 11, 1790, from John Lawrence, the shipper at Norfolk. Lawrence's letter indicated that he had given the master instructions concerning compliance with customs regulations. Lawrence wrote: "I gave the Skipper a most particular Charge to take care to have his vessel and goods cleared out legally and saw him go into the Custom House as I supposed for that purpose and am indeed much astonished that after all he should omit to do it. . . . I am told that [Solomon] Tatham is certainly liable for all Losses that may arise either from his own, of his Skippers Misconduct or Neglect" (copy, Records of the District Court of Virginia, Archives Division, Virginia State Library, Richmond).

deemd, & so did the Court—the remission impossible. Lyle & Mc-Credie had no agency in the business, & were as innocent as children of the transaction by which they lost *their* goods. Hunt was apprized of the hazard to which *his* goods were exposed—enquired into the nature of the risque—askd advice of Colo. Carrington & myself—and was very particularly informd by me, how to save them from seizure, & which he might have done at a very trifling expence—and surely, the Judge transmitted you both Carringtons, & my deposition.[8]

I have Just given Mr Campbell information of the arrival of another American Master, without reporting below—and who produced no paper whatsoever here, but the register—saying that he had "nothing but sand ballast from Bilboa." He appeard to be no more concernd at my telling him he had incurrd a penalty & shewing him the law, than if I had sung him a stave or two of Chevy-chase [9]—and absolutely laughd at every thing that was said. Indeed, before I came to the office, he had treated my clerk with a good deal of contempt, by insinuating that he knew his duty better than he could tell him, that "he knew Congr⟨ess⟩ very well, & could go there and speak to his cause as well as any body." This man comes to the same Merchant that Henry Rust [10] did (who is as guilty of the same offence). He, and his connections are the only people in this District, whom I suspect to be concernd in illicit commerce & this Man may have loaded half a dozen, or more small vessels *under 20 tons*—in the capes as he came up the river. Well persuaded I am, that he came not entirely in Ballast, tho' he has signd & sworn to it. I have *begd* Mr. Campbell to order serch in this case, but, whether he will, or not I

8. No records of the depositions of Edward Carrington, supervisor of the revenue of Virginia, and Heth have been found.

9. The ballad of Chevy Chase commemorated the battle of Otterburn fought on August 19, 1388, between Scottish troops led by the earls of Douglas and Murray and an English force led by Henry Percy, Earl of Northumberland. The ballad was popular in eighteenth-century England and was commended in two issues of Joseph Addison's *Spectator*. The air was used in John Gay's "The Beggar's Opera."

10. At a session of the District Court of Virginia on June 21, 1791, the case of the *United States* v *Henry Rust Master of the Brigantine Columbia* was brought before a jury, and five hundred dollars was awarded to the United States. No record of either a petition or remission appears in the record book of the District Court (D, Records of the District Court of Virginia, Archives Division, Virginia State Library, Richmond).

cant say. Something must be done, or we shall all go wrong. Having written with too much freedom perhaps for an Official letter, I have concluded to make this a private one—and am Dear Sir, with the sincerest wishes for your happiness & prosperity, and the warmest sentiments of affection and friendship

Yrs Will Heth

Colo. A Hamilton

[ENCLOSURE]

William Heth to Alexander Campbell [11]

Collectors Office
Bermuda Hundred [Virginia] Sept 14th 1792

Sir

Samuel Horton entered the Ship Abigail an American Bottom, yesterday as Master or Commander, with a very large Cargo from London, without reporting at Hampton or Norfolk agreeably to the fou[r]th Section of the Collection Law,[12] tho he delivered his Letters to a very great number at the Post Office in the latter Port. The Manifest which he delivered, such as it is—was made at Sea. Besides being defective in point of form as required by the 9th 11th

11. Copy, Hamilton Papers, Library of Congress.

12. "An Act to provide more effectually for the collection of the duties imposed by law on goods, wares and merchandise imported into the United States, and on the tonnage of ships or vessels" (1 *Stat.* 145–78 [August 4, 1790]).

Section 4 of this act reads as follows: "*And be it further enacted,* That the master or commander of every ship or vessel, if bound to the district of Nottingham, shall, before he pass by the port of Town Creek, and immediately after his arrival, deposit with the surveyor of the said port, a true manifest of the cargo on board such ship or vessel: if bound to the district of Tappahannock, shall, before he pass by the port of Urbanna, and immediately after his arrival, deposit with the surveyor for that port a like manifest: if bound to the district of Bermuda Hundred or City Point, shall, before he pass by Elizabeth River, and immediately after his arrival, deposit with the collector of the port of Norfolk and Portsmouth, or with the collector of the port of Hampton, a like manifest: and if bound to the district of South Quay, shall, before he pass by the port of Edenton, and immediately after his arrival, deposit with the collector of the port of Edenton, a like manifest. And the said surveyors and collectors respectively, shall, after registering the manifest, transmit the same, duly certified to have been so deposited, to the officer with whom the entries are to be made. And if the master or commander of any ship or vessel shall neglect or omit to deposit a manifest in manner aforesaid, and as the case shall require, he shall forfeit and pay five hundred dollars, to be re-

12th & 16th Sections of the Collection Law,[13] he has not inserted the Name of a single Consignee in the whole Manifest, so he will have now to make out another report or Manifest before I can possibly enter the Cargo in my Books. He is now in Port.

I am Sir &c. Will Heth

To
Alex Campbell esq
Attorney General
Richmond

[ENCLOSURE]

Alexander Campbell to William Heth [14]

Richmond 1st Nov 1792

Dear sir

I received your favors relating to the Ship Abigail, You will be Pleased to be assured that in all communications from you, I feel myself desiring of pursuing what you think proper to be done: and this because I have had great reason to confide in your judgment with respect to the Subjects of your Office: but it becomes me, in some measure to consider the current of Decisions in the Treasury and where I find a Principle istablished there, to prevent expence to the Individual & mortification to ourselves, in Cases, where if that principle be adhered to, our process wou'd be of none avail.

---

covered with costs of suit, one half to the use of the officer with whom such manifest ought to have been deposited, and the other half to the use of the collector of the district to which the said ship or vessel may be bound: *Provided,* That if manifests shall have been in either of the said cases previously delivered to any officer of the customs, pursuant to the provision herein after to be made in that behalf, the depositing of a manifest as aforesaid shall not be necessary: *And provided also,* That no master of any ship or vessel which was absent from the United States on the first day of May last, and which hath not since returned within the same, or of any ship or vessel not owned wholly or in part by a citizen or inhabitant of the United States, shall incur the said penalty, if he shall make oath or affirmation that he had no knowledge of or information concerning the regulation herein contained, unless it can be otherwise proved that he had such knowledge or information" (1 *Stat.* 153).

13. These sections of the Collection Law concern the duties of masters of vessels on entering from a foreign port and the penalties for failure to have or produce a manifest or to make entry within twenty-four hours of their arrival within the United States (1 *Stat.* 156–59).

14. Copy, Hamilton Papers, Library of Congress.

In a Case like that of the Abigail there are no less than five Cases, in which the Secretary of the Treasury has released. How long he will continue to do so I cannot tell: but it seems to me that he will continue to do so, and that unless Congress interfere, there will be no possibility of judging as to the propriety of instituting process in any Case where he is the ultimate Judge. Indeed I have been o[b]liged, as you know, to take Judgment merely for Costs in a number of Instances, where the parties tho within the mischief & letter of the Congressional Law, wou'd, I was certain, be releaved by the Secretary, either entirely or in such a manner as to bring the Court & its Officers into Contempt. Conversing freely with those who trespass upon the regulations of Congress, I know, certainly, that the Service of process here does not excite in the greater part, of them, one uneasy feeling. They all look forward to a Treasury remission, and as they generally procure that, the Institution of process here becomes a mere Subject of ridicule. I have scrutinized the orders of remission from the Secretary, most carefully, in order to ascertain the principle of them: but their repugnancy is such as to shut out all hope of deriving from them any rule for my government in the Institution of process. The Case of Hunt stands as an high barrier against every rule, which I thought out to operate upon a Case like his. I have therefore declined to issue process in the Case of the Ship Abigail and as I may stand in need of a Justification, I hope you will be so good, as to transmit your letter & a Copy of this, to the Secretary of the Treasury, who, I am sure will find it necessary to adopt some Rule on the Subject to prevent the Confusion and take away that incertainty which have so much clogged the process of our Court in this District.

I am sir with great Esteem & respect your very Obt servt.

Alexr. Campbell

To William Heth esq
Collector
Bermuda Hundred

To Thomas Jefferson

[Philadelphia, November 19, 1792]

Mr. Hamilton presents his Compliments to Mr. Jefferson. On reflection he concluded it to be most in order to address his communication on the subject of Mr Ternant's application to the President.[1] A copy which is sent herewith will apprise Mr. Jefferson of its precise import.

Nov 19. 1792

AL, Thomas Jefferson Papers, Library of Congress.

1. See H to Jefferson, two letters, November 17, 1792; H to George Washington, November 19, 1792.

Report on Several Petitions Seeking Compensation for Property Damaged or Destroyed During the Late War

[Philadelphia, November 19, 1792
Communicated on November 22, 1792] [1]

[To the Speaker of the House of Representatives]

The Secretary of the Treasury, to whom were referred the several petitions in the list hereunto annexed,[2] specified, respectfully makes the following Report, thereupon.

Copy, RG 233, Reports of the Treasury Department, 1792–1793, Vol. III, National Archives; copy, RG 233, Messages from the President, Second Congress, National Archives.

1. *Journal of the House*, I, 625–26. The communicating letter, dated November 21, 1792, may be found in RG 233, Reports of the Treasury Department, 1792–1793, Vol. III, National Archives.

2. H accompanied this report with a "List of petitions referred to in the Report of the 19th of November 1792." The petitioners were: Joseph Beale, whose petition was referred to H on April 13, 1790 (*Journal of the House*, I, 193); Thomas Randall of New York City, whose petition was referred to H on December 15, 1790 (*Journal of the House*, I, 337); Patrick Colvin, whose petition was referred to H on January 5, 1791 (*Journal of the House*, I, 349); John Haverd and others, whose petition was referred to H on January 11, 1791 (*Journal of the House*, I, 352); Israel Jones, whose petition on behalf of Joshua Ashbridge was referred to H on January 17, 1791 (*Journal of the House*, I, 355); sundry citizens of Pennsylvania, whose petition was referred to H on

The said several petitions seek compensation for property of the respective petitioners used, damaged or destroyed by the Army of the United States, during the late War with Great Britain.

In the course of the war, the Officers in the several departments of the civil staff were competent to the purposes of liquidating and compensating similar claims, as far as the nature of military service, and other necessary considerations would permit. But as many circumstances conspire to render this power of compensation and relief not adequate to all the cases, in which it was proper they should be applied, the United States in Congress assembled, on the 20th of February 1782 passed the following resolution.

"That a Commissioner for each State, for the purposes hereinafter expressed, be appointed, as follows. He shall be nominated by the Superintendant of the Finances of the United States, and approved of by the Legislature or the Executive of the particular State, for which he shall have been nominated; and upon the death, refusal or inability to act, of such Commissioner, another person to supply his place shall be nominated by the Superintendant of the Finances, and approved of by the Executive, or the Delegates attending in Congress, of the State, for which he shall be nominated, as the Legislature of the State shall direct: That the said Commissioner so appointed, shall have full power and authority, finally to settle the accounts between the State, for which he shall have been nominated, and the United States; that all accounts of monies advanced, supplies furnished, or services performed, between the United States and a particular State, shall be estimated according to the table of depreciation framed by the Board of Treasury on the 29th day of July 1780, in consequence of the resolution of the 28th day of June preceding, to the time the same is extended; provided always, that specific supplies, furnished pursuant to requisitions of Congress, shall be settled agreeably to the prices mentioned in such requisitions:

January 25, 1791 (*Journal of the House*, I, 362); Ezekiel Conklin and others of Orange County, New York, whose petition was submitted by Ebenezer Hazard and was referred to H on February 8, 1791 (*Journal of the House*, I, 372); Benjamin Fuller, whose petition was referred to H on February 19, 1791 (*Journal of the House*, I, 383); George and Jonathan Hunter, whose petition was referred to H on March 24, 1792 (*Journal of the House*, I, 547); Thomas Grant, surviving partner of Grant and Fine of New York City, whose petition was referred to H on April 4, 1792 (*Journal of the House*, I, 560).

That he be also fully empowered and directed to liquidate and settle in specie value all certificates given for supplies, by public Officers to individuals, and other claims against the United States by individuals, for supplies furnished the Army, the transportation thereof, and contingent expenses thereon, within the said State, according to the principles of equity and good conscience, in all cases, which are not or shall not be provided for by Congress."

"That the said Commissioners respectively give public and early notices of the times and places of their settling, and the districts within which they settle accounts, that as well the public Officers, as private individuals, may have an opportunity to attend."

"And it is hereby further recommended, to the several Legislatures of the respective States, to grant the Commissioner, by a law to be enacted for the purpose, a power to call witnesses, and examine them upon oath or affirmation, touching such claims and accounts as shall be produced, for liquidation and settlement." [3]

On the 3d of June 1784, the following resolutions were passed in Congress.

"That the Commissioners make reasonable allowance for the use of stores and other buildings, hired for the use of the United States, by persons having authority to contract for the same, but that rent be not allowed for buildings which, being abandoned by the owners, were occupied by the troops of the United States."

"That such compensation, as the Commissioners may think reasonable, be made for wood, forage, or other property of individuals, taken by order of any proper officer, or applied to, or used for the benefit of the army of the United States, upon producing to him satisfactory evidence thereof, by the testimony or one or more disinterested witnesses."

"That, according to the laws and usages of nations, a State is not obliged to make compensation for damages done to its citizens, by an enemy, or wantonly or unauthorized by its own troops; yet humanity requires that some relief should be granted to persons, who, by such losses, are reduced to indigence and want; and, as the circumstances of such sufferers are best known to the States to which they belong, that it be referred to the several States (at their own expense) to grant such relief to their citizens, who have been injured,

3. *JCC*, XXII, 84–86.

as aforesaid, as they may think requisite; and if it shall hereafter appear reasonable, that the United States should make any allowance to any particular States, who may be burthened much beyond others, that the allowance ought to be determined by Congress; but that no allowance be made by the Commissioners for settling accounts, for any charges of that kind against the United States." [4]

These resolutions appear to the Secretary to have made provision for the different descriptions of cases, as proper, all circumstances considered, as could well have been devised. If it has not answered every equitable purpose, which ought to have been answered, it must be owing to a defective execution.

It is indeed suggested, that by reason of the Commissioners not having been, a sufficient time, in the execution of their offices, from having been less time, in proportion, in some States that in others, from having used unequal degrees of diligence, many claims have failed of a settlement, as well founded as others that were adjusted, and in a greater degree in some States than in others.

There is, probably, foundation for both these suggestions; yet a remedy is both difficult and dangerous. The discretion vested in the Commissioners was originally a very delicate one. It could only be advantageously exercised by persons immediately in the scenes, where compensations were demanded, who could make a minute enquiry into circumstances, and judge of the personal character and credit of witnesses. The subsequent lapse of time has added to the difficulty of investigating satisfactorily claims, which generally rest on evidence merely oral, and which intrinsically are liable to much vagueness, exaggeration and abuse.

Many of them are barred by the Acts of limitation.[5] It is presumed, that the extreme danger of abuse, with regard to the public, is a sufficient reason for maintaining strictly that bar against claims of such a complexion, though there may be cause to regret individual hardships in consequence.

From the difference in the situation of the Accounting Officers of the Treasury, compared with that of the Commissioners, in respect to the means of investigation, a doubt has been entertained, whether

4. *JCC*, XXVII, 543.
5. *JCC*, XXIX, 866; XXXIII, 392. See also "Report on Sundry Petitions," April 16, 1792.

they were competent to the adjustment of similar claims, as far as they have been recognized by the Acts of Congress, and have been preferred in time. But on more full and mature consideration, it is conceived, that their power is competent to such adjustment, and, unless otherwise directed, they will proceed accordingly; duly impressed, nevertheless, with the necessity of extraordinary caution and circumspection.

The Secretary, upon the whole matter, respectfully submits it, as his opinion, that it is advisable, carefully to forbear a special interposition of the Legislature, in favor of similar claims.

Alexander Hamilton
Secry. of the Treasy.

Treasury Department
November 19th. 1792.

To George Washington[1]

Treasury Department November 19th 1792

Sir

I have carefully reflected on the application of Mr. Ternant, for an additional supply of money for the use of the Colony of St Domingo on account of the Debt due to France;[2] which I regard more and more as presenting a subject extremely delicate and embarrassing.

Two questions arise 1 as to the ability of the UStates to furnish the money, which is stated at about 326000 Dollars,[3] in addition

ADf, Hamilton Papers, Library of Congress; copy, with the closing in H's handwriting, Thomas Jefferson Papers, Library of Congress; LC, George Washington Papers, Library of Congress; copy, RG 233, Messages from the President, Second Congress, National Archives.

1. For earlier plans to defray the cost of supplies for Santo Domingo by using payments on the debt owed to France which the United States had incurred during the American Revolution, see Jean Baptiste de Ternant to H, September 21, 1791, February 21, March 8, 10, 1792; H to Ternant, September 21, 1791, February 21, March 8, 11, 12, 1792; William Short to H, December 28, 1791, January 26, March 24, April 22, 25, May 14, June 28, August 6, 1792; H to Short, April 10, 1792. See also Gouverneur Morris to H, November 2, 1792, note 4.

2. See H to Thomas Jefferson, first letter of November 17, 1792.

3. This figure was given by Antoine René Mathurin de La Forest in a statement of Santo Domingan needs, dated November 12, 1792, and entitled "Etat des subsistances et approvisionnemens nécéssaires, pour les troupes employées à St. Domingue, pendant les mois de Décembre 1792, Janvier et Fevrier 1793,

to the sum remaining of the 400000 Dollars some time since promised 2 as to the propriety of doing it on political considerations.

With regard to ability, I feel little doubt that it will be in the power of the Treasury to furnish the sum; yet circumstanced as we are, with the possibility of more extensive demands, than at present exist, for exigencies of a very serious nature, I think it would not be desireable to be bound by a positive stipulation for the intire amount.

With regard to the propriety of the measure on political considerations more serious difficulties occur.

The late suspension of the King, which is officially communicated, and the subsequent abolition of Royalty by the Convention, which the News papers announced with every appearance of authenticity,[4] essentially change for the moment the condition of France.

If a restoration of the King should take place, I am of opinion, that no payment which might be made in the Interval would be deemed regular or obligatory. The admission of it to our credit would consequently be considered as matter of discretion, according to the opinion entertained of its merit and utility. A payment to the newly constituted power, as a reimbursement in course, or in any manner, which would subject it to be used in support of the change, would doubtless be rejected.

An advance, however, to supply the urgent necessities of a part of the French Empire struggling under the misfortune of an insurrection of the nature of that which has for some time distressed and now exposes to the danger of total ruin by Famine the colony of St Domingo is of a different complexion. Succours furnished in such a situation, under due limitations, would be so clearly an act of humanity and friendship, of such evident utility to the French Empire, that no future government could refuse to allow a credit for them without a disregard of moderation and Equity. But the claim for

---

etabli d'après celui addressé par les administrateurs, calculé pour 4 mois à commencer de Novembre" (letterpress copy, Thomas Jefferson Papers, Library of Congress).

4. The letter which Morris wrote to Jefferson on August 16, 1792, concerning the suspension of the King was endorsed by Jefferson as having been received on October 24, 1792 (ALS, RG 59, Despatches from United States Ministers to France, 1789–1869, June 17, 1792–March 7, 1794, National Archives). An account of proceedings in the Convention concerning the abolition of the monarchy appeared in the November 21, 1792, issue of the [Philadelphia] *Gazette of the United States.*

such credit would not be of a nature to be regularly and of course valid; consequently would be liable to be disputed.

The condition in which the Colony has lately placed itself by espousing the last change which has been made in France,[5] operates as a serious difficulty in the case and may be made a ground of objection to any aid which may be given them.

There is even a question whether there be now any organ of the French nation which can regularly ask the succour—whether the Commission to Mr. Ternant be not virtually superseded.

It is also an objection (in the view of regularity and validity) to the supply asked, that the Decree of the National Assembly, on which it is founded, contemplated a negotiation between the Executive Power in France and our Minister there.[6] The Channel has not been pursued and no substitute has been provided. The business wants organisation in every sense.

From these premisses I deduce, that nothing can be done without risk to the United States—that therefore *as little as possible* ought to be done—that whatever may be done should be cautiously restricted to the single idea *of preserving the colony from* destruction by *Famine*—that in all communications on the subject care should be taken to put it on this footing & even to avoid the explicit recognition of any regular authority in any person.

Under these cautions and restrictions (but not otherwise) I beg leave to submit it as my opinion, that succours ought to be granted; notwithstanding the degree of risk which will attend it. That they should be effected by occasional advances without previous stipulation, and with only a general assurance that the United States dis-

5. H is presumably referring to the defeat of Jean Jacques Pierre Desparbès at the end of October, 1792, and the victory of the commissioners sent from France with the support of the "Amis de la Convention nationale" (Saintoyant, *La Colonisation Française pendant la Révolution*, II, 120–21). The [Philadelphia] *National Gazette* and [Philadelphia] *Gazette of the United States* contain only brief reports of these events. The November 17, 1792, issue of the *National Gazette* contains the following account: "Considerable disturbances have recently happened in Cape-François; in which the patriotic party have been prevalent. One officer of the counter-revolution party was put to death, and about fifty other obnoxious persons shipped off to take their trial in old France, on a charge of having fomented the rebellion of the negroes, in concert with the anti-revolutionists in the mother-country."

6. H is referring to a decree passed by the Legislative Assembly on June 26, 1792. See Morris to H, September 25, 1792, note 8.

posed to contribute by friendly offices to the preservation of an important portion of the French empire and to that of French Citizens from the calamity of Famine will endeavour from time to time as far as circumstances shall permit to afford means of sustenance.

According to a statement of M. Dela Foret [7] the provisions desired to be shipped in the course of November would amount to 83.800 Dollars including the total supply of Fish & Oil. Towards this he computes the application of 50000 Dollars out of the remainder of the 400000 Dollars heretofore promised which would leave a deficiency of 38.800 Dollar. This sum or in round numbers 40000 Dollars can be engaged to be furnished—and in December if no future circumstances forbid a further sum can be engaged to be supplied payable at a future short period. It will be proper that the most precise measures should be taken to ascertain from time to time the investment of the monies supplied in purchasing and forwarding provisions from this Country to the Colony in question.

It has been heretofore understood that the ballance of the sum some time since stipulated was to be furnished; which accordingly has been and is doing.[8]

Engagements for supplies have been entered into upon the basis of that stipulation & payments to as great if not a greater amount are becoming due in which the Citizens of the UStates are materially interested.

The caution which is deemed necessary has reference not only to

7. See note 3. La Forest's statement concludes with a "Résumé général" which reads as follows: "Les fonds nécéssaires pour alimenter St. Domingue jusqu'au ler. Mars 1793 se montent par l'état sy-joint à 178,310 Piastres. En admettant que les traités de l'administration posterieure à l'advertissement mis dans les gazettes le 8 Aout, et qui se montent en total à 140,000 dollars, ne soient acquittées que jusqu'à concurrence du 8. Sepe. et seulment pour fourniture de comestibles faite par les citoyens des Etats unis, ou leurs correspondans, il y en resultera que sur les 100,000 dollars du payement echéant au ler. Xbre., il y en aura seulement 50,000. d'employé à la solde des traites, et que le reste servira aux achats actuels . . . cy . . . 50,000 Piastres. La Trésorerie des Etats Unis auroit donc encore à pourvoir au payement de 128,310 aux epoques fixées dans l'etat cy-joint pour les envoys d'ici à St. Domingue.

"Pe. Me.

"Complement des 4,000,000₶ tournois– 326,000 Piastres
environ à payer comme cy-dessus.... 128,310
difference restant à acquitter........ 197,690."

(Letterpress copy, Thomas Jefferson Papers, Library of Congress.)

8. See Ternant to H, June 26, August 22, October 8, November 15, 1792.

the safety of the UStates in a pecuniary respect but to the consideration of avoiding a dangerous commitment, which may even prove a source of misunderstanding between this Country and the future Government of the French Nation. From all that is hitherto known there is no ground to conclude that the Governing Power by the last advices will be of long duration.

To the President and Directors of the Bank of the United States

Treasury Department
November 20, 1792.

Gentlemen

According to advices received from Amsterdam dated August 30th. 1792,[1] I have good ground to conclude that there is a sum in the hands of our Bankers there,[2] not less than 1,250.000 florins subject to my order; but though there is a moral certainty of this being the case, there are circumstances which admit a bare possibility of the contrary. It is proper to apprise you of this, as a preliminary to the proposition I am going to make—as well on the score of propriety as for the purpose of serving as a guide to your determination and conduct.

If as I understand to be probably the case you have occasion to establish a fund in Europe I propose to you the following arrangement vizt.—

I will cause the Treasurer to draw in favor of whomsoever you shall designate for a sum in guilders equal to 500.000 Dollars at the rate of 36⁴⁄₁₁ pence Pennsyla Curry ℔ Guilder.

His draft or drafts to be at your disposal to be remitted on your own account and the amount to be passed to the Credit of the United States as on the first of January next. If a law shall be passed to authorise the measure, it shall operate as a payment at that period by the United States to the Bank, on account of the loan made to them pursuant to the XIth. Section of the Act which incorporates your institution.[3] If no such law shall be passed it shall remain as a Credit to the Government, but not liable to be made use of, until information shall be received that the Bills have been accepted and paid.

In case of non payment contrary to expectation, the Credit which shall have been given to be refunded; but in such case no damages nor interest on the bills are to be demanded. With respectful consideration, I have the honor to be, Gentlemen,

Your Obedt. Servant

Alexander Hamilton
Secy of the Treasy

The President & Directors
of the Bank of the
United States.

LS, from the Straus Autograph Collection on deposit in the Princeton University Library, with the permission of Mr. Oscar S. Straus, New York City.

1. See William Short to H, August 30, 1792.

2. Willink, Van Staphorst, and Hubbard.

3. "An Act to incorporate the subscribers to the Bank of the United States" (1 *Stat.* 196 [February 25, 1791]). See "Draft of George Washington's Fourth Annual Address to Congress," October 15–31, 1792, note 20.

From Robert Purviance[1]

Baltimore, November 20, 1792. "One hundred and forty six Quarter Casks wine were imported. . . . After they were landed, it was discovered that nine of the Casks had sustained damage during the voyage by leakage. . . . The importer claims a deduction of duties in consequence of the leakage, but as all the ullage casks *together* are worth as much or more than first cost the collecter[2] doubts the propriety [of] making him any allowance, and as this case will often occur he wishes to be instructed by you."

ADf, RG 53, "Old Correspondence," Baltimore Collector, National Archives.

1. Purviance was naval officer for the port of Baltimore.

2. Otho H. Williams.

Report on Several Petitions

[Philadelphia, November 20, 1792
Communicated on November 22, 1792][1]

[To the Speaker of the House of Representatives]

The Secretary of the Treasury, to whom were referred the several petitions specified in the list herewith transmitted,[2] respectfully reports thereupon.

That the objects of the said several petitions have either been subsequently considered and decided upon, by the legislature, or have been comprised in general reports heretofore submitted, whereby a special report thereupon is rendered unnecessary.

Which is humbly submitted, Alexander Hamilton,
Secry. of the Treasry.

Treasury Department
November 20, 1792.

Copy, RG 233, Reports of the Treasury Department, 1792–1793, Vol. III, National Archives.

1. *Journal of the House,* I, 625–26. The communicating letter, dated November 21, 1792, may be found in RG 233, Reports of the Treasury Department, 1792–1793, Vol. III, National Archives.

2. H accompanied this report with a "List of petitions referred to in the report of the 20th of November 1792," which included the names of thirteen petitioners.

James Hubbs petitioned against an action which the United States had brought against him for an infraction of the revenue laws on the grounds that "at the time of committing the offence, he was wholly ignorant" of the Collection Law. Hubb's petition was read in the House of Representatives and referred to H on January 18, 1790 (*Journal of the House,* I, 142). Subsequent consideration of the general problem raised by this petition resulted in "An Act to provide for mitigating or remitting the forfeitures and penalties accruing under the revenue laws, in certain cases therein mentioned" (1 *Stat.* 122–23 [May 26, 1790]).

Several of the petitions which H returned to the House of Representatives at this time had been received before revised revenue legislation had been enacted. Included in this group of petitions were: the petition of merchants and other inhabitants of Portland in the District of Maine, which had been referred to H on January 29, 1790 (*Journal of the House,* I, 147, 149); the petition of sundry inhabitants of Salem, Massachusetts, which had been referred to H on February 9, 1790 (*Journal of the House,* I, 154); and the "memorial of sundry merchants and traders, of the town of Newburyport," Massachusetts, which had been referred to H on April 9, 1790 (*Journal of the House,* I, 191). See also "Report on Defects in the Existing Laws of Revenue," April 22, 1790.

H also returned "A petition of Isaac Osgood and Sons . . . praying that Congress would grant a sum of money, loan, bounty, or other encouragement, to the manufacture of malt-liquors in the United States" (*Journal of the House,* I, 343). The subject of this petition, which was referred to H on December 27, 1790, was considered in H's "Report on the Subject of Manufactures," December 5, 1791.

H also returned four petitions concerning increased compensation for revenue officers, a subject which he had discussed in his "Report on Compensation of Officers Employed in the Collection of the Revenue," April 5, 1792. Three petitions of inspectors of customs from New York, Philadelphia, and Baltimore had been referred to H during January and February, 1791 (*Journal* of the House, I, 352, 357, 363, 366, 376). H returned a similar petition from Joseph Whipple, the collector of customs at Portsmouth, New Hampshire, which had been referred to him on February 27, 1792 (*Journal of the House*, I, 521).

On October 27, 1791, the House referred to H a "petition of sundry persons residing in the Western Territory . . . between Fort Washington and the Little Miami" (*Journal of the House*, I, 441). The Miami Purchase was affected by two acts subsequent to the receipt of this petition: "An Act for ascertaining the Bounds of a Tract of Land purchased by John Cleves Symmes" (1 *Stat.* 251–52 [April 12, 1792]) and "An Act authorizing the grant and conveyance of certain Lands to John Cleves Symmes, and his Associates" (1 *Stat.* 266–67 [May 5, 1792]).

On December 20, 1791, the House referred to H "A petition of Jabez Bowen, Commissioner of Loans in the State of Rhode Island, . . . praying to be allowed the expense of stationery and clerk hire until the first day of October next" (*Journal of the House*, I, 478). See "An Act for making compensations to the Commissioners of Loans for extraordinary expenses" (1 *Stat.* 284 [May 8, 1792]).

On February 25, 1791, the House of Representatives referred to H a "petition of Brown and Francis praying to be reimbursed the amount of the second duty paid by the petitioners on sundry goods of foreign manufacture, which were exported by them from the United States, and afterwards imported into the same" (*Journal of the House*, I, 391). See also Jeremiah Olney to H, October 22, 1790.

From Tench Coxe

Treasury Department, Revenue Office, November 21, 1792. Encloses copy of a letter "this day received from James Read Esquire, Inspector of the Revenue for the first Survey of North Carolina."

LC, RG 58, Letters of Commissioner of Revenue, 1792–1793, National Archives.

From Thomas Jefferson[1]

[Philadelphia, November 21, 1792]

Th: Jefferson has the honour to inclose to the Secretary of the Treasury a copy of his letter to M. de Ternant,[2] communicated to the President & approved by him; also a copy of the note of approbation from the French court of which he spoke to him,[3] with the estimate of M. de la Forest[4] which the Secretary of the Treasury might perhaps wish to keep by him.

Nov. 21. 92.

AL, letterpress copy, Thomas Jefferson Papers, Library of Congress; LC, Papers of the Continental Congress, National Archives.

1. For background concerning the request of Jean Baptiste de Ternant for additional aid for Santo Domingo, see H to George Washington, November 19, 1792. See also H to Jefferson, two letters of November 17, November 19, 1792.

2. Jefferson's letter to Ternant of November 20, 1792, reads in part as follows: "Your letter on the subject of further supplies to the Colony of St. Domingo, has been duly received and considered. When the distress of that Colony first broke forth, we thought we could not better evidence our friendship to that, and to the mother country also, than to step in to it's relief, on your application, without waiting a formal authorization from the national Assembly. As the case was unforeseen, so it was unprovided for on their part, and we did what we doubted not they would have desired us to do, had there been time to make the application, and what we presumed they would sanction as soon as known to them. We have now been going on more than a twelve-month, in making advances for the relief of the Colony, without having as yet received any such sanction; for the Decree of 4 millions of Livres in aid of the Colony, besides the circuitous and informal manner by which we became acquainted with it, describes and applies to operations very different from those which have actually taken place. The wants of the Colony appear likely to continue, and their reliance on our supplies to become habitual. We feel every disposition to continue our efforts for administering to those wants; but that cautious attention to forms, which would have been unfriendly in the first moment, becomes a duty to ourselves; when the Business assumes the appearance of long continuance, and respectful also to the National assembly itself, who have a right to prescribe the line of an interference so materially interesting to the mother country and the Colony.

"By the estimate you were pleased to deliver me, we perceive that there will be wanting to carry the Colony through the month of December, between 30 & 40,000 Dollars, in addition to the sums before engaged to you. I am authorized to inform you that the sum of 40,000 Dollars shall be paid to your orders at the Treasury of the united States, and to assure you that we feel no abatement in our dispositions to contribute these aids from time to time, as they shall be wanting for the necessary subsistence of the Colony: but the want of express approbation from the national legislature must ere long produce a presumption that they contemplate perhaps other modes of relieving the Colony, and dictate to us the propriety of doing only what they shall have regularly and previously sanctioned. . . ." (Letterpress copy, Thomas Jefferson Papers, Library of Congress.)

3. On June 13, 1792, Ternant had sent to Jefferson an extract from a letter dated December 31, 1791, from Claude Antoine de Valdec de Lessart, who was French Minister of Foreign Affairs from November 28, 1791, to March 17, 1792. De Lessart's letter, which Ternant received on June 12, 1792, reads as follows: "J'ai mis sous les yeux du Roi le compte que vous avez rendu de la mission du St. Roustan, et des démarches que vous avez faites pour procurer des Secours à L'Isle de St. Domingue. Sa majesté a autant approuvé votre conduite, qu'Elle a été sensible à l'empressement avec lequel les ministres americains ont accueilli vos demandes; vous voudrez bien le leur faire connaitre et assurer particuliérement M. le Président des Etats unis combien Elle sait apprécier les sentiments qui l'ont dirigé dans cette facheuse occurrence" (letterpress copy, Thomas Jefferson Papers, Library of Congress).

4. See H to Washington, November 19, 1792, note 3.

Report on the Petition of Joseph Ball and Isaac Ledyard

[Philadelphia, November 21, 1792
Communicated on November 22, 1792] [1]

[To the Speaker of the House of Representatives]
The Secretary of the Treasury, to whom was referred by the House of Representatives the petition of Joseph Ball and Isaac Ledyard,[2] respectfully submits the following report thereupon.

The said petition contains the following suggestions.

"That an armed Dutch Ship, named the Renown, owned chiefly by Mr. John Ball, Burgher of St. Eustatius, and employed by him in a trade between that place and Virginia, was, on the 4th. day of March 1781, in the Bay of Chesapeake, having on board her cargo, consisting of one hundred and eighty three hogsheads of Crop Tobacco, manned and equipped for sea, with twenty carriage guns, and a sufficient supply of small arms and ammunition, and then having received sailing orders."

"That at this time, and under these circumstances, the said Ship was impressed by the honorable Thomas Jefferson Esquire, then Governor of the State of Virginia, with the advice of their Council of State, to co-operate with General Baron Steuben, in an attack which was then meditated against a British Army in Portsmouth, under the command of General Arnold." [3]

"That Captain William Lewis,[4] her commander, did enter regular protest."

Copy, RG 233, Reports of the Treasury Department, 1792–1793, Vol. III, National Archives.

1. *Journal of the House*, I, 225–26. The communicating letter, dated November 21, 1792, may be found in RG 233, Reports of the Treasury Department, 1792–1793, Vol. III, National Archives.

2. On February 16, 1791, the House of Representatives received the petition of "Joseph Ball, acting executor of John Ball, deceased, and Isaac Ledyard . . . praying the liquidation and settlement of claims against the United States.

"*Ordered*, That the said . . . [petition] be referred to the Secretary of the Treasury, with instruction to examine the same, and report his opinion thereupon to the House." (*Journal of the House*, I, 380.)

3. In December, 1780, two months after his escape to the British lines, Benedict Arnold had been placed in command of a British force in Virginia.

4. On October 22, 1791, Lewis, who was applying for appointment as keeper

"That her Cargo was relanded to fit her for war, and afterwards destroyed by the British, when they took and burned Norfolk."

"That soon after, a British fleet came to the relief of their troops in Portsmouth. That the ship Renown was pursued up the river, as far as was practicable for ships of her burthen to go, and there taken. That his Excellency Governor Jefferson, in Council, caused the ship and cargo to be valued, and warranted them against all losses and detentions in consequence of the seizure. That the command of the ship was afterwards assumed by General Baron Steuben, with consent of his Excellency Governor Jefferson, and that he did, in like manner, as before by Governor Jefferson, warrant the property in the name and behalf of the United States. All which appears by original and attested papers, copies of which are hereunto subjoined. That Hunter, Banks and Company,[5] who were agents for the said ship in Virginia, did petition the Legislature of that State,[6] praying pay for said Ship and Cargo, and their Committee did report, as above, but more fully, and that order should issue on their Treasurer for payment, which report was not acted upon.[7] That some time

---

of the lighthouse at Cape Henry, wrote to Thomas Jefferson: "I have been a great suffrer in the Impressment of my Ship. I have yours & Baron Steuben's Official letters pledging Payment If any damage should Arise that should be reimbursed. My property was small in the Ship but if I could have obtained it I should have been much more Comfortable than I am at present perhaps your Excellency Can point out some mode, where I can get some redress . . ." (ALS, George Washington Papers, Library of Congress). See H to Jefferson, October 22, 1792; Jefferson to H, October 22, 1792. See also Boyd, *Papers of Thomas Jefferson,* V, 57.

For Lewis's appointment as lighthouse keeper at Cape Henry, see Tobias Lear to H, October 13, 1792; H to Lear, October 18, 1792; Tench Coxe to H, October 31, 1792.

5. Hunter, Banks, and Company had been formed by John Banks and James Hunter of Fredericksburg, Virginia. Secret partners of the firm were Major Ichabod Burnet and Major Robert Forsyth. Charles Pettit was the company's agent in Philadelphia. For the relationship of this firm with Major General Nathanael Greene and the purchase of supplies for the southern army during the American Revolution, see "Report on the Petition of Catharine Greene," December 26, 1791.

6. During the spring, 1782, session of the Virginia Assembly, the petition of John Ball and John Kendall for two ships lost in circumstances similar to those in which the *Renown* was lost was presented to the Assembly (copy, Archives Division, Virginia State Library, Richmond). Hunter, Banks, and Company was agent for Ball and Kendall's ships. The petition is endorsed "May 28th. 1782 referred to propositions."

7. The Library of Congress was unable to find the journals for the spring, 1782, session of the Virginia Assembly when it was compiling its Microfilm Collection of Early State Records.

after Mr. Ball came, himself, to America, renewed the application to the State of Virginia, and continued his solicitations until September 1786, when he died in Virginia. That the State of Virginia did finally refuse to pay for the Ship, but agreed to pay her hire.[8] That Mr. Ball being, for a long time, absent from America, was unacquainted with the propriety of presenting his claim to the Auditors and Comptrollers of accounts of the United States, and looking to them for payment, the ship being lost in their service, and the property warranted by their General, and then Commander in chief in that department. That by the death of Mr. Ball, and derangement of the affairs of Hunter, Banks, and Company, your petitioners could not be in possession of the necessary vouchers and information, to establish their claim against the United States, before the present Session of your honorable House."

The Copy of a Report, (which is presumed to be authentic) [9] of a Committee of the House of Delegates of Virginia, states the transaction which is the subject of the said petition, in the following manner.

"It appears to your Committee, that the said Ball, Hunter, Banks and Company, were on the fourth day of March, in the year of our Lord 1781, owners of the Ship, Renown: That the said Ship was then in port in James River within this Commonwealth, commanded by Captain William Lewis, loaded with one hundred and eighty three hogsheads of Crop Tobacco, from the Warehouses of Shockoes and Birds, mounting twenty guns, provided with a considerable

8. A second petition of John Ball was presented in the Virginia Assembly on December 9, 1785, and referred to the Committee on Claims (*Journal of the House of Delegates of Virginia,* 79–80, Microfilm Collection of Early State Records, Library of Congress). The committee reported on December 31, 1785, that the payment for use of the *Renown* should be made, but that no indemnity for her loss could be made in view of the testimony which indicated that the ship would have been unable to escape the British even if she had not been impressed (*Journal of the House of Delegates of Virginia,* 122, Microfilm Collection of Early State Records, Library of Congress).

9. Although the journals of the spring, 1782, session of the Virginia Assembly have not been found, the copies of the two petitions in the Virginia State Library leave no reason to doubt the authenticity of the report. The words in Ball and Kendall's petition which are not part of the report of the Committee on Claims to which H is referring have been underlined. The cover of Ball's 1785 petition contains a certificate, dated December 8, 1785, the day before the petition was presented, which states: "The Auditors do not conceive themselves authorized to make any allowance for the within Vessel & Cargo, but consider the claims as properly cognizable before the Genl. Assembly."

quantity of good musquets, ammunition and stores, equipped for sea, and destined originally to St. Eustatius, but afterwards to France, when the capture of that Island was announced; That on the said fourth day of March 1781, Thomas Jefferson Esquire, then Governor, meditating a descent upon the garrison of Portsmouth, in conjunction with a French squadron then daily expected within the Capes, issued, with the advice of the Council of State, an Order for engaging voluntarily or impressing all the armed Vessels of private property, which could be immediately collected together, with the whole of the equipments directing them to be employed in the purpose aforesaid. That the said William Lewis obeyed the impress made of the ship, and was assured by a letter from Governor Jefferson, dated in Council on the 8th day of March 1781, that his vessel and her loading were considered, as at the risque of the State, and that a reasonable hire should be paid for the use of the said Vessel and her crew. That the said ship, after having been first appraised, by order of the Governor, was employed in public service, and with the military view aforesaid, for the space of twenty six days, to wit, from the said fourth day of March 1781, to the thirtieth day of the same month in the same year: That during that time, it appears, that the said ship might have proceeded to sea, without the danger of capture, since several vessels did actually sail from James River, and escape into the Ocean, and afterwards arrive at their destined ports in safety, and since the British Cruisers were obliged to confine themselves within the Elizabeth river, from an apprehension of the French naval armament, which remained in the neighborhood of Portsmouth, for a considerable time: That on the said thirtieth day of March 1781, the said ship being discharged from public service, could not prosecute her intended voyage, by reason of the derangement which took place, in consequence of her having been impressed, as aforesaid, and of the arrival of a large fleet of British ships of War in James river. That the said ship attempted to elude their hostility, by proceeding up the said river to Osborne's Warehouses, being the highest point of navigation for vessels of her burthen. That the British fleet also moving up the said river, and the British land forces marching to Osborne's, the said ship was, some time in the month of April 1781, captured, with her rigging, tackle, apparel, furniture and cargo, and was wholly lost to the said Ball, Hunter, Banks and

Company; for which loss, they have neither hitherto received any compensation, nor indeed have they, as yet, obtained any satisfaction for the services rendered to the Commonwealth, by the said Ship, except a small sum on account of the wages of the Marines of the said Ship."

"That the said ship, with her guns, tackle and apparel, was appraised by three merchants, and valued to be worth eight hundred thousand pounds of James River upper inspected Tobacco."

"That her cargo on board amounted to one hundred and ninety five thousand four hundred and ninety six pounds of Richmond Tobacco."

And the same report, upon that state of facts, submits two resolutions, in the following words—

"Resolved, that it is the opinion of this Committee, that the loss of the said ship and her cargo was occasioned by her being impressed into the service of this Commonwealth."

"Resolved, that it is the opinion of this Committee, that the Auditors of public Accounts ought to audit the demand of the said Ball, Hunter, Banks and Company, for the loss of the said ship and her cargo, and to grant a Warrant upon the Treasurer, payable in [10] months, for the amount of what shall appear due to the said Ball, Hunter, Banks and Company thereupon."

It is represented, that this report was referred to a Committee of the whole House, but never acted upon.

No document is produced, as alledged in the petition, shewing that Major General De Steuben "did warrant the property in the name and behalf of the United States."

There is indeed produced a copy of a letter dated the 8th of January 1781,[11] from the Officer, addressed "to the Commodore or commanding Officer of the armed merchant vessels lying at, or above Osborne's," which, after directing him to proceed down the river with the vessels under his command, to endeavor to intercept some small vessels, belonging to the enemy, lying in Appamatox, adds this assurance "Should any damage happen to any part of your fleet, I do hereby assure you, in the name of the United States, that satisfaction shall be made to the Owners, by the public."

But besides that this appears to be a special guarantee for a special

10. Space left blank in MS.
11. Copy, Archives Division, Virginia State Library, Richmond.

enterprize, it is more than two months prior to the impress of the Ship Renown (the first order for which, issued by the Governor of Virginia, was not till the 4th of March following) [12] and could therefore have no reference to that vessel.

As to the assumption of the command of the said Ship by Major General De Steuben, the following facts appear.

1st. That the said General, on the 9th of the same month of March wrote a letter, addressed to the Commodore of the Fleet,[13] lying at Hood's, (who is understood to have been the Commander of the Renown) directing him, in consequence of the Bay and rivers being entirely commanded by the British Vessels, not to proceed lower down the river, than Hood's, but to remain there with all the vessels, that came down, 'till further orders.

2nd. That the said General, on the 14th of the same month of March, wrote a letter, addressed to Captain Lewis of the Renown,[14] among other things, directing him to deliver all the Musquet-cartridges on board the vessels from Richmond, to Mr. Lureman; adding, "if Captain Pryor [15] is arrived, he will take the trouble off your hands."

3d. That the said General, on the 17th of March, wrote another letter, addressed to Captain Lewis of the Renown,[16] in these words,—"Whilst the enemy command the water, the situation of our vessels at Hood's seems not altogether safe. I think it, therefore, advisable, that you order all the vessels to go up as high as Turkey Island. This will make very little difference, in point of time, when they are wanted down, and will ensure them from any danger from the enemy." This letter is accompanied by one of the same date, from John Walker to Captain Lewis,[17] informing him, that the removal to Turkey Island, directed by the said General, was by the desire of the Governor of the State.

4th. That the said General, on the 24th of April following,

12. Copy, Archives Division, Virginia State Library, Richmond.
13. Copy, Archives Division, Virginia State Library, Richmond.
14. Copy, Archives Division, Virginia State Library, Richmond.
15. John Pryor was commissary of military stores.
16. Copy, Archives Division, Virginia State Library, Richmond.
17. Copy, Archives Division, Virginia State Library, Richmond.
Walker, who was an aide-de-camp to von Steuben during the spring of 1781, had been nominated by Jefferson as a liason officer between the Virginia Council and von Steuben because Walker's former membership in the Council made him familiar with its procedures.

wrote another letter, addressed to Captain Lewis of the Renown,[18] in these words.

"The enemy's movements indicate an intention to penetrate up the river, they are now near City point; should they have hazarded a force inferior to what we have, so high up, I think it would be shameful and unpardonable in us to permit it. What is the force of the vessels they have up, I do not yet know; so soon as it is ascertained, I will acquaint you, and, in the mean time, I beg you to have the vessels at Osborne's in readiness, that in case a favorable opportunity should offer, of striking a stroke, you may be able to embrace it, at a moments warning. Any number of militia, that may be necessary, shall be ready to be put on board."

It does not appear, from any of the documents produced, that the said General had been advised of the discharge of the Renown, from the service of the State; which was done by a letter from the Governor in Council, dated the 29th of March 1781.[19]

It appears, that on the 4th of March 1781, a commission issued under the seal of the Commonwealth of Virginia, to Captain Lewis, constituting him Captain of an armed Vessel in the service of the Commonwealth, so long as he should remain within the Bays, rivers, or other waters of the said Commonwealth.[20]

Upon the foregoing state of facts, and a careful attention to the several documents, which accompany the petition, the Secretary is of Opinion.

That nothing has been shewn, amounting to a guarantee of the said vessel, either actual or virtual, on behalf of the United States, and that, consequently, whatever claim of indemnity may exist, is against the Commonwealth of Virginia.

Such, too, appears to have been the clear sense of the parties. Of that Commonwealth only, has relief been sought, 'till the period of the present application to Congress. The Committee of the House of Delegates evidently viewed the State of Virginia, as alone responsible. No allusion is made by them, to any responsibility on the part of the United States.

18. Copy, Archives Division, Virginia State Library, Richmond.
19. Copy, Archives Division, Virginia State Library, Richmond.
20. DS, in the handwriting of Jefferson, Thomas Jefferson Papers, Library of Congress.

The directions, at different times given by Major General De Steuben, wear no other complexion, than that of directions given to a vessel in the service of the State of Virginia. This view of them, on the 17th of March, at least, is confirmed by a letter of Mr. Walker, to Captain Lewis. The presumption is, that the same impression continued on the 24th of April.

The Secretary forbears to urge the objection of the Acts of limitation,[21] which bar the claim, as against the United States; because, if it had been otherwise well-founded, he should be strongly inclined to the opinion, that the circumstances are sufficiently special, to justify an exception in its favor.[22]

All which is humbly submitted. Alexander Hamilton,
Secry. of the Treasry.

Treasury Department,
November 21st 1792.

21. *JCC*, XXIX, 866; XXXIII, 392. See also "Report on Sundry Petitions," April 16, 1792.

22. On March 2, 1793, the House of Representatives considered the petition and "*Ordered*, That the petitioners have leave to withdraw their said petition" (*Journal of the House*, I, 733).

Report on the Petition of George Blanchard

[Philadelphia, November 21, 1792
Communicated on November 22, 1792] [1]

[To the Speaker of the House of Representatives]

The Secretary of the Treasury, to whom was referred by the House of Representatives, the petition of George Blanchard,[2] respectfully submits the following Report thereupon.

The petition seeks compensation for services alleged to have been performed, under the order of the Navy-Board for the eastern department, by Edward Blanchard; stating, that the accounts for those services were rendered, in due time, to the Clerk of that Board; but that, owing to their not being preferred, according to the requisitions of the several Acts of limitation,[3] the accounting Officers of the Treasury now deem themselves restrained from adjusting them.

It has been heretofore stated to the House of Representatives, that the accounts of the said Navy-Board had not been settled.[4]

It is represented to the Secretary, that serious difficulties stand in the way of a final and satisfactory adjustment.

Upon the books of the Board, Edward Blanchard stands charged with sundry sums advanced in old Emission, which together amount to £8.300. money of Massachusetts, but only one entry to his credit appears, for a Bill against the Ship Boston, amounting to £134 like money.

Search has been made among the papers of the Board, deposited in the Treasury, but the accounts, alleged to have been delivered to the Clerk of the Board, have not been found.

It appears, that on the 14th of March 1787, Edward Blanchard wrote to Benjamin Walker, Commissioner for settling the accounts of the Marine Department, informing him, in general terms, of his claim, and stating the exhibition of his accounts to the Clerk of the Board; that in a reply to this letter of the 23d of the same month, the Commissioner informs Mr. Blanchard, that the different sums, paid him, stood against him on the books of the Board, that no accounts of his were to be found among their papers, and that it was necessary, he should furnish his accounts from the beginning (the sooner, the better)—That this intimation of the Commissioner appears to have remained unanswered, 'till the first of April 1789, when Mr. Blanchard wrote to the Commissioner, apologizing for the delay, ascribing it to his ill health, hurry of business, and the hope of again finding the accounts which were delivered to the Clerk of Board; adding, that they were then drawn over and should be forwarded for settlement, when he should please to direct, which accounts were forwarded to the Auditor's Office, some time in .[5]

From these facts it will result, that the case is one, which requires a cautious treatment. Considering the state of the accounts of the Navy-Board, the delay which has ensued, a settlement now on principles safe and satisfactory, in reference to the public, cannot be unattended with material difficulty; but imperfect means of investigation being to be had. In connection, too, with other cases, in which the accounts of the public Officers, which are incapable of being settled, or are destroyed, could alone furnish adequate evidence of the merit of claims, the precedent of a relaxation of the Acts of limitation, if they are a bar in this instance, would be an inconvenient one.

If those Acts present no bar, no special interposition of the Legislature is necessary. The claim will be considered and decided upon, in the course of the Treasury, whenever the state of the accounts of the Navy-Board shall afford sufficient light.

The Secretary, upon the whole matter, is, with all deference, of opinion, that it is advisable to leave the petitioner to the course of Treasury settlement.[6]

Which is humbly submitted, Alexander Hamilton,
Secry of the Treasry.

Treasury Department
November 21st 1792.

Copy, RG 233, Reports of the Treasury Department, 1792–1793, Vol. III, National Archives.

1. *Journal of the House*, I, 625–26. The communicating letter, dated November 21, 1792, may be found in RG 233, Reports of the Treasury Department, 1792–1793, Vol. III, National Archives.

2. On January 13, 1792, the House of Representatives received a "petition of James Blanchard, on behalf of Edward Blanchard, praying the settlement of an account for services rendered by said Edward, as truckman, by order of the Navy Board of the Eastern Department, during the late war.

"*Ordered*, That the said . . . [petition] be referred to the Secretary of the Treasury, with instruction to examine the same, and report his opinion thereupon to the House." (*Journal of the House*, I, 492.)

3. *JCC*, XXIX, 866; XXXIII, 392. See also "Report on Sundry Petitions," April 16, 1792.

4. See "Report on the Petition of the Executors of Edward Carnes," February 28, 1792.

5. Space left blank in MS.

6. On December 18, 1794, the President approved "An Act to authorize the officers of the Treasury to audit and pass the account of the late Edward Blanchard, deceased" (6 *Stat.* 18).

Report on the Petition of Benjamin Brown

[Philadelphia, November 21, 1792
Communicated on November 22, 1792] [1]

[To the Speaker of the House of Representatives]

The Secretary of the Treasury, to whom was referred, by the House of Representatives, the petition of Benjamin Brown,[2] submits the following Report thereupon.

The Act of the last Session, entitled "An Act providing for the settlement of the claims of persons under particular circumstances barred by the limitations heretofore established," [3] removes all obstacles to the claim of the petitioner, arising from the Acts of limitation[4] if otherwise well founded.

But it appears, that Peter Greene, Attorney to Benjamin Brown, received, on the 13th of August 1788, a Certificate from the Commissioner for settling the accounts of the Marine Department, for the balance of pay due to said Brown for his services on board the Frigate Trumbull; which satisfies the claim of the petitioner.

Respectfully submitted, Alexander Hamilton
Secry of the Treasry.

Treasury Department
November 21st 1792.

Copy, RG 233, Reports of the Treasury Department, 1792–1793, Vol. III, National Archives.

1. *Journal of the House,* I, 625–26. The communicating letter, dated November 21, 1792, may be found in RG 233, Reports of the Treasury Department, 1792–1793, Vol. III, National Archives.

2. On July 30, 1790, the petition of Benjamin Brown was "presented to the House and read . . . praying the liquidation and settlement of a claim against the United States.

"*Ordered,* That the said . . . [petition] be referred to the Secretary of the Treasury, with instruction to examine the same, and report his opinion thereupon to the House." (*Journal of the House,* I, 285.)

3. Section 1 of this act reads as follows: "*Be it enacted by the Senate and House of Representatives of the United States of America in Congress assembled,* That the operation of the resolutions of the late Congress of the United States, passed on the second day of November, one thousand seven hundred and eighty-five, and the twenty-third day of July, one thousand seven hundred and eighty-seven, so far as they have barred, or may be construed to bar the claims of any officer, soldier, artificer, sailor or marine of the late army or navy of the United States, for personal services rendered to the United States, in the military or naval department, shall from and after the passing of this act, be suspended, for and during the term of two years. And that every such officer, soldier, artificer, sailor and marine having claims for services rendered to the United States, in the military or naval departments, who shall exhibit the same, for liquidation, at the treasury of the United States, at any time during the said term of two years, shall be entitled to an adjustment, and allowance thereof on the same principles, as if the same had been exhibited, within the term prescribed by the aforesaid resolutions of Congress: *Provided,* That nothing herein shall be construed to extend to claims for rations or subsistence money" (1 *Stat.* 245 [March 27, 1792]).

4. *JCC,* XXIX, 866; XXXIII, 392. See also "Report on Sundry Petitions," April 16, 1792.

Report on the Petition of Pitman Collins

[Philadelphia, November 21, 1792
Communicated on November 22, 1792] [1]

[To the Speaker of the House of Representatives]

The Secretary of the Treasury, to whom was referred, by the House of Representatives the petition of Pitman Collins,[2] respectfully makes the following Report thereupon.

The petition seeks compensation for a vessel alleged to have been impressed into the service of the United States, during the late war, to have been wrecked on her voyage, and to have finally fallen into the hands of the enemy.

The circumstance of the impress, the essential ground of the claim, is supported by no other testimony, than the deposition of the petitioner, which, on general principles, it would be neither regular nor safe to admit.

The claim itself is barred by the Acts of limitation,[3] and is exceptionable from long delay in preferring it; for which delay, no adequate cause is assigned.

On both which accounts, the Secretary respectfully submits an opinion, that the prayer of the petition ought not to be granted.

Alexander Hamilton,
Secretary of the Treasy.

Treasury Department,
November 21st 1792

Copy, RG 233, Reports of the Treasury Department, 1792–1793, Vol. III, National Archives.

1. *Journal of the House,* I, 625–26. The communicating letter, dated November 21, 1792, may be found in RG 233, Reports of the Treasury Department, 1792–1793, Vol. III, National Archives.

2. On March 10, 1790, the House received a "petition of Pitman Collins, of the State of Connecticut, praying to be reimbursed the value of a vessel, the property of the petitioner, which was impressed for the service of the United States, and taken by the enemy during the late war" (*Journal of the House,* I, 172).

On March 11, 1790, the House, "*Ordered,* That the petition of Pitman Collins, which was presented yesterday, be referred to the Secretary of the Treasury, with instruction to examine the same, and report his opinion thereupon to the House" (*Journal of the House,* I, 173).

3. *JCC,* XXIX, 866; XXXIII, 392. See also "Report on Sundry Petitions," April 16, 1792.

Report on the Petition of Hugh Cunningham

[Philadelphia, November 21, 1792
Communicated on November 22, 1792] [1]

[To the Speaker of the House of Representatives]
The Secretary of the Treasury, to whom was referred by the House of Representatives, the petition of Hugh Cunningham,[2] submits the following report thereupon.

Respectfully referring the House of Representatives, to his report of the 17th Instant,[3] on the subject of depreciation generally; The Secretary begs leave to add,

That the claim of the petitioner is in the capacity of an Officer of the State of Pennsylvania, and has reference to that State only, on the part of which it appears to have been rejected.

Which is humbly submitted Alexander Hamilton,
Secretary of the Treasury

Treasury Department,
November 21st 1792

Copy, RG 233, Reports of the Treasury Department, 1792–1793, Vol. III, National Archives.

1. *Journal of the House*, I, 625–26. The communicating letter, dated November 21, 1792, may be found in RG 233, Reports of the Treasury Department, 1792–1793, Vol. III, National Archives.

2. On January 26, 1792, "A petition of Hugh Cunningham was presented to the House and read, praying compensation for his services as a wagon-master, in the service of the United States, during the late war.

"*Ordered*, That the said petition be referred to the Secretary of the Treasury, with instruction to examine the same, and report his opinion thereupon to the House." (*Journal of the House*, I, 498.)

3. See "Report on Several Petitions Seeking Indemnification for Various Sums of Paper Money Received During the Late War," November 17, 1792.

Report on the Petition of Margaret Fisher [1]

[Philadelphia, November 21, 1792
Communicated on November 22, 1792] [2]

[To the Speaker of the House of Representatives]
The Secretary of the Treasury, to whom was referred by the House

of Representatives, the petition of Margaret Fisher,[3] respectfully makes the following Report thereupon.

The petition seeks compensation for expenditures and services, alleged to have rendered and made, by Henry Fisher (the petitioner's deceased husband) he having been stationed, during the late war, at Lewes near Cape Henlopen, under the appointment and instruction of the Council of Safety of the State of Pennsylvania.

As far as may regard a general compensation, for the time and service of the petitioner's late husband, 'tis evident, from the nature of his appointment,[4] that the application can be properly addressed only to the State of Pennsylvania.

Special services, immediately rendered to the United States, and expenses, incurred for their purposes, would be entitled to compensation and reimbursement, according to their nature and extent. But to these also an objection arises, in the present case, from the Acts of limitation,[5] no account having been exhibited against the United States, 'till .[6]

From the face of the account, it appears, that several of the items would not be admissible in the course of the Treasury, if no bar existed; and the propriety of some others could not be safely investigated at so late a day. There is a possibility, that some of the articles charged may have been paid for by the officers, to whom, or to whose order, they may have been furnished.

For so long a delay, no sufficient reason, by way of excuse, is assigned.

Wherefore, though the Secretary is under a general impression, from the documents produced to him, that there are probable grounds of equitable claim upon the United States, on behalf of the petitioner, in some particulars, he does not consider it, as a case, presenting reasons of sufficient force, for making an exception to the operation of the Acts of limitation; the cautious maintenance of which, as a general rule, is recommended by so many weighty considerations.

All which is humbly submitted Alexander Hamilton
Secry. of the Treasry.

Treasury Department,
November 21st 1792.

Copy, RG 233, Reports of the Treasury Department, 1792–1793, Vol. III, National Archives.

1. On April 4, 1777, Congress "*Resolved*, That blank commissions be sent to Mr. Henry Fisher of Lewistown, with orders, to raise, on continental establishment, an independent company . . . that if he chuses to accept the command of the company, Congress will confirm him therein; but, if he should decline . . . [that] he . . . nominate a proper person . . . and in either case, that he nominate the subalterns" (*JCC*, VII, 224).

Fisher declined the command, and on June 2, 1777, he wrote to John Hancock requesting compensation for his expenditures on behalf of the company which he had raised and staffed (LS, signed by Fisher and William Perry, Papers of the Continental Congress, National Archives). No record of any action taken by Congress on Fisher's request has been found.

2. *Journal of the House*, I, 625–26. The communicating letter, dated November 21, 1792, may be found in RG 233, Reports of the Treasury Department, 1792–1793, Vol. III, National Archives.

3. On January 18, 1791, "A petition of Margaret Fisher, administratrix of Henry Fisher, late of Sussex County, in the State of Delaware, deceased, was presented to the House and read, praying that a claim against the United States, for sundry expenditures and services of the deceased, during the late war, may be liquidated and allowed.

"*Ordered*, That the said petition . . . be referred to the Secretary of the Treasury, with instruction to examine the same, and report his opinion thereupon to the House." (*Journal of the House*, I, 357).

4. On September 16, 1775, the Committee of Safety of Pennsylvania resolved that Henry Fisher of Lewistown be appointed to inform the committee of the arrival of any armed British ships at the Cape of Delaware. The resolution and instructions sent to Fisher may be found in *Minutes of the Provincial Council of Pennsylvania, from the Organization to the Termination of the Proprietary Government. Published by the State* (Harrisburg, 1852) (*Colonial Records of Pennsylvania*), X, 337–38.

5. *JCC*, XXIX, 866; XXXIII, 392. See also "Report on Sundry Petitions," April 16, 1792.

6. Space left blank in MS.

Report on the Petition of Aquila Giles

[Philadelphia, November 21, 1792
Communicated on November 22, 1792] [1]

[To the Speaker of the House of Representatives]

The Secretary of the Treasury, to whom was referred the Memorial of Aquila Giles, in behalf of sundry inhabitants of Long Island, by an Order of the House of Representatives of the 12th of February 1791,[2] thereupon respectfully submits the following Report.

The Memorial sets forth, that the provision made by Congress, by their Act passed the 12th of August 1790, for discharging certain debts, contracted by Abraham Skinner, on account of the subsistence of the Officers of the late Army, while in captivity,[3] did not comprise the whole of the claims of the said inhabitants, there remaining still unsatisfied claims, to the amount of near six hundred pounds, similar to those provided for, except, that the said remaining claims had not been included in the general estimate, returned into the Office of Finance, by the late Commissary of prisoners; And the Memorialist prays, that provision may be made to place the Claimants upon an equal footing with those who were provided for by the Act before alluded to.

It must be understood from this statement, that it is presumed to be the case, that the claimants are in possession of certificates issued for them, by the said Commissary of prisoners.

The Secretary respectfully begs leave to refer the House of Representatives, for his opinion respecting the most eligible mode of proceeding in regard to claims similarly circumstanced, to his report upon the Memorial of the Executors of Edward Carnes.[4]

Which is humbly submitted Alexander Hamilton,
Secry. of the Treasry.

Treasury Department,
November 21st 1792.

Copy, RG 233, Reports of the Treasury Department, 1792–1793, Vol. III, National Archives.

1. *Journal of the House*, I, 625–26. The communicating letter, dated November 21, 1792, may be found in RG 233, Reports of the Treasury Department, 1792–1793, Vol. III, National Archives.

2. On February 12, 1792, "A petition of Aquila Giles, on behalf of sundry inhabitants of Long Island, in the State of New York, was presented to the House and read, praying the liquidation and payment of certain claims against the United States. . . .

"*Ordered*, That the said . . . [petition] be referred to the Secretary of the Treasury, with instruction to examine the same, and report his opinion thereupon to the House." (*Journal of the House*, I, 376.)

3. "An Act making certain Appropriations therein mentioned" appropriated the "sum of thirty-eight thousand eight hundred and ninety-two dollars and seventy-five cents, towards discharging certain debts contracted by Abraham Skinner, late commissary of prisoners, on account of the subsistence of the officers of the late army while in captivity" (1 *Stat.* 185).

4. See "Report on the Petition of the Executors of Edward Carnes," February 28, 1792.

Report on the Petition of Udny Hay

[Philadelphia, November 21, 1792
Communicated on November 22, 1792] [1]

[To the Speaker of the House of Representatives]

The Secretary of the Treasury, to whom was referred, by the House of Representatives, the petition of Udney [2] Hay, respectfully makes the following Report, thereupon.

The said petition seeks payment of interest upon a certain promissory note recited therein, from Christopher Greene and Return Jonathan J. Meigs to Simon Frazer,[3] which is understood to have been given, for a sum of money advanced for the use of certain Citizens of the United States, prisoners of war at Quebec, in the year 1776, and which stipulates the reimbursement of the sum advanced, within a year from the date, with lawful interest till paid.

It appears, that some time in August or September 1785, application was made to the United States in Congress assembled, for payment of the principal and interest of the said Note.[4]

It further appears, that Congress, on the 28th of September 1785, passed a resolution, in the words following.

"That the Board of Treasury take order for paying to Return Jonathan Meigs, late a Colonel in the service of the United States, and to the legal representatives of Christopher Greene deceased, late a Colonel in said service, the sum of two hundred dollars, the same having been expended for the use and comfort of the unfortunate prisoners in Quebec, in the year 1776." [5]

The payment of principal, thus directed to be paid, has not been accepted; the payment of interest as well as principal being insisted upon.[6]

As there is an express stipulation of interest on the note, it is clear, that the parties, by whom it was given, are as much bound for the payment of the interest, as of the principal; and that, unless the public indemnification should include both, the relief intended will be partial and defective. The equity of paying the interest, as well as the principal, is, in such a case, without a question. It is not a case, in which, difficulty can arise, from any established principle of Treasury settlement.

The recognition of the debt, by the provision heretofore made, appears to the Secretary to require, that the provision should be so extended, as to complete the relief designed to be afforded.[7]

All which is humbly submitted Alexander Hamilton,
Secry. of the Treasry.

Treasury Department,
November 21 1792.

Copy, RG 233, Reports of the Treasury Department, 1792–1793, Vol. III, National Archives.

1. *Journal of the House*, I, 625–26. The communicating letter, dated November 21, 1792, may be found in RG 233, Reports of the Treasury Department, 1792–1793, Vol. III, National Archives.

2. On February 2, 1792, "A petition of Udney Hay was presented to the House and read, praying to receive payment of a claim against the United States, for an advance of money to two American officers, prisoners in Canada, during the late war.

"*Ordered*, That the said petitions be referred to the Secretary of the Treasury, with instruction to examine the same, and report his opinion thereupon to the House." (*Journal of the House*, I, 501.)

3. DS, RG 217, Miscellaneous Treasury Accounts, 1790–1894, Account No. 3769, National Archives. On April 22, 1784, Charles Hay stated that the note had been endorsed to him (D, Papers of the Continental Congress, National Archives).

4. The application, which was read in Congress on August 9, 1785, is signed by Meigs and Job Greene and is dated August 1, 1785 (D, Papers of the Continental Congress, National Archives).

5. *JCC*, XXIX, 776.

6. Hay's memorial of March 20, 1786, requesting interest on the note may be found in RG 217, Miscellaneous Treasury Accounts, 1790–1894, Account No. 3769, National Archives.

7. On January 14, 1793, the President approved "An Act to provide for the allowance of interest on the sum ordered to be paid by the resolve of Congress, of the twenty-eighth of September, one thousand seven hundred and eighty-five, as an indemnity to the persons therein named" (6 *Stat.* 11).

Report on the Petition of John Jones

[Philadelphia, November 21, 1792
Communicated on November 22, 1792][1]

[To the Speaker of the House of Representatives]

The Secretary of the Treasury, to whom was referred by the House of Representatives, the petition of John Jones,[2] respectfully makes the following Report thereupon.

The petition seeks a compensation for certain storehouses, which, it is alleged, were destroyed by the enemy, during the late war with Great Britain, upon the ground of a contract alleged to have been made with certain persons, on behalf of the State of Pennsylvania, stipulating an indemnification for the stores, if injured or destroyed by the enemy.

By the petitioner's own shewing, the claim belonged exclusively to the cognizance and adjustment of the State of Pennsylvania. Any interference of the United States would be repugnant to the course of similar transactions, and, as a precedent, full of inconvenience.

The assumption of the State debts, on which the petitioner relies, has, for obvious reasons, been confined to liquidated claims. An extension of it to those of an opposite description, would be replete with embarrassment; placing the adjustment of them where there were not competent means of ascertaining their merit.

Had the claim originally been upon the United States, it is barred by the Acts of limitation.[3]

All which is respectfully submitted, Alexander Hamilton,
Secry. of the Treasry.

Treasury Department,
November 21st 1792.

Copy, RG 233, Reports of the Treasury Department, 1792–1793, Vol. III, National Archives.

1. *Journal of the House*, I, 625–26. The communicating letter, dated November 21, 1792, may be found in RG 233, Reports of the Treasury Department, 1792–1793, Vol. III, National Archives.

2. On March 1, 1791, "A petition of John Jones, of Berks county, in the State of Pennsylvania, was presented to the House and read, praying compensation for damages done to his property by the Army of the United States, during the late war. . . .

"*Ordered*, That the said . . . [petition] be referred to the Secretary of the Treasury, with instruction to examine the same, and report his opinion thereupon to the House." (*Journal of the House*, I, 396.)

3. *JCC*, XXIX, 866; XXXIII, 392. See also "Report on Sundry Petitions," April 16, 1792.

Report on the Petition of Prudent La Jeunesse

[Philadelphia, November 21, 1792
Communicated on November 22, 1792] [1]

[To the Speaker of the House of Representatives]

The Secretary of the Treasury, to whom was referred by the House of Representatives, the petition of Prudent La Jeunesse,[2] respectfully submits the following Report,

The petition suggests no specific ground of claim on the justice of the United States, but rather appears to seek a gratuity, in consideration of having espoused the cause of the United States, early in the late war, of having abandoned his residence in Canada, to follow its fortunes, and of being in distress.

No circumstances of merit or suffering are adduced, sufficiently strong or discriminating to call for a special interposition in favor of the petitioner.

Which is humbly submitted. Alexander Hamilton,
Secry. of the Treasry.

Treasury Department,
November 21st 1792.

Copy, RG 233, Reports of the Treasury Department, 1792–1793, Vol. III, National Archives.

1. *Journal of the House*, I, 625–26. The communicating letter, dated November 21, 1792, may be found in RG 233, Reports of the Treasury Department, 1792–1793, Vol. III, National Archives.

2. On August 26, 1789, the petition of La Jeunesse was "presented to the House and read, praying that . . . [his] claims for military services, rendered during the late war, may be liquidated and satisfied" (*Journal of the House*, I, 90).

On September 25, 1789, this petition, incorrectly cited as that of "Monsieur Lajeune," was "referred to the Secretary of the Treasury, to report thereupon . . . to the next session on Congress" (*Journal of the House*, I, 123).

On November 4, 1778, an earlier petition of La Jeunesse had been presented to Congress stating that he had been "employed as an Officer Volunteer in the Army of the United states in Canada during the space of Eighteen months under the Command of Deceased General [Richard] Montgomery General [David] Wooster and General [Benedict] Arnold and was at the Expeditions against St Johns, Chambly, Montreal and the Ceders. That at the retreat of that Army your Petitioner was also obliged to retire from Canada his Native Country" (ADS, Papers of the Continental Congress, National Archives). On the back of this petition a note, dated November 16, 1778, states that the Board of War reported unfavorably on the petition because the period of service was insufficiently supported by evidence.

Report on the Petition of John Lewis

[Philadelphia, November 21, 1792
Communicated on November 22, 1792] [1]

[To the Speaker of the House of Representatives]

The Secretary of the Treasury, to whom was referred the petition of John Lewis,[2] by an Order of the House of Representatives of the 8th of December 1790, thereupon makes the following Report:

The petition seeks to obtain the settlement and payment of a claim, which is barred by the Acts of limitation.[3]

The Secretary, having in his report of the 16th of April last,[4] upon the petitions of several persons, whose claims are in a similar situation, stated the reasons which, in his opinion, operate against the admission of claims so circumstanced, begs leave respectfully to refer the House to that report; there appearing nothing in the present case sufficiently or discriminating to induce a departure from the considerations there suggested.

Which is humbly submitted, Alexander Hamilton,
Secry. of the Treasry.

Treasury Department
November 21st 1792.

Copy, RG 233, Reports of the Treasury Department, 1792–1793, Vol. III, National Archives.

1. *Journal of the House*, I, 625–26. The communicating letter, dated November 21, 1792, may be found in RG 233, Reports of the Treasury Department, 1792–1793, Vol. III, National Archives.

2. On December 7, 1790, the petition of John Lewis was "presented to the House and read . . . praying the liquidation and settlement of claims against the United States" (*Journal of the House*, I, 330).

On December 8, 1790, the House ordered that the petition "be referred to the Secretary of the Treasury, with instruction to examine the same, and report his opinion thereupon to the House" (*Journal of the House*, I, 333).

3. *JCC*, XXIX, 866; XXXIII, 392. See also "Report on Sundry Petitions," April 16, 1792.

4. See "Report on Sundry Petitions," April 16, 1792.

Report on the Petition of William McGilton

[Philadelphia, November 21, 1792
Communicated on November 22, 1792] [1]

[To the Speaker of the House of Representatives]

The Secretary of the Treasury to whom was referred by the House of Representatives, the petition of William M'Gilton,[2] respectfully makes the following Report thereupon.

The petitioner, by his said petition, claims compensation for his services, as a Clerk to John Reynolds, an Assistant Commissary of Issues, from the 14th of October 1780, to the 18th of January 1781.

It appears, that the accounts of the said John Reynolds have never been rendered at any of the proper public Offices; so that it cannot appear with official certainty, that the petitioner was his Clerk, neither can it be ascertained, whether he received compensation or not.

Under these circumstances, the Secretary is of opinion, that it is not advisable to remove the bar, to which his claim is liable, for want of having been presented in time, according to the Acts of limitation.[3]

Which is humbly submitted, Alexander Hamilton, Secry. of the Treasry.

Treasury Department,
November 21st 1792.

Copy, RG 233, Reports of the Treasury Department, 1792–1793, Vol. III, National Archives.

1. *Journal of the House*, I, 625–26. The communicating letter, dated November 21, 1792, may be found in RG 233, Reports of the Treasury Department, 1792–1793, Vol. III, National Archives.

2. On February 10, 1792, "A petition of William M'Gilton was presented to the House and read, praying compensation for his services as Assistant Commissary of Issues, during the late war.

"*Ordered*, That the said petition be referred to the Secretary of the Treasury, with instruction to examine the same, and report his opinion thereupon to the House." (*Journal of the House*, I, 505.)

3. *JCC*, XXIX, 866; XXXIII, 392. See also "Report on Sundry Petitions," April 16, 1792.

Report on the Petition of Reuben Murray

[Philadelphia, November 21, 1792
Communicated on November 22, 1792] [1]

[To the Speaker of the House of Representatives]

The Secretary of the Treasury, to whom was referred, by the House of Representatives, the petition of Reuben Murray,[2] respectfully submits the following Report.

The petition seeks compensation for certain advances, alleged to have been made in Canada, in the year 1776, for the benefit of a detachment of sick soldiers under the charge of the petitioner.

The nature of the claim is a meritorious one, but at this late date, a proper investigation is hardly possible. It is barred by the Acts of limitation: [3] No claim prior to the present petition appearing to have been preferred against the United States.[4]

No proofs accompany the petition.

The Secretary is, therefore, of opinion, that there does not appear sufficient ground for granting the prayer of the petition.

Which is humbly submitted.

Alexander Hamilton,
Secry. of the Treasry.

Treasury Department,
November 21st 1792.

Copy, RG, 233, Reports of the Treasury Department, 1792–1793, Vol. III, National Archives.

1. *Journal of the House*, I, 625–26. The communicating letter, dated November 21, 1792, may be found in RG 233, Reports of the Treasury Department, 1792–1793, Vol. III, National Archives.

2. On November 22, 1791, the petition of Reuben Murray was "presented to the House and read . . . praying to be reimbursed for sundry expenditures in the service of the United States, during the late war. . . .

"*Ordered*, That the said . . . [petition] be referred to the Secretary of the Treasury, with instruction to examine the same, and report his opinion thereupon to the House." (*Journal of the House*, I, 458.)

3. *JCC*, XXIX, 866; XXXIII, 392. See also "Report on Sundry Petitions," April 16, 1792.

4. H appears to have been mistaken, for Murray had presented an earlier petition to Congress which was accompanied by "vouchers and testimonials." The petition was read in Congress on July 15, 1784, and ordered to be considered at the next Congress. On August 2, 1785, the petition was marked for filing (D, Papers of the Continental Congress, National Archives).

Report on the Petition of Ebenezer Prout

[Philadelphia, November 21, 1792
Communicated on November 22, 1792] [1]

[To the Speaker of the House of Representatives]

The Secretary of the Treasury, to whom was referred, by the House of Representatives, the petition of Ebenezer Prout,[2] respectfully makes the following Report thereupon.

The said petition seeks compensation for the services of the petitioner, as Clerk to Joshua Mercereau, Assistant Commissary of prisoners, and William Hunt, Assistant Commissary of Issues.

The accounts of the said Joshua Mercereau have long since been settled. They include no charge for pay to the petitioner, but allowances, it is represented, were made him for compensations to persons, whom he had employed to assist him. Regularly he was entitled to a Clerk. The allowance, at this day, of a compensation to a person, who may have acted in that capacity, would be a very inconvenient precedent.

It is also stated to the Secretary, from the proper Office, that William Hunt received pay for himself and clerks, up to the 31st of October 1779, which, it is to be presumed, included the petitioner. He is not intitled to depreciation, according to the established rules on that head.

The claim is barred by the Acts of limitation,[3] and no special circumstances appear, to recommend an exception to their operation in favor of the petitioner.

Which is respectfully submitted, Alexander Hamilton
Secry. of the Treasry.

Treasury Department
November 21st 1792.

Copy, RG 233, Reports of the Treasury Department, 1792–1793, Vol. III, National Archives.

1. *Journal of the House*, I, 625–26. The communicating letter, dated November 21, 1792, may be found in RG 233, Reports of the Treasury Department, 1792–1793, Vol. III, National Archives.

2. On November 3, 1791, the House received "a petition of Ebenezer Prout, praying to be allowed the balance of his account against the United States, as Clerk to the Assistant Commissary of Prisoners, at Rutland, during the late war.

"*Ordered*, That the said . . . [petition] be referred to the Secretary of the Treasury, with instruction to examine the same, and report his opinion thereupon to the House." (*Journal of the House*, I, 448.)

3. *JCC*, XXIX, 866; XXXIII, 392. See also "Report on Sundry Petitions," April 16, 1792.

Report on the Petition of David M. Randolph

[Philadelphia, November 21, 1792
Communicated on November 22, 1792] [1]

[To the Speaker of the House of Representatives]

The Secretary of the Treasury, to whom was referred the petition of David M. Randolph,[2] respectfully makes the following report thereupon.

Copy, RG 233, Reports of the Treasury Department, 1792–1793, Vol. III, National Archives.

1. *Journal of the House*, I, 625–26. The communicating letter, dated November 21, 1792, may be found in RG 233, Reports of the Treasury Department, 1792–1793, Vol. III, National Archives.

2. On November 4, 1791, "A petition of David Meade Randolph, Executor of Richard Randolph, deceased, was presented to the House and read, praying

The said petition seeks compensation for a quantity of flour, taken by the then enemy, in the year 1776; founding the claim upon the following suggestions.

1st. That Richard Randolph, the petitioner's testator, some time early in the year 1776, contracted to furnish a certain quantity of flour to one Benjamin Baker, for the use of the American troops then stationed in the vicinity of Norfolk; towards the execution of which contract, 240 barrels of flour were put on board a sloop, commanded by a Captain Peck, to be delivered to the said Baker.

2d. That on her way to the intended place of delivery, the Sloop was stopped by an order of Major General Lee,[3] detained under guard for eleven days, and in consequence of the detention, captured by the enemy with her cargo.

The first of these suggestions is satisfactorily supported by the concurrent testimony of Benjamin Harrison junior, Robert Roberts and Benjamin Baker, (Documents A, B, and C).

But the second of them does not appear to the Secretary, to be supported in such a manner, as, officially considered, ought to be deemed entirely satisfactory.

The deposition of Richard Randolph is full and explicit, to the point. But whatever weight this may [be] entitled to, in the private contemplation of persons acquainted with the character of the deponent, it cannot, in an official view, be admitted as a voucher. The principle of excluding the testimony of the party interested, as in support of his own claim, is not less necessary to be observed, for the security of the public, than for the security of individuals. It is also matter of remark, that this deposition is at a distance of near ten years from the circumstance testified,[4] which, with every allowance for the most scrupulous good faith, is of a nature to weaken the reliance on the accuracy of the Statement.

It is true, indeed, that the deposition of Benjamin Harrison, junior,

---

to receive payment for a quantity of flour, supplied by the testator for the use of the Army, during the late war.

"*Ordered*, That the said petition be referred to the Secretary of the Treasury, with instruction to examine the same, and report his opinion thereupon to the House." (*Journal of the House*, I, 449.)

3. Charles Lee.

4. On August 25, 1785, Richard Randolph had written to Congress concerning this claim, but the committee to which his letter was referred did not report (*JCC*, XXIX, 805*n*; XXXIII, 673*n*).

is in affirmance of the same point. But the mode of expression used implies an indefinite and imperfect recollection of the transaction. The words of his deposition, in one place, are these, "This deponent, thinks that in a day or two after receiving information of the detention of the vessel, he went to Williamsburg and procured an order from General Lee to countermand his order for stopping this vessel, which order he gave to the said Peck, then at Williamsburg, with his, the deponent's commands to go immediately to Sandy point, to take charge of his vessel, and proceed to Smithfield or Suffolk, as he should most convenient for avoiding the enemy." In another place, the following clause is added;—"This Deponent perfectly remembers General Lee being at Curl's, the seat of the said Randolph, on his return from South Carolina, to join the northern army, and thinks that, in his presence, General Lee agreed, with the said Randolph, during a conversation on the subject, that the above mentioned Vessel, with the aforesaid quantity of flour, on board, was stopped by his orders, and was taken in consequence thereof, and that he would try to get him paid by Congress, whenever he had leisure."

Interpreting the first clause by the last, the inference seems to be, that the deponent did not mean to state, as an ascertained fact, the alleged agency of General Lee, intending only to assert a persuasion more or less distinct.

And the objection from distance of time is stronger in this, than in the first instance; a period of near fourteen years having intervened.

The following circumstances are of a nature to occasion additional uncertainty.

The letter (document D) which is produced from Richard Taylor, who is stated to have been the Officer commanding at the place, where the vessel was detained, mentions; that the Captain of the vessel was sent for to Williamsburg, by a Committee, which then sat there, though Mr. Taylor did not know what he was detained for (implying that he was detained by the Committee). This intervention of a civil body furnishes an argument, that the detention might have been by their Order.

It does not appear, that General Lee ever made any representation in favor of the claim to Congress.

But admitting, as alleged, that the detention was by his order, the cause of it was wholly unexplained. It cannot be conceded, that the mere detention of a vessel, for some days, by a military Officer, is under all circumstances, a sufficient ground for claiming compensation from the public for any loss, which may have ensued. The position of the enemy, as it regarded the probability of a supply falling into their hands, may have rendered the detention justifiable.

Neither does it appear, except by the concession alleged to have been made by General Lee, at the house of Mr. Randolph, that the loss of the flour was in consequence of the detention; a circumstance equally material with the one last mentioned. It is clear, that there was danger of capture from the enemy in any event. Mr. Harrison states, that the enemy then marauded in small tenders up James river, in which river the capture took place. It is, in the abstract, possible, that the detention might have even given a better chance of escape. The concession by General Lee, supposing it established, not being accompanied by facts or reasons, would hardly be conclusive.

With every disposition personally to confide in the candor and truth of the representations, which are made, as they regard the impressions of the parties concerned, the considerations, which have been noticed, furnish, at this day, weighty official objections to the admission of the claim.

It is, besides, barred by the Acts of limitation.[5]

And it appears from the shewing of the petitioner and the documents produced, that no regular step was taken towards an application to the government, till late in the year 1785, between nine and ten years after the origination of the claim.

All which circumstances being considered, and the difficulty, if not impracticability of a completely satisfactory investigation, at so late a period, an exception to the operation of the Acts of limitation, in favor of the petitioner, is, with all deference, conceived not to be advisable.

Respectfully submitted, Alexander Hamilton,
Secry. of the Treasy.

Treasury Department
November 21st 1792.

5. *JCC*, XXIX, 866; XXXIII, 392. See also "Report on Sundry Petitions," April 16, 1792.

Report on the Petition of Elizabeth Rockwell

[Philadelphia, November 21, 1792
Communicated on November 22, 1792] [1]

[To the Speaker of the House of Representatives]

The Secretary of the Treasury, to whom was referred, by the House of Representatives, the petition of Elizabeth Rockwell, Administratrix of William Rockwell,[2] respectfully makes the following Report thereupon.

The said petition seeks compensation for Scow hire, freight and some small articles of supply, amounting together to £38.13. lawful money of Connecticut, alleged to have been contracted and furnished in the year 1778 and 1779, for the use of the Frigate, the Confederacy, belonging to the United States.

The copy of a Certificate of Joshua Huntington, who had been the Agent for the Confederacy, dated Norwich, March 16th 1790, which accompanies the account annexed to the petition (and which is presumed to be a true copy of an original document) states, that the services, mentioned in the account, were performed for the Continental Ship, Confederacy, and that the account for them would have been settled, and the balance paid, had it been exhibited, before he had made a settlement with the United States.

Upon the examination of the account of the said Agent, on the files of the Treasury, it has not been discovered, that any monies have been paid, or are charged, for the services or supplies in question.

But there is no evidence of any claim having been made in season, according to the requisitions of the Acts of limitation.[3] The claim is, consequently, barred.

And as the only proof of it rests on the Certificate of the public Agent, after the expiration of his Office, (however considerations of public character, and the face of the demand may induce a disposition to suppose it may be well founded) yet the admission of it would be within the danger pointed out by the Secretary, in his report of the 16th of April last.

Nor do there appear to him, otherwise, circumstances sufficiently special, to render a legislative exception to the operation of the Acts of limitation, in this instance, advisable.

All of which is humbly submitted Alexander Hamilton
Secry. of the Treasry.

Treasury Department
November 21st 1792.

Copy, RG 233, Report of the Treasury Department, 1792–1793, Vol. III, National Archives.

1. *Journal of the House*, I, 625–26. The communicating letter, dated November 21, 1792, may be found in RG 233, Reports of the Treasury Department, 1792–1793, Vol. III, National Archives.

2. On April 7, 1790, "A petition of Elizabeth Rockwell, widow of William Rockwell, late of Norwich, in Connecticut, was presented to the House and read, praying that her claim, as administratrix of the said William Rockwell, for his services in the late Navy of the United States, may be liquidated and satisfied.

"*Ordered*, That the said petition be referred to the Secretary of the Treasury, with instruction to examine the same, and report his opinion thereupon to the House." (*Journal of the House*, I, 190.)

3. *JCC*, XXIX, 866; XXXIII, 392. See also "Report on Sundry Petitions," April 16, 1792.

Report on the Petition of Stephen Steele

[Philadelphia, November 21, 1792
Communicated on November 22, 1792] [1]

[To the Speaker of the House of Representatives]

The Secretary of the Treasury, to whom was referred by the House of Representatives, the Memorial of Stephen Steele,[2] submits the following report thereupon.

That the Memorialist prays for the allowance of an Account, exhibited by him, amounting to five hundred and one pounds, eight shillings and seven pence, New York Currency, for work and materials expended in preparing and fitting up field-pieces and howitzers, for the use of the United States, between the ninth of February and seventh of September, 1776.

That he has suggested, that by the removal of many persons, who were Agents in the business which he transacted, and the loss of certain documents, which were taken by the enemy, he has not been able to obtain a settlement in the usual mode, although he has made frequent applications therefor.

The Secretary is informed by the accounting Officers of the Treasury that a due examination has been made, and that no evidence can be found that the claim was exhibited in season; and that it is considered, as barred under the existing limitation Acts of Congress.[3]

It has also been represented to the Secretary, that an account of the Memorialist under the date of September 12th 1776, for services of a similar nature to those, for which compensation is now claimed, amounting to three hundred and sixty pounds New York Currency, was certified by the then Colonel of Artillery, on the 24th of September 1776, and afterwards paid by Nathaniel Cranck, an Officer of the Quarter Master's department.

It also appears, that the Memorialist was a Captain of a Company of Wheelwrights, in the year 1777, and received payment, on sundry rolls, for the services of himself and Company, of John Keese, Esquire, then an Officer in the Quarter Master's department.

From which circumstances, and inasmuch as by the attestation of the petitioner accompanying his memorial, it appears, not only, that his vouchers have been lost, but that the fact of their loss can no otherwise be ascertained, than by his own testimony, strong objections arise to his claim, independent of its being barred by the Acts of limitation.

The zeal of the petitioner in the cause of his country, his having suffered a loss of property, and his present distress, are believed to be truly represented; but circumstanced, as his case is, the special interposition of the legislature in his favor, does not appear to be recommended by any considerations sufficiently special or cogent.

All which is humbly submitted, Alexander Hamilton
Secry. of the Treasry.

Treasury Department
November 21st 1792

Copy, RG 233, Reports of the Treasury Department, 1792–1793, Vol. III, National Archives.

1. *Journal of the House*, I, 625–26. The communicating letter, dated November 21, 1792, may be found in RG 233, Reports of the Treasury Department, 1792–1793, Vol. III, National Archives.

2. On June 10, 1790, "A petition of Stephen Steele, of the city of New York, was presented to the House and read, praying the liquidation and settlement of a claim against the United States" (*Journal of the House*, I, 236).

On June 14, 1790, the House "*Ordered*, That the petition of Stephen Steele . . . be referred to the Secretary of the Treasury, with instruction to examine the same, and report his opinion thereupon to the House" (*Journal of the House*, I, 241).

3. *JCC*, XXIX, 866; XXXIII, 392. See also "Report on Sundry Petitions," April 16, 1792.

Report on the Petition of Sundry Merchants of Wilmington, North Carolina

[Philadelphia, November 21, 1792
Communicated on November 22, 1792] [1]

[To the Speaker of the House of Representatives]

The Secretary of the Treasury, to whom was referred the petition of sundry merchants of Wilmington in the State of North Carolina, by an order of the House of Representatives of the 26th of May 1790,[2] thereupon respectfully reports:

That the case of the petitioners, as appears by their own shewing, is one arising wholly under the laws of the State of North Carolina, prior to its acceding to the present Constitution of the United States,[3] and, of course, is without the reach of relief from the United States.

Which is humbly submitted, Alexander Hamilton,
Secry. of the Treasry.

Treasury Department
November 21st 1792.

Copy, RG 233, Reports of the Treasury Department, 1792–1793, Vol. III, National Archives.

1. *Journal of the House*, I, 625–26. The communicating letter, dated November 21, 1792, may be found in RG 233, Reports of the Treasury Department, 1792–1793, Vol. III, National Archives.

2. On May 26, 1790, "A petition of sundry merchants of the town of Wilmington, in the State of North Carolina, was presented to the House and read, praying relief against the payment of certain duties, which they conceive were unjustly exacted from them, under the operation of a law of the said Sates.

"*Ordered*, That the said petition . . . be referred to the Secretary of the Treasury, with instruction to examine the same, and report his opinion thereupon to the House." (*Journal of the House*, I, 222.)

3. North Carolina ratified the Federal Constitution on November 21, 1789.

Report on the Petition of Thomas Wickes

[Philadelphia, November 21, 1792
Communicated on November 22, 1792] [1]

[To the Speaker of the House of Representatives]

The Secretary of the Treasury, to whom was referred the petition of Thomas Wickes,[2] by an order of the House of Representatives, of the 13th of April 1790, thereupon respectfully reports:

That the case, in which the petitioner seeks relief, is one of those provided for in the Act of Congress, passed the 12th of August 1790.[3]

That the claim, appearing to have been included in a return made to the proper Officer, prior to the operation of the Acts of limitation,[4] there is, in the opinion of the Secretary, in the present instance, nothing to obstruct a regular settlement at the Treasury, in the usual course.[5]

Which is humbly submitted

Alexander Hamilton
Secry. of the Treasry.

Treasury Department
November 21st 1792.

Copy, RG 233, Reports of the Treasury Department, 1792–1793, Vol. III, National Archives.

1. *Journal of the House,* I, 625–26. The communicating letter, dated November 21, 1792, may be found in RG 233, Reports of the Treasury Department, 1792–1793, Vol. III, National Archives.

2. On April 13, 1790, the House received "a petition of Thomas Wickes, praying compensation for services rendered to the United States during the late war.

"*Ordered,* That the said . . . [petition] be referred to the Secretary of the Treasury, with instruction to examine the same, and report his opinion thereupon to the House." (*Journal of the House,* I, 193.)

3. "An Act making certain Appropriations therein mentioned" (1 *Stat.* 185–86).

4. *JCC,* XXIX, 866; XXXIII, 392. See also "Report on Sundry Petitions," April 16, 1792.

5. The vouchers upon which this petition was based and upon which Warrant No. 2487 for one hundred and thirty-five dollars was issued may be found in RG 217, Miscellaneous Treasury Accounts, 1790–1894, Account No. 3648, National Archives.

Report on the Petition of Henry Howell Williams

[Philadelphia, November 21, 1792
Communicated on November 22, 1792] [1]

[To the Speaker of the House of Representatives]

The Secretary of the Treasury, to whom was referred, by the House of Representatives, the petition of Henry Howell Williams,[2] makes the following Report thereupon.

Respectfully referring the House of Representatives, to his general report of the 19th Instant,[3] concerning the provision heretofore made for cases of the property of citizens used, damaged or destroyed by the Troops of the United States.

The Secretary begs leave to add, that it appears by the petitioner's own shewing, that the State of Massachusetts has considered his case, and granted him a conpensation: [4] And that it further appears, from a document, which was produced by the petitioner, that the compensation allowed by the State was meant to be in full.

The State of Massachusetts having decided upon a matter respecting one of its own citizens, having made him a considerable compensation, for the loss which he sustained; that compensation having been made, as in full, and having been accepted by the petitioner, it would be, as far as the information of the Secretary goes, without precedent, in any similar case, to revise the compensation made, on the suggestion of its being inadequate; nor, considering the various incidents of the war, would comparative justice be promoted by doing it.

Though duly sensible of the respectability of the petitioner, and of the extent of the losses, which he originally sustained,[5] the Secretary cannot but regard the considerations, which have been stated, as a bar to the object of his petition.

Which is respectfully submitted

Alexander Hamilton
Secry. of the Treasy.

Treasury Department
November 21st 1792

Copy, RG 233, Reports of the Treasury Department, 1792–1793, Vol. III, National Archives.

1. *Journal of the House*, I, 625–26. The communicating letter, dated November 21, 1792, may be found in RG 233, Reports of the Treasury Department, 1792–1793, National Archives.

2. On February 27, 1792, the House received "A petition of Henry Howell Williams, praying compensation for injuries sustained in his property by the Army of the United States, during the late war.

"*Ordered*, That the said . . . [petition] be referred to the Secretary of the Treasury, with instruction to examine the same, and report his opinion thereupon to the House." (*Journal of the House*, I, 521.)

3. "Report on Several Petitions Seeking Compensation for Property Damaged or Destroyed During the Late War," November 19, 1792.

4. On June 23, 1789, the House of Representatives and the Senate of Massachusetts concurred in a resolution to grant Williams "two thousand pounds & interest by a state note to be charged to the United States" (*Journal of the House of Representatives of the Commonwealth of Massachusetts . . . Commencing 27 May 1789 Ending 9 March 1790*, Microfilm Collection of Early State Records, Library of Congress).

5. An earlier petition to Congress, dated April 7, 1787, states that Williams's eight-hundred-acre farm on Noddles Island in Boston Harbor had been stripped of livestock, grain, and farm implements and that what could not be removed was destroyed in May, 1775, in order to prevent the British from using it. Williams's losses were estimated at twelve thousand dollars (LS, Papers of the Continental Congress, National Archives). The report of the Board of Treasury on this petition states that the property was used by the state and suggests that Williams apply to Massachusetts, adding that "should Claims of a similar description be hereafter allowed by the general Board of Commissioners [for settling the accounts between the states], the State will obtain reimbursement for such sums as shall appear as equitable compensation for the real damage sustained by the Memorialist" (*JCC*, XXXIV, 390–91).

From Ambrose Vasse[1]

[*Philadelphia, November 21, 1792.*] "As a Citizen of the United States I beg leave to solicit through your mediation my Country's protection in an affair which interests not only me personally, but even the American Trade in general. Engaged in the Hispaniola business, I have thro my Correspondents Messrs Coopman & Co [2] of Cape François sold to the Administration of that Colony sundry provisions to a large amount and at such reduced prices as to leave barely a proffit equal to the freight—for the neat proceeds whereof the House at Cape François remitted to me thro the channell of their agents here Bills drawn by said Administration on Mr De la Forest Consul General of France in this City: [3] the acceptance of said Bills has been refused & consequently the payment remains very uncertain. Mr De La Forests Advertisement in the Papers of this day declares positively that they will not be paid as their dates are later than the

9th of September. . . .[4] May I flatter myself that you will honor me with your protection and will use your influence with the minister of France, in order to obtain Justice as well for myself as for my fellow Countrymen and sufferers and to prevail on him to authorise Mr De la Forest to accept & pay all the drafts, drawn on him by the Administration of Hispaniola and most particularly such as have been drawn upon the abovementioned Circumstances."

Letterpress copy, Thomas Jefferson Papers, Library of Congress.

1. Vasse was a Philadelphia merchant in the West Indian trade. This letter was enclosed in H to Thomas Jefferson, December 14, 1792.

2. Francis Coopman, a Frenchman living in the West Indies, was a member of the firm of Zacharie, Coopman, and Company of Baltimore. The other partner, Stephen Zacharie, was a naturalized citizen of the United States. See Otho H. Williams to H, January 23, 1792.

3. Faced with an empty treasury and a hungry population, the government of Santo Domingo had drawn bills on Antoine René Mathurin de la Forest, French consul general, to pay for supplies sent to the island by United States merchants. The bills were drawn on the understanding that they would be paid for out of the debt which the United States owed to France. This understanding between the United States and France was approved by a decree passed by the French Legislative Assembly on June 28, 1792. See Gouverneur Morris to H, September 25, 1792, note 8.

For background on the request for additional United States aid to Santo Domingo, see H to George Washington, November 19, 1792.

4. *The Federal Gazette and Philadelphia Daily Advertiser* carried La Forest's notice on November 21, 1792. Some months before this notice appeared, La Forest advised the government of Santo Domingo to stop issuing these bills. In addition, he placed advertisements in American papers stating that he would not accept any such bills which had been issued after news of his stand on this matter had reached Santo Domingo ([Philadelphia] *National Gazette*, August 11, 1792).

To Otho H. Williams

Treasury Department
November 21. 1792

Sir

Captain Porter of the Revenue Cutter Active having communicated to me,[1] that he has reasons to be dissatisfied with the conduct of his third Mate Mr. James Forbes, I have to desire that you will make proper enquiry into the affair, in which the Naval Officer [2] is requested to assist; communicating to me the result. Enclosed is an extract of Captain Porters letter for your information.

I am Sir Your Obedt. servant Alexander Hamilton

Otho H. Williams Esqr.
Collector, Baltimore.

LS, Columbia University Libraries.

1. See David Porter to H, November 7, 1792.

2. Robert Purviance.

Conversation with George Hammond[1]

[Philadelphia, November 22, 1792] [2]

On the second morning after the receipt of Governor Simcoe's letter,[3] I waited on Mr Hamilton and requested him to inform me whether this government had then learnt the result of the Indian Council held at the Miamis rapids.[4] Upon his answering in the negative, I stated to him loosely and generally that I had received information from Governor Simcoe that the Indians had evinced a willingness to meet early in the spring at Sandusky any persons deputed by the American government to treat with them—and that in consequence of this disposition they had sent a formal message to Governor Simcoe soliciting his Majesty's good offices [5]—not only as mediator, but also as the principal party in the several treaties concluded with them subsequently to the year 1763 and antecedently to the separation of the colonies from Great Britain. I did not enter into any other particulars than merely to express my sense of the propriety of this application to the King—as a power essentially interested in the restoration of tranquillity on the frontiers of his dominions and as the possessor of those treaties that defined the Indian boundaries as existing at the period of ceding the territory comprehended in them to the United States. Which cession could unquestionably *transfer* no other rights of soil or of any other nature than such as his Majesty had actually *enjoyed*. I concluded by requesting that my present communication might be considered as purely *informal*, in the making of which I was actuated by no other motive than a friendly anxiety to give this government intelligence of an event which materially affected it and with which it was unacquainted. Mr Hamilton in reply, thanked me for the confidence which I had placed in him, but expressed his persuasion that this government would not deem it expedient to accede to the Indian proposition of mediation since he conceived that such a proceeding would diminish the importance of the United States in the estimation of the Indians, and might eventually lead to a disagreeable discussion with Great Britain, in the case of any essential difference of opinion arising between her government and that of the United States, in arranging the conditions of the peace. He was proceeding to add other observations of a similar tendency, but I terminated the conversation by saying that I had formerly communicated to him my *personal individual opinion* (to which I still adhered) in favor of this proposition, a recurrence to which on the part of the Indians appeared to me extremely natural, as affording the most feasible mode of adjusting the present unhappy differences. But as he imagined that the American administration would refuse to adopt it, it was at present totally unnecessary for me to enter into any examination of the motives which might dictate that refusal.

D, PRO: F.O., Series 4, Vol. 16, Part V.

1. This conversation has been taken from Hammond to Lord Grenville, December 4, 1792, Dispatch No. 4.

2. Hammond wrote that this conversation took place "on the second morning after the receipt of Governor Simcoe's letter." Earlier in his letter to Grenville, Hammond stated that Simcoe's letter arrived "about a fortnight ago." Assuming that he received Simcoe's dispatches exactly two weeks before December 4, 1792, he would have talked with H on November 22, 1792.

3. John Graves Simcoe was Lieutenant Governor of Canada and Governor of Upper Canada. In the first sentence of his letter to Lord Grenville which reported the above conversation with H, Hammond wrote: "About a fortnight ago Lieutenant [James] Givens arrived here from Niagara with dispatches to me from Governor Simcoe, containing the minutes of the Indian Council assembled at the foot of the Miamis rapids, and the information of a formal message which he had received from the hostile Indians, desiring him to attend at a council to be held early in the spring at Sandusky. . . ." Simcoe's letter to Hammond is dated October 24, 1792.

4. This council was held from September 30 to October 9, 1792, at the Auglaize, at the confluence of the Auglaize and Maumee rivers, and was attended by both the western Indians and the Six Nations. In this period the Maumee River, as well as several other Ohio rivers, was commonly called "Miami." For a discussion of the confusion arising from the names of these rivers, see J. Ross Robertson, *The Diary of Mrs. John Graves Simcoe* (Toronto, 1934), 218–19. The proposed meeting between the commissioners of the United States and the western tribes had been arranged through the offices of the Six Nations. At the council held at the Auglaize representatives of the Six Nations had obtained the reluctant consent of the Ohio Indians to meet the United States representatives at Lower Sandusky the following spring (see "Proceedings of a General Council of the Several Indian Nations . . . held at the Glaize

on the 30th day of September, 1792," *Simcoe Papers,* I, 218–29), and this decision was confirmed at a second council held with Joseph Brant of the Six Nations at the "Foot of Miami Rapids," on October 28, 1792. For the proceedings of this second council, see *Simcoe Papers,* I, 242–43. In spite of their consent to the council with the United States, the western Indians remained skeptical about the value of such a meeting and reiterated their determination to hold to the line of the Ohio River as the boundary between the United States and Indian territory ("The speech of the Cornplanter and New Arrow to Major General Wayne," December 8, 1792, *ASP, Indian Affairs,* I, 337). The agreement of the western tribes to the proposed council was transmitted to the United States Government through the representatives of the Six Nations at a council at Buffalo Creek in November, 1792 (*ASP, Indian Affairs,* I, 323–24). In his reply to the invitation Henry Knox did not refer to the boundary question, but stated: "The President of the United States, embraces your proposal, and he will send Commissioners to meet you at the time and place appointed, with the sincere desire of removing forever all causes of difference so we may always hereafter be good friends and brothers . . ." (Knox to the western Indians, December 12, 1792, *Simcoe Papers,* I, 270). Israel Chapin, United States agent to the Six Nations, had been summoned to attend the Buffalo Creek meeting, but because he was not available at the time, his son, Israel Chapin, Jr., attended in his place. The account of the Buffalo Creek meeting as recorded by Chapin and printed in *ASP, Indian Affairs,* I, 323–24, differs from the account printed in *Simcoe Papers,* I, 256–60. In the former it is stated that the meeting was held on November 16, 1792; in the latter the same meeting is dated November 13–14, 1792. The two accounts also differ on the place designated for the proposed meeting in the spring of 1793. In the account forwarded by Chapin the place is described as the "Rapids of the Miami." In the account sent to Simcoe, as well as in the accounts of the two previous meetings of the Indian council at the Auglaize, the place is described as "Sandusky." This difference aroused the suspicions of the Indians, who believed that Knox was changing the meeting place for the council without consulting them.

5. On October 9, 1792, a deputation of western Indians from the council had delivered to Alexander McKee, deputy superintendent of Indian affairs at Detroit, a message for Simcoe in which the Indians announced their decision to meet with the United States commissioners in the spring and requested Simcoe's presence at the proposed conference. (*Simcoe Papers,* I, 229). Simcoe's reply, promising British aid, is printed in *Simcoe Papers,* I, 230–31.

From Jeremiah Olney

Providence, November 22, 1792. Introduces "the bearer, Mr. Geo. Benson,[1] of the first mercantile House in this Town, under the firm of Brown, Benson & Ives."

ADfS, Rhode Island Historical Society, Providence.

1. Benson had been elected a director of the Providence Bank on October 1, 1792, to replace Nicholas Brown who had resigned ([Philadelphia] *Gazette of the United States,* October 17, 1792).

From William Heth

Collectors Office
Bermuda Hundred [Virginia] 23d. Nov. 92

Sir

Sickness, loss of Clerks—but more especially, the close attention which I have been obligd to pay to the preparing of my last quarters accounts, has prevented me til now, from complying with the order of the Senate enclosed by you the 31st. August last.[1]

The low wages at which, I have hitherto employd my Clerks, has induced me to subjoin a note to my statement of emoluments, which, I hope will not be deemd improper.[2]

You were informed in a private letter, in what manner I was left at a throng season[3]—and how distressing the consequences had nearly proved. The Young Man who served me as an apprentice, I do not expect is alive at this hour. I missd him, much more than the other, who acted as my deputy. So that my application has been, & must continue to be for some time—if *my Head will* permit—as close as it was on the first of my opening of the Office.

You requested me to examine & to send you my remarks on the coasting Act which was prepared at last session. I have never had one moments leisure to look at it since my return. But with respect to the Division of the fees mentioned in the 34th section[4]—lines 9–19—the absurdity is too great to pass unnoticed, and which you readily acknowledged when I pointed it out to you in Phila. As it now stands, it puts me in mind of a vulgar saying, which I hope you will pardon me for repeating—"Whats *yours* is mine, & whats *mine* is my *own.*" The Surveyor is to receive for his *own use* the fees on *all the* business which he is authorised to do—viz enter & clear vessels—& then he is to share wth the Collector the fees, in which he has no agency or concern. As I formerly urged, so I still think, that every man ought to enjoy the fruits of his own labor (this opinion is against my own Interest, for the moiety offers wch. I have recd from the surveyor at Richmond, has been more than all the rest of the fees under the Coasting Act.)[5] But the principle which has obtaind, & which Seems to be preserved in the new act,[6] of giving a moiety of fees to a man, who, from one end of the year to the other, has no agency in the coasting business, who is not at the expence of a single cent, and in short, who has no more concern in discharging the duties prescribd therein than you have—is inconsistent with every principle of Justice, reason & common sense. I mean the Surveyors of the Ports of entry. The Collector—where there is no Naval Officer—does the *whole* duty, & is at the whole expence. Yet, the Surveyor receives his two Dollars for measuring a vessel, wch. is all he does towards her being registerd, & then receives one half of the fees for registering *bonds* & *Trading licence*, the last of which, are found by the Collector, & who is at other expence and trouble, unnecessary to repeat to you. But, if there is to be a division of fees, let them be *general* under this act; I mean, between the superior of the District, and the Surveyor of the Port, who has any agency in the business on which the fees arise; and this perhaps, might be best, & more consistent with the intentions of Congress; for, to Judge from some parts of the law, it would seem, as if they meant that the Collector, being the superior Officer, and in some measure responsible for the Conduct of the Surveyors, having frequently occasion to give them advice & instruction—& thro' whom all prosecutions for offences, are directed—should receive a moiety of all fees under that act. And upon the whole, I believe it would best promote the public service & prevent impositions which might sometimes be committed, but for that check & controul, wch this division of fees produces—only keep the Surveyors of the Ports of entry out of the question, except in cases where they perform service, and all will be right enough.

I have been more troublesome to you in this way lately, than I expected to have been in twelvemonths—but, I could no longer resist the strong impulse of duty. I trust that I shall not feel myself bound to Interupt you again this Winter unless your letters should call for answers.

I am Sir, with very great respect Yr Mo. Ob servt

Will Heth Coll

The Secretary
of the Treasury

ALS, Hamilton Papers, Library of Congress.

1. "Treasury Department Circular to the Collectors of the Customs," August 31, 1792.

2. In a letter dated November 23, 1792, Heth wrote to James Monroe: "I

have just enclosed to the Secretary of the Treasury, a Statement of the emoluments of my office . . . to which, I conceived it proper to subjoin a remark, as concise as the nature & object of it, would admit. But as it is highly probable . . . that such note or remark will be omitted, I must presume . . . to trouble you now with the purport of said remark." Heth's letter amplifies information previously given to H regarding the low financial return of the office, the expense of clerk hire, the poor location of the office, and his illness (ALS, James Monroe Papers, Library of Congress).

3. See Heth to H, October 5, 1792.

4. Section 34 of "An Act for enrolling and licensing ships or vessels to be employed in the coasting trade and fisheries, and for regulating the same" (1 *Stat.* 316–17 [February 18, 1793]) provided for the fees and allowances to be charged for enrolling and licensing vessels and the distribution of these fees among officers of the customs. There is no indication in the printed journals whether this section of the act was the same as that in the bill of the same title which was reported by Benjamin Goodhue of Massachusetts on November 30, 1791 (*Journal of the House*, I, 465; *Annals of Congress*, III, 216).

5. Heth is referring to Section 31 of "An Act for Registering and Clearing Vessels, Regulating the Coasting Trade, and for other purposes" (1 *Stat.* 64 [September 1, 1789]).

6. See note 4. Heth is presumably referring to the proposed act.

From David Ross[1]

Bladensbg [Maryland] Novr. 23d 1792

Sir

I am obliged to you for gratifying my request by sending me a Copy of Co. Mercers letter and of the Certificates of Mr. Hill and Mr. Crawford as it gives me an opportunity of removing any improper impressions that may be made on those who are unacquainted with all the circumstances.[2]

It was taken for granted Co Mercer would deny his charges if ever he should be seriously called on to support them and you will see I advised him to do it or to fritter them away when he could have done it with rather a better grace—but I did not expect he would assume the appearance as he does by his Queries of wishing it believed he had spoken rather honourably of you than otherwise

ALS, Hamilton Papers, Library of Congress.

1. For background to this letter, see the introductory note to H to John F. Mercer, September 26, 1792. See also H to Ross, September 26, November 3, 1792; Ross to H, October 5–10, 1792; Mercer to H, October 16–28, 1792; H to Mercer, November 3, 1792; Uriah Forrest to H, November 7, 1792.

2. The letter in which Ross sent H the enclosures has not been found. The enclosures, however, included Mercer to H, October 16, 1792, and the certificates of Clement Hill and David Craufurd which accompanied that letter.

and that he had only found fault with some of the measures of the Administration—of which he considered you in his Speeches I *heard* as the author and effected by your undue influence over certain members of Congress—and with respect to the purchase of the Debt on account of the Publick I took it for granted from what he said till I received your letter and read the law that you was by the law constituted the sole and direct purchaser as he spoke of you as such & took no notice of any Board [3] or that you had done it *indirectly* as he insinuates in his letter to you. For if he had I should also have taken notice in my Publications of the unjust inference he must necessarily have intended should be drawn against the President as well as the other four Gentlemen that they were under your undue influence—but that he has expressed this Sentiment at other places appears by the enclosed Certificates [4] at least as to two of the Gentlemen of the Board.

That Co Mercer has in his Speeches attacked & admitted he had attacked your Integrity and that too in terms more direct than I was acquainted with till on my late particular enquiry, appears from the Certificates of Mr John Worthington [5] and Captain Campbell,[6] and

3. Section 2 of "An Act making Provision for the Reduction of the Public Debt" provided that purchases of the public debt should be made by a board of commissioners of the sinking fund consisting of "the President of the Senate, the Chief Justice, the Secretary of State, the Secretary of Treasury, and the Attorney General for the time being, and who, or any three of whom, with the approbation of the President of the United States, shall cause the said purchases to be made in such a manner, and under such regulations as shall appear to them best calculated to fulfill the intent of this act" (1 *Stat.* 186 [August 12, 1790]).

4. The enclosures to this letter were: Ross to Charles Wallace, John Davidson, and Major John Davidson, November 14, 1792 (copy, in the handwriting of Ross, Hamilton Papers, Library of Congress); Ross to William Campbell, November 14, 1792 (copy, in the handwriting of Ross, Hamilton Papers, Library of Congress); Ross to William Pinckney, November 18, 1792 (copy, in the handwriting of Ross, Hamilton Papers, Library of Congress); Ross to Philip Barton Key, November 13, 1792 (copy, in the handwriting of Ross, Hamilton Papers, Library of Congress); Campbell to Ross, November 18, 1792 (LS, Hamilton Papers, Library of Congress); Major John Davidson to Ross, November 17, 1792 (ALS, Hamilton Papers, Library of Congress); Key to Ross, November 17, 1792 (ALS, Hamilton Papers, Library of Congress); John G. Worthington to Ross, November 17, 1792 (ALS, Hamilton Papers, Library of Congress); Thomas Cramphin to Ross, November 21, 1792 (ALS, Hamilton Papers, Library of Congress); two statements by Cramphin, October 5 and November 21, 1792 (ADS, Hamilton Papers, Library of Congress).

5. Worthington's statement reads as follows:

"In answer to your Letter of the 14th. Instant, wherein you have requested a Relation, of what I may recollect of Colo. Mercer's Declarations at several public Meetings, during the contested Election in this District, touching the Conduct of the Secretary of the Treasury of the united States, I will with as much Accuracy and Precision, as I possibly can, briefly relate such Declarations as were made by Colo. Mercer in my Presence, at the several public Meetings I attended during the Period aforesaid, as have Relation to the Conduct of the Secretary of the Treasury. Sometime early in the month of September, I was present at a Meeting of the Citizens of Annapolis, called by Capt. [William] Campbell for the Purpose of stating his objections to Colo. Mercer (who was also present) with a View, to show that he was an improper Character to represent again, this District in Congress. Capt. Campbell observed among other objections to Colo. Mercer, that one great Cause of Objection with him, was, that he thought Col. Mercer unfriendly to the Government of the united States, and that his Declarations with Respect to the Secretary of the Treasury, a Man high in Office, had a tendency to destroy the Confidence of the People in, and to render them dissatisfied with the Administration of the general Government, and then, to show why he thought so, he related a Conversation which had taken Place between him, and Colo. Mercer, sometime in the early Part of the Summer; which I will here substantially give. Capt. Campbell observed, that Colo. Mercer had said, that he thought, or had no Doubt, but that the S. of the Treasury was concerned in private Speculations, and that he was friendly to the Interest of Speculators, that he the S. of the Treasury, had as a public Officer, given for Stock, three or four Shillings in the Pound, more than, what it sold for in the Market. Capt. Campbell said, that he then observed, that if this was the Case, the S. was not the only Person to be blamed; but the Board, and that Colo. Mercer answered, that the P. of the united States had declined having any Thing to do in the Business, and that the S. of the T. had been supported by the President of the Senate, and Mr. [John] Jay in opposition to the Secretary of State, and the Atty. General, and that he, the S. of the Treasury was the only chief agent in purchasing the Debt of the U. States under the Act of Congress, and that, therefore he was to blame, and that Mr. Jay had authorised the S. of the T. to vote as his Proxy, and as he thought proper upon one occasion, when the S. wanted an appropriation of Money, and that, therefore 200,000 Dollars were appropriated, in Opposition to the Opinion of the S. of State and the Atty. Genl. which shew that the S. of the Treasury was the governing Person.

"Capt. Campbell observed, that Colo. Mercer mentioned another Thing, which induced him to believe, that the S. of the Treasury was concerned with others in Speculation, which was this, that [Robert] Elliott and [Elie] Williams, the Original Contractors, for Supplies to the western Army, and Theodoseus Fowler, had made their Terms to the S., nearly the same, and that the S. accepted of Fowlers, who was a Friend to [William] Duer, and that he took [John] Cockran and [Walter] Livingston as Fowler's Securities, who were Friends of Duer's, and that soon after the S. of the T., suffered in his Office, the Contract to be assigned to Duer, and that he considered Duer thereafter as responsible for Performance of the Contract, and that all advances of Money were made to him in Consequence of the assignment of the Contract, and which was converted to the Purposes of Speculation, instead of being applied to procure Supplies for the Army. Capt. Campbell after having stated this Conversation, procured a Copy of a Letter from the Secretary's office, in answer to one, written by Duer to the S., wherein it appeared that the S. considered Duer, only as the Agent of Theodoceus Fowler, and not as the Person responsible for the Performance of the Contract, as had been alledged by Colo. Mercer, as stated by Capt. Campbell, a Copy of which

Letter, Colo. Mercer requested, observing he would have probably Occasion for it hereafter. The Charges which Capt. Campbell mentioned to have been made by Colo. Mercer against the S. of the T. in their Conversation, and here related by him, were not denied by Colo. Mercer, before this Meeting, that I heard, but on the contrary, that the Statement of Capt. Campbell was acceded to. On Friday the 14th. of Septr. last, I was also present when Colo. Mercer addressed a Number of the Citizens of Anne Arundel County upon Elk Ridge, and in the course of his Address observed, as well as I recollect, that the S. of T. acting under the Authority of Law, and being entrusted with the public Money, for the Purpose of purchasing the Debt of the U: States, had given for stock 20/. when it was selling in the Market at 18/. when he could have bought it at 14/. in the Pound, and mentioned, that he thought, or had no Doubt (or words to that Effect) that the S. of the T. was connected with, and concerned with others, in speculating in the public Debt and that he was a Friend to Speculation. There were a number of other Declarations fell from Colo. Mercer, which appeared to be calculated to inspire into the minds of the People, a Jealousy and Distrust of the S. of the T. as a public Officer, and to exhibit him as the most dangerous Man in the Government; such as, that he the S. of the T. through his Influence, had fixed upon the People of America, a Tax above all others the most odious, mentioning the Excise, and that he was a Man of so much Influence in the Government, that there were a Number of the Members of Congress, mentioning I think, twenty four, who were always ready to carry into Effect, any Measures, which might be proposed by the S. of the T., and that it became a common Practice in Congress by those Members, when any Measures were proposed respecting the Treasury Department, to ask, whether Hamilton had seen and approved of them, and if answered in the affirmative, they would immediately reply I shall then be for them—after having thus depicted him, as a Man of dangerous Influence in the Government, it was his own Declaration, in nearly the following emphatic words, which caused the preceding Declarations with Respect to the S. of the T., to make probably the deeper Impression on my Mind, to wit, that he Colo. Mercer, was the only Man, who would dare to stand up on the Floor of Congress, and call in question the Conduct of the S. of the T., and that an Opposition or free Discussion of the Conduct of a Man, or Men like him, holding Offices of high Trust, and possessing great Influence in a free Government, was the only Oil, that could keep alive, the Lamp of Liberty." (ALS, Hamilton Papers, Library of Congress.)

Ross added the following note at the bottom of this letter: "Mem. I have mislaid my letter to him which was induced by understanding he had taken Notes of Co Mercers Speech on Elk-ridge—he is modest bred to the Law & in the present assembly."

6. Campbell's statement reads as follows:

"In answer to your letter of the 14 Inst. I will relate a Conversation with Colo Mercer which of itself lent Evidence whether he designed to impeach the Integrity of the Secretary of the Treasury or not. After I had declar'd myself a Candidate in opposition to Colo. mercer we had in June last some Conversation on the subject, at which time, I told him his conduct towards the secretary of the Treasury was one of my Objections to him, that I found considerable prejudices against that officer were sedulously instilled into the minds of the people, very highly injurious to the Interests of Government and which I thought were propagated by himself and warmly enforced by his leading Friends in this District. I further stated that he had impressed an Opinion in the District, that the Secretary was making an improper use of public money to promote Speculations or the Interest of Speculators with whom he was concerned, and observed to him at the same time that I believed the Secretary had taken an Oath that he would not be concerned directly or indirectly in purchases of public Debts. Colo. Mercer in reply observed that he had no doubt the Secretary was in some manner interested that he had given four Shillings in the pound for Stock more than the market price, that a Speculator could buy 3 ℔ Cts @ from 10/ to 10/6 at public auction, and next day sell to the secretary @ 12/; that some alleged this Conduct was to promote the Interest of his Father in law, (Genl. [Philip] Schuyler) but that such strong Circumstances had been communicated to him as to induce him to suspect he had a farther and more immediate Interest in the Business. That Mr. Thomas Fitzsimmons had inform'd him, that during the second session of Congress, Duer, assistant to the secretary, carried his Speculations to such extent as to prevent any Claimant scarcely getting an account passed against the United States, or at least to cause such delay and difficulty in their Business as to oblige almost every one to sell his Claim for whatever could be obtained for it, and that he, Duer, had always his Emissaries ready to become the purchasors. That this Conduct excited an Enquiry by Congress and that he Fitzsimmons as one of the Committee for that purpose, after an Investigation, waited on the Secretary and informed him, he must dismiss Duer, or they would be obliged to report unfavorably, and that accordingly, Duer was in a few days dismissed. In Answer to what Colo. Mercer had said respecting the purchase of a 3 ℔ Cent Stock, I replied that if there was any Censure due on that Subject, it was applicable to the board, which had been appointed, under the controul of the president, to dispose of the sinking funds, and not the Secretary alone, to which Colo. Mercer observed that it was well known the President had declined having any thing to do with the Execution of that Law, that the Secretary of State and the attorney General of the United States were opposed to the appropriations and purchases as made, but that the Secretary of the Treasury was always supported by the two eastern members and that on a particular occasion when the Secretary of the Treasury wished an appropriation of Money and the Secretary of State and the attorney General were opposed to his Views, he wrote to Mr. Jay who was at new york, requesting his attendance at the board of Commissioners, and that instead of attending he wrote a Letter authorizing him as his Proxy to vote as he thought proper on the occasion and that 200,000 Dollars were immediately appropriated, one half thereof to be laid out in New York, and the remainder at Phila. and elsewhere. Colo. Mercer also added that the two eastern Members of the board had always been governed by the Secretary of the Treasury and that therefore, he thought it proper that he, the Secretary should be considered as the author of every thing that had been done and ought to bear the blame. Colo. Mercer added that another Circumstance led him to believe that the secretaries private Interest, was in some manner concerned with his public Measures—that Messrs. Williams and Elliott, who were the former Contractors, and Theodosius Fowler had given their propositions for the Contract for supplies to the western army, which were nearly the same that the Secretary of the Treasury had preferred the latter, who was an intimate Friend of Duers and that Mr. Cochran and Mr. Livingston who were also bosom friends of Duers, were taken as Securities for performance of the Contract and very shortly afterwards the secretary suffered an assignment of the Contract to be made to Duer, in his office, who was always thereafter considered as the accountable person, and received all the Money that was advanced on account of the Contract which, instead of being applied to the performance thereof, was devoted to Speculations, whereby the western Army had suffered to such a Degree as in all probability to occasion our Misfortunes in that Quarter. Colo. Mercer wished

the impressions he appears by the other Certificates to have wished to have made against you and which alone may be sufficient to satisfy you as to the truth of it. Yet I must add some observations on my own account as to what he said at Marlborough to prevent any unjust inference that might otherwise be drawn that I had either misapprehended or misrepresented what he said at that particular place.

I did not apprehend Co Mercer that you was a buyer of Stock with your own money but that as the immediate Purchaser for the Publick you had bought so as to benefit a particular set of men with whom you was privately connected so that in effect you was at the same time both buyer and seller of Stock.

I understand Mr Hill and Mr Crawford [7] both voted for Co Mercer altho he leaves you to infer otherwise yet I have not the most distant inclination to ascribe their Certificates in his language

---

to impress an Idea that the secretary had originally intended the Contract for Duer, and that Fowler and his securities were only made use of to blind the public which the subsequent assignment tended to show as I had heard the secretary censured on this subject, I applied for Copies of the assignment and Letters that had passed between the secretary and Mr. Duer, in order to contradict their assertions on this subject, and obtained them. In September last I called a meeting of the Citizens of Annapolis which Colo. Mercer attended. I then stated the Conversation here related as part of my Charges against him who I conceived wished to destroy the Confidence of the people in the Government by depreciating the Merit of one of its first Officers. He publickly justified the Charge, adding in his History of Duer's Conduct with respect to public Claimants, that a brokers Office was kept next door to the secretarys office for the purpose of buying up their Claims.

"To obviate the Colos. Charge with respect to the Contract assigned to Duer, which he then repeated and justified, as true, I produced the Letter of which I enclose you a copy, and read it to the people; Colo. Mercer requested a perusal of it. I gave it [to] him to read, and he declared he was pleased to see it, as it had not been produced before, and could hereafter be made further use of. Colo. Mercer I find has since spoken of this letter as a copy of one of private Correspondence, and as a proof of the Secretary's interference in his Election. It is in truth a Letter of public access to any Gentleman solicitous of obtaining it, at least I have always supposed so, and so far from being Confidential to me, I have never written or spoken to the Secretary in my Life, directly or indirectly, of which I have more than once informed Colo. Mercer.

"Lest my opposition to Colo. Mercer may be supposed to lend a false colouring to the expressions made use of by him, I will thank you to apply to several respectable persons who were present at that meeting of the Citizens, I have herein alluded to, and am certain that what I have said will be substantially authenticated." (LS, Hamilton Papers, Library of Congress.)

7. Mercer had enclosed copies of statements from Clement Hill and David Craufurd in Mercer to H, October 16–28, 1792.

to "wickedness" or even to improper motives but justice to myself obliges me to show truly my own idea of them that they were derived from inattention and that if there has been any misapprehension of what Co Mercer said at Marlborough it is rather on their part than on mine.[8] I am induced to conclude it was from inattention only, and not coupling the whole of his Speech together as I cannot suppose they had not understanding enough if they had been attentive to his whole speech to descern that his praise of you was that of Anthony to Brutus. And I admit that if I had not taken his whole speech together but had happened to have had my attention called off at particular times and have had it engrossed by that part of it wherein he professed to have been in the habits of intimacy and friendship in the Army and to have even then a very high respect for your abilities; I could certify myself as these Gentlemen have done that he had spoken of you in an honourable manner—but the taking together the whole of his Speech at Marlborough only must I apprehend have compelled every one that heard him with attention to consider this only as proceeding from the art of a Popular Speaker with a design to impress his Audience with an idea of his own Impartiality that his censure might thereby acquire a double force and that the People might be induced to believe that facts and the public Good alone could have induced him to speak in the manner he did against one for whom he had otherwise a friendship & respeck. And I can the more readily conclude his censure of you at Marlborough had escaped the attention of these Gentlemen from a circumstance respecting myself for Co Mercers insinuation agt the President by his observation on General Waynes appointment to the Western

8. In his statement to Mercer, dated October 22, 1792, Craufurd stated that he had "heard Colo. Mercer speak of the Secretary both in private conversation and in a public address to the Inhabitants of this (Meaning Prince Georges County) at the Court house, and I never heard him at either time or in either place say any thing disrespectfully of the Secretarys Character but on the contrary he spoke highly of him as a private Gentleman Colo. Mercer indeed condemn'd the Secretary's conduct as a *public officer* particularly his purchasing in Stock—which I think he thus explain'd that the Secretary could have purchas'd in at two shillings in the pound less than he gave—this Measure Colo. Mercer very much reprobated, and added the United States lost very considerably by such conduct, but throughout the whole of this address he never spoke of the Secretary as a public Officer" (copy, Hamilton Papers, Library of Congress). Hill corroborated Craufurd's statement (copy, Hamilton Papers, Library of Congress).

Army had escaped me [9] & consequently not taken notice of in my Publications till after I was reminded of it by Major Snowden [10] and Mr. John Thomas of Susquehanna who happened to be present. And as to his praise and speaking highly of you in private conversation it could only be with the same view of giving force to his censure unless it might be with a design also of making the very use of it, he now has done if ever he should be called on as to charges he cannot support. And that every unfavourable impression was made even on Mr Hill himself as to your views and conduct as an officer if not as to your Integrity is evident from his own observation to a Gentleman that he was for sending Co Mercer to Congress if it was only to watch the Secretary of the Treasury and the observation of others was what a bad man the Secretary must be if what Co Mercer says is true. But the impressions that were made to your prejudice are wearing off fast and will be entirely removed when it comes to be Publickly known that he has denied having impeached your Integrity but only the Policy of some of the measures of the Administration. These Certificates of Mr Hill and Mr Crawford, also confirm the propriety of my wish to get every thing fixed in writing that there might be no dispute as to what was said. For did not Co. Mercer (as he admits by his Publication) answer when I represented to him the impropriety of charging you without producing some proof, that he thought himself justifiable in saying every thing he believed of you because he could trace the opposition to his election up to yourself, thus supporting his former charges as well as bringing forward a new one instead of seting me right if I had misapprehended him. This was soon after he spoke at Marlborough and before his Speech at Bladensburgh. Therefore can any one believe that Co Mercer could be your friend and could wish to make impressions honourable to you and that there was only a difference of Judgment between you as to the measures of Government when at the very time he spoke at Marlborough he himself thought you was his enemy and had acted so improperly towards him as well as the Publick that altho an officer of the General Government you had meddled in our State election and that too in opposition to him-

9. Major General Anthony Wayne had been appointed in April, 1792, to the command of the newly reorganized United States Army in preparation for a new campaign against the western Indians.

10. This is a reference to either Francis Snowden or Thomas Snowden.

self. And if he had not have intended to charge your Integrity why did he not rectify the mistake as to his intentions, also, on the receipt of your letter in the presence of several Gentlemen instead of making a serious and most direct charge against you of having offered him a bribe to vote for the assumption or at least that you had made the offer to him in such terms that he had a right to take you in jest or earnest which appears by the Certificate of Mr Cramphin [11] which I now send forward and the Certificates of Mr Bayley which I understand has been already forwarded but if it has not on your informing me I will procure it but I do not think I ought to delay this letter for that purpose.[12] It may be proper to mention that I have understood some of Co Mercers friends incline to turn the contents of these Certificates into a joke and that he did not mean any thing unfavourable agt you—but they will find it impossible when they consider the very particular time of making the charge it being on the receipt of your letter calling on him to do you justice by stating what he really did say of you [13]—the painting his own distress for want of money and that you knew this his distress—and when they consider the impressions he made on those present as appears by Mr Cramphins Certificate—and one observed as I am informed what do you think of the Secretary now—and another on being asked if he thought you was in earnest answered he had no doubt you would have given the Money if Co Mercer would have received it—and expressly and at a different time by his own answer to Mr Bayley that your proposition to him was in such terms that he had a right

11. Ross had quoted portions of Thomas Cramphin's certificate of October 5, 1792, in his letter to H of October 5–10, 1792. In a letter to Ross dated November 21, 1792, Cramphin added the following statement: "Since I gave my Certificate of the 5th of October last I mentioned to you some other expressions of Colo. Mercer's, which you requested me to commit to writing, they were as well as my Memory serves me in the following words—Colo. Mercer on the 2d of October after expressing himself in the manner mentioned in my Certificate of the 5th of same month added in the following words 'I was much pushed for Money at the time, for I had a Credit on the Bank, the day of payment was nigh at hand, and had it not been for a Friend I shou'd certainly have been noted and published. Money therefore wou'd have been very acceptable to me at the time, and I have not a doubt but my situation was known.' You are at liberty to make what use you please of this Letter" (ALS, Hamilton Papers, Library of Congress).

12. For William Bayly's certificate, see H to Mercer, September 26, 1792, note 16. A copy of Bayly's certificate had been sent to H by Uriah Forrest on November 7, 1792.

13. See H to Mercer, September 26, 1792.

to take you in jest or earnest. Mr Walter Chandler who was present and may be able to give you additional evidence on this particular subject, I hear is now in Philadelphia.

As concurrent circumstances may perhaps have more weight than charges of the greatest importance agt Co Mercers conduct with those who have no opportunity of informing themselves and who might suppose that what he is alledged to have charged against you has originated in party only where truth is too often sacrificed to the object in view—therefore I shall observe should such a Hero as Co. Mercer represents himself to be, refuse as he does in his Publication [14] to do justice to the innocent Members of Congress for fear of bringing 24 quarrels on his head by giving the names of those corrupt Members who he says are under your influence—on his principle I should have suffered the minds of the People to be poisoned by him against the measures of Government and those who are entrusted with the Administration to be traduced, in silence through fear of his denunciations against his opponents—and that his denunciation was general agt. those that should oppose his election. I have since seen a Certificate of a Gentleman which can be had if necessary. He also asserts in his *off hand Reply* that "it can be affirmatively proved by 200 or 300 persons present a Marlborough" and this relates to his assertion that he there called Capt Campbell a liar rascal and coward whereas I was there 'till both left the place and heard nothing of it nor have I seen anyone that heard him call Capt Campbell so and every one will presume that if it had been the case only before 2 or 3 it must have had an immediate circulation among all the People. And what could he mean by calling you a mushroom excrescence but that you had jumped into wealth by means of an office you was not entitled to. Or why should he have observed at Marlborough that he knew you when you had not a second shirt to your back if he did not mean some impression to your prejudice should remain notwithstanding he told us at the same time that he did not mean it as a reflection and that it was in the retreat through the Jerseys, when he was nearly in the same situation himself. In his Publication he says "a full detail of these and other curious circumstances (relative to Capt Campbell) is lodged with the Printers" and I was much surprised when I applied the 15

14. See the introductory note to H to Mercer, September 26, 1792.

Novr. for a Copy of this detail to be informed by the Gentlemen of the office that no such thing was ever lodged and that on observing this assertion in his Publication a note was sent him from the office that no such detail was lodged and his reply was that it was not ready. He calls your official letter to the Contractor a *private* correspondence a Copy of which I enclose [15] and which Capt Campbell procured from the office for the purpose mentioned in his answer to me and does he not wish from his Publication, that it should be considered a letter as having relation to his election. It may not be improper to observe as he calls some of his opponents a desperate Banditti [16] that there was respectability of character against Co Mercers election in the district at large and in Annapolis the place of his residence there was not only respectability but a considerable number for the place and also a small Majority in his own County at large agt him notwithstanding all his fine Speeches for which he says he received such shouts of applause so that it turned out as I concluded that it only required a knowledge of the man or the subject to defeat all his oratorial powers of Imposition.

I hear Co Mercer has gone on to Congress and as I do not wish to lose another Post in Copying this and the Vouchers I must request you will let Co Mercer have Copies of them. I shall send a Copy of this letter to Mr Hill & Mr Crawford that they may be thereby enabled to put in a different point of view with respect to themselves anything they may suppose has been misapprehended by

Your friend & obedt Servt. David Ross

Alexr. Hamilton Esqr.

15. See H to William Duer, April 7, 1791. For background to this contract, see "Contract for Army Rations," October 28, 1790, note 2. H to Duer, April 7, 1791, note 4.

16. See Mercer to H, October 16–28, 1792.

Catullus No. V[1]

[Philadelphia, November 24, 1792]

For the GAZETTE of the UNITED STATES.

It was my intention to have closed with my last paper, the discussion of Mr. Jefferson's conduct in the particulars which have been suggested; but the singular complexion of the last number* of a series of papers originating in the American Daily Advertiser,[2] obliges me to resume it.

As if bold assertion were capable of imposing any thing for truth, an attempt is made, in the paper alluded to, to impress the following opinions, 1st, That the extract which was given of Mr. Jefferson's letter on the subject of a proposition for the transfer of the French debt,[3] is "false," "deceptive," and "mutilated." These are the epithets in different passages applied to it. 2d, That Mr. Jefferson was the mere vehicle, or to use the precise terms, "only the vehicle of cummunication to Congress." 3d, That he "discountenanced" the proposition. 4th, That the "only" proposition which he made to Congress, was to borrow the money in Holland to discharge the debt.

To give colour to these assertions, I am called upon to produce the entire paragraph from which the extract has been made, and it is suggested, that the whole was deposited in the quarter, from whence the extract is believed to have been taken.

I pledge my veracity that this suggestion is unfounded; as is another—that the information which has been communicated by me

**No. IV.*

[Philadelphia] *Gazette of the United States*, November 24, 1792.

1. For background to this document, see "Catullus No. I," September 15, 1792. The other "Catullus" essays are dated September 19, 29, October 17, December 22, 1792.

2. This is a reference to six articles in a series in the "Vindication of Mr. Jefferson," which appeared in [Philadelphia] *Dunlap's American Daily Advertiser*. For a discussion of these articles, see "Catullus No. IV," October 17, 1792, note 4. "Catullus No. V" was written in reply to the fourth of these articles, which was printed in *Dunlap's American Daily Advertiser*, November 8, 1792.

3. For this extract of Jefferson's letter, see "An American No. I," August 4, 1792, note 10. The "transfer of the French debt" was also discussed in "Catullus No. II," September 19, 1792.

is derived from the opportunities of official situation. I affirm unequivocally, that I obtained through different channels a full knowledge of the transaction in February, 1787—being in no public station whatever—that I then saw the extract, which has been published, and which was at that time taken from the original letter, and has been since preserved, in the most authentic form. That I then also received information equally authentic of the general substance of the letter, as relating to the matter in question, and of all other particulars concerning it, which have heretofore been stated, and which have been preserved, in a manner, that admits no doubt of their accuracy or genuineness.

For this, I again appeal to the letter itself, on the files of the department of state, where alone, as far as I am informed, its entire contents are deposited, and which I entertain no doubt will confirm not only the truth of the extract which has been given, but the justness of the representation of the contents of the letter in all other respects.

Considering the extract as genuine, which undoubtedly it is, it speaks for itself—and unequivocally falsifies the suggestion that Mr. Jefferson was "*only* the *vehicle*" of communication to Congress. It imports, without the possibility of evasion, *advice* to *accede to* the proposition which was made to the Dutch Company, on the dishonorable ground of there being danger, that the public payments *would not be punctual,* and of its being in that case expedient to *transfer the discontents,* which would arise from the want of punctuality, from the court of France, *to the breasts of a private company.* It therefore clearly makes him more than the mere vehicle of communication—the patron and adviser of the measure upon the condition which has been stated. It as clearly refutes the astonishing assertion, that he "discountenanced" the proposition; whatever subterfuge may be brought to colour it. And it equally destroys the other allegation, that the only proposition which Mr. Jefferson made to Congress, was to borrow the money in Holland to discharge the debt.

It has been admitted, that there was another proposition, in the same letter, of that import; but it is denied under the appeal which has been made, that it in any manner derogates from the advice contained in the extract. It is understood to have been offered as an alternative; in case the proposition of the Dutch Company should not be approved—As another mode which might be adopted to effect the payment to France.

It will be remarked by an attentive reader, that while an artful attempt is made to bring into question the genuineness of the extract, a direct denial of its genuineness is not hazarded. Recourse is had to equivocal implications. It is said to be "false and deceptive," not in terms, but "upon a sound construction"—that "the contents of the letter, *even in the extract published*, have been *shamefully misrepresented*"—not that the extract is itself a forgery; but that "other parts of the letter absolutely necessary for the full comprehension of it, are kept back." The jargon of asserting, that a *literal* extract from a paper is "false and deceptive, *upon a sound construction*," is a proof of the embarrassment of the commentator. Whoever will examine the extract will perceive, that as to the purpose, to which it has been applied, it is an *entire* thing. The sentiment reprobated is there complete, and can be affected by nothing collateral. The inferences resulting from it can only be repelled by establishing that the extract is *in terms* false. This I believe will not be pretended.

It is as little true (in the sense in which it is evidently meant to be understood) that the proposition for the transfer of the debt has been imposed upon Mr. Jefferson as his own, as it is that he discountenanced it. It has been acknowledged, that the offer was first made by the Dutch Company; and has only been maintained that Mr. Jefferson advised its acceptance on principles contrary to good morals; a position which can never be overthrown without introducing a new system of ethics. In this sense too, and with the disapprobation, which belonged to it, was it understood by those to whom the advice was addressed, to the honor of the public Councils of the day.

It is suggested that the animadversions upon Mr. Jefferson's conduct, in these papers, proceed from "private revenge." This supposes some *private* injury *real* or *imagined*. The assertor must be not a little embarrassed to support the probability of such a cause. It is affirmed that none such exists. Private revenge therefore cannot be the stimulous. Let Facts speak the true motives. CATULLUS.

George Washington to Edmund Randolph[1]

[United States Novr. 24. 92][2]

Sir

It appears to me necessary, that processes should issue without further delay upon the Indictments found at the last Circuit Court held at York Town in the Commonwealth of Pensylvania, in reference to the laws laying a duty on Spirits distilled within the United States—and proper, that they should be served by the Marshall of the District of Pensylvania,[3] in person. I am to desire that the requisite arrangements [with the Attorney[4] & marshall of the before mentioned District] may be taken for these purposes; [and], you are authorized to signify to the [latter] my expectation of his immediate Agency in the business. [G W]

[The Attorney Genl of the U S]

Df, in the handwriting of H, RG 59, Miscellaneous Letters, 1790–1799, National Archives.

1. For background to this letter, see H to Tench Coxe, September 1, 1792; H to Washington, September 1, 8, first letter of September 9, September 11, 22, 26, 1792; H to John Jay, September 3, 1792; "Draft of a Proclamation Concerning Opposition to the Excise Law," September 7, 1792; Jay to H, September 8, 1792; Randolph to H, September 8, 1792; Washington to H, September 7, two letters of September 17, September 21, October 1, 1792; George Clymer to H, September 28, October 4, 10, 1792; Rufus King to H, September 27, 1792; Washington to Thomas Mifflin, September 29, 1792.
2. Material within brackets is not in H's handwriting.
3. Clement Biddle.
4. William Rawle, United States attorney for the District of Pennsylvania.

From Joseph Whipple

Portsmouth [*New Hampshire*] *November 24, 1792.* "Your Circular letter dated the 25th. Octo. came to my hands the 15th. instant: Comformably to a direction therein contained I enclose you an estimate of the amount of Bounties payable on the 31st. of Decr. next on fishing Vessels that have been licenced in this district, the amount whereof is Dollo. 2091.50. I do not conceive that any claims will be made on this office from any other Vessels, and the probability is that some of these may have failed of such Strict compliance with the law, as will entitle them to the bounty it may therefore to be presumed that the above mentioned Sum will be fully sufficient to be retained in my hands for the payment of those Bounties. . . ."

LC, RG 36, Collector of Customs at Portsmouth, Letters Sent, 1792–1793, Vol. 4, National Archives; copy, RG 56, Letters from the Collector at Portsmouth, National Archives.

From Oliver Wolcott, Junior[1]

Treasury Department, Comptroller's Office, November 24, 1792. "I have prepared a sett of forms for the Superintendents of Indian Affairs, which I have now the honor to transmitt for your consideration, also the draft of a Letter on the same subject. These forms have been calculated with a view to the establishment of an Officer, to superintend the examination & settlement of all deliveries of Stores & public property of the United States; which in my opinion will be an indispensible arrangement to secure the necessary responsibility. If such an Officer should be established, I think he ought to be placed in the same relation to the Treasury as the Accountant of the War Department. . . ."

ADf, Connecticut Historical Society, Hartford.

1. Wolcott was comptroller of the treasury.

To Israel Ludlow[1]

[*Philadelphia, November 25, 1792.* The catalogue description of this letter reads as follows: "Ordering the Original Survey of Lands in Ohio. 'The said tract shall extend from the mouth of the Miami to the mouth of the little Miami, and be bounded by the river Ohio on the South . . . that the President reserves to the U. S., such lands at and near Fort Washington.'[2] Arranges for military protection." *Letter not found.*]

LS, sold at City Book Auction, March, 1942, Lot 191.

1. Ludlow, a native of New Jersey, had been appointed a surveyor under the Continental Congress. On November 20, 1790, H requested him to take charge of the remaining surveys necessary for completion of the boundaries of the Ohio Company purchase, the Scioto Company lands, and the lands of the Miami Company. See Arthur St. Clair to H, May 25, 1791.

2. This quotation with minor changes was taken from "An Act for ascertaining the Bounds of a Tract of Land purchased by John Cleves Symmes" (1 *Stat.* 251–52 [April 12, 1792]). This act also appears in 6 *Stat.* 8.

From Sharp Delany[1]

[*Philadelphia, November 26,1792.* On December 13, 1792, Hamilton wrote to Delany: "I received . . . your letter of the 26th. Ultimo." *Letter not found.*]

1. Delany was collector of customs at Philadelphia.

From William Heth

[*Bermuda Hundred, Virginia, November 26, 1792.* On January 1, 1793, Heth wrote to Hamilton: "I wrote you very fully the 26th Novr. last." *Letter not found.*]

From John Jay

[*New York, November 26, 1792.* On December 18, 1792, Hamilton wrote to Jay: "Your favours of the 26 of November & 16 instant have duly come to hand." *Letter of November 26 not found.*]

From Jeremiah Olney

Providence, November 26, 1792. "As difficulties or losses may occur with respect to the Transmission of Bonds taken for duties, not discharged on the day they fall due, to the District Attorney residing at New Port,[1] it appears to me of considerable importance that you be apprised of the different ways that offer for Transmitting them. . . . I am induced Sir, Respectfully to entreat your advice and particular instructions as to the mode of conveyance which shall appear to you the most proper for the Transmission, of any unsatisfied Bonds to the District attorney, which I Shall invariably observe."

ADfS, Rhode Island Historical Society, Providence.

1. William Channing.

To William Short

Treasury Department
Phila. Novr. 26, 1792.

Sir

Since my last of the 5th. instant a triplicate of which is here inclosed I have received yours of the 30th of August last.

I have only time to inform you that I have directed the sum of 1,250.000 florins to be drawn upon our Commissioners in Amsterdam immediately;[1] which will leave a sum in their hands sufficient to face the Interest and other payments falling due up to the 1st. of March next including the debt due to Spain.[2]

This arrangement is made so as not to affect the sum of 1.625.000 florins which pursuant to Mr. Morris's[3] stipulation with the French Treasury was to be paid in France—because it appears from your letter that it was still possible the payment might be concluded. This possibility will therefore govern until I receive further advice on the subject. But should the payment eventually be stopped, I shall also draw for part, if not the whole, of the sum from hence.

I have the honor to be very respectfully, Sir, Your Obedt. servant Alexander Hamilton

William Short Esquire

LS, William Short Papers, Library of Congress. A copy of this letter was enclosed in H's "Report on Foreign Loans," February 13, 1793.

1. See H to Willink, Van Staphorst, and Hubbard, November 26, 1792.

2. For a description of this debt, see H to Short, September 1, 1790, note 19. See also Joseph Nourse to H, October 9, 1792, and Short to H, October 27, 1792.

3. For the controversy surrounding the payment of this installment on the French debt, see Gouverneur Morris to H, September 25, 1792, and Short to H, September 25, 1792.

Treasury Department Circular to the Supervisors of the Revenue[1]

Treasury Department
November 26. 1792

Sir

The Secretary at War informs me that the arrangement which has been made by him for supplying provisions and other necessaries at the several recruiting rendezvouses within the State of Maryland will expire with the present year; and that a further arrangement will be necessary for the succeeding year.[2]

Convinced that under your care the business would be put upon the most proper footing, I have concluded to ask you to take the trouble of it.

The supplies of provisions are reducible to a precise rate by contract, which is always desirable. Quarter Master's Articles and Medical Assistance appear not to be susceptible of the same regulation. The course consequently has been to contract for provisions at a given Rate ℔ Ration, and to allow the Contract⟨or⟩ for all other supplies, which he also engages to furnish, a Commission of 5 ℔ Cent upon his expenditures. This course, it is presumed, must continue to be substantially followed. It is however left to your discretion, except as to the article of provisions, for which the stipulation of a precise rate ℔ Ration is deemed essential. The Rations to be supplied are to consist of the following Articles—

One pound of bread or flour,
One pound of beef or ¾ of a pound of pork,
Half a gill of Rum, brandy or whiskey
One quart of Salt
Two quarts of Vinegar
Two pounds of Soap
One pound of Candles } per 100 Rations.

The several rendezvouses, the present rates of provisions at each and the commission upon the expenditures for other supplies are as follow—

Places	prices ℔ Ration	Commission
Baltimore	10 Cents	5 ℔ Cent
Hagers Town	12 Cents	

The places will continue as above specified; but it is hoped that the Rations may be reduced in price. Whether an attempt to form a contract for the whole, or the formation of a contract for each place, ought to be preferred, is left to your judgment.

Medical assistance has been a source of abuse and it is desirable that proper care be taken to guard against it.

The provisions must be furnished upon returns of the principal Officer at each rendezvous, specifying the number of men for whom Rations are required and a receipt upon the Return at each delivery for the number of Rations delivered must be obtained from the same Officer. Should a non-commissioned Officer only be at the rendezvous when any delivery is made, the Commissioned Officer charged with the recruiting service at the place must afterwards examine and certify it. Similar *receipts* and *Certificates* must be obtained for all other issues specifying particulars as accurately as the nature of the case admits, and the accounts must finally be settled at the Treasury.

Monies may be paid by you to the Contractor on account, for which duplicate receipts must be taken; one of them, when transmitted to the Treasury, will procure you a Credit for the sum paid, to be charged to the Contractor.

I need not observe to you the great importance of œconomy in the minutest details. The aggregate of saving or expence from attention or inattention to it is immense.

With great consideration, I am, Sir, Your Obed Servt.

Alexander Hamilton

LS, to George Gale, The Indiana Historical Society Library, Indianapolis.

1. A report of May 22, 1794, which Abraham Baldwin of Georgia presented in the House of Representatives, states: "The Secretary of the Treasury, by letter of the 26th of November, 1792, requested the Supervisors of Massachusetts, Connecticut, Vermont, New York, Virginia, and Maryland, to provide, by contract, for the supplying of rations for recruits at certain places of rendezvous, and to pay money to the contractors on account of such supplies, upon duplicate receipts" (D, RG 233, Papers of the Select Committee Appointed to Examine into the State of the Treasury Department, Third Congress, National Archives).

2. For the change in arrangements for Army contracts, see H to George Washington, August 10, 1792.

To Wilhem and Jan Willink, Nicholaas and Jacob Van Staphorst, and Nicholas Hubbard

Treasury Department,
November 26th 1792.

Gentlemen,

You will herewith receive a triplicate of my letter of the 5th instant, and an enclosure for Mr. Short, which you will please to forward.[1]

The Treasurer having been directed to draw upon you, for 1.250.000 florins, I have to request, that his drafts may be duly honored.

I am &c. Alexander Hamilton.

Messrs. Willink, Van Staphorst,
and Hubbard.
Amsterdam.

Copy, RG 233, Reports of the Treasury Department, 1792–1793, Vol. III, National Archives. This letter was enclosed in H's "Report on Foreign Loans," February 13, 1793.

1. H to Wililam Short, November 26, 1792.

From Meletiah Jordan[1]

Frenchman's Bay [*District of Maine*] *November 27, 1792.* ". . . I have also to own receipt of another Thermometer which I am sorry to say has arrived in the same situation as the former. . . .[2] I find that the Letters I receive from your Office are much retarded by being directed to the care of General Lincoln they remain at the Post Office in Boston & never sent to his Office, while they were directed to the care of Robert Haskell[3] of Beverly they came regularly to hand."

Copy, RG 56, Letters to Collectors at Gloucester, Machias, and Frenchman's Bay, National Archives.

1. Jordan was collector of customs at Frenchman's Bay, District of Maine.
2. See H to Benjamin Lincoln, August 2, 1792.
3. See Jordan to H, July 1, 1791.

From Tobias Lear

[*Philadelphia*] *November 27, 1792.* Encloses "a Petition . . . in behalf of the Keeper of the Light House in Portland,[1] to have his salary augmented."

ALS, RG 26, Lighthouse Letters Received, "Segregated" Lighthouse Records, National Archives; LC, George Washington Papers, Library of Congress.

1. Less than a month after this petition was sent to H, an article in the [Portland, Maine] *Eastern Herald* indicated that Joseph Greenleaf, the keeper of the Portland lighthouse, had accepted a sum of money which had been raised by subscription to augment his salary, for Greenleaf did not expect the President to authorize an increase in his salary, although it was a "totally inadequate compensation for his services" (*Eastern Herald*, December 24, 1792). In a letter to Greenleaf on January 17, 1793, Tench Coxe wrote: "Reflexions upon the justice of Government and of the Chief Magistrate too naturally follow from the tenor of these papers, and they are rendered the more unpleasant by the circumstance of the subscription paper being handed round by a gentleman holding a commission under the United States. . . . It is the Opinion of the Secretary of the Treasury with whom I have conferred upon this subject, and it is my opinion that you should refund . . . the Monies . . . paid to you . . . and that you should confide intirely in the equity and wisdom of the President in regard to the compensations for your services" (LC, RG 58, Letters of Commissioner of Revenue, 1792–1793, National Archives). See also H to Benjamin Lincoln, January 23, 1792.

To Jeremiah Olney

Treasury Department
November 27 1792.

Sir

Your letter of the 15th instant[1] has been duly received. Under the circumstances stated, I am pleased with the conduct which you have observed, in relation to the Brig Neptune, from Surinam. Should Mr. Arnold[2] (as you say he threatens) commence a prosecution in the State Court, care must be taken so to conduct your defence as to admit of an appeal to the proper federal one. It will be of course to defray every necessary expence for the purpose.

What you say with regard to the Attorney of the District[3] is duly noticed.

I am, Sir, with consideration, Your Obedt Servant. A Hamilton

Jere. Olney Esqr.
Collr Providence.

LS, Rhode Island Historical Society, Providence; copy, Rhode Island Historical Society, Providence; copy, RG 56, Letters to the Collector at Providence, National Archives; copy, RG 56, Letters to Collectors at Small Ports, "Set G," National Archives.

1. Letter not found, but see Olney to H, November 7, 1792.

2. Welcome Arnold.

3. William Channing was United States attorney for the District of Rhode Island.

From Jean Baptiste de Ternant[1]

Philade. 27 Nove. 1792
l'an 4 de la liberté francaise

Le secretaire d'etat m'ayant informé par une lettre du 20 de ce mois[2] dont vous avez connoissance, que sur ma communication officielle du 8, votre gouvernement a arreté de solder ici à mon ordre quarante mille piastres de plus que les cent mille restant à payer sur les fonds précédemment accordés,[3] je vous prie de vouloir bien faire acquitter entre les mains du Consul general Laforest[4] ou à son ordre, le montant total de ces deux sommes dans la proportion et aux epoques suivantes.

	Dollars
au lr. Decembre prochain	64,935. 1/00
au 15 du même mois	34,558.82/00
au lr Janvr. 1793	10,000.
au 15 du même mois	8,000.
au lr fevr. Suivant	20,958.41/00
au 15 du même mois	380.60/00
et enfin au 15 avril suivant	1,167.16/00
au total	140,000.

LC, *Arch. des Aff. Etr., Corr. Pol., Etats-Unis,* Supplement Vol. 20.

1. For background concerning Ternant's request for additional advances of payments on the debt owed France, see H to George Washington, November 19, 1792; Thomas Jefferson to H, November 21, 1792.

2. ALS, letterpress copy, Thomas Jefferson Papers, Library of Congress. This letter was enclosed in Jefferson to H, November 21, 1792.

3. See Ternant to H, November 15, 1792, note 2. For the basis on which the additional forty thousand dollars had been granted, see H to Washington, November 19, 1792.

4. Antoine René Charles Mathurin de La Forest.

To George Washington[1]

[Philadelphia, November 27, 1792]

The Secretary of the Treasury presents his respects to the President. The execution of the process by the marshal himself is, for many reasons, so important that it does not appear possible to dispense with it.[2] If there should be any failure in the Deputy it would probably furnish a topic of censure and a source of much embarrassment. The impediment in point of health is to be regretted, but, it would seem, must be surmounted.

November 27, 1792.

LC, George Washington Papers, Library of Congress.

1. For background to this letter, see H to Tench Coxe, September 1, 1792; H to Washington, September 1, 8, first letter of September 9, September 11, 22, 26, 1792; H to John Jay, September 3, 1792; "Draft of a Proclamation Concerning Opposition to the Excise Law," September 7, 1792; Jay to H, September 8, 1792; Edmund Randolph to H, September 8, 1792; Washington to H, September 7, two letters of September 17, September 21, October 1, 1792; George Clymer to H, September 28, October 4, 10, 1792; Rufus King to H, September 27, 1792; Washington to Thomas Mifflin, September 29, 1792; Washington to Randolph, November 24, 1792.

2. On November 28, 1792, Tobias Lear wrote to Clement Biddle, United States marshal for the District of Pennsylvania, that in view of Biddle's ill health the President requested that "processes issued at the Circuit Court against the persons indicted for a riot in Washington County" be delayed rather than served by a deputy (ADfS, RG 59, Miscellaneous Letters, 1790–1799, National Archives). On November 27, 1792, in a letter to Washington, Biddle had requested that on account of illness he be permitted to use a deputy (ALS, RG 59, Miscellaneous Letters, 1790–1799, National Archives). The processes were to be served on Alexander Berr and William Kerr. See George Clymer to H, October 4, 1792, note 10.

To the President and Directors of the Bank of the United States

Treasury Department
November 28th. 1792

Gentlemen,

I have to request that you will advance to Messrs. William Young & George Dannaker, the further sum of One thousand Dollars, on account of their Contract[1] with the Public for supplying the Troops of the United States with Clothing for the ensuing year, to be charged as suggested in my letter of the 5th. Instant.[2]

I have the honor to be Gentlemen Your Most Obedient Servant

Alexander Hamilton

The President, Directors & Company
of the Bank of the United States.

LS, Historical Society of Pennsylvania, Philadelphia.

1. See "Contract with George Dannacker and William Young," October 22, 1792.

2. Letter not found.

From Tench Coxe

Treasury Department, Revenue Office, November 28, 1792. Announces the death of the keeper of the Chesapeake lighthouse.[1] Suggests that Lemuel Cornick would be a suitable replacement.

LC, RG 58, Letters of Commissioner of Revenue, 1792–1793, National Archives.

1. William Lewis.

From John Nicholson[1]

[*Philadelphia*] *November 28, 1792.* "In the year 1780 Congress required certain portions of provision called *Specific Supplies* from the different States,[2] in 1781 The late superintendant[3] changed the mode of supplying the Army into Contracts,[4] at which time part of the provisions purchased by Pennsa. for the United states according to the former System remained undelivered in several Mills & places in the state—this so purchased and paid for hath been justly claimed by me in exhibiting the Acct of Pennsa. against the Union, and in support of it I wish to adduce to the Commissioners testimony that information was given by the State of these purchases, this hath been done in part by these provisions at several places having been accounted for by the Contractors per their Accounts,[5] and for what remained I applied to Mr. Morris,[6] but not trusting to his memory he refers me to his letters or official papers for the information.[7] I therefore respectfully request that you would cause an examination of those papers . . . from June 1781 to Novr. 1782. . . ."

LC, Division of Public Records, Pennsylvania Historical and Museum Commission, Harrisburg.

1. Nicholson was comptroller general of Pennsylvania.

2. *JCC*, XVI, 196–201.

3. Nicholson is referring to Robert Morris, who was superintendent of finance from July, 1781, through November, 1784.

4. *JCC*, XX, 734.

5. During 1782 the state of Pennsylvania was given credit in its account of specific supplies for several small sums charged against five contractors for provisioning posts in Pennsylvania (D, RG 217, Journals of the Office of the Register of the Treasury, 1776–1799, Journal "B," October 29, 1781–May 22, 1784, National Archives; D, RG 217, "Ledger B, 1776–1789, Register's Office," National Archives).

6. Under the date of February 7, 1783, the following note appears in Robert Morris's diary: "Mr. John Nicholson Auditor of the State of Pennsylvania applied respecting the Accounts of specific Articles purchased by me and charged in the Account of that State, I soon convinced him how advantageous those Purchases are to the State but told him if the State chose to leave those Purchases for Account of the United States and commute the whole Sum of Money paid to me into the specific Articles at the Prices they bore when the same ought to have been delivered, I would chearfully acquiesce therein" (D, partly in the handwriting of Robert Morris, Robert Morris Papers, Library of Congress).

7. Morris to Nicholson, November 14, 1792 (ALS, Robert Morris Papers, Library of Congress).

From Jeremiah Olney[1]

Custom House
District of Providence 28th. Novr. 1792

Sir

Agreeable to my expectation, as communicated in a former letter;[2] Welcome Arnold Esqr. has commenced a Suit against me for the detention &c. of his Brigantine Neptune, in not granting a permit to Mr. Edward Dexter (who Received from him a *Collusive* Transfer of the Cargo) to unload, while his Bond in Suit remained unpaid.

Mr. Dexter has also commenced a Suit for refusing him the usual Credit on the Transfer of Mr. Arnold. These Suits are brought to the State Court to be held in this Town on the 17th day of December next. I have written Mr. Channing on the Subject, and should he deem it expedient to have another Attorney to assist him in the Prossecution of this Business, I shall think myself authorized to engage one, more especially as it is of great moment that Such Collusive Transfers (ment to seek a Credit in evasion of the Law) be effectually Checked in their infancy.

I have the Honor to be Respectfully Sir Your Most Obed. Hum. Serv. Jereh. Olney Collr.

Alexander Hamilton Esqr.
Secretary of the Treasury

ADfS, Rhode Island Historical Society, Providence.

1. For background concerning Welcome Arnold's "collusive" transfers, see William Ellery to H, September 4, October 9, 1792; Olney to H, September 8, second letter of September 13, October 4, 24, 1792; H to Olney, September 19, 24, October 12, November 27, 1792.

2. This letter, dated November 15, 1792, has not been found. See H to Olney, November 27, 1792.

Report on the Petition of Griffith Jones

[Philadelphia, November 28, 1792
Communicated on November 28, 1792] [1]

[To the Speaker of the House of Representatives]

The Secretary of the Treasury, to whom was referred the petition of Griffith Jones, by an Order of the House of Representatives of the 14th. instant,[2] thereupon respectfully reports:

That the case is one of those stated in a former Report to the House, dated the 16th of April 1792, as barred by the Acts of limitation.[3]

That the present petition is accompanied with a Certificate, recently given by William Mumford, late a Clerk in the Commissioners Office for settling the Accounts of the State of Pennsylvania, with the United States, intended to prove that the claim of the petitioner had been presented at the said office, previous to the time limited for receiving claims.

Admitting the fact to be, as stated in the certificate, it does not appear to amount to such an exhibition of the claim, as would remove the case out of the operation of the Acts of limitation.

But the admission of evidence of the nature of that, which is here offered, after so great a lapse of time, would, it is conceived, be, for obvious reasons, extremely dangerous.

Viewing the matter in this light, nothing of weight occurs to the Secretary, that could lead to an opinion different from that, which he has formerly expressed on the subject.

Which is humbly submitted. Alexander Hamilton,
Secretary of the Treasury.

Treasury Department
November 28th 1792.

Copy, RG 233, Reports of the Treasury Department, 1792–1793, Vol. III, National Archives.

1. *Journal of the House*, I, 629. The communicating letter may be found in RG 233, Reports of the Treasury Department, 1792–1793, Vol. III, National Archives.

2. On November 14, 1792, "A petition of Griffith Jones, of the City of Philadelphia, tanner, was presented to the House and read, praying to receive compensation for a quantity of leather impressed for the use of the Army, during the late war.

"*Ordered*, That the said petition be referred to the Secretary of the Treasury, with instruction to examine the same, and report his opinion thereupon to the House." (*Journal of the House*, I, 619.)

3. *JCC*, XXIX, 866; XXXIII, 392. See also "Report on Sundry Petitions," April 16, 1792.

From Philip Schuyler[1]

New York November 28th 1792

My Dear Sir

Both your letters detailing the conversation held with Mr Willet have been duly received,[2] the contents communicated to a few friends, as I found it unnecessary to extend It, Mr. Willets statement having made no impression with our friends who believed It a Misrepresentation. Mr Van Schaack[3] who was most alarmed at It and who mentioned It to me, was satisfied by my declaration that Willet must have misapprehended or misrepresented what past, as I knew that you was not averse to an examination of the conduct of the Canvassers[4] and that a censure should be conveyed If they had acted corruptly, altho you was decidely of Opinion that the state ought not to be thrown into such a convulsion as might possibly terminate in a manner very painful to the friends of good Government.

When Judge Wilson[5] was here he asked If I had received a line from you on the subject of a proposition he had made you to sell Mr Church[6] lands in Pensylvania, to the Amount of £10000 Sterling at 2/6 per Acre provided double that sum was Advanced him on Loan and for which he proposed giving a mortgage on other lands. I informed him that I had not received a line from you mentioning that business, he pressed me to write you on the Subject. If the lands he proposes to sell were really worth 2/6 per Acre, It might be inconvenient for Mr Church to advance so large a sum as £20000—but as It will be difficult to Asscertain as well the value of the lands Mr Wilson proposes to sell as those he would Mortgage, as the latter would in probability not be productive of an income equal to the Annual interest of the money, as Mr Wilson might not be able to discharge the Interest Annually, Its accumulation might increase beyond the Increase in value of the lands. It therefore does not at present appear to me an Eligible mode of laying out money. I did not mention this to Mr Wilson, but as It may perhaps be better that the negative to his proposition should come from me than from you, I have no Objection that my sense of the business should be communicated unless you should Judge the appropriation an Eligible one.

Our political opponents are evidently embarrassed. The examination into the conduct of the Canvassers, and the testimony of the Wittness and the authenticated documents to prove the general practice of former canvassing committees, they procure, will place Many of the Members in a painful situation on the Question of Censure, and I believe they would be deserted by some should the question be moved, but for three days past the leaders amongst Clintonians have suggested the propriety of an Amendment,[7] and I really beleive they will make the Attempt. If they do, and before the conclussion of the Investigation which is now pursuing, I shall consider it as a victory on our part.

I have a wish to pay you a visit at the Close of the next week, but If the contest is not ended I shall not dare to be absent from absence as my friends would be too much chagrined. I shall however not return to Albany until I have had the pleasure of Embracing you My Dear Eliza and the Little ones, entreat them to Accept my best Wishes, Adieu

Your Ever most affectionately &c &c Ph: Schuyler

Honl Alexander Hamilton Esqr &c

ALS, Hamilton Papers, Library of Congress.

1. Schuyler, who had served as a major general in the American Revolution and as United States Senator from New York from 1789 to 1791, was H's father-in-law.

In this letter Schuyler discusses the report of the committee of canvassers in the disputed New York gubernatorial election of 1792. For background on this subject, see H to Rufus King, June 28, July 25, 27, 1792; King to H, July 10, 29, 1792; William Lewis to H, July 21, 1792; Schuyler to H, May 9, 1792, note 4; H to John Adams, June 25, 1792, note 2; Robert Troup to H, August 24, 1792.

2. Neither letter has been found. The reference is to Marinus Willett and his role in the disputed New York gubernatorial election of 1792. Willett supported the report of the committee of canvassers which awarded the election to George Clinton. Willett's feelings about this matter were so strong that he and William Willcocks, a supporter of John Jay's candidacy, fought an inconclusive duel. See Benjamin Walker to H, July 12, 1792.

3. Peter Van Schaack was chairman of a committee from Kinderhook, New York, which submitted one of many petitions to the New York Assembly against the decision of the committee of canvassers in the 1792 election.

4. As a result of the numerous petitions (including Van Schaack's) which it had received on the report of the committee of canvassers, the New York Assembly instigated an investigation of the committee's report. In the New York Senate, of which Schuyler was a member, the question arose because John Livingston had won a seat in the Senate as a result of the canvassers' decision to reject votes from Clinton County. On November 12, 1792, Schuyler had proposed that the Senate make a thorough investigation of Livingston's claim to a Senate seat (*Journal of the Senate of the State of New York. Sixteenth Session* [New York: Printed by Francis Childs and John Swaine, Printers to the State, 1792], 8).

5. James Wilson, associate justice of the United States Supreme Court, owned extensive tracts of land in western Pennsylvania.

6. H managed the American property of John B. Church, Schuyler's son-in-law and Elizabeth Schuyler Hamilton's brother-in-law, while Church was in England.

7. This is presumably a reference to "an act for electing representatives for this state, in the House of Representatives of the Congress of the United States of America," which was passed by the New York legislature on November 29, 1792, and which provided for changes in the methods of handling and counting votes in elections to the House of Representatives. On November 26, 1792, William S. Livingston had made a motion to insert a clause stating that votes rejected by the canvassers should be counted (*Journal of the Assembly of the State of New York. Sixteenth Session* [New York: Printed by Francis Childs and John Swaine, Printers to the State, 1792], 27–28). This act was vetoed by the Council of Revision as "inconsistent with the spirit of the Constitution and the public good" (Alfred B. Street, *The Council of Revision of the State of New York* [Albany, 1859], 299–301).

From George Washington

United States.
Novemb: 28. 1792.

The Secretary of the Treasury will cause to be paid to the Director of the Mint,[1] the sum of Five thousand Dollars; to be applied to the purposes of said Establishment. Go: Washington.

LC, George Washington Papers, Library of Congress.

1. On November 27, 1792, David Rittenhouse, director of the Mint, had

requested Thomas Jefferson to procure five thousand dollars for current expenses (ALS, RG 59, Miscellaneous Letters, 1790–1799, National Archives). On the following day Jefferson wrote to Washington and enclosed the Rittenhouse letter (ALS, RG 59, Miscellaneous Letters, 1790–1799, National Archives).

To Thomas Willing

Treasury Department November 28th 1792

Sir

I received the resolution of the Directors of the Bank of the united States of Yesterday, relative to my proposition of the 20th instant.[1]

It remains to be determined by the Bank in whose favour the Treasury Bills upon Amsterdam are to be drawn, of which I request to be informed, in order to give the necessary directions.

I have the honor to be very respectfully Sir Your obedt Servt A Hamilton

The President of the Bank of the united States

LS, MS Division, New York Public Library.

1. See H to the President and Directors of the Bank of the United States, November 20, 1792.

From William Short

The Hague Nov. 29. 1792

Sir

I had the honor of addressing you on the 2d. of this month in reply to your letter of the 28th. of August recieved the day before. I was averse to writing to you again before I could transmit at the same time the account I then informed you I had written for to Amsterdam. The commissioners have assured me several times they are pushing forward as fast as they can the general account from the commencement which you have directed, & that they will lose no time in extracting from thence those parts which being posterior to Nov. 1790. regard me. Finding I shall not recieve it for tomorrow's post which is the last in time for the New-York Packet I determine to postpone no longer acknowleging the reciept of your later letters viz: Sep. 13. Oct. 1. & 16.

ALS, letterpress copy, William Short Papers, Library of Congress.

Before I leave the subject of the acct. however I must observe that I had until since the reciept of your letter of Aug. 28. really supposed, (I think the commissioners had given me to understand it) that you recieved regular quarterly accounts from them which settled the reciepts & expenditures. I had not made particular enquiry as to the vouchers & their manner of arranging that part with the treasury, but I took it for granted it was to the satisfaction of government as I heard nothing to the contrary from you. I have been perhaps wrong in not examining more particularly into this subject: if so I must beg you to attribute it to my conviction of the inutility of my interfering between the treasury & the commissioners in the settlement of accounts—my aversion to enter further into the business than was absolutely necessary—& my persuasion that you did not expect it. I am convinced no inconvenience will result from my having recieved the subject in this manner & must beg you to excuse it if it has been improper.

In consequence of your letter of Sep. 13. recieved here the 24th inst. I that day gave directions to the commissioners [1] to appropriate the 105,000 florins agreeably to your orders & to give M. Morris [2] immediate notice of it, which they inform me they did by the first post,[3] & which I also confirmed to him by the same.[4]

It gave me personal satisfaction to find from your letter of Oct. 1 that the late revolution & suspension of the King in France had struck you in the same manner which it had done me, as to payments to that country. That which was made [5] & about which I have so often troubled you & with so much prolixity, though made against my own opinion, & only from respect to that of M. Morris, I find he would endeavour to establish as my act, if any question were to rise on it—& this on the ground of the delay from the 17th. of Aug. to the 5th. of Sept.—& a bill being taken instead of a reciept—circumstances which I explained fully in my letter of Oct. 27th. to you.

1. Short to Willink, Van Staphorst, and Hubbard, November 24, 1792 (ALS, letterpress copy, William Short Papers, Library of Congress).

2. Gouverneur Morris.

3. Willink, Van Staphorst, and Hubbard to Short, November 26, 1792 (LS, Short Family Papers, Library of Congress).

4. Short to Morris, November 27, 1792 (ALS, Columbia University Libraries).

5. See Short to H, August 30, September 25, October 27, 1792; Morris to H, September 25, 1792.

I am persuaded at present however no question will arise on the payment & therefore I will not trouble you farther. M. Morris says now if the payment had been made on the 17th. the U.S. should have credit from the 6th. of Aug. although at present credit is given only from the 5th of Sep. the day of the payment being effected.[6] I know not very well how to reconcile this with his letter[7] which said the bankers might make the payment at liesure, if it was found that so considerable a payment of bank money raised the agio to the disadvantage of the U.S. Be that as it may if his arrangement with the commissioners was such as to entitle the U.S. to credit from the 6th. of August, the delay arising from circumstances not dependent on us, & in part from their own bankers who asked time to consider of the manner they would recieve the payment (in order as our bankers thought that they might write to Paris for instructions) we should certainly have an equal right to insist on the same date as to the credit—& what is still more we have it in our hands to settle this in the allowance of indemnity for depreciation. In like manner the delay occasioned by the suspension of the King as to the payment of the sums on hand, & on which the U.S. are now paying a dead interest, appears to me a just object of consideration in the regulating of the indemnity. As to the delay prior to the 10th. of Aug. it may be in a considerable degree attributed to the French government also & totally to the situation of that country as to the circulating medium they had introduced [which] would have sufficed of itself to occasion the delay though it was not the only cause —a simple state of the progress of this business will I think necessarily ascertain it.

I might leave out of the question myself & the delay which my particular situation so often explained to you, occasioned as to the settling of the indemnity. I have often repeated[8] that knowing a permanent minister was to be appointed for Paris—knowing from the President's instructions to you[9] that arrangements with respect to the debt to France were to be referred to him—& particularly

6. Morris to Short, November 19, 1792 (ALS, William Short Papers, Library of Congress).

7. Morris to Short, August 23, 1792 (ALS, William Short Papers, Library of Congress).

8. See Short to H, September 25, October 9, 27, 1792.

9. George Washington to H, August 28, 1790.

after knowing that another person had recieved this mark of the Presidents confidence—delicacy & propriety forbad me imperiously from taking any steps, in that line, which could admit of delay. It was evident that a short delay could not be injurious to this business, & I had every reason to believe the person designated would be very shortly in Paris after he had announced to me his nomination, & this was very shortly after my return from Amsterdam. I must observe also that I was ignorant during that whole time of your having changed your intention as to the 2½. millions of the precedent six million loan [10] & of course did not know how large sums were on hand destined for France. I only contemplated the 3 million 4 p. cent loan [11] & as that was only coming in monthly the delay as to the payment did not appear to me to be of any importance, supposing daily it would be removed. The original of your letter of Nov. 30. 91. announcing that of the 2½ millions which you had directed to be held to answer your draughts, only one million would be called for which added 1½. million to those in hand for France, was never recieved. I recieved at Paris on the 7th. of May the *triplicate* of your letter of Jan. 28th. in which you say you inclose a *duplicate* of your letter of Nov. 30. It was not however inclosed in the *triplicate*—nor was your report therein alluded to. They came inclosed in the original of your letter of Jan. 28—sent here to the Hague where it was addressed to me—received by M. Dumas [12]—& by what unaccountable stupidity I know not, kept here until my arrival. He says he thought I was in Spain & therefore kept it expecting me here daily, near three months. He says he learned this from the bankers at Amsterdam—they say he dreamed it. Until then I considered the delay of payment as affecting only such sums as were arising on the 1st. 4. p. cent loan [13] (the term of which had not expired, & out of which payments had been at Amsterdam for interest & premium) & the 2d 4. p. cent loan [14] an-

10. For a description of the September, 1791, Holland loan of six million florins, see Short to H, August 31, 1791.

11. The Holland loan of 1792. For a description of this loan, see Short to H, June 28, 1792, note 17.

12. Charles William Frederick Dumas, unofficial agent of the United States at The Hague.

13. The Holland loan of December, 1791. For a description of this loan, see Short to H, December 23, 28, 1791.

14. See note 11.

nounced to me & by me to you just before my leaving Paris. The affair I then considered in M. Morris's hands as to the indemnity & of course as to the time of future payments as settled between him & me & mentioned to you. I am so anxious that you should have a complete view of this subject which has given me so much uneasiness on account of the disadvantage which the U.S. may sustain & the dead interest they have been & still are paying on so large sums, that I undoubtedly give into repetition & prolixity respecting it. It was my intention to shew you here that the delay previous to the 10th. of Aug. may be imputed also to the French government & the situation of that country as to their circulating medium.

When the first 4. p. cent loan was opened & destined to be paid to the French government, the ministry had made a report to the assembly on their colonies & proposed then appropriating the French debt to their succour. The then minister of marine, M. de Bertrand [15] desired that remittances from Amsterdam might be suspended. It is true our apparent interest dictated the same. I then could have no objection as the sums which I contemplated only, viz those arising from the 4. p. cent loan were to be recieved gradually—& the interest & premiums of Feby & March would absorb a part. After my return to Paris this report was expected daily for a long time as I then mentioned to you to be decided on & finally as you have been informed the succeeding Minister, M. de La Coste,[16] did ask for & recieved my consent to his disposition of 800,000 dollars which though not effected may with great justice be stated as a cause of delay on their part—so much for the French government. As to the circulating medium as an impediment to the payment—I have already informed you [17] that on recieving your letter on the subject of indemnity [18] I communicated the intention of our government to the French ministry & desired them to find out some proper basis for adjusting this indemnity. It was certainly a very natural preliminary to any future payment—& as they never did establish any

15. Antoine François, Marquis de Bertrand de Moleville, was French Minister of Marine from October 4, 1791, to March 15, 1792. See Short to H, December 28, 1791.

16. Jean de Lacoste succeeded Bertrand as Minister of Marine. See Short to H, March 24, April 22, 25, May 14, August 6, 1792.

17. See Short to H, November 22, 1791.

18. H to Short, September 2, 1791.

basis they may be considered as the authors of a delay occasioned by the change in the circulating medium which gave rise to the indemnity. This I mean however only as a circumstance to be taken into consideration in fixing the rate of indemnity, & not to push it to the extent it might be carried, as it was not certainly the only real cause of the delay although it might be made to be regarded as a sufficient cause.

After the King's suspension it was impossible to foresee how long that situation of France would continue which should disable us from knowing to whom to make the payments—with such large sums on hand it might have been desirable to have attempted a reduction of the 5. p. cent bonds to 4. p. cent by offering the alternative of re-imbursement—but the then state of the market & of the appearances among European powers shewed evidently it would have been impracticable.

All that could be done was to retard as much as possible the payments still due by the undertakers & to appropriate a part of the sums on hand to the payment of the Spanish debt.[19] The commissioners assured me [20] they took every eligible method of shewing the undertakers they were not to be pressed—adding however that they made a point of honor of not being behind hand with their engagements & that the discount on bills of exchange being exceedingly low at that time, they found their interest in calling for the bonds though they were of a low & dull sale—having been for some time down to 96 or near it. I have renewed this subject to them several times—their last letter relative thereto was of the 22d. inst: [21] they say therein—"You may depend we will continue to prosecute every eligible step to protract the delivery of the bonds of the last loan yet on hand. But you ought not to be surprized that many nay most of the underwriters will fullfill their engagements yielding them 4. p. cent interest while the discount of bills of exchange is but at 1¾ to 2. p. cent: notwithstanding this extreme low rate, the American bonds are but of slow sale, even at very low prices owing to the firm convic-

19. For a description of this debt, see H to Short, September 1, 1790, note 19. See also Joseph Nourse to H, October 9, 1792; Short to H, October 27, 1792.

20. Willink, Van Staphorst, and Hubbard to Short, October 2, 17, November 19, 1792 (LS, Short Family Papers, Library of Congress).

21. Willink, Van Staphorst, and Hubbard to Short, November 22, 1792 (LS, Short Family Papers, Library of Congress).

tion of our money lenders that the situation of politics must bring about a great rise of interest, which will in some degree be felt by the powers least disposed or liable to be involved in the present disturbances, a rise of which they hold themselves ready to profit, by retaining their monies from a permanent employ."

I have already long ago informed you [22] of my having directed the commissioners to provide bills on Madrid for a part of the Spanish debt, & my having written to Mr. Carmichael [23] desiring him to learn of the ministry to whom the bills should be addressed, & whether they would chuse to recieve such part as bills should not be provided for at the time of the answer at Amsterdam. He has made the application both to Count Daranda [24] & M. Gardoqui [25]—but had not an answer when he last wrote to me. The bills are therefore, as their term was approaching, addressed to M. Gardoqui & sent to Mr. Carmichael by the commissioners to the amount I think of 160,000 dollars. I have desired them to extend that sum to 250,000 dollars,[26] which will be only a little under the sum you mentioned—the balance is by way of precaution & will be paid on the final settlement of the account.

For some time also I had considered 2½ millions of the sums on hand as at your disposition & to be drawn for by you, in consequence of my letters to you from Paris [27] in answer to that from you respecting a new loan at 4½. p. cent interest.[28] It was not until the 18th. of Sep. that yours of July 25. shewed me you should call for only a part of that sum.

I inferred from an expression in your letter of Oct 16 that you will find it convenient to employ the sums on hand in the way there mentioned & if it should happen that you find an advantage in their being on hand, it will be some mitigation of the pain which it has given me to see them so long undisposed of (your letter for M. Mor-

22. See Short to H, August 30, 1792.

23. William Carmichael, United States chargé d'affaires at Madrid.

24. Pedro Pablo Abarca de Bolea, Conde de Aranda, member of the Spanish Council of State.

25. Diego de Gardoqui, former Spanish Minister to the United States, was Spanish Minister of Finance.

26. Short to Willink, Van Staphorst, and Hubbard, November 21, 1792 (ALS, letterpress copy, William Short Papers, Library of Congress).

27. See Short to H, May 14, August 6, 30, 1792.

28. See H to Short, March 5, 21, 1792.

ris inclosed in that of the 16th. of Oct. was forwarded to him by last tuesdays post).

On the 9th. of this month I recieved a letter from the commissioners[29] which among other things stated—"The large payments of interest, the drafts of the treasury, remittances to France & to Spain together with M. de Wolf's[30] bills have reduced the unappropriated cash in our hands to about . . . . f 1,460,000
Adding to which the net proceeds of 844. undelivered bonds 801,800

makes . . . . 2,261,800"

They add that the payment of interest to June 1. inclusive together with the reimbursement of the million then—& the 500,000 florins which they understood the French government meant to apply for to pay an instalment due the 5th. of the next month of the loan made for the U.S. by France under the guarantee of the states general[31] would amount to 2,545,000 florins—& of course leave a deficit on the 1st. of June of 283,000 florins. (As yet no application has been made by France with respect to the 500,000 florins). Their object in this statement was to induce me to obtain powers to make a loan at that time at an higher rate than 4. p. cent interest, they supposing I was limited thereto & conceiving an augmentation of interest would be indispensable. Without saying any thing of my powers in my answer[32] I have simply informed them that I was persuaded the U.S. would not be disposed or necessitated to make any future foreign loan at an higher rate than 4. p. cent interest—& that I myself believe, unless there were a very great change abroad, they might count on procuring at that rate such sums as they might have occasion for in future. I think it not amiss to leave this idea to operate with them & let them suppose we should look out elsewhere rather than retrograde in the rate of interest. It seems to me the U.S. should make every

29. Willink, Van Staphorst, and Hubbard to Short, November 9, 1792 (LS, William Short Papers, Library of Congress).

30. Charles John Michael de Wolf, the Antwerp banker who had acted for the United States in negotiating the Antwerp loan of 1791.

31. This is a reference to the French loan of ten million livres borrowed by France for the United States in Holland in 1782. For a description of this loan, see Willink, Van Staphorst, and Hubbard to H, January 25, 1790, note 3.

32. Short to Willink, Van Staphorst, and Hubbard, November 15, 1792 (ALS, letterpress copy, William Short Papers, Library of Congress).

effort to fix this impression on their minds & those of the money lenders. If they should be once fully persuaded of the determination not to raise the rate of interest, it will produce an inestimable effect hereafter in the reduction of the 5. p. cent bonds. By suspending foreign loans for some time which would seem within the power of the U.S. this might certainly be done. Supposing the sums at present on hand called for by you, their present application at home would enable you probably to provide for from thence, the re-imbursement of the million in June next, in addition to the interest payable abroad next year, which you have already informed me would be remitted. I cannot too often repeat how important I think it is not to be forced on the market during its present state & thus obliged to augment the rate of interest—& the resources which I am informed you may find in the bank makes me hope & trust it may be avoided.

M. de Wolf insists still that he can procure money for the U.S. at 4. p. cent—but I find he cannot *secure* the loans as at Amsterdam for large sums. He desires to be employed according to the usage of Antwerp, which is in general if not always different—it is only in fact having bonds for sale which may or may not be taken up. It is a mode wch. with proper restrictions might be used, when a power was not in want of a given sum at a given time. He presses me now to let him open a loan for a million or half a million of florins at 4. p. cent. I have declined it with him on the footing of the U.S. not having any occasion for the money at present. He may be made use of perhaps to impress the idea of the U.S. adhering to the 4. p. cent interest—but this of course will not be for a long time to come. Should loans be made at Antwerp they should be destined to the payments to France—because those payments may be advanced or started without inconvenience. It would be highly dangerous & injurious to depend on Antwerp for the interest & re-imbursements payable at Amsterdam, because they must be to the day.

I recieved yesterday the papers of the Sec. of State, which I sent for to Amsterdam, relative to my sojourn in Spain [33] & I shall set out in a few days. This absence being of course known to you, I have nothing to add respecting it.

33. In January, 1792, Short and William Carmichael had been appointed commissioners for settling the outstanding differences between the United States

I have the honor to be most respectfully, Sir Your most obedient & humble servant W Short

P. S. I omitted mentioning that the commissioners have recd. a letter from the commissaries of the treasury, informing them they have credited the U.S. for 6,000,000₶ [34] on acct of the payment lately made in florins. M. Morris had lately written to me also that he had at length applied to the commissaries on the same subject & forwarded me their answer to the same effect.[35]

The Honble Alexander Hamilton Secretary of the Treasury—Philadelphia

---

and Spain. The papers referred to by Short were Jefferson's letter of March 18, 1792, informing him of his appointment and instructing him to proceed to Spain as soon as possible and two letters from the Secretary of State of October 14, 1792 (one addressed to Short and the other jointly to Short and Carmichael) concerning Spanish activities among the Indians on the southern frontier of the United States. Letter book copies of these letters may be found in RG 59, Diplomatic and Consular Instructions of the Department of State, 1791–1801, January 23, 1791–August 16, 1793, National Archives. Short received both letters on November 28 (Short to Jefferson, November 30, 1792, LC, RG 59, Despatches from United States Ministers to Spain, 1792–1825, August 15, 1792–February 2, 1795, National Archives).

34. Willink, Van Staphorst, and Hubbard to Short, November 14, 1792 (LS, Short Family Papers, Library of Congress).

35. Morris to Short, November 19, 1792 (ALS, William Short Papers, Library of Congress). The letter of the Commissaries of the French Treasury to Morris is dated November 16, 1792, and is printed as an enclosure to Morris to H, December 23, 1792.

From George Washington

United States, Nov: 29. 1792.

It having been represented by the Director of the Mint [1] that the late rise in the price of Copper, and the difficulty of obtaining it, render it improbable that the quantity authorised to be procured can be had, unless some part of it be imported by the United States; it is therefore thought proper that measures should be taken to obtain a quantity from Europe on the public account; and as it is estimated that the sum of Ten thousand dollars will be necessary for this purpose, you are hereby requested, if consistent with the arrangements of the Treasury, to have a bill for the above sum drawn on the

Bankers of the United States in Holland,[2] payable to Mr. Pinckney[3] our Minister in Great Britain. Go: Washington

LC, George Washington Papers, Library of Congress.

1. On November 28, 1792, David Rittenhouse wrote to Thomas Jefferson concerning the requirements of the Mint for copper (ALS, RG 59, Miscellaneous Letters, 1790–1799, National Archives). On the same day Jefferson wrote to Washington about the purchase of copper for the Mint (ALS, RG 59, Miscellaneous Letters, 1790–1799, National Archives).

2. Willink, Van Staphorst, and Hubbard.

3. Thomas Pinckney.

To George Washington

[Philadelphia, November 29, 1792]

The Secretary of the Treasury presents his respects to the president; has the honor to transmit for his consideration the draft of a report pursuant to two references of the House of Representatives, concerning which he will wait upon the President on Saturday, being desireous of sending in a Report on Monday.[1]

Thursday Nov: 29 1792

LC, George Washington Papers, Library of Congress.

1. See "Report on the Redemption of the Public Debt," November 30, 1792.

From Tench Coxe

Treasury Department, Revenue Office, November 30, 1792. Announces "the completion of the light House, Keepers house, oil Vault, and platform on Cape Henry in the state of Virginia." States that extra work has compelled the contractor to submit a bill in excess of the original contract. Asks Hamilton to secure the President's approval of this bill.[1]

LC, RG 58, Letters of Commissioner of Revenue, 1792–1793, National Archives.

1. A copy of one supplementary contract entered into with John McComb, Jr., by Thomas Newton, Jr., for H on July 29, 1791, may be found in RG 26, Lighthouse Deeds and Contracts, National Archives. The existence of another supplementary agreement between McComb and Newton is indicated in McComb's statement of November 10, 1792 (RG 217, Miscellaneous Treasury Accounts, 1790–1894, Account No. 3298, National Archives). The President's approval is copied on the July 29 contract. A note in Coxe's handwriting at the foot of Account No. 3298 indicates that Washington approved both additions to the original contract.

Report on the Petition of Abraham Scribner and Thomas Cable

[Philadelphia, November 30, 1792
Communicated on December 11, 1792] [1]

[To the Speaker of the House of Representatives]
The Secretary of the Treasury, to whom was referred the petition of Abraham Scribner and Thomas Cable,[2] respectfully [submits] the following Report thereupon.

The petition seeks compensation for the hire and value of a sloop, alleged to have been impressed into the public service, in August 1776, by Hugh Hughes, then Assistant Quarter-Master, with an engagement to pay, at the rate of four dollars a day, for the use of the Sloop, and to pay for her, in case of loss by inevitable accident, or capture by the enemy, which loss by capture is stated to have happened.

From the proofs which accompany the petition, there is satisfactory ground to conclude, that the vessel in question was impressed into the public service, at the period mentioned, and that shortly after, she was intercepted and fell into the hands of the enemy.

But it is not equally clear, that her loss was truly owing to her detention in public service. It appears, that she arrived at New York with some Militia and stores on board, the 27th. of August 1776; the day on which she is stated to have been impressed; and it is not alleged, that she was detained more than four days, when the British vessels, which are said to have prevented her safe return, were already in the Narrows above Hell-gate, about eight miles from New York.

Recurring to the known expedition, with which the retreat from Long Island was effected, the probability is, that the detention was still less considerable, than is now, from recollection, suggested: And the presumption, upon the whole, would rather be, that the detention made no difference, as to the eventual fate of the Vessel.

But if there was an unconditional agreement to indemnify in case of loss, that presumption might not be a good objection to the claim. The proof of such agreement (excluding the attestation of one of the petitioners, which, in point of precedent, cannot be received as evidence) is a certificate from Hugh Hughes of the 9th. of April 1790, which comes fully up to the suggestions of the petitioners, except that it would rather appear from it, that the indemnification was to be made only in case of loss by accident, or capture, while in the actual service of the public. If the Certificate is to be understood in this sense, the condition of the indemnification did not happen.

But strong objections otherwise lie against this claim. From the time of its origination to that of presenting the petition under consideration, a period of near fourteen years has intervened. And there is no evidence or suggestion of any prior application. The delay has not only involved a bar from the Acts of limitation,[3] but must render any proof of the agreement relied upon, short of a written cotemporary document, unsatisfactory. The books and vouchers of Mr. Hughes having been destroyed by fire, no aid to his recollection can be supposed to have been drawn from that source. And, as a general rule, it would be extremely unsafe, to admit claims upon the declarations and acknowledgments of public officers, made at so late a day, especially, if founded only upon memory. Reasons of a particular nature, detailed in a report of the Secretary of the 16th. of April last,[4] strengthen the general considerations, which readily occur on this head.

No special excuse for the delay is assigned.

Wherefore, and under all the circumstances of the case, the Secretary does not perceive sufficient ground for an exception to the operation of the Acts of limitation, in favor of the petitioners.

Which is humbly submitted, Alexander Hamilton,
Secry. of the Treasry.

Treasury Department,
November 30th 1792.

Copy, RG 233, Reports of the Treasury Department, 1792–1793, Vol. III, National Archives.

1. *Journal of the House*, I, 639. The communicating letter, dated December 10, 1792, may be found in RG 233, Reports of the Treasury Department, 1792–1793, Vol. III, National Archives.

2. On May 12, 1790, "A petition of Abraham Scribner and Thomas Cable was presented to the House and read, praying payment for the hire and value of a vessel, the property of the petitioners, which was impressed into the transport service of the United States, in the year one thousand seven hundred and seventy-six, and taken by the enemy.

"*Ordered*, That the said petition be referred to the Secretary of the Treasury, with instructions to examine the same, and report his opinion thereupon to the House." (*Journal of the House*, I, 214–15.)

3. *JCC*, XXIX, 866; XXXIII, 392. See also "Report on Sundry Petitions," April 16, 1792.

4. "Report on Sundry Petitions," April 16, 1792.

Report on the Redemption of the Public Debt

[Philadelphia, November 30, 1792
Communicated on December 3, 1792] [1]

[To the Speaker of the House of Representatives]

In obedience to two resolutions of the House of Representatives, one of the 21st instant,[2] directing the Secretary of the Treasury to report a plan for the redemption of so much of the public debt, as by the Act, intituled "An Act making provision for the debt of the United States," [3] the United States have reserved the right to redeem; the other of the 22d instant,[4] directing him to report the plan of a provision for the reimbursement of the loan made of the Bank of the United States, pursuant to the 11th Section of the Act, intituled "An Act to incorporate the Subscribers to the Bank of the United States" [5] The said Secretary respectfully submits the following Report.

The expediency of taking measures for the regular redemption of the public debt, according to the right which has been reserved to the government, being wisely predetermined by the resolution of the House of Representatives, referring the subject to the Secretary, nothing remains for him, but to endeavor to select and submit the most eligible means of providing for the execution of that important object.

With this view, the first enquiry, which naturally presents itself,

Copy, RG 233, Reports of the Treasury Department, 1792–1793, Vol. III, National Archives.

1. *Journal of the House*, I, 631. The communicating letter may be found in RG 233, Reports of the Treasury Department, 1792–1793, Vol. III, National Archives.

2. *Journal of the House*, I, 624.

3. 1 *Stat.* 138–44 (August 4, 1790).

4. *Journal of the House*, I, 625.

5. 1 *Stat.* 196 (February 25, 1791). For the arrangement made by this section, see "Draft of George Washington's Fourth Annual Address to Congress," October 15–31, 1792, note 20.

is, whether the existing revenues are, or are not adequate to the purpose?

The estimates, which accompany the Report of the Secretary of the 14th, instant,[6] will shew, that during the continuance of the present Indian war, the appropriations for interest, and the demands for the current service, are likely to exhaust the product of the existing revenues; though they afford a valuable surplus beyond the permanent objects of expenditure, which, it is hoped, may, ere long, be advantageously applied to accelerate the extinguishment of the debt.

In the mean time, however, and until the restoration of peace, the employment of that resource, in this way, must, of necessity, be suspended: and either the business of redemption be deferred, or recourse must be had to other expedients.

But did no such temporary necessity, for resorting to other expedients, exist, the doing of it would still be recommended by weighty considerations. It would appear, in the abstract, advisable, to leave the surplus of the present revenues free, to be applied to such casual exigencies, as may from time to time occur—to occasional purchases of the debt, when not exhausted by such exigencies, to the payment of interest on any balances, which may be found due to particular States, upon the general settlement of accounts, and finally, to the payment of interest on the deferred part of the debt, when the period for such payment arrives. There is a reasonable prospect, that, if not diverted, it will be found adequate to the two last important purposes.

Relinquishing, then, the idea of an immediate application of the present revenues to the object in view—it remains to examine, what other modes are in the option of the Legislature.

Loans, from time to time, equal to the sums annually redeemable, and bottomed on the same revenues, which are now appropriated to pay the interest upon those sums, offer themselves, as one expedient, which may be employed, with a degree of advantage. As there is a probability of borrowing at a lower rate of interest, a material saving would result, and even this resource, if none better could be devised, ought not to be neglected.

6. "Report on Estimates of the Expenditures for the Civil List of the United States for the Year 1793," November 14, 1792.

But it is obvious, that to rely upon this resource alone would be to do little towards the final exoneration of the nation. To stop at that point would, consequently, be neither provident nor satisfactory. The interests, as well as the expectations of the Union require something more effectual.

The establishment of additional revenues is the remaining resource. This, if the business is to be undertaken in earnest, is unavoidable. And a full confidence may reasonably be entertained, that the Community will see, with satisfaction, the employment of those means, which alone can be effectual, for accomplishing an end, in itself so important, and so much an object of general desire. It cannot fail to be universally felt, that if the end is to be attained, the necessary means must be employed.

It can only be expected, that care be taken to chuse such as are liable to fewest objections, and that in the modifications of the business, in other respects, due regard be had to the present and progressive circumstances of the country.

Assuming it, as the basis of a plan of redemption, that additional revenues are to be provided, the further enquiry divides itself into the following branches:

1st. Shall a revenue be immediately constituted, equal to the full sum which may at present be redeemed, according to the terms of the contract?

2d. Shall a revenue be constituted from year to year, equal only to the interest of the sum to be redeemed in each year, coupling with this operation, an annual loan commensurate with such sum? Or,

3d. Shall a revenue be constituted, each year, so much exceeding the interest of the sum to be redeemed, as to be sufficient, within a short definite term of time, to discharge the principal itself; coupling with this operation also, an annual loan, equal to the sum to be annually redeemed, and appropriating the revenue created, to its discharge, within the terms which shall have been predetermined?

The first plan, besides being completely effectual, would be eventually most œconomical; but considering, to what a magnitude, the revenues of the United States have grown, in a short period, it is not easy to pronounce, how far the faculty of paying might not be strained by any sudden considerable augmentation, wheresoever immediately placed; while the rapid progress of the country in population and resource seems to afford a moral certainty that the necessary augmentation may be made with convenience, by successive steps, within a moderate term of time—and invites to temporary and partial suspensions, as capable of conciliating the reasonable accommodation of the community, with the vigorous prosecution of the main design. For these, and for other reasons, which will readily occur, the course of providing immediately the entire sum to be reduced, is conceived not to be the most eligible.

The second plan, though much more efficacious, that that of annual loans, bottomed on the revenues now appropriated for the payment of interest on the sums to be redeemed, does not appear to be sufficiently efficacious. The Schedule A will shew the effect of it to the first of January 1802, when the deferred debt will become redeemable in the proportions stipulated. Supposing the investment of the interest, which is, each year, liberated, together with that which has been, and will be released by purchases, pursuant to provisions heretofore made, in the purchase of 6 per cent stock; a sum of principal equal to 2.043.837. dollars and 7 cents would be sunk, and a clear annuity, equal to 459.212 dollars and 82 cents would be created towards further redemptions; but the fund then necessary for the future progressive redemption of the debt, according to the right reserved, would be 1.126.616 dollars and 44 cents, exceeding by 667.403 dollars and 62 cents, the amount of the redeeming fund. Something more effectual than this is certainly desirable, and appears to be practicable.

The last of the three plans best accords with the most accurate view, which the Secretary has been able to take of the public interest.

In its application, it is of material consequence to endeavor to accomplish these two points: 1st. The complete discharge of the sums annually redeemable, within the period prefixed, and the reimbursement, within the same period, of all auxiliary loans which may have been made for that purpose. 2ndly. The constituting, by the expiration of that period, a clear annual fund competent to the future redemption of the debt, to the extent of the right reserved.

The period, to which, it is conceived, the plan ought to refer, is the first day of January 1802; because then the first payment, on account of the principal of the deferred debt, may rightfully be made.

In conformity to these ideas, the following plan is most respectfully submitted; premising, that the sum redeemable for the first year of the 6 per cent stock, bearing a present interest, is computed at 550.000 dollars.

Let an annual fund be constituted, during the present session, equal to 103.199 dollars and 6 cents, to begin to accrue from the first of January 1793. Let the sum of 550.000 dollars be borrowed upon the credit of this annuity, reimbursable within five years, that is, by 1st of January 1799. The sum borrowed to be applied, on the 1st of January 1794, to the first payment on account of the principal of the debt.

The proposed annuity will reimburse the sum borrowed with interest, by the first of January 1799, and will thenceforth be free from any further application.

The sum redeemable the second year, that is, on the 1st of January 1795, is computed at 583.000.

Let an annual fund be constituted, during the second session after the present, equal to 109.391 dollars and 60 cents, to begin to accrue from the first of January 1794. Let the sum of 583000 dollars be borrowed upon the credit of this annuity, reimbursable within five years, that is, by the first of January 1800. The sum borrowed to be applied, on the first of January 1795, to the second payment on account of the principal of the debt.

The proposed annuity will reimburse the sum borrowed with interest, by the first of January 1800, and will be thenceforth free from any further application.

The sum redeemable the third year, that is, on the first of January 1796, is computed at 617.980 dollars.

Let an annual fund be constituted, during the third session after the present, equal to 115.955 dollars and 17 cents, to begin to accrue from the first of January 1795. Let the sum of 617.980 dollars be borrowed upon the credit of this annuity, reimbursable within five years, that is, by the first of January 1801. This sum borrowed to be applied, on the first of January 1796, to the third payment on account of the principal of the debt.

The proposed annuity will reimburse the sum borrowed with interest, by the first of January 1801.

The sum redeemable the fourth year, that is, on the first of January 1797, is computed at 655.058 dollars and 80 cents.

Let an annual fund be constituted, during the fourth session after the present, equal to 122.912 dollars and 48 cents, to begin to accrue from the first of January 1796. Let the sum of 655.058 dollars and 80 cents, be borrowed upon the credit of this annuity, reimbursable within five years, that is, by the first of January 1802. The sum borrowed to be applied on the first of January 1797, to the fourth payment on account of the principal of the debt.

The proposed annuity will reimburse the sum borrowed, with interest, by the first of January 1802.

The sum redeemable the fifth year, that is, on the first of January 1798, is computed at 694.362 dollars and 33 cents.

Let an annual fund be constituted, during the fifth session after the present, equal to 152.743 dollars and 12 cents, to begin to accrue from the first of January 1797. Let the sum of 694.362 dollars and 33 cents, be borrowed upon the credit of this annuity, reimbursable within four years, that is, by the first of January 1802. The sum borrowed to be applied on the first of January 1798, to the fifth payment on account of the principal of the debt.

The proposed annuity will reimburse the sum borrowed, with interest, by the first of January 1802.

The sum redeemable, the sixth year, that is, on the first of January 1799, is icomputed at 736.024 dollars and 7 cents.

Let an annual fund be constituted, during the sixth session after the present, equal to 197.680 dollars and 20 cents, to begin to accrue from the first of January 1798. Let the sum of 736.024 dollars and 7 cents, be borrowed upon the credit of this annuity, reimbursable within three years, that is, by the first of January 1802. The sum borrowed to be applied, on the first of January 1799, to the sixth payment on account of the principal of the debt.

The proposed annuity will reimburse the sum borrowed, with interest, by the first of January, 1802.

The sum redeemable the seventh year, that is, on the first of January 1800, is computed at 780.185 dollars and 52 cents.

Let an annual fund be constituted, during the seventh session after the present, equal to 272.848 dollars and 38 cents, to begin to accrue from the first of January 1799. Let the sum of 780.185 dollars, and 52 cents, be borrowed upon the credit of this annuity, reimbursable within two years, that is, by the first of January 1802. The sum borrowed to be applied, on the first of January 1800, to the seventh payment on account of the principal of the debt.

The proposed annuity will reimburse the sum borrowed, with interest, by the first of January 1802.

The sum redeemable, the eighth year, that is, on the first of January 1801, is computed at 826.996 dollars and 65 cents.

Let an annual fund be constituted, during the eighth session after the present, equal to 423.583 dollars and 64 cents, to begin to accrue from the first of January 1800. Let the sum of 826.996 dollars and 65 cents, be borrowed upon the credit of this annuity, reimbursable, within one year, that is, on the first of January 1802. The sum borrowed to be applied, on the first of January 1801, to the eighth payment on account of the principal of the debt.

The proposed annuity will reimburse the sum borrowed, with interest, on the first of January 1802.

The sum redeemable, the ninth year, that is, on the first of January 1802, is computed at 1.126.616. dollars and 44 cents.

The then existing means for the discharge of this sum, arising from the operation of the plan, will be—

1st. The amount of the annuity constituted the third year, which will have been liberated by reimbursement of the third loan. 2nd. The arrears of interest not previously appropriated, and which are computed at 200.000 dollars.

There will consequently be a deficiency, this year, of 810.661 dollars and 27 cents, which will require to be supplied by a temporary loan, to be reimbursed out of the surplus of the fund, which, on the first of January 1802, will exist for future redemptions, and which surplus will be sufficient to reimburse this temporary loan, in about thirteen years and a half.

It may be proper to remark, that this deficiency upon one year is suffered to exist, to avoid an unnecessary augmentation of revenue, materially beyond the sum permanently requisite. No inconvenience ensues, because this temporary deficiency is made up by the surplus of the permanent fund, within the period mentioned. And that fund, from the first of January 1802, is adequate to all future redemptions, in the full proportion permitted by the contrast.

The table in the Schedule B, herewith submitted, will shew, in one view, the principles and operation of this plan.

The Schedule C, will exhibit the means of constituting the several annuities proposed to be established. From it, will be seen, that the proposed annuities are to be composed, partly of taxes to be successively laid, at the respective periods of creating them, partly of the surplus-dividend to be expected on the Stock belonging to the Government, in the Bank of the United States, beyond the interest to be paid on account of it, and partly of the funds heretofore pledged for the payment of interest, which shall have been liberated upon so much of the debt, as will have been extinguished.

The respective amounts of the taxes to be severally laid, will be,

In the first year	43.199, dollars, and 6 cents,
In the second year	109.391, dollars and 60 cents,
In the third year	115.955, dollars and 17 cents,
In the fourth year	102.912, dollars and 48 cents,
In the fifth year	102.743, dollars and 12 cents
In the sixth year	107.680, dollars and 20 cents
In the seventh year	109.649, dollars and 32 cents.
making together	691.530, dollars and 95 cents.

The sum, which will have been redeemed prior to the first day of January, 1802, will be 5.443.607 dollars and 37 cents. The sum redeemable on the first of January, 1802, will be 1.126.616 dollars and 44 cents; and the fund, which will thenceforth exist, for the purpose of future redemption, (as is particularly shewn by the Schedule D) will be 1.210.744 dollars and 34 cents, exceeding the sum strictly necessary, by 84.127 dollars and 90 cents; a fund, which, including the interest, from year to year, liberated, will, as already intimated, be completely adequate to the final redemption of the whole amount of the 6 per cent stock (as well the deferred, as that bearing a present interest) according to the right which has been reserved for that purpose.

In the mean time, a further impression will be made upon the debt, by the investment of the residue of the funds, heretofore established, in the purchase of it; and it is hoped, that the restoration of peace with the Indians will enable the application of the surplus of the existing revenues, together with the proceeds of the ceded lands in our western territory, to the same object. These, whenever they can be brought into action, will be important aids, materially accelerating the ultimate redemption of the entire debt. The employment of these resources, when it can be done, by encreasing the interest fund, will proportionately lessen the necessity of using the resource of taxation for creating the proposed annunities; if the government shall judge it advisable to avail itself of the substitute, which may accrue from that circumstance.

Having now given a general view of the plan, which has appeared upon the whole, the most eligible, it is necessary, in the next place, to present to the consideration of the House, the requisite funds for the execution of it. These will embrace a provision for the first annuity only; that alone requiring, by the plan, immediate provision. With regard to a provision for the subsequent annuities, which is proposed to be successive, the Secretary will content himself, with this general observation, that he discerns no intrinsic difficulty in making provision for them, as fast as shall be necessary, with due convenience to the people, and consistently with the idea of abstaining from taxing lands and buildings (with the stock and implements of farms) reserving them, as a resource for those great emergencies, which call for a full exertion of all the contributive faculties of a country.

The following means for constituting the first annuity are respectfully submitted, Viz.

Annual surplus of the dividend on the stock of government in the Bank of the United States, beyond the interest to be paid out of the said dividend, estimated at 60.000 dollars.

Tax on horses, kept or used for the purpose of riding, or of drawing any coach, chariot, phaeton, chaise, chair, sulkey or other carriage for conveyance of persons; excepting and exempting all horses, which are usually and chiefly employed for the purposes of husbandry, or in drawing waggons, wains, drays, carts or other carriages, for the transportation of produce, goods, merchandize and commodities, or in carrying burthens in the course of the trade or occupation of the persons, to whom they respectively belong, and the horses of persons in the military service of the United States, Viz.

For every horse, not above excepted and exempted, at the rate of one dollar per annum—where only one is used or kept by the same person, with an addition of fifty cents per annum per horse, where more than one and not more than two horses are kept or used by the same person—with an addition of one dollar per annum per horse, where more than two, and not more than four, are kept or used by the same person, and with an addition of one dollar and a half dollar per horse, per annum, where more than four are kept or used by the same person: provided, that this addition shall not be made in respect to horses, usually employed in public stages for the conveyance of passengers.

This progressive encrease of rates on the higher numbers has reference to the presumption of greater wealth, which arises from the possession of such higher number.

The produce of this tax will probably be about equal to the residue of the proposed annuity, which is 43.199 dollars and 6 cents. How near the truth, this estimate may prove, experiment alone can, in so untried a case, decide. An aid to this fund may be derived from the surplus dividend on the Bank stock, for the half year ending the last of December next, which, it is presumed, will be not less than 20.000 dollars. Should a deficiency appear, upon trial, it can be supplied by a future provision.

Proper regulations, for the collection of this tax, will, it is believed, be found not difficult, if the tax itself shall be deemed eligible. Its simplicity has been a considerable recommendation of it. Qualified, as it is, it is not likely to fall on any but such who can afford to pay it. The exemption from the tax, in regard to horses which are appropriated to the purposes of husbandry, or of any trade or occupation, or to the transportation of commodities, seems to obviate all reasonable objection.

If, however, there should appear to the legislature, reasons for preferring a tax on carriages for pleasure, which, it may be observed, will operate on nearly the same description of persons, the sum required may, it is believed, be produced from the following arrangement of rates, Viz. Upon every Coach, the annual sum of four dollars; Upon every Chariot, the annual sum of three dollars; Upon every other carriage for the conveyance of persons, having four wheels, the annual sum of two dollars; and upon every chair, sulkey or other carriage for the conveyance of persons, having less than four wheels, the annual sum of one dollar.

The collection of this tax will be as simple and easy, and perhaps more certain, than that which has been primarily submitted.

With regard to the second Object referred to the Secretary, namely, the plan of a provision for the reimbursement of the loan made of the Bank of the United States, pursuant to the eleventh section of the Act by which it is incorporated; the following is respectfully submitted, (to wit)—That power be given by law to borrow the sum due, to be applied to that reimbursement; and that so much of the dividend on the stock of the Government in the Bank, as may be necessary, be appropriated for paying the interest of the sum to be borrowed.

From this operation, it is obvious, that a saving to the government will result, equal to the difference between the interest, which will be payable on the new loan, and that which is payable on the sum due to the Bank. If the proposed loan can be effected at the rate may be computed at the annual sum of 35.000 dollars; which saving, of those last made in Holland,[7] the nett saving to the government whatever it may be, is contemplated, as part of the means for constituting the proposed annuities.

The benefit of this arrangement will be accelerated, if provision be made for the application of the proceeds of any loans, heretofore obtained, to the payment suggested on the condition of replacing the sums, which may be so applied out of the proceeds of the loan or loans, which shall be made pursuant to the power above proposed to be given.

It will also conduce to the general end in view, if the Legislature shall think proper to authorize the investment of the funds, destined for purchases of the debt, in purchases of six per cent stock, at the market price, though above par. The comparative prices of the several kinds of Stock have been, and frequently may be, such as to render it more profitable, to make investments in the 6 per cents, than in any other species of Stock.

All which is humbly submitted, Alexander Hamilton,
Secry. of the Treasy.

Treasury Department,
November 30th 1792.

7. See "Draft of George Washington's Fourth Annual Address to Congress," October 15–31, 1792, note 17.

A.

TABLE SHEWING THE EFFECT OF A SUM ANNUALLY CREATED, EQUAL TO THE INTEREST OF THE SUM TO BE REDEEMED, WITHIN EACH YEAR, FOR A PERIOD OF NINE YEARS, COMMENCING FROM THE 1st OF JANUARY 1793. ON THE SUPPOSITION, THAT THE INTEREST ON THE SUM ANNUALLY REDEEMED, BE INVESTED, AS IT IS LIBERATED, IN THE PURCHASE OF 6 PER CENT STOCK, AT THE PRICE OF 22 SHILLINGS IN THE POUND.

Periods of redemption		Sums annually redeemable. Dollars. Cents	Interest annually liberated. Dollars. Cents	Sums annually purchased. Dollars. Cents.
January 1st.	1794.	550.000.	33.000.	291.172. 4.
ditto	1795.	583.000.	34.980.	262.523. 5.
ditto	1796.	617.980.	37.078.80.	231.916.56.
ditto	1797.	655.058.80.	39.303.52.	199.233.86.
ditto	1798.	694.362.33.	41.661.73.	164.349.20.
ditto	1799.	736.024. 7.	44.161.44.	127.129.15.
ditto	1800.	780.185.52	46.811.13.	87,432.33.
ditto	1801.	826.996.65.	49.619.79	45.108.90.
ditto	1802.	1.126.616.44.	67.596.41.	61.451.28
Interest on debt paid in and purchased		....	65.000.	573.520.70.
			459.212.82.	2.043.837. 7.

Treasury Department, November 30th. 1792.

Alexander Hamilton. Secy. of the Tresy.

[C]

MODE OF CONSTITUTING THE PROPOSED ANNUITIES.

1793.	Surplus dividend of Bank stock beyond the interest which will be payable, estimated at...	60.000.	
	Tax	43.199. 6	
			103.199. 6.
1794.	Tax		109.391.60.
1795.	Tax		115.955.17.
1796.	Part of annual interest converted into annuity..	20.000.	
	Tax	102.912.48	
			122.912.48.
1797.	Part of annual interest converted into annuity..	50.000.	
	Tax	102.743.12.	
			152.743.12.
1798.	Part of annual interest converted into annuity..	90.000.	
	Tax	107.680.20.	
			197.680.20.
1799.	Part of annual interest converted into annuity..	60.000.	
	Annuity of the first year now liberated by reembursement of 1st. Loan..................	103.199. 6	
	Tax	109.649.32.	
			272.848.38.

B.

TABLE EXHIBITING A VIEW OF THE PROPOSED PLAN OF REDEMPTION.

Periods of redemption or payment.	Sums redeemable.	Temporary Loans. Times of Reimbursement.	Temporary Loans. Years duration.	Amount of sums borrowed with compound interest to the respective periods of reimbursement.	Years when Annuities begin to accrue.	Years Annuities.	Annuities
	Dollars. Cents.			Dollars. Cents.			Dollars. Cents.
January 1st..1794.	550.000.	January 1st..1799.	5.	701.954.	1793...	6.	103.199. 6.
ditto.....1795.	583.000.	ditto.....1800	.........5.	744.071.24.	1794...	6.	109.391.60.
ditto.....1796.	617.980.	ditto.....1801	.........5.	788.715.51.	1795...	6.	115.955.17.
ditto.....1797.	655.058.80.	ditto.....1802	.........5.	836.038.44.	1796.	6.	122.912.48.
ditto.....1798.	694.362.33.	ditto.....1802	4	843.997.41.	1797...	5.	152.743.12.
ditto.....1799.	736.024. 7.	ditto.....1802.	3.	852.021.46.	1798.	4.	197.680.20.
ditto.....1800.	780.185.52.	ditto.....1802	.........2.	860.154.53.	1799.	3.	272.848.38.
ditto.....1801.	826.996.65.	ditto.....1802.	1.	868.346.48.	1800.	2.	423.583.64.
ditto.....1802	1.126.616.44.						
Total sum redeemed by the 1st. of January 1802	... 6.570.223.81.						

Treasury Department, November 30th. 1792
Alexander Hamilton.

N: B: All the calculations in this table proceed upon a rate of five per cent interest.

1800.	Part of annual interest converted into annuity..	220.000.	
	Annuity of second year now liberated by reimbursement of 2d. loan..................	109.391.60.	
	Part of arrears of interest to be applied for balance of annuity of this year................	94.192. 4	
			423.583.64
	But a supplementary provision will be to be made for the second year, equal to the sum of 94.192 dollars, and 4 cents, as the fund in that particular is nöt annual. This may also arise from arrears of interest.		
	The payment to be made on the 1st. of January 1802, may proceed from the following funds.		
	Amount of annuity of 3d. year liberated by reimbursement of 3d. loan..................	115.955.17.	
	Unappropriated arrears of interest............	200.000.	
	Temporary loan..............................	810.661.27.	
			1.266.616.44

Treasury Department, November 30th. 1792.

Alexander Hamilton
Secry: of the Treasy.

D

VIEW OF REDEEMING FUND TO AND UPON THE 1ST. JANUARY 1802.

Interest which will have been liberated by purchases and payments into the Treasury, exclusive of redemptions, according to the proposed plan					65.000.
Jan: 1st.	1794, by redemption	of,	550.000 dols.	rate 6 per cent	33.000.
ditto,	1795, by ditto	of,	583.000,	at ditto	34.980.
ditto,	1796, by ditto.	of,	617.980,	ditto	37.078.80
ditto,	1797, by. ditto,	of	655.058.80	ditto	39.303.52
ditto,	1798, by ditto,	of	694.362.33	ditto	41.661.73.
ditto,	1799, by, ditto,	of	736.024. 7	ditto	44.161.44.
ditto,	1800, by ditto	of	780.185.52	ditto	46.811.13.
ditto,	1801, by ditto,	of	826.996.65	ditto	49.619.79.
ditto,	1802, by ditto,	of	1.126.616.44	ditto	67.596.98.
					459.213.39.

Taxes which have been laid.			
1793,	dollars.	43,199. 6.	
1794,		109.391.60	
1795		115.955.17.	
1796		102.912.48.	
1797		102.743.12	
1798		107.680.20.	
1799		109.649.32.	
			651.530.95.
Surplus dividend of Bank stock beyond the interest which will be payable out of it			60.000.
		Dollars,	1 210.744.34.

Amount of Interest converted into Annuities.		
1796,	Dollars,	20.000.
1797,		50.000.
1798,		90.000.
1800,		220.000.
Annual sum at the end of 1800		380.000.

Treasury Department
November 30th. 1792.

Alexander Hamilton
Secry. of the Treasy.

From Joseph Whipple

Portsmouth, New Hampshire, November 30, 1792. "I have to acknowledge the receipt of your letter of the 1st. instant [1] accompanying Commissions for John Adams as first Mate & Benj Gunnison as second Mate of the Revenue Cutter Scammel. I beg leave to Nominate Samuel Odiorne [2] for the third Mate of Said Cutter. . . ."

LC, RG 36, Collector of Customs at Portsmouth, Letters Sent, 1792–1793, National Archives; copy, RG 56, Letters from the Collector at Portsmouth, National Archives.

1. Letter not found.

2. Odiorne's commission as third mate of the New Hampshire revenue cutter is dated December 18, 1792 ("Register of Acts of the Federal Congress and Communications Received by the Department of State, 1790–1795," D, Papers of the Continental Congress, National Archives).

To Thomas Mifflin [1]

[*Philadelphia, December 1, 1792.* "Mr. Hamilton presents his respectful Compliments to Governor Mifflin and requests he will be so obliging as to send by the bearer the papers [2] he was kind enough to offer a perusal of to Mr. Hamilton." [3] *Letter not found.*]

AL, sold by American Art Association, March 3, 1925, Lot 272.

1. Mifflin was governor of Pennsylvania.

2. The papers, which have not been found, related to the resistance in western Pennsylvania to the Federal excise on distilled spirits. See H to Mifflin, December 3, 1792.

3. Extract taken from dealer's catalogue.

To George Washington

[Philadelphia, December 1, 1792]

The Secretary of the Treasury presents his respects to the President has the honor to submit to him the enclosed communications concerning which he will wait upon The President on Monday.

1st Decemr. 1792

LC, George Washington Papers, Library of Congress.

To the President and Directors of the Bank of the United States

Treasury Department Decr 3d 1792

Gentlemen

I have to request that a further advance of one thousand Dollars may be made by the Bank to William Young & George Dannacker,[1] on account of their Contract with the Publick for supplying the Troops of the united States with Clothing for the ensuing year to be charged as heretofore.

I have the honor to be Gentlemen Your obedt Servt.

Alexander Hamilton

The President & Directors of the
Bank of the united States

LS, Mr. William N. Dearborn, Nashville, Tennessee.

1. See "Contract with George Dannacker and William Young," October 22, 1792; H to the President and Directors of the Bank of the United States, November 28, 1792.

From William Ellery

[*Newport, Rhode Island*] *December 3, 1792.* "No allowance having been made to me for my services from the time I opened my Office to the 30th. of June 1792 by Congress at their last Session, and the addition of an half per centum and fifty dolls. per annum to my other emoluments then granted, to commence on the first of July, being inadequate to a decent maintenance, I have addressed a petition [1] that that Honble Body praying for such an allowance as justice and equity require, and for such an augmentation of Salary as shall added to my fees and other emoluments, afford me a decent support. . . ."

LC, Newport Historical Society, Newport, Rhode Island.

1. On December 27, 1792, "A petition of William Ellery, Collector of the District of Newport, in the State of Rhode Island and Providence Plantations, was presented to the House and read, praying that the compensation allowed him by law may be increased, and rendered more adequate to his services.

"*Ordered,* That the said petition be referred to the Secretary of the Treasury, with instruction to examine the same, and report his opinion thereupon to the House." (*Journal of the House,* I, 655–56.)

H did not report on Ellery's petition, and on January 5, 1795, he returned it to the House of Representatives. See H to Frederick A. C. Muhlenberg, January 5, 1795.

To Thomas Mifflin

Philadelphia December 3. 1792

Sir

I beg you to accept my thanks, for the perusal of the papers you sent me, which I herewith return.[1]

The extracts from the charges to grand Juries are new to me. The correspondence between Mr. Addison and Mr. Clymer, I had before seen.[2]

While I found cause to regret the nature of the discussion, which had taken place, and could not but think the strictures on the Judicial Authority of the Government of the United States and on the System, which had been adopted under that authority, as not unexceptionable in the Judge of a State Court,[3] I concluded, that to avoid a disclosure of the correspondence, would best comport with that careful cultivation of harmony and good humour, between the

General and the particular Governments, and their respective officers, which it is evident is of the greatest importance to the public welfare; and I acted in conformity to this Idea.

How far the same consideration ought to have weight in referrence to the communication, which you mentioned to me, it was your intention to make to the House of Representatives of Pensylvania,[4] or how far there may be considerations of public utility sufficient to overrule any objection which may seem to arise from that source—it is not for me to determine.

With the most perfect respect I have the honor to be Sir Your most obedient & most humble servant Alexander Hamilton

His Excellency Governor Mifflin

ALS, Historical Society of Pennsylvania, Philadelphia.

1. See H to Mifflin, December 1, 1792.

2. See "Draft of a Proclamation Concerning Opposition to the Excise Law," September 7, 1792; George Washington to Mifflin, September 29, 1792.

On October 5, 1792, Mifflin instructed the judges of the Pennsylvania Supreme Court "to charge the Grand Juries of the several counties within your district, to enquire into and present all offences of the nature to which the Proclamation refers" (*Pennsylvania Archives,* 2nd ser., IV, 35). Presumably the charges to which H is referring were those made by the state judges in accordance with Mifflin's orders.

H had learned of the correspondence between Alexander Addison, presiding judge of the County Court of the western district of Pennsylvania, and George Clymer, supervisor of the revenue for the District of Pennsylvania, through several letters that Clymer had sent to H. See Clymer to H, September 28, October 1, 4, 10, 1792.

3. This is a reference to the "strictures" made by Addison. In a letter to Mifflin, enclosing charges to grand juries, Addison wrote: "I have long entertained an opinion which the most serious reflection, (and I have given it a serious reflection,) has not altered but confirmed, that the powers of the federal courts in the extent given them by the judicial laws of the Union are useless or dangerous. Useless, because the State courts are capable in a proper manner of discharging almost all their duties. Dangerous, because if they exercise their powers they must either destroy the essence of the trial by Jury, or swallow up the state courts" (*Pennsylvania Archives,* 2nd ser., IV, 38). See also Clymer to H, October 4, 1792, note 5.

4. See "Extract from Governor Mifflin's Annual Message," December 7, 1792 (*Pennsylvania Archives,* 2nd ser., IV, 52–54).

From Samuel L. Mitchell[1]

[New York, December 3, 1792]

Sir

With great improvement and satisfaction I perused your Report on Manufactures,[2] soon after its publication, and tho I then ardently wished the establishment of such as would render our Country independent of foreign places, for necessary Supplies particularly of naval and military stores, yet I little thought at that time I should ever be placed in a Situation[3] of cooperating with the Secretary of the Treasury in carrying into effect such projects in detail as are comprized in his general Provisions.

I had enjoyed the rural satisfaction of agricultural improvement at Plandome on Long island, had practised Law and tried Causes at the bar, had been appointed an Officer in the Militia; and been a representative of the People in the State Legislature, when I received an Invitation from the Trustees of Columbia College to accept the Chair of Chemical Professor[4] in New York, under the Patronage of the State, which had made provision for the same.[5]

On Reviewing my Stock of knowledge, I thought I could undertake the Duties of the Place consistent with attention to other Business, and accordingly have commenced my Literary and Scientific Operations. The Trustees ordered the Professors to publish each a Syllabus, and accordingly my Outline has been committed to the Press. A Copy of it is herewith forwarded to you;[6] that you may know what is aimed at, and what is a doing under the late legislative sanction, in the State of New York. You will be satisfied I hope, on Perusals that my endeavour in sketching out the Plan, has been to unite philosophical Speculation with improvement in the useful Arts.

The recent Discoveries in Chemistry are so vast and extensive, so fraught with philosophical Truth & so applicable to numberless economical purposes that it is sorely to be lamented, they are so little known in this Country. Yet I feel encouraged to think, Inquiries of this Kind, will have a gradual Progress among us, and keep pace with at least, if not outgo sundry other Improvements. It is greatly to be desired, that Researches and Investigations of the Chemical sort, which have already done so much in advancing and cheapening manufactures, and are capable of doing beneficially so much more, may become fashionable, and be eagerly entered into by Gentlemen of fortune and education, as well as Artists and Manufacturers.

Your manufacturing Society, established at Pasaick falls[7] will require the aid of some Chemical Operations, particularly in the whitening of Cloth and Thread of Cotton, Hemp and Flax. I would hint to you, to have the bleaching done, not by exposure to the Sun Shine in an Open field in the old Way, but to adopt the new Method proposed by Mons. Berthollet,[8] of making Vegetable substances white by means of the *Oxygenated Neuriatic Acid*, as the quickest and cheapest method. In Case this plan should be thought adviseable, I would recommend *Mr. Joseph Russel*[9] of this City, to the Society as a proper person to prepare and oxygenate the Spirit of Salt for the purpose: he being possessed of those qualities as a Man, and that practical skill as a Chemist, which render him in my Judgment, a very fitting Person for the Purpose.

I have received your Communication about the Light House,[10] and am sorry to learn, there is no present Prospect of effecting the erection of such a building at the proposed place. But as Improvements are gradual and progressive, perhaps this part of our Coast may be considered and benefited in its Turn.

I have the Honour to be, with much Respect, Sir, your very obedient Servant Saml. L. Mitchell

New York. Decr. 3. 1792.
The Hon. Alexr. Hamilton

ALS, Hamilton Papers, Library of Congress.

1. Mitchell, who was born near Manhasset Bay, Long Island, New York, served his apprenticeship in medicine under Dr. Samuel Bard and later studied medicine at the University of Edinburgh. On September 29, 1791, he was appointed a captain in the Queens County Militia. From January 5 until March 24, 1791, he was a member of the New York Assembly.

2. "Report on the Subject of Manufactures," December 5, 1791.

3. On November 15, 1792, Mitchell was made secretary of the New York Society for the Promotion of Agriculture, Arts, and Manufactures.

4. Mitchell was Professor of Chemistry, Physics, and Agriculture at Columbia.

5. On April 11, 1792, the New York legislature passed "An Act to encourage Literature by Donations to Columbia College, and to the several Academies in the State." This act provided in part "That the treasurer shall annually for five years, unless otherwise directed by the legislature, pay to the trustees of Columbia College, or their order, . . . the sum of seven hundred and fifty

pounds, to be applied to the payment of the salaries of such additional professors in the said college, as the said trustees shall think proper to appoint" (*Laws of the State of New-York. Fifteenth Session* [New York: Printed by Francis Childs and John Swaine, Printers to the State, 1791], 71).

6. *Outline of the Doctrines in Natural History, Chemistry, and Economics, Which, under the Patronage of the State, are now Delivering in the College of New-York* (New York: Printed by Childs and Swaine, 1792). The first page of this pamphlet, published on September 29, 1792, contains an extract from the minutes of a meeting of the Columbia trustees: "*Ordered*, That every Professor of this College who teaches by LECTURE, do publish, within one year, a SYLLABUS of his Course of lectures." H was at this time a trustee of Columbia College, although he did not attend meetings of the board of trustees while he was Secretary of the Treasury.

7. The Society for Establishing Useful Manufactures, which was located at Passaic Falls in what is now Paterson, New Jersey.

8. Claude Louis Berthollet, who collaborated with Antoine Laurent Lavoisier in the preparation of a systematic chemical nomenclature, was one of the first chemists to adopt Lavoisier's theory of combustion and the first to discover hypochlorites and chlorates. In 1785 he learned that chlorine was a powerful bleaching agent. The use of chlorine spread rapidly from Aberdeen to Glasgow and Manchester in spite of the difficulties in handling the new reagent (Charles Singer, E. J. Holmyard, A. R. Hall, and Trevor I. Williams, eds., *A History of Technology* [Oxford, 1958], IV, 221–22, 247).

9. Russel is listed as a surgeon in *The New-York Directory and Register, for the Year 1792* (New-York: Printed for the Editor, by T. & J. Swords, No. 27, William-Street, 1792), 116.

10. Letter not found.

From Joseph Nourse[1]

Treasury Dept. Registers office 3 Decr. 92

Sir,

I have the Honor to prest. to you the Accounts of the Comrs. of Loans upon which the Estimate for appropriating 35.063 Dollars 28 Cts. was formd being for the Salarys of their Clerks and for stationary in the Loan Offices to 31 March 93[2] the Amount of said accounts the Payment whereof is suspended untill an Appn. shall be made is 18,947.88

The sum requisite for the Payment of the several accounts which may be rend. is stated at 16.115.40

Making the Amt. as p. Estimate Dollars 35.063.28

I have particularizd the Sums which may be required for Each Office—but as this is only by Estimate I would submit a Request that the appn. may be so formed as to cover the General Demand from the several L. O. to that Period.

I have the honor to be &c

Hon: A: Hamilton Esq: Sec: &c

LC, RG 53, Register of the Treasury, Estimates and Statements for 1793, Vol. "135–T," National Archives; copy, RG 233, Reports of the Treasury Department, 1792–1793, Vol. III, National Archives.

1. This letter was enclosed in "Report on the Accounts of the Commissioners of Loans," December 3, 1792.

2. D, RG 53, Register of the Treasury, Estimates and Statements for 1793, Vol. "135–T," National Archives; copy, RG 233, Reports of the Treasury Department, 1792–1793, Vol. III, National Archives. For this statement, see "Report on the Accounts of the Commissioners of Loans," December 3, 1792.

Reports on the Accounts of the Commissioners of Loans

Treasury Department, December 3rd. 1792.
[Communicated on December 3, 1792] [1]

[To the Speaker of the House of Representatives]
Sir

I have the honor to transmit herewith the accounts called for by a resolution of the House of Representatives of Friday last,[2] together with a Statement by the Register exhibiting the detail of the Estimate, to which that resolution relates, and the copy of a letter from him to me of this date.[3] As the accounts are original papers, and necessary documents of the Treasury, I pray that the House will be pleased, after making the use intended of them, to cause them to be returned.

With perfect respect, I have the honor to be, Sir, Your most obedient and humble Servant,

Alexander Hamilton
Secry. of the Treasy.

The Honorable, The Speaker,
of the House of Representatives.

Copy, RG 233, Reports of the Treasury Department, 1792–1793, Vol. III, National Archives.

1. *Journal of the House*, I, 632. The communicating letter, dated December 3, 1792, may be found in RG 233, Reports of the Treasury Department, 1792–1793, Vol. III, National Archives.

2. On November 30, 1792, the House of Representatives "*Resolved*, That the Secretary of the Treasury be directed to lay before the House the accounts of the Commissioners of Loans, for the current year, by which his estimate is formed for appropriating thirty-five thousand and sixty-three dollars and twenty-eight cents, for the salaries of Clerks and for stationery, in the Loan Offices of the United States, to the thirty-first of March, one thousand seven hundred and ninety-three" (*Journal of the House*, I, 631).

3. For the register's letter, see Joseph Nourse to H, December 3, 1792.

LIST OF THE ACCOUNTS OF THE COMMISSIONERS OF LOANS BY WHICH THE ESTIMATE FOR APPROPRIATING THE SUM OF 35.063.28, WAS FORMED, BEING FOR THE SALARIES OF CLERKS, AND FOR STATIONERY IN THE LOAN OFFICES OF THE UNITED STATES, TO 31ST. MARCH 1793.

Number.	States.	Loan Officers.	No. of Treasury Settlement.[4]	Periods.		Amount.	Total.
	New Hampshire	William Gardner		No Account rendered			
1.	Massachusetts	Nat. Appleton.	2533.	1st. January 1792 to 31st. March		1019.27.	
2.	do.	do.	2781.	1st. April to 30th. June 1792		1073.97.	
3.	do.	do.	3141.	1st. July 1792 to 30th. September		1344.14.	3437.38.
4	Rhode Island	Jabez Bowen	2837.	1st. January to 30th. June		588.61.	
5.	do.	do.	3144.	1st. July to 30th. September		190.93	779.54
6.	Connecticut	William Imlay	2906.	1st. Oct: 1790, to 31st. March 1792			1489.13
7.	New York	John Cochran	2591.	1st. Octo: 1790, to 31st. March 1792	5719.70.		
				Deduct provided for on a former Appropriation, for the several L: Officers, as per receipt	4000.	1719.70.	
8.	do.	do.	2938.	1st. April 1792 to 30th. June		2191.92	
9.	do.	do.	3077.	1st. July to 30th. September 1792		1833. 3.	5744.65.
10.	New Jersey	James Ewing.	2520.	1st. January 1792 to 31st. March		160.80.	
11.	do.	do.	2804.	1st. April to 30th. June		88.79.	
12.	do.	do.	3160.	1st. July to 30th. September		90.66.	340.25
13.	Pennsylvania	Thomas Smith.	2429.	1st. January 1792 to 31st March		642.17.	
14.	do.	do.	2677.	1st. April to 30th. June		837.50.	
15.	do.	do.	3108.	1st. July to 30th. September		462.50.	1942.17.
16.	Delaware	James Tilton.	3005.	1st. July 1791, to 30th. September			206.13.
17.	Maryland	Thomas Harwood.	2877.	1st. Octo: 1790, to 31st. Dec. 1791		1519.93.	
18.	do.	do.	2925.	1st. January to 30th. June 1792		523.70.	
19.	do.	do.	3143.	1st. July to 30th. September 1792		245. .	2288.63.
20.	Virginia	John Hopkins.	2482.	1st. January to 31st March 1792			1303.64.
21.	North Carolina	Wm. Skinner.	2480.	to May 1792	2406.48.		.
				Deduct provided for by a former Appropn. as per receipt	2125. .		281.48

22.	South Carolina	John Neufville	3254.	14th. Octo: 1790, to 30th: Sep: 1792	2.552.27.
	Georgia	Richard Wylley		No Account rendered	
				Amount of Accounts, No. 1. to 22	20.365.27.

Deduct a balance which remains, to be applied, of the sum of 21.000 dollars, (included in the sum of 197.119 dollars and 49 cents) appropriated by an Act making Appropriations for the support of Government for the year 1792 [5] — 1.417.39.

18.947.88.

The Accounts of William Gardner for New Hampshire, and Richard Wylley for Georgia, have not been rendered,—the former is estimated at — 650. .

And the latter, at — 364.80.

IN FORMING THE ESTIMATES OF THEIR EXPENSES FROM THE DATE OF THE LAST PERIODS ABOVE STATED, IT WAS SUPPOSED THAT THEIR ACCOUNTS WHEN RENDERED AND SETTLED TO 31ST. DECEMBER 1792, MIGHT BE, AS FOLLOW;

VIZ

Massachusetts	for 3 months		1344.14.	
Rhode Island	do.		293.70.	
Connecticut	9 do.		659.67.	
New York	3 do.		1833. 3.	
New Jersey	3 do.		159.75.	
Pennsylvania	3 do.		467.17.	
Delaware	3 do.		93.87	
Maryland	3 do.		245.	
Virginia	9 do.		2049.53.	
North Carolina	8 do.		562.96	
South Carolina	3 do.		391.78.	
To extend their allowance to 31st. March 1793, estimated, Viz:				
The foregoing Estimate for 50 months amounts to		8000 Dollars.		
3 months for 13 Loan Officers, are 39 months		6240		
Allowance for deficiencies		760.		
			7000.	16.115.40
Total, as per Estimate, Dollars				35,063.28.

5. 1 *Stat.* 226–29 (December 23, 1791).

To George Washington

Treasury Departmt. 3d Decr. 1792.

The Secretary of the Treasury has the honor to submit to the President a communication of the 30th. of Novemr. relating to some additional objects which have been executed towards the completion of the Lighthouse Establishment on Cape Henry.[1]

The Secretary, according to the best information in his possession, considers them as necessary objects, and respectfully submits it as his opinion that it will be advisable to confirm the Contracts which have been entered into by Mr. Newton,[2] in the first instance.

The Secretary, from experience, entertains a confidence in the discretion & judgment of that Gentleman which induces a reliance on the view taken by him of the subject on the spot, with the advantage of a knowledge of local, which cannot be possessed by any person here. A submission to arbitration might not be altogether free from hazard of an increased allowance and it is so apparent that the *whole work* has been accomplished upon such moderate terms, & so probable that it may not even have afforded a due degree of benefit to the Undertaker, as to create a claim on the liberality of the Government in regard to collateral Contracts.

All which is humbly submitted

Alexander Hamilton
Secy. of the Treasury.

LC, George Washington Papers, Library of Congress.

1. See Tench Coxe to H, November 30, 1792.
2. Thomas Newton, Jr., inspector of Survey No. 4 in Virginia.

From Charles Lee[1]

Alexandria [*Virginia*] *December 4, 1792.* Reports that no bounties on fishing vessels will be payable "within this District for the present year."[2]

Copy, RG 56, Letters to and from the Collector at Alexandria, National Archives.

1. Lee was collector of customs at Alexandria, Virginia.
2. See "Treasury Department Circular to the Collectors of the Customs," October 25, 1792.

From Arthur St. Clair

Philadelphia
December 5th 1792

Sir,

Your Letter of the 21st. September [1] enclosing a Copy of an Order of the Senate relative to the Salaries, Fees and Emoluments of Persons holding Offices under the United States, and the actual Expenses and Disbursements attending the Execution of their respective Offices for one Year,[2] came to hand a few days ago. You desire from me an Account of the Offices I hold, as Governor of the western Territory and superintendant of Indian Affairs, embracing those Objects, and for the period therein mentioned to end the first day of October last past. In Answer, Sir, I have to observe that, by the Resolve of Congress of the third of October 1787 [3] the Office of Superintendant of Indian Affairs for the northern Department was united with that of Governor of the western Territory, and the Compensation that had been attached to that Office was added to the Salary of the Governor, making in the whole two thousand Dollars. That, since the establishment of the present Government, there has been no Appointment of a Superintendant and that, hitherto there has been no Fees, nor Emolument of any kind whatsoever beside the Salary.

It is not possible for me to give you, at this time an Account of the Expenses that regularly attend the discharge of the Office annually—nor of the Disbursements I have actually made. The last have been heavy, and have absorbed nearly the whole of the Salary; But, as a part, at least, of those Disbursements are out of the usual Course, having been incurred in the discharge of Duties specially directed by Congress, they cannot be fairly stated as incident to Office, and I expect a reimbursement.

The regular Expenses of the Governor will, however, be considerable for some Years to come; for, the Settlements are so distant and unconnected with each other—the Communications between them so difficult—the Manners of the People so dissimilar, as well as their Languages different, that, it seems to me, to be able to accommodate Laws to their different Situations, it will be necessary for the Governor of that Territory to visit all the Settlements once a Year at least, notwithstanding the extremes of them are nearly a thousand Miles apart. His Expenses on those Occasions cannot be estimated at less than five hundred Dollars especially when it is considered that, in the french Settlements bordering on the Wabash and Mississippi, Money is of less value than, perhaps, in any other part of the World. That, together with a small Sum for Stationery, House Rent, and Postage of Letters will [be] from the whole Disbursement, for the Government property, and should be considered as an annual Expense, altho, in present Circumstances, it may not be incurred. The Disbursements in that part which respect the Indians cannot be conjectured as they depend upon Circumstances entirely unforeseen. There is at present no regular Expense attending it, *that I know of,*[4] except a Salary of sixty Pounds pr. Annum to an Interpreter at Pittsburgh. He was appointed by me; but whether he is continued or dismissed, I am not informed.

I have the honor to be Sir Your most humble Servant

A. St. Clair

The honorable Alexander Hamilton
Secretary of the Treasury

ALS, RG 46, Second Congress, 1791–1793, Reports of the Secretary of the Treasury, National Archives; ADfS, State Library, Columbus, Ohio.

1. Letter not found. See, however, "Treasury Department Circular," September 13, 1792.

2. See "Treasury Department Circular to the Collectors of the Customs," August 31, 1792, note 1.

3. *JCC*, XXXIII, 601.

4. In 1795 St. Clair wrote to George Washington: ". . . I have been very much disgusted for a considerable time, and . . . treatment from some of the departments . . . made such an impression upon me as to determine me to retire from all public service. . . . It began with the War Department, to which the control of Indian affairs is given, and the superintendence to me. That office you know, sir, I held before the establishment of the new Government, and, as such, I was known to the Indians, but, for a very long time I have never been made acquainted with any thing respecting them; numbers of them have been called to the seat of Government from time to time, and by persons employed by the Secretary of War, without the slightest intimation to me. . . . Neither have I ever been informed of the name or residence of my deputy, or received a single line of information or intelligence from him" (William Henry Smith, ed., *The St. Clair Papers: The Life and Public Services of Arthur St. Clair* [Cincinnati, 1882], II, 390–91).

From Tobias Lear

[*Philadelphia*] *December 6, 1792.* "By the President's command, T. Lear has the honor to return to the Secretary of the Treasury, with the President's approbation affixed thereto, the Contract entered into by Thomas Newton junr. on the part of the U.S. with John McComb junr. to execute certain additional objects specified in said Contract, to the Lighthouse lately erected on Cape Henry. . . ." [1]

LC, George Washington Papers, Library of Congress.

1. See Tench Coxe to H, November 30, 1792, and H to George Washington, December 3, 1792.

To John F. Mercer [1]

Philadelphia December 6th. 1792

Sir

In my last letter to you,[2] I informed you of my having transmitted copies of your answer of the 16th of October and of certain certificates accompanying it to Major Ross. I have lately received a letter from him of the 23rd of last month, of which and of the documents, to which it refers, I now send you copies agreeably to the Major's request.

No strictures on the policy or tendency of my public conduct, not connected with an impeachment of my honor or probity, if so understood by me, would have drawn on any correspondence between us. The single cause of the letter from me which introduced it was a belief founded on the strong public declaration of Mr Ross that you had *asserted* or *insinuated* that in the transactions respecting the purchase of public debt on account of the Government,[3] I had been concerned directly or indirectly in some species of Stock-jobbing for my private emolument—or to speak more precisely, that I had as a *buyer for the public* given more than the market price for stock, which I myself or some person or persons, with whom I was connected *in interest, had sold* to the Government.

This was what I understood Major Ross as intending by what he charges you with having said respecting my having been at once the *buyer* and *seller* of Stock (and so he explains himself) [4] not that you had accused me of giving 18/ of *my own money* for Stock which was offered me at 14/.

Upon that understanding of Major Ross's meaning I addressed you, and you will on a revision perceive that it required no infatuation to suppose, that you might have made such an accusation. Nor can you be surprised at my having given credit to Major Ross's statement of what you had said, when you are informed, that I had been before, under the sanction of secrecy, told by more than one person of character of your having made declarations of similar import—and when you reflect that it was not easy for me to imagine that Major Ross would put his name to a publication in a News Paper imputing to you such language as having been used in a public discourse before a numerous auditory, in reference to a point of so much delicacy, if the imputation was not well founded.

Hence the energy of the expressions used in my letter to Major Ross[5]—which however are only hypothetical—applying merely to the statement which had been made by him and having no application if that statement was erroneous.

With regard to the publication of my letter in hand bills[6] though I find on revision that the latitude of my expressions, in the permission I gave Major Ross warranted the use he made of my letter and though I ascribe his having made that use of it to motives the most friendly towards me, yet I am bound in justice to myself to say that such a mode of disclosure was not contemplated by me; my intention reaching no farther than to a free personal communication of the contents of the letter. This may even be inferred from my prohibition of its insertion in a News Paper which became possible by its circulation in a hand bill.[7]

I mention these things solely with a view to the justification of the part I have acted—nor can I believe that any impartial judge will doubt that the situation called for what I did.

Copy, Hamilton Papers, Library of Congress.

1. For background to this document, see the introductory note to H to Mercer, September 26, 1792. See also Mercer to H, October 16–28, 1792; H to Mercer, November 3, 1792; H to David Ross, September 26, November 3, 1792; Ross to H, October 5–10, November 23, 1792; Uriah Forrest to H, November 7, 1792.

2. See H to Mercer, November 3, 1792.

3. For Ross's statement, see the introductory note to H to Mercer, September 26, 1792.

4. See Ross to H, November 23, 1792.
5. See H to Ross, September 26, 1792.
6. H's letter to Ross of September 26, 1792, was circulated in Maryland as a broadside.
7. On the copy this paragraph has been crossed out.

From Jeremiah Olney

Providence, December 6, 1792. "The continued Complaints of the Merchants and Sea-Faring People, residing in this District, That the different Practices of different Collectors occasion an unequal operation of the same Law in the collection of the Revenue; together with the Censures thrown out against me for not conforming to that which is the most favorable to the Importers, constrains me Sir, respectfully, to recall your attention to my Letters of the 17th of Jany. and 28 Feby. 1791, upon the Subject of allowance for Tare on Sugars, Cocoa &c. and the Duty on Oranges, Limes, and Sweetmeats, not brought for Sale, very inconsiderable, and which the Merchants here say is not collected in any other Place; and to entreat that you would be pleased to cause such Measures to be adopted as will tend to produce a speedy uniformity of Practice in those particulars, throughout the United States; rendering thereby the operation of the Revenue Laws equal, and relieving my Mind from the disagreeable Sensations consequent upon such repeated Complaints. . . ."

ADfS, Rhode Island Historical Society, Providence.

To Maria Reynolds[1]

[*Philadelphia, December 6, 1792.* During an interview with Maria Reynolds on December 12, 1792, James Monroe and Frederick A. C. Muhlenberg saw in Mrs. Reynolds's possession "two notes; one in the name of Alexander Hamilton, of the sixth of December." *Letter not found.*]

"Reynolds Pamphlet," August 31, 1797.

1. The statement by Monroe and Muhlenberg is printed as document No. III in the appendix to the "Reynolds Pamphlet," August 31, 1797.

For background to this letter, see James Reynolds to H, November 13–15, 1792.

From James Waters[1]

[Baltimore] Decr 6 1792

Sir

Permit me to inform you, that I shipt several Cargoes, the produce of this state to Cape François there to be sold for my Account, in Augt & Septr last with positive orders, not to sell to Govt, that the French Consul had published he would not pay any Bills drawn on him by the Govt of St Domingo.[2] Notwithstanding my positive Orders, not to sell any property to Government they were compelled to sell to them, and received Bills for payment with the most positive Assurances from the Intendant and National Commissioners just arrived from France who has forwarded the Decree of the National Assembly of France to Mr De Ternant authorising the assembly of St Domingo to draw, and that due honour would be paid to their Draughts, that he had funds in hand to appropriate for that purpose. How great is my surprize! my friends in Philadelphia write that Mr De Ternant says positively that he will not accept, and consequently not pay[3]—the only means I have to do honour to my Credit, the knowledge I have you take at heart the welfare of every Merchant in this State, and of every American, emboldens me to call on you to see justice have its course and that the Commercial Interest of the Country may not sustain a severe blow as many of my Friends are under the same disagreeable situation.

I am &c James Waters

The Secretary of the Treasury
of the U.S.

Copy, Thomas Jefferson Papers, Library of Congress.

1. This copy was enclosed in H to Thomas Jefferson, December 14, 1792. Waters was a Baltimore merchant.

2. For background concerning bills drawn on Antoine René Charles Mathurin de La Forest, see Ambrose Vasse to H, November 21, 1792.

3. Jean Baptiste de Ternant.

From Oliver Wolcott, Junior[1]

T. D.
C. Off Decr. 6th., 1792

Sir

I have the honour to transmit the following statements of disbursements by the Department of War in the years 1790 & 1791.[2]

Number 1. Being a statement of the accounts of Henry Knox Esq. Secretary at War as settled at the Treasury.

No. 2. Being a statement of the accounts of Joseph Howell Esq. from the 10th. of Sept. 1789. to the 1st. of March 1790. as settled at the Treasury.

No. 3. Being a statement of the accounts of Joseph Howell Esq. from March 1st. 1790 to the 31st. of Decr. 1791 as rendered to the Auditor of the Treasury for settlement & depending in his Office.

Some of the expenditures included in these statements, were made previous to the year 1790, but they could not be separated without inconvenience & deranging the order of the Accts. as rendered for settlement.

I enclose duplicates of the accounts at the special request & for the use of the Secy at War.

Hon A Hamilton

ADf, Connecticut Historical Society, Hartford; copy, RG 233, Reports of the Treasury Department, 1792–1793, Vol. III, National Archives.

1. This letter was enclosed in "Report on Disbursements by the Department of War," December 7, 1792.

2. For the enclosures to this letter, see "Report on Disbursements by the Department of War," December 7, 1792.

Report on Disbursements by the Department of War

Treasury Department,
December 7th 1792.
[Communicated on December 7, 1792] [1]

[To the Speaker of the House of Representatives]
Sir,

I have the honor herewith to transmit certain Statements, pursuant to a resolution of the House of Representatives of the 13th ultimo,[2] relative to the disbursements made by the department of War; Also, copy of a letter from the Comptroller of the Treasury on the subject; [3] and to be, with perfect respect, Sir, Your most obedient servant

Alexander Hamilton,
Secry. of the Treasry.

The Honorable The Speaker
of the House of Representatives

A STATEMENT OF THE ACCOUNTS OF HENRY KNOX, ESQUIRE, SECRETARY AT WAR, FOR THE YEARS 1790, AND 1791, AS ADJUSTED AT THE TREASURY OF THE UNITED STATES, AND STATED IN COMPLIANCE WITH THE ORDER OF THE HOUSE OF REPRESENTATIVES OF [4]

Receipts.

1790.
January 1st. A balance remaining in his hands the 31st December 1789, as per accounts settled at the treasury No. 437,[5] dated June 11th: 1790 .... 15.517.47.

Copy, RG 233, Reports of the Treasury Department, 1792–1793, Vol. III, National Archives.

1. *Journal of the House*, I, 635. The communicating letter may be found in RG 233, Reports of the Treasury Department, 1792–1793, Vol. III, National Archives.

2. On November 13, 1792, the House of Representatives "*Resolved*, That the Secretary of the Treasury be directed to cause to be laid before this House a statement of the several disbursements of money made by the Department of War, in the years one thousand seven hundred and ninety, and one thousand seven hundred and ninety-one" (*Journal of the House*, I, 619).

3. Oliver Wolcott, Jr., to H, December 6, 1792.

4. Space left blank in MS. See note 2.

5. D, Massachusetts Historical Society, Boston.

Also a balance on an Appropriation of 20.000 dollars, for Indian treaties, by the Act of Congress of the 20th. August, 1789,[6] as per Account settled at the treasury, No. 406,[7] dated May 18th. 1790..... 3.476.39.

For the following sums received on account of sales of Indian Goods, Viz:

From J Habersham, by W. Baldwin		....	350.	
" 18th.	do	....	400.	
	do	....	550.	
May 24.	do	..........No. 1756, dated Oct: 4th. 1792	470.50.	
				1.770.50.
June 10th.	For Warrant No. 508 in his favor		12.400.	
August 17th.	do........613	....	7.000.	
" 24th.	do........634	....	1 300.	
1791.				
Febry: 4th.	do........868 dated October 4th. 1792		10.000.	
				30.700.
			Dollars.	51.464.36.

Payments.

1791.

June 30th. His several disbursements on account of the War department, from 1st. January 1790, to 30th. June 1791, Viz:

			Dollars Cents.
Contingencies of the War department, included in No. 1756[8]	................dated October 4th. 1792		1.192.21.
Contingencies of the War Office	do	...........do.....	1.234. 6.
Hospital Department	do	...........do.....	2.321.22.
Quarter Master's Department,	do	...........do.....	8 685.68.
Ordnance department, ...	do	...........do.....	15.892. 8
Indian department, ...	do	...........do.....	14.462.89.
Surveyor's department, ...	do	...........do.....	282.80.
Subsistence department	do	...........do.....	3 019.92.
This sum advanced John Meals on account of rations furnished the troops, and for which he is to be held accountable to the United States	do	...........do.....	500.
This sum advanced to W: Sargent, for which Arthur St. Clair is to be held accountable	do	...........do.....	200.53.
Indian department, for amount of sundry deductions, made in the Auditor's Office, which are admitted, Viz:			
Voucher No. 77 in Col.			

6. "An Act providing for the Expenses which may attend Negotiations or Treaties with the Indian Tribes, and the appointment of Commissioners for managing the same" (1 *Stat.* 54).

7. D, Massachusetts Historical Society, Boston.

8. D, Massachusetts Historical Society, Boston.

	Willet's account, for 30 shirts	40.			
	A draft of the Cornplanter on the Secretary at War for carriage of goods	100.	do...........	do.....	140.
	Amount of sundry expenses attending several journies of the Secretary at War, in the years 1785, 1786, 1787 and 1788, for the purpose of inspecting and arranging the stores in the arsenals and magazines of the United States		do...........	do.....	674.13.
July, 21st.	Disbursements for the Ordnance department		do...........	do.....	175.
August 5th.	Do for the contingencies of the War department		do...........	do.....	17.75.
Nov: 30th.	Do. for the contingencies of War Office		do...........	do.....	245.31
	Quarter Master's department, balance due on the settlement of an Account for the purchase of Cartouch boxes, and transportation of clothing		No. 3071[9]......	Octo: 11th.	116.40.
	Amount of a Warrant, No. 83, in favor of Samuel Meredith, for the balance due from H: Knox, Esquire, agreeably to the reports above mentioned				2304.38.
			Dollars, ...		51.464.36.

Treasury Department
Register's Office, 29th. November 1792.

These are to certify that the foregoing statement agrees with the several settlements which have been made at the treasury, of the Accounts of the Secretary at War, and that the same are finally closed (by payment of the above balance) in the books of the United States.

Joseph Nourse, Register.

No. II.

The United States of America, for sundry Expenditures from the 10th. of September 1789, to the 1st. of March, 1790.

To Joseph Howell, junr,
Paymaster General,...... Dr.

9. D, RG 217, Miscellaneous Treasury Accounts, 1790–1894, Account No. 3071, National Archives.

1789.				
Sept.	17th.	No. 28,	Lt. E. Beatty, paymaster 1st. U: S: regt. for one month's pay to Surgeon's mate, and one month's pay to Ensign Sedam ..... dollars,...	65.
		" 29.	Ditto, for three months pay to eleven discharged soldiers	132.
"	19th.	" 30.	Captain Joseph Savage, for one month's pay for himself, Officers, non-commissioned Officers and privates of his Company of Artillery	243.
Octo.	17th.	" 32.	Capt. E: Beatty, paymaster, 1st. U: S: regt. for three months pay to 8 privates, lately discharged from said regiment	96.
	"	" 33.	Capt. Joseph Savage, for two months pay of one Corporal and four privates of his Company	42.
		" 34.	Ditto, for his subsistence, from April 1st. 1788, to September 1st. 1789 .... 204. for do. of Lt. M. Porter, from April 1st. 1788, to April 1st. 1789 .... 96. for do. of Lt. E: S: Fowle, from April 1st. 1788, to September 1st. 1789 ..... 136.	436.
		35.	Capt. E: Beatty, paymaster 1st. U:S: regt. being for three months pay of said regiment, and two companies of Artillery serving in the western department.	11.629.
"		" 36.	Capt. E: Beatty, paymaster 1st. U: S: regt. for subsistence due the Field, Staff and commissioned Officers of the Infantry, from April 1st. 1788, to September 1st. 1789	6.296.
"		" 37.	Ditto, for due one Major, two Captains, and three Lieutenants from April 1st. 1788, to September 1st. 1789	1 156.
"		" 38.	Ditto, for forage due to the field, Staff, and Major Doughty, from do. to do.	1 315.54
		" 39.	Ditto, for forage due the field and Staff Officers, from July 1st. 1787, to April 1st. 1788	702.
"		" 40.	Ditto, being his expenses from 8th. February 1788, to 17th. May 1788, and from December 28th. to 21st. October 1789	398.
Nov.	11th.	" 41.	Capt. Henry Burbeck, being for subsistence due himself, Lieut. John Pierce, and Doctor Heyward, from 1st. April 1788, to September 1st. 1789; and for do. due to Lieut. Wm Moore, from 1st. May 1788, to September 1st. 1789	604.
"	"	" 42.	Contingent Account, for sundry expenses of Office, from October 5th. to November 9th. 1789, as per vouchers, ...	62.60.
"	"	" 43.	William Price, D: C: Military Stores, for his subsistence from 1st. April 1788, to 1st. January 1789	72.
"	"	" 44.	Lieut. Moses Porter, for his subsistence for April, May, June, July and August 1789	40.
"	"	" 45.	Lieut. Colonel Henry Jackson for his pay, subsistence and forage due him from 1st. May to 15th. June 1787	141.

Nov.	11th.	No. 46.	Capt. Henry Burbeck, being for one and a half months pay for himself, two Lieutenants, one Surgeon's mate, three serjeants, two corporals, one musician, and thirty privates; also three months pay for one musician and three privates of his Company, which completes three full months pay to his whole Company, on account of pay due for 1789	450.
"	"	" 47.	Captain Henry Burbeck, being for three months pay due Wm Maloney, a private in Ensign Luse's detachment at Westpoint	12.
"	"	" 48.	Captain Joseph Savage, being for two months pay for himself, two Lieutenants, two Serjeants, two Corporals, one musician and eight privates; Also one and a half month's pay of one musician and fourteen privates of his Company	383.45.
"	"	" 49.	Brigadier General Stark, for his pay, for January and February 1782	250.
"	"	" 50.	Lt. E: S: Fowle, for expenses incurred by him after deserters	13.
"	"	" 51.	Lt. Wm. Moore, for his extra-pay allowed him for doing the duty of Paymaster, for the post of West-Point and Springfield, from the 1st. July to September 30th. 1787	30.
"	"	" 52.	Captain John Smith, being for a half month's pay for recruiting	147.
"	"	" 53.	Contingent Account for sundry Contingencies of Office, from November 6th. to 31st. December 1789	24.10.
1790 Janry.	7th	" 54.	Lt. John Pierce, for a half month's pay to recruits raised for Capt. Burbeck's Company, and Captain Savage's, at West Point	60.
"	"	" 55.	William Hoch, a private in Major Doughty's Company of Artillery, for one month's pay on account	4.
"	22	" 56.	Lt. John Mercer, being for a Warrant drawn in his favor, the 5th. of March 1787, for half month's pay to nineteen recruits, and opposed to his pay in settlement to the 1st. of Jan: 1787, for which Ensign Luse has accounted to the public in his settlement. ..	38.
"	27th.	" 57.	Capt. John Smith, on account of recruiting his Company	100.
Feby.	1st.	" 58.	Lieut. William Moore, for one month's pay ...	26.
				24,967.79/90
			is	24,967.87.
"	9th.	" 59.	Captain A. Paulint, late of Hazen's regiment, for subsistence for May 1786	12.
"	18th.	" 61.	Lieut: John Pierce, being to complete one month's pay to a detachment of recruits at Westpoint	216.50.

Feby. 20th.	No. 60.	Lieut. John Pierce, on account of recruiting Capt. Burbeck's Company	50.
" "	" 62.	Major William North, for his pay and subsistence, of Captain and Inspector from May 1st. 1787, to June 25th. 1788; and also for the pay, subsistence and clothing of his servant, during the same time	1272.62.
		Dollars, ...	26,518.99.

Auditor's Office, March 9th. 1790.

Dr. { The United States of America, in Account Current; with Joseph Howell, jun. P: M: G: since the 10th. September 1789. on the present Government .... Cr.

To Amount of sundry payments since the 10th September 1789, per Abstract..	26.518.99	By balance of an account settled with the United States, ending the 9th. September 1789	107.605. 7
Balance due the United States	105.263.62.	Octo: 10th. By Sam: Meredith Esqr. Treasurer, for a Warrant on him, No. 79, for..	24.177.54.
Dollars..........	131.782.61.	Dollars	131.782.61.

Auditor's Office, March 9th. 1790

Pay Office, New York, March 9th. 1790.
Joseph Howell: p:m: genl.

Treasury Department, Register's Office, November 21st. 1792.

I certify that the above is a true Copy, the Original of which, with the Vouchers therein referred to, are filed on record in this Office.

Joseph Nourse, Register.

No. III.

Joseph Howell, acting paymaster General, in Account with the United States .... Dr.

To Balance of Account ending the 28th. February 1790, as settled at the Treasury, per Auditor's report, No. 171,[10] dated 9th. March 1790 .... 105.263.62.

To Amount of the following Warrants in his favor on Samuel Meredith, Treasurer of the United States, Viz:

No. 269	2242.
506	2500.
612	811.
658	8438.
662	1906.20
714	500.
733	3000.

10. This report is among the accounts dated before September 6, 1790, which are missing from the records in RG 217, Miscellaneous Treasury Accounts, 1790–1894, National Archives.

734	10.000.
737	3000.
739	10.926.
775	15.000.
785	5000.
835	6000.
877	5000.
929	10.000.
930	11.002.20.
935	10.000.
949	15.000.
982	10.000.
1011	18.500.
1031	22.500.
1044	8000.
1065	40.000.
1081	20.000.
1099	13.387.44
1104	32000.
1167	7.500.
1183	4.000.
1220	7.000.
1229	2554.59
1231	5.000.
1240	5000.
1246	8.296.53.
1500	1.500.

325.563.96.

To amount of Warrant, No. 2152, dated 12th. October 1792, being for monies received from the 20th. September 1791, to January 3d. 1792, from the Bank of North America, by virtue of letters of credit from the Secretary of the Treasury .... 156.595.56.

N:B: Six thousand dollars of this sum received by the acting paymaster General, the 3d. January 1792, is not included in his accounts, as the receipt thereof was subsequent to the period, to which they are rendered.

To this sum placed to his debit, on the books of the Treasury, for monies advanced to the following Officers, by John Habersham, Agent for supplying the troops in the State of Georgia, Viz

Captain John Smith	324.
——— Joseph Savage	25.
——— Henry Burbeck	310.

659.

Dollars .... 588.082.14.

Joseph Howell, acting paymaster General, in Account with the United States———Cr.

By Amount of his disbursements from March 9th. 1790, to 31st. December 1791, arranged under the following heads, Viz:

Pay of the troops and militia, including the subsistence and forage of Officers, and arrears of Clothing due to sundry persons .... Dollars 344.823.71.

From which deduct, as follows, Viz:			
This sum repaid by Samuel Armstrong, late paymaster of the 8th. Massachusetts regiment being a balance of pay remaining in his hands on settlement of his accounts	256.40.		
Ditto received of Oliver Beers, administrator to the estate of Isaac Hubbel, for the balance due on settlement of the accounts of the latter, as paymaster to the second regiment of Artillery	977.96.		
Ditto refunded by George Porter, for so much overpaid him, in the balance of pay due to Edward Barnard deceased	10.		
Ditto repaid by Major J: P: Wyllis; being a balance in his hands, on the settlement of an Account, for the pay of troops under his command	752.60.		
Ditto repaid by John Belli, paymaster to the Kentuckey militia, being the pay of sundry guides who had been previously paid	167.66		
Ditto refunded by John Shryer, Assignee to sundry soldiers, for so much paid him on account of Thomas Jones, one of his Assignors, who had been previously paid ..	53.33.		
This sum overcharged in Vouchers, No. 116 and 120	6.		
Ditto returned by William Findley, as pay due to sundry absentees of the Pennsylvania militia, being a part of dollars 5.139$\frac{13}{100}$ received by him, for the pay of said Militia.	394. 9.		
Ditto received of Major General Trescott, for the balance of his account, to the time of his resignation.	22.48		
Amount of errors and overcharges, in the pay of sundry soldiers, per list	56.34.		
		2.690.92	
			342.132.79
By Contingencies of the pay Office			14.93
Ditto of War Department		11.843.98	
From which deduct this sum, being a balance due by Constant Freeman, on the settlement of his Account of Expenditures		243.32	
			11.600.66
By Quarter Master's department			61.166.20.
Indian............. do			32.379.78.
By Hospital Department		4984.23.	
Deduct on error of addition in Doct. M: Scott's account for medicines and attendance		2.68	
			4981.55.
By Surveying Department			1000.
Ordnance..... do		1455.29.	
Deduct an Overcharge in Joseph Cranch's account		80.	
			1454.49.

By Bounties advanced for the recruiting service and premiums to Officers for inlisting men	25.792.	
Deduct this sum repaid by Lieut. Matthew Ernest, being the balance of his recruiting account	124.	
		25.668.
By Subsistence		24.917.32½
By Arrears of pay and subsistence due to sundry Officers and privates of the late Army in the years 1782, and 1783		1.346.10.
By the following sums advanced to the undernamed persons, pursuant to instructions received from the Secretary of the Treasury, Viz:		
John Hopkins, Loan Officer for the State of Virginia, to discharge the arrears of pay and subsistence, due to the Officers and privates of the late line of said State	22.213.51.	
William Skinner, Loan Officer for the State of North Carolina, to discharge the arrears of pay due to the non-commissioned Officers and privates of the late line of said State	17.320.66	39.534.17.
By this sum charged to him for monies advanced the following Officers, by John Habersham, agent for supplying the troops in the State of Georgia, for which he is now entitled to credit, the Officers being respectively held accountable therefor, in the books of the Pay Offic, Viz		
Captain John Smith .... 324.		
——— Joseph Savage .... 25.		349.
By this sum placed to his credit on the books of the Treasury, being so much accounted for by Captain Henry Burbeck, agreeably to the Auditor's report, No. 2929		310.
By Balance due to the United States, 31st. Dec: 1791...........		41.227.14½
		588.082.14

The foregoing is the Copy of a Statement just completed in this Office, although it has not yet been reported on by me to the Comptroller of the Treasury: [11] I believe it to be correct, and now forward it for the information required by the resolution of the House of Representatives of the 13th. instant.

It may be proper to observe, that the credits comprised under the different heads, have been collected and arranged from the Accounts and Vouchers of Mr. Howell, and that they are composed, in part, of advances made to persons, who had not accounted for the application, at the time, to which Statement extends.

Treasury Department, Auditor's Office 24th. November 1792.

R: Harrison, Auditor.

11. The information in Section III of this report may be found in RG 217, Miscellaneous Treasury Accounts, 1790–1894, Account No. 4713, National Archives. The account was not released by the auditor's office until December 20, 1793, and was not approved in the comptroller's office until September 27, 1794.

From Tench Coxe

Treasury Department, Revenue Office, December 8, 1792. Asks if anyone has been appointed keeper of "the Chessapeak Light House." [1]

LC, RG 58, Letters of Commissioner of Revenue, 1792–1793, National Archives.
1. See Coxe to H, November 28, 1792.

To Benjamin Lincoln

Treasury Department, December 10, 1792. "The Collector of Wiscassett [1] has applied to this Office for a supply of blank Certificates of Registry. I have to request that you will, for the present, transmit him a dozen blanks without delay. He has been directed to apply in future to you in due time—naming the quantity required. . . ."

L[S], RG 36, Collector of Customs at Boston, Letters from the Treasury and Others, 1789–1809, Vol. I, National Archives; copy, RG 56, Letters to the Collector at Boston, National Archives; copy, RG 56, Letters to Collectors at Small Ports, "Set G," National Archives.
1. Francis Cook.

From Jeremiah Olney [1]

Custom House
District of Providence 10th. Decer. 1792

The Legislature of the United States having been pleased to Appoint you to the important Office of Superintending a due Collection of the Revenue, I have upon deliberate consideration, deemed it expedient that you should be made acquainted with my particular conduct, as an officer of the Customs, in respect to the late Suit of a Bond taken for duties, complained of by Welcome Arnold Esquire, and which has been the Subject of a Juditial investigation and decision. With this view I take the Liberty Sir, respectfully to enclose for your perusal a Statement of Facts relative to that Transaction, which in my own Justification, I have been compelled to Submit to the consideration of a number of Gentlemen who have heared Mr. Arnolds representation;[2] and I am happy to add, that it has met with general approbation.

I have furnished Mr. Arnold with a Copy of my Statement, but cannot learn that he has made any reply to it, either public or private.

I intreat Sir, that you will consider the Embarrasements I continually meet with from this Gentleman's disposition to oppose the legal execution of my Duty, as my apology for the Trouble I am now about to give you in the perusal of my vindication.

I have the Honor to be with great consideration Sir Your Most Obed. and Most Hum. Servt. Jereh. Olney Collr.

Alexander Hamilton Esqr.
Secretary of the Treasury.

ADfS, Rhode Island Historical Society, Providence.

1. For background concerning Welcome Arnold's collusive transfers, see H to Olney, September 19, 24, October 12, November 27, 1792; Olney to H, September 8, 13, October 4, 25, November 28, 1792; William Ellery to H, September 4, October 9, 1792.

2. Olney is referring to "An Appeal to the Public, on the Disputes with Welcome Arnold," which reads in part as follows:

"If Mr. Arnold's unremitted endeavors to place my official Character in an unfavorable point of view, proceed from motives friendly to the Public Weal, and not from private *Malice* or *revenge*, he surely gives himself a great deal of unnecessary trouble, for if he wishes to have me displaced, he need only prove to the Secretary of the Treasury, that I do not execute the laws, and my Suspension will follow of course. . . .

"As my conduct in the case of Mr. Arnold's Bond has been thoroughly investigated before the District Court, held at Newport on August last; and also before the Circuit Court, held in this Town on the Seventh Instant; And as Judgment in both Trials, was deliberately Rendered in favour of the United States, and in confirmation of the propriety of my Conduct, I entertained a hope that the unfriendly disposition, long manifested in that Gentleman would have Ceased; but unhappily I have been disappointed; for it appears from good authority, that he Still perseveres in his endeavours to prejudice the Worthy Citizens against me; which, Combined with a Consideration that Suggestions were made by Mr. Edwards, Attorney for Mr. Arnold, in the Course of his plea before the Circuit Court, Tending to impress the minds of the Spectators with Ideas unfavorable to my official Character, are Circumstances which, alone, could have Compelled me with painfull reluctance, to appeal to a Candid and impartial Public; whose Confidence and Support I have a right to expect while it shall appear that I have executed the duties of my office consonant to law, and with upright impartiality; and upon no other principles will I claim them. . . .

"From an unwillingness to proclaim Mr. Arnold's delinquency throughout the United States, I forbear to publish this appeal to my fellow Citizens in a Newspaper, especially as the sole object of it is to undeceive those who may have heard his Representation; and for want of leisure to counteract, personally, that Gentleman's repeated uncandid Statement of facts, which I charitably hope, has not reached beyond the limits of this and the district of Newport, I have been induced to adopt a Mode of communication the least exceptionable, as I conceive, by putting this into the Hands of a few disinterested Gentlemen for their perusal." (ADf, Rhode Island Historical Society, Providence.)

To James Waters[1]

Treasury Department Decr 10 1792

Sir

Your communication of the 6th Inst has been duly received.

I regret very much, the dissappointment you mention, and you may be persuaded, if any thing was in my power that could relief in the case it would not be omitted.

But it is presumed that the refusal to pay the Bills in question, is the effect of circumstances too imperious to be controuled, and not to be remedied by any interference which could at present take place.

I am & A H

Mr James Waters
Merchant
Baltimore

Copy, Thomas Jefferson Papers, Library of Congress.

1. This copy was enclosed in H to Thomas Jefferson, December 14, 1792.

From Tench Coxe

Treasury Department,
Revenue Office, December 11th 1792.

Sir,

I have the honor to communicate to you some remarks, upon the laws relative to the duties on distilled Spirits, wines and teas, in regard to points which appear to require legislative interposition.

The Admission of Kentucky (late a Survey of Virginia) into the union as an entire new Member,[1] renders it expedient to consider

LC, RG 58, Letters of Commissioner of Revenue, 1792–1793, National Archives.

1. "An Act declaring the consent of Congress, that a new State be formed within the jurisdiction of the Commonwealth of Virginia, and admitted into

whether the Number of Districts allowed by the 4th. section of the act of March 3d 1791 [2] should not be encreased to fifteen, subject to alterations by the President as before. Clauses giving the power to appoint a Supervisor and Inspectors therefor, with the usual power in the Supervisor (see 18. section) [3] to appoint the subordinate officers of Inspection will become necessary, if Kentucky be erected into a district.

The territory of the United States Northwest of the Ohio, and that South of the Ohio will require that provision be made concerning them, being at present without the territorial limits to which the Presidents power (Section 4. Act of March 3d. 1791) of appointing Supervisors and Inspectors of the Revenue is extended.[4]

Although the Duties should seem to accrue in the North Western and Southern territories under the general Words "*within the United States*" yet the fourth section of the Act of March 1791 creates some question, when it declares that "the United States shall be divided into fourteen districts each consisting of one State" and thus leaves those territories out of the arrangement. There is danger at least that an ill use may be made of this Circumstance with a Jury interested to narrow the law, in a trial for a penalty or forfeiture. It may be well that the words "and the territories thereto belonging" should be added, and that the President of the United States for the time being should be generally authorised to make such temporary provision of districts, surveys and divisions and of Supervisors and other officers as future contingencies might require, untill order could be taken thereon by the legislature. For this purpose it might be well to create a duty to report such temporary arrangement to

---

this Union, by the name of the State of Kentucky" (1 *Stat.* 189 [February 4, 1791]).

Thomas Marshall, inspector of Survey No. 7 in Virginia, had apparently proposed the creation of a separate revenue district for Kentucky (Coxe to Marshall, October 31, 1792, LC, RG 58, Letters of Commissioner of Revenue, 1792–1793, National Archives).

2. "An Act repealing after the last day of June next, the duties heretofore laid upon Distilled Spirits imported from abroad, and laying others in their stead; and also upon Spirits distilled within the United States, and for appropriating the same" (1 *Stat.* 199–214).

3. 1 *Stat.* 203.

4. 1 *Stat.* 133–200.

For Thomas Marshall's discussion of the need for this change, see Coxe to H, October 19, 1792, note 22.

the legislature at the next ensuing session. The Case of North Carolina [5] suggests that this power should apply to alterations of the districts and Surveys within the limits of the fourteen original States, which have been and thereafter may be made.

At present only the lowest rate of duty (seven cents) applies to Spirits distilled in places other than Cities, Towns & Villages, and in distilleries within Cities, Towns & Villages whose Stills are of less capacity than four hundred Gallons, whatever may be the proof,[6] altho' Spirits made in the other Town distilleries are charged with seven, eight, nine, eleven, thirteen & eighteen Cents. This *when perceived* will ruin the trade of the large town distilleries, who now pay more than three fourths of the revenue. On this part of the law two questions arise, whether it be not contrary to the constitution 1st to impose absolutely seven Cents on Spirits distilled in the class of large distilleries in Towns, and to vary and *diminish* it by the election to pay 54 Cents ℔ Annum on the class of small distilleries in Towns and on all stills in the Country, and 2dly to demand 18 Cents for 6th proof Spirits in the larger distilleries in Towns and only seven Cents for the same proof in all other places and distilleries. All excises and other duties are required by the Constitution to be uniform throughout the United States. Should this appear to be a bar against these differences in future, the Idea of a demand by the distillers of reimbursement for the time past will merit reflexion.

Questions having been made whether stills without heads will operate to prevent the extension of the Election to distilleries wherein they may be erected if with such Stills the capacity of the whole be above the privileged size (400 Gallons) and it being possible that the owners of Stills might by the secretion of the head,

5. On October 27, 1792, Coxe wrote to William Polk, supervisor of the revenue for North Carolina, concerning the liability of distillers for taxes accruing after the effective date of the revenue acts but before the appointment of collectors. In this letter Coxe drew a parallel between the North Carolina question and the situation in the western territories (LC, RG 58, Letters of Commissioner of Revenue, 1792–1793, National Archives).

6. Edward Carrington, supervisor of the revenue for Virginia, had raised a question concerning a change inadvertently made by "An Act concerning the Duties on Spirits distilled within the United States" (1 *Stat.* 267–71 [May 8, 1792]) which necessitated this interpretation of the rates (Coxe to Carrington, July 30, 1792, LC, RG 58, Letters of Commissioner of Revenue, 1792–1793, National Archives).

evade the penalties for non-entry and other provisions of the laws, it appears expedient to introduce an explanatory clause relative to such Stills.[7]

It has been thought by some of the officers of the Revenue that licences for terms *less than a Month* are consistent with the law, and by others that licences for one or more months *with a fraction of a Month added* are legal—that is for 1½ or 2½ Months. To prevent erroneous Verdicts the law might be rendered more precisely explicet. See Section 1 Act of May 1792.[8] The same explanation is requisite in regard to the prohibition to distill otherwise than by licence of the Still, during all the remainder of a Year, for any part of which a Monthly licence shall have been granted.[9]

7. On October 29, 1792, Coxe wrote to George Gale, supervisor of the revenue for Maryland: "It would be very agreeable, if the distiller in Baltimore would so dispose of the still without a head as to prevent the discussion and decision of the two questions concerning it. Ingenuity, which, tho' not so designed have a tendency to contravene or diminish the efficacy of any law on the part of the citizen, or which for the security of the Revenue may force the officers to act upon rules apparently too nice and strict, will often produce unpleasant discussions between them. The Still must be more valuable as a still than it can be as a boiler, because cheap Iron Vessels may be procured and copper is very high. It would appear that a distillery with such a Vessel so set up as to be capable of use would be in a situation more dangerous to the Revenue than one which has not such a vessel, and a question arises where is the head? Stills are never made without heads, and the head is a thing not likely to be lost or mislaid. It is more likely to be secreted, or put away for a time in some other part of a distillers possessions from whence it might be brought at Night, and used to the injury of the Revenue. Moreover the 22d. section of the act of the 3d of March 1791, really countenances an opinion that a still set up in a manner admitting its application to boiling, may be considered as one employed because the boiling process is the distilling process. The allegation of the distiller, that altho' the still is *set up* and thereby the *specific* legal Evidence of its employment appears, it is only a boiler and has no worm (which the silence of the law makes an indifferent Circumstance) nor head (upon which a question may arise as the 1st section of the last act is worded) does not appear to satisfy the statute. Other questions have arisen about still heads, and the idea has been suggested by one ingenious distiller of reducing the head comparatively to nothing" (LC, RG 58, Letters of Commissioner of Revenue, 1792–1793, National Archives).

8. 1 *Stat.* 267–68.

9. Carrington wrote to Coxe on May 27, 1792, concerning licenses for fractions of a month. In reply Coxe wrote on June 3, 1792: "That part of your letter which relates to the licenses is under Consideration. It seems doubtful however whether fractions of Months can be taken into View, for the original requisition is to pay fifty four Cents per. Annum with the provision of a right to pay another rate for a smaller term, or any number of that Term. A term less than that specified in the permission does not seem to be allowable" (LC, RG 58, Letters of Commissioner of Revenue, 1792–1793, National Archives).

As the term during which entries of Stills shall be made has elapsed,[10] it merits consideration whether a new term for that duty prior to *June* next should not be established by law, or whether a requisition to enter within a given time all stills which have not been marked, or at least exhibited to an officer of Inspection for the purpose of marking should not be made.

The lien on the Still created by the 8th Section of the Act of May 8th 1792 applies only to Stills paying by the capacity.[11] It appears expedient to extend it to all Stills in which Spirits are manufactured.

The incomplete execution of the 9th section of the Act of May last,[12] and the difficulty and importance of the operation required by that Section, attract particular attention. The exemption from certificates is extended to Casks (and of course to quantities of Spirits) larger perhaps than is necessary. The pack horses in the Western Country have usually two Casks of 10 or 12 Gallons for a load; and it is not uncommon for several to be conducted together. Tho' it is desirable to leave tavern keeper's supplies and family supplies as free from difficulty as is safe, yet it is equally desireable to bring all *traders* spirits under the regulations as far as may be practicable with convenience. It is therefore questionable whether large quantities conveyed in any Waggon, or by any troop of pack horses, or by any boat, should not be subjected to the requisition of certificates &c. tho' in kegs and further, if more than *one* Cask and amounting to 12 gallons or upwards, (as well as if more than 20 gallons in a single cask as now) the Spirits might perhaps be as conveniently connected with Certificates as they are at present. There is however so much difficulty in devising a safe and certain method in which the marking of Spirits out of Cities, Towns and Villages can be effected as the law now requires, that it merits particular consideration and creates a desire that a duty upon the Still might be the only mode of imposing the Tax.[13]

10. Section 2 of "An Act concerning the Duties on Spirits distilled within the United States" provided that entries of stills should be made "between the last day of May and the first day of July in each year" (1 *Stat.* 268).

11. 1 *Stat.* 269.

12. 1 *Stat.* 269–70. For the provisions of this section, see Coxe to H, September 19, 1792, note 3.

13. See Coxe to H, September 19, 1792, note 2.

The drawback is limited by the 11th section of the Act of May 1792 to quantities of 90 gallons and upwards.[14] As a hhd put on board a Vessel for Sea Stores will very generally be from 95 to 120 Gallons, and as hhds or puncheons of 90 gallons and upwards are allways obtainable, it is plain that the drawback will be easily extended to Sea stores, to which it may be objected, that a consumption duty is thus avoided and lost, and a temptation to uncanalised proceedings in regard to drawback Certificates is created.

The 12th. section prohibits the importation of all distilled Spirits in Casks,[15] which have been legally marked which would prevent the return of Spirits distilled in the United States from any foreign unfavorable market: but if this prohibition be repealed as it regards domestic Spirits, then by force of a clause in the impost or collection law no duty will be demandable, as they are Manufactures of the United States,[16] and it is not clear that the law is sufficiently provisional to justify a second demand of excise on certified and marked Spirits, altho' the duty will have been refunded on exportation.

It appears to be worthy of consideration whether the Spirits and Still ought not to be liable to forfeiture in all cases of manufacturing Spirits without having previously complied with the requisitions which the laws make in regard to the antecedent acts of the distiller. The 36th. Section of the act of March 1791 exempts the distillers employing one Still of 50 gallons or of less capacity, from the penalties prescribed for neglecting to report, to mark their houses, Vessels and apartments and to enter in books the Spirits distilled.[17] The operation of this section is such, that, if uncertified Spirits should be proved to have been distilled in such a Still there would be no forfeiture: process could be instituted for the duty. It appears necessary to put such Spirits in regard to forfeiture, on a footing with all others. The extension of the regulations in regard to marking houses, and even as to marking Vessels and keeping books to Stills under or of 50 gallons also merits consideration.

The Supervisors and other officers have recommended strongly

14. 1 *Stat.* 270. 15. 1 *Stat.* 270.

16. Section 24 of "An Act to provide more effectually for the collection of the duties imposed by law on goods, wares and merchandise imported into the United States, and on the tonnage of ships or vessels" (1 *Stat.* 162 [August 4, 1790]).

17. 1 *Stat.* 208.

the allowance of fees for certificates and services in the business of the Revenue. Tho' I mention this for information I cannot do otherwise than express my opinion against it.

The 41st. section of the act of March 1791 provides for Neglects of duty by the officers to the Injury of Individuals.[18] A provision for similar Neglects to the Injury of the United States appears equally reasonable, tho' it may prove more difficult to modify it satisfactorily.

The continuance of the 43d section of the Act of March 1791 being that relative to mitigations,[19] appears to be recommended by the same good policy which dictated it, and the similar provision in the business of the Customs, and which continues in the latter.

Considering the state of things in several of the Surveys it appears to be worth reflexion whether the penalties for injury and opposition to officers should not be encreased and extended to cases of violent menaces and destruction of property. The laws against Arson are highly penal, but there are other modes of injuring the property of an Officer. A wooden house is easily pulled down and goods & chattels may be carried away.

It may be necessary that the regulations and provisions, which are applied to certain matters and cases in the 1st act be extended to similar matters and cases in the second and meditated Act, unless altered by them. There is already a penalty for making and using false certificates, but it is suggested for Consideration whether any pain or penalty should be provided for counterfeiting marks and numbers on Casks, Vessels and on Stills, or for defacing those legally made.

All the pains, penalties and general regulations concerning the certificates for and marks of Casks and Vessels containing foreign and domestic distilled Spirits appear to be applicable to the corresponding Objects in the business of Wines and Teas. Should this prove so on consideration it may be well to apply them by law.

Among the measures which are under consideration to effect the complete execution of the Revenue laws in the Western Counties of Pennsylvania &c the receipt of the duty in Spirits at some reasonable price is again suggested for Consideration.

Doubts have arisen in Connecticut and in some other Districts

18. 1 *Stat.* 208–09. 19. 1 *Stat.* 209.

about the mode of proceeding by distress,[20] wherefore clear and ample legislative directions and authority are desireable, and the more so because the subordinate officers of Inspection, from want of knowlege and Judgment in such proceedings, may innocently transgress in the execution of their Duties.

The Supervisors of some of the districts are desirous that the distillers should be required by law to call on the officers of Inspection at stated times and places to pay the duties on their Stills and Spirits after the manner, which they allege, has been long prescribed in regard to the dues of the State. This idea is strongly recommended and pressed in South Carolina.

It merits consideration whether the officers of inspection ought not to be restrained from granting a new license until the duty accruing under the preceeding one shall have been paid and whether a distiller and Still employed in the manufacturing of Spirits after such accruing of duty, the same being unpaid, ought not to be subjected to a penalty or forfeiture.

There is no doubt that some distillers or importers are in the practice of purchasing second hand marked Casks with the Certificates originally issued to accompany them.[21] A penalty on such *sales* of Casks with certificates, and on the *purchases* thereof would have some good effects. I submit also the Idea of obliging the dealers and others to return their certificates after Casks have been emptied.

20. On October 24, 1792, Coxe wrote to John Chester, supervisor of the revenue for Connecticut: "The mode of proceeding in case of a resort to legal measures under several different Circumstances having been under Consideration a determination in the Case contemplated in the Opinion of John Trumbull Esquire was necessarily post poned. That Opinion appears to be well founded, and it is thought best that you pursue the mode of distraint by the warrant of the Supervisor of the Revenue in such manner and form in all respects as are indicated by the common law of England, as it stood on the 4th day of July 1776. Should you be at a loss about the form of a warrant of distress or any other part of the proceedings it will be well to take the direction of a gentleman of the law acquainted with the practice and statutes of Connecticut and with the common law of England that in pursuing a conformity with the latter, a collision with the two former may be avoided. It would certainly have been better, if the mode of levying had been pointed out and that Idea is noted for attention whenever the Revenue law shall come before the legislature" (LC, RG 58, Letters of Commissioner of Revenue, 1792–1793, National Archives).

21. See Benjamin Lincoln to H, February 25, June 6, 27, 1792; Robert Purviance to H, June 14, 1792. See also "Report on the Difficulties in the Execution of the Act Laying Duties on Distilled Spirits," March 5, 1792.

It remains to be considered whether the officers of Inspection should be prohibited from *owning or working Stills*, and from *buying and selling distilled Spirits, Wines and Teas*. A circular enquiry into the extent in which the facts exist has been made, and it does not appear to be considerable in any District.[22] In some, the connexion between the office and the occupations does not occur at all, so far as advice has been received.

The 42d. section of the act of March 1791 restrains the commencement of actions or suits to three Months after the matter or thing shall have been done or performed, for remedy of which the same shall be brought.[23] This time is short in a country of so sparse a population as the United States is, and especially where such and so many difficulties are thrown in the way of the execution of the Revenue laws.

The United States are in so much danger of suffering in their Revenues from the Drawbacks on the exportation of Spirits, that I submit the propriety of a provision that no greater amount of drawback shall be allowed than shall be proved by the exporter to have been actually paid upon the Spirits exported, deducting therefrom the allowance of half a cent ℔ Gallon, and adding the Value of the duty on Molasses.

It has been represented that the annual and even Monthly licences are too low, and I am of opinion that the representation is justified by a comparison with the rate of Seven Cents (a low duty) with what the commodity will bear with the duties on foreign Spirits and with what is imposed on it by other Nations. A distiller of candor and good character has on application declared that he made

22. On September 27, 1792, Coxe wrote in a circular letter to the supervisors of the revenue: "An intimation has been given in one of the late Gazettes, that an application would be made to Congress to prohibit the Officers of the Revenue from being concerned in Distilleries, Stills &c. One case occurred some time ago, . . . and the requisite steps had been taken to ascertain the precise state of the case in order that such measures might be adopted as would prevent an Officer of the Revenue from being able to injure the United States by reason of his being engaged in a pursuit which would be attended with circumstances of such manifest danger. I am desirous of being informed by you whether any instances exist in your respective districts wherein an Officer of Inspection has any relation to or participation in the ownership or employment of any Still, or Distillery, or to or in the purchase and sale of distilled spirits, foreign or domestic. Early and particular information will be very desirable" (LC, RG 58, Letters of Commissioner of Revenue, 1792–1793, National Archives).

23. 1 *Stat.* 209.

460 gallons of proof brandy in two Months working night and day with a still of 40¾ gallons on cider and peach Maubee or Mauby. His licence cost him of 8.15/100. Dollars, and the duty on the Spirit at seven Cents would have been 32.20/100 Dollars. This is 1.¾ Cents ℔ Gallon. The benefit of his extraordinary industry ought perhaps to be his own, but had he made use of the days only the duties would not have been more than three Cents. It is certain that grain does not admit of near so great a profit to the distiller, and that is much the most usual material. This representation however is only made for information at this time, as there appear to be strong dissuasives against an increase of the duty by licence.

It might be well to provide that a distiller, on rendering up his licence, should make oath that he has not worked beyond the term for which it was granted. No greater hardship occurs in requiring an oath from him than from the distiller who pays by the gallon. In determining on this point the objections to oaths, as well general as those which have been made by the opposers of the excise,[24] will require to be considerably weighed.

A separate communication will be immediately made, in regard to amendments having relation to the Judicial System.[25]

I have the honor to be with great respect, yr. most Obedt. Servt.

Tench Coxe,
Commissr. of the Revenue.

The honble.
The Secretary of the Treasury.

24. See "Report on the Difficulties in the Execution of the Act Laying Duties on Distilled Spirits," March 5, 1792.

25. See Coxe to H, December 14, 1792.

To the President and Directors of the Bank of the United States

Treasury Department
December 12. 1792.

Gentlemen

I have to request that you will furnish Young and Dannacker, upon the principles heretofore agreed upon, with such a further sum of money, as, when added to the advances already made to them,[1] will amount to ten thousand Dollars.

I have the honor to be, Gentlemen, Your Obedt Servt.

Alexander Hamilton

The President and Directors
of the Bank of the U States.

LS, from the original in the New York State Library, Albany.

1. See "Contract with George Dannacker and William Young," October 22, 1792; H to the President and Directors of the Bank of the United States, November 28, December 3, 1792.

To William Channing, Jeremiah Olney, and John S. Dexter

Treasury Department
Decr. 12. 1792

Gentlemen.

I have yet to reply to your letter of the 3d. ultimo,[1] and to acknowledge with approbation the attention which you have paid to the subject communicated in my letter of the 22d. Octr.[2]

I do not clearly understand whether the Stock which was deposited with the Commissioner of Loans,[3] remains still in pledge, or not. If it does, I request that it may be released, and restored to the Bank.

With great consideration I am Gentlemen Your Obed. servant

A Hamilton

The Attorney of the District
the Collector, and
Supervisor of the Revenue
Rhode Island.

LS, Rhode Island Historical Society, Providence; copy, RG 56, Letters to Collectors at Small Ports, "Set G," National Archives; copy, RG 56, Letters to the Collector at Providence, National Archives.

1. Letter not found.

2. See also H to Benjamin Bourne, William Channing, John S. Dexter, and Jeremiah Olney, October 25, 1792.

3. Jabez Bowen was commissioner of loans for Rhode Island.

From Tench Coxe

Treasury Department, Revenue Office, December 12, 1792. "I have the honor to inclose to you a letter from the Supervisor of Massachusetts [1] for the purpose of obtaining the pleasure of the President upon the request contained in its conclusion. I also inclose a letter from the Supervisor of New Hampshire [2] in order that the information relative to the Clothing and accommodation of the troops on which I presume instructions have gone from you,[3] may be in your possession. . . ."

LC, Letters of Commissioner of Revenue, 1792–1793, National Archives.

1. Nathaniel Gorham.
2. Joshua Wentworth.
3. Letter not found, but see "Treasury Department Circular to the Supervisors of the Revenue," November 26, 1792.

From Ernst Frederick Guyer [1]

[Philadelphia, December 12, 1792]

Sir

In obedience to your directions I do myself the honor to lay before you the inclosed estimate of time and expence to establish a compleat Type foundary or such parts thereof as shall be deemed necessary.[2] The sum required in the beginning for this purpose is but small; 600 Dollars would suffice for the first year, and in case the founts could be disposed of as soon as finished, this same sum would be sufficient to establish the whole foundary. If therefore any body could be found who would either advance this sum on a good interest or go into partnership on reasonable terms, I flatter myself to be able to erect in about 8 years time a foundary which will yield honor and profit to me and those concerned and be of benefit to the public in general.

I therefore humbly beg you will be pleased to take my situation into consideration. I cannot begin any for myself; I have been now these two years in a state of the most disagreeable suspence; fed up many a time with the hopes of an establishment and as often disappointed, I lose my time without being useful either to the public or myself. I have some work but neither constant nor sufficient, whereas, if I had encouragement I could begin to work immediately to some purpose, but so it is impossible to work with any degree of content. Deign therefore to assist a young artist who wishes to render himself useful, grant him your powerful protection and he will be sure of success; It will be then his pride to render himself worthy of your goodness and to shew in all his actions the sentiments of gratitude and respect wherewith he is

Sir your most obedient and most humble servant.

Ernst Frederick Guyer.

Philadelphia December 12th.
1792.

The Honorable Alexander Hamilton, Esquire
Secretary of the Treasury of the United States.

ALS, Hamilton Papers, Library of Congress.

1. Guyer, who made mathematical instruments, came from Germany to Philadelphia after the American Revolution. Benjamin Franklin reimbursed him for his passage and placed him in the foundry of Benjamin Franklin Bache (William McCulloch, "Additional Memoranda for the History of Printing," *Proceedings of the American Antiquarian Society* [new series], XXXI [1921], 185–86).

2. "Estimate of Time and Expence requisite to erect a type foundry" (AD, Hamilton Papers, Library of Congress).

From James Reynolds[1]

[*Philadelphia, December 12, 1792.* On this date "Mr. Reynolds sent a letter to Col. Hamilton by a girl; which letter [Jacob] Clingman saw delivered to the girl." *Letter not found.*]

"Reynolds Pamphlet," August 31, 1797.

1. The statement from which this quotation is taken was made by Clingman and is printed as document No. IV (a) in the appendix of the "Reynolds Pamphlet," August 31, 1797.

For background to this letter, see Reynolds to H, November 13–15, 1792.

From Tench Coxe

Treasury Department, Revenue Office, December 13, 1792. "The Supervisor of North Carolina not having yet answered my letter of the 14th September relative to a variation of the arrangement of the State,[1] nor having transmitted the Name of any person as suitable to fill the Office of Inspector of the 1st Survey vacant by the resignation of James Read Esqr.[2] I have the honor to communicate to you the result of my reflexions after a careful examination and particular enquiry of several of the Members of the two houses of Congress from that State. It appeared probable that the three sea Coast Surveys . . . might be converted . . . into two. . . . Enquiry has been made of the honble Mr. Johnson, Hawkins, Steele and Grove[3] (which last Gentleman represents that part of the State) who approve of the suggested alteration. . . . It is . . . to be observed that the Inspector of the 2nd Survey[4] will continue to possess a mark of the public confidence in the office of Collector of the Customs for Newbern and that the Emoluments of the Inspectorship being only a third of a Commission of 2 pr. Cent on 1000 Dollars can be no object. It is indeed plain, that Mr. Daves has never regarded the office as worthy of attention. . . . The persons who have been mentioned as qualified for the office of Inspector of the 1st Survey are Col. Robert Rowan,[5] of Fayetteville, Mr. Callender[6] of Wilmington and Col. Overton[7] . . . who resides on Cape Fear River about 50 Miles above Fayetteville. . . . The extract from the Supervisors letter which I delivered to you will shew the Idea he has of a division of the fifth Survey and his reasons for it. On examination and mature consideration nothing but the increase of *expence* and of *officers* appears against it. . . . Mr. Steele who represents the district and who approves of the division of the fifth survey, also approves of the Supervisors performing by way of experiment the duties of Inspector of that one of the proposed Surveys, in which he resides: namely the eastermost being the district of Salisbury. . . . As the fund assigned for Compensations and expences by the legislature is apparently . . . disposed of, agreeably to the Estimates communicated to both houses by the President,[8] measures which may occasion additions to the disbursement . . . will require a very cautious and very particular preconsideration."

LC, RG 58, Letters of Commissioner of Revenue, 1792–1793, National Archives.

1. On September 14, 1792, Coxe wrote to William Polk: "On the receipt of this letter you will take up the particular consideration of your whole district and give me your Sentiments of any different division of the whole into

surveys which may appear eligible with your reasons in detail" (LC, Letters of Commissioner of Revenue, 1792–1793, National Archives). On November 10, 1792, Coxe wrote to Polk and repeated his request (LC, Letters of Commissioner of Revenue, 1792–1793, National Archives).

2. See Coxe to H, November 21, 1792.

3. Samuel Johnston and Benjamin Hawkins were Senators from North Carolina; John Steele and William B. Grove were members of the House of Representatives from that state.

4. John Daves.

5. Rowan, a merchant in Fayetteville, was married to Susannah Grove, the widow of William B. Grove's father.

6. Thomas Callender was surveyor and inspector of the port of Wilmington, North Carolina.

7. Thomas Overton, who had been a captain in the Fourth Continental Dragoons during the American Revolution, represented Moore County in the North Carolina Assembly.

8. See George Washington to H, October 1, 1792; H to Washington, September 22, first letter of October 31, 1792; Coxe to H, first letter of July 25, September 12–18, October 20, November 19, 1792.

To Sharp Delany

Treasury Department, December 13, 1792. "I received with your letter of the 26th Ultimo[1] an estimate of the Duties which have accrued in your Office during the third quarter of the present year amounting to 402,540 dollars. It does not appear, whether the expences that have occurred during the quarter, are deducted from the sum. If not, I request to be informed of the amount. . . ."

LS, Bureau of Customs, Philadelphia; copy, RG 56, Letters to Collectors at Small Ports, "Set G," National Archives; copy, RG 56, Letters to the Collector at Philadelphia, National Archives.

1. Letter not found.

From Jeremiah Olney

Providence, December 13, 1792. "I have been Honored with your Letter of the 27th Ulto. on the Subject of the Threatned prossecutions in the Case of the Brigantine Neptune,[1] which are now commenced, your Directions shall be Particularly attended to. I have engaged Mr. David Leonard Barnes, as Further Councill in this Business who I have Consulted on the matter of an appeal to the Fœderal Court, and his opinion is enclosed. I have reason to hope a favourable Issue of this business even before the State Court."

ADfS, Rhode Island Historical Society, Providence.

1. For background concerning Welcome Arnold's collusive transfers, see William Ellery to H, September 4, October 9, 1792; Olney to H, September 8, 13, October 4, 25, November 28, December 10, 1792; H to Olney, September 19, 24, October 12, November 27, 1792.

To Jonathan Burrall[1]

Treasury Department Decr 14th 1792

Sir

I request you to invest the sum of fifty thousand Dollars in the funded debt of the united states, bearing a present interest of six per [c]entum; provided it can be obtained at 20 shillings in the pound, with an additional allowance of the Interest that shall be due upon the stock to the time of purchase.

The transfer of the stock which you may purchase must be made to the *President of the Senate*, the *chief Justice*, the *Secretary of State*, the *Secretary of the Treasury*, and the *Attorney General* for the time being.

Enclosed is a letter to the President and Directors of the Office of discount & deposit,[2] requesting them to pay to you the above mentioned sum, of which you will however only avail yourself in proportion to the actual purchase you shall make.

I am Sir Your Obedt Servt Alex Hamilton

Jonathan Burrall Esqr
Cashier of the office of
discount & deposit
N York.

LS, The Andre deCoppet Collection, Princeton University Library.

1. For background to this letter, see "Meeting of the Commissioners of the Sinking Fund," December 14, 1792.

2. See H to the President and Directors of the New York Office of Discount and Deposit of the Bank of the United States, December 14, 1792.

From Tench Coxe

Treasury Department,
Revenue Office, December 14th 1792.

Sir,

In the close of the report, which I had the honor to make on the 11th Instant, concerning the alterations and amendments in the laws relative to distilled Spirits, wines and teas, I intimated, that I should make a separate communication with respect to alterations having relation to the Judicial System.

It has frequently occured in conferences with you, with the Attorney General and the Attorney for the District of Pennsylvania,[1] that there are circumstances in the Judicial System of the United States, in the laws relative to the public Revenues, in the Judicial Systems of some of the States, and in the practice in the State courts, which creating doubts and difficulties, rendered it desirable that they might receive attention, whenever the legislature should have the Business of the Revenue before them. The state of the laws of the Union in regard to bail, the state of the laws of Pennsylvania in regard to costs, in suits wherein the sum recovered does not exceed a certain amount, and the want of a detailed procedure for Cases of distress,[2] are among the matters contemplated. These and other things, which having been only occasionally mentioned in conversation, are not within my recollection have suggested to me and now induce me to submit to you the expediency of an application to the Attorney General for a statement of such amendments of the laws as have occured to him as necessary to give more convenience and promptitude to the execution of the Acts of Congress for raising a revenue on distilled Spirits.

I have the honor to be with great Respect, Sir, your most Obedt. Servant

Tench Coxe,
Commissr. of the Revenue.

The honorable
The Secretary of the Treasury.

LC, RG 58, Letters of Commissioner of Revenue, 1792–1793, National Archives.
1. Edmund Randolph and William Rawle.
2. For an earlier reference to the question of distress, see Coxe to H, December 11, 1792, note 20.

From Tench Coxe

Treasury Department
Revenue Office, Decemr 14th 1792.

Sir,

I have the honor to inform you that the Result of my Enquiries relative to Messrs. Perry,[2] Chamberlain,[3] Richardson [4] and Eccleston [5] have issued as follows.

It appears to be the unanimous opinion of those Gentlemen, among whom are the Senator and Representative who reside in the Survey,[6] that Mr. Chamberlain is a Man of excellent character and of a standing in the community equal to the Office, but that in point of official energy, and particularly of the kind requisite in the Revenue business that he would be excelled by all the other Gentlemen.

I find nothing affirmed of Mr. Perry to give him a preference to Messrs. Richardson, and Eccleston, nor do I perceive any disposition to support him as a candidate. My opinion is from symptoms in one quarter and opinions expressed in the other two, that his appointment would not be considered as advantageous to the public Service. It should be mentioned that he is now of the State Senate.

There appears to be a great deal of decision in favor of Messrs. Richardson and Eccleston's real qualifications, and suitableness in all respects, but a manifest disposition to support Mr. Eccleston.

In regard to Mr. Richardson he has been heretofore in view as the Governor of Maryland, and has been several times in popular employments. His family at present enjoy several places under the State.

In regard to Mr. Eccleston he was a Colonel in the Army, is said to have been in the confidence of General Greene, is a man of pure and extensive public Esteem, lives in the distilling Country, and the centre of the Survey, has been recently sherriff of the County with great satisfaction to the bar, which evinces his punctuality and office talents. He has served in popular offices, but has had nothing lucrative in the executive line. Tho' not at all involved, it is supposed the emoluments of the present Office would be pleasing and convenient to him, and it appears to me that his appointment would carry the impression of remunerating Services and bestowing a benefit where it has been merited, and is likely to be compensated by future official desert.

I have the honor to be with great respect, Sir, your most Obedient Servant

Tench Coxe,
Commissr. of the Revenue.

The honorable
The Secretary of the Treasury.

LC, RG 58, Letters of Commissioner of Revenue, 1792–1793, National Archives.

1. The creation of a third survey of inspection in the Maryland revenue district was a part of the rearrangement of the revenue service which had been drafted by Coxe in July, 1792, and approved by the President on August 4, 1792. See Coxe to H, first letter of July 25, November 19, 1792; Washington to H, August 5, 1792.

2. James McHenry supported William Perry as a candidate for office. See McHenry to H, November 19, 1791; August 16, September 20, November 18, 1792.

3. Samuel Chamberlaine, Jr., had inherited a "very considerable fortune from his father, one of the wealthiest men of his day in the province of Maryland." Before the American Revolution he had been appointed naval officer and collector of the port of Oxford, Maryland (Oswald Tilghman, *History of Talbot County Maryland, 1661–1861* [Baltimore, 1915], I, 552–75).

4. William Richardson.

5. John Eccleston.

6. Senator John Henry and Representative William Vans Murray were both residents of Dorchester County, Maryland, within the newly created third Maryland survey.

To Sharp Delany

Treasury Department, December 14, 1792. "The Revenue Cutter of Georgia being to be provided with Sail Cloth, I have to request that you will purchase upon the most reasonable terms, 9 Bolts equal to No 1 and 3 Bolts equal to No 8 of Boston Manufacture. . . ."

LS, Bureau of Customs, Philadelphia; copy, RG 56, Letters to the Collector at Philadelphia, National Archives; LC, RG 26, Revenue Cutter Service Letters Sent, Vol. "O," National Archives.

To Thomas Jefferson

Treasury Department, December 14, 1792. I . . . enclose . . . copies of two letters to me—with my answers thereto [1]—which concern the Commerce between this Country & St Domingo. . . ."

LS, Thomas Jefferson Papers, Library of Congress.

1. Ambrose Vasse to H, November 21, 1792; H to Vasse, December 14, 1792; James Waters to H, December 6, 1792; H to Waters, December 10, 1792.

Meeting of the Commissioners of the Sinking Fund

[Philadelphia, December 14, 1792]

At a meeting of the trustees of the sinking fund, on the 14th day of December, 1792,

Present: The Vice President, the Secretary of State, and the Attorney General.

The Secretary of the Treasury having informed the Board that he held one hundred thousand dollars at their disposal:

Resolved, That the said sum of one hundred thousand dollars be invested in stock, according to the limits prescribed by the last resolution of the Board; [1] that the money be employed either in Philadelphia or New York, or both; and that Samuel Meredith, the Treasurer of the United States, be the agent at Philadelphia, and that the cashier [2] of the Office of Discount and Deposite at New York, be the agent there.

ASP, Finance, I, 237.

1. See "Meeting of the Commissioners of the Sinking Fund," October 31, 1792.
2. See H to Jonathan Burrall, December 14, 1792.

To the President and Directors of the New York Office of Discount and Deposit of the Bank of the United States [1]

Treasury Department Decr 14th 1792

Gentlemen

I have to request that you will pay to Jonathan Burrall Esquire, Cashier of your institution the sum of fifty thousand Dollars,[2] to be by him invested in the funded debt, on account of the united States.

After the object shall have been effected, the sum will be adjusted by a regular warrant.

I have the honor to be Gentlemen Your obedt Servt

Alexander Hamilton

The President & Directors
of the Office of Discount & Deposit
New York

LS, from the original in the New York State Library, Albany.

1. Philip Livingston was president of the Office of Discount and Deposit in New York.

2. See H to Burrall, December 14, 1792.

To Ambrose Vasse

Treasury Department
Decr 14 1792

Sir

I have duly received your letter without date.[1]

I regret very much the disappointment you mention & you may be assured if any thing was in my power, which could afford relief in the case it would not be omitted.

But it is to be presumed that the refusal to pay the Bills in question is the effect of circumstances too imperious to be controuled; and not to be remedied by any interference which could at present take place.

I have nevertheless inclosed a Copy of your letter to the Secy of State,[2] to which Department the object of your application more immediately relates, but I do not perceive that any thing will be in his power.[3]

I am &c A H

Mr Ambrosse Vasse
Mercht
Philadelphia

Copy, Thomas Jefferson Papers, Library of Congress.

1. Vasse to H, November 21, 1792.

2. H to Thomas Jefferson, December 14, 1792.

3. On December 15, 1792, Jefferson wrote to Vasse: "The Secretary of the Treasury has handed on to me a letter to me complaining of the nonacceptance

of some bills drawn by the government of St Domingo to pay for property of yours. Though I am apprehensive it will not be in my power to procure you a prompt relief, yet the sooner it is taken up, the sooner it will be obtained. If you will do me the honor to call on me any morning convenient to yourself, I shall be ready to confer with you on the subject, in order to consider what best can be done in the case" (copy, Papers of the Continental Congress, National Archives).

Conversation with George Hammond[1]

[Philadelphia, December 15–28, 1792]

Since this conversation with Mr. Jefferson[2] I have had one with Mr. Hamilton upon the same subject, to whom I expressed similar sentiments, and from whom I have received a letter,[3] of which I have the honor of inclosing a copy, as being explanatory of the actual views of this Government upon this particular point, as far as they can now be defined.

Transcript, MS Division, New York Public Library.

1. This conversation has been taken from Hammond to Lord Grenville, January 1, 1793, Dispatch No. 2.

2. In the same letter to Grenville, Hammond described this conversation as follows:

". . . I . . . had a long conversation with Mr. Jefferson on the subject of the disposition manifested by the hostile Indians to enter into a negotiation with the United States for the restoration of peace. The Secretary of State began by observing that as my communication to him of the result of the Council at the Miamis Rapids had been merely *informal,* he requested me to consider the present exposition of his sentiments upon that communication, in a similar point of view. He then informed me that he was authorized by the President to express to me the sense which the members of this government entertained of the candour that I had manifested on this occasion, which they could not but esteem as an additional proof of the sincere solicitude of His Majesty's government to contribute their endeavours towards the effecting of a general pacification between the United States and the Indians now at war with them. From this he proceeded to advert to the solitication, on the part of the Indians of his Majesty's mediation in promoting this desirable object. His general reasoning upon this point was pretty nearly the same as that which Mr. Hamilton has employed upon former occasions. With this addition that he conceived it to be by no means advisable for His Majesty's Ministers to afford their support to the Indian proposition, as in any future misunderstanding that might arise between the government of Canada and any nations of Indians, the latter might deem themselves fully justified from this precedent in requesting the interposition of the American Government in accommodating the dispute. Such a course of proceeding, he imagined, might be a never failing source of disquietude to both governments, the interests of which, according to his opinion, would be best consulted in not regarding the Indians living on their respective frontiers or within their respective territory, as possessing that sort of independent sovereignty which would intitle them to a claim on the intervention of a third power in terminating any differences in which they might be involved. After this general reasoning he noticed the formal application which had been made to Governor [John Graves] Simcoe to attend at the Council to be held early in the Spring at the Glaize. He said that though the members of the American administration reposed the most implicit confidence in the sincerity of that Gentleman's good intentions towards the United States, yet as they had resolved to decline the interposition of Great Britain, his presence at the Council could be viewed in no other light than that of a Spectator. How far his appearance in that character would be compatible with his dignified Station, Governor Simcoe would be best qualified to determine. They should however regret such a circumstance, for if the result of the Council should be unfavorable to a pacification, it would be a very difficult matter for this government, convinced as it might be of the injustice of such a suspicion, to prevent the great mass of the American people, already entertaining prejudices upon this point, from ascribing the ill success of this measure to the interference of the Governor of Upper Canada.

"To these observations I briefly replyed that I considered the solicitation of the King's good offices on the part of the Indians as perfectly natural and just, but as this government did not deem it expedient to concur with them in an application to his Majesty for this purpose, it did not become me to enter into a discussion of the motives which might actuate its conduct. I should however take the liberty of remarking that according to my judgement it would be incumbent upon the government of Canada to state to the Indians explicitly in answer to their formal application, that a compliance with their request had been rendered impracticable, not by any inattention to their interests on the part of His Majesty's government, but by the unwillingness of the United States to admit our interference. In regard to Governor Simcoe's personal attendance, I was persuaded that, even if his other avocations allowed him the opportunity, no considerations could induce him to be present at the Council after the explanations I should give him of the sentiments of the American Government, but that I was too well acquainted with the general disposition of the Indians not to know that *they* would not be satisfied unless Colonel [Alexander] McKee, Colonel [John] Butler, or some other British Agent, in whom they could confide, should be present to explain to them faithfully the nature and tendency of the American offers.

"I therefore thought it my duty, in order to obviate any surmises or suspicions which might otherwise arise, not to conceal my expectation that the presence of some person of the above description would be required for the object I have mentioned. Mr. Jefferson said he conceived such a desire in the Indians to be extremely proper, and that the propositions of the American Government would be so equitable as to make him regardless of the channels, through which the explanations of them might be conveyed.

"Mr. Jefferson concluded the conversation by saying that there was one object, connected with the foregoing circumstances, with respect to the attainment of which he was directed to request my opinion, and, if practicable, my co-operation in accomplishing it. He then stated that the Indians having agreed to meet deputies from the United States at the Glaize early in the Spring, it would be necessary for this government, [to] collect, at their expence, a quantity of provisions sufficient for the support of the Indians during the sitting of the Council. But the winter being so far advanced, and the time of the meeting so near, it would be . . . almost impracticable to obtain and transport through the *American territory alone* the quantity of provisions, which might be required. The attention of this Government was consequently directed to the Lakes of Upper Canada, as offering the most facile means of communication with the place fixed upon by the Indians for the Council. He therefore desired me to inform him whether I imagined that Governor Simcoe would not afford some friendly assistance upon this occasion, by allowing this

Government to form, a contract, for the furnishing of the necessary supplies, with any individuals residing under his jurisdiction, who might be competent to the fulfillment of any engagement of that nature. In that case it was the intention of this government to send a person immediately to Niagara, fully authorized to arrange definitively with any responsible merchants in that quarter all the conditions of any contract into which they might enter—as well with relation to the quantum of provisions requisite, as to the price of them, and the means of transporting them across Lake Erie to the Glaize, which could be affected *solely in vessels belonging to his Majesty's Subjects.* In my answer to Mr. Jefferson I assured him—that his Majesty had seen with the greatest concern the progress and extension of hostilities on the frontiers of his American possessions—that the Governors of Canada in conformity to their instructions, had invariably exerted their best endeavors with the Indians to promote the restoration of tranquility, and that under the influence of these considerations I entertained no doubt, that if the measure at present in contemplation was feasible, Governor Simcoe would most readily concur in granting it his aid and encouragement—and that as to myself, I should, as soon as the American Ministers had come to some final decision upon this matter, lose no time in communicating their wishes to the Governor of Upper and Lower Canada through the medium of a confidential person."

3. See H to Hammond, December 29, 1792.

From Tench Coxe

Treasury Department,
(Private) Revenue Office, December 15th. 1792.

Sir

I have the honor to inclose to you a letter received a last Evening from the Supervisor of Pennsylvania,[1] upon a subject extremely painful in a public and private view. On my expressing to him some time ago my wishes that the returns from that district might be brought forward he observed, that he was apprehensive Mr. Collins would not prove a very regular official Man;[2] and he very lately informed me that he feared he should have difficulty with him in regard to the revenue received. The latter you will remember I mentioned to you, and I have great pain in finding the Supervisors apprehension realized.

When it shall suit your convenience I will attend you upon this unpleasant business.

I have the honor to be, Sir, Your most Obedt. Servt.

Tench Coxe,
Commissr. of the Revenue.

The honble.
The Secretary of the Treasury.

LC, RG 58, Letters of Commissioner of Revenue, 1792–1793, National Archives.

1. The letter from George Clymer has not been found.

2. James Collins, inspector of Survey No. 2 in Pennsylvania.

To Tobias Lear

[Philadelphia, December 15, 1792]

Dr. Sir,

The Supervisor of Massachusetts [1] is desirous of permission to come to Philadelphia on *urgent private business*. I believe the permission may be given him without injury to the service. Will you mention the matter to the President and inform me by a line whether permission may be notified to him or not.

Yours &c.

A: Hamilton

15 Decr. 1792

LC, George Washington Papers, Library of Congress.

1. Nathaniel Gorham. See Tench Coxe to H, December 12, 1792.

On December 18, 1792, Coxe wrote to Gorham stating that the President had approved "your absence from the District for the purpose mentioned in your last letter, provided no injury is likely to arise to the public service" (LC, RG 58, Letters of Commissioner of Revenue, 1792–1793, National Archives).

From John Jay

[*New York, December 16, 1792.* On December 18, 1792, Hamilton wrote to Jay: "Your favours of the 26 of November & 16 instant have duly come to hand." *Letter of December 16 not found.*]

From Samuel Hodgdon [1]

[*Philadelphia, December 17, 1792.* On December 18, 1792, Hamilton wrote to Hodgdon: "I am to acknowledge the receipt of your favor of yesterday." *Letter not found.*]

1. Hodgdon, who had been a member of the commissary department of the Continental Army during the American Revolution, had served as quartermaster general of the United States Army from March, 1791, to April, 1792. At the time this letter was written he was serving as Army storekeeper in Philadelphia.

To Tobias Lear

[*Philadelphia*] *December 17, 1792.* "The Secretary of the Treasury . . . transmits herewith sundry Commissions which from time to time have been returned."

LC, George Washington Papers, Library of Congress.

To James Monroe, Frederick A. C. Muhlenberg, and Abraham B. Venable[1]

Philadelphia December [17] 1792.

Gentlemen

On reflection, I deem it adviseable for me to have Copies of the several papers which you communicated to me in our interview on Saturday evening, including the notes, and the fragment of Mr. Reynolds' letter to Mr. Clingman. I therefore request that you will either cause copies of these papers to be furnished to me, taken by the person in whose hand writing the declarations which you shewed to me were, or will let me have the papers themselves to be copied. It is also my wish, that all such papers as are original, may be detained from the parties of whom they were had, to put it out of their power to repeat the abuse of them in situations which may deprive me of the advantage of explanation. Considering of how abominable an attempt they have been the instruments, I trust you will feel no scruples about this detention.

With Consideration, I have the honour to be, Gentlemen Your Obedient Servant Alexander Hamilton

To Augustus Muhlenburgh
James Monroe, and
Abraham Venable } Esquires

Copy, Hamilton Papers, Library of Congress.

1. This letter appears as document No. XXVI of the "Reynolds Pamphlet," August 31, 1797.

For background to this letter, see James Reynolds to H, November 13–15, 1792.

From William Short

The Hague Dec. 17. 1792

Sir

I had the honor of writing to you on the 29th. ulto by the English packet, the day after I had recieved the letters of the Secretary of State relative to the business in Spain.[1] I expected then to be able, to set out from this place, much sooner. I have been detained by the answer from Paris not arriving as soon as it might have done[2] & by my wish to recieve from the commissioners at Amsterdam[3] & forward to you previously to my departure, the account you had asked of me of the monies paid by my order.[4] I have now the honor of inclosing you that account reduced to the simplest & clearest form possible. It consists of two parts. The monies paid to the French government posterior to Nov. 1790 & The monies paid to me or on my draughts from the time of my being left at Paris as Chargé des affaires (Sep. 24. 1789) up to July 1. 1792.

No. 1. shews the amount of the sums paid to the French government No. 1 (a) & No. 1.(b) are the general account of the commissaries of the French treasury (viz the copy furnished me by M. Morris[5] the original remaining in his hands) in which you will find the same payments comprehended & which vouch them.

No. 2 Is a statement of all the monies that I have recieved or that have been paid on my draughts for any cause whatever, whether on my account or not, up to the 5th. of July last. I chose to have the statement made in that form that there might be no possibility of an omission, although there are several articles which should not enter into my account with the U.S. & which are not entered into the accounts wch. I have transmitted to the department of State. These articles are explained by marginal notes annexed to No. 2. They are for monies which M. Jefferson desired me to pay for him by draughts

ALS, letterpress copy, William Short Papers, Library of Congress.

1. See Short to H, November 29, 1792, note 32.

2. Short was waiting for information on the feasibility of traveling through France on his way to Spain.

3. Willink, Van Staphorst, and Hubbard.

4. See H to Short, August 28, 1792.

5. Gouverneur Morris.

on the commissioners, & which were to enter into his acct. with the U.S. which has certainly been done, as I sent him the accounts of these expenditures made for him, which he approved. That I might not be obliged to keep an account of those draughts I stated in my letters of advice, the purposes for which they were made, desiring that they might be placed in M. Jefferson's account with the U.S. I rather apprehend however that this was not attended to & that the commissioners have placed them in my acct. In that case I must ask the favor of you to advert to Mr. Jefferson's acct. with the U.S. or to M. Jefferson himself, which will immediately shew that these draughts noted in the margin were for him. I wish this reference to be made, because these draughts were not stated in my accts. transmitted annually to the department of state—& also that you may see that I have scrupulously observed a rule which I prescribed to myself as being particularly proper in my situation, namely of never drawing for any part of my salary before it became due. This would not appear to be the case if the draughts made by me on acct. of expenditures for Mr. Jefferson, were to be considered as made on my own acct. for salary & contingencies of stationary, postage &c. I hope & trust that ere this the accts. transmitted by me, on acct of my salary & contingencies will have been carried through the proper process by the department of state, & I ask it as a favor that if any article should not carry the most complete satisfaction with it, that I may be informed of it at present whilst in the way to procure the proper eclaircissements if any should be wanting, although I endeavoured by the accts. themselves & the letters to the Secretary of State accompanying them to leave nothing deficient. I asked his orders with respect to the vouchers for the contingencies disbursed on public account, which remained in my hands, not chusing to venture them across the Atlantic without his directions which I have not yet recieved.

No. 3. Is an account furnished me by M. de Wolf [6] of his draughts on the commissioners at Amsterdam for the payment of the interest due the 1st. inst. on the Antwerp loan. I have had it compared with the books of the commissioners & found it to be just. The draughts

6. Charles John Michael de Wolf, an Antwerp banker who negotiated the Antwerp loan of 1791 for the United States. See Short to H, November 8, 1791, note 4, and November 12, 1791.

were made by M. de Wolf with much care & attention to the interests of the U.S. The favorable moments of the exchange were made use of so as to have obtained a considerable advantage as you will see.

I have formerly mentioned to you that 950 of the bonds of this loan had been suppressed by me, & were left at Paris unsigned in M. Morris's hands.[7] This acct of the payment of the interest will ascertain that they have never been delivered, & that the loan is in fact only 2,050,000 florins. M. de Wolf informs me that these bonds now sell [at] 101½ so that the American credit is higher than that of any other power at Antwerp. I have long ago transmitted you his acct. on the reciepts on this loan & the payments made by him to France,[8] which you will find confirmed also by the acct. of the commissaries inclosed.

Finding that I should be detained both by the necessity of recieving information from Paris as to the certainty of my passage through France, & also by the delay of the commissioners in furnishing me the accts I had asked, I determined to go to Amsterdam for a few days in order to examine myself into the state of American affairs there & give you as just an idea as I could previously to my leaving this country. I have already informed you of what has passed between the commissioners & myself as to the powers they wished me to obtain from you to borrow at an higher rate of interest than 4. per cent.[9] I have not undecieved them as to the limits of my powers, but on the contrary impressed on them how averse I was sure you would be to raise the rate of interest on any occasion whatever. I have recommended it to them particularly to impress this idea on their undertakers & money lenders, if they wished to confine the loans to Amsterdam, letting them understand at the same time that I had better offers made me elsewhere than any rate above 4. per cent interest. They seemed to attend to this part of our conversation with some kind of anxiety, altho' they were unwilling to let me suppose they concieved any danger of our being tempted by offers elsewhere. It will become in future an object of some delicacy to manage this business so as to keep off by means of Antwerp all hope of raising the rate of interest at Amsterdam. The commissioners

7. See Short to H, August 6, 1792.

8. See Short to H, August 6, 1792.

9. See Short to H, November 29, 1792.

would certainly procure a loan at any rate of interest however low rather than see us make use of Antwerp—but they have some motives of much weight for not forcing this rate of interest too low in the first instance if left to themselves. Should the interest be as low as it may be reduced hereafter they lose the profits which they contemplate on the reduction of the rate of interest by opening new loans in future for the same at the reduced rate. By this means you will observe a loan at 4½ or 5. p cent interest, besides the profits it yields immediately holds out the certainty of its producing a second time by its conversion to one of a reduced rate. I mention these as considerations so far as the rate of interest would be under the control of the commissioners—but it might so happen that it would not be under their control—& certainly would so happen if the U.S. were obliged to go on the market at present. The present state of Europe induces all the money lenders to hold back their money on the contemplation of an advanced rate of interest—but above all the present state of the English stocks produces this effect to an incalculable degree. Many people at Amsterdam & other parts of this country have made fortunes by purchasing into the English stocks at the lowest rate & selling out at the highest; so they have been their own witnesses of these ebbs & flows in those stocks, nothing will be so tempting to them as the present prospect of their fluctuation. Every money lender will stand on the watch & hold himself ready for the first turn of the tide. All the borrowing powers at Amsterdam feel the effects of this disposition most sensibly—the American bonds continue the highest but the 4. per cents are down decidedly to 96. & if any person should wish to dispose of any quantity of them they wd. not produce more than 95. The late Spanish loan at 4½ per cent interest hangs an heavy load on those who are interested in it, although supported by Hope's house [10] & all their influence.

You will easily see under this state of the market how essential it is for the U.S. not to be forced on it. I cannot too often repeat how essential it is to ingraft fully the idea of their fixed determination not to retrograde in their rate of interest. Every effort should be made rather than to do this. If once the money lenders were

10. The banking house of Henry Hope of Amsterdam.

allowed to suppose we might be induced to retrograde, it would certainly have an unhappy influence for some time to come—not to mention the double expence to the U.S. of making the loan first at an advanced rate of interest with a view to reduce it hereafter. I flatter myself particularly from your purposing to remit for the payment of interest in future, that there will be no necessity for a new loan for a long time to come—& I derive much pleasure from this consideration. Should you have disposed of the large sums remaining in the hands of the commissioners on recieving information of their being locked up there by the King's suspension, This will enable you I should hope to provide for the million re-imbursement next June from home.[11] It is impossible to say what will be the then state of the market, but it would be dangerous to rely on it lest the U.S. should be forced to make sacrifices in coming on it. The great object is to keep the matter so in our own hands as to be able to come on the market or not—& this is so important that I trust you will excuse the importunity with which I urge it.

As yet no draught of yours on the commissioners has arrived since the suspension except the 100,000 florins you mentioned to me.[12] Should you instead of remitting for the interest due in the first months of the next year, have the payments made from the monies here on hand, & call for the rest—this will enable you to remit for the re-imbursement in June instead of the interest as was your intention, & thus secure the U.S. from being forced on the market against their will. I shall flatter myself at least with this hope as long as I can, as it seems to me to be well founded.

Whilst at Amsterdam I examined also into the state of the Spanish payment.[13] The exchange with Madrid has taken so unfavourable a rise that the commissioners have suspended taking bills. They are persuaded a change will soon take place. As yet no answer has ever been recieved from the Spanish government. These circumstances joined together made me adopt the delay of the commissioners. Should the

11. Short is referring to the payment due in June, 1793, on the Holland loan of five million guilders. For a description of this loan, see Willink, Van Staphorst, and Hubbard to H, January 25, 1790, note 15.

12. See H to Short, October 16, 1792, and H to Willink, Van Staphorst, and Hubbard, October 16, 1792.

13. For a description of the Spanish debt, see H to Short, September 1, 1790, note 19, and Joseph Nourse to H, October 9, 1792.

exchange become more favorable they will remit—if not they will await my orders from Madrid, where I shall be able to learn the cause of the unaccountable silence of the ministry on this subject to Mr. Carmichael.[14]

As you are acquainted with my mission to Spain I need not observe to you how much delay it will occasion if you should continue to transmit through me your orders to the Commissioners. It will probably be more advisable to charge the minister of the U.S. at London or Paris, with a branch so important at this moment & likely to become critical during the next year. A nearer view of the ground than I can possibly have at Madrid may be important & particularly a correspondence more rapid than can take place from thence. I hope you will excuse the liberty I take in suggesting these considerations lest they should escape you in the immense circle you are obliged to embrace.

I shall leave this place the day after to-morrow without fail & pursue my route to Madrid through France. I have the honor to be most respectfully

Sir your most obedient & most humble servant W: Short

The Honble
Alexander Hamilton Secretary of the Treasury Philadelphia

14. William Carmichael who with Short had been appointed commissioner to treat with Spain.

From Tench Coxe

Treasury Department, Revenue Office, December 18, 1792. Encloses "an account of Abraham Hargis the Contractor for sinking and completing the well at the Cape Henlopen or Delaware light House."[1] Discusses the terms of the contract and compares it with the contract for the repair of the lighthouse at Cape Henry in Virginia.[2] Discusses the compensation of the keeper of the Portland lighthouse.[3]

LC, RG 58, Letters of Commissioner of Revenue, 1792–1793, National Archives.

1. Hargis's accounts may be found in RG 217, Miscellaneous Treasury Accounts, 1790–1894, Accounts No. 3179, 3620, National Archives.

See also Coxe to H, May 28, 1792; H to George Washington, June 19, 1792;

H to Tobias Lear, June 22, 1792; Lear to H, June 22, 1792; H to Coxe, June 23, 1792.

2. See Coxe to H, November 30, December 3, 1792, and Lear to H, December 6, 1792.

3. See Lear to H, November 27, 1792.

To Samuel Hodgdon

Treasury Department 18th Decemr. 1792

Sir,

I am to acknowledge the receipt of your favor of yesterday.[1]

That the amount of the Monies received by you for Arms &c. sold to the State of South Carolina,[2] may be ascertained according to the established usage of the Treasury Department, it will be necessary that you present an account thereof with the proper documents at the Auditors Office. A warrant will then issue upon you in favor of the Treasurer, for such sum as may be reported by the Auditor and certified by the Comptroller, to be in your hands on account of the United States.

I am with Consideration Sir Your most Obedt. Servant

Alexander Hamilton

Samuel Hodgdon Esquire

LS, Montague Collection, MS Division, New York Public Library.

1. Letter not found.

2. On October 17, 1792, in reply to a letter from Hodgdon (Hodgdon to Tobias Lear, October 17, 1792, ALS, RG 59, Miscellaneous Letters, 1790–1799, National Archives), Lear reported that the President had approved the issue of six hundred stand of arms from the public store at Philadelphia for the use of South Carolina to be issued "on the terms which . . . will replace them in kind at a short notice" (LC, George Washington Papers, Library of Congress.) On December 21, 1792, Warrant No. 81 for $4,240 was drawn on Hodgdon in favor of Samuel Meredith (RG 217, Miscellaneous Treasury Accounts, 1790–1894, Account No. 5928, National Archives).

To John Jay

Philadelphia Decembr 18. 1792

My Dear Sir

Your favours of the 26 of November & 16 instant have duly come to hand.[1] I am ashamed that the former has remained so long un-acknowleged; though I am persuaded my friends would readily excuse my delinquencies could they appreciate my situation. Tis not the load of proper official business that alone engrosses me; though this would be enough to occupy any man. Tis not the extra attentions I am obliged to pay to the course of legislative manoevres that alone add to my burthen and perplexity. Tis the malicious intrigues to stab me in the dark, against which I am too often obliged to guard myself, that distract and harrass me to a point, which rendering my situation scarcely tolerable interferes with objects to which friendship & inclination would prompt me.

I have not however been unmindful of the subject of your letters. Mr. King [2] will tell you the state the business [3] was in. Nothing material has happened since. The representation will probably produce some effect though not as great as ought to be expected. Some changes for the better I trust will take place.

The success of the Vice President is as great a source of satisfaction as that of Mr Clinton would have been of mortification & pain to me.[4] Willingly however would I relinquish my share of the command, to the Antifoederalists if I thought they were to be trusted—but I have so many proofs of the contrary as to make me dread the experience of their preponderancy. Yr. note to Mrs. Gibbons has been sent.

Very respectfully & Affecly D Sir Yr Obed serv A Hamilton

The Honble J Jay

ALS, Columbia University Libraries.

1. Neither letter has been found.

2. Rufus King.

3. On November 21, 1792, the Senate appointed Oliver Ellsworth of Connecticut, Caleb Strong of Massachusetts, James Monroe of Virginia, Aaron Burr of New York, Samuel Johnston of North Carolina, and Rufus King of New York "a committee to take the Judiciary system into consideration" (*Annals of Congress*, III, 616). Two weeks earlier George Washington had laid before the Senate "a letter and representation from the Chief Justice and Associate Judges of the Supreme Court of the United States, stating the difficulties and inconveniences which attend the discharge of their duties, according to the present Judiciary system" (*Annals of Congress*, III, 611). The committee did not report until January 3, 1793 (*Annals of Congress*, III, 625).

4. For background concerning the 1792 presidential election, see H to John Adams, June 25, 1792; King to H, September 17, 27, 1792; H to ———, September 21, 26, 1792; H to Charles Cotesworth Pinckney, October 10, 1792; H to John Steele, October 15, 1792; Charles Carroll of Carrollton to H, October 22, 1792.

To Tobias Lear

[*Philadelphia, December 18, 1792.*] Sends lists of officers of revenue cutters of New Hampshire, Connecticut, New York, and Pennsylvania.

LC, George Washington Papers, Library of Congress.

From Frederick A. C. Muhlenberg[1]

Philadia. Dec. 18th. 1792

Sir,

I have communicated your Letter of yesterday to Mrs. Venables & Monroe. The latter has all the papers relating to the Subject in his possession, & I have the pleasure to inform you that your very reasonable Request will be speedily complied with. I have the honor to be with much Esteem

Your most obedt. humble Servt Fredk A Muhlenberg

Alexander Hamilton Esqr.

LS, Hamilton Papers, Library of Congress.

1. This letter appears as document No. XXVII in the appendix of the "Reynolds Pamphlet," August 31, 1797.

To James O'Hara[1]

[*Philadelphia, December 18, 1792.* On January 10, 1793, O'Hara wrote to Hamilton: "Being absent on Special business, I had not the honor to answer your letter of the 18th ulto. sooner." *Letter not found.*]

1. O'Hara, who had emigrated from Ireland to the United States before the American Revolution, had served during the war in the quartermaster's department. In the seventeen-eighties he settled in Pittsburgh and in 1790 acted as contractor for the Army during the campaign of Brigadier General Josiah Harmar against the western Indians. On April 19, 1792, O'Hara was appointed quartermaster general of the newly reorganized United States Army.

To George Washington

[Philadelphia, December 18, 1792]

William Richardson of the County of Caroline in the State of Maryland "Inspector of the Revenue for Survey No. 3. of the District of Maryland." [1]

The Secretary of the Treasury has the honor to send above the memorandum which he promised this morning to the President.

18~. Decemr. 1792

LC, George Washington Papers, Library of Congress.

1. See Tench Coxe to H, December 14, 1792.

Report on the Petition of Ludwig Kuhn

[Philadelphia, December 19, 1792
Communicated on December 20, 1792] [1]

[To the Speaker of the House of Representatives]

The Secretary of the Treasury, to whom was referred the petition of Ludwig Kuhn, by an Order of the House of Representatives, of the 28th of November last,[2] thereupon respectfully makes the following Report:

The case is one of those included in a former report to the House, dated the 16th of April 1792,[3] as barred by the Acts of limitation.

To remove the objection, which has been made on that ground to the claim of the petitioner, he has attempt[ed] to prove by his own deposition, that, in the month of March 1786, he exhibited his account and vouchers to Benjamin Stelle, late Commissioner for settling accounts in the State of Pennsylvania.

A Certificate is also produced from William Mumford,[4] late a Clerk in the said Commissioner's Office, intended to prove that the claim had been lodged in the said Office, within the time limited by law; but had not been settled, for want of a certificate from Colonel Magaw: [5] And that at the time, when the Office was closed, the unsettled accounts and certificates were left in the hands of Reading

Howell, and the books and papers of the office had been deposited in the treasury of the United States.

It appears, that the Commissioner before mentioned transmitted to the treasury a number of claims upon the United States, which had been preferred at his Office, and which remained unsettled. The papers have been examined in the Auditor's Office, and no Account in the name of the petitioner can be found.

The evidence with regard to the exhibition of the claim, within the time limited by law, is therefore deficient. The admission of collateral testimony, of the nature of that which is here produced, after so great a lapse of time, it is conceived, would, for obvious reasons, be extremely dangerous; And in this view, nothing of weight occurs to the Secretary, that could lead to a deviation from the opinion expressed in a former report.

Which is humbly submitted Alexander Hamilton,
Secretary of the Treasury.

Treasury Department
December 19th 1792.

Copy, RG 233, Reports of the Treasury Department, 1792–1793, Vol. III, National Archives.

1. *Journal of the House*, I, 651. The communicating letter, dated December 19, 1792, may be found in RG 233, Reports of the Treasury Department, 1792–1793, Vol. III, National Archives.

2. On November 28, 1792, the House received "A petition of Ludwig Kuhn, praying the liquidation and settlement of a claim against the United States, for supplies furnished the Army, during the late war.

"*Ordered*, That the said . . . petition be referred to the Secretary of the Treasury, with instruction to examine the same, and report his opinion thereupon to the House." (*Journal of the House*, I, 628.)

3. "Report on Sundry Petitions," April 16, 1792. In this report H discussed various acts of limitation concerning Revolutionary War claims, including the general acts passed in 1785 and 1787 (*JCC*, XXIX, 866; XXXIII, 392).

4. William Mumford had served as Stelle's clerk from the summer of 1783 until the office closed on April 1, 1787 ("Memorial of William Mumford," May 9, 1790, George Washington Papers, Library of Congress).

5. Robert Magaw, who was appointed a colonel in the Fifth Pennsylvania Rifle Battalion on January 3, 1776, was responsible for purchasing arms for the men under his command (*JCC*, IV, 24, 215). Ordered to New York on June 16, 1776, he was captured at Fort Washington on November 17, 1776 (*JCC*, V, 431).

To George Washington

[Philadelphia, December 19, 1792]

The Secretary of the Treasury, presenting his respects to the President, submits the enclosed papers concerning the execution of a Contract for building a Well on Cape Henlopen.[1] He will in the course of the week wait on the President for his orders.

Decr. 19. 1792

LC, George Washington Papers, Library of Congress.

1. See Tench Coxe to H, December 18, 1792.

To the President and Directors of the Bank of the United States

[*Treasury Department, December 20, 1792.* Letter listed in dealer's catalogue. *Letter not found.*]

LS, sold at Goodspeed's Book Shop, January, 1939, Item 1792.

From George Gale[1]

Baltimore Dec. 20th. 1792.

My Dear Sir

When I was first Officially informed by Mr Coxe of the Division of the District of Maryland into three Surveys I was led to beleive that if the President had conceived he could constitutionally appoint the Inspector during the recess of the Senate the Appointment would have immediately taken place.[2] As nothing has been done in this Business since the Meeting of Congress I am becoming very unhappy least there may be some doubts of the Character on whom the Choice should fall. As it is a point in which I am very Materially interested I have taken the Liberty of recalling your Attention to it. Altho in Compliance with Mr. Coxes Instructions I transmitted the Names of three Gentlemen[3] as very Suitable for the Office I had no Idea that either of the other two Gentlemen Named nor indeed any other person could enter into a Competition with Mr. Perry[4] for the Appointment. He is a Man of Business—is a respectable Character that has served 10 Years in the Senate of Maryland with reputation. He has ever been a Steady friend to the Genl. Government and has an interest in the State which may be very useful. As a proof of his Interest I need only say that he lost but one Vote of the Electors who Chose the last senate. He is the Brother in Law of Mr. Hindman[5] who will soon be a Member of the House of Representatives & has also a considerable influence with another of the new Members. In fine I can assure you that there is no such Character in my Opinion for this appointment 'tho I doubt not there are many presented to the president. Among others that are here Mentioned tis said A Mr. James Tilghman is a Candidate. He is the Friend & Relative[6] of Mr. Coxe and no Doubt will be supported by him Altho I am convinced that if Mr. Coxe knew Mr. Tilghman as well as I do he would not advocate him. If Mr Tilghman is not a Candidate Mr. Coxe may still very probably thro the Channel of his Connexions have received very unfavourable impressions of Mr. Perry—who supported Mr. Hindman against Mr Tilghman (in the last Election to Congress) which a mere candid Statement of the facts that then happened would remove. I repeat that I am convinced if you place Mr. Coxe in my Situation he would determine as I do—tho from the Delicacy of the Connexion I do not think it prudent to Submit the Question to him and therefore beg that you would be pleased to consider this Communication as solely for your own Eye. I have no View in it but the public Interest and I do most solemnly assure you that the promotion of that is the Motive with me for wishing Mr. Perry's appointment.

I am very Sincerely Dr. Sir Your affe & Obt. Servt. Geo. Gale

ALS, Hamilton Papers, Library of Congress.

1. Gale was supervisor of the revenue for the District of Maryland.

2. On August 20, 1792, Tench Coxe had written to Gale asking him to suggest candidates for the position of inspector of the revenue. Coxe stated that "the appointment of an Inspector for the third survey is defered only because the special power to appoint the Revenue Officer, vested in the President by the Act of March 3, 1791, has expired" (LC, RG 58, Letters of Commissioner of Revenue, National Archives). See also George Washington to H, August 5, 1792.

3. See Coxe to H, December 14, 1792.

4. James McHenry had suggested William Perry for office in the revenue department. See McHenry to H, November 19, 1791. McHenry also had re-

ported on Perry's activities in the Maryland election of 1792. See McHenry to H, August 16, September 20, November 18, 1792.

5. William Hindman.

6. Anna Francis, who was Coxe's aunt, had married a James Tilghman.

From James Monroe[1]

[Philadelphia, December 20, 1792]

Sir

I have the honor to inclose you copies of the papers requested in yrs. a few days past.[2] That of the notes you will retain—the others you will be pleased, after transcribing, to return me. With due respect I have the honor to be yr. very humble servant

Jas. Monroe

Every thing you desire in the letter above mentioned shall be most strictly complied with.

Phila. Decr 20. 1792

The honble Alexr. Hamilton Esqr.
Philadelphia.

ALS, Hamilton Papers, Library of Congress.

1. This letter appears as document No. XXVIII of the "Reynolds Pamphlet," August 31, 1797.

2. See H to James Monroe, Frederick A. C. Muhlenberg, and Abraham B. Venable, December 17, 1792.

From William Seton

New York 20th Decemr. 1792

My dear sir

It is a long while since I have had the pleasure of a confidential intercourse with you. I forwarded all the Copies of the Letters that past between us upon the subject of the purchase of Stocks;[1] since which I received a few lines from you covering a letter to forward by the last Packet, but no dispatches for the Minister:[2] my friend in London[3] writes me that the first Pacquet had come to hand and was delivered.

I find Mr. Burrall the Cashier of the Branch is purchasing Stock for the Public.[4] I trust this change is not owing to any fault found with me by the Commissioners, but only to conform to the Bill establishing the Bank.[5]

I often recollect your expression, *that the Branch must ultimately preponderate*. I find this to be the case every day, and indeed it has now such an advantage in its operations over us, that if pusht too far, might be attended with fatal consequences; their Circulation is so great and the reception of their paper so universal, that no one has occasion to drain them of Specie. Our Circulation is so limited, confined merely to the City to pay Duties & discharge Notes in the Branch, the whole almost centers in their hands, & upon every exchange of Bank Notes which we make three times a week, the balance is eternally very large in their favour; we have therefore been obliged to pay them imense Sums in specie, which, and the other great drains we have had for India &ca—has reduced us from upwards of Six hundred thousand Dollars in actual Coin, now down to only Two Hundred thousand; this of course obliges us to cramp our operations, to the very great distress of our Dealers, and in one month to call in near Two hundred thousand Dollars of our Discounts. In the same space of time our Circulation of Bank Notes has lessend Seventy thousand; all the Paper we have now is but a little more than three hundred thousand Dollars, not one third of our Capital; the balance of our Bills Discounted is One Million seven hundred & Ninety thousand, not twice our Capital, & we reduce every week. Yet notwithstanding all this caution, the drain of Specie is so great and we are so much in the power of the Branch (whose direction certainly bear us no good will) that I really at times feel very uneasy. We owe them now Seventy thousand Dollars, the balance of your Treasury account is nearly the same amount. Should these two Sums be suddenly called for, you may easily see from the above detail how distressing & even dangerous it would be to us. Sensible my Dear sir of your attachment to this Institution and desire to serve it, I think it my duty to give you this private and confidential Account of our real situation, and to beg you will at all events prevent our being drawn upon for the Treasurers balance just now, & to save us from the depredations of the Branch if possible. By the 1st. of February I hope our balance of Bills Discounted will be reduced to One Million & an half. If with our Capital we cannot go that length with perfect safety, we might almost as well wind up;

however there must be a certain period or extent of business that would infallibly put us upon a par with the other Bank, but what that extent is, must be found out by experience, & when found out it may perhaps be too small an object to be worth an operation.

When your occupations will allow you one moments leisure, it will be My dear Sir a great comfort to me, to have your sentiments on these points, for I must freely confess to you, that I think the Institution is in danger.[6]

With every sentiment of respect & esteem I am My dear sir Your Obliged Obed Hue Servt. Wm Seton

Alexander Hamilton Esqr.

ALS, Hamilton Papers, Library of Congress.

1. See H to Seton, October 22, 1792; Seton to H, October 26, 1792.

2. See H to Seton, November 5, 1792.

3. Joseph Hadfield.

4. See H to Jonathan Burrall, December 14, 1792.

This is a reference to purchases authorized by the commissioners of the sinking fund. In the spring and summer of 1792, purchases of the funded debt by the commissioners had been made through the agency of the Bank of New York.

5. The act to which Seton is referring has not been determined. Both the Bank of the United States and the Bank of New York were prohibited from trading in stocks either directly or indirectly. See "An Act to incorporate the stockholders of the Bank of New York" (*Laws of the State of New York*, III, 237–41 [March 21, 1791]); "An Act to incorporate the subscribers to the Bank of the United States" (1 *Stat.* 191–96 [February 25, 1791]).

6. H endorsed this letter "no answer."

To Joseph Whipple

[*Philadelphia, December 20, 1792.* On January 19, 1793, Whipple wrote to Hamilton: "I have to acknowledge the receipt of your letter of the 20th December." *Letter not found.*]

From Tench Coxe

Treasury Department, Revenue Office, December 21, 1792. Discusses rearrangement of revenue surveys [1] and compensation for revenue officers in North Carolina.

LC, RG 58, Letters of Commissioner of Revenue, 1792–1793, National Archives.

1. See Coxe to H, December 13, 1792.

To George Washington

Treasury Department, December 21, 1792. "The Secretary of the Treasury has the honor respectfully to submit . . . two Contracts between the Superintendant of the Lighthouse at New London,[1] and Daniel Harris & Nathaniel Richards. . . . The Contract with Danl. Harris is for his compensation as Keeper of the Lighthouse, and that with Nathaniel Richards for supplying it with oil and other necessaries. The terms of both the objects appear to the Secretary reasonable."

LC, George Washington Papers, Library of Congress.

1. Jedediah Huntington.

To Jonathan Burrall

Treasury Department Decr 22d 1792

Sir

I request that you will invest a further sum not exceeding Forty thousand Dollars in the funded Debt of the united States, bearing a present Interest of six per centum, upon the same principles mentioned in my letter of the 14th instant.

The Office of Discount & Deposit will furnish you with the sum, upon the enclosed Letter.[1]

I am Sir Your obedt Servt A Hamilton

Jonathan Burrall Esqr
Cashier of the Office of Discount & Deposit
New York

LS, Lloyd W. Smith Collection, Morristown National Park, Morristown, New Jersey.

1. Letter not found.

Catullus No. VI[1]

[Philadelphia, December 22, 1792][2]

For the GAZETTE of the UNITED STATES.

If perseverance can supply the want of judgment, Mr. Jefferson has an excellent advocate in the writer of his "VINDICATION."[3] But I mistake, if his last attempt is not found to involve still more deeply the character he wishes to extricate.

To repel the imputation on Mr Jefferson, arising from the advice which he gave to Congress respecting the debt to France;[4] he not only labors to shew, that taken in all its circumstances it is not of the exceptionable complexion under which it has been represented, but endeavors to infuse a belief, that the sense of the extract originally communicated, has been altered by the interpolation of certain words as well as by the suppression of a part of the paragraph, from which the extract is derived.[5]

[Philadelphia] *Gazette of the United States*, December 22, 1792.

1. The first five "Catullus" essays are dated September 15, 19, 29, October 17, and November 24, 1792.

2. This essay was written before December 15, 1792. In the [Philadelphia] *Gazette of the United States* of that date a note appeared stating that " 'Catullus' was not received in season for this day's Gazette, but shall appear in our next." In the next issue, December 19, 1792, "Catullus" was again postponed "To make room for the important French intelligence published" on that day (*Gazette of the United States*, December 15, 19, 1792).

3. The "Vindication of Mr. Jefferson" consists of six articles that appeared in [Philadelphia] *Dunlap's American Daily Advertiser*. For a discussion of these articles, see "Catullus No. IV," October 17, 1792, note 4.

4. For background concerning the proposed transfer of the French debt, see "An American No. I," August 4, 1792, note 10. Jefferson's part in this proposal is also discussed in "Catullus No. II," September 19, 1792; "Catullus No. V," November 24, 1792.

5. The fifth article in the "Vindication of Mr. Jefferson" reads in part as follows:

"The following single sentence has been published by him, not only as a literal transcript, but as containing whatever was necessary to explain Mr. Jefferson's sentiments on that head. 'If there is a danger of the public payments not being punctual, *I submit whether it may not be better* that the discontents which would then arise, should be transferred from a court, of whose good offices we have so much need, to the breasts of a private Company.' Some concessions, have it is true, been latterly m[a]de, though reluctantly; but it is still insisted on, that they do not alter the construction contended for, nor vary the import of this single extract; and for its [*l*]*iberal* conformity to the origin[a]l, he has *pledged his veracity*.

It will strike the most careless observer, as not a little extraordinary that a person (who by undertaking to state the contents of a letter, with precise accuracy, and even to detect a minute verbal deviation, must be understood to have access to the original)—should instead of submitting to the public eye a literal transcript of that original, content himself with giving his own paraphrase of it, and should expect that this would be accepted, upon the strength of his assurance, that it exhibits the genuine contents of the letter, on the point in dispute contained in one paragraph only—"That the *arrangement of the idea* is the same, and that *in substance*, nothing has been added to, or taken from it," thus modestly offering his own *construction* of *substance*, the very thing in question, for the thing itself.

That the extract, as given by me, is correct in *every material expression*, is proved by the statement in the VINDICATION. That it is literally correct, I must continue to believe until something more to be depended upon than *constructive substance*, is offered in lieu of it.

The information I possess, is drawn from two sources; one a memorandum in the handwriting of a friend which was given to me as an exact transcript of the words of the letter, and which was copied *verbatim*, in the second of these papers; the other, a document of unquestionable authenticity, not long since consulted, which states the contents of Mr. Jefferson's letter in the following form:

Mr. Jefferson suggests that "if there is a danger of the public payments not being punctual, *whether it might not be* better that the discontents which would then arise, should be transferred from a court, of whose good will we have so much need to the breasts of a private company."

"That the credit of the United States is sound in Holland, and

---

"The variance, then, between us, consists in his *suppression* of the other parts of the paragraph, relating to the same subject, and which should be seen, to enable the reader to comprehend its true import. It consists, likewise, in the *a[l]teration* of a part of the sentence itself, by the *interpolation* of words which do not belong to it. The passage in the letter referred to, reads precisely as I have stated it abo[v]e. Catullus has *altered* it, by the insertion of the following words, '*I submti whether it would not be better*,'—by which the import of that sentence, and especially when standing alone, has been varied. If therefore, the statement which I have given, is correct, it follows that Catullus has been guilty of misrepresentation, and that the extract furnished by him, is *false, deceptive*, and *mutilated*." (*Dunlap's American Daily Advertiser*, December 3, 1792.)

that it would probably not be difficult to borrow in that country the whole sum of money due to the court of France; and to discharge that debt without any deduction, thereby doing what would be grateful to the court, and establishing with them a confidence in our honor." [6]

This statement in the document alluded to, serves to confirm the memorandum, in form as well as substance. Speaking in the third person, it represents Mr. Jefferson as *suggesting*, "*whether* it *might not* be better, &c." whence it is natural to infer, that speaking in the first person in the letter, the terms are, "I submit *whether* it *may not* be better, &c."

The form of conveying the idea by way of question, is common to both vouchers; and the word "whether," which is also common to both, presupposes the words "I suggest," or "I submit," the last being the most accurate, and in that view the most likely to have been used.

It is observable, also, that the same statement disconnects the two propositions, and gives them a distinct and independent aspect. The conjunction "But," which is alledged to be in the original, does not appear in that statement.

It is possible, nevertheless, that some immaterial departures from literal precision, may have found their way into the transcripts, which are relied upon. But while this concession, as a bare possibility is made, it is not intended as an escape from a rigorous responsibility for the essential accuracy of the disclosure. If there be in what has been communicated as a literal extract, any *expression the least material*, tending to the crimination of Mr. Jefferson, which is not to be found in the original, it is admitted to be inexcusable. But not having been possessed of the original, as has been several times stated, any accidental variation of expression, not affecting at all the sense of the quotation, or not affecting it disadvantageously to Mr. Jefferson, cannot be admitted to be of moment; in regard either to the merits of the discussion or to the fairness of procedure. To press such a variance, as an objection, is to cavil, and to betray a consciousness of weakness.

6. In the two preceding paragraphs, H is quoting from the report of the Board of Treasury, February 9, 1787. See "An American No. I," August 4, 1792, note 10.

Now, it happens, that the variance, which is alledged to exist, if it had any influence upon the meaning of the passage, has one favorable to Mr. Jefferson; taking it for granted, that his Apologist has given a true account of it. This will be seen by carefully contrasting the phraseology in the two cases.

The extract, as stated by me, is in these words—"*If there is a danger of the public payments not being punctual,* I submit whether it may not *be better, that the discontents which would then arise, should be transferred from a Court, of whose good will we have so much need, to the breasts of a private company.*" [7]

The statement in the vindication represents, that Mr. Jefferson, "Having stated the proposition as above (referring to the proposition for the purchase of the debt) *observes further upon it,* in its relation to this country, that *if there be a danger our payments may not be punctual, it might be better, that the discontents which would then arise, should be transferred from a court, of whose good will we have so much need, to the breasts of a private company.*" [8]

All the material and exceptionable phrases are the same in the two statements. The only difference between them is, that in the first Mr. Jefferson is made to *submit* in the modest form of a question, "*whether it might not be better.*" the identical sentiment or advice,

7. H is referring to the extract quoted in "Catullus No. IV," October 17, 1792.

8. H is referring to the version of Jefferson's proposal which appeared in the fifth article of the "Vindication of Mr. Jefferson." This version reads as follows: "It [the paragraph in question] states that in 1786, it being known the French court were distressed for money, a Company of Dutch merchants had offered to purchase of them the [A]merican debt, of twenty-four millions of livres, for the sum of twenty, and that their embarrassments inclined them to accept of the proposal: That however a delay was occasioned, on the part of the French court, by the apprehension it might lessen our credit in Europe, and be disagreeable to Congress; whereupon he had been consulted by the agent of the Company, and to whom he had replied, that he was neither authorized to approve or disapprove of the transaction. Having stated the proposition as above, he observes further upon it, in its relation to his country, that if there be a danger our payments may not be punctual, it might be better that the discontents which would then arise, should be transferred from a court, of whose good will we have so much need, to the breasts of a private Company. *But* that it had occurred to him, we might find occasion to do what would be grateful to that court, and establish with them a confidence in our honor: That our credit was good in Holland;—might it n[o]t be possible then to borrow there, the four and twenty millions due to France, and pay them the whole debt at once? This wou[l]d save them from any loss on our account; with some further observations urging the propriety of this latter measure" (*Dunlap's American Daily Advertiser,* December 3, 1792).

which, in the last, he is made to convey in the affirmative tone of an observation, that "*it might be better*"—The last mode of expression is certainly stronger than the first, and if the sentiment conveyed be, as it undoubtedly is, an improper one, the censure due to it is encreased by the greater degree of decision with which it is expressed, as being an indication of a more decided state of mind concerning it. This remark, which might otherwise appear nice and critical, is naturally drawn forth by the attempt to have it understood, that the words "*I submit whether*," which are said to have been interpolated, have an influence upon the sense of the clause injurious to Mr. Jefferson.*

The result is, that the alteration of terms said to have been made, if real, must have been casual, because it either does not vary the sense, or varies it favorably to Mr. Jefferson: and consequently that the charge which has been brought, rests upon him in its primitive force, unmitigated by the alledged change of terms.

In like manner admitting the statement of what is said to follow as a part of the same paragraph, to be truly represented in the vindication—it either corresponds with the view I have heretofore given of the matter, or it implicates Mr. Jefferson in greater reprehensibility than has been yet charged upon him. If either presents an alternative proposition predicated upon the supposition *of a state of things different from that which is the base of the first*, namely, the danger of a deficiency of means for punctual payment, and in that case does not derogate from the first; or proceeding upon the supposition of *the same state of things*, it contains advice to Congress to avail themselves of the yet sound state of their credit in Holland, treacherously to induce individuals upon the invitation of the government to lend them money *on the ordinary terms*, for the purpose of making full payment to France, in order to guard her from loss, and preserve her confidence, in direct contemplation of not being able to render the stipulated justice to those individuals. If this was the advice of Mr. Jefferson, it leaves his conduct without even those slight extenuations which have been supposed to afford a semblance of apology. It takes away the feeble pretexts deduced from the offer

* *The words* "might not be better," *are also said to have been interpolated—though all but the* "not" *are in the quotation made by the Vindicator; a specimen of his accuracy.*

having originated with the Company, and from their gaining a considerable boom in the first purchase.

The last, I acknowledge, is the construction best warranted by the structure of the paragraph as delineated in the vindication. This, as it there stands, would be the most obvious and natural reading. If there be a danger that our payments may not be punctual, it may be better that the discontents which would then arise should be transferred from a Court of whose good will we have so much need to the breasts of a private company. But still it has occurred to me that we may do what is preferable to accepting the proposition of the Dutch Company. We may find occasion to do what would be grateful to the Court of France, and establish with them a confidence in our honor. Our credit is good in Holland—may it not be possible then to borrow there the four and twenty millions due to France, and pay them the *whole debt* at once. This, besides transferring the discontents, to be expected from the want of punctual payments, from the Court of France, to the breasts of individuals would have the farther advantage of saving that court from any loss on our account. It is in this sense only, that the first suggestion can be considered as over-ruled by, or absorbed in the last, and that Mr. Jefferson can be said to have discountenanced the proposition made by the Dutch Company. If this be the meaning intended to be contended for, no pains will be taken to dispute it; and the comment will be left to Mr. Jefferson's most partial admirers.

The writer of the vindication continues to insist, that Mr. Jefferson was only the vehicle of communication, assigning as reasons for this assertion that the transaction had taken place between the parties, before any mention was made of it to him, and that in communicating it to Congress he only made known to that body the desire both of the company and of the French Court; That the *opinion which he gave arose out of the proposition, was in furtherance of the views of the parties*, and that in fact *no decision* could be formed on it, either by the Congress, or himself, without a comparison of the parties as creditors of the United States. But these reasons do not prove that Mr. Jefferson was only the vehicle of communication; they prove the contrary; that he was both the vehicle of communication, and the *patron*, though not the *author* of the proposition. The precise difference between being the mere *vehicle*, and being both the *vehicle* and the *patron* of a proposition consists in this; that in the first case the agent does nothing more than communicate the proposition—in the last *he gives an opinion arising out of it, in furtherance of the views of the proposers;* which is exactly, what is acknowledged to have been done by Mr. Jefferson.

The plea that there could be no *immorality* or *indelicacy*, in espousing a proposition coming from the parties interested, amounts to nothing. The charge is not, that advice was given to accede to the proposition; but that advice was given to accede to it *upon a ground which was dishonorable and unjust.* It is the condition upon which the acceptance is advised, that constitutes the culpability.

In No. 4. of the vindication, the attack upon Mr. Jefferson is said to proceed from *private revenge.*[9] In No. 5. it changes its nature, and becomes an *attack upon principles;* a monarchical plot against the republican character of the community.[10] How long, and how often are the people of America to be insulted with this hypocritical rant? When will these political pharisees learn, that their countrymen have too much discernment to be the dupes of their hollow

9. H is referring to a paragraph in the fourth article in the "Vindication of Mr. Jefferson" which reads as follows: "The person who published the mutilated extract possesses I presume the true one. The whole was deposited in the quarter from whence it is believed to have been taken. I now therefore call upon him to produce the intire paragraph in his defence. In contempt of official duties, as heretofore suggested and not denied, the veil of secrecy has been torn from it, whatever detriment, if any, could be sustained from the exposure of a confidential paper, has been already rendered. It only remains by the publication of the truth, to fix the stigma on him who deserves it. Let this likeness proceed from the same party thus notably distinguished, in gratification of private revenge, for the pernicious example of a gross violation of the duties of a publick trust, and a glaring outrage on the delicacy of a foreign correspondence" (*Dunlap's American Daily Advertiser,* November 8, 1792).

10. H is referring to a paragraph in the fifth article in the "Vindication of Mr. Jefferson" which reads as follows: "Considering this attack upon Mr. Jefferson in the commencement, as an attack upon principles; knowing that the conflicting interests of parties were at work, and that the one which was suspected, with too much reason, to be attached to monarchy, would endeavour, as an obstacle in its way, to undermine not only him, but every other republican character in the confidence of their countrymen; and believing, as well from the duties of his official station as his known delicacy in observing them, he would disregard it, I thought it in some measure a duty I owed to those principles of equality which I venerate, to take up the subject, and place it on its proper ground. So far, then, as any imputation has been raised, against a distinguished and patriot citiz[e]n, I have furnished the reply, and I presume, shewn not only his innocence of any impropriety in the allegations suggested, but likewise the impurity of the motives which dictated as attack" (*Dunlap's American Daily Advertiser,* December 3, 1792).

and ostentatious pretensions? That the citizens of the United States know how to distinguish the men who *serve* them, from those who only *flatter* them, the men who have substantial claims to their confidence, from those who study to conceal the want of qualities, really solid and useful, under the mask of extraordinary and exclusive patriotism and purity?

It is curious to observe the pathetic wailings which have been produced by the animadversions in these papers. It would seem as if a certain party considered themselves as the sole and rightful censors of the Republic; and every attempt to bestow praise or blame not originating with them, as an usurpation of their prerogative, every stricture on any of their immaculate band as a breach of their privilege. They appear to think themselves authorized to deal out anathemas, without measure, or mercy, against all who dare to swerve from their standard of political orthodoxy, which are to be borne without retaliation or murmur. And if any system of either shews itself, they are sure to raise the dismal cry of persecution; themselves the first to assail, and the first to complain. But what is not permitted to men who have so clearly established a title, little less than divine, to a monopoly of all the patriotic virtues!

The only answer, which is due to the feint of offering to enter into arrangements, for ascertaining whether the writer of these papers has in the instance under consideration been guilty of misrepresentation—and the breach of an official duty—is to remind the public that in my first paper I declared myself willing to be known on proper terms to the officer concerned.[11] To this I adhere, in the

11. See "Catullus No. I," September 15, 1792.

The fifth article in the "Vindication of Mr. Jefferson" reads in part as follows:

"Whether the author of these pieces has been guilty of the breach of official duties, in the publication of any thing relative to Mr. Jefferson's letter, I know not. A variety of reasons, of but little importance to the public, and which 'tis not necessary for me to recount, have created a belief, that they proceed from Mr. Hamilton. If so, it will be difficult for him to remove the imputation. The perusal of the extract in 1787, when out of office, and the safe preservation of it since, will not justify its publication by the present acting Secretary of the Treasury; nor does it authorize a belief, if he is the author, that the official document in his possession, has not been resorted to since.—Will it be contended that the conduct of the [o]ffi[c]er at the head of that department, should be scanned in this instance by the duties of the station he held five or ten years past? Or, in other words, that the office imposes on him no particu[l]ar obligations, and which he is bound to regard? . . .

spirit of the original intimation, but I deem a personal disclosure to any subaltern of his, improper; nor do I perceive that it is in the present case necessary to an investigation of facts. The writer of the vindication admits in substance what is alledged, and as to his collateral statements, it has been shewn that they imply more blame on the character meant to be exculpated, than was originally charged. I forbear any comment on the indecency of naming upon conjecture the person who has been named as the author of these papers, or upon the palpable artifice of making an avowal of them, by that *particular* person, the condition of a disclosure of the name of the writer of the vindication. Indecency and artifice are the proper weapons of such adversaries. CATULLUS.

"It now remains only, in justice to the author of the papers under the signature of *An American* and *Catullus*, to settle the fact, whether he has been guilty of misrep[r]esentation, and the breach of an official duty, in the instance alledged, and I have every possible disposition to concur, on my part, in those arrangements which may be necessary to dispell every doubt on that subject. The truth may be ascertained, by a recurrence to the deposits in either of the departments, of State, or the Treasury. If Mr. Hamilton is not the author, and will announce it, I shall consider the subject as unworthy of further notice: if it is neither denied nor owned, but the altercation continued without any proof being produced—for none has yet been—I shall likewise consider it beneath my attention; but if he is the author, and will allow it, my name shall likewise be submitted, and joint measures may then be taken, whereby, and the truth may be placed in a clear, and authentic point of view, before [t]he public." (*Dunlap's American Daily Advertiser*, December 3, 1792).

From Tobias Lear

[*Philadelphia*] *December 22, 1792.* "By the President's command T. Lear has the honor to return . . . with the President's approbation annexed thereto, two Contracts between the Superintendent of the Lighthouse at New London, and Daniel Harris and Nathaniel Richards. . . ." [1]

ALS, RG 26, Lighthouse Letters Received, "Segregated" Lighthouse Records, National Archives; LC, George Washington Papers, Library of Congress.

1. See H to George Washington, December 21, 1792.

From Tobias Lear [1]

[*Philadelphia*] *December 22, 1792.* ". . . T. Lear has the honor to inform the Secretary of the Treasury that the President has appointed Lemuel Cornick to be keeper of the Light House on Cape Henry in Virginia."

ALS, RG 26, Lighthouse Letters Received, "Segregated" Lighthouse Records, National Archives; LC, George Washington Papers, Library of Congress.

1. See Tench Coxe to H, November 28, December 8, 1792; Lear to H, October 13, 1792; H to Lear, October 18, 1792.

To Benjamin Lincoln

Treasury Department, December 22, 1792. "Pursuant to an application from John Lee Esqr, Collector of Penobscot, I have to request that you will supply him with a dozen Certificates of Registry without delay." [1]

LS, RG 36, Collector of Customs at Boston, Letters from the Treasury and Others, 1789–1809, Vol. 1, National Archives; copy, RG 56, Letters to Collectors at Small Ports, "Set G," National Archives; copy, RG 56, Letters to the Collector at Boston, National Archives.

1. Lincoln endorsed this letter "from Alex. Hamilton, Esq. directing a supply of registers to Mr. Lee. never complied with because no opportunity offered, & charity begins at home." See also H to Lincoln, December 10, 1792.

From John Miller[1]

[*Philadelphia, December 22, 1792.* On January 3, 1793, Miller wrote to Hamilton and referred to "your letter of the 22nd ulto." *Letter not found.*]

1. Miller was inspector of clothing for the War Department.

To George Washington

[Philadelphia, December 22, 1792]

The Secretary of the Treasury presents his respects to the President. The name of the person who was employed in superintending the erecting of the Lighthouse by Mr. Newton [1] is *Lemuel Cornick.*[2] The compensation to the Keeper of the Delaware Lighthouse is 266 Dollars and ⅔ of a Dollar.

December 22d. 1792.

LC, George Washington Papers, Library of Congress.

1. Thomas Newton, Jr., inspector of Survey No. 4 in Virginia.

2. See Tobias Lear to H, October 13, 1792; H to Lear, October 18, 1792; Tench Coxe to H, October 17, 1792.

From Gouverneur Morris[1]

Paris 23 December 1792

Dear Sir

I have written to you on the seventeenth of August, twenty-first, and twenty-fifth of September, and second of November. If any of these Letters should be missing, be so kind as to mention it to me, excepting always that of the twenty-first of September, which was on a meer private Affair of a mercantile House at Rouen. I did hope that my last contain'd the End of all Correspondence with Mr. Short, respecting the Payment which at his Request I had agreed for with the Commissioners of the Treasury here; but as soon as the Communication with Holland open'd the Correspondence also open'd as you will see by the Enclosed Copies of Mr. Shorts Letters to me of the 26th. & 27th: of October, with my Answers of the 12th. and 14th. of November. To these I add Copy of the Commrs Letter to me of the 16th. of November. It appears to me proper that you should have in your Office all these Documents, since Time and Change of Circumstances, may render them useful.

I have receiv'd yours of the thirteenth of September, and the Sum of one hundred and five thousand Guilders is (agreably to your Orders) at my Disposition. I will place the Management of this affair in the Hands of Messieurs Grand and Company,[2] who remain very cautious and very solid, if I can prevail on them to come into some regular agreement on the Subject, about which they are very shy lest they should in these perilous Times be exposed to malevolent Insinuation or ungenerous Suspicion.

I fully comprehend the mode of Payment which you recommend, but I must vary from it a little to comply with your just wishes; Otherwise I shall make some Gain to the United States, which is not to be desired or expose them to some Loss which is very much to be avoided. In Order to explain this you must know that the

LC, Gouverneur Morris Papers, Library of Congress.

1. For background to this letter and much of the correspondence between Morris and William Short mentioned in it, see Morris to H, September 25, 1792. See also Short to H, September 25, 1792.

2. The Paris banking house of Ferdinand Le Grand and Company.

Exchange here fluctuates from Day to Day, nay from Hour to Hour, surprizingly. Ten Day, nay six Days, ago one hundred Dollars in Amsterdam would have produc'd little better than eight hundred livres here in Assignats, and yesterday the same Sum would have produc'd above nine hundred; last April it would have produc'd a thousand. The present Exchange is almost as low as that of the Begining of last August, and seems to be going down, but there is no reasoning justly about it. The ablest Bankers are as much at Fault, here, as other People, and it is common to see a variance of five Per Cent in one Day. If therefore I start the Idea of an Exchange on florins, we shall have altercations without End, because the Gentlemen concern'd (knowing nothing of Money Transactions) employ what are call'd here *des hommes d'affaires* who know just enough to be very suspicious, and very troublesome. It was therefore my Plan to procure the precise Specie Dollars, but on proposing it to the acting Partner in Grands House he objected thereto, and prefered the Specie Livres. He has promis'd to make his Estimates and Enquiries, and I ought before the present moment to have known the Result. If I cannot bring them to Act, I will get (if possible) some other person, or else do the Business myself, which will be very *very* disagreable for Reasons which I need not state to *you*; but I am determin'd *if possible* to secure to the Officers[3] *full Value* without *Loss* to the United States.

This same acting Partner in Grands House, to whom I delivered the Letter you enclos'd for them,[4] tells me that the Vouchers you ask for shall be transmitted, as soon as possible, but that the Trouble of finding and selecting them is so much the greater, as they are mingled in the mass of old Papers which (in Order to prepare for Events) had been packed up long ago.

3. See H to Morris, September 13, 1792.

4. Letter not found.

[ENCLOSURE]

William Short to Gouverneur Morris[5]

The Hague Oct 26 1792

Dear Sir

After more than four weeks interruption some of the French mails in arrear were recieved here yesterday & we had hoped therefore that this day, being the regular postday, would have brought us the rest—in this we have been disappointed, & of course conclude that the post communication with Paris is not yet freed from all its obstacles. I therefore send by the way of England my acknowlegement of such of your letters as were recieved yesterday—viz. those dated Sep. 20.–23–24–& 27.

In answer to them I must promise that you cannot desire more ardently than I do the end of our correspondence on the subject in question. I had hoped it would have taken place long ago; & it seems to me a very little effort on your part would have done it—if instead of determining all at once to take no further step in the late payment, you had simply taken the trouble to see that the commissaries gave the U.S. credit for the six millions of livres for which you had agreed & which was a matter altogether between you & them—of course out of my reach & incapable of being settled in Amsterdam. All that could be done there, was done, that is to say the sum you mention in florins was paid & to the persons you desired. Whether the evidence of this payment being effected was a reciept or a bill or any thing else I suppose very immaterial to your arrangement with the commissaries—but it is by no means immaterial to the U.S. that this payment should remain expressed in florins instead of livres. & this for reasons so evident & so often mentioned that I will not fatigue you with repeating them.

I suppose you will dispense me also from examining what mode of effecting this payment would have been best under all the supposable contingencies of French affairs. It is a discussion that would at present be at least useless as to the present affair. I cannot help however observing that I do not pretend to be skilled in futurity,

5. ALS, Columbia University Libraries.

& particularly in matters where so many interests & so many agents out of my knowlege are concerned. I can only see objects which are present & conjecture as to things which are to follow. Whatever may have happened since or may happen in future, yet I think the conjecture which dictated the kind of reciept which I desired from Hogguer,[6] was the most simple at that time & I repeat that I have not the gift of seeing into futurity. I should mention however that there was an error in my expression to you on this subject & that my intention was that it should be expressed as being on account of the debt *due à la France* & to be held (the payment) at the disposition of H. M. C. Majesty. It is true this latter part was not precisely the expression of the day—but it was an inaccuracy which would have been easily forgiven by any succeeding government, as would also, I still imagine, the nature of the reciept required. And this it appeared to me was the point to be obtained—viz. to make the payment so as to stop the interest on six millions of livres & to make it so as that hereafter neither the U.S. nor their agents should be blamed. I hardly think it would have been a disagreeable thing to the government with whom the final settlement should be made to find this sum in the hands of their agents and at that time it might have been expected that this settlement might be made without a very great delay or that the U.S. might have given the orders they judged proper.

Now as to the delay which took place between the time of your agreeing with the commissaries & of the payment made, & which you seem to think denatured the operation—I have already mentioned to you that your letters of the 6th. & 9th. of August were recieved at the same time & by what means, being brought by the same post, they did not get to my hands until the 17th. And as I have said above that I have not the gift of seeing into futurity I must say here I have not the spirit of divination & therefore could not know here before recieving your letter what you had done at Paris. Of course the delay of the month stated by you is not wholly to be attributed to me but only from the 17th. to the 4th. How many days delay you could consider as changing the nature of the affair I can-

6. For Short's attempts to secure a receipt for this payment from Hoguer, Grand, and Company, see Short to Morris, August 21, September 4, 1792, printed as enclosures to Morris to H, September 25, 1792.

not say—but you certainly did consider some delay as optional without this risk since you said the bankers in order to avoid the rise of agio might make the payment *at their liesure.* On the 17th. I gave the orders to the bankers which were reiterated the 19th. Hogguer begged for time to consider of the offer made—our bankers [7] supposed he wrote to Paris for orders—whether he did or not that part of the delay came from him—& when he gave his answer the rest was consumed in letters going & coming between this & Amsterdam, in the hopes of our bankers being able to settle some mode of payment which should avoid the danger I so much apprehended—& I hoped by every post also to recieve more & more information from you, relying really & absolutely on your judgment in this business. On the 4th. of Sep. I recieved yours of the 27th. of Aug. & the same day directed the payment. I think then from the nature of the case & from the expressions of your letters the delay wch. took place cannot be considered either by you or any body else as denaturing it.

Another principle of change which you mention as having been introduced by my doubting, is the bill instead of a reciept or no reciept at all.[8] Now here is a distinction in which there may be a difference but I must own I do not see it—& whether so or not I am entirely innocent; & even if no suspension had taken place of the King or of the payment still this same unfortunate bill would have existed—that being the mode as I am informed which our bankers have constantly used with the French in the payments made at Amsterdam. My usage has been to give them the orders to make the payments, sometimes by remittances—sometimes by payments to the French agents according to the desire of the French government—in both cases I did nothing more than give the orders—leaving the *moyens d'execution* to the bankers supposing them better acquainted with such things than myself—& never enquiring whether it was by entry, reciept, bill, bond or what. Of course when you desired me to direct the payment of f 1,62,5000—& I the bankers, supposing there had been no difficulty as to the suspension, they would have done on the 17th. of Aug. precisely what they did on the 5th. of

7. Willink, Van Staphorst, and Hubbard.

8. See Morris to Short, September 20, 1792, printed as an enclosure to Morris to Short, September 25, 1792.

september. The same doubt as to its being the same payment you had stipulated, would therefore have existed in both cases if it can exist in either. I should have supposed that you would have considered it worth while therefore to see that no doubt should be left, by taking the trouble to satisfy yourself that the U.S. were credited on the books of the treasury for six millions of livres—which was all that was necessary as it can hardly be supposed they will credit the U.S. both for the 6. millions of livres & the 1,625m florins. Your seeing to this consummation of the arrangement appears so natural (& particularly if you concieved the bill instead of a receipt or no receipt introduced doubts as to its identity) that I should have thought you would not have failed to have done it, had there been no suspension—& had you done it in the case of the suspension, you see my dear Sir that you would have saved yourself much ennui & importunity & me much trouble.

So much for the operation being denatured by delay or by the bill. Without enquiring further into this subject I rely on its being susceptible of no question which wd. not equally have existed had that *payment* (which you said the bankers might make at their liesure) *been readily made*. And as in this case you say there can be no difficulty, whether there be change or no change & whether the acts be valid or annulled, I shall repose on your better judgment & hope there will be none.

I should think this still more certain if you would simply take the trouble to remove the doubts of the commissaries if they have any as to this being the identical payment you had stipulated & to see that the U.S. are credited for 6,000,000 ₶. Who my dear Sir can do this so well as yourself? Who else in fact can do it all? I cannot concieve from whence your aversion comes. I have sollicited you in every manner in my power not to leave the matter to future discussion. When the bills were enclosed to you one word from you would have sufficed in presenting these bills—& at that time I did not think there was a moment to be lost & therefore pressed you in the manner I did. I renew here my intreaty that you should put this matter out of doubt. Had you taken no step in it I should have supposed you would do this for the interest & satisfaction of the U.S.—but in a business where you alone have acted with the commissaries —where you alone can remove their doubts if they chuse to have any, where you alone can see the florins converted actually into the livres you agreed for, I repeat it again, I cannot & never could concieve your reason for refusing to do it, & thus risk future discussion.

I shall desire our bankers to write by the next post to the commissaries as you suggest in your letter of the 27th. of Sept. for greater certainty in preventing their giving the U.S. a double credit for the same payment.

I shall not write to the commissaries another letter; the object of that which I inclosed to you was to effect what I wished in the case of your persisting in taking no further step in the business, & there being as I feared then not time enough left to write after recieving your answer. I flatter myself you will for the interest of the U.S. take the last, & as it appears to me, not an inconvenient, step, to have the florins converted into livres according to your stipulation & carried to the credit. I do not consider this as a deviation from what you think proper to be done viz. *to adhere to the original nature & form of the present payment*, but the seeing that that nature & form is adhered to by the commissaries. On no other consideration would I have ordered a payment to be made & expressed in florins than the certainty of their value in livres being previously fixed or the standard for fixing it agreed on—& this was an invariable rule with me.

I thought I had formerly sufficiently explained my wishes as to what you call *certain other things to be done with the same persons whose authority I deny*. My desire was that at a future period when the day of settlement for past payments depreciation &c. came—there should be the fewest questions possible & the business the most possibly in the hands of the U.S. Now to avoid questions it seems to me the first thing is to simplify the subjects as much as possible. The whole of this chapter may be resolved therefore into one simple question to which I leave you the answer. Would this business be more simple & more in the hands of the U.S. if there were book accts. & the obligations paid off still remaining in the treasury or if the only such obligations remained as were still unpaid? I had thought in this latter case the acct. would be more simple & the affair of depreciation more absolutely in the power of the U.S.

I thought another thing also in which it seems from your letters that I was mistaken, & which of course puts an end to this part of the subject; so that I must ask you to regard what I have said on it as an impertinent trouble which I have given you. I had thought I know not why, but supposed I had seen it in the resolves of Congress that the reciepts constituting the debt were for much smaller sums—if they are as you state them only in three, nothing of course can be done of the nature I proposed. I intended to have answered another part of your letters but having been interrupted by persons who have detained me until the hour of the post I must defer it until my next—assuring you at present that I am my dear Sir,

truly yours W Short

M. Morris &c. &c.

[ENCLOSURE]

William Short to Gouverneur Morris [9]

The Hague Oct. 27. 1792

Dear Sir

Notwithstanding the immense length & prolixity of my letter of yesterday it wd. have been continued if I had not been interrupted & detained until the hour of the post. You desire me to consider well before hand as to the obligations, whether I would wish to come to a settlement previously with the ministry, in fixing the value &c. If as you suppose the obligations are only three, nothing more need be said on this business. I had supposed it had been different, & thought I had seen somewhere that the debt of 18. millions [10] consisted of twelve reciepts of 1½ million each. In that case I should have proposed taking up such of these reciepts as were fully paid off—counting the livre tournois as it was paid—& leaving the depreciation out of the question for the present so as to avoid any settlement—the surplus which the U.S. may here after judge proper to pay by way of indemnity to be regulated by them at the time of paying this indemnity. The indemnity being as you justly observe

9. ALS, Columbia University Libraries.

10. This is a reference to the 1782 loan of eighteen million livres from France to the United States. For a description of this loan, see H to Short, September 1, 1790, note 17.

optional with the U.S.—the commissaries could not object to recieving the 31,350 000 ₶ already paid according to your statement for that amount for the present.

You desire me to recollect that you never saw my instructions. They are contained as to this subject in different letters from the Secy. of the treasury, with which I made you acquainted before leaving Paris—& the sentiments contained in a letter I recd. from him soon after arriving here, I extracted & forwarded to you. You therefore knew all I knew as low down as the time of your transacting this business with the commissaries.

I find that I committed an error in mentioning to you yesterday that your letters of the 6th & 9th. of Aug. were not recieved until the 17th—for the sake of accuracy I repeat that they were recd. on the night of the 16th. so that I could not act on them until the 17th.

You say *the present ministers of France complain much of my intention to place the money out of their reach which conduct they consider as evincing a hostile disposition:* As I infer from thence that you see those gentlemen, I cannot help observing thereon that you may notice it to them, if they mean a hostile disposition in the U.S. that their conclusion is a very rapid one & by no means warranted since I could not possibly have any instructions from the U.S. thereon & that what I did would by no means bear the construction they put on it since it was nothing more than the effect of my desire for my own justification to pay the money to that agent or representative of the nation, who alone was known to foreign powers & to whom alone I could have a right to pay the money. If they mean the hostile disposition in me individually—then of course it will not be worth your while to trouble yourself about it. My own disposition is of no importance to any body but it ever will be to follow my instructions & when ordered to pay money or treat with any country, to consider myself bound to do this with the agents whom our government had acknowleged, & whom alone they could have in view at the time of giving me their orders. As to the right of the people to change their government & give it the form they please I do not suppose it will be ever questioned by an American nor that I shall be considered as questioning it. Such considerations may be proper for governments—certainly I had no right to examine them or in this instance do any thing else than follow as near as I could the orders recieved, without any kind of enquiry into the chapter of political rights or the proper mode of exercising them.

I am my dear Sir, truly yours W: Short

M. Morris &c &c.

[ENCLOSURE]

Commissaries of the French Treasury to Gouverneur Morris [11]

Paris 16. Novbre. 1792
L'an premier a la republique

En reponse Monsieur à la lettre que vous nous aves fait L'honneur de nous Ecrire le 14 de ce mois, nous avons celui dernier dire que les Etats unis de l'Amerique ont été Credités sous les Livres a la Tresorerie Pour la datte du 5 Septembre dernier a la Somme de L. 6,000,000. pour le produit des Bco. f 1,625,000. a raison de 34 ⟨–⟩ ℔ 8d. remis le dit Jour par Mess. Wilhem & Jan Willink, & Nicolas & Jacob Vanstaphorst d'Amsterdam, a nos agents &c &c—Hoguer Grand & Compe. le dit. Lieu. . . .

[ENCLOSURE]

Gouverneur Morris to William Short [12]

Paris 12 Novr 1792

My dear Sir

I have received your favors of the twenty sixth and twenty seventh of last month to which I intended to reply this Day but I have been interrupted constantly since I left my Bed to the present Moment in which I have only Time for this Short Acknowledgement of your Letters. I regret it the less as I much fear that in the present Situation of Flanders even these half dozen Lines may miscarry.

adieu I am ever & truly yours Gouv Morris

Wm Short Esqr

11. LS, Columbia University Libraries.
12. ALS, William Short Papers, Library of Congress.

[ENCLOSURE]

Gouverneur Morris to William Short[13]

Paris 14 November 1792

My dear Sir

I have already acknowleged yours of the twenty sixth and twenty seventh of last Month. I will now reply to them. And first I have just written to the Commissaries of the Treasury desiring a Copy of the Entry made in their Books of the Payment in question. Secondly I must inform you that my Reluctance has arisen from a Circumstance highly disagreable and which in my Situation you would have felt I think as I did. The Ministry had taken up the Idea that the Management of what relates to the Debt was in my Hands and that you acted in Consequence of Directions from me. They wish'd me to do things which were by no Means in my Power. I endeavor'd to undeceive them but in vain. Every step I took in Relation to it however indifferent was considered as a Proof of their Hypothesis and they treated my Refusal as a Disavowal of the late Revolution. I assured them that I could neither adopt nor reject it being merely an Agent &ca. &ca. but this answer'd little Purpose and the whole Council are *personally* my Enemies. You may say that they are unreasonable & the like but that does not alter the Thing. This Inconvenience however which is no small one under the Circumstances in which I have liv'd for the last three Months and which has I know excited Representations in America to my Disadvantage,[14] this Inconvenience would not have prevented me from complying with your Wishes if I could have conceiv'd that any valuable End would

13. ALS, William Short Papers, Library of Congress.

14. In a letter dated September 13, 1792, to Jean Baptiste de Ternant, French Minister to the United States, Pierre Henri Hélène Marie Lebrun-Tondu, the French Minister of Foreign Affairs, expressed the following sentiments concerning Morris's behavior: "We have been as much astonished, as piqued at the forms, and tone assumed by the American Minister. We expected to find in him dispositions which would manifest the close union which should prevail between two people animated by the same principles of liberty. . . . It has appeared that Mr Morris is in no wise penetrated with these truths. He has on the contrary demonstrated *humour* (indisposition or dislike) towards us. The Provisory Executive council, informed of these facts, charges you to speak of it to Mr Jefferson in suitable terms, and to express to him our discontent at the conduct of the American minister" (translation, in the handwriting of Jefferson, RG 59, Miscellaneous Letters, 1790–1799, National Archives).

be answerd and I now comply meerly to satisfy you. My Manner of viewing the Object has ever been the same. Either they entered the Sum in question at the Time I wrote or they did not. Enter it in Livres they must if they keep Books of Account like other People. And if they enter it at the Sum I mention'd they give the Credit you desire. If they do not enter it at that Sum there is a question open on their Letter to me and on my Answer. When shall this question be settled, and with whom? In my opinion it would be settled, in common with all other questions relating to the Debt, when the final Settlement thereof is made. And I found that opinion upon the following simple Reason; that in such final Settlement all anterior Payments must of Course come in question, if the United States continue in the Disposition to pay the Depreciation: for if, for Argument Sake, a Stipulation were made *now* (or it had been made at any Time since you left Paris) that a Million of real Money should wipe off two Millions of the Debt, I do suppose that afterwards the Government in claiming the Indemnity would be as well founded in stating the Loss of a Million on that Transaction, as in stating any other Loss sustained. If in one Case we could reply, *there is your Agreement* (to which it might always by the bye be objected that Governments being like orphans ought not to suffer by the Malfeisance of their Guardians) in the other Case we could reply (and I think with far greater Force) *there is your Law according to which you have paid and according to which on every Principle of Justice you are bound to receive.* Observe that I do not put in question here the Authority of the present Government: first because it would only complicate the Subject, and secondly because I do not think it necessary to raise that question. But if it be raised, you will easily see that it must enforce my Observations.

You tell me that in all Events the Evidence of the Payment made in Amsterdam would have been by a Bill on the Commissaries of the Treasury. In that Case the Manner of doing Business is different from that with which I have been hitherto acquainted: and I must add different from what you considered as proper; because you in the first Instance desired a Receipt. I cannot but think that the natural and simple Mode of concluding that Business would have been to have taken the Receipt of Hoguer Grand and Company for bf 1.625.000 paid by Order of Mr. Short in Conformity to the

Agreement made between the Commissaries of the Treasury and Mr. Morris. When the Bankers of the United States made their former Payments at Amsterdam it was perfectly regular to take Bills which of Course ascertaind both the Relation between Florins and Livres and the Period at which the latter should be carried to Account but when by previous Agreement these Points were already adjusted it appears to me that the taking of a Bill of Exchange instead of a Receipt could tend only to undo what had been done. However the Thing is over and it is vain to look back I am oblig'd to repeat because you seem not to have entered fully into the Ideas which I meant to convey. You certainly do not when you contrast that of making Payment *at leizure* with the Delay which took Place without making any Payment at all but with holding it altogether upon a Contingency foreign to the Convention which was by that Payment to be compleated. By Paying at leizure I meant and could only be supposd to mean such Delay as could procure the Bank Money without raising the Agio and this was of Course but a short Period and might be only a Day if on the Exchange there should be more Venders than Purchasers of Bank Money. When I remark on these Things to you it is not that I think the Transaction cannot substantially be supported and I have endeavor'd to support it always on it's true Ground. But I am persuaded that if ever a question be rais'd it will be as follows. The Agreement made by Mr. Morris became void because Mr. Short would not and did not comply with it but withheld the Payment untill a particular Kind of Receipt should be given which the Circumstances of the french nation could by no Means permit. Afterwards a Payment was made which as to the Sum in florins was the same with that agreed on but the Proof that it was not the same in other Respects nor made in pursuance of that Agreement is that a Bill was taken on the Commissaries of the Treasury for the Amount. This Bill passed to a third Person would have constituted a Claim on instead of a Payment to the Government and of Course it was not untill the Bill was receivd by the Commissaries that the Payment was made and of Course that Payment was of the Value of *that* Day and to the *Government of that Day*.

The question you raise respecting the Obligations really and truly appears to me of mere Indifference. If we could purchase these

Obligations for a thousand Guineas would the United States consider that as a Payment would it be so considered by the french Government or by that great Public which judges between Sovereign Powers? I think not. And in like manner tho after full Payment the Obligations should remain where they are no Claim could in my Opinion be rais'd upon them. Now this which may at first Sight strike you perhaps as a Pertness of Reply is connected with some other important Truths. It was propos'd to make over these Obligations to an Individual or Company in Payment of some Contract or otherwise and I was consulted. I declar'd that the United States would never ratify any Bargain respecting those Obligations made without their Concurrence that the Obligations did not constitute but only evidence the Debt which would be acknowleg'd without such Evidence and paid when due not to those who either rightfully or wrongfully might become possest of the Obligations but to our real Creditor who might then settle according to Right and Justice with the Individual or Company. I have Reason to beleive that this also is among the Causes of Disatisfaction which prevails with the Ministry as to me but I care not. I shall pursue the strait Line regardless of Consequences; and I cannot while in the Profession of those which are my real Sentiments and which will I think on Reflection be yours also. I cannot I say higgle about the Possession of Papers which in my Conscience I beleive to be of very little Importance.

However to resume (according to the fashionable Phraseology) you have the best imaginable occasion of setling all these things in your own Way. Mr. Carmichael is very urgent that you should go on to Madrid[15] he has written so to you and mentions it to me in the Fear that his Letters to you may have miscarried. I consider the present Moment as particularly favorable to a Treaty with Spain and I dare say the same thing will strike you forcibly. Of course I shall expect that you will take this City in your Way. You will find it much Changd from what it was; but you will find one Person in it very glad to see you and to reiterate to you the Assurances of the Regard with which he is yours Gouv Morris

15. Short was preparing to join William Carmichael in Madrid, where both men were to act as commissioners to settle outstanding differences between the United States and Spain.

To the President and Directors of the Bank of the United States

Treasury Department Decr 24th 1792

Gentlemen

I request that a further sum of 4034 Dollars & 87 Cents may be advanced to Wm Young & Geo. Dannacker on account of their clothing contract, to be charged as heretofore.[1]

This sum added to the former advances will make up the amount of Twenty thousand Dollars.

I have the honor to be Gentlemen Your obedt Servt

Alexander Hamilton

The President & Directors
of the Bank of the
United States

LS, MS Division, New York Public Library.

1. See "Contract with George Dannacker and William Young," October 22, 1792, and H to the President and Directors of the Bank of the United States, November 28, December 3, 12, 1792.

From George Bush[1]

[*Wilmington, Delaware, December 24, 1792.* On January 4, 1793, Hamilton wrote to Bush: "Your letter under date of the 24th. ulto has been received." *Letter not found.*]

1. Bush was collector of customs at Wilmington, Delaware.

To Henry Knox

Treasury Department 24 December [1792]

Sir,

It being among the duties assigned by Law to the Treasury department, to prescribe forms for keeping and rendering all public accounts, I now address you for the purpose of sugg⟨est⟩ing in what manner it will be hereafter expected that the accoun⟨ting⟩ for ex-

Copy, RG 94, Instructions to David Henley, 1793–1800, National Archives.

penditures in the Indian department be regulated and rendered for settlement.[1] Some forms as essential checks upon the account⟨s⟩ for expenditures relating to the distribution of supplies will accompa⟨ny⟩ the forms [2] for these accounts, and I request that a strict observanc⟨e⟩ of them and of the regulations which are hereafter specified may ⟨be⟩ enjoined on the particular Superintendants in the several departm⟨ents⟩—There being no quarter in which there is greater danger of abuse, proportional care and exactness are called for.

The accounts of the expenditure of money will naturally fall into two divisions, one of which will consist of payments for *services performed* and *contingent expences;* another for *supplies purchased* for the Department—separate accou⟨nts⟩ will be expected for expenditures under these heads.

In relation to the accounts for services it will be necessary that the particulars should be stated in detail and that receipts for the sums paid should be produced. As the rates of allowance for services will in general depend on special circumstanc⟨es,⟩ it is of course confided that every thing will be done to cause them to be regulated by a due attention to œconomy.

It is presumed that all supplies will be procured in consequence of special contracts, or by means of Agents duly authorized by the respective Superintendants, who are to be compensated by a commission on the sums expended. Whenever the nature of the case will admit of it, the former mode under due cautions and restrictions is deemed preferable.

For all supplies which shall be procured by contract, it will be expected that the original agreement or a duplicate thereof will be exhibited at the Treasury, with a particular account from the Contractor of the articles supplied, also a receipt for the sums paid, and a receipt for the specific articles furnished to be signed by some agent authorized and appointed for that purpose, who, it is wished, may be rendered accountable for the issue and delivery thereof in the manner hereafter specified.

1. For earlier references to forms and procedures for the accounting and control of money and supplies used by the Department of War, see H to George Washington, August 10, 1792; Oliver Wolcott, Jr., to H, November 24, 1792.

2. Copies of these forms may be found in RG 94, Instructions to David Henley, 1793–1800, National Archives.

For all articles which shall be purchased by an Agent on commission, a particular account will be required to be supported by the original bills of purchase, with receipts for the sums paid; and also a receipt for the specific articles procured, to be signed by the Agent appointed to issue and deliver the same.

It is also my desire that the Agent who may be appointed to receive the articles which shall be procured under the direction of any Superintendant may also receive all such supplies as shall be procured under the Contracts and arrangements of the Treasury for the use of your department, to be in like manner accountable for the issue and delivery thereof. When any such supplies shall be forwarded, it will therefore be expected that duplicate invoices and receipts therefor will be signed by said Agent one of which to be transmitted to the Comptrollers office.

It is foreseen that in a business so complicated, and exposed to so many casualties as that transmitted to the care of the Superintendants no rules of accounting adapted to all the cases which may occur can be prescribed. The forms herewith transmitted have however been prepared, with a view of reducing the accounts to as uniform a system as the subjects will admit, to which I request you to procure a conformity as far as shall be found practicable.

The accounts for personal services and contingencies are to be stated according to the abstract marked (A) and to be supported by vouchers in the manner before described.

The accounts for all supplies procured on Contract or by purchase are to be classed and arranged agreeably to the examples in the form B which is designed as a specimen, and is to be supported by Vouchers from the Contractors or purchasing Agents. For the articles charged in this Account the receipts of the issuing Agent will be indispensible.

The amount of these abstracts will be transferred to an account current according to the form (C) in which all monies received on public account are to be particularly credited.

In accounting for the issuing and delivery of supplies purchased and received, the greatest caution and accuracy are obviously requisite, to which end it is conceived at the Treasury to be of great importance that the Agent who may be appointed for that purpose, should, in each case, be instructed to observe the following regulations,

All the articles and supplies received to be fairly stated in an abstract or abstracts according to the form marked D.

No delivery on any account to be made except on the written order of the Superintendant, or of a person who is the principal at a Treaty or Conference.

All issues and deliveries to Indians or illiterate persons for their use, to be made in presence of some person to be appointed by the Superintendant, or the principal at a treaty or conference, who shall certify on the orders for delivery, that the articles therein mentioned were in fact issued.

The deliveries so made to be entered in an abstract to be stated according to the form (E), to which deliveries ought to be added all the articles which shall be lost, stolen, or destroyed by accident.

The vouchers for articles charged in the abstract of deliveries as lost, stolen, or destroyed, to be certificates or affidavits from disinterested persons, stating the circumstances of each case and whether the loss was or was not in their judgment, occasioned by the negligence of the Agent or of any other person.

It will be an important guide if at the time of rendering the accounts for settlement, a third abstract signed by the Agent stating the supplies remaining unexpended be rendered to the Treasury agreeably to the form marked (F).

I request that information may be speedily transmitted to the Treasury of the arrangements which may be made under this regulation and your instructions by the respective Superintendants, and that all accounts respecting their several departments may be rendered quarterly for settlement on the last day of March June—September and December annually.

In the instructions which may be given in consequence of this communication it will be adviseable to mark to the respective Superintendants that it is not designed to supercede any restraints which may have heretofore been laid upon them with regard to the procuring of supplies. It is my intention and wish, as far as circumstances shall permit, to have the supplies procured under the immediate direction of the Treasury. These regulations have therefore reference only to those cases in which special authority may have been given to them by you in concert with the Treasury or in which casual exigencies have not admitted the distant provision.

I have the honor to be &c A Hamilton

Henry Knox Esqr
Secretary of War

From Gouverneur Morris

Private: Paris 24 decber 1792

My dear Sir

I wrote to you on the twenty fourth of October and have not since receivd any of your Letters. In that I acknowleged yours of the 22d of June. You will have seen from the public Prints the Wonderful Success of the french Arms [1] arising from the following Causes. 1st. That the Enemy deceiv'd by the Emigrants counted too lightly on the Opposition he was to meet with. 2ly That from like Misinformation instead of attacking on the Northern Frontier back'd by the Resources of Flanders and those which the Ocean could supply, they came across the Ardennes to that Part of Champaign nicknam'd the lousy from its barrenness and misery. 3ly That in this Expedition, where the Difficulty of the Roads Transportation and Communication was the greatest they expected, it so happend that the Season usually dry and fair (when those bad Roads are at the best) was one continued Rain for two Months so that at length they were nearly stuck fast and had as much as they could do to drag back their Cannon &ca. thro the Mud. Lastly that France brought into the Field and has kept up untill very lately the immense Number of 600,000 Troops. This has been done at an Average Expence of about five Millions Sterling per Month beyond their Resources and yet they have ordered a like Army for the next Campaign and talk boldly of Meeting Great Britain also upon his Element. What say you to that Monsieur le Financier? But I will tell you in your Ear that in Spite of that Blustering they will do much to avoid a War with Britain *if the People will let them* but Truth is that the Populace of Paris influence in a great Degree the public Councils.

I think they will have quite as many Men as they can maintain but what that may amount to is hard to determine.

Let me refer now to a Letter I wrote Yesterday. You will see that there is on one Side either a real Want of Comprehension or else a desire to place all Blame on the Shoulders of your Friend. If I may judge by what I have seen from Scipio[2] this latter View is seconded. Now you know that I hate little Things as much as you do and more I cannot. Therefore my good Friend keep me clear of little People. If ever I am destin'd to act in that Business let me have a clear Line drawn and I will go strait forward but do not put me to the Draught with a Horse who looks behind him and tries to get his Neck out of the Collar. I have seen a great Deal of this and tell, I pray you, your friend Paulus[3] that in like Manner as Tarquin[4] has mov'd under the Guidance of Scipio so will others of his Agents. You must observe too that Men sometimes decline thro an apparent modesty to do their Duty when they mean thereby only to shew a resentful Sense of Disappointment and then if the Thing be not well done it is expected that Comparisons will be drawn in their Favor. Read mark learn and inwardly digest these Hints.

The Ministers here are most extraordinary People. They make nothing of Difficulties as you shall judge by a single Trait of Mr. Pache[5] the Minister at War. He had sent Beurnonville[6] to occupy the Moselle River down to Coblentz taking *Treves* and other Places in his Way. Now this Way lies thro a very difficult mountainous Country in which the Snow is already very deep therefore Beurnonville having got a little Neck of Land between the Saar and the Moselle puts his Troops into Winter Quarters pleading their nakedness as an Excuse. The Minister has sent him a Brace of Commissioners who have Power to *impress* in the Neighbourhood whatever may be needful for the Troops and then (their wants supplied) summon him to obey his orders. I have given to Mr. Jefferson a pretty full Account of the State of Things[7] so that if you see that Account (which I take it is of Course) you may Measure by the Standard now given you of all other Affairs.

If I may venture to judge from Appearances there is now in the Wind a Storm not unlike that of the second of September.[8] Whether it will burst or blow over it is impossible to determine.

Adieu I am always truly yours Gouv. Morris

P.S. On looking over this Letter it has occurred to me that I have never yet assigned a Reason why the Completion of the Payment of 6,000,000 ₶ which at Mr Short's Request I had stipulated for with the Government lately abolished appeared to me desirable.[9] In Effect, I left this as I do many other Things to the Sense of the *gentle* Reader but as Readers are sometimes *ungentle* it is not amiss to communicate that Reason to a Friend. I saw that the new Government would be hungry and would urge us for Money in the double View of obtaining an Acknowlegement of *them* as well as of supplying *their* Wants. It was therefore (I thought) right, to take a Position where we might say *There is nothing due*. This would leave open a question which it would be very delicate to answer either Way, as things *appeard* then, and as they *are* now that *appearances* have chang'd. You will have seen the Manœuvres to force me in that Entrenchement, but at last like *your friend* Genl. Lee [10] I was quit at the Worst for a *retrograde Manœuvre*.—But I concluded that Supplies of Money to support the Colony of St Domingo [11] would *in all Events* have been considered *as a good and effectual Payment on our Part* and had my Offer of recommending such Supplies been accepted, I would on *that Ground* have propos'd the Measure which *anticipating the next Instalments* would have still kept open the main Point as long as you should think proper. And thus my *apparent* Retreat was in Effect a Mode of *more permanent Defence* & this is more I believe than poor Lee could say for himself.

Alexander Hamilton Esqr.

ALS, Hamilton Papers, Library of Congress; LC, Gouverneur Morris Papers, Library of Congress.

1. This is a reference to the victory of the French army under General François Duperier Dumouriez at the Battle of Jemappes, November 6, 1792. Dumouriez took Brussels and conquered the Austrian Netherlands.

2. Scipio was Thomas Jefferson. For a list of the "appellations for certain official characters" which H had suggested that he and Morris use in their correspondence, see H to Morris, June 22, 1792.

3. Hamilton.

4. James Madison.

5. Jean Nicolas Pache, French Minister for War from October 20, 1792, to February 3, 1793.

6. General Pierre de Riel de Bournonville.

7. Morris to Jefferson, December 21, 1792 (ALS, RG 59, Despatches from United States Ministers to France, 1789–1869, June 17, 1792–March 7, 1794, National Archives). This letter is printed in part in Morris, *Diary of the French Revolution*, II, 589–93.

8. This is a reference to the September massacres (September 2–7, 1792) at Paris.

9. For a discussion of the payment due on the French debt in the summer of 1792, see Morris to H, September 25, December 23, 1792; Short to H, September 25, 1792; Jefferson to H, October 31, 1792.

10. Presumably this is a reference to the retreat ordered by Major General Charles Lee at the Battle of Monmouth during the American Revolution. In this case Morris's use of "your friend" was sarcastic. H testified against Lee at the latter's court-martial. See "Proceedings of a General Court-Martial for the Trial of Major General Charles Lee," July 4, 1778.

11. For Morris's negotiations with the French Ministry concerning Santo Domingo, see Morris to H, November 2, 1792, note 4.

To Thomas Jefferson

Treasury Department
Decr 26 1792

Sir

I beg leave to suggest, that it would be useful for the Consuls of the United States, every where to be possessed of the Laws of the U States respecting Commerce & Navigation—giving it as a standing instruction, to make known in the best manner possible, in the parts where they reside those regulations, which are necessary to be complied with abroad by Merchants, & the Owners & Masters of Ships.

Prohibitions and penalties in some cases exist as in the 10th & 13th Sections of the Act concerning the duties on spirits distilled within the united States: [1] an ignorance of which is experienced to be a source of embarrassment & in some instances of expence & vexation to foreign Merchants and Navigators.

It would also be of use in the operations of the Treasury if our Consuls in France were directed to transmit, by every opportunity the state of exchange between their respective places of residence and London & Amsterdam and the current difference between specie & assignats: this has reference particularly to the execution of the 17th Section of the Act entitled "an Act for raising a further Sum of money for the protection of the frontiers." [2]

I have the honour to be very respectfully sir your Obed Servt

Alex Hamilton

The Secretary of State

LS, James Madison Papers, Library of Congress.

1. Section 10 of this act reads as follows: "That from and after the last day of April, one thousand seven hundred and ninety-three, no distilled spirits except arrack and sweet cordials, shall be brought into the United States from any foreign port or place, except in casks or vessels of the capacity of ninety gallons and upwards" (1 *Stat.* 270 [May 8, 1792]). Section 13 provided that "if any distilled spirits, except arrack and sweet cordials, shall, after the last day of April next, be brought into the United States in casks or vessels of less capacity than ninety gallons, all such spirits, and the casks and vessels containing the same, shall be subject to seizure and forfeiture" (1 *Stat.* 270).

2. Section 17 of this act reads as follows: "*And be it further enacted*, That so much of the act, intituled 'An act to provide more effectually for the collection of duties imposed by law on goods, wares, and merchandise imported into the United States, and on the tonnage of ships or vessels,' as hath rated the livre tournois of France at eighteen and a half cents, be and the same is hereby repealed" (1 *Stat.* 262–63 [May 2, 1792]).

See also "Treasury Department Circular to the Collectors of the Customs," June 4, 1792.

To Sharp Delany

[*Philadelphia, December 27, 1792.* On the back of a letter which Delany wrote to Hamilton on October 4, 1792, the following words are written: "27 December Answered." *Letter not found.*]

From Antoine René Charles Mathurin de La Forest

[*Philadelphia, December 27, 1792.* On December 29, 1792, Hamilton wrote to George Washington: "The Secretary of the Treasury has the honor to enclose . . . the translation of a letter of the 27 of December, which he has received from mr. de la Forest." *Letter not found.*]

From Jeremiah Olney[1]

Custom House
District of Providence 27th Decer. 1792

Sir

I have the pleasure to communicate for your information, that Judgment was rendered in my favour before the State Court on the 26 Instant, in the Two Suits brought against me by Messrs. Arnold and Dexter in the Case of the Brigantine Neptune. The Gentlemen are extremely mortified and Disappointed in the Issue of their Suits. They have appealed to the Superiour Court of this State to Meet in this Town on the Third Monday of March next. They had four attorneys to manage their Causes, one of whom was from Boston Saml. Dexter Esqr. of distinguished Tallents. The District Attorney [2] will acquaint you with the particular Ground on which these causes were Conducted before the Court.

I have paid forty Two Dollars for the Fees of Two Attorneys whom I found necessary to engage in the Defense of the Suits. The District Attorney has a Demand to make for his particular attention to the Business which I have not yet paid.

Your Letter of the 12th. Instt., relative to the Providence Bank,[3] has come to hand: The Deposit made with the Commissr. of Loans,[4] was returned previous to the date of our last Letter upon this Subject.[5]

I have the Honor to be &c. Jereh. Olney Collr.

Alexr. Hamilton Esqr.
Secy. of the Treasy.

ADfS, Rhode Island Historical Society, Providence.

1. For background concerning Olney's controversy with Welcome Arnold, see William Ellery to H, September 4, October 9, 1792; Olney to H, September 8, 13, October 4, 25, November 28, December 10, 1792; H to Olney, September 19, 24, October 12, November 27, December 13, 1792.

2. William Channing.

3. H to William Channing, Jeremiah Olney, and John S. Dexter, December 12, 1792.

4. Jabez Bowen.

5. Letter not found.

From Tench Coxe

Treasury Department, Revenue Office, December 28, 1792. "In . . . the Communication from the Secretary of the President of the United States to you relative to the appointment of Lemuel Cornick to the duty of Keeper of the light House,[1] I observe no mention is made of the Compensation which is intended to be allowed. It is necessary that the pleasure of the President on that point be known."

LC, RG 58, Letters of Commissioner of Revenue, 1792–1793, National Archives.

1. See Tobias Lear to H, December 22, 1792.

From Tobias Lear

United States, 28 Decr. 1792.

By the President's command T. Lear has the honor to inform the Secretary of the Treasury, that the President requests the Secretary to have a statement prepared, agreeably to the Resolution of the House of Representatives,[1] of which a copy is enclosed, to be laid before the House as soon as it conveniently can be done.

T. Lear. S. P. U. S.

LC, George Washington Papers, Library of Congress.

1. On December 26, 1792, the House of Representatives considered a bill "to provide for a reimbursement of a Loan made of the Bank of the United States." During the debate, William Branch Giles of Virginia made a motion "that the Secretary of the Treasury be directed to lay before the House a statement of the loans and the applications thereof" (*Annals of Congress*, III, 759).

On December 27, 1792, the House "*Resolved*, That the President of the United States be requested to cause this House to be furnished with a particular account of the several sums borrowed under his authority by the United States; the terms on which each loan has been obtained; the applications to which any of the moneys have been made, agreeably to appropriations; and the balances, if any, which remain unapplied. In this statement it is requested that it may be specified at what times interest commenced on the several sums obtained, and at what times it was stopped by the several payments made.

"*Ordered*, That the said resolution be transmitted to the President of the United States by the Speaker." (*Annals of Congress*, III, 761.)

From Thomas Smith

[*Philadelphia*] *December 28, 1792.* Lists "the Stock remaining on the Books of this Office subject to the payment of Interest for the Quarter ending the 31st december 1792."

LC, RG 53, Pennsylvania State Loan Office, Letter Book, 1790–1794, Vol. "615–P," National Archives.

To George Hammond

Treasury Department
December 29. 1792

Sir

From the opinion you have been so obliging as to express that arrangements may probably be made in Upper Canada for procuring a supply, from that quarter, of the Indians expected to assemble at O'glaise in the ensuing spring for the purpose of holding a treaty with this government.[1]

I have the honor to inform you that I have concluded to send an Agent into the territory of Upper Canada, to endeavor to effect contracts for the above-mentioned supply; and, as you have authorized me to do, shall count on your good offices to facilitate the object of his mission. When the person shall be determined upon, it will be made known to you.[2]

It is impossible for us to foresee with certainty the number of persons who will be assembled. We conjecture however that they will amount to about five thousand, men women and children; and that they may remain together six weeks. These are the only data we have as to the quantum of supply, which may be requisite.

Any contract however which may be formed must embrace as much more as may be found necessary.

All details will of course be committed to the Agent who shall be sent.

I have the honor to be with respect &c. Alexander Hamilton

His Excellency
George Hammond Esqr.

Copy, PRO: F.O., Series 5, Vol. 1.

1. In the autumn of 1792 the western Indians agreed to meet representatives of the United States Government in the spring of 1793. The Indians were to assemble not at the Auglaize (O'Glaise) but at Sandusky. Whether the reference to Auglaize as the meeting place instead of Sandusky was a mistake or an intentional change was a matter of dispute. The Indians had stated that Sandusky was to be the meeting place. Secretary of War Henry Knox, however, was informed that the meeting would be held at the "Rapids of the Miami River." See "Conversation with George Hammond," November 22, 1792, notes 4 and 5.

On January 21, 1793, John Graves Simcoe wrote to Hammond: "I cannot but believe that the change of the place in the Speech of Mr. Knox, is in him matter of design, Lower Sandusky, as appointed by the Indians, and the rapids of the Miami, are nearly Ninety Miles apart: the latter is where the States intend to take post, and possibly it might be of material Service to them, to explore the Country by means of their convoys, between this and Fort Jefferson, and Fort Hamilton in particular, as at St. Clair's defeat, They seem to have been so totally ignorant of the intermediate distance" (*Simcoe Papers,* V, 29–30). On January 27, 1793, Simcoe wrote to General Alured Clarke that "in two separate Conversations which Capt. [Edward Baker] Littlehales held with Mr. Hamilton, that Gentleman insisted upon it, in contradiction to him, that *Lower Sandusky,* & the River au Glaize, were one & the same place" (*Simcoe Papers,* I, 280).

The confusion may have arisen from the fact that, although the western Indians had designated Lower Sandusky as the meeting place for the proposed council with the United States commissioners, in transmitting this information to the United States Government during a council at Buffalo Creek in November, 1792, the representatives of the Six Nations stated that the western tribes had requested them "to inform General Washington we will treat with him, at the Rapids of the Miami, next spring, or at the time when the leaves are fully out" (*ASP, Indian Affairs*, I, 323–24). The mistake was corrected on February 28, 1793, when Knox wrote to the western Indians: "When the President of the United States consented to meet you next Spring at the rapids of the Miami, it was under the full conviction that you had appointed that place, as the one most agreeable to you, at which the Council fire should be kindled; but it has since been found that the Interpreter mistook the place you intended. We now find that it is your desire that lower Sandusky should be the place at which the Conference should be held" (*Simcoe Papers*, I, 295).

2. William Hull was the agent appointed by the United States to acquire supplies for the council with the Indians.

From John Jay

New York 29 Decr. 1792

Dear Sir

On my Return this Evening from Rye, I found your Letter of the 18 Inst: at my House.

It is not difficult to perceive that your Situation is unpleasant; and it is easy to predict that your Enemies will endeavour to render it still more so. The Thorns they strew in your way, will (if you please) hereafter blossom, and furnish Garlands to decorate your administration. Resolve not to be driven from your Station; & as your Situation must it seems be militant, act accordingly. Envy will tell Posterity that your Difficulties from the State of *Things*, were inconsiderable, compared with the great, growing and untouched Resources of the Nation. Your Difficulties from *persons* and *Parties*, will by Time be carried out of Sight, unless you prevent it—no other person will possess sufficient facts & Details to do full Justice to the Subject; and I think your Reputation points to the Expediency of memoirs. You want Time, it is true—but few of us know how much Time we can find when we set about it.

Had not your Letter come from the Post office, I should suspect it had been opened. The Wafer looked very much like it. Such Letters should be sealed with wax, impressed with your Seal.

I rejoice with you in the Re-Election of Mr. adams—it has relieved my mind from much Inquietude—it is a great Point gained, but the unceasing Industry and arts of the Anti's, render Perseverance, union, and constant Efforts necessary.

Be so good as to forward the enclosed. Adieu my Dr Sir yours sincerely John Jay

Col. Hamilton

ALS, Hamilton Papers, Library of Congress; ADfS, Columbia University Libraries.

To Susanna Livingston[1]

Philadelphia Decr 29 1792

I am mortified My Dear Miss Livingston that you should have had to write to me[2] on the subject of your Certificates. Of all delinquencies, those towards the Ladies I think the most inexcusable. And hold myself bound by all the laws of chivalry to make the most ample reparation in any mode you shall prescribe. You will of course recollect that I am a married man!

The Certificates have been delayed through the misapprehension of one of my Clerks. They went immediately after you committed them to my care through all the forms of the Treasury; preparatory to a transfer to the Books of Maryland; and do not admit of being reinstated on the Books of New York 'till after a similar process. They are inclosed.

With much esteem & regard Yr. true friend & Obed ser

A Hamilton

Miss Susan Livingston
Baltimore

ALS, Columbia University Libraries.

1. Susanna Livingston was the daughter of William Livingston, who was governor of New Jersey from 1776 until his death in 1790. At this time she was living in Baltimore with her sister, Catherine Livingston Ridley, widow of Matthew Ridley.

2. Letter not found.

To George Washington

[Philadelphia, December 29, 1792]

The Secretary of the Treasury has the honor to enclose for the consideration of the President, the translation of a letter of the 27 of December, which he has received from Mr de la Forest.[1] He will wait upon the President on Monday for his orders concerning the subject of it.

December 29 1792

LC, George Washington Papers, Library of Congress.
1. Letter from Antoine René Charles Mathurin de La Forest not found.

From Tench Coxe

Treasury Department, Revenue Office, December 31, 1792. "The Superintendent of the Establishments on Delaware [1] has occasion for about four hundred and fifteen Dollars to discharge all the balances falling due this day in that part of the public service. I have to ask the favor of a Warrant to him for that Sum. . . ."

LC, RG 58, Letters of Commissioner of Revenue, 1792–1793, National Archives.
1. William Allibone.

From Tench Coxe

Treasury Department,
Revenue-Office, December 31st. 1792

Sir,

I have the honor to represent to you that considerable Inconvenience occurs in the execution of a part of the business of this office, which however may be remedied by placing a limited sum of the Monies appropriated for the Establishments connected with navigation in the hands of the Commissioner of the Revenue for which he will be charged and held accountable. The inconveniencies arise from that part of the expenditures relative to the light houses, Beacons, Buoys and public piers, which are not committed to the execution of any particular Superintendent, or which arise from requests of particular Superintendents, that certain articles, which are better, cheaper, or more expeditiously made in Philadelphia may be procured for them by me in that place. The sums are often so small as to render an antecedent passage of the account or Bill through all the forms of the accountant offices of the Treasury very inconvenient; and warrants for a few dollars would swell the public accounts and give trouble in a greater degree than is agreeable. In instances wherein the Sums are larger, prompt payment easily obtained from a private person, is contrasted with the delay necessarily attending every the smallest case, which passes in the first instance through the official forms.

If no objection to it occurs to you, I would request at this time an advance of two hundred and fifty Dollars, for the purpose abovementioned, which I shall cause to be deposited in the Bank of the United States to the Credit of the Commissioner of the Revenue as Superintendent of the Light Houses &ca to be drawn for only as occasion may require: and I beg leave to add that I shall cheerfully enter into Bond with such surety as the public discretion may appear to require.

I have the honor to be, Sir your most Obedient Servant

Tench Coxe,
Commissr. of the Revenue.

The honble
The Secretary of the Treasury.

LC, RG 58, Letters of Commissioner of Revenue, 1792–1793, National Archives.

From Richard Harison[1]

[*New York, December 31, 1792.* On January 5, 1793, Hamilton wrote to Harison: "Mr. Le Roy[2] has not yet appeared, with the Powers and Receipts mentioned in your letter of the 31 of December." *Letter not found.*]

1. Harison was United States attorney for the District of New York.
2. Herman Le Roy, a New York City merchant and bank director.

From Joseph Nourse

Treasury Department, Register's Office, December 31, 1792. States that the balance "in the Hands of the Cashier of the Bank of the United States" is inadequate. Requests "that a Warrant may issue . . . to be applied in the Payt. of Arrearges of Int. of the Regd. Debt and also of the Dividend becoming due on the first of Jany: 1793. . . ."

ADf, RG 53, Register of the Treasury, Estimates and Statements for 1792, Vol. "134–T," National Archives.

From Joseph Nourse

Treasury Department, Register's Office, December 31, 1792. Transmits "List of the Clerks employd in the Office of the Register of Treasury, the Objects on which they were Employd and their Salary for the last Quarter Ending the 31st. December 1792."

ADf, RG 53, Register of the Treasury, Estimates and Statements for 1792, Vol. "134–T," National Archives.

From Jeremiah Olney

Providence, December 31, 1792. Replies to Hamilton's "circular Letter of the 12th of Octr. last."

ADfS, Rhode Island Historical Society, Providence.

To William Short

Treasury Department
Philadelphia Decer: 31st., 1792

Sir,

Inclosed is duplicate of my letter of the 26th ultimo, mentioning, among other matters, that Treasury drafts had been directed upon the Commissioners in Amsterdam to the amount of 1,250,000 guilders.

It will be proper to inform you that this sum has been reduced to 1,237,500 guilders, to be drawn in lieu of the sum first mentioned;

and that a further sum of 24,750 guilders has since been directed to be drawn.

I have received your letters down to the 9th of October inclusively; but time will not now permit me to enter into any discussion upon the contents.

I have the honor to be, very respectfully, Sir, Your obedt Servant Alexander Hamilton

Copy, RG 233, Reports of the Treasury Department, 1792–1793, Vol. III, National Archives. This letter was enclosed in H's "Report on Foreign Loans," February 13, 1793.

To Wilhem and Jan Willink, Nicholaas and Jacob Van Staphorst, and Nicholas Hubbard

Treasury Department,
December 31st 1792.

Gentlemen,

You will herewith receive a duplicate of my letter to you of the 26th ultimo, advising you of Bills, which the Treasurer of the United States had been directed to draw upon you to the amount of one million and two hundred and fifty thousand guilders.

You will please to observe, that this sum has been reduced to one million and two hundred and thirty seven thousand five hundred Guilders, which will be drawn, in lieu of the sum first mentioned.

In addition to this, I have now to request you to note, that a further sum of twenty four thousand seven hundred and fifty guilders will be drawn by the Treasurer.

I am &c. Alexander Hamilton

Messrs Willink, Van Staphorst
and Hubbard,
Amsterdam.

Copy, RG 233, Reports of the Treasury Department, 1792–1793, Vol. III, National Archives. This letter was enclosed in H's "Report on Foreign Loans," February 13, 1793.

To John F. Mercer[1]

Philadelphia December 1792

Sir

I called upon you this morning, at your lodgings, to resume and finish the subject of our late conversation; but not having seen you, I have concluded to put what I had to say upon paper.

Since our last interview I have perused the papers to which you referred me. They exhibit the affair in a form essentially different from that under which it had come to me; yet they do not entirely free what passed between us from all ambiguity; and consequently do not supersede the necessity of some further explanation. Conscious as you must be, from all the circumstances, which attended the transaction, that what I said to you could bear no other construction than that of a mere pleasantry, I presume you will not hesitate to remove every shadow of doubt which may remain upon it.

The circumstances alluded to, as they rest in my recollection, are as follow—

You met me at the door of my office, in the public street, going from it to dinner, at about three oClock—where there happened to be standing four or five Gentlemen conversing together. You immediately began by telling me that you had a claim upon the public, for some horses killed under you,[2] or lost by you in service, during the late war, which you had not originally thought it worth while to bring forward, but you had concluded to avail yourself of the act[3] lately passed, removing the bar to claims founded on personal service in the army and navy, to obtain an indemnification, and had presented your Account to the Auditor or Comptroller, I forget which, for settlement, which had been refused—adding that you were sure, if it had been the case in any other person, the justice of the claim was so evident, no difficulty would have been made.

I well remember, that I felt a momentary embarrassment from this address, which appeared to me to impeach the partiality of the officers of the Treasury, on the ground of some personal opposition to you—which considering the events of the session, I could not well avoid referring to my self. A question at the instant arose in my mind whether to treat it gravely or with pleasantry. I resolved upon the latter, as well from a disposition to avoid any disagreeable altercation, as from a belief that what you had said was the sudden and inconsiderate effect of disappointment in a matter, which you had persuaded yourself was clearly in your favour.

I assumed therefore an unequivocal tone of pleasantry—and observed to you that the precedent you were endeavouring to establish would suit me very well, for I, also, had lost three or four horses during the war, some of them in consequence of having been wounded under me; but that it appeared to me you would find some difficulty, notwithstanding all your ingenuity, in making it out a claim for personal service, unless you could establish that *yourself* and your *horse* were *one person.*

You answered with some observations aiming at proving to me, that the case might be fairly considered as within the relief intended by the Act—of which not feeling the force, and being disposed to put an end to the discussion at such a time and place—I replied in the same spirit, and with the same air and manner, with which I had begun—that we would take some other opportunity of finishing the argument—but added I—There is one expedient which will shorten the discussion very much—*If you will vote for the assumption tomorrow*, or *if you will change the vote you gave upon the assumption to day,* we'll make the thing very easy, we'll contrive to get your account settled.*

I remember that upon this a laugh went round the persons present, that you joined in it and that we parted in perfect good humour.

I will not assert, that every circumstance here stated is precisely accurate, but I am more than usually misled by my memory, if the narrative is not in every material particular a correct representation of what took place.

I must now ask you to state to me how far it agrees with or differs from your recollection of facts, and particularly whether the circumstances were not such as clearly to forbid what I said being understood in an improper sense. You will readily conceive that I must be solicitous to leave no uncertainty upon my Meaning.

I will barely add that I at the time understood the sum in ques-

* one or the other was the case

tion to be about three hundred Dollars. The reflections, which arise from the consideration of so trifling a sum, are obvious.

I am Sir Your obedient Servant Alex Hamilton

The Honorable
Mr Mercer &c

ALS, Archives of Loyola University, Chicago; copy, Hamilton Papers, Library of Congress.

1. For background to this letter, see the introductory note to H to Mercer, September 26, 1792. See also H to Mercer, November 3, December 6, 1792; Mercer to H, October 16–28, 1792; H to David Ross, September 26, November 3, 1792; Ross to H, October 5–10, November 23, 1792; Uriah Forrest to H, November 7, 1792.

2. See Mercer's statement concerning his claim in the introductory note to H to Mercer, September 26, 1792.

3. See H to Mercer, September 26, 1792, note 20.

From John F. Mercer[1]

Philadelphia Decr. 1792

Sir

I have perused your statement of the conversation between us relative to my Accounts[2] & do not perceive in what it is variant from that which I placed in the hands of the President. In that I declar'd that I did not take what fell from you as a serious proposition but on the contrary—thus far I now repeat—but I can only answer for myself & my own impression—farther I should deem it improper for you to require or me to acquiesce. The Statement that I have already given[3] was the result of my recollection at that time on the subject & my memory now can add to or vary it but little. I mentioned the circumstance originally only to shew the improper advantages that might be taken by relating publickly private conversations & these partially & had not these advantages been taken in a most illiberal manner of me, & had not your letter to Mr. Ross containd a species of similar mistatement[4] this conversation so far from being mentioned would I beleive never have been recollected by me.

I am Sir yr obt hb Ser John F. Mercer

ALS, Hamilton Papers, Library of Congress.

1. For background to this letter, see the introductory note to H to Mercer, September 26, 1792. See also H to Mercer, November 3, December 6, December,

1792; Mercer to H, October 16–28, 1792; H to David Ross, September 26, November 3, 1792; Ross to H, October 5–10, November 23, 1792; Uriah Forrest to H, November 7, 1792.

2. See H to Mercer, December, 1792.

3. For Mercer's statement concerning his claim, see the introductory note to H to Mercer, September 26, 1792.

4. See H to Ross, September 26, 1792.

[The Politicks and Views of a Certain Party, Displayed][1]

[1792]

1. In 1886 Paul Leicester Ford listed this pamphlet among the works which had been erroneously attributed to H and suggested that it was probably written by William Loughton Smith (Ford, *Biblioteca Hamiltoniana* [New York, 1886], vi, 39). In 1887 Joseph Sabin attributed the pamphlet to H (Sabin, *A Dictionary of Books Relating to America* [reprint, Amsterdam, 1961], VIII, 28). In 1914 Charles Evans stated that there were good reasons for attributing the work to Smith (Evans, *American Bibliography* [Chicago, 1914], VIII, 356). In 1917 Albert Matthews settled the controversy by a reference to Smith's copy of the pamphlet, which is now owned by the Charleston Library Society and is inscribed "By William Smith—1792" (Matthews, ed., "Journal of William Loughton Smith, 1790–1791," *Massachusetts Historical Society Proceedings* [Boston, 1918], LI, 77).

The Defence No I[1]

[1792–1795]

Party-Spirit is an inseparable appendage of human nature. It grows naturally out of the rival passions of Men, and is therefore to be found in all Governments. But there is no political truth better established by[2] experience nor more to be deprecated in itself, than that this most dangerous spirit is apt to rage with greatest violence, in governments of the popular kind, and is at once their most common and their most fatal disease.[3] Hence the disorders, convulsions, and tumults, which have so often disturbed the repose, marred the happiness, and overturned the liberties of republics; enabling the leaders of the parties to become the Masters & oppressors of the People.

It is the lot of all human institutions, even those of the most perfect kind, to have defects as well as excellencies—ill as well as good propensities. This results from the imperfection of the Institutor, Man.

Thus it happens, that amidst the numerous and transcendant advantages of republican systems of government, there are some by-asses which tend to counteract their advantages, and which to render these permanent, require to be carefully guarded against. That which has been noticed, a too strong tendency toward party divisions, does not require least a vigilant circumspection.

What then ought to be & will be the conduct of wise and good men? Will it be their constant effort to nourish this propensity—to stimulate the restless and uneasy passions of the community—to sow groundless jealousies of public men—to destroy the confidence of the people in their tried and faithful friends—to agitate their minds with constant apprehensions of visionary danger—to disseminate their own ignorant and rash suspicions as authentic proofs of criminality in those with whom they differ in opinion—to blast with the foulest stains on the slightest pretences reputations which were unsullied till they began to invent[4] their calumnies.

There can be no difficulty in answering these questions in the Negative.

Wise and virtuous men could not fail to pursue an opposite course. They will endeavour to repress the spirit of faction, as one of the most dangerous enemies to republican liberty—to calm and sooth those angry sensations, which in the best administered governments will spring up from the dissimilar manner in which different laws will affect different Interests of the Community. Instead of imputing crime and misconduct to public men where none exists they will rather endeavour to palliate their errors, when connected with good intention and an honest zeal, and will be ready to excuse those lesser deviations from strict rules, which in the complicated affairs of government will more or less occur at all times but which in the infant establishments of a new governmt. were to be calculated upon as inevitable. Instead of labouring to destroy they will endeavour to strengthen the confidence of the people in those to whom they have entrusted their affairs—if there is reasonable evidence that their conduct is in the main guided by upright intelligent & distinterested zeal for the public interest. They will be cautious of censure and the censure which they may be at any time compelled to bestow will be preceded by due examination and tempered with moderation and candour. They would shudder at the idea of exhibiting as a Culprit & Plunderer of the Nation a man who is sacrificing the interests of himself & his family to an honest zeal for

with no motive more selfish than that of acquiring the esteem & applause of his fellow Citizens.

But how it may be asked shall we distinguish the virtuous Patriot, who is endeavouring to inflict punishment upon delinquency and disgrace upon demerit from the factious Partisan who is labouring to undermine the faithful friend of his Country and to destroy the Rival he envies & the Competitor he fears?

There are different ways of making the distinction. From the matter and from the manner of the attack which is at any time made—

ADf, Hamilton Papers, Library of Congress.

1. Although "The Defence No I" is the title given to the first of H's letters signed "Camillus," published in the [New York] *Argus* on July 22, 1795, no similarity other than the title suggests that this document was a draft for the first of those letters.

2. At this point H wrote and crossed out "history and."

3. At this point H wrote and crossed out: "Tis there it finds, at the same time most aliment and fewest restraints. One of the worst tendencies is to divide and agitate the public councils and with them the community, about men more than measures, to cause the public interest to be overlooked or betrayed in the conflict of personal favour on the one hand and personal animosity on the other. Another of its mischievous tendencies is, by keeping the community in a feverish convulsed and anxious state, to dispose the lovers of a more stable and tranquil course of things, to behold with less horror than they would otherwise feel the prospect of a transition."

4. H wrote the word "forge" above the word "invent."

View of the Commercial Regulations of France and Great Britain in Reference to the United States

[1792–1793]

Introductory Note

Although Hamilton's "View of the Commercial Regulations of France & Great Britain in reference to the United States" is undated, it is clear that the documents which comprise it were written by Hamilton at different times during the early part of Washington's Administration. As early as 1789 it was apparent to many Americans that in spite of the apparent prosperity of United States commerce the future of the country in relation to other commercial powers was precarious. It was this realization which led to suggestions for forcing a more favorable policy from other nations through retaliatory tariffs or achieving a permanent system more amicably through the negotiation of commercial treaties.

After the American Revolution, as before, British commercial policy was dominated by the determination to protect British commerce and navigation by the enforcement of the Navigation Laws and the exclusion of foreign powers from trade with the British colonies. At the peace negotiations in 1783 the American emissaries, John Jay, Benjamin Franklin, and John Adams, attempted to secure for the United States some of the commercial advantages which the North American colonies had enjoyed before the Revolution, particularly a share in the carrying trade with the British West Indies. John Jay had inserted in his October 5, 1782, draft of a peace treaty an article which guaranteed that in the ports and possessions of each power the nationals of the other power would be treated in the same fashion as its own nationals. When the final articles of the treaty were drawn up this clause was omitted, chiefly because of the fear that the supporters in Parliament of the British Navigation Laws might prevent acceptance of the treaty if the reciprocity clause was included. A similar proposal by William Pitt for complete reciprocity between the United States and Britain was defeated through the influence of followers of Lord Sheffield who favored a policy of complete mercantile monopoly and vigorous enforcement of the Navigation Laws. These political considerations compelled the negotiators to omit commercial clauses from the final draft of the treaty.[1]

After the American Revolution British trade with the United States had been reopened by an act of Parliament passed in April, 1783, "for the better carrying on of Trade and Commerce between the Subjects of His Majesty's Dominions and the Inhabitants of the . . . United States," which, in addition to permitting United States shipping into British ports without manifests or certificates, invested the King with the power to issue regulations concerning commerce with the United States.[2] This

1. Samuel Flagg Bemis, *The Diplomacy of the American Revolution* (Bloomington, 1957), 235–36, and Setser, *Commercial Reciprocity*, 33–51.

2. 23 Geo. III, C. 39 (1783). Section 3 provided "That, during the Continuance of this Act, it shall and may be lawful for his Majesty in Council, by Order or Orders to be issued and published from Time to Time, to give such Directions, and to make such Regulations, with respect to Duties, Drawbacks, or otherwise, for carrying on the Trade and Commerce between the People and Territories belonging to the Crown of *Great Britain* and the People and Territories of the said United States, as to his Majesty in Council shall appear most expedient and salutary; any Law, Usage, or Custom, to the contrary notwithstanding."

statute was renewed from year to year,[3] and most regulations concerning products imported into Britain from the United States from 1783 to 1788 appeared in a series of orders in council. For example, an order in council issued in 1783 permitted "Oil, or unmanufactured Goods and Merchandises being the Growth or Production of any of the Territories of the United States of *America*, imported directly from thence in British or American Vessels to an Entry upon Payment of the like Duties, as if imported by *British* Subjects in *British* Ships, from any of the *British* Islands or Plantations in *America*." [4] Another order, passed in June, 1783, permitted the importation from the United States of all unmanufactured goods permitted by law on the same terms as if imported from a British colony, such goods to be carried in either British or American bottoms.[5] In December, 1783, a new order in council was passed encompassing all the "several regulations hitherto issued. It permitted the importation of any unmanufactured goods, not prohibited by law (except oil), and pitch, tar, turpentine, indigo, masts, yards, and bowsprits, being the produce of the United states of America, either by British or American subjects, and either in British or American vessels, on paying the same duties as were payable on the importation of such goods from the British colonies by British subjects in British vessels; the production of the documents required by law being also dispensed with, and all drawbacks, exemptions, and bounties, on goods exported from Great Britain to the United states being allowed as fully on such goods exported to the British colonies. Tobacco, the produce of the United states, was allowed to be imported in the same manner into this kingdom. . . ." [6] The British regulations concerning the direct trade between the United States and Britain in the period from 1783 to 1793 generally were favorable enough to enable Great Britain to become the best customer of the United States.[7] This

3. See, for example, 24 Geo. III, C. 45 (1784); 25 Geo. III, C. 5 (1785); 28 Geo. III, C. 5 (1788); 29 Geo. III, C. 1 (1789); 31 Geo. III, C. 12 (1791); 32 Geo. III, C. 14 (1792).

4. Order in council of May 14, 1783. All orders in council cited in the footnotes to this document may be found in *The London Gazette*.

5. Order in council of June 6, 1783.

6. Macpherson, *Annals of Commerce,* IV, 28. This order in council is dated December 26, 1783.

7. Samuel Flagg Bemis has observed: "To the United States the trade was vitally important. It composed by far the greater part of the total volume of American commerce. The precise percentage which Great Britain shared of the total trade of the United States cannot be determined because American customs records do not begin until 1789, and the English statistics have been destroyed by fire. In 1790 of the total American exports valued at $20,194,794 there were sent to British ports $9,246,562; but of a total value of $15,388,409 of imports paying *ad valorem* duties $13,798,168 were from Britain, that is, about ninety per cent. These last figures do not show comparisons with the whole of American imports of that year, because there were other imports, value not estimated, which paid specific duties. If England possessed this amount of the trade in 1790, it is fair to assume that she held at least such a proportion in the six years preceding 1789. Of shipping amounting to 90,420 tons, clearing from

advantage was counterbalanced by the fact that, since the United States had not been able to negotiate a commercial treaty with Great Britain, commercial regulations between the two countries were controlled by temporary regulations which could be changed at any time.

The most important aspect of pre-Revolutionary American commerce had been the trade of the North American British colonies with the West Indies. It was hoped at the time of the peace negotiations that at least some part of the trade could be retained by the United States, but all attempts to gain a foothold in the carrying trade with the West Indies proved fruitless. Postwar British policy toward the United States trade with the West Indies was established by an order in council of July 2, 1783, which, while it allowed the importation into the West Indies of such American products as lumber, flour, and livestock, stipulated that these products were to be brought to the West Indies only in British ships.[8] Although intended as a temporary measure, it was continued by a series of extensions until 1788, when a new act was passed which permanently excluded United States shipping from the West Indian trade.

---

ports in the British Islands for the United States in 463 ships in 1790, 50,979 tons went in 245 British ships; 39,441 tons were classed in 218 American vessels. Of 109,431 tons entering from America, 64,197 tons were in 312 British ships, and 246 American ships carried 45,234 tons" (Samuel Flagg Bemis, *Jay's Treaty, a Study in Commerce and Diplomacy* [New York, 1923], 33–34).

8. The order in council of July 2, 1783, permitted "British subjects to carry in British vessels all kinds of naval stores, spars, and all kinds of lumber, horses, and all other kinds of live stock, and all kinds of corn, flour, and bread from the United States of America to the West-India islands; and to carry rum, sugar, melasses, coffee, chocolate nuts, ginger, and pimento from the islands to the United states, on paying the same duties, and conforming to the same regulations, as if they were cleared out for a British colony" (Macpherson, *Annals of Commerce,* IV, 26). Protests against the prohibition of American ships from the West Indian trade did not come only from the excluded American merchants, for there was also vigorous opposition to the measure from the planters of the West Indies who maintained that the British carrying trade would not be able to supply the islands with provisions. See, for example, *A State of the Allegations and Evidence produced, and Opinions of Merchants and other Persons given, to the Committee of Council; extracted from their Report of the 31st of May 1784, on His Majesty's Order of Reference of the 8th of March last, Made upon the Representation of the* West-India *Planters and Merchants, purporting to shew the distressed State of His Majesty's Sugar Colonies, by the Operation of His Majesty's Order in Council of the 2d of July 1783, and the Necessity of allowing a free Intercourse between the Sugar Colonies and the United States of* America, *in American Bottoms* (n.p., 1784). Macpherson observed: "This order was considered by administration as an indulgence, both to the islands and to the United states: but it was not received as such by either of them. The West-India planters cried out, that the islands must inevitably be ruined, if there were not as free and unrestrained an intercourse between them and the continent, and as free admission of American vessels as there was when the later was under the British dominion; and the Americans were so much offended by it, that the assemblies of three of the states actually made a requisition to the congress that they would prohibit all commercial intercourse with the British colonies" (Macpherson, *Annals of Commerce,* IV, 26).

David Macpherson observed that "the parliament, thinking that the experience of five years had now proved that British vessels were competent to the supply of the West-India islands with the produce of America, enacted a permanent law, instead of the temporary regulations hitherto generally renewed every year." [9]

9. Macpherson, *Annals of Commerce,* IV, 168. This act provided that "no Goods or Commodities whatever shall be imported or brought from any of the Territories belonging to the said United States of *America,* into any of His Majesty's *West India* Islands (in which Description the *Bahama Islands,* and the *Bermuda* or *Somers Islands,* are included), under the Penalty of the Forfeiture thereof, and also of the Ship or Vessel in which the same shall be so imported or brought, . . . except Tobacco, Pitch, Tar, Turpentine, Hemp, Flax, Masts, Yards, Bowsprits, Staves, Heading-boards, Timber, Shingles, and Lumber of any Sort; Horses, Neat Cattle, Sheep, Hogs, Poultry, and Live Stock of any Sort; Bread, Biscuit, Flour, Peas, Beans, Potatoes, Wheat, Rice, Oats, Barley, and Grain of any Sort; such Commodities respectively being the Growth or Production of any of the Territories of the said United States of *America*" (28 Geo. III, C. 6 [1788]).

The only exception to the regulation concerning British bottoms was a minor concession to United States vessels which "arriving in ballast at the Turk's islands, are permitted to load with salt, and no other article, on paying a duty of 2/6 per tun (payable in dollars at 5/6 per ounce) their measurement being determined by a proper officer. Neither can any other article than salt be exported from Turk's islands to any British colony in America or the West-Indies; nor can any goods be exported from them to Great Britain and Ireland, but salt and such articles as may be imported from all countries free of duty.—Such articles, as are allowed to be imported from the United states to the British West-Indies, must not be imported from any foreign West-India island; *except* in cases of distress, when the governor and council of any island may permit the importation of them in British vessels for a limited time.—No goods whatever are allowed to be imported from the United states into Nova Scotia, New Brunswick, Cape Breton, St. John's, Newfoundland, and their dependencies; *except* in cases of distress, when the governor and council of any of the provinces may allow timber and lumber, horses, cattle and other live stock, bread, potatoes, and grain of all kinds, to be imported in British vessels for a limited time. No goods are allowed to be carried away by sea from the United states to the province of Quebec *upon any account whatever*" (Macpherson, *Annals of Commerce,* IV, 168–69).

In his "Report on Commerce," December 16, 1793, Jefferson observed: "*Great Britain* admits in her islands our vegetables, live provisions, horses, wood, tar, pitch, and turpentine, rice and bread stuff, by a proclamation of her Executive, limited always to the term of a year, but hitherto renewed from year to year. She prohibits our salted fish and other salted provisions. She does not permit our vessels to carry thither our own produce. Her vessels alone, may take it from us, and bring us in exchange, rum, molasses, sugar, coffee, cocoa nuts, ginger, and pimento. There are indeed some freedoms in the island of Dominica, but, under such circumstances, as to be little used by us. In the British continental colonies, and in Newfoundland, all our productions are prohibited, and our vessels forbidden to enter their ports. Their Governors, however, in times of distress, have power to permit a temporary importation of certain articles, in their own bottoms, but not in ours. Our citizens cannot reside as merchants or factors, within any of the British plantations, this being

In the Hamilton Papers, Library of Congress, an unaddressed statement dated January 20, 1792, prepared by Phineas Bond, British consul at Philadelphia, presents the British view of Great Britain's commercial policy toward the United States. It is uncertain whether or not Bond addressed this statement to Hamilton. It is, however, endorsed in Hamilton's handwriting "Remarks concerning the Commercial policy of G Britain towards this country by Mr. *Bond* British consul." Bond's statement reads as follows:

"Since the Peace, the Parliament of Great Britain has, annually, given his Majesty Power to make provisional commercial regulations with the United States.

"His Majesty in virtue of this power by his order in Council has permitted the importation of any (unprohibited) Goods, being the Growth or Produce of the United States, directly from thence into Great Britain; not only in British Ships,[10] but in American built ships, owned by American subjects, the Master and at least ¾ of the mariners being American subjects.

"By this regulation his Majesty has put the Commerce of the United States, as far as relates to the Vessels, in which American produce can be imported into Great Britain, upon a footing with every European nation.

"Any unmanufactured goods (except Fish Oil, Blubber, Whale Fins, and Spermaceti) and also any Pig Iron (and other articles enumerated in the order of Council) may be imported into Great Britain on payment of the same duties as the like goods imported from any British Island or Plantation in America—and with respect to Fish-Oil, Blubber, Whale Fins and Spermaceti and all other goods, not enumerated, being the growth, production or manufacture of the United States, they may be imported from the United States into Great Britain subject to such duties of customs and Excise as are payable on the like goods upon their importation from Countries not under the dominion of his Majesty according to the Tables A, D, and F, annexed to the consolidating act,[11] and where differ-

---

expressly prohibited by the same statute of 12 Car. 2, c. 18, commonly called the navigation act" (*ASP, Foreign Relations*, I, 302).

10. At this point Bond inserted the following footnote: "See St. of 12 C. 2. c 18. S. 3 which enacts that no goods &c of the growth &c of any part of America could be imported into the King's European dominions except in British vessels." This is a reference to the Navigation Act of 1660.

11. 27 Geo. III, C. 13 (1787). This act specified the duties to be charged on every product imported into Great Britain, uniting the sums collected by the customs into a "*consolidated fund*, out of which are paid all the annuities or interests upon the various branches of the national debt, and the annual million vested in the commissioners for the reduction of it, the whole national income being moreover engaged as an additional security to the creditors of the public" (Macpherson, *Annals of Commerce*, IV, 124). The tables to which Bond is referring were the detailed schedules of duties and drawbacks which were appended to the act and which were designed to provide a simplified and concise guide for British and foreign merchants to the British customs charges. Except for French imports, the duties imposed by the new act tended to be somewhat higher than those levied earlier (Atton and Holland, *The King's Customs*, 377). An order in council of April 1, 1791, stated that, where the

ent duties are therein imposed upon like goods imported from different foreign Countries, then upon payment of the lowest of such duties—so that with respect to certain enumerated articles, in which the Commerce of the United States is most essentially involved, the same indulgence is granted to the Commerce of the United States, which his Majesty's dominions in North America and the West Indies enjoy. In many of these important articles the Commerce of the United States is most materially benefitted by the indulgence thus given, to the great Injury of other foreign Countries. For instance in the single article of woods of every description (except yards, masts and bowsprits) they may be imported into Great Britain free from duty.

"With respect to every other article of the produce or manufacture of the United States, not enumerated or described in the orders of Council, his Majesty has placed the Commerce of the United States upon a footing with the most favored nations of Europe—except such only with whom Treaties of Commerce have been formed upon principles of reciprocal and mutual advantage. One other material indulgence arises to the Commerce of the United States; By the regulations contained in the orders of Council, all goods and merchandize, being the growth, production or manufacture of the United States, are permitted to be imported into Great Britain exempted *from the Alien's duty;* Whereas goods imported in the Vessels of every other foreign nation, are subject to the payment of Alien's duty.

"A Table of the articles, imported from the United States into Great Britain, under exemptions or reductions of duties, with a comparative estimate of what duties the same articles pay when imported from the most favored nations of Europe, would evince the peculiar advantages gained by the United States—to the great detriment of other foreign nations, and to the immense diminution of the revenue of Great Britain, which in duties on the single article of woods annually receives from other foreign nations near £300,000. Such a table and such an Estimate may be formed by resorting to the export of the favored articles from the United States to Great Britain, and will demonstrate how much America saves in this respect by her commerce with that Country.

"From these combined circumstances it is plain that Great Britain, so far from being considered as the commercial Enemy of these States, has extended benefits and privileges to the Commerce of this Country which originated in colonial indulgence; nor will it be going too far to aver that Great Britain has granted America greater advantages, in point of Commerce than any other nation in Europe can grant." [12]

One of the most lucrative aspects of the trade of the North American colonies before the American Revolution had been the commerce between New England and the French West Indies. Officially the French govern-

tables annexed to the consolidating act specified different duties on the same product when imported from different countries, the lowest duty should be charged on the product when imported from the United States.

12. Copy, Hamilton Papers, Library of Congress.

ment had pursued a policy of complete monopoly of the trade of its West Indian islands and had attempted to enforce this policy by a number of stringent regulations. The *Lettres Patentes* of 1717 and 1727, for example, prohibited foreign trade with the islands and forbade foreign ships to approach within one league of their shores.[13] The need of the French islands for provisions during the Seven Years' War led to some concessions to foreign trade, but in 1763 and 1767 new *arrêts,* while they granted a few privileges to foreign shipping, restored much of the prohibitive policy of the earlier *Lettres Patentes.*[14] In spite of the attempts of both the French and the British government at discouragement, the New England trade—much of it contraband—with the French West Indies flourished during the period preceding the American Revolution.[15] When the Treaty of Amity and Commerce was signed between the United States and France in 1778, provision was made for each power to have most-favored-nation privileges,[16] and in the same year an administrative ordinance permitted foreign vessels into West Indian ports. At the close of the Revolution the demands of French merchants and shipping interests who favored a return to mercantilist regulations made it necessary for the French Ministry to review its West Indian trade policy. In May, 1783, the ordinance of July 20, 1778, opening the West Indies to foreign trade was annulled,[17] and France's postwar policy toward foreign trade with her colonies in the West Indies was enunciated in the *arrêt* of Au-

13. Moreau de St. Méry, *Loix et Constitutions des Colonies Françoises,* II, 557–65; III, 224–36.

14. Moreau de St. Méry, *Loix et Constitutions des Colonies Françoises,* V, 121–26. The 1767 *arrêt* authorized two West Indian ports, Carenage on St. Lucia and Môle de St. Nicholas on Santo Domingo, as entrepôts for foreign commerce but limited the incoming ships to those of more than one hundred tons and enacted stringent inspection procedures to discourage smuggling. The prohibition of ships of less than one hundred tons particularly operated to the disadvantage of the North American colonies since most American ships were considerably below that tonnage.

15. For a discussion of the trade of the North American colonies with the French West Indies before the American Revolution, see Dorothy Burne Goebel, "The 'New England Trade' and the French West Indies, 1763–1774: A Study in Trade Policies," *The William and Mary Quarterly,* 3rd ser., XX (July, 1963), 331–72; Richard Pares, *War and Trade in the West Indies, 1739–1763* (Oxford, 1936), 395–468.

16. Miller, *Treaties,* II, 5. Article 2 of the Treaty of Amity and Commerce also stipulated that each nation should enjoy the privileges granted by the other signatory to any other power "freely, if the Concession was freely made, or on allowing the same Compensation, if the Concession was Conditional."

17. Moreau de St. Méry, *Loix et Constitutions des Colonies Françoises,* VI, 314–15. This ordinance provided that the "Ordonnance du 20 Juillet 1778 cessera d'avoir son exécution, à compter du 1er Juillet prochain, passé lequel temps l'introduction des Bâtimens dans cette Colonie reprendra le cours qu'elle avoit avant ladite Ordonnance. . . ." For the opposition to this prohibitive policy, see Frederick L. Nussbaum, "The French Colonial Arrêt of 1784," *The South Atlantic Quarterly,* XXVII (1928), 64–69; "Lettre du Ministre aux Administrateurs, touchant le Commerce Etranger," June 27, 1784, Moreau de St. Méry, *Loix et Constitutions des Colonies Françoises,* VI, 544–45.

gust 30, 1784. This decree opened eight entrepôts in the French islands in contrast to the two provided for in the *arrêt* of 1767 and added a number of additional products to those permitted by that *arrêt*. The only articles permitted to be exported from the islands were rum, molasses, and goods manufactured in France, and a premium was granted to French industries in the form of a duty of three livres per quintal on foreign salt fish and salt beef. A special advantage to the United States lay in the admission to the West Indies of a number of products on the condition that they be imported in ships of less than sixty tons. The prohibition of American flour, however, was a serious blow to the trade of grain-growing areas in the United States.[18]

Although the *arrêt* represented a liberal trend on the part of the French Ministry, it failed to satisfy all the demands of the United States and aroused opposition among French merchants.[19] Probably because of French agitation, two other decrees were passed the next year which increased the duty on American fish and granted bounties on French cod carried to the French West Indies, and an *arrêt* of 1787 increased both the bounty and the duty.[20]

In the direct trade between the United States and France the French policy was as favorable to the United States as possible in view of the pressure of commercial interests for a mercantilistic policy. Largely through the efforts of Jefferson, who as United States Minister to France pressed strongly for commercial advantages, the French government made a number of concessions to United States commerce during the seventeen-eighties. A considerable reduction on the importation of American whale oil was secured; duties were abolished on skins, potash and pearlash, and beaver skins; provision was made for free importation of ships constructed in the United States; L'Orient and Bayonne were designated free ports specifically for the American trade and access was granted to the other free ports of France; in 1787 a right of entry was granted to American merchandise into all the ports of France; an entrepôt was established on Isle de France especially for the American East Indian trade.[21] Despite these concessions, trade between the United States and France never reached substantial proportions in the years between the American and French revolutions.[22]

18. Moreau de St. Méry, *Loix et Constitutions des Colonies Françoises*, VI, 561–66.

19. Frederick L. Nussbaum, "The French Colonial Arrêt of 1784," 64–69.

20. The *arrêts* of September 18 and September 25, 1785, are printed in Moreau de St. Méry, *Loix et Constitutions des Colonies Françoises*, VI, 847–51, 863–65. A copy of the *arrêt* of February 11, 1787, may be found in the Papers of the Continental Congress, National Archives.

21. Setser, *Commercial Reciprocity*, 81–89; George F. Zook, "Proposals for New Commercial Treaty Between France and the United States, 1778–1793," *The South Atlantic Quarterly*, VIII (1909), 267–83; Boyd, *Papers of Thomas Jefferson*, XIII, 52–91; XIV, 217–25.

22. According to a "General Table of Commerce between France and the United States from 1775 to 1792. . ." France's failure to capture the United States trade from Great Britain after 1783 is indicated by the shift in the balance of trade between the two countries as shown by French customs

Several explanations have been advanced for the failure of France to replace Great Britain in trade with the United States: the fact that habit made Americans prefer British products and that British manufactured articles were generally superior to French; that France could not supply the products needed by the United States and that her merchants were unfamiliar with American commercial arrangements; that French policy was not favorable enough to the United States to offset the advantages offered by Britain.[23] Two factors, however, seem to have been most decisive in circumventing France's efforts to secure the American trade. The first was the inability of French merchants to extend the long-term credit so essential to business operations of American mercantile firms. The British firms' established policy of extending long-term credits often brought a common involvement between creditor and merchant that made severance of ties difficult. Tallyrand observed: "The great capitals of the English merchants enable them to give more credit than those of any other nation; this credit is at least for a year, often for a longer time. The consequence is, that the American merchant who receives his wares from England, employs scarcely any principal of his own in this commerce; but trades almost entirely upon English capitals." [24] The second

---

returns from 1775 to 1792. During the war years, when British ports were closed to American shipping, the value of the balance in favor of France ranged from 2,105,000 livres in 1775 to 8,108,000 livres in 1783. When commerce between the United States and Great Britain was resumed after the war, the balance shifted in favor of the United States from 7,432,000 livres in 1784 to 19,476,000 livres in 1792. By 1793 the balance in favor of the United States had increased to 51,253,330 livres (Edmund Buron, "Statistics on Franco-American Trade, 1778–1806," *Journal of Economic and Business History,* IV [1932], 580).

23. See, for example, Charles Maurice Talleyrand-Perigord, *Memoir Concerning the Commercial Relations of the United States with England* (Boston, 1809), 9. Talleyrand observed that after the American Revolution the United States was "under the necessity of importing from Europe not only a great part of what she consumes internally, but likewise a considerable portion of what she makes use of for her external commerce. Now all these articles are furnished to America so completely by England, that there is reason to doubt whether, in the time of the most severe prohibition, England enjoyed more exclusively this advantage, with what were then her colonies, than she does at present with the independent United States. The causes of this voluntary monopoly are, moreover, easy to be assigned. The immense quantity of manufactured goods which are sent out of England; the division of labor . . . adapted to the different processes of the manufactures, have enabled the English manufacturers to lower the price of all the articles of daily use, below the rate at which other nations have hitherto been able to afford them." See also Boyd, *Papers of Thomas Jefferson,* XIII, 57; Zook, "Proposals for New Commercial Treaty Between France and the United States, 1778–1793," 272; Setser, *Commercial Reciprocity,* 83, 91–92; Henri Sée, "Commerce Between France and the United States, 1783–1784," *The American Historical Review,* XXXI (1926), 732–52.

24. Talleyrand, *Memoir Concerning Commercial Relations,* 9. Talleyrand also observed: "Without doubt the English merchant must, in one way or other, indemnify himself for the interest of the sums of which he allows so

factor which operated to the detriment of French trade with the United States was France's policy toward the importation of tobacco. The right of importation and control of tobacco in France had been sold by the French government in 1721 to the Farmers-General, giving that body absolute control over purchases of foreign tobacco. As a further complication to the sale of American tobacco in France, the Farmers-General in 1785 entered into a contract with the American financier Robert Morris. Under the terms of this contract "Morris undertook to deliver in France sixty thousand hogsheads of tobacco in the three successive years, 1785, 1786, 1787, at the rate of twenty thousand a year, in a specified assortment and quality. The tobacco was to be shipped in American vessels rather than in French. . . ."[25] American merchants shipping tobacco to France thus had to negotiate with Morris as well as abide by the restrictions of the Farmers-General. There were concerted attacks in France both against the Morris contract and, more importantly, against the entire policy of granting the monopoly of the tobacco trade to the Farmers-General. Inspired by Jefferson and led by Lafayette and Vergennes, these attacks were not successful in forcing the cancellation of the Farmers-General monopoly, but they did bring about the appointment of a committee to inquire into the commercial relations with the United States. In the decision of Bernis on May 25, 1785, this committee agreed that, while the contract with Morris could not be canceled, such an agreement should never again be made, and that, in addition to the tobacco purchased from Morris, the Farmers-General should also buy twelve to fifteen thousand additional hogsheads from other American merchants on the same terms as those prescribed by the Morris contract.[26]

---

long a use: but as the orders succeed regularly, and are increasing every year, there is established a balance of regular payments and of fresh credit, which leaves nothing in arrear but the first accommodation, the interest of which is to be gained from the succeeding orders, as well as from the former ones. This first debt establishes, as we see, a connexion between the English and American correspondent, which is difficult to be broken off. The former fears that, if he fail to send the goods ordered, he may overwhelm a debtor whose prosperity is the only security for his advances; the American, on his part is afraid of quitting a creditor, with whom he has too many old accounts to settle. It is almost impossible for any third nation to interfere with these reciprocal interests, strengthened by long habit. Thus France, in her commerce with America, is reduced to the supplying of a few products peculiar to her soil; and does not enter into any competition with England in the sale of manufactured goods, which she would not supply to America either at so cheap a rate, or on such long credit" (Talleyrand, *Memoir Concerning Commercial Relations,* 10).

25. Nussbaum, "American Tobacco and French Politics, 1783–1789," *Political Science Quarterly,* XL (December, 1925), 501. See also Boyd, *Papers of Thomas Jefferson,* XIII, 58–65.

26. For the tobacco monopoly of the Farmers-General, see Nussbaum, "American Tobacco and French Politics," 501–10; Frederick L. Nussbaum, "The Revolutionary Vergennes and Lafayette Versus the Farmers General," *The Journal of Modern History,* III (1931), 592–613 (this article also contains Lafayette's 1786 attack on the tobacco farm, "Resumé de mon avis au Comité du Commerce avec les Etats-unis lorsque la question des tabacs nous a été

Although the Morris contract expired in 1787 and could not be renewed, the control of the Farmers-General over the importation of tobacco continued until the tobacco monopoly was abolished by the Revolutionary government in 1791. Throughout the seventeen-eighties, therefore, the trade in tobacco, one of the most important commodities of the United States, had been stifled by this monopoly.

During the early years of the French Revolution, although American trade was still generally treated more favorably than that of other nations, an increasingly stringent policy was pursued by the French Assembly. Motivated perhaps by disillusion with the failure of the attempt to detach the American trade from Great Britain, sometimes by the pressures of French chambers of commerce and merchant groups which desired a return to mercantilistic policies, particularly in the West Indies, and on occasion simply by ignorance of the implications of its legislation, the Assembly passed a number of decrees to the detriment of American commerce. Although the tobacco monopoly of the Farmers-General was abolished, a heavy duty was placed on the importation of foreign tobacco with considerable distinction in favor of French ships; importation of ships built abroad was forbidden; and the duty on American oils was augmented. William Short, United States chargé d'affaires at Paris, made valiant—but largely unsuccessful—efforts to protect United States commerce against the onslaughts of the Assembly.[27]

On December 16, 1793, Thomas Jefferson submitted to the House of Representatives a report entitled "The Privileges and Restrictions on the

presentée"); Bingham Duncan, "Franco-American Tobacco Diplomacy," *Maryland Historical Magazine*, LI (1956), 273–77; Boyd, *Papers of Thomas Jefferson*, VIII, 385–93, IX, 457–61; Louis Gottschalk, *Lafayette Between the American and the French Revolution, 1783–1789* (Chicago, 1950), 205–08, 215–17, 222–37. For Lafayette's earlier views on the tobacco cartel and on Franco-American commerce generally, see his 1783 "Observations sur le Commerce entre France et les Etats Unis," printed in Gottschalk, "Lafayette as Commercial Expert," *American Historical Review*, XXXVI (1930–1931), 561–70.

27. Writing to Jefferson on March 4, 1791, Short expressed his views on the commercial policy of the Assembly as follows: "I cannot . . . too often repeat to you that it is impossible to form a conjecture either of what the Assembly will do or undo on any subject. Their mode of deliberation & decision renders their being surprized into measures against their intention, unavoidable. Their decree with respect to tobacco may serve as an example. The difference in the duty paid between french & american vessels, suggested probably by some owner of ships, was proposed & passed without its being even suspected that such a proposition would be made—they had no idea certainly that it was a navigation act in a degree of rigor to which it was impossible that any country would submit without attempting to counteract it. . . . I don't doubt that you are fully sensible that the decrees of the Assembly are so essentially the work of accident, of the force of parties & the force of circumstances, that no person in any situation whatever can control them; & of course that no person in my situation could have prevented those which have been passed with respect to the articles of american commerce" (ALS, RG 59, Despatches from United States Ministers to France, 1789–1869, January 16, 1791–August 6, 1792, National Archives).

Commerce of the United States and the restrictions imposed by European countries against United States commerce both in Europe and in the colonies." In this report Jefferson emphasized the severity of British restrictions compared to those of other powers and proposed that the United States impose restrictions on the commerce of any nation which pursued a restrictive policy toward the United States.[28] In an effort to implement Jefferson's proposal, James Madison on January 3, 1794, introduced a series of resolutions which were designed to establish a system of retaliation against nations which enacted discriminatory legislation against American commerce.[29] On January 13, 1794, Senator William Loughton Smith of South Carolina delivered a major speech in the Senate opposing Madison's resolutions.[30] It has been asserted on more than one occasion that Hamilton was the author of this speech, and the document printed below has frequently been cited as proof of this fact.[31] There can be no doubt that Hamilton's notes were used by Smith in his speech. Several sentences in Smith's speech are similar to those in Hamilton's notes, and two of Hamilton's paragraphs appear without change in Smith's speech. On the other hand, it does not necessarily follow that the "View" was prepared specifically for the use of Smith in his attack on Madison's resolutions. Smith's speech is considerably longer than the notes in the "View," and it contains facts and figures not used by Hamilton. At the same time, it does not include information on such topics as whaling and the codfisheries that Hamilton discusses in his notes. Despite the similarities, therefore, the "View" is clearly not a draft of Smith's speech. If indeed Hamilton was the author of Smith's attack, as seems entirely possible from the style and content of the South Carolinian's speech, no draft in his handwriting has been found.

It is possible that Hamilton may have written the notes considerably earlier—before the end of 1792 and perhaps even in late 1791—and either used them himself to prepare Smith's speech or gave them to Smith when the Senator was preparing his criticism of the Jefferson-Madison views on commerce in 1794.[32]

28. *ASP, Foreign Relations,* I, 300–04.

29. *Annals of Congress,* IV, 155–56.

30. *Annals of Congress,* IV, 174–210.

31. John C. Hamilton states that Smith's "elaborate performance was from the pen of Hamilton as appears from his autograph draft" (Hamilton, *History,* V, 450). See also Irving Brant, *James Madison, Father of the Constitution 1787–1800* (New York, 1950), III, 391, and Mitchell, *Hamilton,* II, 290–91.

32. Most of the commercial information given in the "View" appears to apply to the period before the end of 1792. No mention is made, for example, of the French decree of February 19, 1793, which opened the ports of French colonies to American shipping and permitted "All the produce exported or imported by American vessels" into the ports of France on the same terms as French vessels (*ASP, Foreign Relations,* I, 147). Neither does H refer to the decree of March 26, 1793, "exempting from all duties the subsistences and other objects of supply in the colonies" (*ASP, Foreign Relations,* I, 363). This does not, however, necessarily indicate the date of the "View," since the tendency was to look upon the legislation passed during 1793 as temporary measures. In his speech of January 13 Smith observed: "A fair comparison can

There are at least two occasions before the end of 1792 on which Hamilton might have written the "View." He may have prepared it as background material when the cabinet was discussing a proposed commercial treaty with France in late 1791 and early 1792, or it may have been part of a comparative study which Hamilton was preparing during the same period on the commercial systems of Great Britain and France.

The attempt to negotiate a commercial treaty with France was the result of efforts to improve the deteriorating commercial relations between France and the United States. As early as June 2, 1791, the French National Assembly had authorized the King to open negotiations with the United States for a new treaty of commerce.[33] The failure of the French Ministry to act on the authorization led Jefferson to believe that France wanted the first proposals for a new treaty to come from the United States. The Secretary of State, however, was reluctant to take the first steps in negotiation,[34] but Hamilton discussed the matter with Jean Baptiste de Ternant, the French Minister to the United States, in October, 1791.[35] In spite of Ternant's noncommittal attitude, a debate in the cabinet resulted in a decision to draw up the draft for a commercial treaty. In November, 1791, Jefferson drafted a treaty,[36] but Hamilton

---

only be made with an eye to what may be deemed the permanent system of the countries in question. The proper epoch for it, therefore, will precede the commen[ce]ment of the pending French Revolution" (*Annals of Congress*, IV, 175). The conclusions in Jefferson's "Report on Commercial Privileges and Restrictions" of December 16, 1793, do not generally indicate the concessions made by the French government in 1793, although he observes in his letter of transmittal to the House of Representatives that France has "relaxed some of the restraints mentioned in the Report" (*ASP, Foreign Relations*, I, 300–04).

33. *Archives Parlementaires*, XXVI, 710.

34. On November 24, 1791, Jefferson wrote to William Short that "M. [Jean Baptiste] de Ternant tells me he has no instructions to propose to us the negotiation of a commercial treaty, and that he does not expect any" (ALS, letterpress copy, Thomas Jefferson Papers, Library of Congress). For Ternant's reports to his government on his commercial discussions with the United States officials, see Ternant to Comte de Montmorin, October 9, 24, 1791, Ternant to Claude Antoine de Valdec de Lessart, April 8, 1792, and Ternant to the Minister of Foreign Affairs, June 15, 1792 (Turner, "Correspondence of the French Ministers," 57–65, 60–65, 108–14, 126–27).

35. "Conversation with Jean Baptiste de Ternant," October 7, 1791. In late 1791 H wrote to two members of Congress for information on the French policy toward the American fisheries which he may have intended to use either for the proposed Franco-American treaty of commerce or for his comparative study of British and French commercial policy toward the United States. See George Cabot to H, December 8, 18, 1791; Jeremiah Wadsworth to H, December 10, 1791.

36. Jefferson's account of the negotiations is contained in an entry in the "Anas," dated March 11, 1792. Jefferson stated: "Towards the latter end of Nov. H. had drawn Ternant into a conversation on the subject of the treaty of commerce recommdd. by the Natl assembly of France to be negotiated with us, and as he hd nt recd. instrns on the subject he led him into a proposal that Ternant shd take the thing up as a volunteer with me, that we shd arrange condns, and let them go for confirmn or refusal. H. communicated this to the

Presid. who came into it, & proposed it to me. I disapproved of it, observg that such a volunteer project would be binding on us, & not on them, that it would enable them to find out how far we would go, & avail themselves of it. However, the Presidt. thot it worth trying & I acquiesced. I prepared a plan of treaty for exchanging the privileges of native subjects and fixing all duties forever as they now stood. He did not like this way of fixing the duties because he said that many articles here would bear to be raised and therefore he would prepare a tariff. He did so raising duties for the French from 25. to 50 per cent . . ." (Ford, *Writings of Jefferson*, I, 185). A copy of this tariff in Jefferson's handwriting and labeled "The above contains Hamilton's tariff of the duties which cannot be receded from in treaty with France, spoken of in my private note of March 11, 92" may be found in the Thomas Jefferson Papers, Library of Congress. The undated document in H's handwriting from which Jefferson apparently made his notes is in the Hamilton Papers, Library of Congress, and reads as follows:

"An *import* duty, not exceeding 10 per Centum ad valorem, at the place of exportation, may be laid on manufactures of Flax Hemp Wool Cotton silk furs or of mixtures of either, Of Gold Silver, Copper, brass, Iron Steel Tin Pewter or of which either of these metals is the material of chief value, upon flour, salted beef pork and fish, & Oils of every kind. Bar-Iron and bar-lead nails and spikes steel unwrought, cables cordage, yarn twine and pack thread shal⟨l⟩ not be deemed to be included, in the foregoing enumeration.

"An *import* duty not exceeding 15 per centum ad valorem at the place of exportation may be laid upon Porcelaine or China wares Glass and all manufactures of glass, Stone and earthen wares and generally upon all manufactures of which stone or earth is the principal material.

"An import duty not exceeding 50 per Centum ad valorem at the place of exportation may be laid on all spirits distilled from fruits. [This is computed on a Gallon of brandy costing 2/ Stg 20 Cents ⅌ G]

"An import duty not exceeding 25 per Centum ad valorem, at the place of exportation, may be laid on all wines. [20 Cents ⅌ Gall]

"Grain of every kind, peas and other vegetables, live Cattle Pitch Tarr and Turpentine, unmanufactured wood, Indigo, Pot and pearl-ash, Flax Hemp Cotton silk wool shall be free from duties both on exportation and importation.

"Neither party shall impose any duty on the exportation to the countries of the other ⟨of⟩ any raw material whatsoever. This prohibition ⟨shall⟩ be deemed to extend to molasses and Tobacco.

"An *export* duty not exceeding five per Centum ad valorem at the place of exportation may be imposed on all brown and clayed sugars.

"All articles not specified or described in the foregoing clauses may be rated according to the discretion of each party both as to exportation and importation but neither party shall lay any higher duty upon any production or manufacture of the other imported into any part of the dominions of such party than shall be laid upon the like or a similar production or manufacture of any other nation imported into the same or any other part of the dominions of said party.

"Neither party shall subject the vessels cargoes or Merchants of the other to any greater charges or burthens within its own ports, than its own vessels cargoes and merchants shall be subject to within the ports of the other; except as to duties by way of revenue, to the Government which may be regulated as either party pleases within the limits and in conformity to the principles established in this Treaty. [⟨Cha⟩rges alluded to are ⟨no⟩t charges ⟨co⟩mmissions for Agents ⟨all⟩owances for guards &c]

"Neither party shall grant any bounties or premiums upon its own ships, nor upon commodities imported in its own ships, which shall not extend to the

opposed it on the ground that the rates were too low. The negotiations were finally dropped.

Although Hamilton may have drawn up the "View" as background for the abortive Franco-American commercial treaty, the possibility also exists that the notes were part of a comparative study of the commercial systems of Britain and France in relation to the United States, for Hamilton had undertaken such a project in late 1791 and in 1792. On December 19, 1791, George Hammond, the British Minister to the United States, reported to Lord Grenville that "Mr. Hamilton informed me that he was preparing a report upon the actual state of the navigation and commerce of this country, whence it would appear that the present system of France was more favorable to the former, and that of Great Britain to the latter." [37] On January 1, 1792, Hamilton wrote to Jefferson that he was "engaged in making a comparative statement of the Trade between the U S & France & between the U S & G Britain" and requested any pertinent information Jefferson might have concerning French commercial regulations.

The possibility also exists that Hamilton wrote these notes in anticipation of Jefferson's report on commerce. As indicated above, this report was not made to Congress until December 16, 1793. The report, however, had been requested by the House of Representatives on February 23, 1791, and throughout 1791 and 1792 it was known that the Secretary of State was drawing up such a report.[38] Whatever may have been the spe-

---

Ships nor to commodities imported in the Ships of the other party nor upon any commodities whatsoever with special reference direct or indirect to an exportation to the countries of the other.

"Neither party shall prohibit an importation into its own dominions or the vent there of any of the productions or manufactures of the other.

"Neither party shall grant or allow in consequence of any former grant any privilege or exemption in Trade to another nation which shall not be ipso facto communicated to the other party.

"Neither party shall grant to another nation the peculiar privileges and exemptions stipulated by this treaty except for the peculiar considerations upon which they are herein stipulated. Peculiar privileges and exemptions and peculiar considerations shall be deemed to be those only which are contained in the stipulation of the   articles.

"Neither party shall reduce any existing duties upon the ships productions or manufactures of other countries except by virtue of a treaty founded on a reciprocation of equal privileges and exemptions with those mutually stipulated in the present Treaty."

The material within brackets was written by H in the margin opposite the paragraphs in which it is printed above. In *JCHW*, IV, 555–57, and *HCLW*, V, 129–31, this document is dated 1794 and is printed as an enclosure to H to John Jay, May 6, 1794.

Jefferson maintained that H intended to use the proposed treaty with France as "a pretext to engage us on the same ground with Hammond, taking care at the same time, by an extravagant tariff to render it impossible that we should come to any conclusion with Ternant" (Ford, *Writings of Jefferson*, I, 186).

37. "Conversation with George Hammond," December 15–16, 1791.

38. On February 23, 1791, the House of Representatives requested that Jefferson report to Congress on "the nature and extent of the privileges and

cific occasion for Hamilton's writing of the "View," it was prompted in general by the commercial problems which had arisen as a result of the failure of the United States to negotiate commercial treaties with Britain and France.

View of the Commercial Regulations of France & Great Britain in reference to the United States.[39]

Preliminary remarks

I The Table which is annexed takes the year 1790 as the proper period to shew the commercial policy of France previous to the Revolution just terminated. The Notes accompanying that table explain the alterations which have since taken place. There is however no mention of the expiration of the time limited for the Premium on French Fish imported into the French Colonies which happened in 1790;[40] because this makes no alteration in the general complexion of the policy of France in this particular. It is usual for greater caution to limit the duration of premiums to a certain period, even where it is supposed that a further continuation may be necessary, and if the premium in question has not been removed it affords no proof of an intention to relinquish it as the situation of France at the time of the cessation, and since may be presumed to have precluded arrangements respecting the Trade of her Colonies.

---

restrictions of the commercial intercourse of the United States with foreign nations, and such measures as he shall think proper to be adopted for the improvement of the commerce and navigation of the same" (*Journal of the House,* I, 388). In a letter to the Speaker of the House of Representatives on February 20, 1793, Jefferson explained the delay in presenting his report: "The report was . . . prepared during the ensuing recess ready to be delivered at their next Session. . . . It was thought possible at that time, however, that some changes might take place in the existing state of Things, which might call for corresponding changes in measures. I took the liberty of mentioning this in a letter to the Speaker of the House of Representatives, to express an opinion that a suspension of proceedings thereon for a time, might be expedient, and to propose retaining the Report 'till the present session . . ." (letterpress copy, Thomas Jefferson Papers, Library of Congress). Jefferson then requested a second postponement to which the House agreed (*Journal of the House,* I, 710, 718).

39. ADf, Hamilton Papers, Library of Congress.

40. Article 1 of the French *arrêt* of September 18, 1785, gave a premium of ten livres per quintal on dried fish imported in French bottoms into the French West Indies for the following five years (Moreau de St. Méry, *Loix et Constitutions des Colonies Françoises,* VI, 847).

If any have been made it may be inferred from *Commeres*' pamphlet[41] that though the duty on foreign Fish has been reduced from three to five livres, the premium on French Fish has been raised from 10 to 12 which makes the aggregate of duty and premium, operating as a bounty on French Fish the same as before namely 15 livres.[42]

General observations.

I The Commercial system of Great Britain makes no discriminations to the *prejudice* of the UStates as *compared* with other foreign powers.

There is therefore no ground for a complaint on the part of the UStates that the system of G Britain is particularly *injurious* or *unfriendly* to them.

II. The Commercial system of Great Britain makes important discriminations in favour of the United States as compared with other foreign Nations. This is exemplified in the instances of Tobacco Lumber Pot and Pearl Ash, Tar and Pitch, Pig & bar Iron; which when carried from the U States to G Britain are either exempt from duties which are paid on the same articles brought from other foreign Countries or pay so much less duty as to give them a clear advantage in the competition for the British Market. Our Vessels too in the *direct Trade* with G B are in various instances exempted from the duties which are paid by the Ships of other Nations; and in general are on the same footing in that Trade with the Vessels of the British Colonies.[43] Admission is also given to a variety of the

41. Guillaume François de Mahy Cormeré, *Observations Importantes sur les Colonies de l'Amérique* (Paris, 1791).

42. H obviously meant to write "reduced from five to three." The passage to which he is referring reads as follows: "L'importation des morues, par le commerce de France, n'est que de 2,500 barils; celle du poisson salé de 1,300 barils, année commune, à Saint-Domingue. Les Etats-unis importent annuellement dans cette colonie, plus de 30,000 barils de morue & de poisson salé, quoique cet article soit soumis à un droit de 3 livres par quintal, & que le commerce de France jouisse d'une prime de 12 livres par quintal" (Cormeré, *Observations*, 50).

43. Article 5 of the French colonial *arrêt* of August 30, 1784, had laid a duty of three livres per quintal on salted fish imported into the French West Indies "et sera le produit dudit droit de trois livres, converti en Primes d'encouragement pour l'introduction de la morue et du poisson salés, provenans de la pêche françoise" (Moreau de St. Méry, *Loix et Constitutions des Colonies Françoises,* VI, 562). On September 25, 1785, a new *arrêt* raised the duty on

commodities of the UStates in the British West Indies which is not given to similar commodities of other foreign Countries.

There is therefore ground to assert that the commercial system of G B is more favourable & friendly to the UStates than to other foreign Countries.

III. The Commercial system of France previous to the Revolution made fewer and less important discriminations in favour of the United States as compared with other foreign Nations than that of Great Britain. In the West Indies our privileges were the same. The same commodities only and upon the same terms might be carried thither & brought from thence from & to the UStates which might be carried thither and brought from thence from & to other foreign Nations. The discriminations in favour of the United States in the direct Trade with France are not known to have extended beyond the articles of Fish Oils [44]

and vessels of the build of the UStates, when *owned by French subjects,* which were admitted to naturalization and so far promoted the building of Ships as an article of Trade with France. This last discrimination is now abolished & no new ones have been made in our favour.[45]

---

foreign fish imported into the French West Indies to five livres per quintal. The *arrêt* also provided that "le produit dudit droit de *Cinque livres* sera versé chaque année au Trèsor-Royal, pour être employé d'autant, au complément de la Prime de *Dix livres* accordée par Sa Majesté, en l'Arrêt de son Conseil du 18 de ce mois, par quintal de Morues sèches provenantes de la Pêche Françoise qui seront importées auxdites Colonies" (Moreau de St. Méry, *Loix et Constitutions des Colonies Françoises,* VI, 864). The *arrêt* of September 18, 1785, had granted a premium of ten livres per quintal on fish imported in French bottoms into the French West Indies (see note 40). This bounty was increased to twelve livres and the duty on foreign fish to eight livres by the "Arrêt du Conseil d'Etat du Roi, Qui porte à Huit livres de droit de Cinq livres par quintal, établi par l'Arrêt du 25 septembre 1785, sur la Morue sèche de pêche étrangère importée aux Isles du Vent & sous le Vent; & à Douze livres la Prime de Dix livres accordée par l'Arrêt du même mois, par quintal de Morue sèche de pêche françoise, importée aux mêmes Isles." A printed copy of this *arrêt* of February 11, 1787, may be found in the Papers of the Continental Congress, National Archives.

44. This and subsequent spaces in MS were left blank by H. John C. Hamilton filled in some of the spaces with figures taken from Smith's speech (*JCHW,* V, 80–91).

45. Article 5 of the "Arrêt du conseil pour l'encouragement du commerce avec les Etats-Unis d'Amerique" of December 29, 1787, had provided that

There is therefore ground to assert that the Commercial system of France toward the United States, as compared with other foreign Nations, has been and now is less favourable and friendly than that of Great Britain.

Particular observations

I As to flour. This article previous to the Revolution in France was subject to but a very light duty on its importation there. At present it is free to all the world.[46] But unless material changes take place in the state of France the UStates are likely to derive little benefit from this circumstance.

The ordinary price of flour in France is about per barrel.[47]

In Pensylvania it may be stated at upon an average; the freight to France is ;[48] other charges amount to about which would make the cost and charges of a barrel of American flour in France of course, it cannot except on extraordinary occasions be sent there without loss.

In Great Britain it has been stated that flour was subject to a prohibitory duty till the price there was above 48/ the quarter.[49]

"Tout navire qui ayant été construit dans les Etats-Unis, sera ensuite vendu en France ou acheté par des Français, sera exempt de tous droits, à la charge de justifier que ledit navire a été construit dans les Etats-Unis" (Isambert, *Recueil Général des Anciennes Lois Françaises,* XXVIII, 490). On March 4, 1791, however, a decree was introduced forbidding "L'importation des navires et autres bâtimens de construction étrangère, pour être vendus dans le royaume, sera prohibée; lesdits navires et bâtimens ne pourront en conséquence jouir des avantages réservés à la navigation française, à l'exception toutefois de ceux desdits bâtimens qui, à la promulgation du présent décret, se trouveront être de propriété française." This decree was sanctioned on March 13, 1791 (Duvergier, *Lois,* II, 287).

46. Under the terms of the March, 1791, *Tarif Général,* flour of all kinds was admitted into France duty free (*Archives Parlementaires,* XXIII, 609). In his speech Smith noted that wheat and flour were imported into France free, "that is to say, under a duty of one-eighth per cent. as a Custom-house regulation, merely for ascertaining the quantity imported" (*Annals of Congress,* IV, 219).

47. John C. Hamilton completed this statement as follows: "The ordinary price of flour in France is about $5 66 cents per barrel (of Pennsylvania)" (*JCHW,* V, 82).

48. John C. Hamilton completed this statement as follows: ". . . American flour in France $6 33 cents" (*JCHW,* V, 82).

49. Under the provisions of the Corn Law of 1773, when the domestic price was above forty-eight shillings, wheat imported from abroad paid only a nominal duty of sixpence a quarter. Exportation was forbidden when the price reached forty-four shillings. In addition, the 1773 law permitted the storing of

The flour of the UStates can therefore only be carried occasionally to Great Britain as well as to France; but the occasions have hitherto been more frequent in Great Britain than in France.

Accordingly in the course of the years the whole quantity of flour sent from Pensylvania to France amounted to that sent to Great Britain to [50]

But the Act of Parliament of the puts this article upon a worse footing than heretofore and experience only can decide whether flour can be henceforth sent with most advantage to G Britain or to France.

The Quarter, however, which in relation to both Nations, it most interests the U States to have access to, as a market for their flour, in the West India Islands. Here the comparison is decidedly in favour of G Britain. The general system of France is to *prohibit* the reception of our Flour in her West India Markets—that of G Britain to *permit* it.

It is true that *occasional* suspensions of the prohibition take place; but these suspensions being confined to *cases of necessity*, the system of France, *which excludes us as far as possible*, cannot on this account be viewed as less unfavourable to the UStates, than if no such suspensions took place.

Flour appears to be the principal staple of the U States. This principal staple is on the whole more favoured by the Regulations of G B than of France. Accordingly in the year the exportations

---

foreign grain in warehouses in Great Britain without the payment of duty until such time as it should be sold. It could then either be held until the domestic price of grain reached a point where the import duty was nominal or, upon the posting of bond that it would not be relanded in England, it could be reexported. Similar regulations were applied to peas, rye, beans, barley, and oats (13 Geo. III, C. 43). By 1791 opposition to the 1773 law forced passage of a new law dealing with the importation of grain into Great Britain. Under the provisions of the 1791 Corn Law, when the domestic price of wheat was under fifty shillings a quarter, a duty of twenty-four shillings threepence was levied on imported wheat; when the price was between fifty and fifty-four shillings, a duty of two shillings sixpence was charged; and, when the domestic price rose above fifty-four shillings, the duty was reduced to a nominal sixpence. When the price reached forty-six shillings, exportation was forbidden (31 Geo. III, C. 30). See also the orders in council of January 5, February 18, and March 23, 1791.

50. This paragraph in *JCHW*, V, 82, reads as follows: "Accordingly, in the course of the years 1786 and 1788, the whole quantity of flour sent from Pennsylvania to France amounted to 2396 barrels; that sent to Great Britain, to 828 barrels."

to the British dominions amounted to to the French dominions to .[51] The comparison is the stronger in favour of G Britain from the circumstance that this year was one of extreme scarcity in France. In ordinary years the difference must be far greater.

II. As to Tobacco

It may be premised that this is an article of such a nature that it is immaterial to the UStates what duty is laid upon it in either of the two Countries if the same duties affect all other imported Tobacco. Tis a case in which neither of the Countries produces itself the article to enter into Competition with that of the UStates. The duty therefore must essentially fall upon the Buyers not the sellers.

Previous to the French Revolution there was no import duty in France upon Tobacco but it was under a monopoly of the Farmers General;[52] a situation far more disadvantageous to the UStates than any tolerable duty could be; by destroying a free competition among purchasers.

The Decree of January 1791[53] has laid a duty upon this article if brought from the UStates to France in American Vessels of 25

51. This sentence in *JCHW,* V, 83, reads as follows: "Accordingly, in the year 1790, the exportations to the British dominions, amounted to $1,534,276; to the French dominions to $1,483,195."

52. See the introductory note to this document.

53. In the early months of 1791 discussion of a new decree concerning the importation of tobacco began in the French Assembly. The resulting decree, passed March 1, 1791, reads in part as follows:

"Art. 1er. L'entrée, dans le royaume, du tabac fabriqué sera prohibée et il ne pourra être importé du tabac en feuille autrement qu'en boucauts, et par les ports et bureaux qui seront ci-après désignés.

"Art. 2. L'importation par mer des tabacs en feuille n'aura lieu que pour les tabacs des Etats-Unis d'Amérique, des colonies espagnoles, de la Russie et du Levant.

"Lesdits tabacs devront être importés directement, savoir: ceux des Etats-Unis d'Amérique, par navires desdits Etats, ou par vaisseaux français. . . .

"L'importations desdits tabacs par les bâtiments des autres nations est défendue. . . .

"Art. 5. Le . . . droit de 25 livres par quintal sera perçu sur les tabacs qui seront importés par les bâtiments des Etats-Unis d'Amérique, espagnols ou russes.

"Art. 6. Il ne sera perçu que 18 l. 15 s. par quintal sur les tabacs importés par bâtiments français, venant directement des Etats-Unis d'Amérique, des colonies espagnols, de Russie et du Levant." (*Archives Parlementaires,* XXIII, 595.)

This duty was incorporated into the *Tarif Général* passed by the National Assembly on March 2, 1791 (*Archives Parlementaires,* XXIII, 618–19).

livres ℔ Kental; if brought in French Ships of only 18 livres and 15 sous. The Tobacco of the United States has been and is upon no better footing than that of some other foreign Nations.

In Great Britain, as had been stated, a considerably higher duty is paid on *other* foreign Tobacco than on that of the United States; and it may be carried to G Britain in Vessels of the UStates upon the same terms as in British Bottoms while the Ships of other Nations bringing Tobacco are subject to a greater duty on the Tobacco which they bring than the Ships of Great Britain.[54]

Although, therefore, there is a higher duty on Tobacco in Great Britain than in France; yet as in France the duty is the same on other foreign Tobacco as on ours; as in Great Britain a higher duty is

54. The Consolidating Act of 1787 had provided that tobacco "of the Growth or Production of Ireland, or of the Growth or Production of his Majesty's Colonies, Plantations, Islands, or Territories in America, or of the growth or production of the United States of America" should pay a duty of one shilling threepence per pound. A duty of three shillings sixpence was levied upon tobacco "of the Growth, Production, or Manufacture of the Plantations or Dominions of Spain or Portugal" (27 Geo. III, C. 13 [1787]). See also 19 Geo. III, C. 35 (1779); 25 Geo. III, C. 81 (1785); 26 Geo. III, C. 52 (1786). Tobacco might be imported directly from the United States to Great Britain in either American or British ships. It might be imported from the British colonies only in British vessels. American tobacco, however, might be imported from the colonies to Great Britain if it had been brought to the colony from the United States in British vessels (25 Geo. III, C. 81 [1785]). See also the order in council of March 24, 1786. An order in council of April 3, 1789, provided that "any Tobacco, being the Growth or Production of any of the Territories of the said United States of America, may (until further Order) be imported . . . upon Payment of the same Duties as Tobacco imported by British Subjects from any British Colony or Plantation is or may hereafter be subject to; but under and subject nevertheless to all and singular the Regulations of an Act made and passed in the Twenty-fifth Year of the Reign of His Present Majesty. . . ." In 1789 an act of Parliament placed a duty of one shilling sixpence and an excise duty of two shillings on tobacco imported from the dominions of Spain or Portugal, while "For every Pound Weight of Tobacco, of the Growth or Production of *Ireland*, or of the Growth or Production of his Majesty's Colonies, Plantations, Islands, or Territories in *America*, or of the United States of *America*, imported into *Great Britain*, there shall be paid a Custom Duty of Sixpence; and also an Excise Duty of Ninepence." The act further provided that tobacco from the United States should be imported only in British or United States ships. Article V of this act stipulated that from October 10, 1789, "no Tobacco whatever shall be imported or brought into *Great Britain*, from any Port or Place whatever, other than some Port or Place within his Majesty's Colonies, Plantations, Islands, or Territories in *America*, or some Port or Place within the United States of *America*" (29 Geo. III, C. 68). See also 30 Geo. III, C. 40 (1790). The order in council of April 1, 1791, stipulated that American tobacco might be imported in either British or American ships upon payment of the same duty as if imported by British subjects from British possessions.

charged on other foreign Tobacco than upon ours; as the comparative rate, not the quantum of the duty in either Country, is the only thing which concerns us; it is evident that our Tobacco is much more favoured by Great Britain than by France. Indeed the difference of Duty operates as a positive bounty upon the Tobacco of the UStates.

As it regards our navigation, the comparison is still more striking. Here too, we are more favoured by G Britain, than other Countries. While the existing regulation of France is in the degree the most exceptionable to be found in the code of any Country. It amounts to a *prohibition* of carrying our own Tobacco to France in our own Ships.[55]

Several European Nations have aimed at a Monopoly of the carrying Trade of their Colonies; but this spirit has not extended to their home dominions. Slight differences have been made between foreign & National Ships in favour of the latter; but a difference amounting to an exclusion of the former is perhaps without example except in the Regulation in question.

The principle of this Regulation would prostrate the Navigation of the UStates more effectually than any which is to be found in the system of any other Country.

Hence in respect to the Article of Tobacco, the staple of the UStates which may be deemed second in importance, the Regulations of Great Britain are far more favourable than those of France

G Britain took from us in the year while France took only [56]

Hence also it appears that Great Britain is a far better Customer for this Article than France.

III. As to Fish & Fish Oil

The Regulations of France as to these articles are incomparably more favourable in their operation than those of Great Britain; though there is no material difference in principle.

Great Britain lays a prohibitory duty on Oil which excludes all but the finest kinds occasionally and absolutely prohibits Fish.[57]

55. See note 53.

56. In *JCHW*, V, 84, this paragraph reads as follows: "Great Britain took from us in the year 1790, $2,777,808, while France took only $427,746."

57. Under the provisions of the Consolidating Act of 1787, "Train Oil, or Blubber, or Fish Oil, of British fishing" paid a duty ranging from 9*s.* 11*d.* to £1.15*s.*3*d.* "the Ton containing 252 gallons" depending upon the conditions

France lays such duties on the Fish & Oil of other countries and grants such premiums and encouragements in relation to the products of her own fisheries, as amout completely to a prohibition so far as her Capacity to supply her own dominions extends.[58]

---

under which it was taken or caught. The same product of "foreign fishing" paid a duty of £18.3*s*. (27 Geo. III, C. 12). British spermaceti was entered duty free, while that of foreign fisheries paid 17*s*.8*d*. per hundredweight if "coarse and oily" and 8*d*. per pound if fine. For further benefits conferred on British fishing, see 26 Geo. III, C. 41 (1786); 26 Geo. III, C. 50 (1786); 26 Geo. III, C. 26 (1786). See also the order in council of October 6, 1790. The order in council of April 1, 1791, permitted the importation of these products in American ships on the same terms as if imported in "British-built Ships, owned by His Majesty's Subjects, and navigated according to Law, from any British Island or Plantation in America."

58. After this paragraph in the MS, H wrote and crossed out the following: "In France these regulations have the effect of a prohibition.

"In the French West Indies the case is different because there is a total incapacity to supply them and the regulations are necessarily relaxed in their execution; so as to allow a beneficial market to our Fish to a very great extent."

See note 43. The "Arrêt du Conseil d'Etat du Roi, Pour l'encouragement du Commerce de France avec les Etats-Unis d'Amérique" of December 29, 1787, had provided that "Whale-Oils and spermaceti, the produce of the fisheries of the citizens & inhabitants of the United States of America, which shall be brought into France directly in French vessels or in those of the United States shall continue to be subjected to a duty only of seven livres ten sols the barrel of five hundred and twenty pounds weight, & whale fins shall be subject to a duty of only six livres thirteen sols four deniers the quintal with the ten sols per livre on each of the said duties; which ten sols per livre shall cease on the last day of December one thousand seven hundred & ninety; His Majesty reserving to himself to grant further favors to the produce of the whale fisheries carried on by the fishermen of the United States of America which shall be brought into France in French vessels or in those of the United States, if, on the information which His Majesty shall cause to be taken thereon, he shall judge it expedient for the interest of the two Nations.

"The other fish-oils and dry or salted fish, the produce in like manner of the fisheries of the citizens & inhabitants of the United States, & brought also directly into France, in their, or in French vessels, shall not pay any other nor greater duties than those to which the oils & fish of the same kind, the produce of the fisheries of the Hanseatic towns, or of other the most favored Nations, are or shall be subject in the same case. . . .

"The entrepot (or storing) of all the productions and merchandize of the United States shall be permitted for six months in all the ports of France open to the Commerce of her Colonies; and the said entrepot shall be subject only to a duty of one eighth per cent." (Printed document, Papers of the Continental Congress, National Archives.) This decree is also printed in Isambert, *Recueil Général des Anciennes Lois Françaises*, XXVIII, 489–92.

Because of the opposition of French merchants and chambers of commerce to this decree, on February 22, 1788, another decree was passed which modified the favors granted to the United States by excluding the products of the American fisheries from the right of entrepôt granted by the December 29, 1787, *arrêt* (printed document, Papers of the Continental Congress, National Archives). A much more stringent decree against foreign fisheries was passed

The duty on foreign Fish in the French west Indies & the premium on French Fish as stated in the Table [59] amount virtually to a bounty on French Fish, of nearly 100 ℔ Cent of the value. In France the duty alone is about 75 ℔ Ct and it is understood that the premiums and bounties in favour of the French Fisheries are enormous.

The distinctions nevertheless which have been made in favour of the Whale fisheries of the United States have been of material aid to them; but there is reason to apprehend that the means which have been successfully used to detach our Fishermen and the vast encouragements which are given by the Government that the Whale Fishery of France is establishing itself on the ruins of that of the UStates.[60]

The Codfishery stands on a different footing. Our natural ad-

---

on September 28, 1788, prohibiting "dans toute l'étendue du Royaume, des Huiles de Baleine & de Spermacéti, provenant de Pêche etrangère" (printed document, Papers of the Continental Congress, National Archives). For a short time it was uncertain whether or not the French government intended to apply this decree to the products of the American fisheries (see Jefferson to John Jay, November 19, 1788, Boyd, *Papers of Thomas Jefferson,* XIV, 213–14), but on December 7, 1788, largely as a result of Jefferson's efforts, a decree was passed "Qui excepte de la prohibition portée par l'arrêt du 28 septembre dernier, les Huiles de Baleine & d'autres Poissons, ainsi que les fanons de Baleine, provenant de la pêche des États-unis de l'Amerique" (printed document, Papers of the Continental Congress, National Archives).

During the discussions in the Assembly preceding enactment of the tariff of March 2, 1791, it was decided that American oils would pay a duty of twelve livres per quintal, but by a decree of March 2 this duty was reduced to six livres per quintal (*Archives Parlementaires,* XXII, 470–71, 475; XXIII, 602, 611). William Short described the situation as follows: ". . . the National Assembly have changed their decree with respect to the american oils imported to France, on the representation of the committees they have reduced the duty from 12 ₶. to 6 ₶. the quintal. . . . The committees calculate that the internal duties hitherto paid on oils & to which the american were subject (independent of the duty of 11 ₶. 5s. the barrel on entering the kingdom) were upwards of 5 ₶. the quintal. By the *arret du conseil,* the duty would have been at present only 7 ₶. 10. the barrel of 500 lb. Still the 6 ₶. being in lieu of all other duties is considered as giving greater facilities to the importation of the american oils than they would have had under the former government" (Short to Jefferson, March 11, 1791, LC, RG 59, Despatches from United States Ministers to France, 1789–1869, January 16, 1791–August 6, 1792, National Archives). Although this view was not shared by the friends of the United States in France, the duty of six livres tournois per quintal was recognized by the *Tarif Général* passed March 2, 1791 (*Archives Parlementaires,* XXIII, 611).

59. See enclosure.

60. See note 58. H's observation on the attempt of the French government to "detach" American fishermen is a reference to the migration of American whalemen to France during the seventeen-eighties. See George Cabot to H, December 18, 1791, note 3.

vantages are so great as to render it difficult to supplant us; but as far as we have been able to maintain in this respect a competition with the French fisheries in the French Markets it is to be attributed to their incapacity to supply themselves which has counteracted the effect of a system manifestly prohibitory in its principle.

The real spirit of the system of France on this head not only appears from what has been done but from the manner of doing it.

In August 1784 the arret giving admission to *foreign* Fish in the W India Markets was passed.[61] In September 1785 another arret was passed granting a premium of 10 livres ℔ Kental on French Fish. Seven days after, so great was the anxiety, another arret was passed raising the duty on foreign fish from *three* to *five* livres.[62] An Arret of the 29 of December 1787 grants a right of *storing* for six months in France all the productions of the United States in order to re-exportation paying only a duty of 1 ℔ Cent. In February following another arret passes excepting from this right *all the products of the Fisheries;* [63] evidently from a jealousy of interference with the French Fisheries.[64]

A further explanation of the Spirit of the French system on this point is to be found in a passage of a Report to the National Assembly in the year 1789 from the Committee of Agriculture & Commerce. After stating a diminution of the product of the French Cod Fishery during the year 1789 the Report proceeds thus "This diminution ought to be attributed to the Collusion of the English and Free Americans who contrived to disappoint the French Fisheries, by finding means to supply us with their Fish while they eluded the payment of the duty imposed on importation; *in order to establish a preference in favour of the Cod of the French Fishery*." [65]

But however similar the *principle* of the French and English Regulations may be in regard to their Fisheries the result to the UStates is vastly different.

61. Importation of foreign fish into designated entrepôts in the French West Indies was permitted by article 2 of the *arrêt of* August 30, 1784 (Moreau de St. Méry, *Loix et Constitutions des Colonies Françoises,* VI, 562).

62. For the *arrêts* of September 18 and September 25, 1785, see note 43.

63. For the December 29, 1787, and February 22, 1788, *arrêts,* see note 58.

64. This paragraph was quoted almost verbatim in Smith's speech of January 13, 1794 (*Annals of Congress,* IV, 182).

65. This paragraph was quoted by Smith in his speech of January 13, 1794 (*Annals of Congress,* IV, 183–84).

The dominions of France take of the Fisheries of the UStates to the extent of . Those of Great Britain to the extent only of [66]

IV As to Wood particularly Lumber.

The Regulations of France have not made & do not make any distinction as the articles of this kind in favour of the United States.

Those of Great Britain make material distinctions in favour of the UStates and their Ships; putting the citizens and Ships of the UStates in this respect upon the same footing as those of their own colonies, as far as regards the European Market.[67]

Great Britain is also a much better customer than France for articles of this kind.

The amount in value taken from us by the dominions of the former in was [68]

That of the latter

V As to Rice

This Article has stood and now stands upon a better footing in France than in Great Britain being free in the former Country and subject to a high duty in the latter.[69] And there being no discrimination in either Country in favour of the Rice of the UStates.

66. In *JCHW*, V, 86, this paragraph reads as follows: "The dominions of France take of the fisheries of the United States to the extent of $724,224; those of Great Britain to the extent only of $88,371."

67. In regard to wood Smith observed in his speech of January 13, 1794: "This article (the fourth in importance as an export) stood and stands on a decidedly better footing in the British than in the French system. In Great Britain it was and is free from duty, while other foreign rival woods are subject . . . to considerable, and, in several instances, high duties. The observations with regard to this difference, as applied to tobacco, apply to this article in full force, with this additional circumstance, that some of the Northern nations could afford to undersell us, were it not for the protection derived from the high duties on their woods.

"In the French West Indies, our wood is subject to a duty of one per cent. ad valorem, with no distinction for or against us. In the British West Indies it is free, with a distinction in our favor, by the prohibition of other foreign wood. The duty, it is true, is of no great consequence, but it is not so of the prohibition in the British West Indies of all foreign wood, but from the United States." (*Annals of Congress*, IV, 181.)

68. In *JCHW*, V, 87, this paragraph reads as follows: "The amount in value taken from us by the dominions of the former in 1790 was $622,635; that of the latter, $476,039."

69. The British Consolidating Act of 1787 laid a duty of seven shillings fourpence on rice (27 Geo. III, C. 13). The French *Tarif Général* of March, 1791, admitted rice free (*Archives Parlementaires,* XXIII, 609).

It is to be observed however that as the article is produced in neither Country and as the Rice of the U States is on the same footing in the British Market with that of other Countries the observation made in respect to the duty on Tobacco may in some sort be applied to this Article.

But it applies with far less force; because Tobacco has no competition; while Rice as far as it is a substitute for bread or vegetables has competitors in all the articles which fall under either description.

This article however stands upon a somewhat better footing in the British than in the French West Indies being free in the former and subject to a duty of 1 ℔ Cent in the latter.[70] The difference is not considerable.

The British dominions took in of this article in value Dollars the French [71]

V As to grain namely Wheat Rye Indian Corn Oats.

As they respect the European dominions of France & Great Britain they may be considered nearly in the same light with flour.[72]

All these articles are free in the British West Indies. Wheat & Rye are prohibited in the French; but Indian Corn & Oats are admitted upon a duty of 1 ℔ Cent. The result upon the whole is that the English have been better customers than the French.

The British dominions took ⟨of these⟩ articles in the year in value . The French .[73]

The Act of Parliament of is likely to make a difference hereafter in the British European Market. According to that Act

70. In his speech of January 13, 1794, Smith observed: "In the French West Indies, rice was subject to a duty of one per cent. ad valorem, with no distinction for or against us. In the British West Indies, it was and is free, with a distinction in our favor, resulting from the prohibition of other foreign rice. . . . In the West Indies . . . Rice there makes a part of the common food. A duty upon it tends to prevent its being such, by letting in cheaper substitutes. This reflection operates in favor of the British against the French system, in respect to the West Indies, there being a duty upon it in the French, none in the British West Indies. But that duty is so light that, from this cause, and its extending to other articles, it ought scarcely to be counted. The prohibition of other foreign rice, however, is a circumstance of some value, assuring to this article from the United States a monopoly of the British West India market" (*Annals of Congress,* IV, 180–81).

71. In *JCHW*, V, 87, this paragraph reads as follows: "The British dominions took in 1790 of this article, in value, $953,939; the French $322,926."

72. See notes 46 and 49.

73. In *JCHW*, V, 87, this paragraph reads: "The British dominions took of these articles in the year 1790, in value, $685,071; the French $280,792."

But experience alone can determine with certainty the effect.

VI As to Pot & Pearl Ash.

These articles have stood and still stand upon a better footing by the British Regulations than by the French.

By the Regulations of the France the Pot & Pearl Ash of other Countries are upon the same footing with those of the U States.

But by the regulations of G Britain those of the U States are free while those of other Countries are subject to a duty of about 5 ℔ Cent.[74]

Great Britain in took from the United States of these Articles in value . France [75]

VII As to Indigo [76]

VIII As to live Animals

The regulations of both Countries may be considered as pretty

74. An act of 24 Geo. II, C. 51 (1751) permitted potash and pearlash from British colonies in America to be imported into England in English ships without the payment of duty. After the American Revolution successive orders listed potash and pearlash among the products which might be imported from the United States in American ships upon the same terms as if imported from British colonies in America in British ships. For examples see orders in council of April 4, 1787, April 3, 1789, April 1, 1791. Under the Consolidating Act of 1787, potash and pearlash from other foreign countries paid a duty of two shillings threepence (27 Geo. III, C. 13).

The duties upon the importation of potash and pearlash into France were abolished by the *Tarif Général* of March, 1791, making the importation of these products free to all countries (*Archives Parlementaires*, XXIII, 617).

75. In *JCHW*, V, 88, this paragraph reads as follows: "Great Britain, in 1790, took from the United States of these articles in value $747,078: France, $20,720."

76. John C. Hamilton filled in the space left by H for a discussion of this product with a statement from Smith's speech (*JCHW*, V, 88). Smith's statement reads as follows: "This article (eighth in value of our exports) stands upon a decidedly better footing in the system of Great Britain than in that of France. France is herself our competitor in the supply of her own market, and she aims at securing to herself the monopoly of it by adding to the advantage of a superior quality of her own indigo, as asserted by the Secretary of State, the discouragement to ours of double the duty paid on her own. Great Britain admits the article into her home market free of duty. Both countries exclude it from their West India market. Neither make any distinction for or against us" (*Annals of Congress*, IV, 183). John C. Hamilton added at the conclusion of this paragraph: "In 1790 Great Britain took of this article in value $479,530: France, $12,649" (*JCHW*, V, 88).

equal in respect to these Articles; the duty of one per Cent paid in the French West Indies while none is paid in the English being of no consequence in relation to articles in which the French themselves can maintain no competition.[77]

The dominions of France took in of these articles in value

Those of Great Britain [78]

IX As to Naval Stores namely Pitch Tar & Turpentine

The regulations of Great Britain are more favourable than those of France; for though the duties are higher in the former than in the latter; yet France places these articles from all countries on the same footing while England lays higher duties on them when brought from other Countries than when brought from the U States.[79] The difference as remarked in other cases is a bounty upon the productions of the UStates. The rate of duty here is of no consequence for the reason assigned in respect to Tobacco.[80]

X As to salted provisions

The regulations of France as to these Articles are evidently more

77. By the order in council of July 2, 1783, Great Britain permitted "Horses, Neat Cattle, Sheep, Hogs, Poultry, and all other Species of Live Stock and Live Provisions . . . being the Growth or Production of any of the United States" to be imported into the British West Indies, but only in ships owned and navigated by British subjects.

The *arrêt* of August 30, 1784, permitted the importation into the designated entrepôts in the French West Indies "d'animaux et bestiaux vivants de toute nature" (Isambert, *Recueil Général des Anciennes Lois Françaises*, XXVII, 460).

78. In *JCHW*, V, 88, this paragraph reads as follows: "The dominions of France took in 1790 of these articles in value $352,795: those of Great Britain, $62,415."

79. After the American Revolution Britain permitted pitch, tar, and turpentine to be imported into Great Britain in United States ships on the same terms as in British vessels. See the orders in council of December 26, 1783, April 16, 1784, April 8, 1785, April 1, 1791. Article 6 of the French *arrêt* of December 29, 1787, provided that "Les thérébentines, brais & goudrons provenant des États-Unis de l'Amérique, apportés directement en France par Vaisseaux François ou des États-Unis, ne payeront qu'un droit de Deux & demi pour cent de la valeur, & seront les droits mentionnés, tant au présent article qu'en l'article IV, exempts de toute addition de sous pour livre" (printed document, Papers of the Continental Congress, National Archives).

80. In *JCHW*, V, 89, an additional sentence at the end of this paragraph reads: "Great Britain, in 1790, took from us of these articles, $196,832: France, $7,366."

favourable than those of G Britain; being tolerated by the former & prohibited by the latter.[81]

The duties however are high and even in respect to Beef are a serious incumbrance upon the sale with a living profit. In respect to Pork they amount essentially to a Prohibition in France, which has great means of internal supply, & in the French West Indies the article is prohibited.

The Dominions of France took of these articles in in value

Those of Great Britain only [82]

XI As to Flax seed

It does not appear that any difference exists in the Regulations of the two countries in respect to this Article; but G B is far the better Customer.

Her dominions took in value in [83]

The French

XII As to Iron

The Regulations of G Britain are more favourable to the UStates in respect to this Article than those of France; for France admits the Iron of other Countries upon the same footing with that of the U States and lays a small duty upon Bar Iron.[84]

81. Jefferson stated in his "Report on Commerce" that in France "Salted beef is received freely for re-exportation; but if for home consumption, it pays five livres the quintal. Other salted provisions pay that duty in all cases, and salted fish is made lately to pay the prohibitory one of 20 livres the quintal." In Great Britain "Our salted fish, and other salted provisions, except bacon, are prohibited" (*ASP, Foreign Relations*, I, 301–02).

82. In *JCHW*, V, 89, this paragraph reads as follows: "The dominions of France took of these articles in 1790, in value $318,454: those of Great Britain only $7,557."

83. In *JCHW*, V, 89, this sentence reads: "Her dominions took in value in 1790, $219,924: the French, $3,290."

84. In his "Report on Commerce," Jefferson observed that, although Britain permitted American bar iron to enter Great Britain free while that of other nations paid a duty, this advantage was qualified by the fact that the United States did not produce enough for its own use (*ASP, Foreign Relations*, I, 301).

At the end of this sentence in *JCHW*, V, 90, the following sentence appears: "Great Britain took from us of this article in to the amount of $196,832: France to the amount of $2,143."

G B admits the Iron of the U States ⟨free from⟩ duty & lays a considerable duty on the article ⟨brought from other⟩ Countries.[85]

XIII As to Ships built in the UStates

The Regulations of France did favour more the building of Ships for sale than those of G B; for Ships built in the UStates & purchased by French subj [86]

85. Britain admitted both pig iron and bar iron from the United States in either British or American vessels upon the same terms as if imported in British-built ships owned by British subjects. See, for example, the order in council of April 1, 1791.

86. The MS is incomplete.

FOOTING OF THE COMMERCE OF THE UNITED STATES WITH THE DOMINIONS OF FRANCE AND GREAT BRITAIN IN THE YEAR 1790[87]

	Articles of the United States	France		Great Britain & Ireland		French America		British America	
I	Flour	Duty ⅛ ⅌ Ct ad valorem	A	Duty of 3d Sterling the quarter when Price above 48/ but 24/3 when under	A	prohibited	A	Free	A
II	Tobacco	No duty but *under Monopoly*	B	Duty ⅓ ⅌ lb	A	prohibited	A		
III	Wood namely Timber or wood for building except Masts Spars	Duty ⅛ ⅌ Ct. ad valorem	A	Free	A	Duty 1 ⅌ Ct. ad valorem and local duties unknown if any	B	Free	A
	Other wood including all called Lumber	Unknown but believed to be free		Free	A	Duty as above	B	Free	A
IV	Fisheries								
	Whale Oil	Qr 7 livres 10 sous ⅌ barrel of 520 lbs	A	Duty of £18. 3 Sterling ⅌ Ton of 252 Gallons	A				
	Spermaceti	do do		17/8 ⅌ Cwt.					
	Whale Fins	6 livres 13 sous 4d. the Kent							

V	Salted Fish	A same duty as Hanseatic Towns or other most favoured Nation said to be	A Prohibited except Stockfish which is subject to a duty of 2/1 sterling ⅌ 120 lb	C Duty 5 ₶ ⅌ Quintal with a premium of 10 ₶ p Quintal on French Fish equivalent to a duty of 15 ₶ ⅌ Kental about 80 ⅌ Ct ad valorem	Prohibited	A	Qr. Mr. Coxe [88]
VI	Rice	A ⅛ ⅌ Cent ad valorem	A 7/4 Stg ⅌ Cwt.	B duty 1 ⅌ Ct. ad valorem & local duties *if any*	Free	A	
VII	Grain namely Wheat	....	A 6d Sterling when price above 48/ ⅌ quarter 24/3 when under	A prohibited	Free	A	
	Rice	A ⅛ ⅌ Cent ad Valorem	A 3d. when above 32/ & 22/ when under	A prohibited	Free	A	
	Indian Corn	....	1d when above 24/ ⅌ Qr 11/ when under	B Duty 1 ⅌ Ct. and local duties if any	Free	A	
	Oats	....	A 2 when at or above 16/ ⅌ Quarter 6/7 when under		Free	A	

87. AD, Hamilton Papers, Library of Congress.

John Church Hamilton substituted for the table printed above a table entitled "Comparative Footing of the United States with the Dominions of France and Great Britain prior to the pending Revolution of France" (*JCHW*, V, 92–95). A copy of this statement in the Oliver Wolcott Papers, Connecticut Historical Society, Hartford, is endorsed as follows: "This Statement was prepared for Wm. Smith Esqr of So. Carolina upon which data his Speeches against Mr Madisons resolutions for restraining & regulating Commerce were founded." The table also appears at the end of the version of Smith's speech which was printed as a pamphlet in 1794 (Smith, *The Speeches of Mr. Smith, of South-Carolina, Delivered in the House of Representatives of the United States, in January, 1794, on the Subject of Certain Commercial Regulations, Proposed by Mr. Madison, in the Committee of the Whole, on the Report of the Secretary of State* [Philadelphia: Printed by Thomas Dobson, at the Stone House, No. 41, South Second-Street, 1794]).

88. Concerning these and other matters which H queried in this document, see H to Tench Coxe, January 1, 1794, and Coxe to H, January 3, 1794.

	Articles of the United States	France	Great Britain & Ireland	French America	British America
VIII	Pot & Pearl Ash	⅛ ꝑ Cent ad valorem A	Free	....	....
IX	Indigo	5 livres ꝑ Kental B	Free	....	....
X	Live Animals	....	....	Duty 1 ꝑ Ct. ad valorem & local duties if any B	Free A
XI	Naval Stores namely				
	Pitch	.... A	11/ Stg the Last		
	Tar	Duty 2½ ꝑ C ad valorem	ditto—Qr A	Duty 1 ꝑ Ct. ad valorem & local duties if any B	Free A
	Turpentine	....	2/3 ꝑ Cwt.		
XII	Salted Provisions				
	Beef	Duty 5 livres ꝑ Kental B	Prohibited A	Duty 1 ꝑ C ad valor & 3 livres per Kental B	Prohibited A
	Pork	Duty 5 livres ꝑ G Kental some ports & prohibited in others B	Prohibited A	Prohibited A	Prohibited A qr.
XIII	Flax seed	⅛ per Cent ad valor A	Free A	....	....

XIV Iron				B			
Pig	Unknown	free		A			
Barr		free		qr			Qr. Qr. Qr.
Ships	When owned by French subjects naturalized	partially subject	B				
	Productions of the West Indies						
Rum & Taffea	....	....			Duty 1 ℔ Ct. ad Valorem		
Sugar	....	....			Prohibited	D	
Molasses	....	....			Duty 1 ℔ Ct. ad valorem		Free from Jamaica & Grenada—Duty 4½ ℔ Ct. ad valorem on Sugars from other Islands
Coffee	....	....			Prohibited	D	
Cocoa	....	....			Prohibited	D	
Ginger	....	....			Prohibited	D	
Pimento	....	....			Prohibited	D	
Salt	....	....			ditto	D	Permitted from Turks Island
other productions	....	....			Prohibited	D	Prohibited

A

Authorities as to France [89]

A Arret 29 Decr. 1787 [90]

B Mr. Jeffersons Table which is here followed & believed to be right [91]

Authorities as to Great Britain

A Proclamation 26 December 1783 explained by the following Statutes of

Charles II		Chap 2	20th. Ch 7
	32	Ch	2
Georg 1 [92]	24	C	51
	30	C	16
Geor 3	5	C	45
	11	C	42
	12	C	60
	19	C	35
	23	C	29 [93]
	25	C	81
	26	C	41. 50. 52. 53. 60
	27	C	13

Authorities as to French West Indies

A. Letters Patent of Oct 1727 [94]

B Arret 30 of Aug 1784 [95]

C Arrets of the 18th & 25 Sepr 1785 [96]

D Letters Patent of October 1727
Arret of 30 Aug 1784

Authorities as to British W I.

A. Proclamation above cited explained by Statutes

Notes

I Flour — This article by a Decree of the National Assembly of 31 of January 1791 is free of duty on *its importation into France*. The UStates have stood & now stand, on the same footing with other foreign Nations as to this Article.[97]
By an Act of parliament of [98]

II Tobacco — By the abovementioned decree this article is now subject to a duty of 25 livres ℔ Kental if imported into France in Vessels of the UStates; & to a duty of 18 livres and 15 sous if imported in French Ships.[99] In this respect the U States stand on the same footing with the Colonies of Spain and the *Ukraine*. The difference of duty amounts to a prohibition of carrying in Ships of the U States.

		In Great Britain there is a difference of duty of 100 ℔ cent in favour of the Tobacco of the UStates compared with that of Spain and Portugal which pays 3/6 ℔ lb. The Ships of the U States carry on the same footing with those of G Britain.[100]
III	Wood	All the kinds of this Article which interest the UStates are by the decree of January 1791 admitted into France duty free; but so are the same kinds from other foreign Countries. In Great Britain a preference is given to the Wood of the United States by considerable duties on wood of the same kinds from other countries.[101] Deal Boards of other Countries are rated from £12.2.2 Sterling down to £5.6 the 120. Staves from 17/7 Stg to 4 the 120[102] Masts spars & bowspritts also pay a higher duty if imported in the Ships of other countries & all nonemureated woods if brought from any part of Europe pay 33 ℔ Cent ad valorem.
IV	Salted fish	Great Britain prohibits the Fish of all the world. The arrets of France of the 30th. of Aug 1784 18 & 25 Sepr 85 (which are the only ones known) admit foreign Fish into their Island on the conditions shewn on this Table; but the US enjoy no particular privilege. Their Fish & the Ships which bring it are exactly on the same footing with the Fish & the Ships of other Nations.[103] A pamphlet published at Paris in 1791 by Mr. Commerè[104] states that the duty on this article in the F W Indies is 3 livres with a premium of 12 on French Fish but no such regulation has appeared.

89. In the space above the words "Authorities as to France" H wrote the following words: Breads & biscuits prohibited French Is. Free B."

90. See note 58. A printed copy of this *arrêt* may be found in Papers of the Continental Congress, National Archives.

91. H is referring to a table prepared by Jefferson in December, 1791, as a comparative study of British and French trade policies toward the United States. This table is printed in Ford, *Writings of Jefferson*, V, 412–13. A manuscript copy of the table is in the Hamilton Papers, Library of Congress.

92. The reference should be to George II.

93. The reference should be to chapter 39.

94. "Lettres-Patentes du Roi, en forme d'Edit, concernant le Commerce étranger aux Isles et Colonies de l'Amérique" (Moreau de St. Méry, *Loix et Constitutions des Colonies Françoises*, III, 224–36).

95. Moreau de St. Méry, *Loix et Constitutions des Colonies Françoises*, VI, 561–66.

96. Moreau de St. Méry, *Loix et Constitutions des Colonies Françoises*, VI, 847–52, 863–65.

97. See note 46. 98. See note 49. 99. See note 53.

100. See note 54. 101. See note 67. 102. 27 Geo. III, C. 13 (1787).

103. See note 43. 104. See notes 41 and 42.

In Europe this article as a commodity of the United States was placed by the Arret of the 29 of December 1787[105] on the same footing with the fish of the Hanseatic Towns or other favoured Nations.

The Decree of January 1791 imposes a duty on the Fish of the U States imported into France in common with all foreign Fish of 20 livres about 4 Dollars ꝑ Kental. No distinction in Favour of the UStates.[106]

V Fish Oil

The decree of January 1791 imposes a duty of 6 livres ꝑ Kental on this Article imported into France being of the product of the Fisheries of the UStates very considerably lower than the British Duty.[107] Introduced through the departments of the Upper and Lower Rhine, Meurthe & Moselle it is rated at 12 livers ꝑ Kental.

In other cases foreign Fish Oil is prohibited.

VI Rice Grain[108]
Pot & Pearl Ash[109]

The decree of January 1791 makes these Articles on their importation into France free of duty. No distinction in favour of UStates.

An Act of Parliament prohibits the importation into Great Britain of

The UStates in respect to these Articles stand on the same footing with other Nations.

In respect to Pot & Pearsh Ash Great Britain makes a distinction in favour of the U States by a duty on the same articles brought from other foreign Nation of about 5 ꝑ Cent.[110]

VII Indigo

VIII Naval Stores

The Decree of January 1791 lays a duty on Tar of 15 sous ꝑ Kental, on Pitch of 5 sous ꝑ Kental on Turpentine of 35 sous ꝑ Kental. No distinction in favour of the UStates.[111]

Great Britain makes a distinction upon Tar & Pitch in favour of the U States by about ⅕ more duty on the same articles brought from other countries.[112]

IX	Beef & Pork	The decree of January 1791 lays a duty of 5 livres ℔ Kental on these Articles imported into France from the U States as well as other foreign countries. No distinction in our favour. G B prohibits them in respect to all foreign countries. No distinction to our prejudice.
X	Flax & Flax Seed	
XI	Pig & Bar Iron	The Decree of January 1791 lays a duty of 1 livre ℔ Kental on bar Iron but leaves Pig free.[113] No distinction in favour of the UStates. G Britain makes a considerable difference in favour of the U States by a duty on Russian Bar Iron of £3.9.1 ℔ Ton on the bar Iron of other countries of £2.16.2 on Pig Iron of other countries of 5/6 ℔ Ton.[114]
XII		Vessels built in the UStates & belonging to French subjects were capable of being naturalized in France. This distinction in our favour is now done away.[115] In England Ships built in the U States have been & are intitled to be recorded & being recorded & owned by B subjects enjoy the same ⟨pri⟩vileges as B. built ⟨sh⟩ips in the Trade between the U S & Britain.
XIII		A general distinction in favour of the U States runs through the regulations of G B in this particular that most articles of foreign Countries brought in foreign Ships pay a higher Duty than if brought in British Ships; but not so of the same Articles if brought in Ships of the UStates.

105. See note 58.

106. This duty on foreign salted fish was imposed by the *Tarif Général* of March, 1791 (*Archives Parlementaires*, XXIII, 616–17).

107. See notes 57 and 58.

108. See notes 69 and 70.

109. See note 74.

110. Under the Consolidating Act of 1787 other foreign nations paid a duty of two shillings threepence per hundredweight on potash and pearlash (27 Geo. III, C. 13).

111. These duties were incorporated into the *Tarif Général* of March, 1791 (*Archives Parlementaires*, XXIII, 610, 619).

112. See note 79.

113. See *Tarif Général* of March, 1791 (*Archives Parlementaires*, XXIII, 609).

114. 27 Geo. III, C. 13 (1787).

115. Under the *Tarif Général* of March, 1791, the importation of foreign-built ships into France was prohibited (*Archives Parlementaires*, XXIII, 623). See also note 45.

XIV

In the West India Trade of France the U States stand upon the same footing with other foregn Nations; in one instance perhaps upon a worse as it regards the operation of the thing namely as to salted beef which *though foreign* if brought from France in French Ships is exempted from the duty which is paid on the same article carried from the UStates directly to the Islands. The proximity of Ireland to France seems to render this an advantage to her over the U States.

In the West India Trade of G B the United States have the peculiar advantage of their commodities being introduced upon the same footing as if brought from the B Dominions in America except as to the Article of carrying in Ships of the United States. Here is a distinction in favour of the U States & none against them.

Note[116] The Notes (g) and (h) of Mr. Jeffersons Table[117] refer to an arret of 9th of May 1789 as making certain alterations in the trade of the U States with the French W Indies.

But this Arret (which is merely an Ordinance of the Governor General of St Domingo) is confined *wholly* to the *South part* of the Island of St. Domingo on very special reasons relative to the improvement of that particular spot and with very severe restrictions to prevent an extension. It is no part of the permanent system of France, no part of the general system of the West Indies & is not known to have received the sanction of the King.[118] It was besides past at a Moment of Revolution.

116. This note was written on a separate page and obviously was intended to be distinct from the notes that preceded it.

117. See note 91. Note "g" in Jefferson's table states: "There is a general law of France prohibiting foreign Flour in their Islands, with a suspending power to their Governors, in cases of necessity. An *Arret* of May 9, 1789, by their Governor makes it free till 1794, August; and in fact it is generally free there." Note "h" reads as follows: "The *Arret* of Sept. 18, 1785, gave a premium of 10 ₶ the Kental on fish brought in their own bottoms, for 5 years, so that the law expired Sept. 18, 1790. Another *Arret*, past a week after, laid a Duty of 5 l. the kental on fish brought in foreign vessels, to raise money for the premium before mentioned. The last *Arret* was not limited in time; yet seems to be understood as only commensurate with the other. Accordingly an *Arret* of May 9, 1789, has made fish in foreign bottoms liable to 3 l. the kental only till Aug. 1, 1794." (Ford, *Writings of Jefferson*, V, 412–13). See also note 43.

118. The "Ordonnance Concernant La Liberté du Commerce pour la Partie du Sud de Saint-Domingue" of May 9, 1789, which granted liberal concessions to foreign shipping, is printed in Saintoyant, *La Colonisation Française pendant la Revolution,* I, 452–53. It was annulled on July 2, 1789, by the "Arret du Conseil d'Etat du Roi Cassant et Annulant L'Ordonnance du Gouverneur Général de Saint-Domingue du 9 Mai 1789, Laquelle Accordait aux Etrangers la Liberté du Commerce pour la Partie Sud de Saint-Domingue" (Saintoyant, *La Colonisation Française pendant la Révolution,* I, 453).

1793

To the President and Directors of the Bank of the United States

Treasury Department
January 1. 1793.

Gentlemen

I presume it to be your understanding of the matter, as well as mine, that the first installment on account of the two Millions due from the Government to the Bank of The United States, becomes payable, as on this day.[1] A proposition to the Legislature, for a more extensive reimbursement, having produced discussions which have retarded a provision for that installment [2]—I think it incumbent upon me, founding myself on the necessity of the case, to inform you, that I shall consider two hundred Thousand Dollars of the monies in your possession belonging to the United States, as a *deposit* with you, for the payment of the installment in question; to receive its final and more formal shape as soon as Legislative provision shall be made concerning it.

With respectful consideration I have the honor to be Gentlemen Your most Obedient servt Alex Hamilton

The President & Directors
of the Bank of The United States

ALS, Historical Society of Pennsylvania, Philadelphia.

1. This sum had been borrowed under the terms of Section 11 of "An Act to incorporate the subscribers to the Bank of the United States" (1 *Stat.* 196 [February 25, 1791]), which provided "That it shall be lawful for the President of the United States, at any time or times, within eighteen months after the first day of April next, to cause a subscription to be made to the stock of the said corporation, . . . on behalf of the United States, to an amount not exceeding two millions of dollars; to be paid out of the monies which shall be borrowed by virtue of either of the acts, the one entitled 'An act making provision for the debt of the United States;' and the other entitled 'An act making provision for the reduction of the public debt;' borrowing of the bank an equal sum, to be applied to the purposes, for which the said monies shall have been procured; reimbursable in ten years, by equal annual instalments; or at

any time sooner, or in any greater proportions, that the government may think fit."

2. In his "Report on the Redemption of the Public Debt," November 30, 1792, H had proposed in relation to the debt owed the Bank of the United States that "power be given by law to borrow the sum due, to be applied to that reimbursement; and that so much of the dividend on the stock of the Government in the Bank, as may be necessary, be appropriated for paying the interest of the sum to be borrowed." H's report was received by the House of Representatives on December 3, 1792, and on December 21 a bill was presented providing for "the reimbursement of a Loan made of the Bank of the United States." On December 24 in the course of the debate William B. Giles of Virginia observed that he "was averse to increasing the Debt of the United States by additional loans. . . . He therefore moved that the section should be stricken out which provides for a loan, in order to substitute a clause providing for the sale of the shares in the Bank, owned by the United States, that the proceeds may be applied to the reimbursement of the Loan." The debate continued on December 26, but on December 27 a motion that "the House do now proceed to the further consideration of the bill providing for the reimbursement of a Loan made of the Bank of the United States" was defeated (*Annals of Congress,* III, 733, 751, 753–61).

From William Heth

Bermuda Hundred [Virginia] 1st. Jany 1793

Dear Sir

Private

Pardon me I beseech you, for interrupting you, to beg an answer to my Official letter of the [1] Decr. last, respecting the receiving money in Richmond.[2] With respect to my private concerns, I am in a painful situation because I am in suspence—for, if the scheme of paying, & receiving money, *in* Richmond, cannot be adopted, the Office *must* be removed from this place to Petersburg. In which case, I must remove my family to that neighbourhood and the arrangements necessary to be made in my affairs, between such a step, & remaining where I am, is of such moment to me, as to create a great anxiety to hear from you.

Mr. Campbell,[3] our U. States Atty. drew upon me some time ago for fifty pounds, without rendering any thing like an Account. It was impossible for me to pay it. Decisions & Judgts. have passd upon most of the Suits instituted by me—the Costs are therefore, or ought to be, in the Clerks or Marshals hands. Yet these Officers talk of holding fast my Moieties of the penalties which you have imposed in certain cases, until they pay themselves. Will not this be hard? They will not render Accounts in manner directed by the Comptroller,[4] on which subject I wrote you very fully the 26th Novr. last [5] and I have now mentioned these circumstances, with a hope that, you will consider said letter as really deserving an answer. Yet, My dear sir, I would not have presumed so much upon that condescension which you have ever manifested towards me, as thus to call your attention for a moment, from more important duties, if it was not, that I am asked by those Officers every time I meet them, whether I have recd. your answer.

I am Dear Sir, with great affection & respect Yrs W Heth

ALS, Hamilton Papers, Library of Congress.

1. Space left blank in MS.
2. Letter not found.
3. Alexander Campbell.
4. Oliver Wolcott, Jr., was comptroller of the Treasury.
5. Letter not found.

From Meletiah Jordan

Frenchman's Bay [District of Maine] January 1, 1793. "Your Circular Letter of 25th October 1792 I have this day received. In consequence of which I have transmitted to the Comptroller of the Treasury the different returns I was in use to send to your Office, those only excepted which you desire should be forwarded to you. . . . I cannot possibly ascertain the Estimate of Money due from this District to the Fishermen, . . . & until they make their appearance can form no idea of the money likely to be due on that head, although I imagine there is enough to the Office to answer the purpose."

Copy, RG 56, Letters to Collectors at Gloucester, Machias, and Frenchman's Bay, National Archives.

To John Kean

Treasury Department
January 1 1793

Sir

The Treasurer of the United States has this day been directed to draw on the Office of Discount and Deposit at Baltimore for Twenty thousand Dollars, and to deposit the bill, as usual, in the Bank of the

United States. I have therefore to request that you will deliver it to Messrs Elliott and Williams,[1] or to their Agent, Colo Smith,[2] upon the payment of the Cash.

I am, Sir, very respectfully, Your Mo. Obedt Servant.

Alexander Hamilton

John Kean Esqr.
Cashier of the Bank of the US.

LS, The Huntington Library, San Marino, California.

1. Robert Elliot and Elie Williams were contractors for the supply of the Army on the western frontier.

2. Samuel Smith, who had served as a lieutenant colonel in the American Revolution and was a member of the Baltimore merchant firm of Samuel and John Smith, Jr., had been elected to Congress in 1792. See James McHenry to H, August 16, 1792. The Smith firm supplied Elliot and Williams with goods for the Indian trade and in 1791 was drawn into the latter firm's conflict with the Treasury over the settlement of accounts. See, for example, Samuel Smith's letters to Otho H. Williams, who was collector of customs at Baltimore and Elie Williams's brother, abstracted in *Calendar of the General Otho Holland Williams Papers in the Maryland Historical Society* (Baltimore, 1940), 239, 241, 242.

From Charles Lee

Alexandria [*Virginia*] *January 1, 1793.* Transmits a statement of "Tonnage, Duties, payments, and drawbacks, during the last quarter." [1]

Copy, RG 56, Letters to and from the Collector at Alexandria, National Archives.

1. This letter was written in reply to H's "Treasury Department Circular to the Collectors of the Customs," October 12, 1792.

From George Washington

Philadelphia Jany 1st. 1793

Dear Sir

After reading the enclosed letter [1] return it to me. My sentiments on the *general* principle your are acquainted with. With the one handed, under this cover, do as shall seem best to you in the case before us, & let me know the result; or, if you chuse it, I am ready to confer further with you on the subject.

I am always Your Sincere frd & sr Go: Washington

ALS, Hamilton Papers, Library of Congress.

1. The enclosure is presumably Thomas Jefferson's opinion on the request made by Antoine René Charles Mathurin de La Forest in a letter to H, December 27, 1792, which H had transmitted to Washington on December 29. La Forest had requested that advances be made on the salaries of the French consuls in the United States from the payments owed France. Jefferson's letter to Washington, dated January 1, 1793, reads in part as follows: "I have duly considered the translation of the letter of Dec. 27 from M. de la Forest stating that the French Consuls here have a right to receive their salaries at Paris, that under the present circumstances they cannot dispose of their bills, and desiring that our government will take them as a remittance in part of the monies we have to pay France. . . . I do not observe any objection from the treasury that this channel of remittance would be out of the ordinary line and inadmissible on that account. Taking it therefore on the ground merely of an advance unauthorized by the French government, I think the Bills may be taken. We have every reason to believe the money is due to them, and none to doubt it will be paid every creditor being authorized to draw on his debtor. They will be paid indeed, in assignats, at the nominal value only, but it is previously understood that these will procure cash on the ⟨receipt⟩ of the real value we shall have paid for them. The risk, if any, is certainly very small, and such as it would be expedient in us to encounter in order to oblige these gentlemen. I think it of real value to produce favorable dispositions in the agents of foreign nations here" (ALS, letterpress copy, Thomas Jefferson Papers, Library of Congress).

To George Washington

[Philadelphia, January 1, 1793]

Mr. Hamilton wishing the President a happy New-Year & presenting him his affectionate respects, returns the inclosed.[1] He will wait on the President tomorrow on the subject, for a few minutes.

1st January 1793.

LC, George Washington Papers, Library of Congress.

1. See Washington to H, January 1, 1793, note 1.

To the President and Directors of the Bank of the United States

Treasury Department
January 2 1793.

Gentlemen

I have to request that you will advance to Tench Coxe Esqr, Commissioner of the Revenue, the sum of nine hundred and sixty five Dollars and forty seven Cents, upon the same principles as mentioned in my letter to you of the 10th of October last.[1]

It will be necessary to take a receipt from Mr Coxe, specifying that this money is for his own, Clerks and Messenger's salaries from the 1st of October 1792 to the 31st of December following.[2]

I have the honor to be, Gentlemen, Your Obedt Servt.

Alexander Hamilton

The President and
Directors of the Bank
of the US.

LS, Amherst College.
1. Letter not found.
2. A receipt in Coxe's handwriting accompanies this letter.

To Tench Coxe

[*Philadelphia, January 2, 1793.* On January 3, 1793, Coxe wrote to Hamilton: "In compliance with the direction in your letter of the 2d. instant." *Letter not found.*]

From Tench Coxe

Treasury Department, Revenue Office, January 2, 1793. "I have the honor to inclose to you for the purpose of submission to the President, three Contracts Made by the Collector of the District of Washington in North Carolina [1] for the stakeage of all the shoals, sounds &c. within that state and North of the District of Wilmington, which have heretofore been staked. . . . I have only to observe that as the sums are larger [than] heretofore, it may be because they are for a whole year, which has not been the Case in the former Contracts. . . . the immediate necessity of the Case appears to operate strongly in favor of the acceptance of the Contracts. . . ." [2]

LC, RG 58, Letters of Commissioner of Revenue, 1792–93, National Archives.
1. Nathan Keais.
2. These contracts, dated December 10, 1792, were signed by Keais with Green Parker and Walter Hanrahan, with John Bragg and John Wallace, and with John Wallace and John G. Blount. They were approved by George Washington on January 21, 1793 (copies, RG 26, Lighthouse Letters Received, Lighthouse Deeds and Contracts, National Archives).

From George Latimer

Introductory Note

This letter from Latimer, a Philadelphia merchant, concerns one phase of the involved question of using portions of the debt owed France by the United States for the relief of Santo Domingo. After the outbreak of the slave insurrection in Santo Domingo in August, 1791, the plight of the French colonists on the island became increasingly desperate. In September, 1791, Jean Baptiste de Ternant, the French Minister to the United States, applied to the United States Government for aid. Although Ternant did not have formal authorization from his government, several relatively small sums were advanced as emergency assistance.[1] On December 19, 1791, Antoine François, Marquis de Bertrand de Moleville, the French Minister of Marine, proposed to the National Assembly that the American debt to France be applied to the purchase in the United States of supplies for the relief of Santo Domingo, and in anticipation of this new arrangement William Short suspended payments to France on the United States debt.[2] Although in March, 1792, the French Assembly authorized the sum of six million livres for aid to Santo Domingo, this decree did not contain any direct reference to the United States.[3] After a series of delays the French Assembly decreed on June 26, 1792, that "Le pouvoir exécutif est authorisé à traiter avec le ministre des Etats-Unis, afin d'en obtenir des fournitures pour Saint-Domingue, en comestibles et matières premières propres à la construction, jusqu'à la concurrence de 4 millions de livres tournois, imputables sur la dette américaine." [4]

On March 3, 1792, before this decree had been issued, Ternant wrote to Jefferson and requested the sum of four hundred thousand dollars for the relief of Santo Domingo as an advance on the sums owed to France.[5] The President agreed to the advance, even though Ternant still lacked formal authorization from the French government, and directed the French Minister to open negotiations with Hamilton.[6] The plan worked out by Hamilton and Ternant in an exchange of letters on March 8, 1792, provided for a series of one hundred thousand dollar advances, the first to be made immediately, the second on June 1, 1792, the third on September 1, and the fourth on December 1. During the year, however, the schedule for these payments was disrupted by minor changes requested by Ternant on behalf of the French consul general, Antoine

Copy, Thomas Jefferson Papers, Library of Congress.

1. See Ternant to H, September 21, 1791.
2. See Short to H, December 30, 1791, January 26, 1792.
3. *Archives Parlementaires*, XL, 577–78.
4. *Archives Parlementaires*, XLV, 594.
5. LC, *Arch. des Aff. Etr., Corr. Pol., Etats-Unis*, Supplement Vol. 20.
6. Jefferson to Ternant, March 7, 1792 (ALS, letterpress copy, Thomas Jefferson Papers, Library of Congress).

René Charles Mathurin de La Forest, for convenience in meeting expenses.[7]

In November, 1792, Ternant requested an additional sum of approximately three hundred twenty-six thousand dollars beyond the original advance of four hundred thousand dollars. In view of the unstable political situation in France, Ternant's lack of authorization to negotiate for advances on behalf of the French government, and the likelihood that future governments in France might refuse to acknowledge payments on the debt made to the present regime, it was Hamilton's opinion that "as *little as possible* ought to be done—that whatever may be done should be cautiously restricted to the single idea *of preserving the colony from* destruction by *Famine*—that in all communications on the subject care should be taken to put it on this footing & even to avoid the explicit recognition of any regular authority in any person." Emergency aid to Santo Domingo should nevertheless be granted, but as "occasional advances without previous stipulation." [8] Consequently, Jefferson informed Ternant that the United States would continue to make advances for aid to Santo Domingo but only on an *ad hoc* basis. In conclusion he stated that in the decree of June 26 the French Assembly "contemplates purchases made *in the United States only*. In this they might probably have in view, as well to keep the business of providing supplies under a single direction, as that these supplies should be bought where they can be had cheapest, and where the same sum will consequently effect the greatest measure of relief to the Colony. It is our wish, as undoubtedly it must be yours, that the monies we furnish, be applied strictly in the line they prescribe. We understand, however, that there are in the hands of our Citizens, some bills drawn by the administration of the Colony, for articles of subsistence *delivered there*. It seems just that such of them should be paid as were received before bona fide notice that, that mode of supply was not bottomed on the funds furnished to you by the United States, and we recommend them to you accordingly." [9]

The bills referred to by Jefferson had been issued by the administration of Santo Domingo. In September, 1791, agents of the colonial government had arrived in Philadelphia and attempted to negotiate directly with the United States Government for aid to Santo Domingo. Because Ternant objected to this procedure, negotiations were transferred to the accredited representatives of France—Ternant and La Forest.[10] The Santo Domingan administration, however, continued to purchase supplies from United States merchants trading to the island and to issue in payment bills both on the French Treasury and on La Forest in Philadelphia.

7. See Ternant to H, August 22, October 8, November 15, 1792.

8. For H's opinion on Ternant's request, see H to Washington, November 19, 1792.

9. Jefferson to Ternant, November 20, 1792 (letterpress copy, Thomas Jefferson Papers, Library of Congress).

10. Ternant to Montmorin, September 28, 1791 (Turner, "Correspondence of French Ministers," 45–51). For a detailed account of this incident, see Jefferson to Short, November 24, 1791 (LC, Papers of the Continental Congress, National Archives).

At first the bills drawn on La Forest were honored by the French consul general, but the expenditures of the colony for supplies continued to increase, and on June 16, 1792, Ternant wrote to the French Minister of Foreign Affairs that, since he had received no instructions from his government on aid to Santo Domingo, he had ordered La Forest to suspend payment on all drafts of the Santo Domingan administration in excess of the first two payments which he had received from the United States Treasury. On June 25 he announced that, in spite of his remonstrances, Santo Domingan officials were showing no restraint in issuing drafts.[11] As a result, in August, 1792, La Forest inserted a notice in United States newspapers which stated: "The Administration of the French colony of St. Domingo, continuing to draw bills upon me, though advised more than two months ago to suspend drawing; I am under the necessity, in order to avoid exposing the credit of France, of informing the public, that from the date of this advertisement, I will not accept nor pay any of those bills beyond No. 138, of the 17 of July. . . ." [12] Protests by American merchants were so vigorous, however, that in November, 1792, La Forest published the following notice:

"*The public are forewarned* anew against taking any drafts from the administration of the French colony of St. Domingo on the subscriber, as none will be either accepted or paid, but such as will be issued, after a public notice given by the Subscriber, that funds are or will be provided for the discharge of the same.

"And as drafts of the above mentioned colonial administration on the subscriber, have been received in payment of supplies by several merchants, before the advertisement of the 9th of August last was known in St. Domingo, the bearers of such bills drawn to the 9th of September 1792, inclusively, are informed that they may apply for payment as soon as the said bills shall become due respectively." [13]

Philadelphia Jany 2 1793

Sir

In June last a French Merchant from Hispaniola, who had entered into a contract with the administration of that Colony, to supply at Port au Prince a large quantity of Flour, and other Articles, was introduced to me, by a mercantile House of this City, his Contract

11. Turner, "Correspondence of French Ministers," 131, 139–40, 153.

12. [Philadelphia] *National Gazette*, August 11, 1792.

13. *The Federal Gazette and Philadelphia Daily Advertiser*, November 21, 1792. For correspondence concerning the application of the debt owed to France by the United States, see Ternant to H, September 21, 1791, February 21, March 8, 10, 1792; H to Ternant, September 21, 1791, February 21, March 8, 11, 12, 1792; H to Jefferson, November 17, 1792; H to Washington, November 19, 1792; Short to H, December 28, 1791, January 26, March 24, April 22, 25, May 14, June 28, August 6, 1792; H to Short, April 10, 1792. See also Gouverneur Morris to H, November 2, 1792, note 4.

was explained by his Correspondent here. Payment of part was to be made in Specie on delivery of the Flour &c at Port au Prince. Fully confiding that said contract would be faithfully adhered to, I furnished him with fifteen hundred Barrells of Flour which he shipped about the latter end of July for Port au Prince where it was unloaded. Then the administrators found it impossible (as I understood) to fullfill their engagment of payment in ready money, their funds being totally exhausted. At that very period the French Commissioners[14] & General Desparbes[15] arrived from France, who published a decree which gave reason to expect that the Minister of France to the United States of America, was making provision for the support of the Colony and for the payment of the Bills, drawn by the Administration on Mr De la Forest influenced thereby, and the more so, as those at the head of the Administration convinced that gentleman, that these Bills upon Mr De la Forest would unquestionably be paid, he received (in lieu of the specie engaged by contract to be paid him) in payment, Administration Bills on Mr De la Forest. Of these Bills I received 7927 Dollars—say seven thousand nine hundred & twenty seven dollars, thirty seven Cents—which when presented for Acceptance were protested and I have since been told that those Bills notwithstanding the repeated exertions of the Gentleman—who was the Contractor, and had personally delivered the cargo at Port au Prince and returned with the Bills—will not be paid because they were drawn on the 10th of Septemr, but that if they had been of the 9th of Septr they would have been honoured. It is true Mr De la Forest⟨'s⟩ advertisements in the News Papers fixed the 9th in preferance to any other day, but why the Bills of the 9th should be paid & those of the 10th refused, I know not. It is strang⟨e⟩ that the Administration having no Authority to draw Bills either in Augt or Septemr should take such license, but it seems stranger still that assuming such liberty, Bills drawn on the 9th should be paid & those of the 10th (one day later) be rejected. I have been advised to apply to you & solicit your mediation and protection in this business and I have no doubt of

14. This is a reference to the three civil commissioners for Santo Domingo appointed by the French government in the spring of 1792. The new commissioners, Étienne Polverel, Léger Félicité Sonthonax, and Jean Antoine Ailhaud, arrived at Cap-Français on September 18, 1792.

15. Jean Jacques Pierre Desparbès, commander of the six thousand French troops that accompanied the civil commissioners to Santo Domingo.

your interferance being of the greatest consequence. Please to pardon the freedom of this application and believe me to be &c

Geo Latimer

The Secretary of the Treasy

From Tench Coxe

Treasury Department,
Revenue Office, January 3d. 1793.

Sir,

I have the honor to inclose to you an authenticated copy of an Act of the legislature of New York[1] received this day from Mr. Lawrence,[2] one of the Representatives in Congress from that State. I have to observe on this Act that the reservation of Jurisdiction contained in the proviso appears to be inconsistent with the intention of the last clause but one of the 8th. Section of the 1st. Article of the Constitution of the United States,[3] and with the Act of Congress entitled an Act to erect a Light House on Montok point &c. passed the 12th. day of April last.[4]

I have the honor to be with great Respect, Sir, your most Obt. Servt.

Tench Coxe
Commissr. of the Revenue.

The honble.
The Secretary of the Treasury.

LC, RG 58, Letters of Commissioner of Revenue, 1792–1793, National Archives.

1. On December 18, 1792, the New York legislature passed "An Act to cede the jurisdiction of certain lands on Montaack Point, to the United States of America, for the purposes therein mentioned." The cession of land to the United States contained the following limitation: "*Provided nevertheless,* that such jurisdiction so ceded . . . shall not extend, or be construed to extend, so as to impede or prevent the execution of any process at law, under the authority of this State, except so far forth, and such process may affect any the real or personal property of the United States within the said tract . . ." (*Laws of the State of New York,* III, 385).

2. John Laurance, a New York City lawyer, had served in the Continental Congress and the New York Senate from 1785 to 1787 and was a member of the New York Senate in 1789. He was elected to Congress in the same year.

3. This section of the Constitution authorized Congress "To exercise exclusive Legislation in all Cases whatsoever, over such District (not exceeding ten Miles square) as may, by Cession of particular States, and the Acceptance of Congress, become the Seat of the Government of the United States, and to exercise like Authority over all Places purchased by the Consent of the Legislature of the State in which the Same shall be, for the Erection of Forts, Magazines, Arsenals, dock-Yards, and other needful buildings."

4. This act reads as follows: "*Be it enacted by the Senate and House of Representatives of the United States of America in Congress assembled,* That as soon as the jurisdiction of such land on Montok Point in the state of New York as the President of the United States shall deem sufficient and most proper for the convenience and accommodation of a lighthouse shall have been ceded to the United States it shall be the duty of the secretary of the treasury, to provide by contract which shall be approved by the President of the United States, for building a lighthouse thereon, and for furnishing the same with all necessary supplies, and also to agree for the salaries or wages of the person or persons who may be appointed by the President for the superintendence and care of the same; and the President is hereby authorized to make the said appointments. That the number and disposition of the lights in the said lighthouse shall be such as may tend to distinguish it from others, and as far as is practicable, prevent mistakes" (1 *Stat.* 251).

From Tench Coxe

Treasury Department
Revenue Office, January 3d. 1793.

Sir,

In compliance with the direction in your letter of the 2d. instant,[1] I have the honor to inform you that the following persons are employed in this office.

William Barton, principal	Clerk at	800 Dollars ℔ Annm.
John Mease	Clerk at	400.
Peter Footman	do. at	400
Ezekiel Forman	do. at	400
Michael Gitts, Messenger & Office keeper		200
	Dollars.	2200

The Establishment of this Office having been made at a stage of the last session,[2] when there was not time to place the Clerks upon as good a footing as the legislature have been pleased to ordain in regard to the others, I take occasion to observe that at a convenient opportunity I could wish in Justice to the persons employed it may be submitted to Congress.

I have the honor to be with great respect Sir, your most Obt. Servant

Tench Coxe,
Commissr. of the Revenue

The honble.
The Secretary of the Treasury.

LC, RG 58, Letters of Commissioner of Revenue, 1792–1793, National Archives.
1. Letter not found.
2. The office of commissioner of the revenue had been established on May 8, 1792. See Section 6 of "An Act making alterations in the Treasury and War Departments" (1 *Stat.* 280–81).

To John Miller

[*Philadelphia*] *January 3, 1793*. "It is perfectly agreeable to me that Nathaniel Waters and Peter Cooper, the two persons mentioned in your letter of the 22nd ulto.[1] should be employed as Inspectors at the prices following—Vizt. for Inspecting the Hats 7/6 ℔ day and for inspecting the Boots and Shoes at the rate of half a Cent per pair round."

Extract, RG 217, Miscellaneous Treasury Accounts, 1790–1894, Account No. 4377, National Archives.
1. Letter not found.

To the President and Directors of the New York Office of Discount and Deposit of the Bank of the United States

[*Philadelphia, January 3, 1793*. The dealer's catalogue description of this letter reads: "Revoking the credit requested in favor of the bank's cashier." [1] *Letter not found.*]

LS, sold at Anderson Galleries, February 3–5, 1913, Lot 345.
1. See H to the President and Directors of the New York Office of Discount and Deposit, December 14, 1792.

From Timothy Pickering[1]

General Post Office
Philadelphia Jany 3d 1793

Sir

Since the close of the last War with Great Britain the Mails for Canada, brought by the British Packets to New York have been transmitted to Albany by the carriers of the Mails of the United States; and from Albany by a Courier to Montreal. Mr Lansing[2] the postmaster at Albany, was the agent in this business in behalf of the Deputy postmaster General for Canada.[3] Mr Lansing made some propositions to me for continuing his agency, by a Contract for carrying the Mail from Albany thro' Vermont; a post road being established by law, as far as Burlington on Lake Champlain. I declined his proposals. Afterwards, in March last, Mr Edwards Deputy postmaster in Montreal,[4] came to this City, and manifested the desire of Mr Finlay, the Deputy postmaster General for Canada to have some arrangement made for the regular conveyance of the Canada Mail. I then made the propositions contained in the inclosed paper, which have since been agreed to by Mr Finlay; and the Mail is now conveyed in the manner therein described: [5] Some accidents occasioned delays: but the plan is now in operation. The sentiments expressed in that paper will show my sense of such a connection with our neighbours in Canada and how readily I shall enter into any negociation for a similar connection with any other part of that extensive province.

With respect to a communication by post with Niagara, which you mentioned to me yesterday, I now enclose a statement which will show the accomplishment of that object to be exceedingly easy: & am Sir &c. T. P.

LC, RG 28, Letter Books, 1789–1794, National Archives.

1. Pickering was appointed postmaster general on August 19, 1791.

2. Abraham G. Lansing.

3. This is a reference to Hugh Finlay, who had been deputy postmaster general for the British provinces in North America under Benjamin Franklin. After the treaty of peace Finlay was appointed director general of the post office for the provinces of Quebec, Nova Scotia, New Brunswick, and their dependencies.

4. Edward Edwards.

5. See Pickering to Edwards, September 28, 1792; Pickering to Finlay, September 28, 1792, January 11, 1793 (LC, RG 28, Letter Books, 1789–1794, National Archives).

Report on Foreign Loans[1]

Treasury Department.
January 3d. 1793.
[Communicated on January 4, 1793][2]

[To the Speaker of the House of Representatives]
Sir,

In obedience to an Order of the President of the United States, I have the honor to transmit sundry Statements, No. 1, 2, 3, 4, respecting the several foreign Loans, which have been made under his authority, by the United States, shewing, in conformity to the resolution of the House of Representatives of the 27th of December,[3] as far as the materials in the possession of the Treasury will now permit, the several particulars specified in that resolution; these Statements will equally fulfil the object of the Resolution of the House of the 24th of December.[4]

With perfect respect, I have the honor, to be, Sir, Your most obedient and Humble Servant, Alexander Hamilton.

The Honorable the Speaker
of the House of Representatives.

Copy, RG 233, Reports of the Treasury Department, 1792–1793, Vol. III, National Archives.

1. A supplement to this report was sent to the House of Representatives on January 10. See "Report on Foreign Loans. Supplementary Statement Showing the Sums Borrowed in the United States," January 10, 1793.

2. *Journal of the House*, I, 662.

3. The House "*Resolved*, That the President of the United States be requested to cause this House to be furnished with a particular account of the several sums borrowed under his authority, by the United States; the terms on which each loan has been obtained; the applications to which any of the moneys have been made, agreeable to appropriations; and the balances, if any, which remain unapplied. In this statement it is requested that it may be specified at what times interest commenced on the several sums obtained, and at what times it was stopt, by the several payments made" (*Journal of the House*, I, 655).

4. The House "*Resolved*, That the Secretary of the Treasury be directed to lay before this House an account of the application of the moneys borrowed in Antwerp and Amsterdam, for the United States, within the present year" (*Journal of the House*, I, 653).

I

STATEMENT OF THE SEVERAL SUMS WHICH HAVE BEEN BORROWED FOR THE USE OF THE UNITED STATES BY VIRTUE OF THE ACTS OF THE FOURTH AND TWELFTH OF AUGUST 1790,[5] SHEWING THE PARTICULAR APPLICATION OF THE MONIES, TO THE FIRST OF JANUARY 1793, INCLUSIVELY, AND THE BALANCE REMAINING UNAPPLIED.

Loans (A)

		Florins. Sts. d.
First Loan,	made at Amsterdam, commencing on the 1st of February 1790, at 5 per cent interest, and 4½ per cent charges[6] …………………	3.000.000.
Second Loan,	made at Amsterdam, commencing on the 1st day of March 1791, at 5 per cent interest, and 4 per cent charges[7] …………………	2.500.000.
Third Loan,	made at Amsterdam, commencing on the 1st of September 1791, at 5 per cent interest, and 4 per cent charges[8] …………………	6.000.000.
Fourth Loan,	made at Antwerp, commencing on the 1st of December 1791, at 4½ per cent interest, and 4 per cent charges[9] …………………	2.050.000.
Fifth Loan,	made at Amsterdam, commencing on the 1st of January 1792, at 4 per cent interest, and 5½ per cent charges[10] …………………	3.000.000.
Sixth Loan,	made at Amsterdam, commencing on the 1st of June 1792, at 4 per cent interest, and 5 per cent charges[11] …………………	3.000.000.
		19.550.000.

5. "An Act making provision for the (payment of the) Debt of the United States" (1 *Stat*. 138–44 [August 4, 1790]) and "An Act making Provision for the Reduction of the Public Debt" (1 *Stat*. 186–187 [August 12, 1790]).

6. For a description of this loan, see H to Willink, Van Staphorst, and Hubbard, November 29, 1790, note 1.

7. For a description of this loan, see William Short to H, February 17, 1791.

8. For a description of this loan, see Short to H, August 31, 1791.

9. For a description of this loan, see Short to H, November 8, 1791, note 4; November 12, 1791.

10. The Holland loan of December, 1791. For a description of this loan, see Short to H, December 23, 28, 1791.

11. The Holland loan of 1792. For a description of this loan, see Short to H

Charges upon the Loans.

On 3.000.000. Florins ...... at 4½ per cent	135.000.	
2.500.000 " .... at 4 per cent	100.000.	
6.000.000 ... " .... at 4 per cent	240.000.	
2.050.000 ... " .... at 4 per cent	82.000.	
3.000.000 ... " .... at 5½ per cent	165.000.	
3.000.000 ... " .... at 5 per cent	150.000.	
		872.000.
Net amount of the Loans		18.678.000.

Payments made to France. (B.) 12

			Livres tournois S. d.	Florins. Sts. d.
1790 Dec:	3d:	Remittance from Amsterdam,	3.611.950.	1.500.014. 9.
1791. June	1st.	do ... do	2.696.629. 4.	1.005.000.
Aug:	11th.	do ... do	941.176. 9.	352.187.10.
Sept.	12th.	do ... do	642.896. 9. 9.	238.233. 6.
	15th.	do ... do	1.080.874.12. 6.	400.531.12.
"	22d.	do ... do	1.457.734.15. 4.	539.414.10.
"		do ... do	907.280.15. 2.	335.726.14.
"	29th.	do ... do	616.212.14. 7.	229.500.15.
Octo.	3d.	do ... do	220.680.10.	81.957.10.
"	6th.	do ... do	806.420. 3. 3.	300.951. 9
"	13th.	do ... do	1.139.053.14. 1.	429.550.16.
"	20th.	do ... do	811.154. 2. 8.	302.291. 4.
"	24th.	do ... do	487.692. 2. 8.	180.608.13.
Nov:	10.	do ... do	1.540.909. 2.	567.825.
Dec:		do. from Amsterdam	5.367.272.14. 6.	1.968.000.
1792. Aug:	9th.	do. from Amsterdam	6.000.000.	1.641.250.
				10.073. 1.
Charges on the Remittances to France. Brokerage on Florins 10.073.043.8. at 1 per mille.			28.327.937. 9. 6.	10.073.043. 8.

12. For descriptions of the French loans, see H to Short, September 1, 1790, notes 17 and 26; Short to H, November 30, 1789, note 3; Willink, Van Staphorst, and Hubbard to H, January 25, 1790, note 3.

Payments on account of other foreign Loans made and to be made to the 1st of January 1793, inclusively.

1791....February 1st	289.783. 6.			
June 1st	350.000.			
1792....February 1st	230.000.			
" March 1st	119.879. 4			
" June. 1st	350.000.			
" September 1st	294.566.13			
" December. 1st	92.250.			
1793. January 1st	106.709.19. 8.			
	1.833.189.			
From which, deduct so much remitted to the Commissioners from the Treasury, pursuant to special appropriations by the Acts, intituled "An Act making appropriations for the support of Government for the year 1790;"[13] and, "An Act making certain appropriations therein mentioned."[14]	100.000			
		1.733.189. 2. 8.		
Commission on the payment of 1.917.250, florins interest, at 1 per cent		19.172.10.		
For postage and advertising		613. 8. 8.		
For interest on the debt due to certain foreign Officers, payable in Paris,[15] (C)		105.000.		
Reimbursement of the Spanish debt, estimated at (D)[16]		680.000.		
Bills drawn upon the Commissioners in Amsterdam, by the Treasurer. (E)		5.649.621. 2. 8.		
			18.270.712.12. 8.	
Leaving a Balance in the hands of the Commissioners, of				407.287. 7. 8.

13. 1 *Stat.* 104–06 (March 26, 1790). 14. 1 *Stat.* 185–86 (August 12, 1790).

15. For a description of this debt, see Short to H, August 3, 1790, note 5. Section 5 of "An Act supplementary to the act making provision for the Debt of the United States" (1 *Stat.* 282 [May 8, 1792]) authorized the President "to cause to be discharged the principal and interest of the said debt, out of any of the monies, which have been or shall be obtained on loan." Although originally the interest on this debt was payable in Paris, H had made arrangements in September, 1792, to have the principal or both the principal and interest paid in the United States beginning on October 15, 1792. See H to Gouverneur Morris, September 13, 1792; H to Short, September 13, 1792. For the negotiations on the payment of these officers, see also H to Short, August 16, 1792; H to George Washington, August 27, 1792; Washington to H, August 31, 1792.

16. For a description of this loan, see H to Short, September 1, 1790, note 19; Joseph Nourse to H, October 9, 1792. See also Samuel Flagg Bemis, *Pinckney's Treaty* (Reprinted: New Haven, 1960), Appendix II, "The Fi-

Remarks.

(A) The dates here mentioned are those for commencing payments on account of the respective loans. The usage is, to allow a certain time to the subscribers (ordinarily from three to six months) to pay in the sums subscribed, the sums paid in, in each month, bearing interest from the beginning of the month. The Schedule No. II, shews the monthly periods of actual payment. The first of these loans was set on foot by our Bankers in Holland,[17] without previous authority, for reasons of weight, respecting the interests and credit of the United States. A due regard to the motives, and considerations relative to the yet unascertained effect of our financial arrangements in their first stages led to an acceptance of that loan on account of the government. The fourth of these loans was originally contracted for three millions of florins, but nine hundred and fifty thousand florins were afterwards suppressed,[18] in consequence of its being found, that money had become obtainable at a lower rate of interest.

(B) The conversion of florins into livres, in each case, is regulated by the actual market rate of exchange, at the time of payment. It is, however, understood, that there is to be a reliquidation, with a view to certain equitable considerations. The rate of exchange, for the proceeds of the Antwerp loan, is stated by analogy—no more certain rule being, at present, in possession of the Treasury.

(C) The actual payment of this interest is not yet known at the Treasury, but an appropriation has been made for it, at the disposal of the Minister Plenipotentiary of the United States in France.

(D) Advice is received, that this payment was going on, though it had not been completed. There is no cause to doubt, that it has been since carried into full effect.

(E) The produce of the Bills drawn for this sum, and others particulars respecting it, will appear from the Schedules, No. III and IV.

According to the terms of all these loans, the United States are bound to reimburse, in fifteen years, by equal instalments, the first beginning the eleventh year; but the United States have reserved a right upon all, except the two last, to reimburse, at any time, at their pleasure; The reimbursement of the two last (according to the general usage of the country, observed in all loans by the United States, prior to the present government) cannot begin 'till the eleventh year.

Treasury Department, January 3d: 1792

Alex. Hamilton, Secry. of Treasy.

17. Willink, Van Staphorst, and Hubbard.

18. See Short to H, March 24, August 6, 1792.

No. II

STATEMENT SHEWING THE PARTICULAR PERIODS, WHEN THE BONDS WERE DISTRIBUTED, AND THE MONIES RECEIVED UPON THE DIFFERENT LOANS.

On the first Loan, dated the 1st. of February 1790.

			florins.	
1790.	February.	Received by the Commissioners	1.167.000.	
"	March	ditto	515.000.	
"	April	ditto	232.000.	
"	May	ditto	230.000.	
"	June	ditto	191.000.	
"	July	ditto	191.000.	
"	August	ditto	32.000.	
"	September	ditto	39.000.	
"	October	ditto	39.000.	
"	November	ditto	39.000.	
"	December	ditto	170.000.	
"	January	ditto	155.000.	
				3.000.000.

On the Second Loan, dated the 1st. of March 1791.

1791.	February.	Received by the Commissioners	669.000.	
"	March	ditto	1.058.000.	
"	April	ditto	317.000.	
"	May	ditto	456.000.	
				2.500.00.

On the Third Loan, dated the 1st. of September 1791.

1791,	August 31st.	Received by the Commissioners	1.905.000.	
"	September 30th.	ditto	1.816.000.	
"	October 31st.	ditto	1.379.000.	
"	November 30th.	ditto	870.000.	
"	December 31st.	ditto	30.000.	
				6.000.000.

On the fourth Loan, made at Antwerp, dated the 1st. of December 1791	paid, as received, to France	2.050.000

The details of this Loan are deficient

On the fifth Loan, dated the 1st. of January 1791.

1791.	December 31st.	Received by the Commissioners		509.000.	
1792.	January 31st.	ditto		701.000.	
"	February	ditto		524.000.	
"	March	ditto		439.000.	
"	April	ditto		378.000.	
"	May	ditto		285.000.	
"	June	ditto	112.000.	164.000.	
"	July	ditto	52.000		
					3.000.000.

On the Sixth Loan, dated the 1st. of June 1792.

1792.	June 1st.	Received by the Commissioners	705.000.	
"	do	ditto	761.000.	
"	July	ditto	468.000.	
"	August	ditto	222.000.	
"	September*	payable	281.000.	
"	October	ditto	281.000.	
"	November	ditto	282.000.	
				3.000.000.

* These three sums are stated upon conjecture, the Accounts received not coming lower down, than the sixth of September.

Treasury Department,
January 3d. 1793.

Alexander Hamilton,
Secretary of the Treasury.

No. III.

A STATEMENT OF THE BILLS WHICH HAVE BEEN DRAWN BY THE TREASURER OF THE UNITED STATES, UPON THE COMMISSIONERS IN AMSTERDAM, SHEWING THE APPLICATION OF THE MONIES ARISING FROM THE SALES OF THOSE BILLS, AND THE BALANCE WHICH REMAINS UNAPPLIED.

		Florins Sts. d.	Dollars. Cts.
The Amount of Bills sold by the Banks of North America and New York, as settled at the Treasury, is		2.468.673.12. 8.	997.443.53
Amount of Interest which has arisen on the credit allowed to the Purchasers			8.082.83
Amount of Bills furnished the Secretary of State	99.000. .		
Ditto..........ditto	95.947.10.		
		194.947.10.	78.766.67.
		2.663.621. 2. 8.	1.084.293. 3.

Amount of Bills disposed of by the Bank of the United States.

			florins		dollars. Cts.		
1792.	April	17th.	500.00.	favor J. Kean at 36⁴⁄₁₁ d.	202.020.20		
	June	30th.	123.750	T. Jefferson ....do........	50.000.		
From	July	12th.					
to	Octo:	15th	1.100.000.	J. Kean ......40⁷⁄₁₀ cents	447.700.		
	Nov.	30th.	1.237.500.	T. Willink 36⁴⁄₁₀ g.	500.000.		
	Dec.	28th.	24.750.	J. Kean......do	10.000. .		
						2.986.000.	1.209.720.20.
Interest which will accrue on the Sales computed according to the terms aforesaid							10.755.90.
						5.649.621. 2. 8.	2.304.769.13.

Payments made on account of the French Debt principally for the supply of the French Colony at St. Domingo.[19]

				Dollars. Cts.
1792	February,	21st.	To the Minister plenipotentiary of France	8.325. .
	December,	15th.	..........ditto..............	5445. .
	February,	21st.	the Consul General of France	22.000. .
	March,	12th.	..........ditto..............	100.000. .
	May,	31st.	..........ditto..............	100.000. .
	September,	17th.	..........ditto..............	26.088. .
	"	28th.	..........ditto..............	17.936. .
	October,	15th.	..........ditto..............	24 660. . .
	November,	1st.	..........ditto..............	19.961. .
	"	16th.	..........ditto..............	2.358. .
	"	22d.	..........ditto..............	8.997. .
	"	30th.	..........ditto..............	64.935. 1.
	December	15th.	..........ditto..............	34.558. .
	"	31st.	..........ditto..............	10.000. .

445.263.83*

Payment of the debt due to certain foreign Officers made and to be made[20] .... 191.316.90†

Dollars,...... 636.580.73

Remarks.

* The continuing necessity of the Colony of St Domingo will call for further supplies. A decree of the National Assembly of France of the 26th. of June 1792,[21] contemplates a supply from the United States of 4.000.000 of livres, or 720.000 dollars.

† Provision has been made for the payment of the principal part of the interest of this debt, at Paris, according to stipulation. Interest upon the whole ceased on the 1st of January 1793.

The residue of the sum drawn for is applicable to the purchase of the public debt. There remains to be received, according to the terms of sale, ...Dollars,...... 632.132. 2.

Treasury Department, January 3d. 1793.

Alexander Hamilton
Secretary of the Treasury.

19. The United States had advanced money to France to purchase supplies to suppress the insurrection which had begun in Santo Domingo in August, 1791. For the negotiations on the application of payment on the French debt for the relief of Santo Domingo, see the introductory note to George Latimer to H, January 2, 1793.

20. See note 15.

21. On June 26, 1792, the Assembly decreed that "Le pouvoir exécutif est authorisé à traiter avec le ministre des Etats-Unis, afin d'en obtenir des fournitures pour Saint-Domingue, en comestibles et matières premières propres à la construction, jusqu'à la concurrence de 4 millions de livres tournois, imputables sur la dette américaine" (*Archives Parlementaires*, XLV, 594).

No IV.

A PARTICULAR STATEMENT OF THE BILLS DRAWN BY THE TREASURER OF THE UNITED STATES, SHEWING THE DIFFERENT PERIODS WHEN DRAWN —AND PAID IN AMSTERDAM—AND THE BALANCE REMAINING UNPAID ON THE SIXTH OF SEPTEMBER, 1792.

Date of the Secretary's direction.	Amount of Bills directed to be drawn	When drawn.	In whose favor.	Amount of Bills drawn by the Treasurer.	When paid in Amsterdam.	Amount of Bills paid in Amsterdam.
	Florins. Sts. d.			Florins St. d.		Florins. St. d.
1790. Dec: 15th:	25.000. . .	1790. Dec: 17th:	Tench Francis.	25.000. . .	from 21: to 28: Febry:	276.978.12. .
do.	25.000. . .	—	Wm. Seton......	25.000. . .	14-to 22 Mar:	154.608.10. .
20.	3.052.10. .	20.	Tench Francis	3.052.10. .	4-to 30: Ap:	339.786.10. 8.
22:	7.000. . .	23.	ditto	7 000. . .	16-to 26. May.	95.000. . .
30.	8.340. . .	30.	ditto	8 340. . .	31. do.	99.000. . .
31.	25.000. . .	31.	ditto	25.000. . .	6-to 27 July.	323.340. . .
1791. Jan: 1:	110.000. . .	1791.	ditto		1-to 24 Aug:	186.002.11. .
6:	100.000. . .		Wm. Seton.....		12-to 26 Sept:	40.956.11. .
13	100.000. . .	January	T: Francis......		6-to 31: Oct:	45.000. . .
27.	100.000. . .		ditto	71.000. . .	6-to 28: Dec:	39.540. . .
—	200.000. . .		Wm. Seton.....		1792 3-to 31: Jan:	792.414. 5. .
29:	100.000. . .		T. Francis......		11-to 20. Feb:	32.544.15. .
Mar. 18.	99.000. . .	March 19:	Th. Jefferson.	99.000. . .	6-to 30 Mar:	138.500. . .
May 3.	200.000. . .		T: Francis......		10: April	95.947.10. .
—	200.000. . .	—	Wm. Seton.	600.000. . .	2: May.	4.000. . .
21.	100.000. . .		ditto			
—	100.000. . .		T: Francis......			
Verbal direction	65.281. 2. 8.	June	ditto	65.281. 2. 8.		
Octo: 31:	500.000. . .	Octo &	ditto			
—	500.000. . .	Nov.	Wm. Seton.....	100.000. . .		
1792. Jan: 27:	95.947.10. .	1792 Jan: 27:	Th: Jefferson.	95.947.10. .		
	2.663.621. 2. 8.			2.663.621. 2. 8.		2.663.621. 2. 8.

Date of the Secretary's direction.	Amount of Bills directed to be drawn	When drawn.	In whose favor.	Amount of Bills drawn by the Treasurer.	When paid in Amsterdam.	Amount of Bills paid in Amsterdam.
April 17:	500.000. . .	April.	John Kean..	500.000. . .	from 2–25. July.	376.946.19. .
June 29:	123.750. . .	June 30:	Th: Jefferson.	123.750. . .	3–27. Aug:	246.803. 1
July 12:	500.000. . .	July.	John Kean.......	500.000. . .	Balance remaining	
Aug: 30:	200.000. . .	Aug:	ditto	200.000. . .	to be paid on the	2.362.250. . .
Oct. 8.	300.000. . .	Octo:	ditto	300.000. . .	6th of September	
15:	100.000. . .	—	ditto	100.000. . .	1792.	
Nov: 30:	1.237.500. . .	Dec:	Th: Willing.....	1.237.500. . .		
Decr. 28:	24.750. . .	—	John Kean.......	24.750. . .		
	2.986.000. . .			2.986.000. . .		2.986.000. . .

Remarks.

The Bills drawn from the 15th December 1790, to June 1791, inclusively, have been sold at 36⁴⁄₁₁ ninetieths of a dollar per guilder, payable in sixty days—or in ninety, with interest for thirty days.

Those drawn in October and November, 1791, have been sold at the same rate of Exchange, for cash; or on a credit not exceeding ninety days—the purchaser paying interest for the whole term of the credit.

The terms, upon which the Bills in April, 1792, have been disposed of, were a credit of six months; the first two months without interest, and the last four months with an allowance of six per cent by the purchaser—the rate of exchange as before.

In July, August and October, 1792, the rate of exchange was 40 cents and seven mills per guilder; one moiety to be paid in two, and the other moiety, in four months, with interest from the time of each sale.

In November and December 1792, the exchange was 36⁴⁄₁₁ ninetieths of a dollar.

Alexander Hamilton.
Secretary of the Treasury.

Treasury Department,
January 3d. 1793.

Report on the Several Persons Employed in the Treasury Department

Treasury Department,
January 3d. 1793.
[Communicated on January 4, 1793] [1]

[To the Speaker of the House of Representatives]
Sir,

I have the honor to transmit herewith, six lists, No. 1, 2, 3, 4, 5, 6, shewing the several persons employed in the different Offices of the Treasury Department, with the Salary allowed to each,[2] And to be, with perfect respect,

Sir, Your most obedient and humble servant,

Alexander Hamilton
Secry. of the Treasy.

The Honorable,
The Speaker of the House of Representatives

No. 1.

LIST OF PERSONS EMPLOYED IN THE OFFICE OF THE SECRETARY OF THE TREASURY OF THE UNITED STATES, WITH THEIR SALARIES ANNEXED.

Names.	Rank.	Salary.
Alexander Hamilton	Secretary of the Treasury	Dollars, 3.500.
John Meyer	principal Clerks, at	800.
Edward Jones	800 dollars each	800.
Leighton Wood	Clerk	600.
Andrew G: Fraunces	ditto	500.
Daniel Brent	ditto	500.
George Walker	ditto	500.
Sylvanus Bourne	ditto	500.
Aaron S. Lawrence	ditto	400.
George F. Bauman	Messenger and Office-keeper	250.

Treasury Department,
January 3d. 1793.

Alexander Hamilton,
Secy. of the Treasy.

Copy, RG 233, Reports of the Treasury Department, 1792–1793, Vol. III, National Archives.

1. *Journal of the House*, I, 662.
2. On December 31, 1792, the House "*Resolved,* That the Secretary of State,

No. 2.

LIST OF THE SEVERAL PERSONS EMPLOYED IN THE OFFICE OF THE COMPTROLLER OF THE TREASURY OF THE UNITED STATES ON THE 31ST. OF DECEMBER 1792, AND OF THE SALARIES PER ANNUM ALLOWED TO EACH.

Names of the persons employed.	Their rank.	Their Salary.
Oliver Wolcott, junior,	Comptroller of the Treasury	Dollars 2400.
Henry Kuhl	principal Clerk	800.
William Brodie	Clerk	600.
William M. Biddle	ditto	600.
James Shoemaker	ditto	500.
William Irvine	ditto	500.
James Graham	ditto	500.
Alexander Brodie	ditto	500.
Charles Jarvis	ditto	500.
Gervas Hall	ditto	500.
John P: Ripley	ditto	300.
John Borrows	Messenger and Office-keeper.	200.

Treasury Department,
Comptroller's Office, January 3d. 1793.
Oliv: Wolcott, junr. Comptroller

No. 3.

LIST OF PERSONS EMPLOYED IN THE OFFICE OF THE COMMISSIONER OF THE REVENUE.

Names.	Station.	Salary ꝑ ann.	
Tench Coxe,	Commissioner of the revenue,	1900.	
William Barton	principal Clerk	800.	
			2.700.
John Mease	Clerk	400.	
Peter Footman	"	400.	
Ezekiel Forman	"	400.	
			1.200.
Michael Gitts	Messenger and Office-keeper	200.	200.
		Dollars.	4.100.

Treasury Office,
Revenue Office January 3d. 1793.

Tench Coxe
Commr. of the Revenue.

---

the Secretary of the Treasury, and the Secretary of War, be directed to lay before this House lists of the several persons employed in the offices of their respective Departments, with the salaries allowed to each" (*Journal of the House*, I, 658).

No. 4

LIST OF PERSONS EMPLOYED IN THE OFFICE OF THE AUDITOR OF THE TREASURY OF THE UNITED STATES.

Names.	Station.	Salary ℔ annum	Total Amount
		Dollars.	
Richard Harrison.	Auditor	1900.	
William Simmons.	Principal Clerk	800.	2700.
George Nixon	Clerk	540.	
Robert Underwood	"	540.	
James Burnside	"	600.	
William Blackburn	"	450.	
Ezekiel Freeman	"	500.	
John Crosby	"	500.	
Doyle Sweeny	"	640.	
Clement C. Brown	"	800.	
Morgan Sweeny	"	350.	
Richard Reddy	"	450.	
John White	"	500.	
John Gibson	"	420.	
John Stapleton	"	420.	
William Aldricks	"	420.	
Michael Forrest	"	350.	7480.
Joseph Bowman,	Messenger	250.	250.
			10.430 Dollars.

Treasury Department,
Auditor's Office, January 3d. 1793

R. Harrison.

No. 5.

LIST OF PERSONS EMPLOYED IN THE OFFICE OF THE TREASURER OF THE UNITED STATES, WITH THEIR SALARIES ANNEXED.

Names.	Rank.	Salary.	
Samuel Meredith.	Treasurer of the United States	Dollars,	2400.
Andrew Graydon,	Chief Clerk		800.
John Thomson	Clerk		500.
Samuel Brook	ditto		300.
Alexander Frazier	Messenger & Office keeper		100.

Treasury of the United States
January 3d. 1793.

Samuel Meredith
Treasurer of the United States.

No. 6.

LIST OF THE SEVERAL PERSONS EMPLOYED IN THE OFFICE OF THE REGISTER OF THE TREASURY, WITH THE SALARIES ALLOWED TO EACH.

Clerks.	Joshua Dawson	Dollars.	700.
	William Banks		700.
	Joseph Stretch		700.
	Miles F. Clossy		700.
	Jacob S. Howell		700.
	John Woodside		650.
	Thomas O:Hara		600.
	Charles Tomkins		550.
	John Finley		550.
	Matthew Walker		500.
	John Little		500.
	John Hindman		500.
	John Burchan		500.
	William P. Gardner		500.
	John Woodward		400.
	Edward O:Hara		400.
	John Boyd		400.
	Richard Banks		400.
	Gabriel Nourse		400.
	William Storey		400.
	George Sibbald		400.
	Michael Kennedy		400.
	William James		400.
	Stewart Cummin		400.
	John Matthews		400.
	Charles Wilson		400.
	William Sheppard		300.
	James Stewart		300.
	Samuel Clindonnon		300.
	George Mitchell		266.66
	David Rittenhouse		266.66
	William Nourse		250.
	Michael Nourse		200.
	John Woodside junior		150.
		Total for Clerks, Dollrs.	15.183.32
	Leonard Hideley, Andrew Wright	Keepers of the several Offices at 175. Dollars, each, is	350.
	Joseph Nourse, Register		1750.
		Dollars,	17.283.32

Treasury Department,
Register's Office, 3d January 1793.

Joseph Nourse, Register

To George Bush

Treasury Department, January 4, 1793. "Your letter under date of the 24th. ulto [1] has been received. What you observe in regard to the . . . mercantile interest in your district, shall be duly attended to."

Copy, RG 56, Letters to Collectors at Small Ports, "Set G," National Archives.

1. Letter not found.

From Tench Coxe

Treasury Department, Revenue Office, January 4, 1793. "I have the honor to inform you that on the receipt of Mr. J. N. Cummings's letter to you [1] relative to the case of Mathias Brewer, I wrote to him for information on certain points, which appeared necessary.[2] I desired him to communicate the same, with a general State of the Case, to the Supervisor. . . .[3] I am in daily expectation of the papers and letters when I shall proceed in the adjustment of the matter."

LC, RG 58, Letters of Commissioner of Revenue, 1792–1793, National Archives.

1. Letter not found. John N. Cumming of Newark, New Jersey, the operator of a stagecoach line, was active in procuring workmen for the Society for Establishing Useful Manufactures and in 1793 was elected a director of the society. He also served as a revenue officer in Newark.
2. The "case of Mathias Brewer" concerned a distillery in New Jersey. On December 31, 1792, Coxe asked Cumming for information on this case, requesting him to state "whether the distillery is in a city, town or village, and what is the aggregate of the contents of all the Stills therein, also furnish copies of the entry by him made, and of the License by you granted" (LC, RG 58, Letters of Commissioner of Revenue, 1792–1793, National Archives).
3. Aaron Dunham.

From Tench Coxe

Treasury Department, Revenue Office, January 4, 1793. Discusses a "plan of repairs of the light House on Tybee Island at the Mouth of the Savannah River." [1]

LC, RG 58, Letters of Commissioner of Revenue, 1792–1793, National Archives.

1. According to a notice in the [Philadelphia] *National Gazette* for December 5, 1792, "Savanna Light House on Tybee island took fire about a month since, when the wooded work was entirely consumed."

To Thomas Jefferson

Treasury Department
Jany: 4 179[3] [1]

Sir

I have the honor to inclose you the Copy of a letter I have received from Mr Geo Latimer of this City relating to some concerns of his, with the Govt of St Domingo,[2] to which I have answered in substance as heretofore communicated to you on a similar subject.[3]

I have the honour to be with Respect Sir Your Obed Servt
A Hamilton

The Secretary of State

LS, Thomas Jefferson Papers, Library of Congress.

1. H misdated this letter "1792."
2. Latimer to H, January 2, 1793.
3. See Ambrose Vasse to H, November 21, 1792; H to Vasse, December 14, 1792; James Waters to H, December 6, 1792; H to Waters, December 10, 1792. These letters were transmitted to Jefferson on December 14, 1792. No letter from H to Latimer has been found.

To Tobias Lear

[*Philadelphia*] *January 4, 1793.* ". . . The Statements [1] went in yesterday, and are copying for the President."

LC, George Washington Papers, Library of Congress.

1. This is a reference to copies of the statements enclosed in "Report on Foreign Loans," January 3, 1793.

From Joseph Nourse

Treasury Department, Register's Office, January 4, 1793. Encloses "three Statemts. from the Treasury Books of the Appropriation of Ten Thousand Dollars granted 26 March 1790 [1] for the Purpose of defraying the Contingent Expences of Governt. leaving a Balance due thereon the first of this Month of Eight thousand Three hundred and two Dollars and fifty Cents." [2]

LC, RG 53, Estimates and Statements for 1793, Vol. "135–T," National Archives; LC, RG 53, dated January 3, 1792, Estimates and Statements for 1793, Vol. "135–T," National Archives. At the top of the copy dated January 3 the following note is written: "This letter was not sent." The wording of this copy differs slightly from the copy printed above.

1. Section 3 of "An Act making appropriations for the support of government for the year one thousand seven hundred and ninety" reads: "That the President of the United States be authorized to draw from the treasury a sum not exceeding ten thousand dollars, for the purpose of defraying the contingent charges of government, to be paid out of the monies arising as aforesaid from the duties on imports and tonnage; and that he cause a regular statement and account of such expenditures to be laid before Congress at the end of the year" (1 *Stat.* 105).

The enclosures mentioned in this letter may be found in RG 53, Estimates and Statements for 1793, Vol. "135-T," National Archives.

2. At the bottom of this letter the following statements appear:

"By Direction of the Secy of the Treasury the aforesaid Amount is to be drawn out Yearly.

"By Direction of the President of the United States the aforesaid Amount was varied being drawn out so as to comprise the Actual Expenditures of the Year 1792 only."

To George Washington

Treasury Department, January 4, 1793. Submits to the President two communications from Tench Coxe "suggesting certain alterations in the arrangement heretofore made, within the Revenue, District of North Carolina." [1] Proposes minor changes.

LC, George Washington Papers, Library of Congress.

1. See Coxe to H, December 13, 21, 1792.

To Richard Harison

Philadelphia January 5 1793

Dear Sir

Mr. Le Roy [1] has not yet appeared, with the Powers and Receipts mentioned in your letter of the 31 of December.[2] Every practicable facility will be given to the business, when it comes forward. But I believe, according to the course of the Treasury, a Certificate, not money, will be given for the ballance.

Your account is returned with directory remarks upon it. I am sorry you should have the trouble of so many different applications; but the course of public business requires it.

I am more sorry that we have been deprived of the pleasure of seeing you. Every friend I see, from a place I love, is a cordial to me—and I stand in need of something of that kind now and then.

The triumphs of Vice are no new things under the sun. And I fear, 'till the Millenium comes, in spight of all our boasted light and purification—hypochrisy and Treachery will continue to be the most successful commodities in the political Market. It seems to be the destined lot of Nations to mistake their foes for their friends; their flatterers for their faithful servants.

Adieu Believe me with true esteem and regard
Your obedient ser A Hamilton

Richard Harrison Esqr
New York

ALS, New-York Historical Society, New York City; copy, Hamilton Papers, Library of Congress.

1. Herman Le Roy was a New York City merchant.

2. Letter not found.

Report on the Petition of Timothy de Monbreun[1]

[*Philadelphia, January 5, 1793.* An entry in the *Journal of the House* for January 5, 1793, reads as follows: "The Speaker laid before the House a letter and report from the Secretary of the Treasury on the memorial of Timothy de Monbreun[2] which were read." *Letter and report not found.*]

Journal of the House, I, 662.

1. On December 7, 1792, "A memorial of Timothy de Monbreun was presented to the House and read, praying compensation for supplies furnished, and services rendered, to the United States, whilst a Lieutenant in Colonel Clark's, or the Illinois regiment, raised by the State of Virginia, during the late war.

"*Ordered*, That the said memorial be referred to the Secretary of the Treasury, with instruction to examine the same, and report his opinion thereupon to the House." (*Journal of the House*, I, 635.)

After H's report was read on January 5, 1793, the House "*Resolved*, That the memorialist have leave to withdraw his said memorial" (*Journal of the House*, I, 662).

2. Jacques Timothé Boucher, Sieur de Monbreun, a former resident of Kaskaskia, had joined George Rogers Clark's Illinois regiment on May 12, 1780, as a lieutenant. On March 5, 1782, he wrote to Clark requesting either his "pay of Lieutenant in good money or in merchandise" or a discharge from the Army, but did not ask for money due for supplies (James, *Clark Papers*, 41–42). No mention has been found of supplies furnished by De Monbreun in Clark's accounts, and the statement of the Virginia commissioners appointed to examine Clark's accounts states that only the sum of six hundred and forty

dollars in back pay was due to De Monbreun and recommends payment (James, *Clark Papers*, 320).

Although the Virginia commissioners ignored the question of money owed him for supplies furnished during the American Revolution, De Monbreun indicated in a memorial addressed to the Virginia House of Delegates on November 11, 1794, that he had incurred obligations for supplies delivered to the Indians when he was commandant of Kaskaskia shortly after the American Revolution. His memorial defines his services as follows: ". . . your memorialist was a Lieutenant in Colonel Clark's or the Illinois Regiment raised by this State during the late war; that after the disbanding of that Regiment, to wit, on the 18th of January 1783, he was appointed Commandant of KasKaskias and the neighbourhood in which post he continued until the 14th day of August 1786. . . . These operations were attended with considerable expence to your Memorialist, who, as there was no provision made by law to defray those contingent charges, was absolutely compelled to entertain and supply with provisions all the Indians, of the several tribes who came to KasKasKies; besides, policy required, that small presents should be made to them, in order to preserve their friendship." De Monbreun's letter and accounts are printed in Clarence Walworth Alvord, *Kaskaskia Records, 1778–1790*, "Collections of the Illinois State Historical Library," V, Virginia Series (Springfield, 1909), 355–58.

To George Washington

Treasury Departmt. 5 Jany. 1793.

The Secretary of the Treasury has the honor respectfully to enclose to the President of the United States copies of certain statements No. 1. 2. 3 & 4, which have been rendered to the House of representatives pursuant to a resolution of the House of the 27 of Decembr. last.[1]

A Hamilton

LC, George Washington Papers, Library of Congress.

1. See "Report on Foreign Loans," January 3, 1793.

To William Rawle[1]

[Philadelphia] Jany 6. 1793

Dr Sir

I think you have a paper shewing the manner in which, the tracts to which Judge Sims & his associates are intitled were to be located—put into your hands for the purpose of drawing up a declaration &c concerning it.

Be so good as to let Mr. Ludlow, who on behalf of the UStates is preparing a map,[2] have a view of any such paper which may be in your possession.

Yrs. with esteem A Hamilton

Mr. Rawle

ALS, Historical Society of Pennsylvania, Philadelphia.

1. Rawle was a prominent Philadelphia lawyer and United States attorney for the District of Pennsylvania.

2. John Cleves Symmes of Morristown, New Jersey, who had served in the Continental Congress in 1785 and 1786, had been a judge of the Northwest Territory since 1788. Under the Confederation Symmes had applied for a large tract of land in the Ohio country, and on October 15, 1788, "the late Board of Treasury, by virtue of resolutions of Congress of the twenty-third and twenty-seventh of July, and twenty-third of October, one thousand seven hundred and eighty-seven, contracted with John Cleves Symmes and his associates, for a tract of land lying in the Western country, and bounded westwardly by the Great Miami, southwardly by the Ohio, eastwardly by a line beginning on the Ohio, at a spot twenty miles distant, and above the mouth of the Great Miami, and extending from the said spot in a course parallel with the general course of the Great Miami, and northwardly by a line running due east and west, from the last mentioned line to the Great Miami, so as to include one million of acres" (*ASP, Public Lands,* I, 75). In November, 1790, in response to a Congressional resolution of August 12, 1790, H had authorized Israel Ludlow to survey the Symmes purchase (Arthur St. Clair to H, May 25, 1791, note 2), but the unsettled conditions on the frontier resulting from the Indian war of 1791 and the continued depredations of the Indians during 1792 made it impossible for Ludlow to complete his survey (Ludlow to H, May 5, 1792). Because Symmes both claimed and sold land not included in his contract, Congress on April 12, 1792, passed "An Act for ascertaining the bounds of a tract of land purchased by John Cleves Symmes." This act authorized the President to "alter the contract, made between the late board of treasury and the said John Cleves Symmes, for the sale of a tract of land of one million acres" and defined the boundary "so as to comprehend the proposed quantity of one million of acres" (6 *Stat.* 7–8). On May 5, 1792, another act of Congress transferred ownership to Symmes and his associates "in fee simple, such number of acres of land as the payments already made by the said John Cleves Symmes, his agents or associates, under their contract of the fifteenth day of October one thousand seven hundred and eighty-eight, will pay for," together with a further tract of 106,837 acres ("An Act authorizing the grant and conveyance of certain Lands to John Cleves Symmes, and his Associates" [1 *Stat.* 266]). In November, 1792, H again ordered Ludlow to undertake the survey of the Miami lands (H to Ludlow, November 25, 1792).

From Edmund Randolph[1]

Philadelphia Jany. 7. 1793.

Sir

When I first read your letter, inclosing the cession of Montok-point,[2] I suspected, that it would be necessary to travel into a wide constitutional field. I was apprehensive, that I should be obliged to inquire, whether congress, even if they were so disposed, could accept a cession, with a reservation of state-jurisdiction. But when I adverted to the act, which directs a light-house to be built on Montok-point, it became obvious, that congress did not mean to accept this cession, with a mutilated jurisdiction. The words are: "As soon as the jurisdiction shall have been ceded:" that is, as soon as New-York shall have relinquished her jurisdiction. It is manifest, that this has not been done; and therefore the act of New-York is not commensurate with the act of congress.[3]

I have the honor, sir, to be with great respect Yr. mo. ob. serv.
Edm: Randolph.

The Secretary of the Treasury.

ALS, RG 26, Lighthouse Letters Received, Vol. "C," Connecticut and New York, National Archives.

1. For background to this letter, see Tench Coxe to H, January 3, 1793.

2. Letter not found.

3. H transmitted this opinion to Coxe. In a letter dated January 11, 1793, Coxe sent Randolph's opinion to John Laurence, Representative from New York, and concluded: "Under these circumstances it is the opinion of the Secretary of the Treasury, that the copy act of the legislature of the State of New York, should be returned to you from whom it was received with a statement of what has occured upon the subject" (LC, RG 58, Letters of Commissioner of Revenue, 1792–1793, National Archives).

From Jean Baptiste de Ternant

[*Philadelphia, January 7, 1793.* On January 13, 1793, Hamilton wrote to Ternant: "drafts cannot be made at the Treasury as desired by your letter of the seventh instant." *Letter not found.*]

From Thomas Pinckney

London 8th. Janry 1793.

My dear Sir

I am informed by Messrs: Bird, Savage and Bird[1] Merchants of this City that a scheme is in agitation for the payment in London of the interest on that part of the American funds which is in Europe through the medium of Agents to be appointed by the Bank of the United States;[2] as they wish in conjunction with another respectable house to obtain this Agency they very judiciously think that your support would greatly strengthen their application to the President & Directors of the Bank & have requested of me a letter of recommendation to you on the Subject—& I accede to the proposal without reluctance as I am persuaded that private application never influences your mind in public appointments at the same time that the testimony of those acquainted with the applicants will have such weight as it merits. With respect to the present business I can only inform you that the gentlemen who compose this house are respectable in their private capacities as well as in their mercantile transactions, & as far as my information goes very well connected here; they are known to have had considerable concerns in the American funds already which it is their present object to continue & to evince that I do not recommend where I have not a confidence all my transactions in the money line pass through their hands; which tho' not considerable are of importance to me.

Your letter to Messrs: Vanstaphors [3] &c was brought to me yesterday by the Captn of the New Pigon & shall be sent by this days mail.

I have the honor to be with the utmost respect dear Sir Your most obedient and most humble Servant Thomas Pinckney

ALS, Hamilton Papers, Library of Congress.

1. The firm of Henry Martins Bird, Benjamin Savage, and Robert Bird.

2. This may have been the plan referred to by H in his letter of November 5, 1792, to William Short.

3. H to Willink, Van Staphorst, and Hubbard, November 5, 1792. This letter had been enclosed in H to Pinckney, November 5, 1792.

To Tench Coxe

[*Philadelphia, January 10, 1793.* On January 12, 1793, Coxe wrote to Hamilton: "Agreeably to your Note of the 10th instant, I have the honor to inclose to you a draught of an Act." *Letter not found.*]

From James O'Hara

Pittsburgh January 10, 1793

Sir,

Being absent on Special business, I had not the honor to answer your letter on the 18th ulto.[1] sooner.

Your regulation respecting the settling of my Accounts shall certainly be as strictly observ'd as the nature of the service will admit of.

The various sums of money which I am Obliged to advance for collecting the necessary supplies from the extensive Frontiers, and the scatter'd situation of the troops render'd it impossible to exhibit the Accounts to the Treasury of the United States at the expiration of every quarter, regular as I could wish. They shall be immediately attended to and furnished as soon as possible.

I have the honor to be Sir Your Mst. Obt. humble Servant

James O'Hara, QmG

LC, RG 92, Journal of the Quartermaster General James O'Hara, April 19, 1792–May 17, 1794, National Archives.

1. Letter not found.

Report on Foreign Loans. Supplementary Statement Showing the Sums Borrowed in the United States

Treasury Department,
January 10th. 1793.
[Communicated on January 11, 1793][1]

[To the Speaker of the House of Representatives]
Sir,

The Resolution of the House of Representatives of the 27th of December last,[2] having been considered as contemplating foreign Loans only, the Statements rendered to the House on the 3d instant, were confined merely to those objects.

But lest a greater latitude should have been intended by that resolution, I have the honor to transmit herewith a supplementary Statement, No. V, which contains the several sums that have been borrowed in the United States, under the authority of the President; and to be, with perfect respect,

Sir, Your most obedient servant, Alexander Hamilton,
Secretary of the Treasury.

The Honorable, The Speaker
of the House of Representatives.

V

A STATEMENT OF THE MONIES WHICH HAVE BEEN BORROWED IN THE UNITED STATES, BY THE GOVERNMENT, AND APPLIED PURSUANT TO SEVERAL ACTS OF CONGRESS.

Under the Act, intituled "An Act making appropriations for the support of Government for the year 1790," [3] the following sums were borrowed from the Bank of New York, and applied, as specified in the said Act, Viz:

1790, March 31st	30.000. dollars.
April 8th	25.000.
	55,000. dollars,

at the rate of six per centum per annum, from the respective dates mentioned, to the 14th. May 1790, when the loan was reimbursed.

Pursuant to the Act, intituled "An Act for raising a farther sum of money for the protection of the frontiers, and for other purposes therein mentioned," [4] a loan has been obtained from the Bank of the United States, agreeably to a contract with the said Bank, dated the 25th of May 1792, of 523,000* dollars, at the rate of five per cent per annum, reimbursable at the pleasure of the United States; upon which loan, there has been received in the treasury, in the following instalments, and applied to the purpose, for which it was appropriated,

100.000. dollars, on the 1st of June, 1792.
100.000. do. 1st of July, do.
100.000. do. 1st of August do.
100.000. do. 1st of September do.†

The interest accruing on the said instalments to the 1st of January 1793, was made payable on that day and thenceforth until the reimbursement of the principal, the interest on the whole is to be paid half-yearly, namely, on the 1st of July, and on the 1st of January in each year.

The surplus of the duties laid by the Act before mentioned, to be applied, as the same shall accrue, to the reimbursement of the principal and interest.

Errata. *The true Sum, agreeably to contract, was 523,500. dollars.
† This sum was not received 'till the 28th of September.

Pursuant to the Act, entitled "An Act to incorporate the subscribers to the Bank of the United States," [5] a loan has been made by the said Bank to the United States, of 2.000.000 dollars, at the rate of six per cent per annum, reimbursable, in ten years, by equal annual instalments, or at any time sooner, or in any greater proportions that the Government may think fit.

This loan has been applied, as directed by the Act, under which it was borrowed.

The time, when the interest commenced, on one million of dollars of the said loan, is coincident with the time, when the dividend upon the Stock of the Bank began to accrue, namely, the 20th of December 1791—upon the remaining one million of dollars, interest commenced on the 1st of July 1792.

Treasury Department. Alexander Hamilton,
January 10th 1793 Secretary of the Treasury.

Copy, RG 233, Reports of the Treasury Department, 1792–1793, Vol. III, National Archives.

1. *Journal of the House*, I, 668.
2. See "Report on Foreign Loans," January 3, 1793, note 3.
3. 1 *Stat.* 104–06 (March 26, 1790).
4. 1 *Stat.* 259–63 (May 2, 1792).
5. 1 *Stat.* 191–96 (February 25, 1791).

Remarks on a Request by Jean Baptiste de Ternant

[Philadelphia] Friday, January 11th: 1793.

The Secretary of the Treasury waited upon the President on the subject of the papers which were put into his hands yesterday,[1] and observed.

That the advance required by the French Consuls could be made without any inconvenience to the Treasury of the U. S. but as the U. S. had already paid to France the amot. of what was due to her *at present*, and as the unsettled State of things in France made it uncertain whether, when they shall have formed a permanent government, they will agree to allow of the advance thus made, the Secretary thought it was a matter which required weighty consideration and gave it as his opinion, that the President had better take the sentiments of the heads of the Departments on the subject. Which meeting the President's ideas, the Gentlemen were requested to attend the President tomorrow morning at nine O'clock.[2]

JPP, 5.

1. On January 10, 1793, Thomas Jefferson "laid before the President a letter from the Minister of France, and certain papers relative to an advance of money which the Consul Genl. of France had requested from the Treasury of the U. S. in behalf of himself and the other French Consuls in the U. S. for their support, as they found it impracticable to obtain their allowance by disposing of Bills on Paris. This advance, if made, they suggest, may be placed to the Acct. of the Debt due from the United States to France.

"These papers were put into the hands of the Secretary of the Treasury, with a request that he would take them into consideration, and see the President upon them tomorrow morning." (JPP, 4–5.)

See also H to George Washington, December 29, 1792; Washington to H, January 1, 1793.

2. An entry in JPP for January 12, 1793, reads as follows: "The Heads of the Departments and the Attorney General of the United States, waited on the President this morning at nine o'clock, according to appointment, and took into consideration the request of the French Consul General for an advance of money for the support of the French Consuls residing in the U.S. when it was thought proper to comply with the request" (JPP, 7).

From Tench Coxe

Treasury Department, Revenue Office, January 12, 1793. "Agreeably to your Note of the 10th instant,[1] I have the honor to inclose to you a draught of an Act of the President of the United States, calculated to establish certain alterations of the Revenue Arrangement in the District of North Carolina,[2] conforming with what I presume from your said note to be the pleasure of the President. . . ."

LC, RG 58, Letters of Commissioner of Revenue, 1792–1793, National Archives.

1. Letter not found.

2. See Coxe to H, December 13, 21, 1792; H to George Washington, January 4, 1793.

To Jean Baptiste de Ternant[1]

Treasury Department
January 13. 1793

Sir

I think it proper to apprise you that under the existing circumstances the Registry of your "delegations" or drafts cannot be made at the Treasury as desired by your letter of the seventh instant.[2]

With respect I have the honor to be Sir Your obedient servant
Alexander Hamilton

The Minister Plenipotentiary
of the Republic of France

ALS, *Arch. des Aff. Etr., Corr. Pol., Etats-Unis*, Vol. 20.

1. For background to this letter, see the introductory note to George Latimer to H, January 2, 1793.

2. No letter of this date from Ternant to H has been found. This may be a reference to Ternant to Thomas Jefferson, February 7, 1793 (letterpress copy, Thomas Jefferson Papers, Library of Congress) concerning Santo Domingo. In his letter to Jefferson of January 7, Ternant transmitted a request made to him by Léger Félicité Sonthonax, one of the civil commissioners of Santo Domingo, for additional aid (Sonthonax to Ternant, December 9, 1792, letterpress copy, Thomas Jefferson Papers, Library of Congress). Ternant also requested that the United States assume responsibility for the drafts which had been issued by the government of Santo Domingo and had not yet been settled, and for a further sum of money to complete the four million livres voted by the French Assembly in its decree of June 26, 1792.

On January 14 Jefferson wrote to Ternant to inform him that the President had approved the French Minister's proposal. Jefferson then added: "I have however, Sir, to ask the favor of you to take arrangements with the Administration of St. Domingo, so as that future supplies from us, should they be necessary, may be negotiated here, before they are counted on and drawn for there. Bills on the French Agents here to be paid by us, amount to Bills on us; and it is absolutely necessary that we be not subject to calls, which have not been before calculated and provided for . . ." (letterpress copy, Thomas Jefferson Papers, Library of Congress).

Washington's approval of this arrangement was given in Tobias Lear to Jefferson, January 14, 1793 (ALS, RG 59, Miscellaneous Letters, 1790–1799, National Archives).

Draft of Instructions for William Hull[1]

[*Philadelphia, January 14, 1793.* On January 14, 1793, George Washington recorded in the "Journal of the Proceedings of the President" that "The Secretary of the Treasury submitted . . . a draft of Instructions to be given to General Hull who is to go into Canada to purchase provisions for the treaty to be held with the hostile Indians in the Spring at Au Glaize."[2] *Draft not found.*]

JPP, 13.

1. Hull, a native of Derby, Connecticut, had served as a lieutenant colonel in a Massachusetts regiment during the American Revolution. After the war he settled in Newton, Massachusetts, where he practiced law. In 1784 Congress sent him to Canada on an unsuccessful mission to demand the surrender of the posts held by the British in violation of the terms of the 1783 treaty. In January, 1793, Hull was appointed the agent to arrange with Governor John Graves

Simcoe for the purchase of supplies for the proposed meeting with the western Indians in the spring.

2. For the proposed meeting between the commissioners of the United States and the western Indians, see "Conversation with George Hammond," November 22, 1792, note 4. See also "Conversation with George Hammond," December 15–28, 1792; H to Hammond, December 29, 1792.

Although H's draft has not been found, Hull's instructions are described by his biographer as follows: "His instructions were, to explain to Governor Simcoe, then Governor of Upper Canada, the manner in which the savages were supplied with the munitions of war, provisions and clothing, by the Agents of Indian Affairs, and the commanding officers of the British garrisons at Detroit, Michilimackinac, and other places conveniently situated for the purpose. He was likewise authorized to hold treaties with the Indians, and inform them that the President of the United States would appoint Commissioners the next summer to meet them at Sandusky or any other convenient place, with full authority to settle all differences and to bury the hatchet. He was further directed to make arrangements with Governor Simcoe, that there should be no impediment in the passage of the Commissioners over Lakes Ontario and Erie, with the supplies for the treaty" (Maria Campbell, *Revolutionary Services and Civil Life of General William Hull; Prepared from His Manuscripts, by His Daughter, Mrs. Maria Campbell: Together with the History of the Campaign of 1812, and Surrender of the Post of Detroit, by His Grandson, James Freeman Clarke* [New York, 1848], 254–55).

From James Tillary[1]

[New York, January 14, 1793]

Sir

Mr Mulligan[2] will have the honor of seeing you in Phila. & promised to deliver this letter personally. It incloses 200 Dolls, which I have been indebted to you a most unconscionable length of time. When Mr Childs[3] was in Phila. about a year ago, he was commissioned by me (having then the needful of my property) to discharge my pecuniary obligations to you. But disappointments pressed so severely upon him that he excused himself to me in the best way he could for not doing as I directed him.

The Baron[4] who is now with you, took up his note a few days before he left us & paid me every farthing. But what need I trouble you with a long story.

You lent me some money to serve me at a time when an act of friendship had embarrassed me, & I now return it to you with a Thousand thanks, the only Interest, I shall offer at present. The fact is I have had your money so long that I don't recollect when my note was given—besides on *such occasions* I am a very bad Accountant. I might give you a dish of Local Politics, but your supplies on that score issue from many sources of more competent information. I flatter myself that I have been, & shall be, in some measure, useful in keeping from Congress that Whore in Politics ⟨– –⟩.[5] The Chancellor is removed from the Presidency of the Scotch Socty.[6] & that has been ascribed to my interference.

The truth is I wish't to make the whole family unpopular, because in my Judgement, by their apostacy[7] they had rendered themselves quite odious.

If you can lay your hands on my *Note* you will oblige me by sending it.

Success, Honor, & long life to you James Tillary

N. York Jany. 14

ALS, Hamilton Papers, Library of Congress.

1. Tillary was a New York City physician and politician.

2. John W. Mulligan was a graduate of Columbia College who in 1791 had become Baron von Steuben's private secretary.

3. Francis Childs was publisher of *The* [New York] *Daily Advertiser.*

4. After the American Revolution Steuben had settled in New York City where he engaged in various business enterprises. After the New York State legislature in 1786 had granted him sixteen thousand acres of land near Utica, he divided his time between New York City and his estates. While in New York City he lived in an apartment owned by Tillary. See Tillary to H, March 6, 1792.

5. The name on the MS has been inked over, but presumably the reference is to William S. Livingston, the Republican candidate for Congress from New York City in 1792. When he had been elected to the New York Assembly in 1791, he had received considerable Federalist support, but during 1792 he had become closely allied with the family of Robert R. Livingston of Clermont, the chancellor of the state of New York, and generally supported the chancellor's policies. Tillary's epithet may also refer to Livingston's unsuccessful attempt to secure the political support of the Mechanic's Society with a claim that while serving in the Assembly he had secured legislative approval of its charter.

6. The St. Andrew's Society of New York City.

7. This is a reference to the defection of the Livingston family from the Federalist party. Although Robert R. Livingston, political leader of the Clermont branch of the Livingston family, had supported the Federalists in 1789, he allied himself with Governor George Clinton in 1790. The dissatisfaction of the Livingston family with the Federalists has generally been attributed to the fact that the members of that family received no patronage under the new Federal Government.

From Wilhem and Jan Willink, Nicholaas and Jacob Van Staphorst, and Nicholas Hubbard

[*Amsterdam, January 14, 1793.* On March 15, 1793, Hamilton wrote to Willink, Van Staphorst, and Hubbard: "I received . . . the letter . . . of the 14 of January last." *Letter not found.*]

From Alexander Dallas[1]

[Philadelphia, January 15, 1793]

Sir.

I have received the enclosed letter from Mr. Gallatine,[2] one of the Members of the General Assembly, of this State, respecting the subject, on which we conversed some days ago; and I will esteem it a particular favour, if you will enable me to make an early answer to the questions which he proposes.

I am, with the sincerest esteem and respect Sir, Your most obedt. serv A. J. Dallas Secy

Secretary's Office
Phila., 15th Jany 1793

Be pleased to return the letter after perusal.

To Alexander Hamilton, esqr.

Copy, Division of Public Records, Pennsylvania Historical and Museum Commission, Harrisburg; LC, Division of Public Records, Pennsylvania Historical and Museum Commission.

1. Dallas was secretary of the Commonwealth of Pennsylvania. For background to this letter, see John Nicholson to H, July 26, 1792, note 1.

2. In 1780 Albert Gallatin emigrated from his native Geneva and settled in Fayette County, Pennsylvania. In 1788 he took part in the Harrisburg convention which had been called to find means of amending the Federal Constitution. The following year he sat in the convention which revised the Pennsylvania constitution. From October, 1790, until his election to the United States Senate in February, 1793, Gallatin was a member of the Pennsylvania House of Representatives, and at the time this letter was written he was a member of the committee on ways and means in the Pennsylvania House. It was to this committee that a letter written to the Pennsylvania House by Christian Febiger, treasurer of Pennsylvania, on January 1, 1793, was referred. Febiger's letter accused John Nicholson, comptroller general of Pennsylvania, of speculating in "new loan" certificates on which Febiger calculated that Nicholson had made a profit of approximately twenty-five percent. Febiger's letter led to the impeachment proceedings against Nicholson in the Pennsylvania legislature (Hogan, *Pennsylvania State Trials*, 67–69).

[ENCLOSURE]

Albert Gallatin to Alexander Dallas [3]

[Philadelphia, January 14, 1793]

Sir,

I have read with attention the letter of the Secretary of the Treasury of the U. S. dated 21 December, 1791,[4] and the two letters of the Comptroller-General dated 24th December, 1791,[5] and 29th of February, 1792,[6] relative to the construction of the 18th section of the Act of Congress making provision for the debt of the U. S.[7] It appears to me that the word "*those*" in the enacting part of the clause can only apply to the certificates issued by the State, but as that never could be the meaning of the Act of Congress, I agree that the construction given by the Secretary is the only rational one. Be that as it may, it is very certain that neither the New-Loan certificates of *Pennsylvania*, remaining in circulation, nor the Continental certificates in exchange for which these New-Loans had been issued, have been surrendered to the U. S. It is not less certain that the payment of interest, whether to the state or to individuals has not been suspended, the present suspension to the state is but temporary, and arises merely from the extension of the former law of Congress by their Act of last May, and will of course cease on the first of March next, (if the former objections are not revived) and of course it must have appeared to the satisfaction of the Secretary of the Treasury that all the New-Loan certificates have been re-exchanged or redeemed. To have considered them as such is I suppose, what the Comptroller means by the "equitable decision" [8] of

3. Hogan, *Pennsylvania State Trials*, 74–76.
4. H to Thomas Mifflin, December 21, 1791.
5. See Mifflin to H, December 27, 1791, note 1.
6. See Nicholson to H, January 18, 1792, note 1.
7. Section 18 of "An Act making provision for the (payment of the) Debt of the United States" (1 *Stat.* 138–44 [August 4, 1790]) reads as follows: "Be it further enacted, that the payment of interest whether to states or to individuals, in respect to the debt of any state, by which such exchange shall have been made, shall be suspended, until it shall appear to the satisfaction of the secretary of the treasury, that certificates issued for that purpose by such state, have been re-exchanged or redeemed, or until those which shall not have been re-exchanged or redeemed, shall be surrendered to the United States."
8. Gallatin is referring to the opinion expressed by Nicholson in his letter to Mifflin, February 29, 1792. See Nicholson to H, January 18, 1792, note 1.

the Secretary. It is however of importance to us to know what were the real grounds of that decision, as it is possible that the subscription made lately in New-Loan certificates to the loan of the U. S. may affect it materially. For if the Secretary considered the whole of the New-Loan certificates as actually re-exchanged or redeemed, it must have been, because the state law which entitled the holders to such an exchange might been supposed to have been altogether carried into effect, since not a single of those certificates had been offered for subscription to the loan of the U. S. But as some have been offered since the extension of the loan took place, that circumstance may induce him to alter his opinion, and indeed I cannot well understand how he may suppose himself justifiable in looking upon the whole amount as being actually re-exchanged, whilst he has got it in proof, that some of them are not so. Upon the first impression I should be led to think that the Secretary having once declared (by his allowing the interest not to be suspended) that the whole amount was re-exchanged (and that upon the information of the state officer) will now look upon them in the same light and return them as not assumable, an opinion which I think, may also be supported on different ground both from the nature of the certificates themselves and from the state law of 1789,[9] which declared the state not to be liable for the payment of the principal.

However as the whole of this reasoning is mostly conjectural, as the decision of the Secretary may, under the present circumstances, lead him to suspend the payment of interest to the subscribers to the loan (since it was extended at least) unless some legislative measures can prevent that inconvenience, permit me to suggest to you the propriety of procuring as soon as possible the necessary information on that subject, as I have no doubt the House or the committee of ways and means will soon apply to you in an official manner for the same. The questions which appear to me the most necessary to be solved are the following—

1st. What were the grounds of the decision of the Secretary of

9. Gallatin is referring to the Pennsylvania act of March 27, 1789, "An Act to Repeal so Much of Any Act or Acts of Assembly of This Commonwealth as Directs the Payment of the New Loan Debt or the Interest Thereof Beyond the First Day of April Next, and for Other Purposes Therein Mentioned" (James T. Mitchell and Henry Flanders, eds., *The Statutes at Large of Pennsylvania from 1682 to 1801* [Harrisburg, 1908], XIII, 263–67).

the Treasury relative to the intended suspension of interest in Feb. 1791, and what construction did he give to the 18th section of the funding Act of Congress?

2d. Does he look now on the New-Loan certificates offered for subscription to the loan of the U. S. as assumable, if so, upon what ground? if not, upon what grounds also? and will he return them soon to the subscribers?

3d. Will his decision relative to the suspension of interest be the same now as last winter, and if it is not, what measures on the side of the Legislature of *Pennsylvania*, will remove the difficulties that may in his opinion now prevent the payment of interest?

I have chosen to communicate to you my ideas on that subject as an individual, rather than to wait for the formalities of official application taking place, in order to prevent delays; which I hope will be a sufficient apology for this letter.

With sincere esteem, &c. Albert Gallatin.

Philadelphia, Jan. 14, 1793.

A. J. Dallas, Esq.

To Thomas Jefferson

[Philadelphia, January 15, 1793]

The Secretary of the Treasury presents his respectful compliments to The Secretary of the State—requests he will meet the Comms. of the Sinking Fund at ten oClock tomorrow forenoon at the house of the Secy of the Treasury. The V President has been so obliging as to accommodate the place to the indifferent state of Mr. Hamilton's health.

Jany. 15. 1793

AL, Thomas Jefferson Papers, Library of Congress.

To Thomas Jefferson

Treasury Department January 15th 1793

Sir

Major Rochefontaine [1] has presented at the Treasury an authenticated copy of a Register Certificate in his favour, from which it appears, that the original has been deposited with Mr Delamotte, vice consul of the united States at Havre in France.

It being necessary, that the Treasury should be in possession of the original certificate, I have in the enclosed letter [2] desired Major Rochefontaine to cause it to be forwarded hither. This letter will probably be transmitted to Havre, and will therefore require to be authenticated by your signature; it being presumed, that mine is not familiar to the Consul. [I request some proper Memorandum on the inclosed for this purpose.] [3]

It will be requisite, that Mr Delamotte [and other consuls and Vice Consuls of the UStates] should be directed to forbear in future taking any deposits of original certificates of the like nature. This direction I conceive will come properly from your department.[4]

I have the honor to be very respectfully Sir your obedt Servt

Alexander Hamilton

The Secretary of State

LS, Thomas Jefferson Papers, Library of Congress.

1. Etienne Nicolas Marie Béchet, Chevalier de Rochefontaine, had served with the United States forces during the American Revolution. After the Revolution he returned to France, where he played a leading part in promoting the Scioto enterprise. In 1792 he fled France and settled in the United States. The certificate mentioned in this letter was one issued to Rochefontaine as part of the debt owed to foreign officers who had served in the American Revolution. For a description of this debt, see William Short to H, August 3, 1790, note 5. H wrote to Gouverneur Morris on September 13, 1792, describing the procedure for the retirement of this debt and stated that payment would be upon "demand and the production of the certificate by the party or his legal representative. . . . As the certificates will be required to be produced here; the payment of Interest at Paris must be made without the production of them." Rochefontaine had left his certificate with the Sieur de La Motte, the vice-consul of the United States at Le Havre. A statement in the records of the State Department reads as follows:

"Col. Rochefontaine came to begg Mr. Gefferson to write to M. delamotte vice consul of america at havre de Grace, to order him to send immediately to M hamilton secretary of the treasury of the United states of america, the original title of M. Rochefontaine against the United states; which has been deposited by him in the consul's office last February. M. hamilton had agreed with M. Rochefontaine to Speack to Mr. Gefferson on the subject, and M. Rochefontaine hope he has done it; but as he has an opportunity of a Gentleman sayling wednesday next, from this port to proceed by the way of Belfast to france, M. Rochefontaine will be much obliged to Mr. Gefferson to write the said letter, and he will call to morrow morning to get it" (AL, RG 59, Miscellaneous Letters, 1790–1799, National Archives). This statement is marked "recd. in the office 15 Jany 1793."

2. Letter not found.

3. The bracketed words in this and the next paragraph are in H's handwriting.

4. On January 15, 1793, Jefferson wrote to La Motte: "I am informed by Colo. Rochefontaine that he deposited with you in February last the original certificate from the treasury of the U. S. of the sum of money due from them to him. As the rules of the Treasury office require that these originals should be returned on paiment, I am to desire that you will transmit the same by some safe conveyance to Mr. Hamilton, Secretary of the Treasury, for which this shall be your warrant" (ALS, letterpress copy, Thomas Jefferson Papers, Library of Congress).

To Thomas Jefferson

[Philadelphia, January 15, 1793]

Mr Hamilton presents his Compliments to Mr. Jefferson. The enclosed letter, written by his Clerk, will, it is hoped, express his wish sufficiently to render it unnecessary to remodel it. As Col Rochefontaine informs him The vessel, by which the letter is intended to be sent, departs tomorrow Morning he will be obliged by its being returned to him with the proper certificate this Evening.

Jany 15 179[3] [2]

AL, Thomas Jefferson Papers, Library of Congress.

1. For background to this letter, see the second letter which H wrote to Jefferson on January 15, 1793.

2. H misdated this letter "1792."

To George Washington

Treasury Department, January 15, 179[3].[1] "The Secretary of the Treasury has the honor to submit to the President of the United States the enclosed Letter from the Commissioner of the Revenue [2] respecting the Lighthouse on Tybee Island. The arrangement which he proposes appears to the Secretary an adviseable one. . . ."

LC, George Washington Papers, Library of Congress.

1. This letter is misdated "1792."

2. See Tench Coxe to H, January 4, 1793.

From Tobias Lear

[*Philadelphia*] *January 16, 1793.* "By the President's command T. Lear has the honor to return to the Secretary of the Treasury the letter from the Commissioner of the Revenue respecting the Light

House on Tybee Island; [1] and to inform the Secretary that the President approves of the arrangements therein suggested. . . ."

LS, RG 26, "Segregated" Lighthouse Records, National Archives; LC, George Washington Papers, Library of Congress.

1. See H to George Washington, January 15, 1793.

Meeting of the Commissioners of the Sinking Fund

[Philadelphia, January 16. 1793]

At a meeting of the trustees of the sinking fund, January 16th, 1793, Present: The Vice President, the Secretary of State, the Secretary of the Treasury, and the Attorney General.

The Secretary of the Treasury having informed the Board that there are, at their disposal, a balance of the dividends of interest on the stock heretofore purchased, and the further sum of two hundred thousand dollars:

Resolved, That the balance aforesaid be applied to the purchase of stock, according to the instructions given, and the limitations prescribed, by the last resolutions of the Board.[1]

Resolved, That the said two hundred thousand dollars be applied to the purchase of six per cents only, within the space of ten days; and that the Board will meet on the expiration thereof, to wit, on Saturday, the 26th inst. to take further order, concerning the said two hundred thousand dollars, if necessary.

ASP, Finance, I, 237.

1. See "Meeting of the Commissioners of the Sinking Fund," December 14, 1792.

From Gouverneur Morris

Paris 16 January 1793.

Dear Sir

I shall transmit herewith Copy of what I had the Honor to write to you on the twenty third of last Month. I have since after much difficulty or rather many difficulties adjusted the Mode of payment on Certificates to foreign Officers.[1] Messieurs Grand and Company could not be prevail'd on to deal in Specie because it might have exposed them to Plunder and personal Danger. Similar Feelings would I find operate on others therefore I was oblig'd to relinquish that Idea or convert myself into a Banker which would I found besides other Inconveniences consume all my Time and after all produce little Benefit either to the Public or to the Parties. The best Plan which after all Investigation suggested itself to my mind is as follows. The Dollars being already converted into livres at a very Advantageous Exchange for the Parties I have directed payment to them at the Rate of 54 g. (or half pence) banco for the Crown of three livres which is as near the Par of Exchange as can be without Fractions. For the Value of the Dutch florin being taken according to the Assays of their Coin at 2. ₶—4s. of France we have the following proportion as 44s is to 40g. so is 60s to 54g. 54d the Value of the Ecu in current Money; and if from this be deducted one per Cent for the Agio between the Bank and Current, which is the Ratio that has ruled for some time past, we have just the 54g banco which I have fixed on. Thus no Complaint can exist and the Exchange being fixed according to the Ideas which People here have been used to it is much more satisfactory than if I had taken the Dollar as a Standard because the Dollar being always a Commodity here and the Price of course fluctuating the Exchange would have been to them a double one and of Course a double Source of Altercation and Disquietude. It remains for me to shew that the Fixation above mentioned corresponds with your Orders. The Dollar at 50 Stivers or 100 Gros gives banco 99g And as the Dollar (worth according to the Assays 5.33 livres) is carried out in the Certificates at 5.40 livres or 5.₶ 8 we have the following Proportion as 3 ₶ is to 54g. so is 5 ₶ 8 to 97g. 2. This leaves to the United States a Difference 1g. 8 to pay the Bankers Commissions Postages and the Stamp duties here on the Bills of Exchange. These will very nearly absorp that little Difference so that in round Numbers the 50 Sous or Stivers current which you counted on will about pay the Dollar which is due.

LC, Gouverneur Morris Papers, Library of Congress.

1. See H to Morris, September 13, 1792.

Report on Bank Deposits, Surplus Revenue, and Loans

Treasury Department
January 16. 1793
[Communicated on January 18, 1793] [1]

[To the President of the Senate]
Sir

I have the honor to transmit herewith, pursuant to the order of the Senate, of yesterday,[2] the following documents, viz:

Books, No 1 and 2, containing the current Cash Account between the United States and the Bank of the United States from the commencement of the operations of that Institution until this day.

Files A, B, C, D

A containing a series of accounts beginning the 16th of June 1792 and ending the 5th of January 1793, shewing the Cash Account of the United States with the Office of Discount and Deposit of the Bank of the United States, at Boston.

B Containing a series of accounts beginning the 23d of May 1792 and ending the 5th of January 1793 shewing [the Cash Account of the United States with the office of Discount and Deposit of the Bank of the UStates] [3] at New York.

C Containing a series of accounts beginning the 9th of August

DS, RG 46, Second Congress, 1791–1793, Reports of the Secretary of the Treasury, National Archives.

1. *Annals of Congress*, III, 630.

2. On January 15, 1793, the Senate "*Ordered*, That the Secretary of the Treasury lay before the Senate the account of the United States with the Bank of the United States, specifying the precise sums, with the dates of the debits and credits, from the institution of the Bank to the day the return is made. That the Secretary of the Treasury also lay before the Senate the account of the surplus of revenue appropriated to the purchase of the Public Debt, to the same period, specifying the sums and dates. That he lay before the Senate a statement of the money borrowed by virtue of the law passed August 4, 1790, with the appropriation of the amount, and the precise dates. That he lay before the Senate the amount and application of the money borrowed by virtue of the law of August 12, 1790; and that he also lay before the Senate an account exhibiting the probable surplus and unappropriated revenue of the year 1792, stating, as far as possible, the dates and the sums" (*Annals of Congress*, III, 629).

3. This and the other bracketed portions of this letter are in H's handwriting.

1792 and ending the 5th of January 1793 [shewing similar Acots. with the Office of Discount & Deposit at] Baltimore.

D Containing a series of accounts beginning the 9th of June and ending the 22d of December 1792 [shewing similar Cash Account with the Office of Discount & Deposit at] Charleston.

Statement E being an Abstract of the balances remaining in the several Offices of Discount and Deposit at the respective periods of the last Returns.

Statements A B and No 1, 2, 3, being Accounts of the sales of Bills on Amsterdam by the Bank of the United States and the several Offices of Discount and Deposit.

These documents fulfil the first object of the order abovementioned.

Statement F Shewing the Surplus of Revenue appropriated to the purchase of the public debt. This surplus arose at the end of the year 1790, and was appropriated by an Act of the 12th of August 1790.[4]

This fulfils the second object of the order, as I understand its meaning.

Statements (printed) No. I, II, III, IV.[5]

These have been heretofore presented to the House of Representatives and shew with as much detail and accuracy, as is now in the power of the Treasury, the different loans which have been made pursuant to the Acts of the 4th [6] and 12th of August 1790, and their application, as far as it has gone.

These loans having been contracted, in virtue of the powers communicated by both Acts, without particular reference to either, a specification of the loans made upon each is of course not practicable. This mode of proceeding was indicated 1st by an intimation from our Bankers in Holland that a distinction might prove an embarrassment (being a novelty, the reason of which would not be obvious to the money lenders), 2dly, by the consideration, that if the loans were made upon both acts indiscriminately, their application could

4. "An Act making Provision for the Reduction of the Public Debt" (1 *Stat.* 186–87).

5. See "Report on Foreign Loans," January 3, 1793.

6. "An Act making provision for the (payment of the) Debt of the United States" (1 *Stat.* 138–44).

be regulated, as circumstances, from time to time, should render advisable.

These documents fulfil, as far as is practicable, the 3d and 4th objects of the order.

Statement G shewing the probable unappropriated surplus of the public Revenue during the year 1792.

This fulfils, as far as can now be done, the last of the objects comprised in the order of the Senate.

But by way of explanation, I beg leave to refer to the printed statement D which accompanied the estimate for the service of the present year, reported to the House of Representatives, on the 14th of November last,[7] and which is herewith transmitted.

The Books, No 1 and 2, the papers contained in the files A B C & D and those marked A B No 1, 2, 3, are originals. They are sent, rather than transcripts, to avoid delay; as it is understood that the statements called for have reference to the deliberations of the Senate on the Bill making appropriations for the service of the current year.[8]

I supposed it would be most agreeable to the Senate to be enabled, as soon as possible, by the receipt of the information they have required, to proceed to a decision on that important subject. And exposed as I am to very perplexing Dilemmas, for the want of the requisite appropriations, in consequence of arrangements which it was my duty to enter into, to be able to keep pace with the exigencies of the public service, I could not but feel a solicitude to hasten the communication.

As the Originals, which have been mentioned, are necessary Documents of Office, I request that the Senate will be pleased to cause them to be returned, as soon as they shall have answered the purpose, for which they have been required.

With the most perfect respect, I have the honor to be, Sir, Your Obed [and humble] Servant. Alex Hamilton

[Secy of the Treasy]

[The vice President of the U States &]
The President of the Senate.

7. "Report on Estimates and Expenditures for the Civil List for the Year 1793," November 14, 1792.

8. This is a reference to the debate on "An Act making Appropriations for the support of Government for the year one thousand seven hundred and ninety-three" (1 *Stat.* 325–29 [February 28, 1793]).

No. 1

SALES OF GOVERNMENT BILLS ON AMSTERDAM, AT THE OFFICE OF DISCOUNT AND DEPOSIT IN NEW YORK. VIZT, 225,000 GUILDERS @ $36\frac{4}{11}$ NINETIETHS OF A DOLLAR ⅌ GUILDER, ON A CREDIT OF SIX MONTHS, WITH INTEREST FOR THE LAST FOUR MONTHS.

When sold.	To whom sold.	Amount in Guilders	Amount in Dollars.	When paid	Amount of Interest.	Sums paid.
April 25th.	Rowlett & Corp.	162,000	65,454. 54	Octor. 15th	1201. 36	66,655. 90.
26th.	Norman Butler	8,000	3232. 32	Augt. 6	21. 54	3,253. 86
May 4	William Edgar	1,000.	404. 4.	July 4th		404. 4
" 10th.	Saml Ward & Brs.	26,000	10,505. 5	Novr. 13th.	215. 35	10,720. 40
18th.	George Scriba	28 000	11,313. 13	" 21st.	231. 92	11,545. 5
		225 000	90,909. 8		1670. 17.	92,579. 25

Office of Discount & Deposit
NewYork January 12th. 1793.

Errors Excepted
Jonthn. Burrall Cashr

N.B. The Secretary of the Treasury gave permission to receive payment of the Notes that were on Interest at any time before they became due.

No. 2

SALE OF GOVERNMENT BILLS ON AMSTERDAM, AT THE OFFICE OF DISCOUNT AND DEPOSIT IN NEW YORK VIZT. 250,000 GUILDERS AT 40 CENTS 7 MILLS ℔ GUILDER PAYABLE THE ONE HALF IN 2 MONTHS, AND THE OTHER HALF IN 4 MONTHS, WITH INTEREST.

When sold	To whom sold.	Amount in Guilders	Amount in Dollars.	When paid.	Amount of Interest	Sums paid
1793						
July 27	Saml. Ward & Brothers	25,000	5087. 50	Sepr. 29th	53. 37	5 140. 87
"	ditto		5087. 50	Novr. 28th.	104. 29	5,191. 79
"	Obadiah Bowen	25,000	5087. 50	Sepr. 29th	53 37	5,140. 87
"	ditto		5087. 50	Novr. 28th	104. 29	5,191. 79
Augt. 7th	Nicholas Cook & Co.	25 000	5087. 50	Octor. 9th	53. 37	5 140. 87
"	ditto		5087. 50	Decr 3rd	104. 29	5 191. 79
"	Josiah Adams & Co.	25,000	5087. 50	Octor 9th	53. 37	5 140. 87
"	ditto		5087. 50	Decr 8th	104. 29	5 191. 79
21st.	Jacob & Philip Mark	25,000	5087. 50	Octor 23d	53. 41	5 140. 91
	ditto		5087. 50	Decr 22d	104. 29	5,191. 79.
27th.	John Murray	15,000	3055	Octor 29th	32. 7	3,087. 7
	ditto		3050	Decr 27th	62. 53.	3,112 53
Sepr 3d.	Daniel Badcock	25,000	5087. 50	Novr 4th	53. 42	5 140. 92
	ditto		5087. 50	1793 Jany 5th.	104. 30	5 191. 80
4th.	Matthew Clarkson	10,000	2035	Novr 5th	20. 35	2 055. 35
"	ditto		2035	1793 Jany 5th	40. 70	2,075. 70
"	LeRoy & Bayard	25,000	5087. 50	Novr 5th	50. 87	5,138. 37
"	ditto		5087. 50	1793 Jany 5th	101. 74	5,189. 24
5th	Van Horne & Clarkson	25,000	5087. 50	Novr. 7th.	53. 41	5 140. 91
"	ditto		5087. 50	1793 Jany. 6th	104. 29	5 191. 79
7	Nicholas Hoffman	3,000	610. 50	Novr 9th.	6. 40	616. 90
"	ditto		610. 50	Jany 8th	12. 51.	623. 1
10th	John P. Mumford & Co.	22,000	4,477	Novr. 12th	47. 1.	4,524. 1
"	ditto		4,477	1793 Jany 12th.	91. 77.	4,568. 77
		250,000	101,750		1 569. 71	103,319. 71

No. 3

ACCOT. SALES OF 50,000. GUILDERS, GOVERNMENT BILLS ON AMSTERDAM, AT THE BALTIM OFFICE OF DISCT. & DEPT.

Date	Number.	Purchasers.	Amot. Guilds.	Price ℔ Guilder	Time of Credit	Principal in Dollars & Cents	Interest in Dollars & Cents	Total in Dollars & Cents.	
				Cents & Mills					
1792 July 26	653	Ghequeire & Holmes	4.000	@ 40.7	60 days	1.628. 00	16. 28	1,644 28	
"	654	Ditto	4.000	@ do.	120 do.	1.628. 00	32 56	1,660 56	
"	{631 684	George Grundy	8,000	@ do.	60 & 120 do.	3.256. 00	29. 34	*3,285. 34	* of which 1300. dollrs. was paid at the time of Sale,
"	641	William Van Wyck	3.000	@ do.	60 & 120 do.	1.221. 00	18 31	1,239 31	which is the reason for
"	685	Rutien & Konecke	6.000	@ do.	60 & 120 do.	2.442. 00	36 63	2,478 63	the Interest on this, ap-
August 6	660	Henry Schroeder	4.000	@ do.	60 & 120 do.	1.628 00	24 42	1,652. 42	pearing less, than the
"	664	William Taylor.	5.000	@ do.	60 & 120 do.	2.035 00	30 52	2,065 52	same sum, immediately above.
"	696	Adrian Valck	7.000	@ do.	60 & 120 do.	2.849 00	42. 74	2,891 74	
"	713	Nicholas Slubey & Co.	9.000	@ do.	60 & 120 do.	3.663 00	54 94	3,717 94	
			50,000			20,350 00	285. 74	**20.635 74	** Total, and paid agreably to the Credit given.

Baltimore Office of Discount & Deposit.
January 12th. 1793
David Harris
Cashr.

Statement AB

ACCOT. OF TREASURY BILLS ON AMSTERDAM SOLD BY THE BANK OF THE UNITED STATES & OFFICES OF D & D

Date of Sale	Guilders	Purchasers Names	Monies received		Notes remg. unpaid		Remarks
			Amt of Note	Int on do	Amount	when payble	
1792							
April 25	88.053. 1	Matthew McConnell	35,577	931 4			
27	156,543 15	Jonathan Williams	63.250.	1,326. 30			
	5.403. 4	Anthony Butler	2.183 16	43. 66			
28	225,000	Office at New York	. . .	. . .			
	25,000.	Thomas Fitzsimons	10.101. 2.	314 91			
July 2d.	24,000	Pragers & Co.	9.758	156 52			
21	50,000	Office of New York	. . .	. . .			
	25 000	Office of Baltimore	. . .	. . .			
31	612	Saml. Meredith	249 9	6. 91			
	25,000	Joseph Anthony & Son	10.175.	152. 62			
	25,000	Ward & Brothers	10.175.	152. 62			
	15,000.	Anthony Butler	105 } 6 000 }	. . . 93.			paid 105 Dolls. at the time of Purchase
	24,000.	William Bell	9,768.	146 52			
Augt. 1	50.000	Office New York	. . .	. . .			
2	25,000	Do. Balto.	. . .	. . .			
9	1,386	Willm. McPherson	564 2	8 78			
10	8.332. 10	Henry Hill	3,391 33	52. 11			
14	50,000.	Office of New York	. . .	. . .			
15	3,000	Bake & Co.	1,221	18 33			
16	50,000.	Office of New York	. . .	. . .			
21	2,000	Leond. Jacoby	814	12 24			
	12,658 10	Fredk. W. Starrman	5,152 22	79 85			
	2 000	Cash	814.	. . .			
22	12.000	Ditto	4,884.	. . .			
24	10,000	Bohlen	4.070.	59 5			
31	50,000.	Office at New York	. . .	. . .			
	20.000	Thos. Ketland	8,140	126 16			

Septr.	5	12,000	George Meade	4,884	75 70		
	14.	25,000	Geo: Sweetman	10,175	157 71		
	15	25,000	Nixon & Foster	10,175	157 71		
	29	25,000.	Geo: Ord	10,175	157 71		
		25,000	Thos. M Willing	10,175	157 71		
		6,000.	Leonard Jacoby	1,221	13.	1,221.	29th Jany
Octr.	2	15,000	Geo: Harrison	3,052 50	32 4	3 052 50	" do.
		6,800	F. W. Starrman	1,383 80	14 52	1,383 50	2 Feby.
	3	25,000	Willing Morris & Swanwick	5,087 50	53 40	5,087 50	3d. do
	4.	10,000	Jos: Anthony & Son	2,035	21 36	2,035.	4th. do
	6.	13,000	T. Dalton	2,645 50	27 77	2,645 50	7th. do
		15,000.	Geo: Bickham	3,052 50	32 4	3,052 50	" "
		12,211	John Donaldson	2,484 94	26 7	2,484 94	" "
	10	7,116	Conyngham Nesbitt & Co.	1,448 11	15 20	1,448 11	8 do.
		25,000	Pragers & Co.	5,087 50	53 41	5,087 50	" "
		25 000	F & J. West	5,087 50	53 41	5,087 50	" "
		25,000	Jas. & W Miller	5,087 50	53 41	5,087 50	" "
	11	3,000	John Donaldson	610 50	6. 40	610 50	10th. do
	13	15,289	Berthier & Co.	3,111 32	32 67	3,111 32	12th. do
		20.000	Robert Morris	4.070.	42 72	4,070.	" "
		15.000	Lewis Deblois	3,434. 59	146 67	1,669 67	" "
		120,000	Cash	48,840.	. . .	. . .	. . .
	15	5,000	John Nixon	1,017 50	10 68	1 017 50	14th do
		16,000	Anthony Butler	3,256.	34 18	3 256.	" "
		8,595	Cash	3 498 17	. . .	. . .	. . .
	17.	1.000	do.	407.	. . .	. . .	. . .
	18.	35,000	do.	14,245	. . .	. . .	. . .
	19	34,000	do.	13,838	. . .	. . .	. . .
		10,000	do.	4,070.	. . .	. . .	. . .
	20	10,000	do.	4,070	. . .	. . .	. . .
	24	10.000	do.	4,070	. . .	. . .	. . .
	26	15.000.	do.	6,105	. . .	. . .	. . .
		1,600,000		384,292. 27	5,056. 11	51,408 4	

146.67 is the Amt. of the whole Int. on the two Periods of 60 & 120 days for Bills sold L. Deblois.

	Amount of Monies recd. at the Bank of the U.S. for Amsterdam Bills		
	Bills to the 15th Jany 1793 as above	384,292. 27	
	Interest recd. on do. as above	5.056. 11	
			389,348. 38
Total Amt. of Guilders sold at the Office at New York is . . . 475,000	Amount of Monies recd at the Office of Discount & Deposit at New		
	York ⅌ Acct No 1	92,579. 25	
	do ⅌ Acct No 2	103,319. 71	
			195,898. 96
Total Amt. of Guilders sold at the Office at Baltimore 50,000	Amount of Monies recd. at the Office of Discount & Deposit at Baltimore ⅌ Acct. No 3		20,635. 74
	Total Amt. of Monies recd. by the Bank & Offices, for Amsterdam Bills		605.883. 8
	There still remain due on Acct. of Amsterdam Bills, Notes payable at Bank, as above		51.408. 4
N. B:	As these Notes are not always paid the day they fall due, the Interest is not carried out		

Bank of the United States Jany. 15th. 1793
Davd. S. Franks
Asst. Cashier

Statement E.

STATEMENT OF BALANCES IN THE SEVERAL OFFICES OF DISCOUNT & DEPOSIT.

Dates of Returns	Offices of Discount & deposit				Balances
1793					Dollars cents
Jany 5	Boston			156 028. 67	
		Amount of draughts not yet paid		70.375.	
					85.653 67
Jany 5	New York			224 734. 51	
		Received for Bills sold on Amsterdam		190.700. 78	
				415.435. 29	
		Draughts unpaid	60.000.		
		Invested in the Public debt	50.000.		
				110,000.	
					305,435 29
Jany 5	Baltimore			55,058. 64	
		Amount of draughts not yet paid		10,000.	
					45.058. 64
1792 Decembr. 22	Charleston			93.015. 85	
		Amount of draughts not yet paid		63.350.	
					29.665 85
					465.813. 45

Treasury Depart. January 6. 1793
Alexander Hamilton

Statement F

A STATEMENT SHEWING THE SURPLUS OF THE REVENUE APPROPRIATED TO THE PURCHASE OF THE PUBLIC DEBT BY THE ACT OF CONGRESS OF THE 12TH OF AUGT. 1790

Net amount of Duties arising from Imports and Tonnage, from the first day of August 1789 to the last day of December 1790, inclusively	3,131,667. 94
Amount of monies received from Nathaniel Gilman, late receiver of continental taxes	3,225. 70
	3,134,893. 64

Appropriations. vizt.

Date		Act	Amount	Total
1789 Aug	20	An Act providing for the expenses which may attend Negotiations or Treaties with the Indian Tribes and the appointment of Commissioners for managing the same[9]	20,000.	
Sepr.	29	An Act making appropriations for the present Year[10]	639,000.	
1790. Mar	26	An Act making Appropriations for the support of government for the Year 1790[11]	*754,658.99	
July	1	An Act providing the means of intercourse between the United States and Foreign Nations[12]	80,000.	
	"	An Act to satisfy the claims of John McCord against the United States[13]	1,309.71	
	22	An Act providing for holding a treaty or treaties to establish peace with the Indian Tribes[14]	20,000.	
Aug	4	An Act to provide more effectually for the collection of duties imposed by Law on Goods Wares and Merchandize[15]	10,000.	
	10	An Act authorizing the Secretary of the Treasury to finish the light house on Portland head in the District of Main.[16]	1,500.	
	11	An Act for the relief of Disabled Soldiers and Seamen lately in the service of the United States, and of certain other persons[17]	548.57	
	12	An Act making certain appropriations therein mentioned[18]	233,219.97	
				1,760,237. 24
		Surplus of the Revenue on the last day of December 1790.		1,374,656. 40

* The amount of the expenses arising from, and incident to the Sessions of Congress which happened in the Year 1790, being 203,167.22/100 Dollars, is included in this sum.

9. 1 *Stat.* 54.
10. 1 *Stat.* 95.
11. 1 *Stat.* 104–06.
12. 1 *Stat.* 128–29.
13. 6 *Stat.* 2–3
14. 1 *Stat.* 136.
15. 1 *Stat.* 145–78.
16. 1 *Stat.* 184.
17. 6 *Stat.* 3–4
18. 1 *Stat.* 185–86.

A Statement of the Sums which have been applied to the purchase of the Public Debt

	Dollars Cents
The Amount heretofore reported to Congress by the Commissioners for purchasing the Public Debt, down to the 17th of November 1792 is in Specie	967,821. 65
Since that date there has been applied to the same purpose through the agency of Samuel Meredith the sum of	15,098. 11
And through Jonathan Burrall in New York	50,000. ..
Total Amount in Specie	1,032,919. 76

Treasury Department
January 16th 1793

Statement G

A STATEMENT SHEWING THE PROBABLE SURPLUS OF THE REVENUE OF THE UNITED STATES FOR THE YEAR 1792

		Dollars Cents
Net product of Duties on Imports and Tonnage from the 1st of January to the 31st of December 1792, as estimated*		3,900,000.
Ditto on home made Spirits as estimated		400.000.
Appropriations		4,300.000.
Interest on the Public Debt for the year 1792	2.849.194.73	
For the Support of Government for the same Year appropriated by the act of the 23d of December 1791 [19]	600.000.	
Towards carrying into execution the act intitled "An Act for making farther and more effectual Provision for the Protection of the frontiers" appropriated by the act of the 2d of may 1792.[20]	523.500.	
To defray any expense incurred in relation to the intercourse between the united States and foreign Nations appropriated by the Act of the 8th of may 1792 [21]	50 000.	
		4.022.694. 73
Surplus		277.305. 27

Treasury Department January 16. 1793
Alex Hamilton

*This sum is estimated by adding to the ascertained product of the year 1791 an ascertained excess of the product of the first two quarters of the year 1792, beyond the product of the first two quarters of the year 1791 being 252,319 dollars and eleven cents, and the estimated product for a half year of the additional duties on imports laid during the last session of Congress and commencing on the 1st. of July last, being 261,750 dollars. According to the information hitherto received at the Treasury, there is every probability that the amount of the duties for the last half year of 1792 will fully equal this calculation of their product; if in the ratio of the first half year, will exceed it.

19. 1 *Stat.* 226–29. 20. 1 *Stat.* 259–63.

21. This is a reference to Section 3 of "An Act making certain appropriations therein specified" (1 *Stat.* 285).

To William Edgar[1]

Philadelphia Jany 17.
1793

Sir

This will be handed you by General Hull,[2] whom I have charged with a Commission to be executed in Upper Canada, that is the contracting for supplies for an Indian Treaty expected to be held at Au Glaise the Ensuing Spring. I wish him to be possessed of Letters of Introduction to respectable Merchants of the Country to which he is going and believing that no one can answer this purpose better than yourself & Mr. Macombe I take the liberty to ask the favour of you both to do it. I do not write to Mr. Macombe but I will be obliged to you to mention the subject to him & my request. With much esteem & regard

I am Dr sir Your Obed servant A Hamilton

Wm. Edgar Esqr

ALS, MS Division, New York Public Library.

1. Edgar was a New York City merchant. Edgar and Alexander Macomb, both of whom had come from northern Ireland, had settled before the American Revolution in Detroit where they became traders and land speculators. During the Revolution they became partners with Alexander Macomb's younger brother William in the Detroit firm of Macomb, Edgar, and Macomb and conducted a lucrative business supplying the Indian department of the British army.

2. For information on William Hull's trip, see H to George Hammond, December 29, 1792, and "Draft of Instructions for William Hull," January 14, 1793.

To Samuel Hodgdon

[*Philadelphia, January 17, 1793.* The catalogue description of this letter reads "in reference to army pay." *Letter not found.*]

LS, sold by Stan V. Henkels, Jr., June 24, 1927, Lot 134.

Receipt to Benjamin Walker[1]

[Philadelphia, January 18, 1793]

Received January 18th. 1793 of Benjamin Walker Agent for Baron De Steuben Three thousand Dollars in full of all claims and demands against the said Baron De Steuben to this day.

Alexander Hamilton

ADS, Mr. Hall Park McCullough, North Bennington, Vermont.

1. Walker was naval officer for the port of New York. During the American Revolution he had served as aide to Baron von Steuben. After the war he was a close friend of the Baron and on frequent occasions helped him with his involved financial problems.

From Tench Coxe

Treasury Department,
Revenue Office, January 19th. 1793

Sir,

In examining a report concerning the commencement, progress and present state of the establishments in Massachusetts for the direction and safety of navigation made to this office by the Superintendent thereof,[1] in pursuance of a late circular instruction,[2] I perceive a proviso in the copy of the Act of cession,[3] which appears to render the same of no effect, under the Act of Congress of the 7th. of August 1789, "for the establishment, and support of light houses, Beacons, Buoys and public piers"[4] and which also appears to be inconsistent with the Constitution of the United States.[5]

The proviso of the Act of the legislature of Massachusetts is in the words following—

"Provided also that all civil and criminal process issued under the authority of this commonwealth or any officers thereof may be executed on any of said Lands or in any of said buildings, in the same way and manner as if the Jurisdiction had not been ceded as aforesaid."

I have the honor to make you this communication for the purpose of obtaining the Attorney generals opinions—

1st Whether the cession contemplated in the Act of the legislature of Massachusetts is made in such manner as to be availing and of effect under the Constitution of the United States, And

2dly Whether the said Cession is made in such manner as to be availing and of effect under the Act of Congress of the 7th day of August 1789, refered to above.[6]

I have the honor to be with great respect Sir, your most Obt. Servant

Tench Coxe
Commissr. of the Revenue.

The honorable
The Secretary of the Treasury.

LC, RG 58, Letters of Commissioner of Revenue, 1792–1793, National Archives.

1. Benjamin Lincoln.

2. Coxe to the Superintendents of Lighthouses, October 23, 1792 (LC, RG 58, Letters of Commissioner of Revenue, 1792–1793, National Archives).

3. "An Act for Granting to the United States of America the Several Public Light-Houses Within This Commonwealth" (*Acts and Laws of the Commonwealth of Massachusetts, 1790–1791* [Boston, 1795], 7–9). This act was passed on June 10, 1790.

4. Section 1 of this act stipulated that the expenses arising after August 15, 1789, for the "maintenance and repairs of all lighthouses, beacons, buoys and public piers erected, placed, or sunk before the passing of this act, at the entrance of, or within any bay, inlet, harbor, or port of the United States, for rendering the navigation thereof easy and safe, shall be defrayed out of the treasury of the United States: *Provided nevertheless*, That none of the said expenses shall continue to be so defrayed by the United States, after the expiration of one year from the day aforesaid, unless such lighthouses, beacons, buoys and public piers, shall in the mean time be ceded to and vested in the United States, by the state or states respectively in which the same may be, together with the lands and tenements thereunto belonging, and together with the jurisdiction of the same" (1 *Stat.* 54).

5. See Coxe to H, January 3, 1793, note 3.

6. For a similar case of jurisdiction reserved by a state, see Coxe to H, January 3, 1793; Edmund Randolph to H, January 7, 1793.

To George Washington

Treasury Department, January 19, 1793. "The Secretary of the Treasury has the honor to transmit herewith to the President of the United States three provisional Contracts made by the Collector of Washington in North Carolina, for the stakage of the shoals, sounds &c. within that State, north of the District of Wilmington, accompanied with a letter from the Commissioner of the Revenue relative to the subject. . . ."[1]

LC, George Washington Papers, Library of Congress.

1. See Tench Coxe to H, January 2, 1793.

From Joseph Whipple

Portsmouth [*New Hampshire*] *January 19, 1793.* Acknowledges "the receipt of your letter of the 20th December" [1] enclosing commissions for officers of the New Hampshire revenue cutter.

LC, RG 36, Collector of Customs at Portsmouth, Letters Sent, 1792–1793, Vol. 4, National Archives; copy, RG 56, Letters from the Collector at Portsmouth, National Archives.

1. Letter not found.

To George Washington

Treasury Dept. 20 Jan: 1793.

The Secretary of the Treasury has the honor to submit the Draft of a supplementary Act for making certain alterations in the District of North Carolina, heretofore considered & approved by the President.[1]

A Hamilton

LC, George Washington Papers, Library of Congress.

1. See Tench Coxe to H, December 13, 21, 1792, January 12, 1793; H to Washington, January 4, 1793. Washington's "abstract of a supplementary arrangement made in the District of North Carolina, in regard to certain surveys, to facilitate the execution of the law laying a duty on distilled spirits" was received in the Senate on January 26, 1793, and in the House on January 28, 1793 (*Annals of Congress*, III, 634, 851).

From Tobias Lear

[*Philadelphia*] *January 21, 1793.* "By the President's command T. Lear has the honor to return to the Secretary of the Treasury, three contracts made by the Collector of Washington in North Carolina for the stakeage of the shoals, sounds &c. in that State; [1] which contracts are ratified by the President."

LC, George Washington Papers, Library of Congress.

1. See Tench Coxe to H, January 2, 1793, and H to Washington, January 19, 1793.

Treasury Department Circular to the Collectors of the Customs

Treasury Department,
January 22d, 1793.

Sir,

Enclosed is an act, entitled, "An act concerning the registering and recording of ships or vessels," passed the 31st of December last.[1]

This act is to take effect after the last days of March next. The forms of the certificates of Registry therein prescribed, will be immediately prepared and transmitted by the Register of the Treasury.

Copies of all certificates which shall be granted pursuant to the said act, are directed to be transmitted to the Register of the Treasury, once in three months. Memorandums of changes of masters, and all original certificates which shall be surrendered to be cancelled, are after the last day of March next, likewise to be transmitted to the said Register. But this must be done from time to time as such incidents shall occur; conforming with regard to the last mentioned originals to my circular instruction of the 2d of January 1792.

The Schooner Fame, of Newbury Port, having met with an accident in the West-Indies in August last, proof has been made by the master, of the loss of her Certificate No. 10, which was granted by the Collector of Newbury Port[2] on the 25th of April 1791, to William Coombs, owner, Solomon Haskel, master. But as it is reported that the vessel has since been taken up and carried into the Island of Tortola, there is a probability of the certificate being saved. This information is therefore given, in case the document should again make its appearance in any way, that it may be detained and the circumstance communicated to me.

With great consideration, I am, Sir, Your obedient Servant,

A Hamilton.

LS, Office of the Secretary, United States Treasury Department; LC, to Samuel R. Gerry, Essex Institute, Salem, Massachusetts; L[S], RG 36, Collector of Customs at Boston, Letters from the Treasury and Others, National Archives; LS, sold at Kingston Galleries, Inc., 1962, Lot 78; copy, RG 56, Circulars of the Office of the Secretary, "Set T," National Archives; copy, United States Finance Miscellany, Treasury Circulars, Library of Congress.

1. 1 *Stat.* 287–99.
2. In 1791 the collector at Newburyport, Massachusetts, was Stephen Cross.

From Tobias Lear

United States 23d Januy. 1793.

By the President's direction T. Lear has the honor to transmit to the Secretary of the Treasury a Copy of the Resolution of the House of representatives relative to the Loans made in Holland;[1] with which the President requests the Secretary to comply as soon as he conveniently can.

Tobias Lear.
S.P.U.S.

LC, George Washington Papers, Library of Congress.

1. The enclosed resolution, passed by the House of Representatives on January 23, 1793, reads as follows: "*Resolved*, That the President of the United States be requested to cause to be laid before this House copies of the authorities under which loans have been negotiated, pursuant to the acts of the fourth and twelfth of August, one thousand seven hundred and ninety, together with copies of the authorities directing the application of the moneys borrowed" (*Journal of the House*, I, 677).

Washington may have enclosed a second resolution of the same date which reads as follows: "*Resolved*, That the President of the United States be requested to cause this House to be furnished with the names of the persons by whom, and to whom, the respective payments of the French debt have been made in France, pursuant to the act for that purpose; specifying the dates of the respective drafts upon the Commissioners in Holland, and the dates of the respective payments of the debt. A similar statement is requested respecting the debts to Spain and Holland" (*Journal of the House*, I, 677).

To John Adams

Treasury Department
January 24. 1793

Sir

An order of yesterday from the House of Representatives[1] renders it necessary that I should have recourse to the Treasury Bank Books and the Accounts of the several Offices of Discount and Deposit which were lately transmitted to the Senate.[2]

I request that the Senate will be pleased to cause them to be returned. After the purpose has been answered they will be sent again to the Senate for such further examination as they shall deem requisite.[3] With perfect respect

I have the honor to be Sir Your obedient & humble servant

Alexander Hamilton

The Vice President of The United States
& President of the Senate.

ALS, RG 46, Second Congress, 1791–1793, Reports of the Secretary of the Treasury, National Archives.

1. The House "*Resolved,* That the Secretary of the Treasury be directed to lay before this House an account exhibiting, half-monthly, the balances between the United States and the Bank of the United States, including the several Branch Banks, from the commencement of those Institutions, to the end of the year one thousand seven hundred and ninety-two.

"*Resolved,* That the Secretary of the Treasury be directed to lay before this House an account of all moneys which may have come into the Sinking Fund, from the commencement of that Institution to the present time; specifying the particular fund from which they have accrued, and exhibiting, half-yearly, the sums uninvested, and where desposited.

"*Resolved,* That the Secretary of the Treasury be directed to report to this House the balance of all unapplied revenues at the end of the year one thousand seven hundred and ninety-two, specifying whether in money or bonds, and noting where the money is deposited; that he also make report of all unapplied moneys which may have been obtained by the several loans authorized by law, and where such moneys are now deposited." (*Journal of the House,* I, 677–78.)

2. See "Report on Bank Deposits, Surplus Revenue, and Loans," January 16, 1793.

3. This request was received in the Senate on January 24, 1793, and it was "*Ordered,* That the Secretary of the Senate return the papers . . . to the Secretary of the Treasury" (*Annals of Congress,* III, 633).

To Henry Knox

Treasury Department January 24th 1793

sir,

I send you a letter of this day from Mr Miller,[1] Inspector of Cloathing, suggesting the necessity of certain precautions for the preservation of the Hats which have been delivered. You will be fully sensible of the importance of due care on this point, and will I doubt not give the necessary direction to Mr Hodgsdon.[2]

I have the Honour to be very Respectfully Sir, Your obedient servt.

A Hamilton

The Secretary at War

Copy, RG 94, Hodgdon and Pickering Papers, National Archives.

1. John Miller to H, January 24, 1793.

2. Samuel Hodgdon.

From Tobias Lear

United States 24 Jany 1793

By the President's command T. Lear has the honor to transmit to the Secretary of the Treasury a Resolution of the Senate respecting Loans made in Holland &c. with which the President requests the Secretary to comply.[1]

Tobias Lear.
S.P.U.S.

LC, George Washington Papers, Library of Congress.

1. The Senate resolution, adopted on January 23, 1793, reads as follows: "*Resolved*, That the President of the United States be requested to lay before the Senate, copies of the powers given by him for the negotiation of the loans authorized by the laws of the 4th and 12th of August, 1790, and of the communications from the Public Commissioners in Holland" (*Annals of Congress*, III, 633).

From John Miller[1]

Philadelphia 24 January 1793

Sir,

Since I had the honor of addressing you a few days ago,[2] all the Hatts at present finished have been inspected and are now delivering at the public Store to the Amount of 1500. As there is no place fitted for their Reception otherwise than in bulk on the Floor, and no article is more liable to damage from the Moath than a wool hatt, I cannot but regret that those, which are undoubtedly the best parcel that ever were made for the army, should be put in this danger. The only mode I can Suggest is to have them well pack'd in cases or dry Casks and shut up, before the dust collects on them. Some directions may be necessary to Col. Hodgdon[3] on this Subject. Although this is out of my province, yet I could not refrain from the communication of my ideas viewing the interest of the poor Soldier, and the credit of the inspection involv'd therein. With perfect respect,

I am, Sir, Your Most Obedt. Servt. Jno. Miller.

The Secretary of the Treasury

Copy, RG 94, Hodgdon and Pickering Papers, National Archives.

1. For the action which H took on this letter, see H to Henry Knox, January 24, 1793.
2. Letter not found.
3. Samuel Hodgdon.

To George Washington

Treasury Department. Jany 24 1793.

Sir,

As the Law appropriating Ten thousand Dollars for the purpose of defraying the contingent charges of Government (tho' in that respect not very precise in it's terms) seems to contemplate the rendering an account from time to time of the disbursement of that sum;[1] I have the honor to enclose three copies of a statement to the end of the year 1792,[2] in order that if it be judged expedient, one may be sent to each House of Congress.

With the highest respect and the truest attachment, I have the honor to be Sir, Your mo: Obedt, Servt. A Hamilton
Secy. of the Treasy.

LC, George Washington Papers, Library of Congress.

1. This is a reference to Section 3 of "An Act making appropriations for the support of government for the year one thousand seven hundred and ninety," which provided that "the President of the United States be authorized to draw from the treasury a sum not exceeding ten thousand dollars, for the purpose of defraying the contingent charges of government, to be paid out of the monies arising as aforesaid from the duties on imports and tonnage; and that he cause a regular statement and account of such expenditures to be laid before Congress at the end of the year" (1 *Stat.* 105 [March 26, 1790]).
2. See Joseph Nourse to H, January 4, 1793.

To George Washington

[Philadelphia, January 25, 1793]

Mr. Hamilton presenting his respects to The President, submits the enclosed Drafts.[1]

25 January 1793

LC, George Washington Papers, Library of Congress.

1. The enclosures have not been found, but on January 25, 1793, "The Secretary of the Tresy sent to the President the supplimentary arrangemt. respectg the Surveys of No. Carolina" (JPP, 28). See also H to Washington, January 20, 1793.

From Wilhem and Jan Willink, Nicholaas and Jacob Van Staphorst, and Nicholas Hubbard

[*Amsterdam, January 25, 1793.* On February 26, 1793, Willink, Van Staphorst, and Hubbard wrote to Hamilton: "We had the honor to address You the 25 Ulto." *Letter not found.*]

To Tench Coxe[1]

[Philadelphia] Saturday. [January 26, 1793]

Dear sir,

I mentioned one or two things yesterday, which were urgent. One was the papers for the enquiry. You will see by the enclosed, that they are to go to the house of representatives. Will you be so good as to have a letter prepared this morning. I stay at home to-day, to look over petitions. Let the warrants, &c., be sent me.

Yours, affectionately. A. Hamilton.

George S. White, *Memoir of Samuel Slater, the Father of American Manufactures, Connected with a History of the Rise and Progress of the Cotton Manufacture in England and America* (Philadelphia, 1836), 290.

1. This letter concerns information which Coxe was to furnish H for the latter's "Report on the Balance of All Unapplied Revenues at the End of the Year 1792 and on All Unapplied Monies Which May Have Been Obtained by the Several Loans Authorized by Law," February 4, 1793.

Meeting of the Commissioners of the Sinking Fund

[Philadelphia, January 26, 1793]

At a meeting of the trustees of the sinking fund, on Saturday, the 26th of January, 1793,

Present: The Vice President, the Secretary of State, the Secretary of the Treasury, and the Attorney General.

The Secretary of the Treasury having informed the Board that one hundred and fifty thousand dollars remain unexpended, under the order of the sixteenth day of this instant (January:)[1]

Resolved, That the said one hundred and fifty thousand dollars be applied to the purchase of six per cent. stock and the deferred debt, on the principles of the resolutions of August, 1791;[2] that the agent prefer the one or the other, according as a greater or less rate of interest may be redeemed; and that the purchases be made either at Philadelphia, under the direction of Samuel Meredith, Treasurer of the United States; or at New York, under the direction of the cashier of the Office of Discount and Deposite of the Bank of the United States there.

ASP, Finance, I, 237.

1. See "Meeting of the Commissioners of the Sinking Fund," January 16, 1793.
2. See "Meeting of the Commissioners of the Sinking Fund," August 15, 1791.

From Tench Coxe

Treasury Department,
Revenue Office, January 29th 1793.

Sir,

I have the honor to enclose to you first draughts of several documents, agreably to the Note at the foot of this letter, containing a part of the information relative to the Revenue on distilled Spirits[1] indicated by your verbal communication of the 26th inst. Others are in preparation and will be sent when finished. It is supposed that an early view of these documents may be useful in the general preparation, which occasions their present transmission. Should any or all of these papers be necessary for transmission to the legislature they shall be fairly copied, and officially signed.

I am, sir, with great respect your most Obt. Servt.

Tench Coxe,

The Secretary of the Treasury

Commissr. of the Revenue.

LC, RG 58, Letters of Commissioner of Revenue, 1792–1793, National Archives.

1. A note at the bottom of Coxe's letter describes the enclosures as follows:

"A. General account of Bonds taken to secure the Duties on Spirits distilled in the United States whereon the Duty is payable by the gallon, commencing on the first day of July 1791 and ending on the 30th day Septemr. 1792. beyond which period no quarterly returns of Bonds have been received.

"B. General abstract of Duties arising on Stills in places other than Cities, Towns and Villages employed in distilling Spirits from domestic materials, commencing on the 1st day of July 1791 and ending on the 30th of June 1792, beyond which no half yearly abstracts have been received.

"C. Schedule of Monies paid by the several Supervisors into the Treasury of the United States from 1st July 1791 to the 31st day of December 1792."

The materials that Coxe enclosed were to be used by H for his "Report on the Balance of All Unapplied Revenues at the End of the Year 1792 and on All Unapplied Monies Which May Have Been Obtained by the Several Loans Authorized by Law," February 4, 1793.

To Charles Lee

[*Philadelphia, January 31, 1793.* On February 7, 1793, Lee wrote to Hamilton: "In answer to your letter of the 31st. of last month." *Letter not found.*]

From John F. Mercer[1]

Philadelphia Jany. 31. 1793.

Sir

I receiv'd a letter from you containing several enclosures[2] the Evening before I left Annapolis, & in the hurry of departure the package was left behind. I have since repeatedly written to have it forwarded to me but as this has not yet been done, I conclude that it is mislaid & that I shall not receive it whilst here. I must rely altogether therefore on my memory for the contents & will only suppress a wish that this Controversy might draw to a conclusion, as protraction has given room for many injurious calumnies—such as that I had denied at Philadelphia what I had asserted in Maryland—this I was told had been explicitly declar'd at the State House in Annapolis where the Legislature were then in Session during my absence, & I felt it ⟨therefore necessary⟩ to place every paper that had in any manner passed between us & relative to the subject in

ALS, Hamilton Papers, Library of Congress.

1. For background to this letter, see the introductory note to H to Mercer, September 26, 1792. See also H to Mercer, November 3, December 6, December, 1792; Mercer to H, October 16–28, December, 1792; H to David Ross, September 26, November 3, 1792; Ross to H, October 5–10, November 23, 1792; Uriah Forrest to H, November 7, 1792.

2. See H to Mercer, December 6, 1792, in which H enclosed copies of certificates concerning remarks made by Mercer during the Maryland campaign in the fall of 1792.

the hands of Mr. George Mann [3] for the perusal of any person, on whom he coud rely for their return.

After premising thus, I now declare generally that the Statements & Certificates Contain'd in your last exhibit full as much candor & much more truth, than I coud have expected from the preceding violence of the parties, all of whom excepting Mr. Key & Mr. Cramptin [4] (who also voted against me) were the principal partizans in the late opposition. In my general observations I mean to exclude Majr. Ross's own statements & Remarks. I have invariably declin'd answering directly any letter from him or expressing any sentiment relative to his Conduct on my Election unless when calld on in the public prints & I shall in this indirect manner commit myself as little as possible. It may not however be amiss to observe that it [is] not a *legal* attempt, to prove words declard to be spoken at Marlbrough by evidence of what was said at Annapolis, for the very obvious reason that there is not an opportunity of producing opposite testimony. However Capn. Campbells statement may perhaps set this in a clear light.[5] He brought your transactions in the purchase of Stock forward himself & produced the Law under which you acted sanction'd by the implied approbation of the President & a Majority of the Board.[6] He states this conduct to have arisen from a conversation I had with him on the subject of the procedure of that Board, & in fine that conversation & the discussion turning on yr. Conduct under the Law & his not suggesting that I exhibited you in any manner as dealing in Stocks on yr. own Acct. must evidence, that no such surmise was entertain'd there, as Majr. Ross is supposed to have brought forward in his publication [7] viz. that you dealt in Stock on your own acct. directly or indirectly. It will be also proper to remark that altho' the Questions in which you were involv'd were the leading or ostensible reasons originally assigned for the opposition to me as stated by Capn Campbell which however cannot be reconcild with his avow'd intention of offering for my District

3. Mann was the owner of an inn in Annapolis.

4. Philip Barton Key and Thomas Cramphin. Both men sent statements of their recollection of Mercer's remarks during the Maryland election campaign to Ross. See Ross to H, November 23, 1792.

5. See Ross to H, November 23, 1792, note 6.

6. See Ross to H, November 23, 1792, note 3.

7. For Ross's statement, see the introductory note to H to Mercer, September 26, 1792.

before I ever came to Congress, yet as brought before the public they were but a small part of his charges—these related chiefly to my conduct as a Member of the State Legislature & only gave way to the introduction of ye. subject as the Capital ground, after Major Ross took up his pen, & as my observations were all in reply to Capt. Campbells charges which I had Stated by impartial Persons in writing in Order to comment on whenever I spoke, it will account for the reiteration of similar observations in several distinct parts of the District.

With regard to the particular Certificates after remarking the uncandid insinuation that I had procurd Certificates from persons friendly to my Election & had meant to infer the contrary,[8] & stating what appears evidently on the fact of the Letter that the Gentlemen whom I had selected for moderatn & integrity, two on each side were furnished with a Copy of that Letter before I receiv'd any answer or coud possibly divine, that Mr. Rozier & Mr. Young[9] woud not be as willing & as explicit as the other two Gentlemen. I must fully admit that what Mr. Key states[10] who was present at

8. See Ross to H, November 23, 1792.

9. Mercer had written to Henry Rozier and Notley Young, among others, requesting statements on their recollection of Mercer's remarks concerning H. On October 23, 1792, Young replied to Mercer that, as he was "but partially present during your address to the people of Prince Georges County, and the greater part was unheard by me, I can not with propriety answer your Queries" (copy, Hamilton Papers, Library of Congress). At the bottom of a letter from William Paca, dated October 26, 1792, Mercer wrote: "No answer has yet been receivd from Mr. Henry Rozier" (copy, Hamilton Papers, Library of Congress).

10. Key's statement, dated November 17, 1792, was sent to Ross. See Ross to H, November 23, 1792. It reads as follows:

"In answer to your favor, I must inform you that I was present at Marlborough and at Annapolis *the second time,* that Col. Mercer addressed the People on the subject of his Election, in Opposition to Mr. Campbell. I was not in Annapolis at the first meeting.

"The general impressions made by Col. Mercer on Me were very unfavorable to the secretary of the Treasury. I can not detail particular expressions, for they have escaped my Memory, but two of his Charges were, 'that the secretary had interfered in our State Elections in favor of Campbell against him;' And that the secretary had lavish'd the public Money by purchasing *equal* Portions of Stock from *different Persons;* at *different Prices,* When He might have purchased the same from one, at the lowest Price, to answer better the Views and Object of Government.

"The Inference to be drawn from this was, that the secretary of the Treasury encouraged Speculation, and protected Speculators. He further declared that there were a Considerable Number of Persons in congress Who always *voted* with the Treasury, from undue Treasury Influence as I infered.

Marlbrough is the fact as far as it states facts. It shoud have gone farther & stated that I had explain'd that this conduct was founded on what I conceiv'd false principles of supporting public credit. The conclusion is Mr. Key's it was not mine. Mr. Cramptin's [11] did not appear to me to be explicit it only seems to corroborate Majr. Ross's publication by a general kind of warranty without descending to any particulars. There is no Certificate that insinuates that I wished to impress the public Mind with the Idea that you were a speculator in any sense of the word; unless it may be a part of Mr. Worthingtons [12] Certificate & this is not explicit & certainly admits of a different exp[la]nation. To say you were the head of the speculators, coud fairly be construed that they were under your patronage, & If I used any language of this kind which I cannot recollect that must have been the idea. For the contrary if it had been the case must have appeared explicitly from some one person as I spoke several times & pains have not been spared & the selection not such as to promise a very candid statement. Messrs. Wallace & Davidson,[13] state generally that I meant to make unfavorable impressions with respect to you & that people must have taken me as a great Enemy from what I said. I neither did nor do mean to impress any one that what I said was intended to raise your reputation as Member of the Government, not did I mean to promote it in any manner, but this I repeat that I spoke nothing that coud tend in my opinion to wound your honesty or integrity—which at that time I thought unimpeach'd & which I do not at this moment intend to insinuate any thing against. I certainly used language in every respect much more

---

"I do not recollect any expressions of Col. Mercer reflecting on *Mr Hamiltons* private Life. But as I consider public Dishonor of Character incompatible with private Integrity, and as those Charges, if true, are a stain on the secretary of the Treasury, I confess the Impressions on my Mind made by Col. Mercer Were very unfavorable to the secretary. A direct Interference in an Election would be very highly improper in him, and if the purchase of stock as related, was earnestly intended to encrease his Influence, It was dishonorable." (ALS, Hamilton Papers, Library of Congress.)

11. See note 4.

12. For John Worthington's statement, see Ross to H, November 23, 1792, note 5.

13. Ross had asked Charles Wallace and Major John Davidson to state their recollections of Mercer's remarks concerning H. See Ross to H, November 23, 1792. Davidson's reply is dated November 17, 1792 (ALS, Hamilton Papers, Library of Congress). Wallace's statement has not been found.

favorable than I had done before on the floor of Congress, & which had been very generally promulgated.

Capt. Campbell has stated the substance of private conversation in which he acknowledges that ye. subject was introduc'd by himself & he has committed several errors perhaps from want of recollection—particularly with regard to a precise Sum of 200,000 dollars.[14] I never knew the sum & he must have got this else where. Some of the errors I recollect to have contradicted before the first assemblage at Annapolis, but in general the conversation is such as really passed & altho' my authorities may have not been accurate, yet they were such as warranted my language in the manner in which the thing actually came forward. I recollect to have particularly declard that I never had said or thought that you were any how personally or pecuniarily interested with Duer,[15] & particularly stated my idea on that subject, that Duer was favor'd from motives of personal friendship in whatever transactions he was concern'd in that were connected with your office. With respect to the whole opposition agt. me, wherever it commenc'd it will ever be a disgrace to the opponents in its conduct & its event—deduct Mr. Thomas's[16] personal Warm friends & Relatives & a numerous Religious Society who heretofore attach'd to me & my politics were seperated by the Negro business in the State Legislature.[17] There never was a more feeble & contemtable Opposition for Numbers Wealth & Character. After this

14. See Ross to H, November 23, 1792, note 6.

15. For the statements of William Campbell and John Worthington concerning Mercer's remarks on William Duer's Army contract, see Ross to H, November 23, 1792, notes 5 and 6.

16. John Thomas, Mercer's opponent in the 1792 Maryland election campaign.

17. By "the Negro business in the State Legislature" Mercer is referring to the debates on the status of slaves which had taken place in 1791 when he had been a member of the Maryland House of Delegates. In December, 1791, the House of Delegates had considered complaints "respecting the conduct of the society in Baltimore county, who style themselves the Maryland Society for promoting the Abolition of Slavery and the relief of free Negroes and others unlawfully held in Bondage" and examined the society's memorial to the legislature. The society had been sponsoring petitions brought by slaves and freed Negroes in the criminal court of Baltimore County. On December 21, 1791, the House of Delegates resolved "That the memorial of the said society is indecent, illiberal, and highly reprehensible, and moreover is as untrue as it is illiberal." At the same time the House passed additional resolutions circumscribing the right of slaves to file manumission petitions in the Maryland courts (*Votes and Proceedings of the House of Delegates of the State of Maryland. November Session, 1791. Being the First Session of this Assembly*, 105–06, Microfilm Collection of Early State Records, Library of Congress).

detail I here again repeat what I formerly said that I neither did directly or indirectly represent you as any wise pecuniarily concern'd in purchasing or Selling Stock or impeach your honor or honesty. That I have been led into this business with provocation & that the attack has not been on my side—that altho I am infinitely above retorting the terms you have used, because it woud be but a paltry compromise with a delicacy really offended. Yet I again place myself on the ground of my original reply & without fearing or provoking any personal difference, I shall let it rest with you to decide whether any or what further steps the present controversy may require.

I am with due respects &c John F. Mercer

Idea Concerning a Lottery[1]

[Philadelphia, January, 1793]

In concerting a lottery, with a view to the best success of the undertaking—the following points seem necessary to be attended to—

1 That it be simple and summary; because it will be more readily understood by every body & the imagination will see fewer obstacles between *hope* and *gratification.*

2 That the Tickets be at a low price and within the reach of great numbers. The Rich or adventurous can then purchase a greater number to bring their chances to the same ratio with higher prices; and the less rich or more cautious can take a chance without putting much to risk. Every body, almost, can and will be willing to hazard a trifling sum for the chance of a considerable gain.

3 That there be rather a *small* number of *large* prizes or a *considerable* number of *considerable* prizes than a great number of *small* prizes; for adventurers would as leave lose altogether as acquire trifling prizes and would prefer a small chance of winning *a great deal* to a great chance of winning little. Hope is apt to supply the place of probability and the Imagination to be struck with glittering though precarious prospects. It may be suspected that in this country the middle course will best succeed; that is a *considerable* number of *considerable* prizes. Moderate sums will appear here great to far the greatest number of adventurers. And if the sum which may

be raised should be raised successively, it may be well to have such a number of prizes as will raise conversation of winnings within a number of little circles.

Taking these principles as guides and supposing 30000 Dollars (including charges) the sum to be raised—the following scheme may perhaps not be ineligible.

50000 Tickets each at 4 Dollars	200 000
Deduct sum to be raised	30 000
Difference will be the Total amt. of the prizes [2]	170 000

Prizes

1			20 000
3	each	10000	30 000
6	each	5000	30 000
10	each	1000	10 000
10	each	500	40 000
400	each	100	40 000
500			170 000

It will probably be found easier to raise the sum allowed to be raised in different portions than in an entire sum. I should not think 30 000 likely to be beyond the reach of pretty easy accomplishment.

Offices for the sale of Tickets ought to be opened at Powles Hook on the North River and at [3] on the Delaware. This will render Philadelphia & New York the *markets.*

Perhaps it will be most adviseable to draw the lottery at Powles Hook.

It is not certain that the following scheme would not succeed much better.

Prizes

1			50 000
1.			20 000
5.	each	10 000	50 000
50	each	1 000	50 000
			170 000 [4]

AD, Hamilton Papers, Library of Congress.

1. This lottery plan was drawn up by H for the use of a committee appointed on January 1, 1793, by the directors of the Society for Establishing

Useful Manufactures "to form a Plan for a Lottery to raise a part or the whole of the Monies authorized by the Charter for the use of the Society, and report the same to this Board at their next meeting ("Minutes of the S.U.M.," 78).

Joseph Stancliffe Davis describes the lottery experiment of the Society for Establishing Useful Manufactures as follows: "In April the outlines of the scheme were approved and a long list of prominent citizens of New York, New Jersey, and Philadelphia appointed 'Superintendents,' any three of whom (always including the governor of the Society) were empowered to modify the scheme in detail and carry it into execution. . . . at New Year's, 1794, public announcement was widely made. In brief the scheme was to sell 38,000 tickets at $7 each ($266,000); to give 14,539 prizes. . . . From the prizes fifteen per cent was to be deducted, thus raising $39,000 for the Society. . . . Before publishing the plan the board appointed a committee to attend the New York legislature at its next meeting with a petition requesting liberty to sell tickets of the lottery in that state. This was not accomplished. In April, 1794, the board . . . [recommended] 'to the superintendants to send on Tickets to the New England States as far as Boston. . . .' All efforts were fruitless. The drawings, announced 'positively' to take place, were repeatedly postponed. At last, in November, 1795, the failure of the scheme was faced, and a new plan for raising only $6667.50 was substituted. The drawings for this too were postponed, but they did actually take place in the summer and fall of 1796. It is gravely to be doubted, however, whether the proceeds covered the expenses which had been entailed" (Davis, *Essays*, I, 477–79).

2. In the margin opposite this paragraph H wrote:

"1.		30 000
1.		20 000
1.		10 000
2	e 5000	10 000
4	ea 2500	10 000
5	ea 1000	5 000
6"		

3. Space left blank in MS.

4. The following "Scheme for a Lottery" in an unidentified handwriting may be found among the Hamilton Papers, Library of Congress:

"Scheme for a Lottery

2 of 30,000		60,000	
2 " 20,000		40,000	
4 " 10,000		40,000	
8 " 5,000		40,000	
10 " 2,000		20 000	
15 " 1,000		15,000	
20 " 500		10,000	
40 " 200		8,000	
60 " 100		6,000	
100 " 50		5,000	
1 first Drawn		2,000+	transpose this to last drawn because the Sales will be promoted by the expectations at the close. Qu: would it not be well to transpose of 20 or 30,000 Drs. to *the last drawn.*
5 first Drawn last 5 Days		10,000	
1 last Drawn		2 000	
16400 of 30		492 000	
16668 prizes			
33232 Blanks			
50,000 Tickets @ 15 Ds. each		750,000	

The Tickets all to be sold by Contract the Contractors giving security for keeping their engagements. The time of drawing to be fixed by *Law* and Commissioners appointed also by *Law* to attend the same. The payments to be made by *installments*. The *Law* that authorizes the drawing of the Lottery must also fix *the time of payment* of the *prizes*. There must also be a *Law* Authorizing proper persons who apply for the privilege to devide the Tickets in halves, quarters, Eights &c. first depositing *the Ticket so divided* in the hands of some responsible *public* officer who will by some signature *Identify* the shares so divided and stamp a Value upon them in the public opinion that *nothing else* will give them. The Tickets to be delivered to the Subscribers at 17.25 each Ticket and *no deduction* whatever made from the prizes. This will cover the 100,000 Dr and leave a handsome allowance for the expences attending the conducting drawing &c."

On James Blanchard[1]

[Philadelphia, January, 1793]

That the spirit of Faction is a common and one of the most *fatal* diseases of Republics, one which has most frequently wrought their destruction, is a truth witnessed by all history and by all experience.

ADf, Hamilton Papers, Library of Congress.

1. Blanchard had served as quartermaster and regimental paymaster of the Third New Hampshire Regiment during the American Revolution. In 1791 and 1792 he was a persistent opponent of the funding system and an advocate of discrimination in favor of those Revolutionary War soldiers who through necessity had alienated their certificates. Blanchard's letters suggest that he was a self-appointed delegate to persuade the soldiers of the Revolutionary Army in the various states to demand from the United States Congress a settlement of their claims. See Blanchard to H, May, 1791, February 29, 1792.

This essay by H was prompted by the following exchange of letters between Blanchard and John N. Cumming, a businessman from Newark, New Jersey, which appeared in the [Philadelphia] *National Gazette* on January 5, 1793:

"Mr. Freneau,

"Please to give the two following letters a place in your paper, and you will oblige

"Your humble servant, James Blanchard

"Phila. Jan. 4 1793.

"Sir,

"I received your's of November 15, a few days since. Your information by Capt. Donald was true respecting both your and Gen. [William] Hull's circular letters. The Cincinnati, as a society, voted against taking up the consideration, but had nothing against the merits of the memorial of Gen. Hull, as officers. A number of our leading characters, from fortunate circumstances, kept their certificates, and perhaps purchased some in addition, and feel themselves very comfortable. The officers of inferior ranks have mostly moved out of the state, or by marriage or business got Into tolerable circumstances. It is said our members of Congress, at least two of them, viz. [Elias] Boudinot and [Jonathan] Dayton, have made money by speculation. As for my own part, thank God, I am able to live by the sweat of my brow: almost all my certificates I sold at about 3/4 for 20/.—throwing in the interest. I thought from the disposition of the officers, at their last meeting, that it would be difficult to obtain a meeting of one half on the subject—my business requiring my constant attention, induced me to lay aside any thoughts on the subject. I have at the same time no doubt but about one half of our officers, were they collected, would join with you and the rest of our brethren, in asserting claims founded in perfect justice.

"I am, Sir Your obedient servant, J. N. Cumming.

"New-Ark, Dec. 5, 1792.

"Philadelphia, Dec. 19, 1792.

"Sir,

"I received your favor of the 5th instant, and wrote you a few lines in answer; but on a second reading, I beg leave to inform you, that I lament your senior officers declining to come forward in behalf of those of inferior rank and the soldiery, who have not ability to come forward for themselves.

"Notwithstanding those gentlemen have been so fortunate as to retain their own certificates, and perhaps to make an addition, the remnant petitioned for would not affect their purchases, but do justice to their private stock.

"With regard to your members, Captain Dayton was not in Congress when the funding law passed, and cast his bread upon the waters with other speculators. But Mr. Boudinot was in Congress, and having a large sum in fictitious certificates, had an opportunity to fund a large sum of debt for a small sum in specie.

"The representatives from the Eastern States are endeavoring to persuade the agents that are here, that they will see the fallacy of their application; for the representatives of the states of Virginia and Georgia do not mean, by advocating the cause of the army, that they should receive any payments, but to bring on a division, in hopes to overthrow the government.

"This would be an unpopular doctrine in Virginia, as they have the fullest confidence in the justice and ability of their members.

"The farmers in the southern states conceive they have been swindled out of their certificates by the New-England speculators. This belief has been corroborated on the information of a letter from Mr. Amasa Learned, a member from Connecticut, in the beginning of the last session to Mr. Jedidiah Leeds, of Richmond, soliciting him to be an agent in Virginia (either on commissions, or as a partner) for the purpose of purchasing the deferred and state debts; advising that those certificates could be purchased at a low rate, and that the Secretary of the Treasury was bringing forward a plan to make the whole debt at 6 per cent. stock, which was then selling at 25 shillings in the pound. But Mr. Leeds doubted the propriety of the transaction, and declined the concern.

"At present I can form no conjecture of the sequel. Col. Hamilton, notwithstanding his appointment in the continental army, secured to himself a place from danger, and was indulged two years previous to the treaty of peace, to be absent on his private concerns, and in the advantages of speculation: since he has been Secretary of the Treasury, he is against any payments, except the depreciated paper which the army have received, that netted them only one eighth of the sum stipulated in specie for their monthly wages: And the President, notwithstanding his pathetic promises in general orders, at New-Windsor

That this spirit would make its way into the American Republic was a thing to have been looked for, as well from the nature of man, as from the experience which has been had in every other case. But that it would so soon have attained the extreme violence at which it has arrived—that at so early a stage of our public affairs, we should have seen a powerful party formed in our councils actuated wholly by the springs of personal rivalship jealousy and animosty—considering men only and not measures resisting constantly whatever is proposed, by others—and proposing nothing themselves for the public interest or advantage—exhibiting a perpetual conflict of principles, true only to the point of personal opposition, maligning today this measure because it contains a particular quality or does not permit a particular thing; and tomorrow quarrelling with that very quality and rejecting that very thing when it is presented to them in another measure—labouring incessantly to obscure the clearest objects and to excite fears doubts and distrusts in the community which they cannot themselves feel—always industriously sowing and fostering discontents, artfully inviting to their standard the discontented of every description—countenancing and using as instruments of the foulest calumny and detraction the most worthless characters among us—and in the desperate game of ambition putting every thing that is dear in Society to the hazard of the die—that we should so soon have been witnesses to such a scene was not within the ordinary course of probality. Yet such is the true picture of our situation—a situation which ought to be viewed by every sober and virtuous citizen as the melancholy prognostic of future convulsion and calamity—a situation nevertheless far from being as extensively understood as it ought to be and which, except with a few, who have better opportunities of observation has not hitherto excited a due degree of alarm or attention. The pernicious designs meditated against the public tranquillity & happiness are cloaked under so thick a veil of hypocrhisy, that the real conspirators against

(That a country rescued by their arms from impending ruin, will never leave unpaid the debt of gratitude) is now silent.

"The writings for public information on the funding system are nearly finished, and a part are sent to the counties of Berkshire and Hampshire, in Massachusetts.

"I am, Sir, most respectfully, Your humble servant, James Blanchard.

"To Col. J. N. Cumming—Newark"

the public weal pass with a large proportion of the community as its best friends and guardians.

Such alas has been the usual good fortune of the same description of men in all countries and at all times! Happy thrice happy will be it for the People of America if they shall finally vindicate their character for discernment, by avoiding the snares which are spread for them by these wiley hypochrites—these crafty and abandonned imposters!

One of the principal engines, which is imployed by the party alluded to, is an unremitting effort to destroy, by every expedient they can devise, no matter how base, the public confidence in those, who are the most powerful obstacles to their machinations.

General and indiscrimate charges, dark and mysterious hints of speculation and corruption in the characters they wished to pull down were for a long time the weapons they have employed to effect their favourite purpose. But grown bolder of late and finding other means necessary to forward the work they have at length adopted the expedient of employing persons as public Accusers—who having no characters to lose, do not scruple to affix their names to the calumniating falshoods which are dictated to them.

A gross and disgustful instance of this exists in the case of James Blanchard; a man absolutely bankrupt both in fortune and fame. This Desperado comes forward the Apostle of purity, the Champion of the injured Soldier, the professor of a holy zeal against speculation and speculators—and to bestow an air of authenticity upon the slanders he wishes to propagate, he gives them the sanction of his name. See publication on the Signature of JB in the NG.[2] Other instruments of the party are at the same time employed, in order to give importance to his communications, to make the panygeric of his independence and virtue. And Mr. Blanchard finds himself the theme of encomiastic addresses.[3]

Who is this virtuous Champion? Let the following narrative answer.

2. See note 1.

3. In the margin opposite this sentence H wrote: "See: address to JB in the NG." This is a reference to a letter to James Blanchard, signed "A Fellow Laborer," which had appeared in the *National Gazette* on January 9, 1793.

(History of Blanchard & his tricks & falsehoods accompanied with a plan & distinct reference to the proofs?) [4]

Now let the Public judge what regard is due to the ridiculous tales of this worthless man. And what respect to a party which countenances and puts into action such vile and detestable instruments.

Among the characters he has attempted to asperse is found the Secretary of the Treasury. I pass by as unworthy of notice the insinuations he throws out to the prejudice of that Gentleman's military merit. Let the appeal be here to recorded facts and to the knowlege of the whole army.

I confine myself to those suggestions which endeavour to throw upon him the suspicion of being what is generally understood by the word Speculator. The immaculate Blanchard says [5]

Mr. Hamilton finished his Military service with the seize of York, at which he commanded a corps of Light Infantry composed of detachments from different Regiments; and being attached to no permanent corps of the army the event of that seige which was in fact the termination of military operations in all but S C & Georgia left him without the opportunity of being further useful in the army. He however did not *resign* but obtained a *furlough* or *leave of absence* from the commander in Chief; with the declared intention of rejoining the army if circumstances, contrary to expectation, should call for farther exertions in that line. Mr Hamilton then went to Albany where he had left Mrs. Hamilton in the house of her father, and resumed the study of the law which he had but began at the time of his entrance into the army in the early part of 1776—a

4. The following document, in an unidentified handwriting, dated "Philadelphia Jany 8th 1793," in the Hamilton Papers, Library of Congress, is part of the evidence collected by H: "Mr. Blanchard in conversation with Mr. Isaac Bronson, mentioned that his last journey to Virginia was unsuccessful, he not being able to raise money by the sale of Lands as he expected; so as to profit by a List of bounty Lands due to the Virginia Line. Being asked how he obtained the List, he replied that it was '*by stealth from the War Office*'—but that the Office was now more careful & that another List could not be obtained. He admitted that he had not personally suffered by the depreciation of Certificates, his own being *lately* obtained. Mr. Bronson understood from Blanchard that he had not seen Mr. Learneds Letter to which he had alluded in the Newspaper publication but that there was a Man in Philadelphia who had seen it. This conversation was this day."

5. At this point H left a space of several lines blank in the MS. See note 1.

pursuit which it will readily be conceived engaged his whole time and attention.

In [July, 1782] [6] the Legislature of New York elected him a Member of Congress, which body he joined at an interesting period of the public affairs and continued with in until [July, 1783] when he left it, returned to Albany and resumed the pursuit of the Law.

In [December, 1783] the City of New York was evacuated. Mr Hamilton removed with his family to that City; and was constantly afterwards, except when diverted from it by temporary public avocations, sedulously engaged in the practice of the Law.

It is well known to all his fellow Citizens (and candid men of all parties will confess it) that Mr. Hamilton scrupulousness forebore being concerned in what is termed speculation (the most familiar objects of which in the state of New York were Public Securities and confiscated property). In fine he came into his present Office, with a character in pecuniary respects, as pure as any man in the UStates. Such was the general opinion & voice of his fellow Citizens?

Is it probable then that since he has been in Office, when under a positive and explicit prohibition of law, he should not only have abandonned all the maxims of his former life—but should disgrace himself by a perjured violation of his Official duties? Is such a suspicion to be entertained upon the surmises of a virulent and persecuting Faction or the insinuations of a man who is proved to be destitute of Truth and honor?

Mr. Blanchard has not indeed directly charged the Secretary of the Treasury with being concerned while in Office in speculation; but he has stated [7]

and has left it to be inferred that there was an interested understanding between Mr. H and Mr Larned in relation to a plan intended to be brought before Congress.

With sensible men the absurdity of the things refutes the suggestion. It is destitute of all probability that Mr. H should ever have had it in contemplation to propose to Congress to raise the three to 6 ℔ Cents to six and make the deferred bear a present interest of 6 ℔ Cent which is the allegation of Mr. Blanchard. Such a plan would have contradicted all the principles Mr. H had laid down in his re-

6. The dates enclosed in brackets in this document were omitted in MS.

7. At this point H left a space of several lines blank in the MS. See note 1.

ports would have called immediately for great additional resources of taxation which he has uniformly manifested his opinion could not be commanded and would have had not the least chance of success with Congress. It is certain that no such plan has ever been hinted to Congress by the Secretary; and considering what manner of man Mr Blanchard is, the natural conclusion must be that the whole tale is an aukward and malicious forgery.

From Tench Coxe

Treasury Department, Revenue Office, February 1, 1793. Encloses "for the purpose of submission to the President, a contract between the Superintendent of the light House at Portsmouth [1] in New Hampshire and Titus Salter [2] for six months." Discusses the terms of the contract.

LC, RG 58, Letters of Commissioner of Revenue, 1792–1793, National Archives.

1. Joseph Whipple, collector of customs at Portsmouth, was also superintendent of the Portsmouth lighthouse.

1. Salter was keeper of the Portsmouth lighthouse.

To Thomas Jefferson

Treasury Department Febry 1st 1793

Sir

The following is an extract from a letter of Mr Short to me, dated Hague November 2. 1792.

"I should repeat perhaps what I formerly mentioned to you, that Mr. Jefferson on his departure from Paris left with me bills of exchange to the amount of I think 66,000 ₶. This was destined to a particular object with which you are aquainted.[1] He expected it would be immediately applied and therefore wished me to be the instrument instead of deposing it in a Bankers hands, to avoid the Commission. When the term of these bills arrived, finding less probability of their being immediately applied, and not chusing to keep by me such a sum at my risk in an house which was robbed regularly two or three times a year, I gave the bills to Mr Grand[2] to receive their amount, and to hold it appropriated to the object in question. It remains still in his hands, having never been called for. I wrote more than once respecting it on finding the depreciation commencing, but never received an answer. It remains now to be considered whether you would chuse to receive it in its depreciated State or wait for the change of circulating medium in France."

This communication is made with a request to know, whether the fund in question continues to be necessary for its original purpose or may be withdrawn.

I have the honor to be very respectfully Sir Your obedient Servant Alex Hamilton

The Secretary of State

LS, Thomas Jefferson Papers, Library of Congress.

1. This money was intended for the ransom of American captives at Algiers. See William Short to H, November 2, 1792, note 10; Jefferson to H, February 4, 1793.

2. Ferdinand Le Grand.

To William Short

Treasury Department February 1st 1793

Sir

Since my last letter to you dated the 31st of December last, of which a Duplicate is enclosed, I have received yours of the 27th of October and 2d of November.

It was not intended by mine of the 28th of August, that the account to be rendered by you should extend to any of the payments made by the Commissioners [1] on account of the Debt to France, or the foreign loans, or the bills drawn from hence. But merely to your particular Transactions—your Salary &a; or to any monies which may have been drawn from the Commissioners and put under your disposition for ulterior expenditure.

I presume a duplicate of the accounts transmitted by you to the Secretary of State will answer the purpose.

With respectful consideration I have the honor to be Sir Your obedient Servant Alexander Hamilton

William Short Esqr

LS, William Short Papers, Library of Congress.

1. Willink, Van Staphorst, and Hubbard.

To Wilhem and Jan Willink, Nicholaas and Jacob Van Staphorst, and Nicholas Hubbard

[*Philadelphia, February 1, 1793.* On May 1, 1793, Willink Van Staphorst, and Hubbard wrote to Hamilton: "We received your Respected favors of 1 February, 15 & 16 March." *Letter of February 1 not found.*]

From Tench Coxe

Treasury Department, Revenue Office, February 4, 1793. Transmits a statement "of the Revenue on Spirits distilled in the United States from foreign and domestic materials from the commencement of the duty thereon to the thirty first of December 1792." Emphasizes that the statement is "founded in some degree upon informal documents and information derived from official correspondence."

LC, RG 58, Letters of Commissioner of Revenue, 1792–1793, National Archives.

From Thomas Jefferson

Philadelphia, February 4th. 1793.

Sir,

The details respecting the Sum of 66,000 ₶., which are the subject of Mr. Short's letter of Nov. 2d. 1792; and of yours of the 1st instant, and which he observes still remains in the hands of Mr. Grand, are as follow.

On the 14th. of February 1785, Congress appropriated a sum of 80,000 Dollars, for the purpose of effecting Treaties with the Barbary States.[1] The missions of Mr. Barclay to Morocco, and of Mr. Lamb, to Algiers, were made on this fund.[2] On the 18th. of July, and 12th. of October 1787, they gave orders to their Minister Plenipotentiary at Versailles to take measures, through the agency of a particular religious order, for ransoming their citizens in captivity at algiers, and constituted the Balance of the appropriation of

February 14. 1785, as a fund for this purpose.[3] On the 21st. of February 1789, the Commissioners of the Treasury, drew an order on their Bankers in Holland in favor of the minister Plenipotentiary of the United States, at Versailles for 30,000 florins, supposed to be the Balance aforesaid, which order came to my hands, on the 5th. of April. I left Paris in September following, at which time a part of the Bills for this sum, had been remitted to me; but were not yet due. These I delivered to Mr. Short, to whom bills for the residue were also sent by the Bankers: and the Religious order, which I had engaged to commence the negotiation were notified that the business had devolved on Mr. Short.[4] Letters received in 1790, left little to hope from their agency. The State of this business was reported by me to Congress December 28, 1790,[5] and I submitted the expediency of adopting some more promising measures, without relinquishing the chance of success by the former: of which, however, having little hope, you will recollect that I proposed to you the application of this money to the payment of our foreign Officers at Paris,[6] rather than let it lie idle there, and, more especially, as we might then presume on commanding that sum at any time, should the negotiations at Algiers, call for it, contrary to expectations. You observed to me that you did not think yourself authorized to change the appropriation of this money, without an Act of Congress, but that you were then preparing a report for Congress, which would necessarily comprehend this object. I, accordingly wrote to Mr. Short, on the 23rd. of January 1791,[7] in these words "We must still pursue the redemption of our captives, through the same channel, till some better means can be devised. The money, however, which is in Mr. Grand's hands, will be the subject of a letter to you from the Secretary of the Treasury, as soon as he can have an act of Congress, authorizing the application of it, to the debt of the foreign officers." Mr. Short, in a letter of March 30. 1791,[8] acknowledged the receipt of this letter of mine, which, probably had escaped his recollection, when in that to you of Nov. 2d. 1792, he said he had never received an answer, unless he meant a definitive answer. The subsequent appropriation of 50,000 Dollars by Congress in their act of may 8. 92. c. 41. § 3.[9] being a substitute for the sum in the hands of Mr. Grand, the latter became unnecessary for it's original purpose, and therefore open to any other application.

I must apologize for the minuteness of these details, by the desire I felt of availing myself of the occasion furnished by your letter of possessing the Treasury office with a full statement of a transaction, in which I, among others, had been entrusted, while the particulars are yet in my mind, and on papers in my possession.

I am, with due respect Sir, Your most obedt servant,

The Secretary of the Treasury

Copy, Thomas Jefferson Papers, Library of Congress; LC, RG 59, Domestic Letters, 1792–1795, National Archives.

1. *JCC*, XXVIII, 65.

2. Thomas Barclay, who was appointed in October, 1785, as an agent of the United States to negotiate a treaty with Morocco, had successfully concluded a treaty with the Emperor of that country in January, 1787. John Lamb had been appointed agent to Algiers in October, 1785, with instructions to negotiate a treaty with that country. The demands of the Dey of Algiers, however, proved so exorbitant that in September, 1786, Lamb was ordered to return to the United States without concluding an agreement. For material relating to the missions of Barclay and Lamb, see Boyd, *Papers of Thomas Jefferson*, VIII, 610–24, and *ASP*, *Foreign Relations*, I, 100–04.

3. On February 1, 1787, Jefferson, at that time United States Minister Plenipotentiary to France, had written to John Jay: "If these pyrates find that they can have a very great price for Americans, they will abandon proportionably their pursuits against other nations to direct them towards ours. That the choice of Congress may be enlarged as to the instruments they may use for effecting the redemption, I think it my duty to inform them that there is here an order of priests called the Mathurins, the object of whose institution is to beg alms for the redemption of captives. They keep members always in Barbary searching out the captives of their own country, and redeem I beleive on better terms than any other body, public or private. It occured to me that their agency might be obtained for the redemption of our prisoners at Algiers. I obtained conferences with the General and with some members of the order. The General, with all the benevolence and cordiality possible, undertook to act for us if we should desire it. . . . I informed the general that I should communicate the good dispositions of his order to those who alone had the authority to decide whatever related to our captives" (Boyd, *Papers of Thomas Jefferson*, XI, 101–02).

On July 18, 1787, Jefferson's letter was read in the Continental Congress, and he was "authorised to take such measures as he may deem most adviseable for redeeming the American Captives at Algiers, and at any expence not exceeding that which European Nations usually pay in like cases" (*JCC*, XXXII, 364–65). On October 12, 1787, Congress resolved: "That the balance of the appropriation for the Barbary treaties of 14 feby 1785 not hitherto applied to that Object be and it is hereby constituted a fund for redeeming the American captives now at Algiers and that the same be for this purpose subject to the direction of the Minister of the United States at the Court of Versailles" (*JCC*, XXXIII, 664). See also *ASP*, *Foreign Relations*, I, 100–02.

4. Jefferson's letter, addressed to "Monsr. Chauvier, General et grand ministre des Chanoines reguliers de l'Ordre de la Sainte Trinité. Rue des Mathurins," is printed in Boyd, *Papers of Thomas Jefferson*, XV, 430–31.

5. Jefferson's report on the prisoners at Algiers was presented to Congress on December 30, 1790. It is printed in *ASP, Foreign Relations*, I, 100–04.

6. For a description of the debt due the foreign officers, see William Short to H, August 3, 1790, note 5. Section 5 of "An Act supplementary to the act making provision for the Debt of the United States" (1 *Stat.* 282 [May 8, 1792]) authorized the President "to cause to be discharged the principal and interest of the said debt, out of any of the monies, which have been or shall be obtained on loan." For the negotiations on the payment of these officers, see H to Short, August 16, September 13, 1792; H to George Washington, August 27, 1792; Washington to H, August 31, 1792; H to Gouverneur Morris, September 13, 1792.

7. ALS, letterpress copy, Thomas Jefferson Papers, Library of Congress.

8. ALS, Thomas Jefferson Papers, Library of Congress.

9. Section 3 of "An Act making certain appropriations therein specified" reads as follows: "*And be it further enacted,* That a sum of fifty thousand dollars in addition to the provision heretofore made be appropriated to defray any expense which may be incurred in relation to the intercourse between the United States and foreign nations, to be paid out of any monies, which may be in the treasury, not otherwise appropriated, and to be applied under the direction of the President of the United States, who, if necessary, is authorized to borrow, on the credit of the United States, the said sum of fifty thousand dollars; an account of the expenditure whereof as soon as may be, shall be laid before Congress" (1 *Stat.* 285).

Report on the Balance of All Unapplied Revenues at the End of the Year 1792 and on All Unapplied Monies Which May Have Been Obtained by the Several Loans Authorized by Law

[Philadelphia, February 4, 1793]

Introductory Note

Republican leaders in Congress were determined to demonstrate that Hamilton's administration of the Treasury Department was at worst corrupt or at best irregular. His opponents in Congress thought that they could discredit him by investigating the way in which he had handled the proceeds from two loans which Congress had authorized in 1790. "An Act making provision for the (payment of the) Debt of the United States" [1] provided for a twelve-million-dollar loan, the proceeds of which were to be used for the payment of interest and installments of the foreign debt. "An Act making Provision for the Reduction of the Public Debt" [2] provided for a two-million-dollar loan, the proceeds of which were to be used for the purchase of the domestic debt. On the basis of these two acts loans were floated at Amsterdam and Antwerp.[3]

Copy, RG 233, Reports of the Treasury Department, 1792–1793, Vol. III, National Archives.

1. 1 *Stat.* 138–44 (August 4, 1790).

2. 1 *Stat.* 186–87 (August 12, 1790).

3. For an account of the negotiation of these loans, see H's correspondence with William Short and the Amsterdam banking firm of Willink, Van Staphorst, and Hubbard.

In using the money obtained through these loans, the Republicans in Congress charged that Hamilton had ignored the congressional stipulation that the first loan should be used exclusively for payment of the foreign debt and the second loan for payment of the domestic debt. In sum, they stated that he had employed a part of the twelve million dollars to pay the domestic debt and a part of the two million dollars to pay the foreign debt.

The Republicans in Congress first became suspicious of Hamilton's handling of these funds when he proposed that the Government pay its entire debt to the Bank of the United States by floating a new loan abroad.[4] On December 24 and 27, 1792, the House of Representatives passed resolutions calling for information on the Government loans.[5] Hamilton replied with his "Report on Foreign Loans" on January 3, 1793. The House, however, was not satisfied with this report, and on January 23, 1793, it adopted five resolutions proposed by William Branch Giles, a Virginia Republican, who frequently served as Thomas Jefferson's spokesman in the House. The famous "Giles resolutions" read as follows:

"*Resolved,* That the President of the United States be requested to cause to be laid before this House copies of the authorities under which loans have been negotiated, pursuant to the acts of the fourth and twelfth of August, one thousand seven hundred and ninety, together with copies of the authorities directing the application of the moneys borrowed.

"*Resolved,* That the President of the United States be requested to cause this House to be furnished with the names of the persons by whom, and to whom, the respective payments of the French debt have been made in France, pursuant to the act for that purpose; specifying the dates of the respective drafts upon the Commissioners in Holland, and the dates of the respective payments of the debt. A similar statement is requested respecting the debts to Spain and Holland.

"*Resolved,* That the Secretary of the Treasury be directed to lay before this House an account exhibiting, half-monthly, the balances between the United States and the Bank of the United States, including the several Branch Banks, from the commencement of those Institutions, to the end of the year one thousand seven hundred and ninety-two.

"*Resolved,* That the Secretary of the Treasury be directed to lay before this House an account of all moneys which may have come into the Sinking Fund, from the commencement of that Institution to the present time; specifying the particular fund from which they have accrued, and exhibiting, half-yearly, the sums uninvested, and where deposited.

"*Resolved,* That the Secretary of the Treasury be directed to report to this House the balance of all unapplied revenues at the end of the year one thousand seven hundred and ninety-two, specifying whether in money or bonds, and noting where the money is deposited; that he also make report of all unapplied moneys which may have been obtained by the several loans authorized by law, and where such moneys are now deposited." [6]

4. See "Report on the Redemption of the Public Debt," November 30, 1792.
5. *Annals of Congress,* III, 753, 761.
6. *Annals of Congress,* III, 835–36.

Giles's speech to the House of Representatives in support of these resolutions reads as follows:

"The resolutions . . . have grown out of the embarrassments I have met with in attempting to comprehend the Report of the Secretary of the Treasury, made in pursuance of an order of this House of the 27th of December, 1792, exhibiting sundry statements respecting foreign loans.[7] These embarrassments have increased in proportion to the attention which I have bestowed on the subject; and a number of official papers to which I have had reference for information, instead of elucidating, seem rather to obscure the inquiry. To obtain necessary information, therefore, is the object of these resolutions, and no one can doubt the immediate applicability of this information to a bill now lying upon your table, for the purpose of reimbursing the loan of $2,000,000,000 made of the Bank of the United States, by opening a new loan for that sum abroad, and by changing the application of the like sum already borrowed and appropriated to the discharge of the debt to France from its original destination to the immediate discharge of the debt to the Bank.[8]

"The first resolution has arisen from that part of the printed Report of the Secretary of the Treasury which exhibits the terms upon which various loans have been made abroad, but neither presents the precise authorities under which those negotiations have been made, nor the precise amount of the sums borrowed for the separate and distinct objects of the two acts mentioned in the resolution.

"Another reason has more strongly suggested the propriety of calling for the information requested by this resolution. The bill now upon your table, which has been before alluded to, contemplates the whole of the moneys borrowed from abroad, and now on hand, as being originally appropriated to the discharge of the French debt, and proposes to change the original destination of these identical moneys; and the reason assigned for this measure has been the unsettled state of affairs in France.

"In the printed Report of the Secretary of the Treasury, he remarks that the same moneys are *applicable* to the Sinking Fund. It appears strange, that after express and distinct appropriations by law, that any misunderstanding relative to this object should exist, and the information called for may possibly explain this seeming contradiction.

"The second resolution has arisen from that part of the printed Report marked B, and which exhibits the payments made to France, but does not furnish the names of the persons engaged in those negotiations, nor does it present to view the length of time those persons have been possessed of the public moneys, by stating the dates of the respective drafts in Holland, and the dates of the actual application of the moneys to the discharge of the debt; and it is evident that from the time the loans are respectively created, to the times of the actual application of the moneys

7. See "Report on Foreign Loans," January 3, 1793.

8. "A bill providing for the reimbursement of a loan made of the Bank of the United States" had been introduced in the House on December 21, 1792 (*Journal of the House*, I, 652).

borrowed, the United States are paying the usual interest upon the debt intended to be redeemed, and the stipulated interest upon the moneys borrowed for the redemption. This remark is equally applicable to the payments of other foreign debts with the payments of the debt to France.

"The third resolution has arisen from calculations drawn partly from the last page of the printed report, and from the original Bank book of the United States, from which it appears that the balances in Bank in favor of the United States were as follows:

In Bank, Philadelphia, 30th May, 1792, and 16th June, same year, in branch banks	$676,952	55
1792, June 30th, in all banks in the United States	555,271	22
July 28th and 31st, in all banks in the United States	511,423	91
August 25th, 30th, and 31st, in all banks in the United States	740,903	87

"On the 1st of June, a loan was negotiated with the Bank of the United States on the part of the United States, for $100,000, at 5 per cent. per annum. On the 1st of July, another loan was made upon the same terms for the like sum. On the 1st of August, another loan was made upon the same terms for the like sum. On the 1st of September, another loan was made upon the same terms for the like sum. It appears from the last page of the printed Report, that there had been drawn into America, from the 15th of December, 1790, to the 27th of January, 1792, of the moneys borrowed abroad, the sum of 2,663,621 florins, 2 stivers, and 6 deniers. If this sum were unexpended, and lodged in the bank at the times of making these loans, (and Congress have never yet been informed of any deficiency of revenue,) the United States will, of consequence, have paid upon the moneys borrowed from the Bank of the United States, from 15 to 17 per cent. per annum, to wit: they will have paid 5 per cent. upon the original debt to France, 5 per cent. upon the moneys borrowed for its redemption, exclusive of douceurs and other charges, and 5 per cent. upon the sum borrowed of the bank, which may be deemed part of this deposite made in the Bank by the United States. But, discarding these inferences, it must at least be admitted that the United States are paying 5 per cent. for the loan of moneys from the Bank, when a sum larger than the loan itself, is actually deposited in Bank. It is here to be remarked, that a balance of cash is admitted, by the Treasurer's return, to have been in his hands on the 31st of December, 1790, amounting to $973,342 43, and in July 30, 1791, the sum of $582,189 54.

"I am informed that bills are often drawn in favor of the Bank for moneys in the hands of the revenue officers in distant parts of the United States, and that credit is entered in the Bank book upon the receipt of such bills, although the moneys may not actually be in Bank for some time after the credit is entered, and hence it is inferred that the Bank-book does not conclusively show the real sum in Bank, not to mention that such bills answer all the purposes of cash, and ought therefore to be credited upon the receipt of them. It is to be remarked that there is a regular and continual influx of moneys into the Bank by the operation of these bills. It is not very material whether a bill lodged in Bank to-day, should be paid to-day, provided something like the same sum should be paid in consequence of a bill lodged in Bank one or two months ago, and the bill of to-day should be paid one or two months hence. The following statement will, in some measure, explain this idea, by exhibiting half-monthly the balances of public money in all the banks, about the middle and end of each month, beginning with May, 1792, and ending with December of the same year:

May	$340,322 11
May	332,116 35
June	776,107 65
June	523,272 22
July	441,637 13
July	521,426 91
August	743,470 19
August	740,903 08
September	695,302 23
September	367,961 25
October	456,895 52
October	473,388 99
November	681,250 09
November	811,212 51
December 15	1,020,824 73
December 22, and January 5—last returns	790,642 11

"The fourth resolution has arisen from that part of the printed Report which remarks that the *residue of the sum drawn from Holland*, amounting to $1,668,188 27 *is applicable to the purchase of the public debt.* It is known that the sum of $1,374,656 40, being the surplus of the revenue up to the end of December, 1790, was originally appropriated to the Sinking Fund; that the surplus of other appropriations have been applied to this fund, and that the interest of the debt purchased has also been wholly appropriated to its increase. It is also known that between $1,100,000 and $1,200,000, and no more, of the original appropriation, have been really invested in the purchase of the debt; it is, therefore, somewhat unaccountable that so large a sum as $1,668,188 should be drawn from the loans abroad, when the Sinking Fund has always overflowed from domestic resources, and when the probability of purchasing is extremely lessened by the rise in the price of paper and the limitations of the last act of Congress upon that subject.[9] It would not be deemed an economical arrangement to make a loan of so large a sum of money upon terms by no means honorable or advantageous, and appropriate it to the purchase of the debt under limitations which would forbid its investiture. The information called for in this resolution may possibly explain these difficulties.

"The fifth and last resolution has arisen from that part of the printed Report . . . which states the whole sums drawn from Holland to amount to $2,304,769 13; but neither immediately presents to view the balance

9. Sections 6, 7, and 8 of "An Act supplementary to the act making provision for the Debt of the United States" described the conditions under which the commissioners of the sinking fund were to purchase the debt of the United States (1 *Stat.* 282–83 [May 8, 1792]).

on hand, nor informs where that balance is deposited. It appears by the Bank-book, that the whole deposite of the United States in Bank at this time, from all resources, amounts to $790,642 11. Hence, it will appear from a statement partly conjectural, and partly founded upon the statements in the printed Report, and some official documents, that $1,554,851 43 remain unaccounted for, as will appear from the following account:

"*Sums which ought to be in the Treasury.*

Whole moneys drawn from Holland, as stated in the printed Report,	$2,304,769
Deduct paid for St. Domingo, as stated in printed Report,	455,263
Leaves a balance of	1,859,506
Deduct to foreign officers, if paid	191,316
Leaves a balance of	1,668.190
Add surplus of Sinking Fund, conjectural	400,000
Add surplus of revenue of 1792, reported at	277,385
Whole amount	2,345,495

"Sums not taken into this estimate: First. Any moneys not paid of the $191,316, due to foreign officers. Second. So much moneys in Bank as arose from the revenues. Third. The receipts of the current year.

From this aggregate sum of	$2,345,495
Deduct in Bank	790,642
Balance not accounted for	1,554,853

"In this last estimate, cents have not been taken into calculation, which makes an inconsiderable variation in some of the sums.

"Another circumstance appears somewhat singular: in the printed Report, 2,986,000 florins are stated to have been drawn from Holland in the year 1792. In the Bank-book, it appears from the list of bills drawn, that 8,695,237 florins were drawn for in the same time. This difference, I presume, may admit of explanation probably from the manner of negotiating this matter, or from some casual mistake. It deserves, however, to be explained.

"It appears from another statement, made up to the 1st of April, 1793, that there ought to be at that time a sufficient sum of money in the Treasury to reimburse the loan of 2,000,000 dollars to the Bank, and to answer all the other purposes of Government.

"*Treasury*	Dr.
April 1, 1793. Balance of foreign loans	$1,668,182 27
Surplus of Sinking Fund, conjectural	400,000 00
Bonds payable in December, 1792	460,126 00
Bonds payable in January, 1793	129,332 00
Bonds payable in February	87,057 00
Bonds payable in March	202,447 00
Surplus of the revenue of 1792	277,305 27
All the revenue of the current year, estimated at	1,000,000 00
These sums make the sum of	4,224,389 54

"Treasury	Cr.
Debt to Bank, if paid	$2,000,000 00
One quarter's interest, to April, 1793	700,000 00
Bonds payable in December, if applied to the last quarter's interest	460,126 00
One quarter's expenses of Army and Government, estimated at	400,000 00
	3,560,136 00
Deduct this sum from	4,224,389 54
Balance in favor of the Treasury, if the debt of the Bank be paid	664,263 54

"The papers from which I have collected these statements may be deceptive in themselves, or may be subject to explanations from others. Candor, however, induces me to acknowledge that impressions resulting from my inquiries into this subject, have been made upon my mind, by no means favorable to the arrangements made by the gentleman at the head of the Treasury Department. But I shall keep myself open to conviction, in case of any sufficient explanation which may be hereafter given, and I now avow that my acknowledgment of mistake shall be at least commensurate to any conviction produced.

"I cannot help remarking, before I sit down, that we have been legislating for some years without competent official knowledge of the state of the Treasury, or revenues; in the course of which time, we have been engaged in the most important fiscal arrangements; that we have authorized a loan of the Bank of the United States for more than $500,000,[10] when probably a greater sum of public money was deposited in the Bank; that we have passed a vote this session, authorizing a further loan for $800,000,[11] and that we were upon the point of authorizing a loan abroad for $2,000,000,[12] without knowing the extent of the authorities at present existing for borrowing, the amount of moneys on hand in consequence of loans already made, or the application of the moneys which may have been used; and I conceive it is now time that this information be officially laid before this House." [13]

Although historians of the Washington Administration have devoted considerable attention to the Giles resolutions, less attention has been paid to the fact that on January 23, 1793, the Senate also adopted resolutions similar in content to the five resolutions adopted by the House. These resolutions read as follows:

"*Ordered,* That the Secretary of the Treasury lay before the Senate

10. This loan was authorized by Section 16 of "An Act for raising a farther sum of money for the protection of the frontiers, and for other purposes therein mentioned" (1 *Stat.* 262 [May 2, 1792]).

11. Section 3 of "An Act making appropriations for the support of Government for the year one thousand seven hundred and ninety-three" authorized the President to borrow eight hundred thousand dollars from the Bank of the United States (1 *Stat.* 328 [February 28, 1793]). The House had approved the bill and sent it to the Senate on January 9 (*Journal of the House,* I, 665).

12. See note 8.

13. *Annals of Congress,* III, 836–40.

a general account, exhibiting the amount of all the public funds and moneys (loans included) up to the end of the last year, and what remains of each appropriation, either in cash, bonds, certificates, or other securities, and stating where the balances are deposited, as far as the same can at present be done. That he particularly state the amount which has been drawn into the United States, of the moneys borrowed in Europe, under the acts of the 4th and 12th of August, 1790, the purposes for which drawn, how any part thereof hath been applied, with the balance now on hand, and where deposited. . . .

"*Resolved,* That the President of the United States be requested to lay before the Senate, copies of the powers given by him for the negotiation of the loans authorized by the laws of the 4th and 12th of August, 1790, and of the communications from the Public Commissioners in Holland." [14]

The reports submitted by Hamilton to the Senate as a result of its January 23 resolutions are dated February 5 and 14, 1793. In the first of these reports Hamilton also replied to the following section from the first resolution which was deleted from the resolution as passed: "That [the Secretary of the Treasury] . . . also lay before the Senate a copy of the powers under which he negotiated the loans made under the laws of the 4th and 12th of August, 1790, and the original communications from the Public Commissioners in Holland, stating the difficulties of making separate loans under the same acts, as mentioned in his letter of January, 1793." [15]

Hamilton replied to the charges made by the House resolutions in a series of reports that were completed by February 19, 1793. But Republicans in and out of Congress were still not satisfied, and another set of resolutions was drafted criticizing Hamilton's administration of the Treasury. According to Paul Leicester Ford, the "rough draft" of these resolutions was in Jefferson's handwriting.[16] Giles modified these resolutions somewhat and submitted them to the House of Representatives on February 27, 1793. The resolutions read as follows:

"1. *Resolved,* That it is essential to the due administration of the Government of the United States, that laws making specific appropriations of money should be strictly observed by the administrator of the finances thereof.

"2. *Resolved,* That a violation of a law making appropriations of money, is a violation of that section of the Constitution of the United States which requires that no money shall be drawn from the Treasury but in consequence of appropriations made by law.

"3. *Resolved,* That the Secretary of the Treasury has violated the law passed the 4th of August, 1790, making appropriations of certain moneys authorized to be borrowed by the same law, in the following particulars,

14. *Annals of Congress,* III, 632–33.

15. *Annals of Congress,* III, 632. For H's explanation of the difficulties of separating the loans, see "Report on Bank Deposits, Surplus Revenue, and Loans," January 16, 1793.

16. Ford, *Writings of Jefferson,* VI, 168–71. Ford states that the original document was loaned to him by Sarah N. Randolph.

viz: *First,* By applying a certain portion of the principal borrowed to the payment of interest falling due upon that principal, which was not authorized by that or any other law. *Secondly,* By drawing part of the same moneys into the United States, without the instructions of the President of the United States.

"4. *Resolved,* That the Secretary of the Treasury has deviated from the instructions given by the President of the United States, in exceeding the authorities for making loans under the acts of the 4th and 12th of August, 1790.

"5. *Resolved,* That the Secretary of the Treasury has omitted to discharge an essential duty of his office, in failing to give Congress official information in due time, of the moneys drawn by him from Europe into the United States; which drawing commenced December, 1790, and continued till January, 1793; and of the causes of making such drafts.

"6. *Resolved,* That the Secretary of the Treasury has, without the instructions of the President of the United States, drawn more moneys borrowed in Holland into the United States than the President of the United States was authorized to draw, under the act of the 12th of August, 1790; which act appropriated two millions of dollars only, when borrowed, to the purchase of the Public Debt: And that he has omitted to discharge an essential duty of his office, in failing to give official information to the Commissioners for purchasing the Public Debt, of the various sums drawn from time to time, suggested by him to have been intended for the purchase of the Public Debt.

"7. *Resolved,* That the Secretary of the Treasury did not consult the public interest in negotiating a Loan with the Bank of the United States, and drawing therefrom four hundred thousand dollars, at five per cent. per annum, when a greater sum of public money was deposited in various banks at the respective periods of making the respective drafts.

"8. *Resolved,* That the Secretary of the Treasury has been guilty of an indecorum to this House, in undertaking to judge of its motives in calling for information which was demandable of him, from the constitution of his office; and in failing to give all the necessary information within his knowledge, relatively to the subjects of the reference made to him of the 19th January, 1792, and of the 22d November, 1792, during the present session.

"9. *Resolved,* That a copy of the foregoing resolutions be transmitted to the President of the United States." [17]

Of the nine resolutions presented by Giles, seven were incorporated from Jefferson's draft without substantive change. The sections of the Jefferson draft which were either modified or omitted by Giles read as follows:

"3. *Resolved,* That the Secretary of the Treasury, in drawing to this country and lodging in the bank the funds raised in Europe, which ought to have been applied to the paiments of our debts there in order to stop interest, has violated the instructions of the President of the United States for the benefit of speculators and to increase the profits of that institution.

17. *Annals of Congress,* III, 900.

"9. *Resolved,* That at the next meeting of Congress, the act of Sep 2d, 1789, establishing a Department of Treasury should be so amended as to constitute the office of the Treasurer of the United States a separate department, independent of the Secretary of the Treasury.

"10. *Resolved,* That the Secretary of the Treasury has been guilty of maladministration in the duties of his office, and should, in the opinion of Congress, be removed from his office by the President of the United States."[18]

On February 28 and March 1 the House defeated the second set of Giles's resolutions. Only six of the nine resolutions were committed for discussion, and only five Republicans, including Giles and Madison, voted in favor of all six resolutions.[19] On March 2 Congress adjourned *sine die.*

A word should be added concerning the timing of the two sets of resolutions proposed by Giles. When he introduced his first set of resolutions on January 23, he and other Republicans in Congress undoubtedly thought that Hamilton would be unable to assemble the materials for a reply before Congress adjourned in early March and that voters would, therefore, believe that Hamilton was guilty of the charges implied in the resolutions. This strategy failed when Hamilton by a prodigious effort drew up the necessary reports and submitted them to Congress before the end of February.[20] The resolutions of censure proposed by Giles on February 27 were introduced so late in the session that, if they had passed, Hamilton could not conceivably have replied to them before Congress adjourned. But they did not pass, and for the second time Giles and his Republican supporters in and out of the House were thwarted.

18. Ford, *Writings of Jefferson,* VI, 169–71.

19. *Annals of Congress,* III, 899–963.

20. Between February 4 and February 19, 1793, H presented the following reports in response to the House and Senate resolutions: "Report on the Balance of All Unapplied Revenues at the End of the Year 1792 and on All Unapplied Monies Which May Have Been Obtained by the Several Loans Authorized by Law," February 4, 1793; "Report Exhibiting the Amount of All the Public Funds up to the End of 1792 and Statement of What Remains of Each Appropriation," February 5, 1793; "Report on Foreign Loans," February 5, 1793; "Report on Foreign Loans," February 13, 1793; "Report Relative to the Loans Negotiated under the Acts of the Fourth and Twelfth of August, 1790," February 13–14, 1793; "Report on Revenue, Appropriations, and Expenditures," February 14, 1793; "Report on the State of the Treasury at the Commencement of Each Quarter During the Years 1791 and 1792 and on the State of the Market in Regard to the Prices of Stock During the Same Years," February 19, 1793.

Treasury Department, February 4th, 1793.
[Communicated on February 4, 1793] [21]

[To the Speaker of the House of Representatives]

Sir,

I have lost no time in preparing, as far as has been practicable, consistently with the course of facts, the several statements required by the resolutions of the House of Representatives, of the 23d. of last month,[22] and I have concluded to add to them such further statements, as appeared to me necessary to convey fully the information, which is understood to be the object of those resolutions. It was my first intention to submit these statements collectively, with such explanatory remarks, as the occasion might demand, but finding, on experiment, from the extent and variety of the matter, involved in the resolutions, that more time will be requisite for a full developement of it, than I had anticipated, considerations of weight in my mind have determined me to present the different parts of the subject successively. Among other advantages, incident to this course of proceeding, will be that of having it in my power to give a more accurate and mature view of the entire subject, without too great a dereliction of current business of the department. In executing the task I propose to myself, I shall rely on the indulgence of the House, to a latitude of observation, corresponding with the peculiar circumstances of the case.

The resolutions, to which I am to answer, were not moved without a pretty copious display of the reasons, on which they were founded. These reasons are before the public through the channel of the press. They are of a nature, to excite attention, to beget alarm, to inspire doubts. Deductions of a very extraordinary complexion may, without forcing the sense, be drawn from them.

I feel it incumbent on me to meet the suggestions, which have been thrown out, with decision and explicitness. And, while I hope, I shall let fall nothing inconsistent with that cordial and unqualified respect, which I feel for the House of Representatives, while I acquiesce in the sufficiency of the motives, that induced, on their part,

21. *Journal of the House*, I, 689.

22. See the introductory note to this report.

the giving a prompt and free course to the investigation proposed—I cannot but resolve to treat the subject, with a freedom, which is due to truth, and to the consciousness of a pure zeal for the public interest.

I begin with the last of the four resolutions;[23] because it is that, which seeks information, relating to the most delicate and important of the suggestions, that have been hazarded.

Here, however, I have to regret the utter impossibility of a strict compliance with the terms of the resolution. The practicability of such a compliance would suppose nothing less than that, since the last day of December 1792, all the accounts of the Collectors of the Customs, and other Officers of the revenue, throughout the whole extent of the United States, could be digested, made up, and forwarded to the Treasury, could be examined there, settled and carried into the public books, under their proper heads. In a word, that all the revenues, receipts and expenditures of this extensive country could have passed through a complete exhibition, examination, and adjustment, within the short period of twenty three days.

It was made, (as I presume, from the result) satisfactorily to appear to a Committee of the House of Representatives, who were charged, during the last session, with framing a direction to the treasury for bringing forward an annual account of receipts and expenditures, that the course of public business would not admit of the rendering of such an account, in less than nine months after the expiration of each year; in conformity to which idea, their report was formed, and an Order of the House established.[24]

23. There were five resolutions, and the discussion which follows in the text deals with the fifth resolution of the House. See the introductory note to this report.

24. The order to which H is referring was adopted on December 30, 1791. It reads as follows: "*Resolved*, That it shall be the duty of the Secretary of the Treasury to lay before the House of Representatives, on the fourth Monday of October in each year, if Congress shall be then in session, or if not then in session, within the first week of the session next following the said fourth Monday of October, an accurate statement and account of the receipts and expenditures of all public moneys, down to the last day inclusively of the month of December immediately preceding the said fourth Monday of October, distinguishing the amount of the receipts in each State or District, and from each officer therein; in which statements shall also be distinguished the expenditures which fall under each head of appropriation, and shall be shown the sums, if any, which remain unexpended, and to be accounted for in the next statement, of each and every of such appropriations" (*Journal of the House*, I, 484).

I need do nothing more, to evince the impracticability of an exact compliance with the resolution in question, than to observe that it is even more comprehensive, though with less detail, than the order of the House, to which I have alluded.

To evince, nevertheless, my readiness to do all in my power, towards fulfilling the views of the House, and throwing light upon the transactions of the department, I shall now offer to their inspection sundry Statements, marked A, B, C, D, E, F, which contain, as far as is, at this time, possible, the information desired, and with sufficient certainty and accuracy, to afford satisfaction on the points of inquiry involved in the resolution.

The Statement A, shews, in abstract, the whole of the receipts into, and expenditures from the Treasury, commencing with the first of January, and ending with the last day of December 1792, corresponding with the accounts of the Treasurer. These accounts have been regularly settled up to the end of September, and copies have been laid before the two Houses of Congress.[25] The account for the quarter terminating with the year has not yet passed through the forms of settlement but it is under examination, and will, no doubt, be settled as it stands, the manner of conducting the business, and the usual care and accuracy of the officer concerned, leaving very little room to apprehend mis-statement or error. A copy of this account is herewith submitted in the Schedule, marked, C.

This Statement takes up the balance of the general account of receipts and expenditures, to the end of the year 1791, as reported to the House of Representatives, within the first week of the present Session,[26] and continuing it down to the end of the year 1792, shews a balance then in the treasury, of seven hundred and eighty three thousand, four hundred and forty four dollars and fifty one cents.

The Statement, B, is a more comprehensive document. It is a general account of Income and Expenditure. It shews, not merely, the

25. On November 7, 1792, the Speaker of the House "laid before the House a letter from the Treasurer of the United States, accompanying his accounts of the receipts and expenditures of the public moneys, from the first of January, one thousand seven hundred and ninety-two, to the thirtieth of September following, inclusive" (*Journal of the House,* I, 614). The letter was also presented in the Senate on November 7 (*Annals of Congress,* III, 611).

26. See "Report on the Receipts and Expenditures of Public Monies to the End of the Year 1791," November 10, 1792. This report was presented in the House on November 12, 1792 (*Journal of the House,* I, 618).

actual receipts of money into the Treasury, but the whole amount of the national revenues, from the commencement of the present government to the conclusion of the year 1792, as well outstanding, as collected—the proceeds of the domestic loans—the whole amount of the sums which have been drawn into the United States, on account of the foreign loans—and all other monies, for whatever source, which have accrued within the period embraced by the Statement.

Those items form the debit-side of the account, amounting to seventeen millions eight hundred and seventy nine thousand, eight hundred and twenty five dollars and thirty three cents.

The Credit-side consists of two items. 1st. The whole amount of the actual expenditures, to the end of the year 1791, as stated in the general account of receipts and expenditures before referred to. 2nd. The whole amount of the actual expenditures during the year 1792, as specified generally in the Statement A, and particularly in the several quarterly accounts of the Treasurer, amounting to twelve millions seven hundred and sixty five thousand one hundred and twenty eight dollars and eighty three cents.

The balance of this account of income and expenditure is consequently five millions one hundred and fourteen thousand six hundred and ninety six dollars and fifty cents; which corresponds with the excess of the public income (including the proceeds of loans, foreign and domestic) beyond the actual expenditure, or, more properly speaking, disbursement, to the end of the year 1792. This of course, is exclusive of those parts of the proceeds of foreign loans, which have been left in Europe, to be applied there; the amount, application and balance of which are exhibited, as far as they are yet known in the treasury, in the Statement, No. I, of my late report on foreign loans.[27]

This balance, as noted in the Statement, B, is composed of the following particulars:

1st.	Cash in the treasury, per Statement A. . . . Dollars	783.444.51
2d.	Cash in the Bank of the United States, and the offices of discount and deposit of New York and Baltimore, not yet passed to the credit of the Treasurer, per Statement AB[28]	605.883. 8.

27. See "Report on Foreign Loans," January 3, 1793.
28. Copy, RG 233, Reports of the Treasury Department, 1792–1793, Vol. III,

3d.	Proceeds of Amsterdam Bills remaining in deposit, in the Bank of North America, including the sum of one hundred and fifty six thousand five hundred and ninety five dollars and fifty six cents, advanced by the Bank without interest, which is credited in the general Account of receipts and expenditures, Statement A..........	177.998.80.
4th.	Proceeds of Amsterdam sold, but not yet received	614.593. 2
5th.	Cash in hands of Collectors of customs, per Abstract D	151.851.25.
6th.	Bonds unpaid at the end of the year one thousand seven hundred and ninety two, on account of the duties on imports and tonnage, and falling due between that time and May one thousand seven hundred and ninety four, per Abstract E..	2.442.069.15.
7th.	Uncollected residue of duties on Spirits distilled within the United States, per Abstract F.......	341.057.19.
	Making together ....Dollars	5.116.897.

This aggregate somewhat exceeds the balance of the account; but in a case where estimates must necessarily supply the deficiency of ascertained results, differences of this nature are of course. It is, at the same time, satisfactory to observe, that the estimates, which have been heretofore communicated, are proved by the official documents, already received, to have been essentially correct.

It will, no doubt, readily occur to the House, that a very small part of the excess, which has been stated, is a real surplus of income. There remain to be satisfied numerous objects of expenditure, charged upon the fund by the appropriations, which have been made, that cannot fail ultimately to exhaust it, probably within four or five hundred thousand dollars; which will be embraced in the appropriations for the service of the year one thousand seven hundred and ninety three. A further explanation on this point is reserved for future communication.

A due comprehension of the Statements now presented must ob-

National Archives. "Statement AB" had also been sent to the Senate and is printed in these volumes as an enclosure to "Report on Bank Deposits, Surplus Revenue, and Loans," January 16, 1793.

viate every idea of a balance unaccounted for, in whatever sense the allegation may have been intended to be made.[29]

If there was before any obscurity on the subject, it was certainly not the fault of this department. 'Till the last resolutions, no call has been made upon it, which rendered it proper to exhibit a general view of the public monies and funds—or to shew the amount and situation of such as were unapplied. Particular calls for particular objects were made, which, as I conceive, were complied with; but they were not comprehensive enough to embrace a disclosure of that nature.

It could not, therefore, with propriety, have been alleged, that there was a balance unaccounted for. To infer it, from documents, which contained only a part of the necessary information, was not justifiable. Nor could it otherwise happen, than that conclusions, wholly erroneous, would be the consequences of taking such imperfect data for guides.

It may be of use, by way of elucidation, to point out some of the most palpable features of the error which has been entertained.

The following items are stated, as the basis of the supposed deficiency: [30]

Residue of the proceeds of the foreign bills supposed to be unapplied, after deducting the sums furnished for St. Domingo,[31] and the amount of the debt to the foreign Officers [32] ....Dollars, 1.668.190.

29. At this point H is referring to part of the speech which Giles made in the House of Representatives in support of his resolutions. See the introductory note to this report.

30. The items listed by H are taken from the account which Giles presented to the House to prove that the Treasury Department had failed to account for $1,554,851.43. See the introductory note to this report.

31. The United States had supplied France with funds to purchase supplies needed to deal with the insurrection which had occurred in Santo Domingo in August, 1791. See William Short to H, December 28, 1791, January 26, April 22, 25, May 14, June 28, August 6, 1792; H to Short, April 10, 1792; Jean Baptiste de Ternant to H, February 21, March 8, 10, 1792; H to Ternant, February 22, March 8, 1792; H to Jefferson, November 17, 1792; H to George Washington, November 19, 1792.

32. For a description of this debt, see Short to H, August 3, 1790, note 5. Section 5 of "An Act supplementary to the act making provision for the Debt of the United States" (1 *Stat.* 282 [May 8, 1792]) authorized the President "to cause to be discharged the principal and interest of the said debt, out of any of the monies, which have been or shall be obtained on loan." For the negotia-

Surplus of the sinking fund, meaning, I presume, that part of the surplus of the revenue to the end of the year 1790, which hath not been applied in purchases........	400.000.
Surplus of revenue of the year 1792, as reported......	277.385.
Deduct in Bank, meaning, I presume, the balance of the Treasurer's Cash Account..............................	790.642.
Balance not accounted for...............	1.554.933.

It appears, in the first place, to have been overlooked, that in Statement, No 3, of my late report concerning foreign loans,[33] mention is made, that on the 3d of January there remained to be received of the proceeds of the foreign Bills, six hundred and thirty two thousand one hundred and thirty two dollars and two cents; consequently, that sum could not be considered, as in the treasury, and ought to be deducted from the supposed deficiency.

Among the official papers, which, it is intimated, were consulted, was an original Account rendered by the Bank of the United States, of the sales of Amsterdam Bills, shewing a sum of six hundred and five thousand eight hundred and eighty three dollars and eight cents, as having been received by the Bank, and two of its Offices of discount and deposit, for the proceeds of those Bills.[34] Had that document been understood, it would have been known, that this sum was in bank over and above the balance of the Treasurer's Cash account; and this also would have served to account for a large part of the supposed deficiency namely, six hundred and five thousand eight hundred and eighty three dollars and eight cents. The course of this transaction will be hereafter explained.

But among the misconceptions, which have obtained, what relates to the surplus of revenue of the year 1792, is not the least striking. The laws inform, (and consequently, no information on that point from this department could have been necessary) that credits are allowed upon the duties on imports, of four, six, nine, twelve months,

---

tions on the payment of these officers, see H to Short, August 16, September 13, 1792; H to Washington, August 27, 1792; Washington to H, August 31, 1792; H to Gouverneur Morris, September 13, 1792.

33. See "Report on Foreign Loans," January 3, 1793.

34. See "Statement AB" of "Report on Bank Deposits, Surplus Revenue, and Loans," January 16, 1793.

and in some cases, of two years.[35] Reason dictates, that a surplus in such case must be considered as postponed in the collection or receipt, 'till all the appropriations upon the fund have been first satisfied. The account of receipts and expenditures to the end of 1791, in possession of the House, shews, that at that time, no less a sum than one million eight hundred and twenty eight thousand two hundred and eighty nine dollars and twenty eight cents, of the antecedent duties, were outstanding in bonds.[36] How, then, could it have happened, that the surplus of 1792 was sought for in the Treasury, at the very instant of the expiration of the year? I forbear to attempt to trace the source of a mistake so extraordinary.

Let me, however, add, that of the surplus in question, one hundred and seventy two thousand five hundred and eighty four dollars and eighty two cents are not payable 'till April and May 1794, as will be seen by the Abstract E.

Thus have I not only furnished a just and affirmative view of the real situation of the public account, but have likewise shewn, I trust, in a conspicuous manner, fallacies enough in the Statement, from which the inference of an unaccounted for balance is drawn, to evince, that it is one tissue of error. In this, I might have gone still further, there being scarcely a step of the whole process, which is not liable to the imputation of misapprehension. But I wish not unnecessarily to weary the patience of the House.

Another circumstance, to which importance has been given, and which was noticed in connection with the suggestion last discussed, is a disagreement between a memorandum in the Treasurer's Bank book, and the Statement reported by me of the amount of Bills drawn at the treasury upon the foreign fund.[37] A disagreement, no

35. For example, see Sections 41 and 42 of "An Act to provide more effectually for the collection of the duties imposed by law on goods, wares and merchandise imported into the United States, and on the tonnage of ships or vessels" (1 *Stat.* 168 [August 4, 1790]); Section 3 of "An Act repealing, after the last day of June next, the duties heretofore laid upon Distilled Spirits imported from abroad, and laying others in their stead; and also upon Spirits distilled within the United States, and for appropriating the same" (1 *Stat.* 199 [March 3, 1791]); Section 1 of "An Act making farther provision for the collection of the duties by law imposed on Teas, and to prolong the term for the payment of the Duties on Wines" (1 *Stat.* 219–20 [March 3, 1791]).

36. See note 26.

37. In this paragraph H is referring to remarks made by Giles in the House of Representatives in support of his resolutions. See the introductory note to this report.

doubt, exists, and to the extent of five millions seven hundred and sixty thousand one hundred and thirty eight florins or guilders.

But the following circumstances contain the solution of this disquieting appearance.

There will be found in the Statement A, two several credits, each for two millions of dollars, as for monies received into the treasury, with corresponding debits of equal sums, as for monies paid out of the treasury.

But neither the one nor the other did, in reality take place. The whole is a mere operation to accomplish the purposes of the eleventh Section of the "Act to incorporate the Subscribers to the Bank of the United States," [38] without an inconvenient and unnecessary displacement of funds.

That Section authorizes a subscription to the Stock of the Bank, on account of the Government, not exceeding in amount two millions of dollars, and provides for the payment of it, out of the monies, which should be borrowed, by virtue of either of the Acts of the fourth and twelfth of August 1790, the first making provision for the public debt, the last for reducing it; [39] enjoining, at the same time, that a loan should be made of the Bank, to an equal amount, to replace the monies, which were to be applied to the payment of the subscription.

It is evident, that nothing could have been more useless, (at the same time that it would have been attended with obvious disadvantages to the Government) than actually to draw from Europe out of the monies borrowed there, the sum necessary for the payment of the subscription to the Bank, and again to remit out of the loan,

38. Section 11 of "An Act to incorporate the subscribers to the Bank of the United States" provided "That it shall be lawful for the President of the United States, at any time or times, within eighteen months after the first day of April next, to cause a subscription to be made to the stock of the said corporation, as part of the . . . capital stock of ten millions of dollars, on behalf of the United States, to an amount not exceeding two millions of dollars; to be paid out of the monies which shall be borrowed by virtue of either of the acts, the one entitled 'An Act making provision for the debt of the United States;' and the other entitled 'An Act making provision for the reduction of the public debt;' borrowing of the bank an equal sum, to be applied to the purposes, for which the said monies shall have been procured; reimbursable in ten years, by equal annual instalments; or at any time sooner, or in greater proportions, that the government may think fit" (1 *Stat.* 196 [February 25, 1791]).

39. 1 *Stat.* 138–44, 186–87. See the introductory note to this report.

which was to be obtained of the Bank, a sufficient sum, to replace such monies, or such part of them, as may have been destined for the foreign object. Loss upon exchange in consequence of overstocking the market with Bills, Loss in interest by the delays incident to the operation; and which would necessarily have suspended the useful employment of the funds for a considerable time. These are some of the disadvantages to the Government. To the Bank alone could any benefit have accrued, which would have been in proportion to the delay in restoring or applying the fund to its primitive destination. Such an operation, therefore, could only have been justified by an indisposition, on the part of the Bank, to facilitate the principal object, without the intervention of actual payment.

But no such disposition existed. On this, as on every other occasion, a temper, liberal towards the government, has characterized the conduct of the Directors of that institution.

It was accordingly proposed by me and agreed to by them, that the object to be accomplished should be carried into effect by a merely formal arrangement. In this, however, it was necessary to consult the injunctions of law, and the principles of the constitution of the Treasury Department.

These points then were to be effected—a payment of the subscription money, to vest the Government with the property of the Stock—possession of the means of paying it, which were to be derived from the foreign fund, and, of course, were first to be in the treasury, before payment could be made—the replacing what should be taken from that fund, by a loan of the Bank.

The following plan for these purposes was devised an executed by previous concert.

The Treasurer drew bills upon our Commissioners in Amsterdam, for the sums requisite to complete the payment on account of the subscription: these bills were purchased by the Bank, and Warrants in favor of the Treasurer upon the Bank served to place the proceeds in the treasury. Warrants afterwards issued upon the Treasurer, in favor of the Bank, for the amount of the subscription money, which was receipted on the part of the Bank, as paid. Other Warrants then issued in favor of the Treasurer upon the Bank, for equal sums, as upon account of a loan to the Government, which Warrants were satisfied by a redelivery to the Treasurer of the Bills which had been drawn upon the Commissioners. In the first place, warrants were drawn upon the Treasurer, to replace the monies supposed by the arrangement, to be drawn from the foreign fund, which perfected the operation. But from the detail, which has been given, it will be seen, that in fact, no monies were either withdrawn from, or returned to that fund. The Bills were cancelled, annexed to the warrants, and are lodged in the treasury, as vouchers of the transaction.

These Bills were for two separate sums, each two millions four hundred and seventy five thousand guilders, equal to a million of dollars; the payment having been divided into two parts, upon certain equitable considerations, relative to the dividend of the first half year.

This transaction explains four millions nine hundred and fifty thousand guilders, equal to the sum, which forms the disagreement, between the memorandum in the Treasurer's Bank-book, and the Statement reported by me.

The residue is thus explained. The sum of one million two hundred and thirty seven thousand five hundred guilders, directed to be drawn for, on the thirtieth of November, was directed to be comprised in one or more Bills, as the Bank should desire. It was at first placed in one Bill; but this Bill was afterwards returned, with a request that it might be converted into smaller sums. The Bill returned was cancelled, and in lieu of it, there had been furnished, prior to the first of January, of the present year, nine hundred and thirty four thousand five hundred guilders—the balance, three hundred and three thousand, then remaining to be furnished. The sum of nine hundred and thirty four thousand five hundred guilders, consequently appears twice in the memorandum.

These two sums of four millions five hundred and ninety thousand, and nine hundred and thirty four thousand guilders, exceed the difference in question, by one hundred and twenty four thousand three hundred and sixty two guilders.

The Treasurer informs me that there are two bills not included in the memorandum; one for one hundred and twenty thousand seven hundred and fifty, and the other for six hundred and twelve guilders; which make up the above mentioned excess. The former of those two bills was furnished to the Secretary of State, for the purpose contemplated by the third Section of the Act of the last

Session, entitled "An Act making certain appropriations therein specified." [40]

Is it not truly matter of regret, that so formal an explanation on such a point should have been made requisite? Could no personal enquiry of either of the Officers concerned, have superseded the necessity of publicly calling the attention of the House of Representatives, to an appearance in truth, so little significant? Was it seriously supposable, that there could be any real difficulty in explaining that appearance, when the very disclosure of it proceeded from a voluntary act of the head of this department?

With perfect respect, I have the honor to be, Sir Your most obedient and most Hble Servt. Alexander Hamilton.

Secretary of the Treasury.

The Honble. Jonathan Trumbull Esqr.
Speaker of the House of Representatives.

P:S: Another Statement of income and expenditure having been made, which presents the subject under aspect, but agreeing in the result with the Statement (B) is herewith also submitted, marked (Ba).

40. Section 3 of that act provided that, "to defray any expense which may be incurred in relation to the intercourse between the United States and foreign nations," the sum of fifty thousand dollars might be "paid out of any monies, which may be in the treasury, not otherwise appropriated" (1 *Stat.* 285 [May 8, 1792]).

A

GENERAL ACCOUNT OF RECEIPTS AND EXPENDITURES OF PUBLIC MONIES, COMMENCING THE 1ST. OF JANUARY 1792, AND ENDING THE 31ST. DECEMBER 1792.

Dr.

1792.		Dollars. Cts.
September 30th.	To the amount of Expenditures from the 1st. of January, to the 30th. of September 1792, agreeably to the Treasurer's Accounts settled at the Treasury, copies of which have been by him transmitted to the House of Representatives, Viz:	
	In the Quarter ending the 31st. of March, 1792	1.191.909. 38.
	*In the Quarter ending the 30th. of June, 1792	3.552.430 25.
	*In the Quarter ending the 30th. of September, 1792	2.972.759. 81.
December 31st.	To the account of Expenditures, from the 1st. of October, to the 31st. of December 1792, agreeably to the Treasurer's Accounts rendered for settlement	1.250,592. 61.
	Balance remaining in the hands of the Treasurer,	783.444 51.

Cr.

1792.		Dollars Cts.
January 1st.	By balance in the treasury, agreeably to the general Statement of receipts and expenditures to the end of the year 1791	973.905. 75.
Decemr. 31.	By amount of monies received into the treasury, from the first day of January 1792, to this date. Viz:	
	For balances due by sundry persons on monies advanced to them under the present government	5.629. 88.
	For balances due by sundry persons on accounts which originated under the late government	4.702. 82.
	For arms and accoutrements sold to the State of South Carolina out of the public stores, by direction of the President	4.240.
	For amount received for fines, penalties and forfeitures	118.
	For amount received on account of a loan of 523.500 dollars, made by the Bank of the United States, in pursuance of an Act passed on the 2d. day of May 1792 [41]	400.000.
	For amount of a loan made by the Bank of North America, without interest, for the use of the department of War	156.595. 56.
	For amount received on account of proceeds of Bills of exchange drawn by the Treasurer, on the Commissioners in Amsterdam	540.002. 80.

	[For the purpose of effecting a] subscription to the Capital Stock of the Bank of the United States, agreeably to an Act passed February 25th: 1791 [42]	2.000.000.
	For amount of a loan obtained from the Bank of the United States, agreeably to the last mentioned Act	2.000.000.
	For the excess of the first half yearly dividend on the capital stock of the Bank of the United States, held by the United States, beyond the interest payable to the Bank	8.028.
	For amount received from sundry Supervisors, on account of duties on distilled Spirits	208.942. 81.
	For amount received from the Collectors of the Customs, on account of duties on imports and tonnage	3.443.070. 85.
9.751.136. 56		9.751.136. 56.

Treasury Department
Register's Office, January 28th. 1793.
Stated by,. . . . . Joseph Nourse, Register.

* Note. In the expenditures for the Quarter ending June 30th. and September 30th. 1792, are included Warrants to the amount of four millions of dollars, which were drawn for the purpose of effecting the subscription of five thousand shares to the Capital Stock of the Bank of the United States, and to cover the loan obtained in consequence thereof—Two millions of dollars being drawn to effect the subscription, and two millions for the amount of the loan. The Bills of exchange drawn by the Treasurer, on which these transactions were predicated, have been cancelled at the Treasury.

41. Section 15 of "An Act for raising a farther sum of money for the protection of the frontiers, and for other purposes therein mentioned" provided "That the sum of one hundred and fifty thousand dollars, out of the surplus of the duties, which accrued to the end of the year one thousand seven hundred and ninety-one, and a farther sum of five hundred and twenty-three thousand five hundred dollars, out of the surplus of the duties hereby established as the same shall accrue, making together the sum of six hundred and seventy-three thousand five hundred dollars, shall be, and are hereby appropriated and applied, in addition to any former appropriation for the military establishment of the United States" (1 *Stat.* 259–63).

42. See note 38.

B

GENERAL ACCOUNT OF INCOME AND EXPENDITURE.

Dr.

To net amount of duties on imports and tonnage, and of fines, penalties and forfeitures, as per Account of receipts and expenditures to the end of the year 1791, reported to the House of Representatives the 10th. November, 1792.[43] — 6.534.263. 84

To amount of monies which came into the Treasury, to the same end of the year 1791, from other sources than the general revenues, as per the same Account of receipts and expenditures. Viz:

Total of receipts — 4.771.342.43.

Deduct this sum received for duties on imports and tonnage, being included in the net Amount above charged — 4.339.472.99.

— 371.869. 44

To product of duties on spirits distilled within the United States, for a half year, ending the 31st. December 1791 — 150.000.

To product of duties on impost and tonnage for the year 1791, as estimated — 3.900.000.

To product of duties on spirits distilled within the United States, for the same period, as estimated — 400.000.

To amount of monies which came into the treasury, during the year 1791, from other sources than the general revenues, as per general account of receipts and expenditures herewith transmitted, marked A, Viz:

Total receipts including the balance in Cash at the end of 1791, as credited in said Account — 9.751.136.56.

Deduct this sum which was the balance in the treasury at the end of 1791, the same being included in the above totals of revenues and receipts for the same period — 973.905:75.

Cr.

By amount of expenditures to the end of the year 1791, as per account of receipts and expenditures to the end of that year, reported to the House of Representatives, the 10th. of November 1792. — 3.797.436. 78.

By amount of expenditures, during the year 1792, as per general account of receipts and expenditures herewith transmitted, marked A, viz:

Total Debit side of said Account — 9.751.136:56.

Deduct Cash on hand — 783.444.51.

— 8.967.692 5.

the revenue, on account of duties on distilled spirits, being included in the total products above charged	208.942.81.				
Deduct this sum received from Collectors of Customs, on account of duties on imports and tonnage, being also included in the total above charged	3.443.070.85.				
		4.625.919.41			
			5.125.217. 15.		
To proceeds of Bills drawn and disposed of upon our Commissioners in Holland, on account of foreign loans, as per Statement No. III reported to the House of Representatives, the 3d. instant,[44] Viz:	2.304.769:13				
To which add for an error in stating the amount of interest which arose on the credit allowed to purchasers of Bills, by the Banks of North America and New York	1 000.			Balance being the excess of Income beyond the expenditure to the end of the year 1792	5.114.696. 50.
		2.305.769.13.			
Deduct this sum included in the receipts into the treasury to the end of the year 1791, as per account of receipts and expenditures, reported to the House of Representatives the 10th. November 1792.	361.391:34				
Deduct also this sum included in the receipts during the year 1792, per general account of receipts and expenditures herewith transmitted, marked A.	545.902:89.				
		907.294.23.			
			1.398.474. 90.		
			17.879.825. 33.		17.879.825. 33.

43. See "Report on the Receipts and Expenditures of Public Monies to the End of the Year 1791," November 10, 1792.

44. See "Report on Foreign Loans," January 3, 1793.

The foregoing Balance is composed, as follows;

I.	Of Cash in the treasury, as per general account of receipts and expenditures, marked A		783.444.51.
II	Of Cash in the Bank of the United States, and the Offices of Discount and Deposit of New York and Baltimore, per Account rendered by the Bank herewith, marked AB[45]		605.883. 8.
III	Of the proceeds of Bills on Amsterdam remaining in deposit in the Bank of North America, including the sum of 156.595.56 dollars, loaned without interest, which loan is credited in the general account of receipts and expenditures, marked A		177.998.86.
IV.	Of the proceeds of Amsterdam bills, not yet received		614.593. 2.
V.	Uncollected residue of duties on spirits distilled within the United States, Viz:		
	Total as estimated	550.000.	
	Deduct sums received into the treasury, and credited in account of receipts and expenditures, marked A	208.942.81.	
			341.057.19.
VI.	Cash in hands of Collectors of Customs, per Abstract of weekly returns herewith, marked D		151.851.25.
VII.	Bonds unpaid at the end of the year 1792, on account of duties on imports and tonnage, and falling due between that time and May 1794. See Abstract marked E		2.442.069.15.
	Dollars		5.116.897.

Notes.

Places of deposit of the above mentioned Cash, No. I and II.

I.	Cash being balance of Treasurer's Account			
	Bank of United States, Philadelphia		109.169.45.	
	Bank of North America, do.		61.601.30.	
	Bank of New York, New York		69.019. 8.	
	Bank of Providence, Providence		28.157.87.	
	Office of discount and deposit, Boston		154.860.67.	
	Ditto	New York	224.734.51.	
	Ditto	Baltimore	73.653.64	
	Ditto	Charleston	62.015.85.	
	In hands of Treasurer		232.14.	
				783.444.51.
II.	Cash on account of foreign Bills			
	Bank of United States, Philadelphia		398.348.38.	
	Office of discount and deposit, New York		195.898.96	
	Ditto	Baltimore	20.635.74.	
				605.883. 8.
	Dollars			1.389.327.59.

III. Of this sum, 156.595.56 dollars, are considered as in deposit by way of counterbalance to an advance made by the Bank, for the use of the department of war, for the purposes of the Act passed the 3d. of March

45. This account was also sent to the Senate and is printed in this volume as an enclosure to "Report on Bank Deposits, Surplus Revenue, and Loans," January 16, 1793.

1791, for raising and adding another regiment to the military establishment of the United States, and for making further provision for the protection of the frontiers.[46] It has remained without final adjustment, from a doubt, whether the funds, upon which the appropriations, which comprehend the surplus of duties to the end of 1791 are bottomed, are fully sufficient. A sum of about 50.000 dollars, must depend on the existence of certain surpluses upon antecedent appropriations, which, it is believed, will not require the full sums appropriated; but the purposes of those appropriations not being yet fully satisfied, the real state of the business is not yet completely ascertained. An example of this exists in the case of a sum of forty thousand dollars, appropriated for paying off certain specie claims on the Quarter Master's department, incurred during the late war.[47] It is known that further claims exist, but not to what extent. There are several other cases attended with similar uncertainty. A recent examination leaves some doubt, whether warrants can safely issue to wind up the transaction.

V. Whether the sum stated here, as outstanding, be correct, must, in a great degree, depend on the accuracy of the estimated product of the duties. It will be observed, that the product, as carried into the Statement, was originally fixed by estimation, and even now the materials in possession of the Treasury, respecting a branch of revenue, for known reasons not yet reduced to perfect order, are unavoidably imperfect, and liable to some error. The estimate may exceed or fall short of the reality, and proportionally affect the outstanding balance. But, however this may turn out, it cannot affect the merits of the Statement. The excess or deficiency of one side of the account would correspond with a like excess or deficiency on the other. The auxiliary Statement, however, marked F, serves to shew, that there can be no material error in the estimate.

VI} VII} These two items are also liable to some degree of uncertainty. The Cash returns of the Collectors are not being all received up to the end of the year, and some disbursements, which were to be made to that time, not having been completed, the account, which was then in their hands, cannot be pronounced with precision. The difference, however, which may appear, upon a settlement of their accounts, cannot be material. In like manner as monthly abstracts of bonds, up to the end of the year, have not yet been received from some parts, and it has been found necessary to supply the deficiency by a comparative estimate, the result may vary somewhat from the fact. But enough is ascertained, to pronounce that the difference must be inconsiderable, and in reference both to the cash and bonds in the hands of the Collectors, whatever difference may hereafter appear, is liable to the same remark, as to the merits of the Statement, which has been made in regard to the duties on distilled spirits. The differences, in both cases, must resolve themselves into the circumstance of the estimated amounts of the duties proving greater or less than the real amounts (See Abstracts D and E.)

Treasury Department
February 4th. 1793.

Alexander Hamilton,
Secretary of the Treasury.

46. 1 *Stat.* 222–24.

47. "An Act making certain Appropriations therein mentioned" appropriated "The Sum of forty thousand dollars, towards discharging certain debts contracted by colonel Timothy Pickering, late quartermaster general, and which sum was included in the amount of a warrant drawn in his favour by the late superintendent of the finances of the United States, and which warrant was not discharged" (1 *Stat.* 185 [August 12, 1790]).

Ba

A STATEMENT OF THE INCOME AND EXPENDITURE OF THE UNITED STATES FROM THE COMMENCEMENT OF THE PRESENT GOVERNMENT TO THE END OF THE YEAR 1792.

		Dollars.	Cts.
Amount of duties on imports and tonnage, and of fines, penalties and forfeitures, as per Account of receipts and expenditures, to the end of the year 1791, reported to the House of Representatives, the 10th. of November 1792,[48]		6.534.263.	84
Sundry Contingent funds received, Viz:			
For fines and forfeitures &c.	334.82		
For balances due on Accounts which originated under the Government	11.001.11.		
		11.335.	93
Product of duties on spirits distilled within the United States, for a half year, ending the 31st. of December 1791, as estimated		150.000.	
Product of duties on imports and tonnage, for the year 1792, as estimated		3.900.000.	
Product of duties on spirits distilled within the United States, for the same period, as estimated		400.000.	
Receipts into the Treasury, as stated in the general Abstract of receipts and expenditures herewith transmitted, marked A. Viz:			
A loan from the Bank of North America, without interest.	156.595.56.		
A loan from the Bank of the United States, on interest.	400.000.		
A loan from do do	2.000.000		
Value of Bills of exchange drawn by the Treasurer on the Commissioners in Amsterdam, for the purpose of effecting a subscription to the Capital Stock of the Bank of the United States	2.000.000.		
Excess of the first half yearly dividend on the Capital Stock of the Bank of the United States, beyond the interest payable to the Bank	8.028.		

	Dollars.	Cts.
By Amount of expenditures, to the end of the year 1791, as per Account of receipts and expenditures to the end of that year, reported to the House of Representatives, the 10th. of November 1792.	3.797.436.	78.
Amount of expenditures during the year 1792, as per general Account of receipts and expenditures, herewith transmitted, marked A	8.967.692.	5.
	12.765.128.	83.
Cash in the Treasury, as per general Account of receipts and expenditures, herewith transmitted, marked A	783.444.	51.
Cash in the Bank of the United States, and the Offices of discount and deposit, of New York and Baltimore, per Account rendered by the Bank, herewith transmitted, marked AB	605.883.	8.
Amount remaining in deposit in the Bank of North America, being the proceeds of Bills on Amsterdam, and including the sum of 156.595. 56/100 dollars, loaned without interest, stated as a receipt per Contra	177.998.	80.
Proceeds of Bills on Amsterdam, not yet received	614.593.	2.

Balances due on Accounts which originated under the late government		4.702.82	
For Arms and Accoutrements		4.240.	
For fines, penalties and forfeitures		118.	
For balances on monies advanced under the present Government	5629.88.		
Deduct repayments made by Jeremiah Olney and Joseph Nourse, as stated in the account of receipts and expenditures, to the end of the year 1791,[49] which repayments are deducted from the expenditures of 1791, and are also credited in the general Account of receipts and expenditures herewith transmitted, marked A	857.83.		
		4.772. 5.	
			4.578.456. 43
Amount of Bills drawn and disposed of upon our Commissioners in Holland, on account of foreign loans, as per Statement, No. III, reported to the House of Representatives, January 3d. 1793 [50]		2.304.769.13.	
To which add for an error in stating the amount of interest which arose on the credit allowed to purchasers by the Banks of North America and New York		1.000.	
			2.305.769. 13
Total Amount			17.879.825. 33.

Amount of duties on spirits distilled within the United States uncollected, and remaining in the hands of the Revenue Officers, being the difference between the estimated product of said duties, and the sums received to the end of the year 1792	341.057. 19.
Cash in hands of Collectors at the close of the year 1792, agreeably to the last returns received at the Treasury	151.851. 25.
Amount of Bonds for duties on imports, unpaid at the end of the year 1792, and falling due between that time and May 1794. See Abstract marked E.	2.442.069. 15.
	17.882.025. 82.

Treasury Department
February 4th. 1793.

Alexander Hamilton,
Secretary of the Treasury.

48. See "Report on the Receipts and Expenditures of Public Monies to the End of the Year 1791," November 10, 1792.

49. See references to repayments by Olney and Nourse in "Report on the Receipts and Expenditures of Public Monies to the End of the Year 1791," November 10, 1792, which may be found on pages 87, 108, and 109 in this volume.

50. See "Report on Foreign Loans," January 3, 1793.

[C] [51]

PAYMENTS TO THE TREASURER OF THE UNITED STATES.*

No.	Paid Warrant		
1503.	To David Allison, agent for Robert King and Richard Fields, for their compensation going Express to the Cherokee nation	64.	
1818.	Robert Forsyth, for his compensation as marshal for the district of Georgia	130.	15.
1970.	Edward Blake, superintendent of the lighthouse in South Carolina, to defray the expenses of said establishment	681.	36.
1999.	Arnold Willis, balance due to him from the United States, for a bill of exchange returned unpaid	594.	50.
2036.	Sharp Delany, assignee of Lieut. Col: de Touzard, for his pension	180.	
2056.	Jonathan Williams, junr. for a bill of exchange on the late commissioners at Paris, returned	12.	
2074	William Allibone, for his services and expenses in examining and surveying the light-house at Bald Head, North Carolina	212.	
2077.	William Bill, for sundry setts of Exchange on the late Commissioners at Paris, returned	168.	
2083	Joseph Anthony, agent for John Brown Cutting, being in full for a sum of money granted him by Congress	1,580.	46.
2084	William Allibone, superintendent of the light-house at Cape Henlopen, to defray expenses in support of said Establishment	430.	
2096.	Oliver Wolcott, junr: for the salaries of his office, as Comptroller of the Treasury	1,850.	
2097	Samuel Meredith, on account of the War department	2,500.	
2098	Ditto ditto	500.	
2099	Henry Knox, for the salaries of his office, as Secretary at War	1,762.	50.
2100.	William Simmons, Attorney for John Cochran, for his salary as Commissioner of loans for New York	375.	
2101.	Nehemiah Tilton, agent for James Tilton, for his salary as commissioner of loans for Delaware	150.	
2102.	Joseph Nourse, for the salaries of his office as Register of the Treasury	4,500.	
2103.	John Meyer, agent for Alexander Hamilton, for the salaries of his office, as Secretary of the Treasury	2,306.	
2104.	Richard Harrison, for the salaries of his office as Auditor of the Treasury	2,608.	58.
2105.	George Taylor, agent for Thomas Jefferson, for the salaries of his office as Secretary of State	1,621.	67.

* See Report of the Secretary of the Treasury, dated February. 4th. 1793 Reference C.

51. At this point in the MS the following note appears: "For Reference C, containing an Account of Receipts and Expenditures by the Treasurer of the United States, from 1st. October to 31st. December 1792, See Record of Treasurer's Accounts. Vol. 2: page to ." The manuscript for the accounts printed above as enclosure "C" may be found in RG 233, Records of Reports from Executive Departments, Reports from the Treasurer, 2d Congress, 2d session, to 3d Congress, 2d session, National Archives.

No.	Paid Warrant		
2106.	John Jordan, for his pension	10.	
2107.	James Mathers, for his salary as door keeper to the Senate of the United States	125.	
2108.	Thomas Claxton, for his salary as assistant door keeper to the House of Representatives	112.	50.
2109.	Isaac Sherman, for his salary as a clerk employed in the Treasury department in counting money	125.	
2110.	David Henley ditto ditto	125.	
2111.	W. Irvine, J. Kean, and W. Langdon, for the salaries of their office, as commissioners for adjusting claims of individual states with the United States	3,075.	
2112.	Gifford Dally, for his salary as door keeper to the House of Representatives	125.	
2113.	George Turner, for his salary as one of the Judges of the Western territory	200.	
2114.	John Kean, Attorney for Frederick William de Steuben, for his pension	625.	
2115.	John Inskeep, Attorney for Joseph Anderson, for his salary as one of the Judges of the territory south of the Ohio	200.	
2116.	Matthew McConnell, Attorney for Arthur St. Clair, for his salary as governor of the Western territory	500.	
2117.	Bernard Webb, agent for John Beckley, for his salary as Clerk of the House of Representatives	375.	
2118.	Thomas Fitzsimons, agent for James Wilson, for his salary as one of the Associate Judges	875.	
2119.	Bernard Webb, agent for John Beckley, attorney for Harry Innes, for his salary as district judge of Kentucky	250.	
2120.	John Kean, Attorney for Thomas Bee, for his salary as district Judge of South Carolina	450.	
2121.	Ditto, Attorney for John Neufville, for his salary as Commissioner of loans for South Carolina	250.	
2122.	John Bard, agent for Nathaniel Pendleton, for his Salary as Judge for the district of Georgia	375.	
2123.	Samuel Meredith, for the salaries of his office, as Treasurer of the United States	775.	
2124.	Robert Morris, agent for Edmund Randolph, for his salary as Attorney General of the United States	375.	
2125.	Hugh Williamson, Attorney for William Blount, for his salary as governor of the territory south of the Ohio	500.	
2126.	Ditto, Attorney for Daniel Smith, his salary as Secretary of the territory south of the Ohio	187.	50.
2127.	Ditto, Attorney for William Skinner, for his salary as Commissioner of loans for North Carolina	250.	
2128.	Ditto, Attorney for John McNairy, for his salary as one of the Judges of the territory south of the Ohio	200.	
2129.	Samuel Meredith, Attorney for John Blair, for his salary as one of the Associate Judges	875.	
2130.	Thomas Smith, for his salary as Commissioner of loans for Pennsylvania	375.	
2131.	John Sitgreaves, Attorney for John Sitgreaves, for his salary as Judge for the district of North Carolina	375.	
2132.	Robert Smith, Attorney for David Campbell, for his salary as one of the Judges of the Western territory	200.	

No.	Paid Warrant		
2133.	Richard Peters, for his salary as Judge for the district of Pennsylvania	400.	
2134.	Samuel A. Otis, for his salary as Secretary to the Senate	375.	
2135.	Joseph Nourse, attorney for John Sullivan, for his salary as Judge for the district of New Hampshire	250.	
2136.	Ditto, attorney for Cyrus Griffin, for his salary as Judge for the district of Virginia	450.	
2137.	William Cushing, for his salary as one of the associate judges	875.	
2138.	Samuel Meredith, on Account of the War department	3,000.	
2139.	Ditto ditto	1,000.	
2140.	Clement Biddle, agent for Thomas Johnson, for his salary as one of the associate Judges	875.	
2141.	Alexander and James Parker, Agents for Samuel McDowell, junior, compensation to the Assistant Marshal for the district of Kentucky	40.	79.
2142.	Alexander Parker, agent for Samuel McDowell, junior, compensation to John Eakin, as assistant in taking a census of the inhabitants of Kentucky	50.	4.
2143.	Joseph Howell, for extra services of a clerk employed in his office as accountant to the War department	229.	16.
2144.	Tobias Lear, on account of the President's compensation	3,000.	
2145.	William Allibone, superintendent of the light house at Cape Henlopen, to defray expenses in support of said establishment.	400.	
2146.	John Kean, Attorney for Richard Law, for his salary as judge for the district of Connecticut	250.	
2147.	Elliott and Williams, for provisions issued, and sundry supplies furnished the Quarter master's department	2,760.	67.
2148.	James Mazurie, assignee of Pierce Manning, agent for Abner Neale, for attending the circuit and district courts of North Carolina.	20.	
2149.	Joseph Anthony, attorney to James Iredell, for his salary as one of the associate Judges	875.	
2150.	Robert Underwood, agent for Joseph Bindon, attorney to Dominique L'Eglize, for his pension	30.	
2151.	Samuel Hodgdon, Attorney for James O'Hara, for the use of the Quarter master's department	2,000.	
2152.	Joseph Howell, on account of the department of War	156,595.	56.
2153.	George Meade, agent for Richard Wylly, commissioner of loans for Georgia, for the salary of a clerk employed in his office	91.	20.
2154.	James Boggs, agent for Robert Morris, for his salary as judge for the district of New Jersey	250.	
2155.	Joseph Howell, for the salaries of his office, as accountant of the War department	625.	
2156.	Henry Knox, assignee of Michael Hillegas, for the amount of a warrant, No. 485, returned unpaid	33.	33.
2157.	Robert Elliott and Elie Williams, being on account of supplies furnished, and to be furnished, for the use of the Army	20,000.	
2158.	Tobias Van Zandt, agent for William Allen, for 80 horsemen's swords, furnished Capt. Stake's troop	400.	
2159.	Clement Biddle, balance due to him on account of provisions issued to the recruits	114.	13.

No.	Paid Warrant		
2160.	George Bickham, attorney for Samuel McDowell junior, his compensation as marshal for the district of Kentucky	83.	
2161.	John Templeman, for a sett of exchange on the late commissioners at Paris, returned	12.	
2162.	Samuel Meredith, on account of the War department	10,000.	
2163.	Ditto ditto	2,000.	
2164.	William Porter, assignee of Daniel Hale, for sundry rations issued to the recruits at Albany, &c.	169.	79.
2165.	John Kean, attorney for Henry Marchant, for his salary as Judge for the district of Rhode Island	200.	
2166.	A. R. C. M. de la Forest, being on account of the debt due from the United States to France	24,660.	
2167.	Joseph Nourse, agent for John Hopkins, for his salary as Commissioner of loans for Virginia	375.	
2168.	Robert Underwood, assignee for Joseph Bindon, attorney for Joseph Traversie, for his pension	30.	
2169.	Samuel Emery, agent for Nathaniel Appleton, for his salary as Commissioner of loans for Massachusetts	375.	
2170.	Charles Young, assignee of Nathaniel Chipman, for his salary as Judge for the district of Vermont	200.	
2171.	Melancton Smith, for provisions issued to the troops at Westpoint	128.	72.
2172.	David Allison, agent for William Blount, for the use of the War department, in the territory southwest of the Ohio	5,000.	
2173.	Abraham Witmer, assignee of Joseph Dicker, and others, for 100 rifles delivered for the use of the army	1,200.	
2174.	Robert Forsyth, being in full of his own and assistant's compensation for taking an enumeration of the inhabitants of Georgia	336.	61.
2175.	Robert Forsyth, his compensation for attending several sessions of the district and circuit courts of Georgia	231.	90.
2176.	Melancton Smith, for provisions issued to the troops at New York	268.	86.
2177.	Tobias Lear, on account of the President's compensation	1,000.	
2178.	Henry Drinker, attorney for Chauncey Whittlesey, for rations issued to the troops at Connecticut	879.	44.
2179.	Thomas Billington and Charles Young, on account of a contract for furnishing the troops with clothing	4,500.	
2180.	Abraham Wilt, attorney for major de Bert de Majun, a foreign officer, late in the service of the United States	7,371.	
2181.	George Meade, agent for Richard Wylly, for his salary as Commissioner of loans for Georgia.	175.	
2182.	John Kean, attorney for William Imlay, for his salary as Commissioner of loans for Connecticut	250.	
2183.	Tench Coxe, for oil purchased for the use of the light house at Cape Henry, in the State of Virginia	380.	80.
2184.	Samuel Howell, for supplies furnished the dragoon recruits at Elkton, under the command of Major Rudolph	162.	85.
2185.	Samuel Smith, agent for Elliott and Williams, on account of the expenses of the recruiting service	4,000.	
2186.	Samuel Hodgdon, attorney for James O'Hara, being for the use of the Quarter master's department	1,000.	
2187.	Reed and Forde, assignees of captain Sharpe, a foreign officer, late in the service of the United States	1,229.	11.

No.	Paid Warrant		
2188.	Edmund Randolph, attorney General, for his expenses to, and from York town, in attending the circuit courts held there	54.	
2189.	Ferdinand Gourdon, assignee of William Paca, for his salary as Judge for the district of Maryland	375.	
2190.	Samuel Hodgdon, attorney for James O'Hara, being for the use of the Quarter master's department	35,000.	
2191.	John Stagg, junr. agent for Thomas Randall, superintendent of the light house at Sandy-hook, for the support of said establishment	231.	86.
2192.	George Taylor, Attorney for John Jay, for his salary as chief Justice of the United States	1,000.	
2193.	Abraham Miller, for rations and other supplies furnished to a detachment of recruits at Bridgetown	48.	86.
2194.	Christian Lybrandt, for 30,000 bricks, for the purpose of finishing the light house at Bald head, North Carolina	150.	
2195.	Peter Bob, for 3,000 ditto ditto	15.	
2196.	John Brown, attorney for Robert Irwin, for his compensation as assistant to the marshal for the district of Kentucky	51.	27.
2197.	Patrick Ferrall, for defraying the contingent expenses of the Commissioner's office	150.	
2198.	Philip Nicklin and Co. assignees of Samuel Smith, agent for Elliott and Williams, on account of supplies furnished for the use of the army	20,000.	
2199.	Samuel Meredith, on account of the War department	6,362.	
2200.	Antoine R. C. M. de la Forest, on Account of the debt due from the United States to France	19,961.	
2201.	William Allibone, superintendent of the light house at Cape Henlopen, to defray expenses in support of said establishment	534.	
2202.	Thomas Billington and Charles Young, for sundry pattern articles of clothing, deposited in the War office	128.	46.
2203.	John Hopkins, commissioner of loans for Virginia, to pay interest on the several species of stock	3,600.	
2204.	Ditto, to enable him to pay invalid pensions	400.	
2205.	John Lamb, balance due to him, on account of sundry expenditures to invalid pensioners in New York	498.	54.
2206.	James Burnside, attorney for James Ewing, for his salary as Commissioner of loans for New Jersey	175.	
2207.	Thomas Harwood, Commissioner of loans for Maryland on account of interest on the several species of stock	7,000.	
2208.	Edward Carrington, assignee of Matthew Harvey, for rations issued to the troops at Fincastle, Virginia	517.	36.
2209.	Ditto, assignee of James Roberts, for rations issued to the troops marching from Richmond to Winchester	354.	4.
2210.	Joseph Nourse, agent for Elizabeth Bergen, for her pension	13.	33.
2211.	John Hopkins, commissioner of loans for Virginia, on account of the interest due on the several species of stock	1,200.	
2212.	Tobias Lear, on account of the President's compensation	2,000.	
2213.	Thomas Billington and Charles Young, balance due to them on account of a contract for supplying the troops with clothing	705.	11.

No.	Paid Warrant		
2214.	Joseph Nourse, agent for paying the contingent expenses of the Treasury department	800.	
2215.	John Wilkins, Assignee of Alexander Scott, balance due for supplies furnished the troops at Lancaster	668.	47.
2216.	Samuel Meredith, agent for James Read, assignee of John Skinner, his compensation as marshal for the district of South Carolina	156.	
2217.	Ditto, agent for ditto, assignee for ditto ditto	285.	60.
2218.	Jonathan Trumbull, to enable him to make payments to the members of the House of Representatives	12,000.	
2219.	Samuel A. Otis, to be applied towards the payment of the Senators, for their compensations	2,384.	40
2220.	Roger Sherman, attorney for Philip B. Bradley, his compensation as marshal for the district of Connecticut	337.	7
2221.	William Allibone, Superintendant of the light-house at Cape Henlopen, for support of said establishment	144.	
2222.	Alexander Humphries, balance due on account of provisions furnished to captain Gibson's company at Staunton	385.	71.
2223.	Benjamin Connor, balance due on account of rations furnished and supplies in the Quarter master's department	387.	57.
2224.	John Kean, Attorney for Richard Law, for his salary as judge for the district of Connecticut	250.	
2225.	George Thatcher, Attorney for David Sewall, for his salary as Judge for the district of Maine	500.	
2226.	Tench Francis, to be applied towards the purchase of certain Indian supplies	2,000.	
2227.	Samuel Meredith, on Account of the War department	8,000.	
2228.	Ditto ditto	2,000.	
2229.	Jedidiah Huntington, for payments made to invalid pensioners at Connecticut	57.	12.
2230.	Samuel A. Otis, to be applied towards the payment of the Senators, for their compensations	268.	80
2231.	Jeremiah Smith, attorney for Daniel Warner, for his compensation as deputy marshal for the district of New Hampshire	96.	14.
2232.	William Imlay, Commissioner of loans, Connecticut, to pay interest due on the several species of stocks	4,750.	
2233.	William Imlay, agent for paying the invalid pensioners in the State of Connecticut	2,000.	
2234.	Antoine R. C. M. de la Forest, being on account of the debt due from the United States to France	2,358.	
2235.	Richard Wylly, commissioner of loans, Georgia, on account of interest due on the several species of stock	1,300.	
2236.	John Hopkins, Commissioner of loans, Virginia, on account of interest due on the several species of stock	1,250.	
2237.	Ditto, Commissioner of loans, Virginia, on account of interest due on the several species of stock	1,800.	
2238.	William Gardner, commissioner of loans, New Hampshire, on account of interest due on the several species of stock	5,050.	
2239.	Winthrop Sargent, for his salary as Secretary of the territory north west of the Ohio	750.	
2240.	Hugh Williamson, Attorney for William Blount, for the use of the War department, within the territory South West of the Ohio	6,000.	

No.	Paid Warrant		
2241.	Clement Biddle, for provisions issued to the recruits, and various supplies furnished in the Quarter master's and hospital department	997.	87.
2242.	Benjamin Lincoln, superintendant of light house, Massachusetts, amount of sundry expenses in support of said establishment.	9,617.	96.
2243.	Benjamin Bayley, agent for John Paulding for his pension	100.	
2244.	Clement Biddle, for sundry supplies furnished Joseph Brandt, chief of the six nations of Indians, during his stay in Philadelphia	466.	33.
2245.	Jedidiah Huntington, superintendant of light house, New London, amount of sundry expenditures in support of said establishment	1,093.	21.
2246.	Otho H. Williams, amount of sundry payments to invalid pensioners, at Baltimore	1,603.	79.
2247.	Antoine R. C. M. de la Forest, being an account of the debt due from the United States to France	8,997.	
2248.	John Hopkins, Commissioner of loans, Virginia, on account of interest due on the several species of stock	7,350.	
2249.	Ditto, Commissioner of loans, Virginia, on account of payments made to invalid pensioners	2,750.	
2250.	Samuel Hodgdon, attorney to James O'Hara, for the use of the Quarter master's department	1,000.	
2251.	Joseph Nourse, for the purpose of stating and printing certain public accounts	220.	
2253.	Samuel Hodgdon, Attorney for James O'Hara, for the use of the Quarter master's department	1,500.	
2254.	Samuel Meredith, on account of the War department	5,500.	
2255.	Ditto ditto	1,500.	00.
2256.	Adam Anstat, for 17 rifles made by order of the Secretary at War	204.	
2257.	John McIntire, for sundry rations issued to the militia of Ohio County, State of Virginia	318.	64.
2258.	Samuel Millish, junr., attorney for Israel Chapin, balance due for supplies furnished, and expenses incurred for the five nations of Indians	27.	33.
2259.	James B. Smith, for making three large wampum belts for the use of the Indian department	43.	
2260.	Wheelen and Miller, agents to Jacob Dickert and others, for 67 rifles made for the use of the United States	804.	
2261.	Henry Drinker, for three sinkers for the beacon boats directed to be stationed in the bay of Chesapeak	74.	44.
2262.	John Nicholson, for 26 rifles made by order of the Secretary at War	312.	
2264.	Tobias Lear, on account of the President's compensation	1,000.	
2265.	John Kean, to be applied towards discharging unclaimed dividends	2,671.	99.
2267.	Antoine R. C. M. de la Forest, on account of the debt due from the United States to France	64,935.	1.
2268.	John Miller, junr. for his attendance inspecting the clothing for the army	200.	
2269.	Tench Francis, on account of the incidental and contingent expenses of the War department	1,000.	
2270.	Samuel A. Otis, to be applied towards payment of the Senators, for their compensations	3,840.	

No.	Paid Warrant		
2271.	Samuel Meredith, on account of the War department	1,500.	
2272.	Ditto ditto	1,500.	
2273.	David Ridgway, for 30,000 bricks, for the completion of the light house at Bald head, North Carolina	150.	
2274.	John Kean, to be applied towards discharging unclaimed dividends	90.	10.
2275.	Ditto ditto	32.	66.
2276.	James Ewing, Commissioner of loans, New Jersey, to pay interest on the several species of stock	4,000.	
2277.	Samuel Meredith, on account of the War department	6,000.	
2278.	Joseph Anthony and son, Assignees for John Habersham, agent for James Seagrove, for a bill of exchange drawn on account of the War department	900.	
2279.	James Wilson, attorney for James Duane, for his salary as Judge for the district of New York	375.	
2280.	Ditto, Attorney for James Duane, for his salary as Judge for the district of New York	1,125.	
2281.	John Kean, to be applied towards discharging unclaimed dividends	770.	17.
2282.	Gabriel Blakeney, for sundry rations issued to the militia of Washington county, Pennsylvania	947.	84.
2283.	John Hopkins, on account of payments made to invalid pensioners	400.	
2284.	William Imlay, agent for paying invalid pensions in the State of Connecticut	1,500.	
2285.	Ditto, Commissioner of loans, Connecticut, to pay interest due on the several species of stock	1,500.	
2286.	Jonathan Burrall, assignee of John McComb, agent for John McComb, junior, on account of a contract for erecting a light house on Cape Henry	2,000.	
2287.	James McKenzie, for his pension	30.	
2288.	Samuel Meredith, on account of the War department	34,878.	
2289.	Solomon Maxwell, balance due on account of supplies furnished the recruits in the State of Delaware	250.	60.
2290.	John McComb, junior, balance due on account of contract for erecting a light house of Cape Henry, Virginia	3,350.	
2291.	Thomas Billington and Charles Young, on account of sundry articles of clothing for the use of the army	2,000.	
2292.	James Poupard, for sundry seals for the use of the public offices of the territory north west of the Ohio	123.	80.
2294.	The State of Maryland, for payments made by said State to invalid pensioners	2,343.	63.
2295.	John Adams, on account of his compensation as Vice president of the United States	340.	
2296.	Tobias Lear, for so much paid by the President to an express rider	12.	
2297.	Samuel A. Otis, on account of the contingent expenses of the Senate, and of his office	655.	50.
2298.	John Kean, to be applied towards discharging unclaimed dividends	548.	10.
2299.	Jonathan Burrall, agent for Nicholas Hoffman, to be applied to the purpose of purchasing certain Indian supplies	640.	56.
2300.	George Benson, Agent for Jabez Bowen, for his salary as Commissioner loans, Rhode Island	150.	

No.	Paid Warrant		
2301.	Jean de Ternant, being on account of the debt due from the United States to France	5,445.	
2302.	Ditto, for his pay and services as a foreign officer late in the service of the United States	9,754.	68.
2303.	John Hopkins, on account of payments made to invalid pensioners	1,150.	
2304.	Ditto, Commissioner of loans, Virginia, on accot: of interest due on the several species of stock	750.	
2305.	Nathaniel Appleton Massachusetts ditto	3,000.	
2306.	Jonathan Trumbull, to enable him to make payments to the members of the House of Representatives	12,000.	
2307.	Antoine R. C. M. de la Forest, being account of the debt due from the United States to France	34,558.	82.
2308.	Clement Biddle, balance due to the State of Pennsylvania on account of rations issued to the militia of said State	1 447.	93.
2309.	Tobias Lear, agent for Jonathan Steele, his compensation as Clerk of the circuit and district Courts of New Hampshire	52.	20.
2310.	Ditto, attorney for Nathaniel Rogers, his compensation as marshal for the district of New Hampshire	329.	93.
2311.	Robert Crawford, agent for John Stuart, balance due for supplies furnished the riflemen in Virginia	1 753.	6.
2313.	Tobias Lear, on account of the President's compensation	1,000.	
2314.	Samuel Hodgdon, Attorney for James O'Hara, for the use of the Quarter master's department	8,090.	67.
2315.	Tench Francis, to be applied to the purpose of purchasing sundry military stores	1,000.	
2316.	Aaron Robinson, balance due on account of supplies furnished to the recruits at Bennington	322.	62.
2317.	William Allibone, superintendant of the light house at Cape Henlopen, for support of said Establishment	966.	50.
2320.	Clement Biddle, for his compensation as marshal for the district of Pennsylvania	545.	51.
2321.	Ditto ditto	622.	95.
2322.	John Cochran, commissioner of loans for New York, to be applied towards the payment of interest on the several species of stock	93,000.	
2323.	Thomas Harwood, Maryland, ditto	11,000.	
2326.	Thomas Smith, Pennsylvania ditto	25,402.	83.
2328.	Samuel Meredith, for purchases made him, as agent to the Trustees for the reduction of the public debt	15,098.	11
2333.	John Kean, to be applied towards payment of interest on the funded six and three per cent stocks	304,303.	27.
2338.	Edward Blake, Superintendant of the lighthouse at South Carolina, for defraying the expenses of said establishment	163.	27.
2339.	Ditto ditto	1,253.	52.
2340.	John Habersham, for amount of sundry payments made to Invalid pensioners	526.	77.
2341.	Nathaniel Appleton, commissioner of loans for Massachusetts, to pay interest due on the several species of stock	62,000.	
2342.	William Ellery, superintendant of the light house at Rhode Island, to defray expenses of said establishment	754.	58.

No.	Paid Warrant		
2343.	Jabez Bowen, Commissioner of loans for Rhode Island, to pay interest on the several species of stock	6,000.	
2344.	Ditto ditto	6,000.	
2345.	William Imlay, Commissioner of loans for Connecticut, do.	4.050.	
2346.	Samuel Meredith, to defray contingent expenses of his own and Henley and Sherman's office	158.	97.
		1,250,592.	61.
	Balance in my hands this day, as explained below	783,444.	51.
		2,034,037.	12.
	Cash in the Bank of the United States	109,169.	45.
	Ditto North America	61,601.	30.
	Ditto New York	69,019.	8
	Ditto Providence	28,157.	87.
	Ditto, office of discount and deposit, Boston	154,860.	67.
	Ditto New York	224,735.	51.
	Ditto Baltimore	73,653.	64.
	Ditto Charleston	62,015.	85.
	Amount of contingencies paid, for which there is no appropriation	142.	14.
	Amount paid Saml. Brook, a clerk in the office, for which there is no do.	90.	
	Dollars	783,444.	51.

RECEIPTS BY THE TREASURER OF THE UNITED STATES.

No.	Received for Warrant —				
	Balance of Account furnished to the 1st. of October last			420, 914.	51.
1520.	On Isaac Holmes	Collector	Charleston	480.	
1535.	ditto	ditto	ditto	201.	36.
1685.	John Habersham	ditto	Savannah	231.	90.
1686.	ditto	ditto	ditto	130.	15.
1687.	ditto	ditto	ditto	336.	61.
1688.	Charles Lee	ditto	Alexandria	4,000.	
1689.	John Lamb	ditto	New York	498.	54.
1690.	William Lindsay	ditto	Norfolk	1,200.	
1691.	James Read	ditto	Wilmington (N. C.)	441.	60
1692.	Jedidiah Huntington	ditto	New London	57.	12.
1693.	ditto	ditto	ditto	4,750.	
1694.	ditto	ditto	ditto	2,000.	
1695.	John Habersham	ditto	Savannah	1,300.	
1696.	William Lindsay	ditto	Norfolk	300.	
1697.	William Heth	ditto	Bermuda hundred	1,800.	
1698.	Joseph Whipple	ditto	Portsmouth	3,000.	
1699.	ditto	ditto	ditto	2,050.	
1700.	Benjamin Lincoln	ditto	Boston	9,617.	96.
1701.	Jedidiah Huntington	ditto	New London	1,093.	21.
1702.	Otho H. Williams	ditto	Baltimore	1 603.	79
1703.	George Biscoe	ditto	Nottingham	700.	
1704.	Otho H. Williams	ditto	Baltimore	23,000.	
1705.	Sharp Delany	ditto	Philadelphia	3,040.	96.

No.	Received for Warrant —				
1706.	John Lamb	ditto	New York	13,219.	26.
1707.	Jedidiah Huntington	ditto	New London	1,700.	
1708.	Hudson Muse	ditto	Tappahannock	450.	
1709.	William Heth	ditto	Bermuda Hundred	1,310.	
1710.	ditto	ditto	ditto	1,725.	
1711.	James McC. Lingan	ditto	George town, Maryland	1,115.	
1712.	William Lindsay	ditto	Norfolk	400.	
1713.	Jedidiah Huntington	ditto	New London	1,000.	
1714.	ditto	ditto	ditto	1,000.	
1715.	ditto	ditto	ditto	500.	
1716.	ditto	ditto	ditto	500.	
1717.	ditto	ditto	ditto	500.	
1718.	ditto	ditto	ditto	500.	
1719.	ditto	ditto	ditto	500.	
1720.	ditto	ditto	ditto	500.	
1721.	ditto	ditto	ditto	500.	
1722.	ditto	ditto	ditto	500.	
1723.	ditto	ditto	ditto	500.	
1724.	ditto	ditto	ditto	500.	
1725.	ditto	ditto	ditto	500.	
1726.	ditto	ditto	ditto	500.	
1727.	Jonathan Fitch	ditto	New Haven	2,000.	
1728.	ditto	ditto	ditto	500.	
1729.	ditto	ditto	ditto	500.	
1730.	ditto	ditto	ditto	500.	
1731.	ditto	ditto	ditto	500.	
1732.	ditto	ditto	ditto	500.	
1733.	ditto	ditto	ditto	500.	
1734.	Samuel Smedley	ditto	Fairfield	300.	
1735.	ditto	ditto	ditto	300.	
1736.	ditto	ditto	ditto	300.	
1737.	ditto	ditto	ditto	100.	
1738.	ditto	ditto	ditto	200.	
1739.	John Halsted	ditto	Perth Amboy	2,714.	24.
1740.	James McC. Lingan	ditto	George town, Maryland	400.	
1741.	Abraham Archer	ditto	York town, Virginia	200.	
1742.	Hudson Muse	ditto	Tappahannock	1,500.	
1743.	Richard M. Scott	ditto	Dumfries	200.	
1744.	ditto	ditto	ditto	200.	
1745.	Charles Lee	ditto	Alexandria	3,000.	
1746.	ditto	ditto	ditto	1,000.	
1747.	ditto	ditto	ditto	1,000.	
1748.	ditto	ditto	ditto	1,000.	
1749.	ditto	ditto	ditto	500.	
1750.	ditto	ditto	ditto	500.	
1751.	ditto	ditto	ditto	500.	
1752.	ditto	ditto	ditto	500.	
1753.	ditto	ditto	ditto	1,000.	
1754.	William Gibb	ditto	Foley landing	200.	
1755.	Thomas Benbury	ditto	Edenton, N. Carola.	250.	
1756.	ditto	ditto	ditto	250.	
1757.	ditto	ditto	ditto	250.	
1758.	ditto	ditto	ditto	250.	
1759.	ditto	ditto	ditto	250.	
1760.	ditto	ditto	ditto	250.	

No.	Received for Warrant —				
1761.	ditto	ditto	ditto	250.	
1762.	ditto	ditto	ditto	250.	
1763.	ditto	ditto	ditto	250.	
1764.	ditto	ditto	ditto	250.	
1765.	ditto	ditto	ditto	250.	
1766.	ditto	ditto	ditto	250.	
1767.	ditto	ditto	ditto	400.	
1768.	ditto	ditto	ditto	400.	
1769.	James Read	ditto	Wilmington, N. C.	500.	
1770.	ditto	ditto	ditto	500.	
1771.	ditto	ditto	ditto	500.	
1772.	ditto	ditto	ditto	500.	
1773.	ditto	ditto	ditto	500.	
1774.	ditto	ditto	ditto	500.	
1775.	ditto	ditto	ditto	500.	
1776.	ditto	ditto	ditto	500.	
1777.	ditto	ditto	ditto	500.	
1778.	ditto	ditto	ditto	500.	
1779.	ditto	ditto	ditto	400.	
1780.	John Daves	ditto	Newbern	500.	
1781.	ditto	ditto	ditto	500.	
1782.	ditto	ditto	ditto	500.	
1783.	ditto	ditto	ditto	500.	
1784.	ditto	ditto	ditto	500.	
1785.	ditto	ditto	ditto	500.	
1786.	ditto	ditto	ditto	500.	
1787.	ditto	ditto	ditto	500.	
1788.	ditto	ditto	ditto	200.	
1789.	ditto	ditto	ditto	200.	
1790.	Nathan Keais	ditto	Washington	250.	
1791.	ditto	ditto	ditto	250.	
1792.	ditto	ditto	ditto	250.	
1793.	ditto	ditto	ditto	250.	
1794.	ditto	ditto	ditto	500.	
1795.	Isaac Gregory	ditto	Camden	250.	
1796.	ditto	ditto	ditto	250.	
1797.	ditto	ditto	ditto	250.	
1798.	ditto	ditto	ditto	250.	
1799.	ditto	ditto	ditto	250.	
1800.	ditto	ditto	ditto	250.	
1801.	ditto	ditto	ditto	300.	
1802.	William Heth	ditto	Bedmuda Hundred	1,150.	
1803	ditto	ditto	ditto	750.	
1804.	Francis Cook	ditto	Wiscassetts	250.	
1805.	Isaac Holmes	ditto	Charleston	163.	27.
1806.	ditto	ditto	ditto	1,253.	52.
1807.	John Habersham	ditto	Savannah	526.	77.
1808.	Abraham Archer	ditto	York town, Virginia	250.	
1809.	ditto	ditto	ditto	250.	
1810.	ditto	ditto	ditto	250.	
1811.	ditto	ditto	ditto	250.	
1812.	ditto	ditto	ditto	400.	
1813.	Hudson Muse	ditto	Tappahannock	800.	
1814.	ditto	ditto	ditto	500.	
1815.	ditto	ditto	ditto	500.	

No.	Received for Warrant —			
1816.	Charles Lee	ditto	Alexandria	500.
1817.	ditto	ditto	ditto	300.
1818.	ditto	ditto	ditto	1,000.
1819.	ditto	ditto	ditto	1,000.
1820.	ditto	ditto	ditto	1,000.
1821.	ditto	ditto	ditto	1,000.
1822.	ditto	ditto	ditto	1,000.
1823.	James Read	ditto	Wilmington, N: Carol.	500.
1824.	ditto	ditto	ditto	500.
1825.	ditto	ditto	ditto	500.
1826.	ditto	ditto	ditto	500.
1827.	ditto	ditto	ditto	500.
1828.	ditto	ditto	ditto	500.
1829.	Isaac Gregory	ditto	Camden	500.
1830.	William Lindsay	ditto	Norfolk	2,000.
1831.	ditto	ditto	ditto	2,000.
1832.	ditto	ditto	ditto	2,000.
1833.	ditto	ditto	ditto	2,000.
1834.	ditto	ditto	ditto	2,000.
1835.	ditto	ditto	ditto	1,000.
1836.	ditto	ditto	ditto	1,000.
1837.	ditto	ditto	ditto	1,000.
1838.	William Heth	ditto	Bermuda Hundred	1,000.
1839.	William Lindsay	ditto	Norfolk	1,000.
1840.	ditto	ditto	ditto	500.
1841.	ditto	ditto	ditto	500.
1842.	ditto	ditto	ditto	500.
1843.	ditto	ditto	ditto	500.
1844.	ditto	ditto	ditto	500.
1845.	ditto	ditto	ditto	500.
1846.	ditto	ditto	ditto	500.
1847.	ditto	ditto	ditto	500.
1848.	ditto	ditto	ditto	500.
1849.	ditto	ditto	ditto	500.
1850.	ditto	ditto	ditto	2,000.
1851.	ditto	ditto	ditto	2,000.
1852.	ditto	ditto	ditto	2,000.
1853.	William Heth	ditto	Bermuda Hundred	2,000.
1854.	William Lindsay	ditto	Norfolk	1,000.
1855.	ditto	ditto	ditto	1,000.
1856.	William Heth	ditto	Bermuda hundred	1,000.
1857.	ditto	ditto	ditto	1,000.
1858.	ditto	ditto	ditto	500.
1859.	ditto	ditto	ditto	500.
1860.	William Lindsay	ditto	Norfolk	500.
1861.	ditto	ditto	ditto	500.
1862.	ditto	ditto	ditto	500.
1863.	ditto	ditto	ditto	500.
1864.	William Ellery	ditto	Newport	754. 58.
1865.	Epes Sargent	ditto	Gloucester	1,500.
1866.	Joseph Hiller	ditto	Salem	8,000.
1867.	Stephen Hussey	ditto	Nantucket	130.
1868.	Joseph Otis	ditto	Barnstable	49.
1869.	Edward Pope	ditto	New Bedford	600.
1870.	Benjamin Lincoln	ditto	Boston	137,000.

No.	Received for Warrant —				
1871.	Hodijah Baylies	ditto	Dighton	1,000.	
1872.	Jeremiah Hill	ditto	Biddeford & pepperellboro'	1,966.	28
1873.	Nathaniel F. Fosdick	ditto	Portland	5,854.	
1874.	William Webb	ditto	Bath	2,177.	90
1875.	Francis Cook	ditto	Wiscassetts	76.	46.
1876.	John Lee	ditto	Penobscot	594.	12.
1877.	Stephen Smith	ditto	Machias	400.	
1878.	L. T. Delesdernier	ditto	Passamaquody	140.	
1879.	Jeremiah Olney	ditto	Providence	31,800.	
1880.	ditto	ditto	ditto	4,000.	
1881	Jediidiah Huntington	ditto	New London	7,150.	
1882.	Jonathan Fitch	ditto	New Haven	950.	
1883.	Samuel Smedley	ditto	Fairfield	690.	
1884.	Henry P. Dering	ditto	Sagg Harbour	300.	
1885.	John Lamb	ditto	New York	325,150.	7.
1886.	ditto	ditto	ditto	32,196.	61.
1887.	ditto	ditto	ditto	8,799.	50.
1888.	John Halsted	ditto	Perth Amboy	1,080.	
1889.	Sharp Delany	ditto	Philadelphia	327,415.	42.
1890.	ditto	ditto	ditto	17,750.	92.
1891.	George Bush	ditto	Wilmington, Del.	5,573.	92.
1892.	Otho H. Williams	ditto	Baltimore	97,977.	35.
1893.	ditto	ditto	ditto	20,000.	
1894.	John Gunby	ditto	Snowhill	100.	
1895.	John Davidson	ditto	Annapolis	2,026.	57.
1896.	George Biscoe	ditto	Nottingham	1,514.	64.
1897.	John C. Jones	ditto	Cedar point	500.	
1898.	James McC. Lingan	ditto	George town, Maryland	4,823.	16.
1899.	William Heth	ditto	Bermuda hundred	18,630.	4.
1900.	Richard M. Scott	ditto	Dumfries	500.	
1901.	Charles Lee	ditto	Alexandria	11,841.	3.
1902.	Thomas Benbury	ditto	Edenton, North Carola.	600.	
1903.	Charles Brown	ditto	George town, S. Carolina	1,501.	55.
1904.	ditto	ditto	ditto	1,500.	
1905.	William Lindsay	ditto	Norfolk	21,708.	2.
1906.	Isaac Holmes	ditto	Charleston	4,757.	69.
1907.	ditto	ditto	ditto	6,798.	7.
1908.	ditto	ditto	ditto	2,550.	55.
1909.	ditto	ditto	ditto	11,121.	71.
1910.	ditto	ditto	ditto	36,816.	10.
1911.	Edward Wigglesworth	ditto	Newburyport	14,830.	50.
80.	William Shippen			2,547.	38.
82.	The President, Directors and Company of the Bank of North America			156,595.	56.
83.	Henry Knox			2,304.	38.
84.	Samuel Hodgdon			4,240.	
85.	Clement Biddle			118.	
15.	Edward Carrington	Supervisor	Virginia	871.	40.
16.	ditto	ditto	ditto	2,750.	
17.	ditto	ditto	ditto	7,350.	
18.	John Chester	ditto	Connecticut	1,500.	
19.	ditto	ditto	ditto	1,500.	
20.	Andrew Barrett	ditto	Delaware	700.	
21.	John Chester	ditto	Connecticut	1,720.	

No.	Received for Warrant —			
22.	Richard Morris	ditto	New York	8,349. 11.
23.	John S. Dexter	ditto	Rhode Island	12,200. 22.
24.	George Gale	ditto	Maryland	4,320. 57.
25.	Nathaniel Gorham	ditto	Massachusetts	44,000.
			Dollars	2,034,037. 12.

Treasury of the United States }
Philadelphia, January, 1st, 1793. }

Samuel Meredith,
Treasurer of the United States.

D

STATE OF THE BALANCES IN THE HANDS OF THE COLLECTORS, TAKEN FROM THE WEEKLY RETURNS, 7TH. JANUARY 1793.

		Dollars	Cts
Joseph Whipple	Portsmouth	8.824.	49.
Stephen Cross,	Newbury port	4.019.	77.
Epes Sargent	Gloucester	1.808.	7.
Joseph Hiller	Salem	14 785.	74.
Samuel R. Gerry	Marblehead	1.924.	70.
Benjamin Lincoln	Boston	18.340.	69.
Benjamin Watson	Plymouth	957.	51.
Joseph Otis	Barnstable	181.	8.
Stephen Hussy	Nantucket	144.	14.
John Peas	Edgar town	133.	53.
Edward Pope	New Bedford	436.	99.
Hod: Baylies	Dighton	192.	20.
Rich. Trevett	York	224.	86.
Jere. Hill	Biddeford	850.	77.
N. F. Fosdick	Portland	3.146.	92.
Will. Webb	Bath	1.171.	51.
Francis Cook	Wiscassett	2.031.	48.
John Lee	Penobscot	252.	39.
Melat. Jordan	Frenchman's Bay	513.	40.
Stephen Smith	Machias	374.	40
L. F. Delesdernier	Passamaquody	75.	15.
Will. Ellery	Newport	2.086.	14
Jer: Olney	Providence	2.315.	31.
J. Huntington	New London	6.916.	45.
Jona: Fitch	New Haven	6.581.	74
Sam: Smedley	Fairfield	2.227.	38
Steph: Keyes	Vermont	29.	43
H: P: Dering	Sagg Harbour	252.	76
John Lamb	New York		
John Halsted	Perth Amboy	114.	33.
John Ross	Burlington	402.	48.
Eli Elmer	Bridgetown		
D: Benezet junr	Great Egg Harbour	131.	30.
Sharp Delaney	Philadelphia	37.892.	88.
[George Bush	Wilmington	958.	76] 52

52. The material within brackets was omitted in this copy of the report. It has been inserted in *ASP, Finance*, I, 199.

O: H: Williams	Baltimore		
Jere: Nicholls	Chester	30.	75.
Jere: Banning	Oxford	52.	80.
John Muir	Vienna	2.235.	27.
John Gunby	Snowhill		
John Davidson	Annapolis	471.	33.
George Biscoe	Nottingham	560.	76.
John C. Jones [53]	Cedar Point	168.	84.
James M: Lingan	George Town	181.	23.
George Wray	Hampton	13.	90.
William Lindsay	Norfolk	12.263.	33.
William Heth	Bermuda Hundred		
Abraham Archer	York Town	230.	4.
Hudson Muse	Tappahannock	723.	35
Vin. Redman	Yeocomico	33.	52.
Richard M. Scott	Dumfries		
Charles Lee	Alexandria	725.	70.
William Gibb	Folly Landing	76.	12.
Nath: Wilkins	Cherrystone		
Thomas Bowne	South Quay	87.	9.
Richard Taylor	Louisville		
James Read	Wilmington	2.535.	36.
John Daves	New Bern	1.370.	90.
Nathan Keais	Washington	414.	4.
Thomas Benbury	Edenton	1.699.	88.
Isaac Gregory	Camden	487.	43.
Charles Brown	Charleston, S: C:	1 904.	76.
Isaac Holmes	Charleston	2 839.	98.
Andrew Agnew	Beaufort		
John Habersham	Savannah	1 968.	38.
Cornelius Collins	Sunbury	109.	20.
Christopher Hillary	Brunswick		
James Seagrove	St. Mary's		
	Dollars,	151.851.	25.

Copied from the Original state of balances
the above date, February 1st. 1793.

L. Wood, junr.

E

AMOUNT OF BONDS BECOMING DUE FOR DUTIES IN THE SEVERAL STATES, FROM THE FIRST OF DECEMBER 1792, TO MAY 1794, INCLUSIVE, VIZ:

State of Massachusetts	485.124.29.
Rhode Island	69.627.99.
Connecticut	77.531.18.
New York	665.229.78.
Pennsylvania	471.809.51.
Delaware	252.
Jerseys	2.282.42.
Maryland	309.715.60.

53. In MS, "Coles." The mistake has been corrected in *ASP, Finance*, I, 199.

Virginia	188.527.63.	
North Carolina	28.275.13.	
South Carolina	26.694.80.	
Georgia	20.539.99.	
		2.345.610.32
Amount due in April 1794, at New York	155.118. 6.	
Amount due in May 1794, at Philadelphia	17.466.76.	
		172.584.82.
Amount of Schedules received,		2.518.195.14

The following not having returned Schedules, the several amounts are taken from the Schedules for the year 1791, Viz:

Massachusetts,	Salem Schedule for December 1791	6.079.22.	
Connecticut,	New London, do	1.902.14.	
New York,	New York, Novemr. and Decemr. 1791.	66.478.75.	
Pennsylvania,	Philadelphia, Octo: Nov: and Dec: 1791	155.889.92.	
Delaware,	Wilmington Dec: 1791.	1.978. 9.	
Virginia, Norfolk, Bermuda Hundred and	Alexandria do	1.142.59.	
North Carolina,	Wilmington and New Bern do. } Edenton, Nov: and Dec: 1791. }	3.010.60.	
South Carolina,	Charleston, Oct: Nov: and Dec: 1791.	84.337.86.	
Georgia,	Savannah, Nov: and Dec: 1791.	4 870.83.	
			336.000.
	Dollars,		2.854.195.14.

Taken from the Originals
February 1st. 1793

L. Wood. junr.

Amount of the above Abstract	2.854.195.14.
Add for the increase of duties by virtue of the Act of the last Session, for raising a farther sum of money, for the protection of the frontiers and for other purposes therein mentioned, computed on the foregoing sum of 336 000, dollars, being the amount of duties for certain periods of the year 1791, for which, returns have not been received as above mentioned—say one seventh	48.000.
	2.902.195.14.
Deduct amount of duties for the month of December, as per Abstract	460.125.99.
Amount of outstanding and unsatisfied Bonds on the 1st. of January 1793, for duties to that period Dollars,	2.442.069.15.

F

THE REVENUE ON SPIRITS DISTILLED IN THE UNITED STATES, PRIOR TO THE YEAR 1793,

Dr.		Dollars.	Cts.			Dollars.	Cts. Cr.
1792. December 31st.	To the amount of monies received into the treasury from the several Supervisors of the revenue, since the last day of June 1791, the particulars whereof have been compared with the Records of Warrants in the Office of the Secretary of the Treasury, and with the books of the Treasurer	208.942.	81.	1792. Decr. 31st.	By amount of duties arising on Spirits distilled in the United States, from foreign and domestic materials, since the last day of June 1791, so far as the returns thereof have been received at the Treasury	403.720.	20 3/20
	To the amount of the allowances made by the President for compensations and expenses (including the first cost of books, office-furniture, marking instruments &c. and certain compensations relative to foreign distilled spirits, wines and teas, since the last of June 1791, agreeably to the Communication of the President to both Houses of Congress, on the 22d. day of November 1792[54]	80.785.			By the estimated amount of duties arising on spirits distilled on the United States, from foreign and domestic materials, since the last day of June 1791, during certain terms, the returns wherefor have not been received at the Treasury	227.450.	
	The balance of the above revenue, which remained on the 31st. day of December 1792, in credits and bonds outstanding	341.442.	39 3/20				
	Dollars,	631.170.	20 3/20		Dollars,	631.170.	20 3/20

Treasury Department,
Revenue Office, February 2d. 1793.

Tench Coxe,
Commissioner of the Revenue.

54. *Annals of Congress*, III, 616, 723.

INDEX

COMPILED BY JEAN G. COOKE